Defending the Rights of Others

When the Cold War ended between 1989 and 1991, statesmen and scholars reached back to the period after World War I when the victors devised minority treaties for the new and expanded states of Eastern Europe. This is the first study of the entire period between 1878 and 1938, when the Great Powers established a system of external supervision to reduce the threats in Europe's most volatile regions of irredentism, persecution, and uncontrolled waves of westward migration. It examines the strengths and weaknesses of an early stage of international human-rights diplomacy as practiced by rival and often-uninformed western political leaders, by ardent but divided Jewish advocates, and also by aggressive state minority champions, in the tumultuous age of nationalism and imperialism, Bolshevism and Fascism, between Bismarck and Hitler.

Carole Fink is Professor of European International History at The Ohio State University. She has written *The Genoa Conference: European Diplomacy, 1921–22* (1984), which was awarded the George Louis Beer Prize of the American Historical Association, and *Marc Bloch: A Life in History* (Cambridge University Press, 1989), which has been translated into five languages.

Defending the Rights of Others

THE GREAT POWERS, THE JEWS, AND INTERNATIONAL MINORITY PROTECTION, 1878–1938

CAROLE FINK
The Ohio State University

CAMBRIDGE UNIVERSITY PRESS
Cambridge, New York, Melbourne, Madrid, Cape Town, Singapore, São Paulo

Cambridge University Press
The Edinburgh Building, Cambridge CB2 2RU, UK

Published in the United States of America by Cambridge University Press, New York

www.cambridge.org
Information on this title: www.cambridge.org/9780521838375

First published 2004
This digitally printed first paperback version 2006

A catalogue record for this publication is available from the British Library

Library of Congress Cataloguing in Publication data

Fink, Carole

Defending the rights of others : the great powers, the Jews, and international
minority protection, 1878–1938 / Carole Fink.

p. cm.

Includes bibliographical references and index.

ISBN 0-521-83837-1 (hb)

1. World Politics – 19th century.
2. World Politics – 1900–1945.
3. Minorities – Legal status, laws, etc. – Europe – History.
4. Jews – Legal status, laws, etc. – Europe – History.
5. Minorities – Europe – History.
6. Europe – Ethnic Relations. I. Title.

D359.7.F56 2004
323.1192′404′09034 – dc22 2003056914

ISBN-13 978-0-521-83837-5 hardback
ISBN-10 0-521-83837-1 hardback

ISBN-13 978-0-521-02994-0 paperback
ISBN-10 0-521-02994-5 paperback

To my students

Contents

PART THREE: A NEW ERA OF MINORITY RIGHTS?

Maps

Photographs

Preface

"... There once was a time when we deplored criminal acts."[1]

After the Soviet empire disintegrated between 1989 and 1991, there were immediate comparisons with the period after World War I when four empires collapsed and a belt of new and enlarged polyglot states emerged in Eastern Europe between Germany and Russia.[2] As succession states were formed and dissolved in the 1990s, and as peoples stuck on the "wrong side" of new borders were once more vulnerable to persecution, violence, and ethnic cleansing, Mikhail Gorbachev and others recommended the reinstitution of the special treaties written in Paris in 1919 to protect minority rights.

This book elucidates the history of international involvement in the minorities question between 1878 and 1938. During that tumultuous sixty-year period, the Great Powers grappled with this thorny problem in Eastern Europe, spreading a mantle of protection over specific populations considered at risk either because of a past history of persecution or a recent transfer of sovereignty. Before World War I, the international system was developed primarily to protect the Jews in the new Balkan states; in 1919, more elaborate guarantees were placed over 25 million Jews, Germans, Ukrainians, Hungarians, Bulgarians, Albanians, and others who fell within the new frontiers of Eastern Europe.

1. Albert Einstein to Stephen Wise (handwritten), Princeton, Jan. 5, 1937, American Jewish Historical Society Archives, Stephen S. Wise Papers (hereafter abbreviated as Wise followed by the microfilm reel numbers) 74–68.
2. Michael Burns, "Disturbed Spirits: Minority Rights and New World Orders, 1919 and the 1990s," in Samuel F. Wells Jr. and Paula Bailey Smith, eds., *New European Orders, 1919 and 1991* (Washington, DC: Woodrow Wilson Center Press, 1996), pp. 42–61.

How did the international community define these minorities? It was fairly simple in 1878, when religion was still the main identifying element. However, by 1919, the existence of national minorities, which included formerly dominant groups along with long-subject peoples, was also recognized. To avoid the explosive term "national," with its politically dangerous overtones of failed or future claims to self-determination, the Paris Peace Conference adopted the descriptive formula of "race, language, and religion" to subsume all the possible characteristics of a minority.[3] Moreover, the peacemakers took pains to deny a group identity to minorities, identifying their new charges either as "persons" belonging to such groups or as "inhabitants who differed from the majority population in race, language, and religion." As this book shows, these cautious formulations not only failed to protect Eastern Europe's "unmeltable" minorities but may also have worsened their plight.

Although most of the world's minorities were excluded from international protection during this period, their existence undoubtedly shaped the minority treaties and their implementation. Every great power ruled heterogeneous, restive populations and was sensitive to their demands for equality, increased rights, autonomy, and even independence. Moreover, as magnets for the bulk of foreign immigrants from Eastern Europe, the liberal democracies, Great Britain, France, and the United States, were as alert to the domestic as to the diplomatic repercussions of international minority protection.

The era covered by this book falls into three parts. The first, an age of European and global empires and emerging Balkan states, commences at the 1878 Congress of Berlin and ends with the Great War; the second centers on the diplomacy of the Paris Peace Conference; and the third, dealing with the world's first minorities system devised by the League of Nations, ends with its destruction at the Munich Conference in September 1938.

By 1878, the Great Powers had accepted responsibility for imposing minority protection on all new and expanded states in order to maintain order in Eastern Europe. Britain and France, facing a rising domestic clamor over abuses to religious and national minorities in the East, also feared that a mass exodus westward would produce dire economic, political, and social consequences. At the other end of Europe the newly independent and expanded Balkan states in 1878, joined by those carved out of the four defeated empires between 1919 and 1923, resisted these attempts to limit their sovereignty and groaned over the taint on their national honor. Above all,

3. Articles 86 and 91, Treaty of Versailles.

they protested the dual standard that enabled "older" outside powers to interfere in their internal affairs while rejecting a universal minorities system.[4]

The much-contested Paris Peace Conference stands as a watershed in the history of minority rights and is the central part of this book. In 1919, a new era was supposed to dawn in European and world politics. The peacemakers devised an international system that included history's first collective human-rights treaties under the guarantee of the League of Nations, an endeavor that set a model, both negative and positive, for future international efforts.[5]

Looming always in the background were the threats of abuse and irredentism from states that styled themselves minority champions. Before 1914, there were the pan-Slav politicians of tsarist Russia who, claiming to speak for the Slavs and Orthodox Christians, meddled repeatedly in Balkan politics while also pursuing anti-Semitic and Russification policies inside their realm.[6] During World War I, it was Wilhelmian Germany that preached a pan-Germanic mission to cover its annexationist policies in the East while practicing intolerance within its own borders. In the 1920s, it was Weimar Germany that ardently championed its lost population but failed to establish a liberal minorities regime at home. And, after 1933, it was the Third Reich, fiercely racist in its domestic policies, but expansionist abroad, that delivered the coup de grâce to an already-frayed international minorities system.

The most ardent nonstate proponents of international minority protection during this period were the Jews of Western Europe and the United States. During this crucial period of Jewish history, marked by turmoil and misery in Eastern Europe, the emigration of huge numbers to the United States and smaller ones to Palestine, and the growing religious and national divisions in the Jewish world, three generations of intercessors moved onto the stage of world diplomacy as advocates for their endangered coreligionists, often with fateful consequences.[7]

This is not the first book to investigate the international dimensions of the minorities question in Eastern Europe. In 1934, the distinguished English historian and analyst of ethnic and religious questions in Eastern Europe,

4. The most recent defense of the Minority States' position, and an ardent one it is, is Peter D. Stachura, "National Identity and the Ethnic Minorities in Early Inter-War Poland," in Peter D. Stachura, ed. *Poland Between the Wars, 1918–1939* (Houndmills/London: Macmillan, 1998), pp. 60–86.
5. Carole Fink, "The Minorities Question at the Paris Peace Conference," in Manfred F. Boemeke, Gerald D. Feldman, and Elisabeth Glaser, eds. *The Treaty of Versailles: A Reassessment after 75 Years* (Cambridge: Cambridge University Press, 1998), pp. 249–74.
6. Before World War I, Russia's stance was emulated by Italy, Romania, Serbia, Bulgaria, and Greece, all claiming the mission of liberating their captive people in either the Habsburg or the Ottoman empires and all, except for Italy, noticeably intolerant of their own minorities.
7. Carole Fink, *The Jews and Minority Rights During and After World War I* (Cape Town University, South Africa: Kaplan Centre for Jewish Studies and Research, 2001), Occasional Paper No. 3.

Carlile Aylmer Macartney, published his magisterial study tracing the history of minority protection from medieval Europe to the modern period, with special emphasis on the nineteenth and twentieth centuries.[8] Several earlier works had provided extensive detail on the minorities question at the Paris Peace Conference.[9] In 1933, Oscar I. Janowsky published his still-valuable Columbia University doctoral dissertation on the role of Jewish nationalists in the drafting of the minority treaties[10]; three years later in Berlin, Kurt Stillschweig augmented the story by analyzing the Jews' participation in the League of Nations system.[11] Except for Janowsky, who had access to unpublished Jewish records, all these authors based their studies on printed sources. During World War II, Jacob Robinson's collection[12] and Pablo de Azcárate's semiofficial account[13] evaluated the interwar system and vainly anticipated its revival.

As the Cold War descended on Eastern Europe, there were a few critical appraisals of the minority treaties and their implementation, most notably by Tennent H. Bagley (1950),[14] Innis L. Claude (1955),[15] and Erwin Viefhaus (1960),[16] but none drew on new or unpublished materials. After the opening of the German diplomatic records came two studies of the Reich's minority policies[17]; and the opening of the League of Nations' archives in the 1970s enabled two critical investigations of its interwar system.[18]

8. C. A. Macartney, *National States and National Minorities* (London: Royal Institute of International Affairs, 1934); 2nd ed. (London: Russell & Russell, 1968).
9. Among them, Jacques Fouques Duparc, *La protection des minorités de race, de langue et de religion: Étude de droit des gens* (Paris: Dalloz, 1922); Dragolioub Krstich, *Les minorités, l'état et la communauté internationale* (Paris: Rousseau, 1924); and Nathan Feinberg, *La question des minorités à la conférence de la paix de 1919–1920* (Paris: Rousseau, 1929).
10. Oscar I. Janowsky, *The Jews and Minority Rights (1898–1919)* (New York: Columbia University Press, 1933).
11. Kurt Stillschweig, *Die Juden Osteuropas in den Minderheitenverträgen* (Berlin: Jastrow, 1936).
12. Jacob Robinson et al., *Were the Minorities Treaties a Failure?* (New York: Institute of Jewish Affairs of the American Jewish Congress and the World Jewish Congress, 1943).
13. Pablo de Azcárate, *League of Nations and National Minorities: An Experiment*, trans. Eileen E. Brooke (Washington: Carnegie Endowment for International Peace, 1945). Azcárate was a former League Minorities Director.
14. Tennent H. Bagley, *General Principles and Problems in the International Protection of Minorities: A Political Study* (Geneva: Imprimeries Populaires, 1950).
15. Innis L. Claude, *National Minorities: An International Problem* (Cambridge: Harvard University Press, 1955).
16. Erwin Viefhaus, *Die Minderheitenfrage und die Entstehung der Minderheitenschutzverträge 1919* (Würzburg: Holzner, 1960).
17. Carole Fink, *The Weimar Republic as the Defender of Minorities, 1919–1933: A Study of Germany's Minorities Diplomacy and the League of Nations System for the International Protection of Minorities* (Ann Arbor, MI: University Microfilms, 1969); Helmut Pieper, *Die Minderheitenfrage und das Deutsche Reich, 1919–1933/34* (Hamburg: Institut für Internationale Angelegenheiten der Universität Hamburg, 1974).
18. Christoph Gütterman, *Das Minderheitenschutzverfahren des Völkerbundes* (Berlin: Duncker und Humblot, 1979); Christian Raitz von Frentz, *A Lesson Forgotten: Minority Protection Under the League of Nations: A Case of the German Minority in Poland, 1920–1934* (New York: St. Martin's, 1999).

In sum, until 1989, the broad subject of international minority protection fell into relative obscurity, leaving many gaps and some myths about this sixty-year period. Since the fall of Communism and the creation of a new order in Eastern Europe, almost every treatise on international minorities protection has reserved at least an introductory chapter to its history, either as a model or a cautionary tale. Based on older works, these chapters and essays lack documentary evidence and rigorous analysis of a complex diplomatic practice before World War II.[19]

Thus this is the first book to examine international minority protection over a long period and in a broad compass. Based on archival research in eleven countries as well as a huge amount of primary and secondary literature, this work recounts the complexity of transnational minority protection, including the political, economic, and social dimensions as well as the human and group dynamics of the problem. It is both a traditional diplomatic history in the form of a narrative and a topical study centered on specific incidents in specific places. It focuses primarily on the Jewish minority question in Eastern Europe within the larger context of the origins and development of international minority protection.

Throughout this book runs the thread of the three main parties, the minority defenders, the Great Powers, and the minority states, interacting before an often-aroused world public opinion. From this struggle, three related themes emerge: the strengths and weaknesses of minority champions, the pretensions and ambivalence of Great-Power statesmen, and the fierce resistance and vulnerability of all the minority states.

As long as concerned voices urge their governments to protect oppressed groups, as long as governments strive to coordinate their humanitarian actions, and as long as their leaders remain cautious over stirring irredentism and destabilizing states and regions, this history of the attempts and failures between 1878 and 1938 may have some usefulness.

Long in the making, this book owes much to many people. First, I should like to acknowledge with gratitude the research support I have received from the American Council of Learned Societies, the American Philosophical Society, the National Endowment for the Humanities, and the German Marshall Fund of the United States as well as the College of Humanities of The Ohio State University (OSU). I should also like to express thanks for the residential fellowships I have been awarded at the Woodrow Wilson International Center for Scholars, the Rutgers Center for Historical Analysis,

19. See, for example, Kristin Henrard, *Devising an Adequate System of Minority Protection* (The Hague: Nijhoff, 2000), pp. 3–8; N. Rouland, S. Pierre-Caps, and J. Poumarède, *Droit des minorités et des peuples autochtones* (Paris: Presses Universitaires de France, 1996), pp. 35–54; P. Thornberry, *International Law and the Rights of Minorities* (Oxford: Oxford University Press, 1991), pp. 25–37.

and the School of Historical Studies of the Institute for Advanced Study in Princeton as well as to Mishkenot Sha'ananim, a residence in Jerusalem for writers and artists, for a memorable three-month stay during the snowy winter of 1992. In addition, I should like to acknowledge the OSU History Department and my two other intellectual homes, the Melton Center for Jewish Studies and the Slavic and East European Studies Center, for their research and travel support, and to single out Chris Burton, Maurea al'Khouri, and Marianne Keisel for many years of genial assistance.

I have appreciated the invitations to discuss the subject of international minority protection before many audiences who provided helpful comments and suggestions. These have included the universities of Copenhagen, Leeds, Tübingen, and Vienna; the Hebrew University in Jerusalem; the International Christian University in Tokyo; the Central European University in Budapest; the University of Cape Town in South Africa; the Center for Historical Analysis of Rutgers University; the Peace Studies Program of Cornell University; the Remarque Institute of New York University; and the Center for German and European Studies at the University of California, Berkeley, as well as the World Congress of Jewish Studies.

Among the joys of historical research is the opportunity to "get one's hands dirty" in the archives. All the specialists I have worked with have been extremely helpful, but let me mention with special thanks Leo Greenbaum of the YIVO Institute of Jewish Research and Lyn Slome at the American Jewish Historical Society, both now housed in the Center for Jewish History in New York; Kevin Proffit at the American Jewish Archive in Cincinnati; Cyma Horowitz at the American Jewish Committee Archive in New York; Bernhardine Pejovic at the League of Nations Archive of the UN Library in Geneva; and Monique Constant, director of the Archive of the French Ministry of Foreign Affairs in Paris as well as the unfailingly helpful staff of the Political Archive of the German Ministry of Foreign Affairs, formerly in Bonn and now in Berlin, the Modern Documents Archive in Warsaw, and the Central Zionist Archive in Jerusalem. In three libraries I received exceptional assistance: OSU, the Institute for Advanced Study in Princeton, and the University of North Carolina at Wilmington (UNCW); let me single out David Lincove and Joseph Galron of the OSU Library and Louise Jackson and Sue Ann Cody at UNCW for special thanks.

Among those who contributed greatly to this book, I start with thanks to Terry Benjey and Andrew Blank, who patiently and expertly guided my work on the computer; Joan Huber, who proofread many of the chapters and gave encouragement throughout; Eve Levin, who read the entire book with an expert eye; Margaret Popovich, who produced the maps with great skill; Edward Kołodziej and Adam Kozuchowski, who provided first-rate research assistance in Warsaw; Sumiko Otsubo, who prepared excellent translations of numerous Japanese documents; Terry Thompson, who long ago assisted my investigations of cultural and national autonomy; Paul Hibbeln and Matthew Romaniello, who helped in the final preparation of the manuscript; La Gretia Copp for her work on the Index; the two anonymous readers who made wise and essential suggestions; Victoria Danahy, who has been a dedicated copy editor; Ken Karpinski and Catherine Felgar, who put all the parts together; and Frank Smith, who represents the highest standard of history editors. I am deeply indebted to John Chambers, Michael Hogan, William Keylor, Jack Matlock, and Melton McLaurin for their long and enthusiastic support of this project and to Fritz Stern and Gerhard Weinberg for many years of unstinting assistance and inspiration.

Thanks also to Hedva Ben Israel, Kathleen Burk, Krystyna Cieliszak, Sandi Cooper, Emily Davidson, Inga Floto, Verdianna Grossi, Hilda and Ralph Godwin, Françoise Pradelet, and Marion Schubert, for their generous hospitality; to Catherine Cline, Harriet Green, Hilda Godwin, Susan Hartmann, Joan Huber, Dorothy Kahn, Joyce Kuhn, Sherrill Martin, Félix and Lilo Messer, Françoise Pradelet, Sophia Radcliffe, Helena Schlam, Goldie Shabad, Marion Schubert, Judith Snider, Joy Totten, Juanita Winner, and Ruth Winter, for marvelous conversations and fine adventures away from the books and the keyboard; to the late Ali Andrusier for the joyous times in Jerusalem; to the late Jarmil Sochor for his indomitable optimism and patience; to Judith Woodall for numerous acts of warmth and friendship; and to my children, Stefan Harold Fink and Jolie Fink Parrish for their wonderful selves.

Finally, to those to whom this book is dedicated, I offer praise for your commitment and achievements and my thanks for the lessons you have imparted.

Columbus, Ohio, August 2003

Abbreviations

The following abbreviations are used in the footnotes. Full details of the works cited below and of other works referred to by abbreviated titles in the footnotes are given in the Bibliography.

AA	Auswärtiges Amt [German Foreign Ministry]
AAN	Poland, Archiwum Akt Nowych [Modern Documents Archive], Warsaw
ADAP	*Akten zur Deutschen Auswärtigen Politik*
Adler, Diary	Cyrus Adler Diary, American Jewish Committee Archives, New York
Adler papers	Cyrus Adler papers, American Jewish Committee Archives, New York
AGND	Records of the Adjutantura Generalna Naczelnego Dowództwa [Polish Supreme Command], Piłsudski Institute of America, New York
AIU	Alliance Israélite Universelle, Paris
AJA	American Jewish Archives, Hebrew Union College, Cincinnati, OH
AJC	American Jewish Committee Archives, New York
ALW	Papers of Leon Wasilewski [Akta Leona Wasilewskiego], Archiwum Akt Nowych, Warsaw
AMZV	Czech Republic [formerly Czechoslovakia], Archiv Ministerstva Zahrančních Večí [Archive of the Foreign Ministry], Prague

ARA	American Relief Administration
ARC	American Red Cross
Baker	R. S. Baker papers, Library of Congress
BDBJ	Board of Deputies of British Jews, London
CAHJP	Central Archives for the History of the Jewish People, Hebrew University, Givat Ram, Jerusalem
Cecil, Diary	Robert Cecil Diary, British Library, London
CDPS/CNS	Conferenza della Pace (1919). Segretario [Peace Conference 1919. Secretariat] Commissione dei nuovi Staati [Committee on New States] Archive. Italian Foreign Ministry, Rome
Council of Four	Arthur S. Link, trans. and ed., *The Deliberations of the Council of Four, Mar. 24–June 28, 1919: Notes of the Official Interpreter Paul Mantoux*
CZA	Central Zionist Archives, Jerusalem
DBFP	*Documents on British Foreign Policy, 1919–1939*
DD/CB	France, Ministère des Affaires Étrangères. *Documents Diplomatiques: Affaires d'Orient: Congrès de Berlin 1878*
DDF	*Documents Diplomatiques Français (1871–1914)*
DDI	*I Documenti Diplomatici Italiani*
DGFP	*Documents on German Foreign Policy*
Dulles	Allen W. Dulles papers, Seeley G. Mudd Manuscript Library, Princeton University
DZA	Deutsches Zentralarchiv [(East) Germany, Central Archive], formerly Potsdam, now incorporated in Bundesarchiv, Berlin
FMAE	France. Ministère des Affaires Étrangères [Ministry of Foreign Affairs]
FRUS PPC	*Foreign Relations of the United States: The Paris Peace Conference*
GB CAB	Great Britain, Cabinet documents, Public Record Office, Kew
GB FO	Great Britain, Foreign Office records, Public Record Office, Kew
Germ. AA	Captured records of the German Foreign Ministry, T-120 on microfilm, U.S. National Archives, College Park, MD

Germ. PA AA	Germany. Politisches Archiv des Auswärtigen Amtes [Political Archive of the Foreign Ministry], formerly in Bonn, now in Berlin
Gibson	Hugh Gibson papers, Hoover Institution on War, Revolution, and Peace, Stanford University, Stanford, CA
HM CC	Sir James Headlam-Morley papers, Churchill College, Cambridge
HM UU Col.	Sir James Headlam-Morley papers, University of Ulster at Coleraine
Headlam-Morley, *Memoir*	Sir James Headlam-Morley, *A Memoir of the Paris Peace Conference 1919*
Hoover	Herbert Hoover Presidential papers, West Branch, IA
House, Diary	Edward M. House, Diary, Yale University
Hudson	Manley O. Hudson papers, Law Library, Harvard University
IMAE	Italy. Ministero degli Affari Esteri [Ministry of Foreign Affairs]
JDC	Joint Distribution Committee; also American Joint Distribution Committee; Archive, New York, NY
JFC	Joint Foreign Committee [of British Jews]
KNP	Komitet Narodowy Polski [Polish National Committee]
LC	Library of Congress, Washington, Manuscript Division
LGP	Lloyd George papers, House of Lords, London
LH	Leland Harrison papers, Library of Congress,
LM	Louis Marshall papers (either American Jewish Archives, Hebrew Union College, Cincinnati, OH, or American Jewish Committee Archives, New York)
LNA	League of Nations, Archives, United Nations Library, Geneva
LNOJ	League of Nations, *Official Journal*
Miller, *Covenant*	David Hunter Miller, *The Drafting of the Covenant*
Miller, *Diary*	David Hunter Miller, *My Diary at the Conference of Paris*

Morgenthau	Henry Morgenthau papers (microfilm), Library of Congress, Washington, DC
MSZ	Poland. Ministerstwo Spraw Zagranicznych [Ministry of Foreign Affairs]
NA	National Archives, College Park, MD
PA-AP	Papiers d'Agents, Archives Politiques, FMAE, Paris
Paderewski	Paderewski papers, AAN
PIA	Piłsudski Institute of America, New York, NY
PRM	Poland, Protocol of the Council of Ministers, AAN, Warsaw
PWW	*The Papers of Woodrow Wilson*, ed. Arthur Link. Other editions specified in notes.
Receuil	France. Ministère des Affaires. Conférence de la Paix, 1919–1920. *Receuil des actes de la conférence*
Schiff	Jacob Schiff papers, American Jewish Archives, Hebrew Union College, Cincinnati, OH
Stephen S. Wise	*Stephen S. Wise: Servant of the People. Selected Letters*
Tardieu	André Tardieu papers, FMAE Paris
USDS	U.S. Department of State Records, National Archives, College Park, MD
W/M	Lucien Wolf–David Mowschowitch papers, Microfilm ed., YIVO Institute for Jewish Research, NY
Warburg	Felix Warburg papers, American Jewish Archives, Hebrew Union College, Cincinnati, OH
White	Henry White papers, Library of Congress
Wise	Stephen S. Wise papers, microfilmed copy American Jewish Historical Society, Center for Jewish History, NY
Wolf, Diary	Lucien Wolf Diary, Mocatta Library, University College, London
WWP	Woodrow Wilson papers, Library of Congress
YIVO	YIVO Institute for Jewish Research, Institute of Jewish History, NY

A Note on Place and Personal Names

Any work covering sixty years of East European history will encounter the difficulty of naming the places concerned. In an attempt to be as consistent as possible I have followed the following practices: (1) Names such as Bucharest, Cracow, Kovno, Prague, Salonika, Vilna, and Warsaw as well as Bessarabia and Galicia are rendered in the standard English spelling; (2) other cities, regions, and rivers are rendered in the name they held at the time; thus Lemberg in 1918, and Pinsk in 1919, but also Poznań for the entire period 1918–39; (3) places still under Turkish sovereignty in the nineteenth century, such as Jassy (Iaşi) are given two names; (4) in cases in which the orthography has changed (Shantung/Shandong), both spellings are initially given; and (5) where there is any possible confusion, for example, Zbrucz (Zbruch) River, both names appear.

In discussing the struggle in Eastern Galicia, I have used the term Ukrainians, although some of the combatants identified themselves as Ruthenians.

I have used the expression Eastern Europe to designate the entire region between the Baltic and Adriatic and Aegean Seas.

I have also made every attempt to make the English spelling of personal names as consistent and recognizable as possible.

CF

PART ONE

From Empires to New States

1

Prologue

The Congress of Berlin

"We can only do a human work, subject like all such work, to the fluctuations of events."

Otto von Bismarck

International minority protection, which reached its apogee after World War I, had nineteenth-century roots. At the Congress of Berlin in 1878, the delegates combined the two principles of territorial readjustments and external control over internal affairs. The Great Powers not only checked tsarist Russia's drive into Southeastern Europe by imposing the old rules of compensation and the balance of power; perceiving the dangers lurking within the new borders they had drawn, the Powers also placed a stiff price on the recognition of four successor states of the Ottoman Empire. The heated debates, the conditions they imposed, and the subsequent results all mark the beginning of a new stage of modern European diplomacy.

CURBING RUSSIAN IMPERIALISM

Tsarist Russia went to war with the Ottoman Empire on April 24, 1877. The immediate cause was the Turks' crushing of the Slavic uprisings in Bosnia and Herzegovina, suppression of the Bulgarian insurrection, and the rout of Serbia and Montenegro. This eighth Russo–Turkish War, extending over almost two centuries, was not only the continuation of Russia's efforts to seize the Straits but also represented a new form of tsarist expansionism. Spurred by the rise of Balkan nationalism, Russia's leaders espoused the pan-Slav and Orthodox mission to liberate the lands and peoples of European

Turkey, with the goal of transforming the land bridge to Constantinople into a region of satellite states.[1]

The nine-month war, which lasted until January 1878, was an unexpectedly evenly matched contest.[2] After the Turks held the fortress of Plevna for five long months against Russia and its reluctant ally Romania,[3] the exhausted tsarist army reached the gates of Constantinople. But failing to achieve a decisive military verdict – a Königgrätz or a Sedan – Russia had neither seized the Straits and Constantinople nor evicted Turkey from Europe.

Russia's newest *Drang nach Suden* also challenged the three Great Powers. Great Britain and France, the nominal protectors of the Ottoman Empire, were determined to deny Russia access to the eastern Mediterranean, whereas Austria–Hungary, with its own large Slav and Orthodox population, was insistent on retaining the status quo in Southeastern Europe.[4] All three were outraged by the Treaty of San Stefano (March 3, 1878), dictated by pan-Slav General Nicholas Ignatiev, which rearranged the map of the Balkans, creating a huge Bulgarian client state that stretched from the Danube to the Aegean and from the Black Sea to Albania and split European Turkey in two.[5] Faced with British threats and keenly aware of Russia's economic and military weakness, Tsar Alexander II retreated from the pan-Slav gambit at San Stefano and submitted to Europe's demands.[6]

Europe's third major congress of the nineteenth century opened in Berlin on June 13, 1878. It lasted only one month because its agenda was limited and almost everything had been prepared in advance. Among the participants were the two exhausted combatants and five fresh bystanders determined to solve the "Eastern Question" – the disintegration of the Ottoman Empire –

1. Full details of works with abbreviated titles are given in Sections 1B and 2 of the Bibliography. The standard study is Sumner, *Russia and the Balkans*; see also Geyer, *Russian Imperialism*, pp. 64–79; Durman, *Time of the Thunderer*, pp. 158–206; Jelavich, *Russia's Balkan Entanglements*, pp. 143–73; MacKenzie, *Tsarist Russian Foreign Policy, 1815–1917*, pp. 68–81; LeDonne, *The Russian Empire*, pp. 137–40, 265–9, 324. A revisionist work by Weeks, "Russia's Decision for War With Turkey," describes a weak, politically divided regime that reluctantly took up arms against an obdurate Ottoman Empire, primarily to salvage its "national honor."
2. Despite the dire state of Ottoman finances, British loans enabled the Porte to purchase armaments from Germany and the United States. Rich, *Great Power Diplomacy*, p. 224.
3. Lying across Russia's most expeditious southward invasion route, the United Principalities (Romania's official name until 1878) tried to limit the damage of tsarist occupation and war with the Turks by characterizing its actions as a struggle for national independence.
4. Haselsteiner, "Zur Haltung der Donaumonarchie," and Dioszegi, "Die Anfänge der Orientpolitik Andrássys."
5. Among the treaty's other terms, Serbia, Montenegro, and Romania were to gain independence, Bosnia and Herzegovina were to become semiautonomous provinces within the Ottoman Empire, and Russia's Romanian ally was to return southern Bessarabia to Russia.
6. Durman, *Time of the Thunderer*, pp. 219–44; Jelavich, *Russian Foreign Policy*, pp. 181–2; Goraíainov, *La question d'Orient*, pp. 229–51.

by a calibrated multinational partition, thus setting the tone for the next Berlin Conference on Africa seven years later.[7]

The results were a triumph of Disraelian firmness and Bismarckian discipline. Reaping the main rewards of its aggression, Russia extended its Black Sea coastline by regaining southern Bessarabia in the West and by annexing Ardahan, Kars, and Batum in the East. As to the Balkans, the congress agreed on full independence for Serbia, Montenegro, and Romania, and autonomy for a greatly reduced Bulgaria. But the other side profited as well. The Ottoman Empire retained Macedonia[8] as well as control over the Straits, through which the British Fleet could pass at will into the Black Sea. Moreover, the Turks' defenders amply rewarded themselves, with Britain taking Cyprus, Austria–Hungary occupying Bosnia–Herzegovina, and France given the green light to occupy Tunisia.

The congress modified the Treaty of San Stefano in another significant way. Whereas Russia's dictated treaty had been silent over minority rights, the Powers were determined to impose conditions regarding religious freedom and civic rights in all the new states.[9] In bringing forth a new political order in the Balkans, the Great Powers added a major new ingredient to the agenda of European diplomacy[10] (see Map 1.1).

THE DANUBIAN PRINCIPALITIES, THE JEWS, AND THE GREAT POWERS

Among the four newly liberated states, Romania was by far the principal object of international concern over the issue of minority rights. The principalities of Wallachia and Moldavia, which formed the strategic triangle separating Russia and the Habsburg monarchy from the mouth of the Danube and the Straits, had over the past generation established the region's most dismal record.

Romania's ethnic and religious problems were shaped by its geography, history, and national culture. Following four centuries of Ottoman rule, the

7. See the critical appraisals by Munro, *The Berlin Congress*, and by Lord, "The Congress of Berlin," pp. 47–69, prepared on the eve of the Paris Peace Conference by a key participant in the Polish Commission of 1919.
8. As distinct from the ancient kingdom of Alexander the Great, this Ottoman province since the fourteenth century was a heavily mixed region of Greeks and Slavs as well as of Christians, Jews, and Muslims, which, after 1878, became a caldron of national rivalries, repression, and terrorism.
9. The accord between Austria–Hungary and England signed on June 6 made this statement: "Les deux Gouvernements se réservent la faculté de proposer au Congrès des mesures tendantes à assurer la protection des populations." Austria. Haus- Hof- und Staats Archiv, Great Britain, VIII, fasc. 170, quoted in Gelber, "German Jews at the Berlin Congress," p. 221.
10. Preconference agreements in Medlicott, *The Congress of Berlin and After*, pp. 4–35; pessimistic verdict in Sumner, *Russia and the Balkans*, p. 565.

Map 1.1. Southeastern Europe after the Congress of Berlin, 1878.

Danubian provinces in 1828 came under Russian control. Over the next four decades, tsarist officials introduced laws and administrative practices that promoted economic modernization but also imposed an exceptionally harsh regime over Romania's sizable Jewish population.[11] During this critical incubation period of local nationalism, the poets and publicists, following the trends of European romanticism, defined "Romanianism" in terms of native virtues (blood, soil, and orthodoxy). These they contrasted with the negative images of pagan Turks, avaricious Hungarians, Austrians, and Russians, predatory Greeks, and, especially, the alien Jews whose numbers had swelled under Ottoman rule to about 10% of the population and almost half the population of the Moldavian capital Jassy (Iaşi).[12] For a brief period in 1848, liberal and patriotic Jews and Romanians joined in the struggle for freedom and a unified country, only to be crushed by tsarist and Ottoman troops.[13]

In 1856, the Romanian question moved to Europe's center stage. Russia, after its humiliating defeat in the Crimean War, was forced to evacuate the Principalities, cede the mouth of the Danube (southern Bessarabia) to Moldavia, and renounce its claim as the protector of Christians in the Ottoman Empire.[14] However, when the victors failed to agree on a new government, the Romanians took matters into their own hands. In 1858 the assemblies in Wallachia and Moldavia established identical regimes and a year later elected a single ruler, Alexander Ion Cuza. Despite the fiction of Ottoman suzerainty and the blandness of the new official name ("The United Principalities"), Romanianism had triumphed. Europe, preoccupied elsewhere, followed France's lead and bowed to this peaceful defiance[15] (see Map 1.2).

But not without reservations. Since 1815, general statements on national rights, religious toleration, and civil equality had become a standard condition in international diplomacy. For example, in the Final Act of the Congress of Vienna, Britain and France had induced a pledge from the three partitioning powers to "preserve the Polish nationality"[16]; in 1830, in return for recognizing Greece's independence, the Powers had mandated freedom

11. Iancu, *Juifs en Roumanie*, pp. 46–50.
12. Volovici, *Nationalist Ideology and Antisemitism*, pp. 4–5.
13. Iancu, *Juifs en Roumanie*, pp. 50–4; Djordjevic and Fischer-Galati, *Balkan Revolutionary Tradition*, pp. 111–12; Cohen, "The Jewish Question," p. 202.
14. Schroeder, *Austria, Great Britain, and the Crimean War*; Curtiss, *Russia's Crimean War*; Baumgart, *The Peace of Paris*.
15. Hitchins, *Rumania*, pp. 6–7; Iancu, "Napoléon III et la politique française."
16. Webster, *British Diplomacy*, pp. 287–8, 290–1, 306–7; Müller, *Quellen zur Geschichte des Wiener Kongresses*, pp. 203–97; Straus, *Attitude of the Congress of Vienna Toward Nationalism*, pp. 123–45.

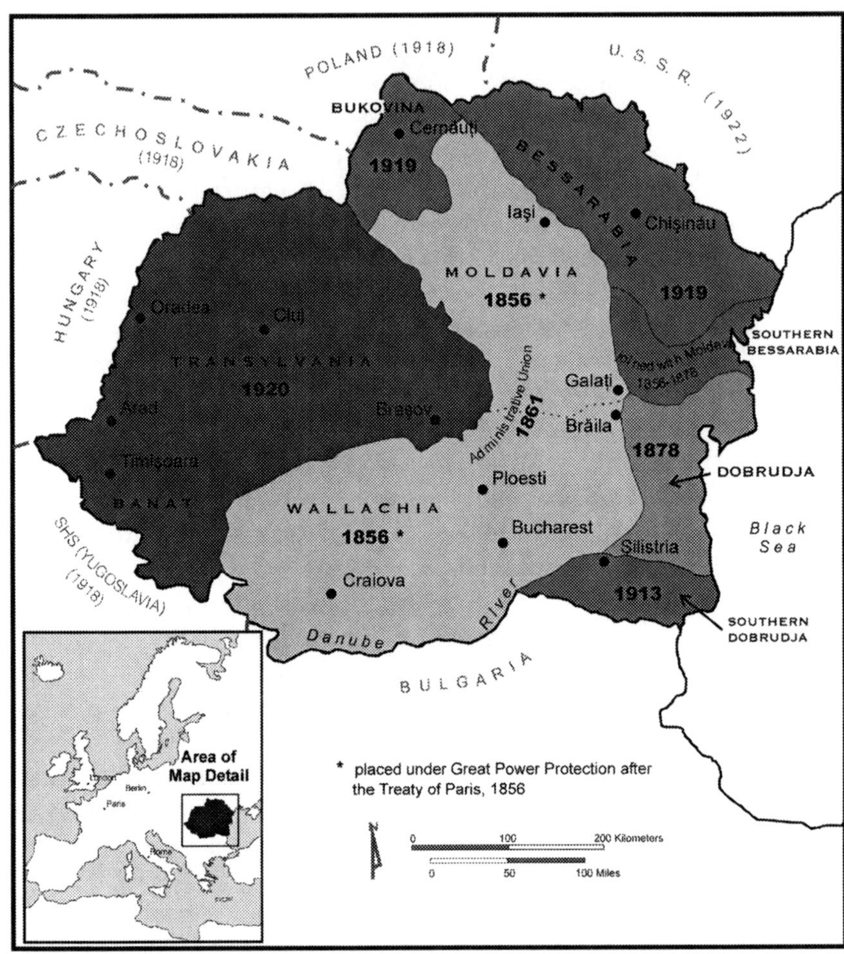

Map 1.2. Evolution of Romania's frontiers, 1856–1920.

for all religions; and in 1856, the Powers bound the Ottoman Empire to respect the rights of non-Muslims.[17]

To be sure, these humane stipulations were largely unenforceable. Not only were powerful states such as Russia and Turkey fiercely resistant to outside interference, but also small states were jealous of their sovereignty.[18] Moreover, even a powerful guarantor, such as Great Britain, was more reluctant to sow disorder than to fight for justice and human rights in

17. Claude, *National Minorities*, pp. 7–8; Macartney, *National States and National Minorities*, pp. 159–60.
18. Pearson, *National Minorities in Eastern Europe*, pp. 130–1.

the East.[19] Thus, against Russia's egregious violations of Polish freedom in 1830 and 1863, there were only sterile diplomatic protests; and when several thousand Maronite Christians were massacred in Lebanon in 1860 and hundreds of rebels slaughtered in Crete in 1866, the western powers were silent. Only the threat of Russian intervention over the "Bulgarian horrors" sent western emissaries scurrying to Constantinople in a futile plea for reforms.[20]

The Jewish question in European diplomacy was an entirely different matter. It too begins at the Congress of Vienna, where German–Jewish notables had sought international support in their vain struggle to maintain the rights they had gained under the French occupation.[21] Instead of state power, Jewish diplomacy relied on the talents, courage, and connections of private individuals who believed in the solidarity of their people. Newly emancipated themselves, and having only recently achieved economic and political success, these West European Jewish intercessors set out to support the rights of their coreligionists in Central, Eastern, and Southern Europe and to persuade their rulers to introduce more liberal regimes. By the mid-nineteenth century, two leaders stood out, the British stockbroker–philanthropist, Sir Moses Montefiore (1784–1885) and the French jurist and statesman, Adolphe-Isaac Crémieux (1796–1880), who had joined forces in 1840 to combat a ritual-murder accusation in the Ottoman Empire.[22] During the Crimean War, the Rothschild bankers in

19. After several candid interviews with Alexander II over the repression in Poland in 1863, during which the tsar parried expressions of public outrage in England and in France with his accusations of the Socialist and Democratic plots against Russia hatched in Britain, British Ambassador Lord Napier gave this advice to Earl Russell: "I prefer what I believe to be the interest of England and Germany to the aspirations of the Polish race . . . The Russian Empire is passing through a great transformation . . . under a respectable Sovereign and an improving administration. A great error, nay a great crime, has been committed in Poland, but we are justified in hoping that it was an exceptional wrong in a general course of justice and conciliation . . . I see in the cessation of the Polish revolt, in the subordination of European interference to moderate aims, and in the maintenance of peace, the best guarantees for the solid progress of representative principles of government in Poland and in Russia." Napier to Russell, St. Petersburg, April 6, 1863, in Bourne and Watt, *British Documents on Foreign Affairs*, Part I, Series A (Russia), p. 36. For the diplomacy of the 1863 Polish crisis, see Taylor, *Struggle for Mastery*, pp. 133–41.

20. Krstitch, *Les minorités*, pp. 172–7, 181–4; also Harris, *Britain and the Bulgarian Horrors*; Pundeff, "Bulgarian Nationalism," especially pp. 118–9.

21. Although the Jewish emissaries gained Prussian, Austrian, and even Russian support for an emancipation article in the constitution of the new German Confederation, the opposition of key German states and the lack of British support produced the empty, unenforceable Article 16. Kohler, *Jewish Rights*; Baron, *Die Judenfrage*; Wolf, *Diplomatic History of the Jewish Question*, pp. 12–15, 17–18.

22. Frankel, *The Damascus Affair*. Montefiore and Crémieux also interceded, unsuccessfully, in the case of Edgardo Mortara of Bologna, who was seized by the Catholic Church in 1858 after an alleged baptism by a servant girl and subsequently became a priest. Kertzer, *Edgardo Mortara*; Iancu, "Adolphe Crémieux et la défense des droits des juifs," pp. 252–4.

Britain and France urged their governments and the Porte to include Jewish rights in the peace treaty.[23]

Romania's clash with the Great Powers began in 1856. On the eve of the Congress of Paris, Austria, Britain, France, and the Ottoman Empire met in Constantinople to draft peace terms with Russia. Without warning, French Ambassador Edouard Thouvenel introduced several clauses pertaining to Moldavia and Wallachia that called not only for equal treatment and protection of all religions, but also for equal access to public employment, equality of civil rights, particularly the right to property in all its forms, for natives *and* foreigners, and equal political rights for all inhabitants not under foreign protection. Although mentioning no specific groups, Napoleon III's emissary had clearly endorsed full Jewish emancipation in Romania.[24]

Hailed by the British and French Jewish press, this proposal created an uproar in the Danubian provinces. The ruling princes of Wallachia and Moldavia bombarded the diplomats in Paris with protests and complained directly to the British and French governments that granting civil, political, and property rights to the Jews would "bring the country to certain ruin." These threats, strongly endorsed by the French and British consuls in Jassy (Iaşi) and Bucharest, struck a sympathetic chord among the Powers, which beat an unceremonious retreat.[25]

Having won the first round, Romania revealed its future course by forbidding the Jews to vote for the two assemblies that decided the country's future. The National Liberals, deserting their 1848 Jewish allies, assumed a strongly anti-Jewish stance in their "practical politics."[26] In Moldavia, with its larger Jewish population, political leaders called for restricting citizenship to Christians, halting Jewish immigration, and even curtailing Jewish religious practices.[27]

Two years later, in response to the merging of the two principalities, the European powers tried again to dictate terms to Romania. Once more it was France, prodded by Baron James de Rothschild, which called for full civil and political rights to all inhabitants without distinction of origin

23. Feldman, "Jewish Emancipation"; on the Rothschilds' importance in the financing of the Crimean War, see Ferguson, *House of Rothschild*, pp. 71–82.
24. Feldman, "Jewish Emancipation," pp. 46–7; texts in Ubicini, *Principautés devant l'Europe*.
25. Article 23 of the Treaty of Paris in 1856 contained only the conventional provision on freedom of religion without specifying equality of civil and political rights. Feldman, "Jewish Emancipation," pp. 48–9; Iancu, *Juifs en Roumanie*, p. 57. Compare Riker, *Roumania*, pp. 22–108.
26. On the growth of Romanian chauvinism, see Emerit, *Victor Place et la politique française en Roumanie*, pp. 80–1; Iancu, *Juifs en Roumanie*, pp. 59–61; Fischer-Galati, "Romanian Nationalism," especially pp. 384–6.
27. Feldman, "Jewish Emancipation," pp. 50–4.

or religion.[28] This time it was tsarist Russia that thwarted the effort by castigating the "moral and social" deficiencies of the Moldavian Jews.[29] In an awkward compromise, Article 46 was inserted into the 1858 Convention of Paris:

> All Moldavians and Wallachians are equal before the law and in matters of taxation, and shall have equal access to public employment in each of the principalities... Moldavians and Wallachians of all Christian faiths shall equally enjoy political rights. The enjoyment of these rights can be extended to other religions by legislative enactment.[30]

Not unexpectedly, Romanians and Jews interpreted this text in opposite ways. Whereas the former denied that any special form of Jewish protection had been granted, the latter insisted that their existence and legal rights were now recognized.[31] To be sure, the seven signatory powers had cloaked their disagreement over Jewish emancipation in ambiguity. After excluding Jewish inhabitants from the category of "Moldavians and Wallachians" entitled to full civil and political rights, in the last sentence they proposed a specific, if unattainable, remedy.[32] For the next two decades, this terribly vague article locked Romanians, Jews, and the Great Powers in a public debate over its meaning.

The reign of Alexander Cuza between 1859 and 1866 brought a brief golden age to the United Principalities. The compromise candidate of the conservative landowners and the more-Nationalist-than-Liberal Forty-Eighters, Cuza quickly alienated his patrons by promoting a series of progressive, modernizing measures.[33] A protégé of Napoleon III, he also

28. On July 16, 1858, the son of Baron James de Rothschild forwarded the petition of seventeen Moldavian Jews to Foreign Minister Count Alexandre Walewski, chair of the Conference of Paris, who offered firm assurances of France's support; Ibid., p. 57; Iancu, *Juifs en Roumanie*, pp. 57–8.
29. Iancu, *Juifs en Roumanie*, p. 58.
30. Text in *British and Foreign State Papers*, Vol. 48, p. 120; minutes, pp. 81–132.
31. Text of petition to the Romanian Chamber of Deputies in 1872, in Kohler and Wolf, *Jewish Disabilities in the Balkan States*, App. I, pp. 98–101. Western Jews went even further, maintaining that the article not only recognized the existence of non-Christians and accorded them civil rights but also constituted an international obligation by the United Principalities; *Allgemeine Zeitung des Judenthums*, Oct. 11, 1858, pp. 571–2.
32. Feldman, "Jewish Emancipation," pp. 58–63.
33. These included fairly sweeping electoral, legal, and agrarian reforms; the expansion of public education and establishment of universities in Bucharest and Jassy (Iaşi) and the nationalization of the estates of the monasteries, which placed a quarter of the country's territory under state control. Fischer-Galati, "Romanian Nationalism," especially pp. 384–5; Hitchins, *Rumania*, pp. 7–10.

    Despite Cuza's reforms, the state and the landowners still held about 66% of the land whereas the peasants only a little over 33%, and usually the poorest properties in marshlands, sandy soil or the steepest terrain. Otetea, *Romanian People*, pp. 388–9.

attracted foreign capital that built up the provinces' railways, harbors, and industries.[34]

Cuza's reign also brought about some minor improvements in the condition of Romanian Jews.[35] The Civil Code of 1864 granted the right of certain categories of Jews to participate in municipal elections[36]; but no progress was made on the issue of citizenship, and restrictions in rural areas mounted.[37] The Cuza era also witnessed an escalation of verbal and physical violence. In April 1859, a ritual-murder charge triggered a bloody pogrom in Galaţi (Galatz), during which the synagogue was destroyed, its torah burned, and numerous Jewish houses sacked. Instead of disciplining the culprits, the authorities arrested eleven Jews who were freed only after the protests of foreign consuls. In 1865, twenty years before Éduard Drumont's notorious book, *La France juive*, A. Kălimănescu published the brochure, *Jidanii în România*,[38] which termed the Jews "corrupt and corruptors," the destroyers of the wealth and soul of Romania; Kălimănescu pleaded with his readers to retrieve their nation's industry, capital, and commerce from the Jews. Another influential anti-Semite, Dionisie Pop Martian, attacked the Jews as "foreigners, exploiters, and usurers."[39]

The seven tumultuous years of Cuza's reign also altered the structure of Romanian Jewry. In 1862, his government dissolved the local Jewish councils that had regulated the community's fiscal and legal affairs without replacing them with an arrangement similar to the French *Consistoires*. The result was to fracture the Jewish community into religious, social, cultural, and ethnic factions, with traditionalists vying against progressives and the more numerous Yiddish-speaking masses of Moldavia contesting their less numerous, more assimilated coreligionists in Wallachia, who aspired to emulate their western counterparts in becoming "Romanians of the Jewish faith."[40]

In February 1866, a coalition of disgruntled radicals and conservatives ousted the reformer. Cuza's French patron, distracted by his embroilments

34. Cameron, *France and the Economic Development of Europe*, pp. 322–4, 498–500; Riker, *Roumania*, p. 436.
35. At the beginning of 1864, the prince assured a Jewish delegation, "I would give you everything but I cannot," while promising to work for "gradual emancipation." Segel, *Rumänen und seine Juden*, p. 38.
36. These included individuals who had performed military service and obtained the rank of junior officer, graduated from a Romanian college or university, received a certificate or doctoral degree from a foreign university, or founded a factory or manufacturing plant useful to the state and employing at least fifty workers.
37. Iancu, *Juifs en Roumanie*, pp. 59–60.
38. *Jidan* was a pejorative expression comparable to *Yid*.
39. Iancu, *Juifs en Roumanie*, pp. 60–1, 281–2.
40. *Monitorul Oficial*, Dec. 7, 1864, quoted in Iancu, *Juifs en Roumanie*, p. 62.

in Mexico, Italy, and Germany, acquiesced in the coup and in the election of a foreign ruler. The chosen candidate was the shrewd and ambitious twenty-seven-year-old Prince Charles of Hohenzollern-Sigmaringen, who not only drew the Principalities into the Prussian orbit but also onto the local and European stage.[41]

Charles' arrival in the Principalities, which coincided with the convocation of a constitutional convention, stirred a momentary hope among Romania's Jews that emancipation was at hand. In June 1866, the aged Crémieux journeyed to Bucharest to plead with the legislators and the prince.[42] The response was an immediate eruption of "spontaneous" anti-Jewish demonstrations, which included attacks on the new Bucharest synagogue and a virulent press campaign against "selling Romania to the Jews" that fueled legislative opposition to the modest measures proposed by Prince Charles. Ion C. Brătianu (1821–91), the former Forty-Eighter who had become Romania's most powerful nationalist politician, inaugurated the era of official anti-Semitism. The Jews, according to Brătianu's passionate speech to the chamber, were a "wound" and a "plague" to Romania not because of their low level of civilization,[43] but because their huge numbers created social disorder; Romania's salvation lay in discriminatory legislation.[44] The appeals by Romanian Jews to the Protector Powers, who were absorbed in the Austro–Prussian war, were of no avail. The notorious Article 7 in the Romanian Constitution of 1866 not only excluded foreign Jews from ever becoming citizens but also worsened the status of indigenous Jews by reducing their civil liberties and civil protection.[45]

Worse was to come. In September 1866, the Romanian government revived the clause in the tsarist Organic Statute providing for the expulsion of native *and* foreign Jews on the grounds of "vagabondage." The ensuing wave of roundups and deportations in the towns and countryside created an

41. Chiriță, "România și Conferința de la Paris"; older works include Djordjevic and Fischer-Galati, *Balkan Revolutionary Tradition*, p. 140; Otetea, *Romanian People*, p. 390; Taylor, *Struggle for Mastery*, p. 160; Henry, *L'abdication du Prince Cuza*.

 The assemblies' first choice in the spring of 1866 had been Count Philip of Flanders, the brother of the king of Belgium, who declined the offer. Charles, who was distantly related to Napoleon III, was the second son of Charles Antony of Hohenzollern-Sigmaringen, the head of the southern German and Catholic branch of the ruling house of Prussia who had entered its service. A Catholic with a Protestant wife, Charles, whose election was almost unanimously ratified in a national plebiscite, agreed to bring his children up in the Orthodox faith. Kremnitz, *Aus dem Leben König Karls von Rumänien*, Vol. 1, pp. 3–100.

42. Crémieux, reminding his interlocutors that in 1848, as a minister in a provisional government, he had drafted the legislation freeing the black peoples in the French empire, urged generosity at this significant moment for Romania. Posener, *Adolphe Crémieux*, p. 186.

43. Brătianu reminded the legislators that the gypsies were to be granted citizens' rights.

44. *Monitorul Oficial*, June 20, 1866, quoted in Iancu, *Juifs en Roumanie*, p. 68.

45. Welter, *Judenpolitik der rumänischen Regierung*, pp. 17–46.

uproar among French and British Jews who demanded Brătianu's resignation and the restoration of basic civil rights. Backed by the British and French governments, the eighty-three-year-old Montefiore journeyed to Bucharest in August 1867, only to receive empty assurances from Prince Charles and criticisms from the local reactionary press for his attempt to create a "new Palestine" in Romania.[46]

For the next decade, the Jews of Romania became targets of a "cold pogrom" of systematic exclusion by laws, edicts, and restrictions as well as of disenfranchisement and threats of expulsion. Under the aegis of Mihail Kogălniceanu, another Forty-Eighter who had once helped draft the emancipation edict in Moldavia, circulars were drafted to "purge" the villages of Jews. Prohibited from residing permanently in the countryside, Jews could not own farms, vineyards, houses, or taverns; the bankrupt rural families who poured into the towns were arrested for spreading crime and infection. No better off were the urban Jews, who were restricted in their rights to own homes and movable property, barred from pleading in the courts, and prevented from becoming professors, lawyers, pharmacists, state doctors, and railroad employees. Although subject to military service, Jews could not become officers.[47]

After 1866, the exclusive mission of Romanianism gave precedence to state creation over economic and social reform, thus sacrificing the peasants as well as the Jews. Anti-Semitism offered an easy excuse for the principalities' poverty, corruption, and despotism. Under the slogan "Romania for the Romanians," Romanian nationalism became synonymous with a virulent anti-Semitism based on ancient religious prejudice and contemporary economic competition, political power struggles, and xenophobia.[48]

To the outside world, Romania became the prime exemplar of Balkan despotism and violence. Its actions not only defied the norms of tolerance and enlightenment that were being established in Western and Central Europe[49]; they represented as brutal a regime as in the dark days of Nicholas I of Russia.

Yet despite its German prince, Latin heritage, and Francophile tendencies,[50] Romania was an essentially small, undeveloped Balkan country located in a remote, but strategic corner of Southeastern Europe. Still under

46. Kremnitz, *Aus dem Leben König Karls von Rumänien*, Vol. 1, p. 201; Iancu, *Juifs en Roumanie*, pp. 69–85.
47. Welter, *Judenpolitik der rumänischen Regierung*, pp. 46–64; Iancu, *Juifs en Roumanie*, Chap. 5.
48. Iancu, *Juifs en Roumanie*, pp. 119–34; Fischer-Galati, "Romanian Nationalism," especially pp. 385–6; also Chirot, *The Creation of a Balkan Colony*; Iancu, "Races et nationalités en Roumanie," especially pp. 405–7.
49. Hobsbawm, *Age of Empire*, p. 87; Stern, *Gold and Iron*, p. 355.
50. By the 1870s Bucharest referred to itself as the "Paris of the Balkans."

multilateral control and nominal Turkish sovereignty, its leaders waited impatiently for full independence, which could be granted only by the Great Powers. Nevertheless, in the decade of Romania's informal entry into the European arena, a distinctive diplomatic pattern of interventionism and defiance had developed.

"A TEST CASE FOR JEWISH POWER"

In 1860, the *Alliance Israélite Universelle* (*Alliance*, or AIU) was founded to provide an international defender for the beleaguered eastern Jews, and Romania was its prime concern.[51] Crémieux, the *Alliance*'s first president, assembled copious evidence of discrimination and violence, confirmed by foreign emissaries, and implored the signators of the Paris Convention to protest.[52] In a letter on August 3, 1867, to Prince Charles' private secretary, the French jurist Émile Picot, Crémieux vented his outrage and frustration, giving this warning:

> Romania is a recent creation.... [There is] much to be done in this new country, above all measures of conciliation not acts of violence and hatred.... If there is no immediate solution to this brigandage against the Jews we shall have to expose this entire affair to all of Europe and to all the civilized nations; we will demand an active intervention, which will not be refused.[53]

Romania became "a test case for Jewish power" just as a radical transformation was occurring within the international Jewish community. Following Prussia's victory over France in 1871, the *Alliance* ceased to be the exclusive spokesman of Jewish diplomacy, which was now dispersed among individuals and organizations in London, Vienna, Berlin, Frankfurt, Rome, Brussels, Amsterdam, New York, Boston, and Philadelphia, as well as in Paris. This burgeoning Jewish leadership, animated by the liberal values of the era between 1789 and 1871, insisted that universal Jewish emancipation was just, practical, and inevitable.[54]

Special committees for Romanian Jewry sprang up, with the main one in Berlin. On the initiative of German–Jewish leaders, an international congress was convened in Brussels in October 1872 to coordinate their efforts. Thirty deputies from eight countries[55] dedicated themselves to the goal of achieving

51. Szajkowski, "Jewish Diplomacy."
52. Iancu, "Races et nationalités en Roumanie," p. 398.
53. Quoted in Iancu, *Juifs en Roumanie*, p. 77. The occasion for this protest was the murder of a Jewish prisoner in Galaţi on the pretext of his attempt to flee. See also Iancu, "Adolphe Crémieux, l'Alliance Israélite Universelle et les juifs de Roumanie."
54. Stern, *Gold and Iron*, p. 369.
55. Austria, Belgium, Britain, France, Germany, the Netherlands, Romania, and the United States.

"by all legal means, civil and political equality" for their coreligionists in Romania. Their three-part program consisted of direct political action by Romanian Jews (petitioning Parliament for rights); humanitarian aid and melioration efforts from outside to combat the backwardness of Romanian Jewry through education and "moral improvement"; and the acceleration and coordination of their lobbying efforts with their governments and with Bucharest.[56] This first "Jewish summit" in modern times provided as much a grist for Romanian and other European anti-Semites as a demonstration of Jewish power and Jewish influence.[57]

Another "solution" came from an unexpected source. The United States, which was neither party to the various treaties nor a major trading partner with Romania, had been a bystander until 1870. But following a direct appeal by Jewish leaders, President Ulysses S. Grant dispatched an unpaid Jewish consul, subsidized by the American–Jewish community, to do "missionary" work among his oppressed coreligionists in Romania. The emissary, Benjamin Peixotto, a thirty-six-year-old Jewish lawyer of Sephardic background from Cleveland and an activist in Jewish affairs, became imbued with the mission of emancipating Romanian Jews.[58]

Immediately after his arrival in Bucharest in February 1871, Peixotto dedicated himself to improving the condition of Romanian Jewry. Despite cautions from the State Department, huge expenses, and the attacks of the anti-Semitic press, the novice diplomat plunged into local and national affairs. In the winter of 1872, it was Peixotto who sparked the protests by foreign emissaries and foreign Jewish organizations over the riots in Ismail and Cahul and the wrongful sentencing of several Jews.[59] An advocate of "self-defense," Peixotto preached the virtues of Jewish dignity and Jewish solidarity. His most notorious deed occurred in August 1872, when he impulsively sounded out the Romanian government on a proposal by American benefactors to facilitate the emigration of Romanian Jews to America. The Romanian Council of State gave a clever, noncommittal response and offered free passports. The Jews of Romania and abroad were shocked by Peixotto's initiative, which was roundly condemned by the Brussels Conference in October.[60]

56. Iancu, *Bleichröder et Crémieux*, pp. 28–9.

57. Stern, *Gold and Iron*, pp. 370–1.

58. Gartner, "Consul Peixotto"; Iancu, "Benjamin Franklin Peixotto"; also Quinlan, "Early American Relations with Romania"; Funderburk, "United States Policy Toward Romania," especially pp. 309–11.

59. Both Ismail and Cahul were in southern Bessarabia, ceded by Russia and joined with Moldavia in 1856.

60. Gartner, "Consul Peixotto," pp. 79–92; Iancu, *Juifs en Roumanie*, pp. 109–11, 115.

Population removal was not a new idea. Throughout the Middle Ages, Europe's Christian kingdoms had expelled the Jews; and in the seventeenth century, Louis XIV had forced the Huguenots to leave France. In the nineteenth century, it was the nation-state that turned an unfriendly eye on seemingly "unassimilable" religious and ethnic groups that stood in the path of political and economic progress. The United States, for example, not only initiated the forced removal of its indigenous peoples but periodically contemplated the possibility of returning black Americans to Africa. In Europe, government officials on the one hand and philanthropists, businessmen, and religious leaders on the other devised colonization schemes to remove dissident religious groups or to rescue the oppressed by filling the distant, "empty" lands of Russia and Palestine.[61]

Peixotto's endorsement of large-scale emigration to America created a crisis in the Jewish world. By ignoring the problems of logistics and expense, his rash initiative led to confusion and disappointment among potential immigrants. It also delivered a precious propaganda weapon to the Romanian anti-Semitic press, which rejoiced in the Jews' dilemma and the inevitable benefits to the homeland: By leaving for foreign shores, the Jews would free the land of their scourge; and by remaining they offered a public denial that they were being persecuted.[62] But the most damaging aspect of Peixotto's scheme was its blow to the *Alliance*'s long struggle for political and civil equality in Romania and Eastern Europe. Indeed, the prospect of uncontrolled hordes of impoverished, unassimilable immigrants struck as sensitive a nerve among western Jews as among non-Jews.[63]

The European governments, which had midwifed the United Principalities' birth and remained Romania's legal guardians, continued to monitor its internal turmoil. Their consuls were far more active in Romania than in other parts of the Ottoman Empire as observers, critics, mentors, and

61. See Staudenraus, *African Colonization Movement*, and Fredrickson, *Black Image in the White Mind*, pp. 1–42. On Russia, see Breyfogle, *Heretics and Colonizers*, Chap. 1; on Palestine, see Nawratzki, *Jüdische Kolonisation Palästinas* especially pp. 110–20; also, Ferguson, *House of Rothschild*, pp. 278–80.

62. "The American initiative places the Jewish invaders of Romania . . . before a dilemma which is most favorable for Romania: if the Jews emigrate in sufficient numbers to relieve the country of hundreds of thousands of parasites who live off the work of the Romanians, the country will be saved from its greatest scourge; if they do not emigrate, which, unfortunately, is quite probable, they will thus prove to the world that they are not so unhappy and persecuted here and prefer to remain instead of departing, even at our expense, to America rich and egalitarian par excellence". *Românul*, Aug. 7–8, 1872, reprinted in Iancu, *Juifs en Roumanie*, pp. 296–8.

63. Until the end of the nineteenth century, western Jewry opposed anything but a "controlled movement of selected, vocationally trained young men." Gartner, "Consul Peixotto," pp. 93–4; also Gartner, *Jewish Immigrant in England*, pp. 40–56; Szajkowski, "Attitude of American Jews to East European Immigration." Peixotto left Romania on June 18, 1876, on the eve of the next Balkan crisis. Burks, "Romania and the Balkan Crisis."

spies as well as the official spokesmen of their governments.[64] But given the three predatory empires on Romania's borders, these foreign emissaries were often more favorable to the majority than to the threatened Jews. For example, Britain's emissary suspected that Russia had instigated the Ismail–Cahul riots in order to undermine the remnants of Ottoman rule in the Balkans.[65]

Not surprisingly, the guarantor powers took no joint initiatives in Romanian affairs. In 1872, deputies in several West European parliaments protested the incidents in Ismail and Cahul; but their governments simply followed the American lead. When Romania passed laws barring Jews from selling tobacco (1872) and spirits (1873), Britain's efforts to organize a collective démarche were undermined by Russia's categorical refusal; and Romania rejected any incursion in its "internal affairs."[66]

The rift among the Powers was widened further in 1875 when Austria–Hungary became the first government to sign a commercial treaty with Romania. This agreement included a clause relegating the Dual Monarchy's Jewish citizens to the same "special" abject status as Romanian Jews in regard to their personal, legal, and property rights. Responding to protests in the Austrian and Hungarian parliaments, the government justified its capitulation on the purely pragmatic grounds that extending Habsburg influence in the Balkans was more important than a futile fight over Jewish rights. From the Romanian perspective, this treaty brought more than economic benefits; Vienna's recognition of its internal regime shattered the facade of the High Contracting Parties. Soon after, Russia readily signed a trade agreement with the same restrictions, although France, Britain, Italy, and Germany held back as a means of keeping pressure on Bucharest.[67]

During the next two years there was a new wave of riots and expulsions in the two principalities and new restrictions against the Jews.[68] In 1876, at a second international meeting in Brussels of sixty-five Jewish leaders from nine countries, there was another futile appeal to Romania's guarantors.[69] But the Bucharest government retained a free hand in its domestic affairs not only because of the Powers' disaccord but because

64. Riker, *Roumania*, pp. 289, 343.

65. Gartner, "Consul Peixotto," pp. 68–9.

66. Loëb, *Israélites en Turquie, en Serbie et en Roumanie*, pp. 439–42.

67. Details in Iancu, *Bleichröder et Crémieux*, pp. 40–7.

68. "The Jews in Roumania," *The New York Times*, Jan. 16, 1876; also June 23, 1877, which on the same page reported the "Hilton–Seligman" controversy over the refusal of a Saratoga Springs, NY, hotel to admit a prominent Jewish banker.

69. At that moment the seven powers were assembled in Constantinople, summoned by Britain to press reforms on the Ottoman Empire and to avert another Russo–Turkish War, both of which they failed to do. Rich, *Great Power Diplomacy*, pp. 222–3.

none held the principle of Jewish rights ahead of its political and economic interests.[70]

The outbreak of the Russo–Turkish War provided the occasion for Romania's long-awaited declaration of independence on May 10, 1877. Opposed by the Great Powers, which refused to guarantee Romania's neutrality, the declaration came with the heavy price of another Russian occupation.[71] Romania's "war of liberation" was greeted with popular enthusiasm. Among its 58,000-strong army were almost 900 Jews, conscripted under the law of 1876, who won numerous decorations for bravery in combat; in addition, many Jewish civilians supported the war effort in the hope of a dramatic change in their status.[72] After six months of heavy fighting, casualties, and matériel losses, Romania's struggle ended abruptly with the Russo–Turkish Armistice of January 31, 1878.[73] As a nonsovereign belligerent, Romania was neither invited to attend the peace negotiations nor asked to sign the Treaty of San Stefano.[74]

Even before the firing stopped, western Jewish leaders began preparing a campaign for the emancipation of the Jews of Romania.[75] This was their last chance to lobby the Great Powers before Romania and the other Balkan states gained international recognition. The various national organizations consulted among themselves, coordinated their programs, and consulted their governments. The three-part strategy established in Brussels in 1872 was refocused and concentrated in the diplomatic realm.[76]

A new and powerful figure emerged in international Jewish diplomacy, Gerson von Bleichröder (1822–93), who was Bismarck's banker and confidant and had been an avid defender of his coreligionists since the persecutions began in 1866 in Romania. In 1871, the Iron Chancellor had charged Bleichröder with the task of salvaging the fortunes of highly placed Prussians who had invested in the defunct Romanian railroad-building scheme of a converted Jewish entrepreneur, Bethel Henry Strousberg.[77] Bismarck, who loathed the Romanians and considered their German prince one more pawn

70. Iancu, *Juifs en Roumanie*, pp. 104–6, 116–17.

71. Burks, "Romania and the Balkan Crisis," p. 129.

72. Iancu, *Bleichröder et Crémieux*, p. 31, details the Jews' contributions.

73. Otetea, *Romanian People*, pp. 408–12.

74. Iancu, *Juifs en Roumanie*, p. 154.

75. See *Jewish Chronicle* [London], Jan. 4, 1878: "As soon as peace negotiations begin, we must be ready to urge on the Powers concerning the claims of the Jews in the Danubian Principalities."

76. Iancu, *Bleichröder et Crémieux*, pp. 37–40; Gelber, "German Jews at the Berlin Congress," especially pp. 228–31.

77. The Strousberg consortium, formed in 1868 to build 942 kilometers of track linking the entire country from north to south, was personally approved by Prince Charles and also by Bismarck, as a means of replacing the French influence of the Cuza regime as well as bypassing Austria's monopoly over navigation on the Danube; Iancu, *Bleichröder et Crémieux*, pp. 72–3.

Photograph 1.1. Adolphe Crémieux (from *Adolphe Crémieux: A Biography* [1941]; reprinted with the permission of the Jewish Publication Society).

on his diplomatic checkerboard, had failed in his efforts to bully Charles and his government. Within a year Bleichröder devised a German successor company linked to a reputable Austrian railway builder and mobilized international pressure on Romania to accept the new arrangement.[78]

Almost immediately after receiving his patent of nobility in March 1872, Bleichröder intensified his lobbying of Bismarck on behalf of Romanian Jews along with his discreet contacts with Jewish leaders at home and abroad.[79] Bleichröder's prestige enhanced the visibility and confidence of Germany's newly emancipated German Jews. His first major success occurred in 1876 when the Reichstag postponed a German–Romanian trade treaty, which would have imposed the same restrictions on German as on Habsburg Jews.[80]

On the eve of the Congress of Berlin, Bleichröder suddenly came into the limelight of European international politics. Before him were two great

78. Details in Iancu, *Bleichröder et Crémieux*, pp. 74–6.
79. Stern, *Gold and Iron*, pp. 355–71; Iancu, *Bleichröder et Crémieux*, pp. 34–7.
80. Gelber, "German Jews at the Berlin Congress," especially pp. 225–7. A key opposition figure was Bleichröder's friend, Liberal leader Eduard Lasker.

Photograph 1.2. Gerson von Bleichröder (photograph of the 1888 painting of Bleichröder by Emile Wanters; reproduced with the permission of Arnhold and S. Bleichroeder Advisers, New York).

challenges: to lead the campaign for Jewish emancipation in Romania and to force Romania to rescue Reich stockholders by agreeing to take over the bankrupt railways and by assuming their debts.[81]

On his first assignment, Bleichröder and the Berlin Romania Committee mobilized the Jewish world. The Jewish communities of Germany, Britain, Austria–Hungary, and Italy as well as of Switzerland and The Netherlands petitioned their governments on behalf of Romanian Jewry and received warm expressions of support. Jewish leaders also encouraged parliamentary deputies in Italy, Germany, Britain, Austria–Hungary, and France to elicit positive statements from their governments.[82]

But there was also disagreement over Bleichröder's strategy. Crémieux, on behalf of the *Alliance*, prudently advised that the local Jewish communities

81. Stern, *Gold and Iron*, pp. 369–71. In a letter to Bismarck at the end of December 1877 Bleichröder made this plea: "For twenty-two years I have served your Excellency faithfully without seeking any compensation. Now the time has arrived for my reward and it is equal rights for the Romanian Jews." Quoted in Gelber, "German Jews at the Berlin Congress," p. 229, n. 16, but not in Stern.

82. Details in Iancu, *Bleichröder et Crémieux*, pp. 48–9; see, e.g., Waddington's statement in *Journal des Débats*, June 7, 1878.

negotiate directly with Serbia and Romania before pressing their case with the Great Powers, but Bleichröder hotly refused.[83] In Romania, the Jews were now deeply divided between the impoverished Moldavian masses in the towns and countryside who appealed for outside support and the less numerous, more prosperous inhabitants of Bucharest and the rest of Wallachia who strongly opposed foreign interference in "their" government's internal affairs.[84] Indeed, some German Jews voiced their fears of the consequences for themselves as well as for Romanian Jewry of forcing Bismarck to coerce Romania.[85]

In his capacity of chief railways negotiator, Bleichröder met in April 1878 with Ion Brătianu, who was on a diplomatic tour of the major capitals, but he made little headway with the Romanian prime minister. Indeed, it was widely suspected that Romania, if forced by Bismarck's "Jewish financiers" to buy the railroads, intended to purchase them as cheaply as possible and immediately offer them to Russia or to Austria.[86] As expected, Brătianu rebuffed Bleichröder's remarks about "Europe's interest" in the emancipation of the Jews, warning that, once enfranchised, these "immense hordes would be a permanent danger" to the Romanian people.[87]

On May 14, 1878, Bleichröder and his colleagues celebrated another triumph when the Reichstag again rebuffed a German–Romanian trade treaty.[88] Under Bleichröder's steady direction and with his patron's apparent support, the Bismarckian Reich had formed an alliance, if only temporary, between Jewish and German interests. And Germany had suddenly moved to the forefront of an international démarche on behalf of Romanian Jewry.[89]

ARTICLE 44

The other Great Powers at the Congress of Berlin regarded the Jewish question in Romania as a marginal but unavoidable issue. France, Romania's former imperial patron, was now under a shaky parliamentary regime, which

83. Crémieux to Bleichröder, Feb. 19, 1878, Bleichröder to Crémieux, Feb. 21, 1878, quoted in Iancu, *Bleichröder et Crémieux*, pp. 133–5.
84. See Isidore Loëb, for the Central Committee of the *Alliance Israélite Universelle* (hereafter AIU), to Adolph Weinberg, President of the Zion Association of Bucharest, Paris, Mar. 19, 1878, in Iancu, *Bleichröder et Crémieux*, pp. 140–1.
85. *Allgemeine Zeitung des Judenthums*, Mar. 8, 1878, quoted in Stern, *Gold and Iron*, p. 375.
86. W. E. Medlicott, "Roumanian Independence," especially pp. 574–5. Bleichröder's partner, Adolph von Hansemann, was incorrectly believed to be Jewish.
87. Bleichröder to Crémieux, Apr. 12, 1878, in Iancu, *Bleichröder et Crémieux*, pp. 146–7.
88. Bleichröder to Central Committee (Lehmann), AIU, May 19, 1878; Central Committee (Loëb) to Bleichröder, May 20, 1878; Bleichröder to Crémieux, May 23, 1878, in Iancu, *Bleichröder et Crémieux*, pp. 151–3, 155–6.
89. See Corti to Cairoli, Berlin, June 22, 1878, *I Documenti Diplomatici Italiani* (hereafter *DDI*), Ser. 2a, Vol. 10, pp. 190–1; Stern, *Gold and Iron*, pp. 371–2, 375–7.

had only recently survived a royalist coup. Eclipsed by Germany in 1871, the Third Republic had lost its enthusiasm for supporting European nationalist movements and aimed instead at pursuing an imperial mission overseas, for which it needed Bismarck's support. Although the Quai d'Orsay maintained its close ties with the AIU[90] and refused to sign a commercial treaty with Romania, it also dutifully followed the Iron Chancellor's lead in Eastern Europe.[91]

The new Italian kingdom, with its anti-Habsburg, anti-Russian biases and shared Latin heritage, considered itself the natural ally and mentor of Romania. Nonetheless, "mother Rome," with numerous assimilated Jews in its legislature, diplomatic corps, press, and commerce, could not sanction Bucharest's exclusionary policies. On the eve of the Congress of Berlin, an Italian–Romanian commercial treaty, which had been laboriously negotiated over three years, was withdrawn from parliamentary consideration because of strong internal and external pressures.[92] For the time being, Italy too would line up behind Bismarck.[93]

Britain and Austria–Hungary were cautious actors in regard to Romania. Both suspected Bismarck's sudden zeal to police Romania's internal affairs, fearing that it might force the Bucharest government into a greater dependency on Russia. Thus the two joined France in overriding Russia's objections, enabling Romania to send an emissary to the Berlin Congress, not as a member but only as a supplicant.[94]

Against huge odds and without any reliable allies, Romania carefully prepared its diplomatic debut.[95] The price of independence was expected to be the loss of southern Bessarabia and the imposition of new forms of

90. For examples, see Crémieux to Saint-Vallier (French ambassador in Berlin), Mar. 24, 1878, Saint-Vallier to Crémieux, Mar. 27, 1878, Crémieux to Saint-Vallier, Apr. 16, 1878, Crémieux to Waddington, June 30, 1878, in Iancu, *Bleichröder et Crémieux*, pp. 141–2, 142–3, 148, 158–9.

91. See Saint-Vallier to Waddington, Apr. 15, 1878, *Documents Diplomatiques Français* (hereafter *DDF*), 1re Sér., Vol. 2, p. 297; Dufaure to Waddington, June 16, 24, July 4, 1878, Waddington to Dufaure, June 10, 16, 27, July 9, 12, 1978, Comte de Voguë to Waddington, June 8, July 6, 1878, France, Ministère des Affaires Étrangères (hereafter FMAE), Papiers d'Agents (hereafter PA-AP), Waddington 176. In general, Waddington renounced the unsure advantages of siding with Russia at the Congress of Berlin for the benefits of joining the Anglo–German–Austrian coalition; and Bismarck, on his part, cast Waddington as the conference's "chief mediator." Taylor, *Struggle for Mastery*, p. 253, n. 2.

92. See Loëb to Armand Levy (Rome), Paris, Mar. 31, 1878; Crémieux to Italian Prime Minister Benedict Cairolli, Paris, Apr. 8, 1878, texts in Iancu, *Bleichröder et Crémieux*, pp. 143–5; also *L'Opinione*, May 6, 1878: "Following numerous protests throughout the Kingdom, the President of the Council of Ministers has announced that the treaty with Romania will not be presented to parliament until the deplorable gaps are filled which assure the equality of treatment for all Italians in Romania without distinction of religion."

93. Corti, "Bismarck und Italien."

94. Hitchins, *Rumania*, p. 49.

95. On Brătianu's unsuccessful visits to Vienna and Berlin to press Romania's claims, see Vogüé to Waddington, Vienna, Apr. 13, 1878, Saint-Vallier to Waddington, Berlin, Apr. 15, 1878, *DDF*, 1re Sér., Vol. 2, pp. 295–7.

foreign control. Foreign Minister Mihail Kogălniceanu, author of the expulsion measures against the Jews a decade earlier, drafted an ambitious memorandum for the Congress of Berlin, naively claiming, among other things, a share in any Ottoman indemnity, an international guarantee of Romanian neutrality, and full independence and full national integrity. Romania's case was undermined not only by Russia's overwhelming might but also by its own dismal record of persecution, which only Russia could endorse.[96] The two Romanian delegates, who arrived on June 13, the opening date of the congress, cooled their heels for two and a half weeks while the Great Powers bickered over the removal of Bulgaria and Bosnia from the Ottoman Empire.

In the halls and corridors of Berlin there was an assemblage of European Jews who, recalling their disappointment in 1856, hand-carried their petitions and met personally with the delegates.[97] In the absence of the aged, ailing Crémieux, Bleichröder and the Berlin Romania Committee were in charge. Bleichröder's office became the headquarters for the Jewish delegations, and his privileged relationship to Bismarck gave him special access to the other statesmen.[98] The Jews of Romania sent two groups, with the larger, from Moldavia, urging internationally guaranteed rights and freedom, the smaller, from Wallachia, opposing any diplomatic action.[99]

Under Bismarck's firm direction, the question of Jewish rights was handled deftly, in stages, at the Congress of Berlin. Once the partition of Bulgaria was settled, France on June 24 proposed an article granting complete freedom of religion and equality of rights to all inhabitants of this new, autonomous principality.[100] Bismarck's clever piecemeal strategy was applied

96. Romania's special relationship to Russia is discussed in Oldson, *Providential Anti-Semitism*, pp. 29–30.

97. See "Mémoire de l'Alliance Israélite Universelle adressé au Congrès de Berlin (9 juin 1878)" and "Appel du Comité Roumain de Berlin adressé au Congrès à la veille de la discussion de la question roumaine (1 juillet 1878)" in Iancu, *Bleichröder et Crémieux*, pp. 235–41.

98. Stern, *Gold and Iron*, p. 377; more details in Iancu, *Bleichröder et Crémieux*, pp. 49–54 and Gelber, "German Jews at the Berlin Congress," pp. 233–41.

99. Gelber, "German Jews at the Berlin Congress," pp. 234–5.

100. Protocol No. 5, June 24, 1878, in *Documents Diplomatiques: Affaires d'Orient: Congrès de Berlin 1878* (hereafter *DD/CB*), p. 98. Waddington also introduced a second article pertaining to the protection of foreign Catholics in Bulgaria *and* Eastern Rumelia that, because of Turkish objections, he withdrew a day later. The Congress of Berlin contented itself with accepting the statement of Carathéodory Pacha that complete religious freedom existed throughout the Ottoman Empire, including Eastern Rumelia. Ibid., Protocol No. 7, pp. 124–5.

Host Bismarck – as a convenience and a courtesy – had assigned the role of introducing the minority clauses to France's inexperienced foreign minister, who otherwise occupied a minor role at the conference. This unwelcome assignment produced an ironic outcome; the Third Republic, although far less solicitous of Jewish rights abroad than its imperial predecessor, long celebrated its human-rights defense in Berlin. See Marshall, "William Henry Waddington"; Dianoux, "L'émancipation des juifs" p. 343.

first "where it hurt least," to a land of fewer than 9,000 Jews, primarily Sephardic, who, until recently, had flourished under the relatively safe conditions of the Ottoman Empire.[101] The congress unanimously adopted the French motion.[102]

The initiative in regard to Bulgaria established an important precedent, which could not be ignored by Messrs. Brătianu and Kogălniceanu. Just days before, the two ministers had rebuffed the appeals of two French officials of the AIU, challenged the competence of the Great Powers to regulate Romania's affairs, and insisted that Romania's sole purpose in Berlin was to protect its territorial integrity and political independence.[103]

Serbia's turn came next. In 1830, it had gained international recognition as an autonomous principality under Ottoman suzerainty and also fell under Russian "protection," which lasted until the end of the Crimean War. Ruled by the native Obrenović and Karadjordjević dynasties, whose feuds were fueled by Turkish, Russian, Austrian, and French agents, Serbia's political struggles were punctuated by conspiracies, coups, and assassinations as well as by schemes for a Balkan League and military adventures against the Ottoman Empire.[104]

Serbia's climactic struggle for independence began in 1875. Belgrade had secretly supported the revolt in Bosnia–Herzegovina in the hope of becoming the "Sardinia of the Balkans," the liberator of its people from Ottoman control and creator of a giant Balkan state. During its brief, bloody war with Turkey, Serbia was deserted by its Russian patron, which failed to save its fellow Slavs from inglorious defeat.[105]

When Russia finally took the field against the Ottoman Empire, it had already bought Austrian neutrality with the promise of Bosnia–Herzegovina. In the peace of San Stefano, in which Serbia was also excluded, Russia repaid Belgrade's brief, but critical, military support with recognition of Serbia's independence and a strip of territory, but it also created a huge Bulgarian rival to block Serbia's Balkan ambitions. In June 1878, Serbia

101. Barely 1% of a population of approximately 1,800,000, Bulgarian Jews had played a major role in the export trade and commerce and, under Ottoman rule, had even filled local administrative and judicial posts. However, the Jews' declaration of neutrality during the Bulgarian uprising in 1876 led to anti-Jewish outbursts, raising alarm among British Jews and stirring the Liberal opposition leader William Gladstone also to champion the cause of Jewish rights in the Balkans. Gelber, "La question juive." The quotation is from Stern, *Gold and Iron*, p. 379.

102. Waddington to Dufaure, Berlin, June 26, 1878, *DDF*, 1re Sér., Vol. 2, pp. 342–3.

103. *Le Temps*, June 21, 1878. On June 24, Brătianu and Kogălniceanu sent their official memorandum and renewed their plea to be heard by the congress. Novotny, *Geschichte des Berliner Kongresses*, Vol. 1, p. 95.

104. Jelavich, *The Balkans*, Vol. 1, pp. 193–204, 238–47, 332–5,

105. MacKenzie, *The Serbs*.

and its ally, Montenegro, sent deputations to the Congress of Berlin in quest of international recognition and adequate territorial compensation as well.[106]

Despite the smallness and long residence of its Jewish population, Serbia had established as bleak a record of persecution as Romania's.[107] Over four and a half decades under Russian guidance, with only brief periods of toleration, the principality had imposed severe restrictions on the Jews' residence, property, and professional rights. Under pressure by Serbian merchants, the Karadjordjević rulers had condoned, if not abetted, the riots and expulsions in the countryside that forced most of the Jews into a desolate quarter of Belgrade. The government also endorsed the budding Palestine colonization movement as the ideal solution to a minority problem, which, like Russia's, would inevitably grow with the state's expansion in the Balkans.[108]

On a historic date, June 28, 1878, Serbia's case came before the Congress of Berlin. After the acrimonious debate over assigning Bosnia–Herzegovina to Austrian occupation,[109] the diplomats discussed the terms of Serbia's recognition. The Turkish and British delegates proposed the identical guarantees of religious freedom that had been imposed on Bulgaria, and Waddington added, "complete equality of rights" to the proposal.[110]

Suddenly Foreign Minister Alexander Gorchakov, harking back to Russia's reservations of twenty years earlier, announced his objections. While not contesting the sacred principle of religious freedom "which had always been applied in Russia," he opposed giving civil and political rights to the Jews, warning his colleagues not to

> confuse the *israélites* of Berlin, Paris, London or Vienna, to whom one would assuredly not withhold these rights, with the *juifs* of Serbia, Romania, and several Russian provinces who, in his opinion, were a veritable scourge [*un véritable fléau*] to the indigenous population.[111]

In a heated exchange, Bismarck suggested that the Jews' "deplorable condition" might be the result of the denial of their civil and political rights,

106. Georgévitch, "La Serbie au Congrès de Berlin."
107. Serbia had about 1,800 Jews, one-fifth the size of the Bulgarian community, in an only slightly smaller total population of approximately 1,700,000; of these, almost 1,600 lived in Belgrade. Gelber, "La question juive," p. 98.
108. Gelber, "La question juive," pp. 92–9; Alcalay, *The Jews of Serbia*, pp. 75–6.
109. *DD/CB*, Protocol No. 8, pp. 129–41. As in the case of Bulgaria, there were no Serbian delegates present.
110. Ibid., p. 142; see also Waddington, "La France," p. 472.
111. *DD/CB*, Protocol No. 8, p. 152. In his communication to Emperor Franz Joseph on June 29, Andrássy (another Forty-Eighter turned *Realpolitiker*) underscored Gorchakov's distinction between "Israeliten und Juden"; quoted in Gelber, "German Jews at the Berlin Congress," p. 242. Compare Novotny, *Geschichte des Berliner Kongresses*, p. 104.

but Gorchakov and Shuvalov insisted that in certain parts of Russia such restrictions were necessary for the protection of the local population.[112]

Unable to overcome the Russian objections, Bismarck settled on an innocuous clause promoting the principle of religious freedom. The congress maintained the precept that Serbia's entry into the community of nations required its satisfying the Great Powers' conditions.[113] And unlike Romania, Serbia was prepared to acquiesce.[114] Subsequently, with Austrian and French support, Serbia's frontiers were considerably expanded at the expense of Bulgaria, although these fell short of Belgrade's maximum territorial goals.[115] Serbia was also forced to assume a portion of the Ottoman debt as well as financial responsibility for the railways under construction by an Austrian company headed by Baron de Hirsch.[116]

Europe's warning to Romania was clear and unequivocal.[117] Yet Bleichröder made a last futile effort to elicit concessions from Brătianu and Kogălniceanu. He also received this remarkable assurance from Bismarck, that the Jews of Romania would obtain "the same basic recognition of equal rights . . . as are enjoyed by subjects of the Reich."[118] From Paris, an anxious Crémieux dispatched a last-minute plea to Waddington: "In the name of God, cede nothing to . . . Romania."[119]

On July 1, 1878, the two Romanian representatives were allowed to address the congress over the strong objections of Gorchakov but with the support of Bismarck's western partners, Britain, France, and Italy.[120] Their diplomatic debut, badly prepared and apathetically received, repeated the doleful petition for southern Bessarabia, neutrality, and a war indemnity, but omitted any specific reference to the Jewish issue.[121]

112. In this exchange, both used the expression "*israélites*"; *DD/CB*, pp. 142–3.
113. Waddington to Dufaure, Berlin, June 30, 1878, *DDF*, 1re Sér., Vol. 2, p. 346.
114. *DD/CB*, Protocol No. 12, July 4, 1878, p. 188.
115. With Austria's support, Serbia received an additional 10,800 square kilometers of territory as compared with 150 square kilometers in the Treaty of San Stefano.
116. *DD/CB*, pp. 143–7; Georgévitch, "La Serbie au Congrès de Berlin"; Gelber, "La question juive," pp. 101–2.
117. Bleichröder to Crémieux, June 30, 1878, in Iancu, *Bleichröder et Crémieux*, pp. 159–60.
118. Gelber, "German Jews at the Berlin Congress," especially pp. 243–4.
119. Crémieux to Waddington, June 30, 1878, in Iancu, *Bleichröder et Crémieux*, pp. 158–9.
120. On the chancellor's "western entente," see Winckler, "Bismarcks Rumänienpolitik und die europäischen Grossmächte," pp. 65–6. Discussion of Romanian representation, June 28, *DD/CB*, p. 146, and debate on June 29, ibid., pp. 154–6.
121. *DD/CB*, Protocol No. 10, July 1, 1878, pp. 162–6. Because of the delegates' nervousness or resignation, their speeches were almost inaudible; indeed, Brătianu had already telegraphed Bucharest on June 23 that southern Bessarabia was lost. Jelavich, "Romania at the Congress of Berlin," p. 199. Waddington, "La France," pp. 476–9, scored Romania's refusal to negotiate directly with Russia, as well as its expectation that the congress, led by France, would compensate its loss of southern Bessarabia.

Once Brătianu and Kogălniceanu had been dismissed, Waddington proposed the conditions for Romania's joining the "great European family." Although acknowledging the "difficult local conditions" in Romania, the French foreign minister deemed it essential that this new state observe "the grand rule of equality of rights and freedom of religion" that had already been affirmed by the Ottoman Empire and had now been imposed on Bulgaria and Serbia. A chorus of affirmation for the principle of religious freedom arose from Germany, Austria, Britain, Italy, Russia, and the Porte; only Bismarck alluded to the delicate issues of public law and politics.[122]

Shuvalov raised another discordant note by announcing that Russia's approval of Romanian independence was conditional on the latter's acceptance of the loss of southern Bessarabia. Although the other powers had more or less acquiesced in the tsar's obsession with this strategic scrap of territory at the mouth of the Danube, there was a certain amount of dismay over Russia's plunder of its small ally. Indeed, southern Bessarabia had a sizable Jewish population, which would lack any form of international protection.[123]

Waddington, in an attempt to stave off a feud between the obstreperous Balkan progeny and its huge imperial neighbor, proposed to expand Romania's territorial compensation in northern Dobrudja, a larger area than southern Bessarabia but with no Romanian inhabitants. When the Russians balked over reducing Bulgaria further, Waddington, joined by Andrássy, Corti, Bismarck, and Salisbury, appealed to Russia's sense of honor, justice, and generosity to alleviate their "harsh" treatment of Romania. Thus, thanks to its old French patron, Romania acquired additional territory at the mouth of the Danube as well as the Black Sea port of Constanta.[124]

The Treaty of Berlin, signed by the seven Great Powers on July 13, 1878, contained sixty-six articles; of these, eleven, scattered throughout the text, dealt with religious freedom and civil and political rights in Bulgaria, Serbia, Montenegro,[125] and Romania, and also in the Ottoman Empire.[126]

122. *DD/CB*, pp. 166–7.

123. With the ironic result that Russian Jews would have more rights in Romania than in their own country: D'Avril, *Négociations relatives au Traité de Berlin*, p. 391.

124. Waddington to Dufaure, Berlin, July 1, 1878, *DDF*, 1re Sér., Vol. 2, pp. 347–8. By this maneuver France succeeded in putting more physical distance between Russia and Bulgaria; but the Romanians were not grateful. Waddington to Voguë, Berlin, July 10, 1878, underscored Bismarck's nervousness over this squabble and his own "great intervention" for civil equality and religious freedom in Romania, FMAE PA-AP Waddington 176; also, Waddington, "La France," pp. 480–1.

125. During the session of July 1, Montenegro's independence was recognized under identical internal conditions as those of Bulgaria, Serbia, and Romania. And according to the prior Russo–Austrian agreement and over strong Turkish objections, Montenegro's annexation of Ottoman territory, which included numerous Albanians, was approved; *DD/CB*, pp. 171–5; also Corti to Cairoli, Berlin, July 1, 1878, *DDI*, Ser. 2a, Vol. 10, p. 252.

126. On the Ottoman Empire: Articles 20 (religious liberty in Eastern Rumelia), 61 (guarantee of security for the Armenians against the Circassians and the Kurds), and 62 (general religious freedom

Article 44 read

In Romania the difference of religious creeds and confessions shall not be used against any person as a ground for exclusion or incapacity in matters relating to the enjoyment of civil and political rights, admission to public employments, functions and honors, or the exercise of the various professions and industries in any locality whatsoever.

The freedom and outward exercise of all forms of worship shall be assured to all persons belonging to the Romanian state [*tous les ressortissants de l'état roumain*] as well as to foreigners, and no hindrance shall be offered either to the hierarchical organization of the different religious communities nor to their spiritual leaders.[127]

Unlike the clauses pertaining to Bulgaria, Serbia, and Montenegro, Article 44 contained a third paragraph, which read

Nationals of all the Powers, businessmen or others, will be treated without distinction of religion on a complete level of equality.[128]

However, missing from the final text of Article 44 was a key addition, proposed in the drafting stage by the Italian delegate, the Count de Launay, which read

The Jews of Romania who do not belong to a foreign nationality have the right to acquire Romanian citizenship.[129]

Bismarck had summarily vetoed this suggestion, which represented an effort to "alter the Congress's earlier decisions."[130] The other powers concurred, reluctant to underline Romania's transgressions.[131] By rejecting this sole, specific reference to the Jews, which doomed them to another generation of discrimination, Bismarck not only beat a retreat in the face of Gorchakov's hostile remarks and disavowed his pledge to Bleichröder; he may also have signaled that his main purpose was not to provide the Jews of Romania with an internationally recognized claim to citizenship but simply to

throughout the empire, French control over the Holy Places, and equality of rights for monks at Mount Athos); *DD/CB*, pp. 282–3, 294–5.

127. *DD/CB*, pp. 290–1; Article 43 granted Romania's independence, Articles 45 and 46 dealt with southern Bessarabia and Dobrudja.
128. A clause that clearly reflected the Great Powers' distrust as well as their own economic interests.
129. *DD/CB*, Protocol No. 17, July 10, 1878, pp. 248–9. After Bismarck vetoed changing the original formula, Gorchakov took the opportunity to reiterate his objections to granting the Jews of Romania political and civil rights. A year later, de Launay characterized his initiative as a reflection of his government's stated policy on "religious equality." De Launay to Depretis, Berlin, July 2, 1879, *DDI*, Ser. 2a, Vol. 10, p. 592.
130. "Il est nécessaire que le Congrès s'oppose à toute tentative de revenir sur le fond." *DD/CB*, Protocol No. 17, July 10, 1878, p. 248.
131. Thirty-five years later, Wolf to Montefiore, Oct. 8, 1913, YIVO Institute for Jewish Research, Lucien Wolf-David Mowshowitch papers (hereafter YIVO W/M) 35, explained that the Italian amendment had been dropped not, as generally believed, because it was offered "too late," but because the Powers desired the citizenship clauses in the Treaty of Berlin to be uniform.

establish a form of leverage over Bucharest.[132] Under Bismarck's leadership, the Congress of Berlin had made anodyne statements on political and civic equality and religious toleration in the Balkans without providing sanctions or guarantees for either.[133]

Jewish leaders nevertheless rejoiced in what they considered a "victory" for their own people and for the cause of "humanitarianism and justice."[134] Bleichröder, who had provided lavish entertainment for the delegates and ostensibly won a great triumph, sent an effusive letter of thanks to his patron.[135] Expressions of gratitude from Jewish communities poured in to Bismarck and to Waddington. The pope congratulated the French Republic's Protestant foreign minister for his stout defense of religious freedom.[136]

For Romania, the trip to Berlin had meant defeat over every issue of national importance. "Europe," it concluded, wanted "peace at any price," and used small states as pawns in the balance of power. At Berlin, Romania had shed its Great-Power guardianship but also had its first, brutal experience of isolation, ostracism, and Great-Power domination. For practical reasons, the government made Article 44 the focus of public outrage, directing its fury and threats against the Jews.[137]

AFTERMATH

The diplomatic maneuvers following the Congress of Berlin revealed Europe's rapid retreat from the facade of humanitarian interventionism back to the ways of traditional *Realpolitik*.[138] Immediately after the close, the Romanian Foreign Ministry requested a formal exchange of ministers with the major governments of Europe. Without awaiting the fulfillment of Article 44, Austria–Hungary, Russia, and the Ottoman Empire immediately obliged. Although France and Germany held firm, Bismarck had to stop Italy and then Britain from granting "premature" recognition. Throughout the fall and winter of 1878–9, as persecutions against Romanian Jews

132. Geiss, "Die jüdische Frage," especially pp. 415–17. On the other hand, Iancu, *Juifs en Roumanie*, p. 161, minimizes the importance.
133. Macartney, *National States and National Minorities*, pp. 108–9.
134. Gelber, "German Jews at the Berlin Congress," especially pp. 245–6.
135. Excerpts in Stern, *Gold and Iron*, p. 379; also, Heilbrunn, "Bismarcks blinder Hofjude," p. 307.
136. Iancu, *Juifs en Roumanie*, pp. 161–2; Stern, *Gold and Iron*, pp. 378–9.
137. Consul-General Fava to Cairoli, Bucharest, July 3, 1878, *DDI*, Ser. 2a, Vol. 10, p. 269; *The Times* [London], July 5, 1878.
138. "Unless some of the treaty powers can be induced to actively interfere, it is likely that the Roumanian Jews will be no better off in the immediate future than they have been in the past," *The New York Times*, Nov. 29, 1878; also Dec. 4, 1878 on the dire situation of Romanian Jewry.

mounted and the Romanian Parliament balked at convening a constitutional convention, Berlin kept its "western entente" in line.[139]

Nonetheless, the "champion of humanity,"[140] Otto von Bismarck, had little inclination to enforce the implementation of Article 44 as the Jews, the Romanians, and most of his diplomatic colleagues interpreted it. The Iron Chancellor, in a major political shift, was in the process of abandoning the German Liberals, courting the pope, and preparing a secret alliance with Austria–Hungary. He had been drawn into Romanian affairs by the railway issue, and its favorable settlement became one of his primary goals after the Congress of Berlin.[141]

Prince Charles and his ministers recognized that Romania had to do something, even on the symbolic level, to meet Europe's demands for Jewish rights; but they faced an intransigent parliament dominated by anti-Semitic deputies who were reluctant to revise the 1866 constitution.[142] For over a year and a half a great debate raged in Romania over the inequities of European statesmen, the conspiracy of world Jewry, and the perils of Jewish emancipation. In the meantime, Serbia, once its parliament had dutifully adopted the religious-toleration clauses, was granted full and complete recognition by all the Great Powers in the spring of 1879.[143]

Romania rejected the simplest solution, which was to insert the text of Article 44 into its constitution.[144] Instead, the government, taking the hint from Berlin, decided to accept the article in principle but defer its application, gambling on the fact that the Great Powers would appreciate a "sincere effort" and not impose an absolute solution contrary to Romania's "vital interests."[145]

The new version of Article 7 of the Romanian constitution, adopted by the Romanian chamber in October 1879, was audaciously defiant. Insisting

139. See Bleichröder to Crémieux, Sept. 18, 1878, in Iancu, *Bleichröder et Crémieux*, pp. 179–80; Bülow to German ambassadors in London, Paris, Rome, and Vienna, Berlin, Oct. 6, 1878, U.S. National Archives, Captured Records of the German Foreign Ministry on microfilm (hereafter Germ. AA T-120) K688/4327/K173065–66; De Launay to Cairoli, Berlin, Nov. 16, 1878, *DDI*, Ser. 2a, Vol. 11, pp. 61–2.

140. The term by which he was addressed by the Berlin Jewish community on July 11, 1878, quoted in Stern, *Gold and Iron*, p. 379.

141. See De Launay to Depretis, Berlin, July 7, 1879, *DDI*, Ser. 2a, Vol. 11, pp. 610–11; Waller, *Bismarck*, pp. 56–8; Stern, *Gold and Iron*, pp. 382–3.

142. *Românul*, Aug. 20, 1878, in Germ. AA T-120 K688/4327/K173065–66; Kremnitz, *Aus dem Leben König Karls von Rumänien*, Vol. 4, pp. 88–9; also Oldson, *Providential Anti-Semitism*, pp. 47–65, 99–125.

143. De Launay to Depretis, Berlin, March. 17, 1879, *DDI*, Ser. 2a, Vol. 11, pp. 311–12, compares Berlin's acceptance of Serbia's "good faith" with its suspicions of Romania.

144. De Launay to Cairoli, Berlin, May 16, 1879, Maffei to Fava [Bucharest], Rome, September 26, 1879, *DDI*, Ser. 2a, Vol. 12, pp. 10–13, 181.

145. Iancu, *Bleichröder et Crémieux*, p. 70, quoting from Prince Charles' message to the Chamber on June 3, 1879.

that all the Jews in the country were "foreigners,"[146] it provided for the emancipation of only a few privileged categories and forced the rest to undergo highly restrictive procedures for individual naturalization.[147] The Romanian government invoked two pertinent examples: The negative one was Algeria, where the collective naturalization imposed by France had given 30,000 Jews dominance over millions of Arabs; the positive one was imperial Russia, where the government protected its native population by withholding equal rights to the Jews. Neither a colony nor a great empire, but a new sovereign state, Romania pleaded with Europe not to force a "small Latin nation to incorporate *en bloc* so large and so alien an element."[148] Brătianu had also dispatched his Finance Minister Dimitrie Sturdza to Berlin to negotiate on the railways and the Jews.[149]

It was an undoubtedly unequal struggle between Romania and the Jews. The Jewish position was weakened by the imminent danger to its Romanian kin; the *Alliance* received numerous reports of expulsions from several Moldavian villages.[150] Moreover, western Jews were now retreating from their support of full emancipation. Earlier, Montefiore had urged Bleichröder to temper his pleas on behalf of the Jews of Russia, insisting that they must demonstrate "confidence" in the tsar's desire to "ameliorate the condition of the Jews," that the social and political improvement of the eastern Jews (*Ostjuden*) must be gradual, and that the latter must enlist their own rich kindred to "educate and raise" their less fortunate coreligionists.[151] In the case of Romania, Bleichröder's Viennese friend and fellow banker, Moritz Ritter von Goldschmidt, had advised against an immediate emancipation, deeming these Jews, who threatened to offend Christian sensibilities, less worthy than western Jews.[152]

146. The text of paragraph 1 referred to the Jews as "foreigner[s] . . . whether or not subject to foreign protection."
147. Those who had served in the army could be naturalized collectively on the initiative of the government. Individuals who had established commercial or industrial enterprises, produced useful inventions, or demonstrated distinguished talents might be naturalized "in stages." See Germ. AA T-120 K688/4328/K174517–540. *The Times* [London], Sept. 25, 1879, had termed these "vague and insidious conditions."
148. Iancu, *Bleichröder et Crémieux*, pp. 83–4. It was the *Décret Crémieux* of Oct. 24, 1870, when Crémieux was Minister of Justice in the Government of National Defense (1870–1), which had enfranchised the Jews of Algeria.
149. Medlicott, "Roumanian Independence," pp. 582–3.
150. Central Committee AIU to Waddington, Aug. 10, Sept. 10, 1879, Bleichröder to Central Committee, Sept. 3, 1879, in Iancu, *Bleichröder et Crémieux*, pp. 205, 216–18, 214; Bleichröder to AA, July 25, Aug. 7, Sept. 9, 1879, Germ. AA T-120 K688/4327/K174068–71, K174417–18, K174451.
151. Stern, *Gold and Iron*, p. 379. Significantly, it had been Montefiore who had initiated the campaign in Britain on behalf of Serbia's Jews; see Gelber, "La question juive," pp. 93–5.
152. Stern, *Gold and Iron*, p. 368.

After a year-long struggle, Bleichröder's ardor for full emancipation had undoubtedly diminished. Indeed, he was shocked when a few prominent Wallachian Jews endorsed the new Romanian legislation and solicited his support in their efforts to gain personal naturalization.[153] Fending off the *Alliance*'s pleas for "firmness," Bleichröder appealed for "realism." Acutely sensitive to his master's moods and to shifting political and international currents, Bleichröder, with his huge personal financial stake in the Romanian railways, by the fall of 1879 was moving toward a compromise on Article 44.[154]

Bismarck too was weary of the struggle. It is possible that his strategy had always been to deploy the Jewish question to force Romania to settle the railroad question[155]; but the mercurial *Junker* often applied several forms of pressure to coerce stubborn opponents and control ephemeral allies. Formally, at least, Bismarck continued to demand Romania's full compliance with Article 44 in order to set a good standard for the other Balkan states and ensure guarantees for German nationals.[156] But he was clearly unhappy with the international consequences of delaying Romania's recognition: France and Britain had become restive and suspicious; Italy broke ranks in November 1879; and Austria and Russia were gaining influence in Romania.[157] At home, the kaiser not only opposed Article 44 but was reportedly irritated over the delay in sending an emissary to his relative's court in Bucharest.[158] Moreover, the advent of Germany's noisy new anti-Semitic party created a serious impediment for Bismarck's claim to set tolerance standards abroad.[159]

153. Bleichröder to Central Committee AIU, Oct. 12, Oct. 25, Nov. 16, 1879, in Iancu, *Bleichröder et Crémieux*, pp. 223, 226–7, 228–9.
154. Bleichröder to Crémieux, July 9, 15, 29, Aug. 11, 1879, excerpt of letter from Saint-Vallier to Waddington, July 31, 1879, in Iancu, *Bleichröder et Crémieux*, pp. 193–4, 196–7, 199–200, 200–1, 206–7. Dianoux, "L'émancipation des juifs," p. 43, underlines Bleichröder's recognition of the limits of his power to intercede in favor of his coreligionists.
155. This was the general sentiment at the time (*DDI*, Ser. 2a, Vol. 12, pp. 315, 331–2, 363–4, 372–3) and later argued in Meisl, *Die Durchführung des Artikels 44*, p. 81, Winckler, "Bismarcks Rumänienpolitik," and Burks, "Romania and the Balkan Crisis," p. 318.
156. The animating force was Bleichröder who hoped to "save what could be saved," even by indirect means; see Bleichröder to Crémieux, Oct. 25, Nov. 16, 1879, in Iancu, *Bleichröder et Crémieux*, pp. 227–8.
157. Bleichröder to Crémieux, Oct. 1, 25, 1879, in Iancu, *Bleichröder et Crémieux*, pp. 218–19, 226–7; Saint-Vallier to Waddington, Varzin, Nov. 14, 1879 (confidential), Berlin, Dec. 10, 1879, *DDF*, 1re Sér., Vol. 2, pp. 589–92, 597–8; Cairoli to Marochetti, Rome, Nov. 24, 1879, Tosi to Cairoli, Berlin, Nov. 24, 1879, Di Robilant to Cairoli, Vienna, Nov. 27, 1879, *DDI*, Ser. 2a, Vol. 12, pp. 303–4, 304–5, 313–14; Radowitz to German Ambassador, Rome, Dec. 10, 1879, Germ. AA T-120 K688/4329/K174810; Medlicott, "Roumanian Independence," pp. 584–8.
158. Meisl, *Die Durchführung des Artikels 44*, pp. 85–6, quoting from records of the cabinet meeting of Nov. 10, 1879; also Stern, *Gold and Iron*, pp. 380–92.
159. Oldson, *Providential Anti-Semitism*, pp. 81–94; Pulzer, *Political Anti-Semitism*, pp. 92–8.

Faced with Europe's disunity, Romania might have held out, but with meager prospects and rewards. Instead, Romania chose the lesser evil, which was to relent over the railways and not over Jewish emancipation, whereupon Bismarck's antagonism and obstruction suddenly evaporated.[160] In the beginning of 1880 Brătianu convinced the recalcitrant parliament to vote the acquisition of the railways on extremely favorable terms to the German stockholders.[161] On February 20, 1880, without having made any serious effort to fulfill the terms of Article 44, Romania received formal, unconditional recognition by Britain, France, and Germany, accompanied by a collective note acknowledging its incomplete compliance with the treaty.[162] The Great Powers were relieved of their burden with this long-delayed, formal settlement.[163]

Prince Charles and his people recognized Romania's victory and Europe's capitulation over Article 44. One of its most prominent writers and politicians, C. A. Rossetti, wrote at the end of 1881 that Romania had settled "its most burning and dangerous question . . . contrary to the manifest will of the powers and even contrary to the spirit of the Treaty of Berlin."[164] Until the eve of World War I only 1,500 Romanian Jews were emancipated, a figure that included the approximately 900 veterans honored collectively in 1879 and an average of fourteen individual naturalizations over the next thirty-five years. The rest, who remained in the invidious category of "aliens not under foreign protection," suffered mounting forms of discrimination, violence, and expulsions.[165]

160. Saint-Vallier to Waddington, Berlin, Dec. 10, 1879, *DDF* 1re Sér., Vol. 2, pp. 597–8. To be sure, Britain, with its own commercial and political aims in the Balkans, had been impatient to establish relations with Romania, but, as recompense for Cyprus, had dutifully followed Bismarck's lead. *British and Foreign State Papers*, Vol. 71, pp. 1137, 1140, 1143, 1145, 1149–56; Oldson, *Providential Anti-Semitism*, pp. 81–7.

161. The estimated purchase price was approximately nine times the value of their holdings. Details of the final negotiations in Iancu, *Bleichröder et Crémieux*, p. 92; Oldson, *Providential Anti-Semitism*, pp. 76–81; Winckler, "Bismarcks Rumänienpolitik und die europäische Grossmächte," pp. 74–88; Stern, *Gold and Iron*, pp. 382–92; Medlicott, "Roumanian Independence," pp. 587–9.

162. [H. von] Bismarck to German Ambassadors, in London and Paris, Berlin, Feb. 11, 1880, Germ. AA T-120 K688/4329/K174907–10; also France, Ministère des Affaires Étrangères, *La Reconnaissance de la Roumanie*, pp. 13–18; *British and Foreign State Papers*, Vol. 71, pp. 1186–8. Tornielli to Cairoli, Bucharest, Feb. 20, 1880, *DDI*, Ser. 2a, Vol. 12, p. 514, stated that Italy's "impatience to escape from a false situation could not have been better justified."

163. Freycinet to Saint-Vallier, Paris, Feb. 22, 1880, France, Ministère des Affaires Étrangères, *La Reconnaissance de la Roumanie*, pp. 18–19.

164. *Românul*, December 25, 1881, quoted in Iancu, *Juifs en Roumanie*, p. 180; also Kremnitz, *Aus dem Leben König Karls von Rumänien*, Vol. 4, pp. 293–6.

165. Naturalizations ranged from a high of fifty-two in 1880 to zero in 1884–5, 1887–8, 1890–1, 1898–9, and 1909; Iancu, *Juifs en Roumanie*, pp. 186–9, based on the figures of the AIU; forms of oppression, pp. 189–205.

Bismarck rewarded Romania's submission on the railways question by ending its diplomatic isolation and transforming it into a German satellite. He sponsored the creation of a Romanian kingdom in 1881 to raise its international prestige, reduce Russian pressure, and stave off the forces of "revolution"; a year later Charles was crowned as Romania's first king, Carol I.[166] And in 1883, as the French had anticipated, Brătianu secretly led Romania into the Austro–German Alliance.[167]

With Romania's virtually unconditional recognition, Bleichröder and his Jewish colleagues had received a stunning defeat, greatly intensified by Crémieux's death on February 10, 1880. The German intercessor tried to rationalize their failure, insisting that they had rescued Romanian Jews from new outbursts of hatred and persecution.[168] No excuse, however, could conceal the miscarriage of the Jews' elaborate strategy of mobilizing the press, legislators, and governments of Central and Western Europe as well as their financial and economic resources to force Jewish emancipation on Romania. The celebrated Article 44 became an icon of miscalculation and betrayal.[169]

To be sure, Jewish leaders had been divided over the desirability of immediate and complete emancipation. Not only were Romanian Jews distant, different, and more numerous than their western kin, but they were not a unified "modern" community with their own political program. Romania had cleverly exacerbated these disagreements by harping on the "scourge" of its Jews to the native peasantry, on their "Germanic" [Galician] and "Slavic" [Russian] origins, and on their unassimilability. Such charges stirred the latent insecurities of western Jews and reinforced their old, fundamental conviction that emancipation "had to be earned."[170]

166. De Launay to Cairoli, Berlin, March 22, 1880, *DDI*, Ser. 2a, Vol. 12, pp. 622–3; Kremnitz, *Aus dem Leben König Karls von Rumänien*, Vol. 4, pp. 392–407. Charles, whose marriage was childless, in 1880 designated his nephew, Prince Ferdinand of Hohenzollern, as his heir.

167. "Vertrag mit Rumänien 1883," Germany, Auswärtiges Amt, *Die Grosse Politik der Europäische Kabinette*, Vol. 3, pp. 263–82. Also, Saint-Vallier to Freycinet, Berlin, Mar. 19, 1880, Ducros-Aubert to Barthélemy Saint-Hilaire, Bucharest, Mar. 26, 1881, Barthélemy Saint-Hilaire to Ducros-Aubert, Paris, Apr. 3, 1881, *DDF*, 1re Sér., Vol. 3, pp. 57–9, 393–4, 395–6. Compare Medlicott's "Roumanian Independence," pp. 588–9 with Iancu, *Juifs en Roumanie*, pp. 177–80, on Romania's treatment by the Great Powers.

168. Bleichröder to Central Committee, AIU, Feb. 14, 1880, in Iancu, *Bleichröder et Crémieux*, pp. 233: "La solution de la question se trouve ainsi dans une phase très favorable, car ceux qui connaissent la situation dans laquelle se trouve la Roumanie, doivent reconnaître avec moi qu'une émancipation plénière et subite aurait, en présence des agitations qui troublent le pays et ameutent la populace, conduit à la persécution de nos coreligionnaires, tandis que de cette manière le but est atteint sans provoquer de convulsions dans le pays qui auraient nui en première ligne à nos amis."

169. Central Committee AIU to Bleichröder, Feb. 22, 1880, in Iancu, *Bleichröder et Crémieux*, pp. 233–4; Meisl, *Die Durchführung des Artikels 44*, pp. 86–8; Chirot, *Romanian Anti-Semitism*.

170. Iancu, *Bleichröder et Crémieux*, p. 130.

Romania's rhetoric of stigmatization and exclusion not only echoed the opponents of emancipation in France between 1789 and 1791; it also resounded with the new, virulent anti-Semitism emerging from the crash of 1873, the end of the liberal era, and the growing popularity of racist sentiments throughout Europe.[171] Even the liberal Waddington, without condoning Gorchakov's invective against Jewish predators in Eastern Europe, had acknowledged Romania's "local difficulties," much as enlightened reformers a century earlier had deplored the special "conditions" in Alsace. The fact that the Jews of Vienna and Bucharest, like the French–Sephardic notables ninety years earlier,[172] had begun to apply a "quality" standard to the teaming hordes of Moldavian Jews undoubtedly undermined their crusade for justice and equity. Romania's tokenism and pseudo-emancipation, its privileging of exceptionalism over the rights of all inhabitants, were almost as damaging to Jewish solidarity as its implacable opposition to Article 44.

During the Congress of Berlin and its aftermath, European Jews were forced to take stock not simply of the progress and pace of Jewish emancipation but also of the material and practical conditions within such developing countries as Serbia and Romania, both former colonial societies about to enter complex international networks of finance, trade, railroads, and resource development. In Romania, as in most of the successor states, the host of Jewish artisans, small entrepreneurs, moneylenders, and laborers, once welcomed by the rulers, had become the hated competitors of Romanians at the same time that the economic modernization promoted by the West was rendering the Jews' skills obsolete and their situation desperate. Despised and betrayed by their government, their coreligionists, and the Great Powers, the impoverished Jews of Romania reacted after 1878 with a mass, largely uncoordinated, emigration to Western Europe, America, and Palestine.[173]

In their struggle against Article 44, Romanian leaders often complained over the machinations of international "Jewish power" to an increasingly receptive European audience. Indeed, the high-profile humanitarian activities of Montefiore and Goldschmidt, Crémieux and Bleichröder, reached their peak at the Congress of Berlin in their campaign to achieve religious freedom and emancipation in Romania. Nevertheless, the fact that between

171. Already in 1871, after decades of relative harmony, a major anti-Jewish riot suddenly broke out in Odessa in which six people were killed and several hundred houses and businesses were destroyed. Herlihy, *Odessa*, pp. 299–303.

172. Schwarzfuchs, *Les juifs*, Chap. 13 ("Une émancipation difficile"), pp. 205–18; also Badinter, *Libres et égaux*.

173. Iancu, *Juifs en Roumanie*, pp. 249–64; between 1899 and 1914, close to 90,000 Jews left Romania.

1878 and 1880 the strongest and most secure elements of European Jewry had patently needed, attempted, and ultimately failed to help their weak and disparaged coreligionists constituted a clear, if unrecognized, lesson in the limits of persuasion, the power of prejudice, and the heightened vulnerability of a small but visible minority scattered among a growing number of nationalist states. The decision to rely on their divided, distracted, and indifferent governments was fateful. Neither Romania's obstreperousness nor Gorchakov's cunning differentiation between western *Israeliten* and eastern *Juden* was as damaging to "Jewish power" as the tergiversations of western statesmen and the unscrupulousness of Otto von Bismarck.[174]

In 1878 the Concert of Europe embarked on a new course in the Balkans. Neither as liberators nor occupiers, seven major powers had dictated conditions on the internal governance of four new states. There were no formal negotiations with the affected parties. The imposed clauses on minority rights became requirements not only for recognition but were also, as in the cases of Serbia, Montenegro, and Romania, conditions for receiving specific grants of territory.

According to custom, prudence, and practicality, the Great Powers in 1878 issued no universal pronouncements on religious freedom or Jewish emancipation. Instead, they inserted their conditions in the form of separate clauses within a multilateral treaty, which contained no stipulations for individual or collective enforcement. The Powers were not only reluctant to elaborate specific minority rights; but they were also hesitant to cast a protective mantle over all vulnerable inhabitants – citizens and noncitizens – in the new Balkans.

The Berlin Treaty represented a paper threat. Theoretically, Russia could protest over Romania's ill-treatment of its non-Christian citizens and the Porte over the treatment of Muslims in Serbia, Montenegro, or Bulgaria; but they did not. Great Britain, a disinterested power, perennially abstained from interfering in "local" Balkan affairs.[175] Indeed, only the United States, which had no rights under the Treaty of Berlin, protested its infringement.[176] Until the end of World War I, all seven signatory powers formally recognized their rights and responsibilities toward minorities under the Treaty of Berlin, which they neither implemented nor revised.

174. Geiss, "Die jüdische Frage," pp. 418–21.
175. Kiderlen to AA, Bucharest, Apr. 28, 1910, Germ. AA T-120 K688/4329/K175444.
176. See copy of US. Secretary of State John Hay's circular to the signatory powers on Aug. 11, 1902, in Germ. AA T-120 K688/4329/K175062–65, which *The Times* [London] on Sept. 23, 1902, called a "great surprise."

Nonetheless, to restrict the diplomatic significance of Article 44 to Bismarck's machinations, his colleagues' submission, Jewish weakness, and Romania's noncompliance ignores its full impact then and since. The decision at the Congress of Berlin to impose internal conditions on four new states in 1878 undoubtedly placed a new burden on international statecraft and produced results that a new generation of leaders were forced to confront. By expanding the principle of internationally dictated, nonreciprocal minority rights in the Balkans, the Great Powers created an onerous legacy of resentment, defiance, and frustration.

2

Bucharest, August 1913

"Things are very confused in the international field and I have good reasons for believing that the understanding among the Great Powers is nothing like as complete as the papers make out."[1]

"I cannot refrain from expressing regret that we Jews with all our power are not as strong today as Montenegro, the entire population of which is not half as large as the Jewish population of New York City."[2]

Exactly thirty-five years after the Congress of Berlin, another peace settlement was negotiated pertaining to the succession states of the Ottoman Empire. This time, however, the Great Powers were not present. After a generation of stunning material progress and relative peace in Europe, the outbreak of the Balkan Wars delivered a warning of brutal future contests and also brought a major setback to the cause of minority rights.

THE BALKAN WARS

In 1912, four former rivals, Serbia, Bulgaria, Montenegro, and Greece, formed an alliance to evict the Ottoman Empire from Europe. The Great Powers, now divided into two hostile camps, had failed to check this menacing enterprise. Neither a distracted imperial Britain nor an increasingly assertive France counseled Russia, the Balkan League's original sponsor, to restrain its bellicose clients. On the other side, a vacillating Germany ignored the league's threat to Austria–Hungary, while Italy, which was currently at war with Turkey, welcomed the newest "Balkan storm."[3]

1. Wolf to Montefiore, Dec. 3, 1912, YIVO W/M 35.
2. J. L. Magnes to Louis Marshall, President, AJC, Dec. 27, 1912, copy in AJC Adler papers.
3. Taylor, *Struggle for Mastery*, pp. 483–90; Rich, *Great Power Diplomacy*, pp. 425–27.

The First and Second Balkan Wars (October 8–December 3, 1912 and June 29–July 30, 1913, respectively), Europe's first serious combat since the fall of Plevna in 1877, were brief but exceedingly violent episodes. The initial war of liberation rapidly deteriorated into an internecine struggle that included widespread atrocities against the noncombatant population. Particularly in Macedonia, "the megalomania of the national ideal" exposed Muslims, Jews, Armenians, Greeks, Bulgarians, Serbs, and Albanians to pillage and forced requisitions, assault and rape, collective reprisals and forced conversions, torture and mutilation, and expulsion and massacre by foreign troops as well as by their local enemies.[4] The two Balkan Wars produced huge numbers of casualties, vast material destruction, and a flood of refugees; there were egregious infractions of the new codes established at the First and Second Hague Conferences of 1899 and 1907 to protect civilians as well as prisoners of war.[5]

Once hostilities threatened to erupt in October 1912, the Great Powers were forced to respond. Austria–Hungary and Russia had each tried to forestall the fighting but could not prevent the almost total rout of the Turkish army in Europe. A panicked Vienna government called for outside intervention to block Serbia's aggrandizement; the Russians, anxious over Bulgaria's expansion toward Constantinople, agreed.[6] On December 16, 1912, the emissaries of the Triple Entente and the Triple Alliance convened in London under the chairmanship of British Foreign Secretary Sir Edward Grey, who was anxious to revitalize the old Concert of Europe, to mediate the Balkan crisis and determine its territorial outcome.[7]

The London Conference of Ambassadors turned out to be a feeble, slow-moving agency for controlling Balkan affairs, a pale shadow of its Berlin predecessor thirty-five years earlier.[8] Not only were Europe's two blocs incapable of reconciling their national aims or coordinating effectively with their allies, but the objects of their diplomacy, brimming with nationalist ambitions and military arms, were determined to defy Great-Power dictates. Indeed, the main purpose of the London Conference was to contain the Balkan conflict without, however, ensuring more than a temporary truce.[9]

4. Detailed in Carnegie Endowment for International Peace, *Causes and Conduct of the Balkan Wars* (the work of a six-member international fact-finding commission with representatives from Austria, France, Germany, Great Britain, Russia, and the United States), pp. 71–207.
5. Ibid., pp. 208–64.
6. Ronald Bobroff, "Behind the Balkan Wars."
7. Grey to Bertie, Dec. 16, 1912; Gooch and Temperley, *Origins of the War*, Vol. 9, p. 290.
8. Above all, it was an ambassadors' meeting, not a convocation of heads of state, and it was plagued by delays in communication as well as by the participants' inability to forge compromises on the spot.
9. Grey, *Twenty-Five Years*, Vol. 1, pp. 262–3. A detailed, and still useful, description of the tedious negotiations between Dec. 16, 1912 and May 30, 1913, is found in Helmreich, *Diplomacy of the Balkan Wars*, pp. 249–340.

On paper at least, the Treaty of London signed on May 30, 1913 did produce one resounding success for the revived Concert of Europe. Austria–Hungary, Italy, and Russia teamed up to deny Greece, Montenegro, and, especially, Serbia the major spoils of victory by creating an independent Albania along the Adriatic coast. But this remotely devised strategic buffer state, with its unspecified boundaries, provoked attempts by Albania's three angry neighbors to impose its frontiers by force; in the end, almost a million Albanians were left outside, and a permanent source of ethnic conflict was created in the Balkans.[10]

The Great Powers were even less effective in determining the fate of Macedonia, the province retained by Turkey in 1878, whose 3 million inhabitants contained Europe's most religiously and ethnically diverse population. About two-thirds of the Macedonians were either Muslim (Turks or Albanians) or Orthodox (Greeks, Serbs, and Bulgarians). The remainder consisted of some 70,000 Jews and smaller numbers of Kutzo–Vlachs (who were distantly related to Romanians), Armenians, Gypsies, and Circassians.[11]

Macedonia, the chief contested prize of the Balkan Wars, had long been a hotbed of rebelliousness and repression, which foreign states had been powerless to restrain.[12] After the Young Turks seized power in 1908, they rebuffed the West's mediation efforts and threatened to submerge Macedonia into a Turkish national state, whereupon Greece, Serbia, and Bulgaria resolved to seize as much of the province as possible. All three governments, along with those of Romania and Turkey, had long interfered in Macedonia in disputes over schools and church appointments; and each had financed their own secret terrorist organizations, which set the stage for the atrocities of 1912–13.[13]

Within a month of the signing of the Treaty of London, the Balkan League fell apart. Bulgaria had sustained the most intense combat against the Turks only to see Greece and Serbia requite their losses to Albania by snatching the lion's share of Macedonia and to see Russia demand territorial compensation for Romania, which had sat on the sidelines. In a hapless gesture of revenge, Bulgaria attacked Serbia and Greece, which were joined by Romania and Turkey, and it was soundly defeated in three weeks. Without a word of protest from the Conference of London, the combatants conducted

10. Costa, *Albania*; Duda, *Der Fall Albanien*. Historical background is given in Skendi, *Albanian National Awakening*.
11. Great Britain. Foreign Office. Historical Section, *Macedonia* (London: His Majesty's Stationery Office, 1920), pp. 28–38.
12. Lange-Akhung, *The Macedonian Question*; Bridge, *The Macedonian Struggle*; Sowards, *Macedonian Reform*; Aptiev, *Die mazedonische Frage*.
13. Dakin, *Greek Struggle in Macedonia*; Perry, *Politics of Terror*.

their own negotiations in Bucharest and signed a peace treaty on August 10, 1913.[14]

The Treaty of Bucharest, followed by a series of bilateral treaties with Turkey, signaled a critical change in the European balance of power. This militant display of Balkan nationalism had undermined the two most vulnerable, multinational pillars of the system (the Ottoman Empire and Austria–Hungary), rewarded recklessness and insouciance in two others (Russia and Germany), and produced a marked passivity, and even fatalism, in Paris and London over the possibility of resisting local acts of force. The Balkan Wars also produced a misreading of the nature of future wars.[15] As a reward for their aggression, Serbia and Greece had almost doubled in size, each gaining 1.5 million inhabitants. Romania received the prize of Silistria. Bulgaria, the major loser, won only a narrow strip of Macedonia as well as Western Thrace on the Aegean Sea but was forced to cede the bitterly contested Adrianople to Turkey. The Great Powers, except for supporting Vienna's pressure on Serbia and Greece to evacuate Albania, had tacitly acquiesced in major strategic and demographic changes in the Balkans[16] (see Map 2.1).

Moreover, the precepts of international supervision of minority rights established at the Congress of Berlin were largely ignored during the Balkan Wars of 1912–13. Despite the efforts of Austria–Hungary as well as of several Jewish groups, the Treaty of London made no reference to rights to be granted to populations acquired by the Balkan League. The Treaty of Bucharest contained only minor stipulations protecting the religious rights of Balkan Christians. And in the subsequent treaty between Bulgaria and Turkey, a new element was introduced, the transfer of minority populations.[17]

This negative development reflected an alteration in the international climate since the age of Bismarck. Not only had Europe embarked on the global expansion known as the "new imperialism"; in the past decade it had become divided into two heavily armed military alliances that had barely averted a general war. Moreover, two outside powers, the United States and Japan, now challenged Europe's military and economic hegemony in the Americas and Asia. On the continent itself, between 1878 and 1914 the

14. Helmreich, *Diplomacy of the Balkan Wars*, pp. 341–406.
15. Especially because the battles of the Balkan Wars only *seemed* "swift and decisive." Taylor, *Struggle for Mastery*, p. 500; also Hall, *The Balkan Wars*; Herrmann, *The Arming of Europe*; and Gerolymatos, *The Balkan Wars*.
16. Two useful contemporary studies are Jacob Schurman, *The Balkan Wars,* and Trotsky, *The Balkan Wars*, which contains the passionate, astute observations of the *Kievskaya Mysl*'s war correspondent.
17. Macartney, *National States and National Minorities*, 2nd ed. pp. 172–5.

Map 2.1. Southeastern Europe after the Balkan Wars, 1913.

growth of industry and cities, mass transportation and communication, nationalism and popular democracy had all transformed the peoples of Europe. Still the world's leading banker, producer, and merchant, Europe had also spawned racist ideologies, religious persecutions, and social and economic discrimination, which sent millions of its ambitious and threatened peoples to distant lands where, far more than earlier exiles, they changed national and international politics.[18]

THE MINORITY QUESTION IN THE AGE OF EUROPEAN IMPERIALISM

Between the Congress of Berlin and World War I the plight of Europe's minorities had significantly worsened. In the Balkans, the Christians of the Ottoman Empire suffered more frequent persecutions and repression, while Romania continued to exclude the Jews from its public life. Throughout Europe, anti-Semitism suddenly became a major political and social movement.[19] After 1881, the Jews of Russia suffered a wave of pogroms along with the old crippling legal restrictions and a growing economic plight.[20] In Wilhelmian Germany, social and legal barriers undermined and even threatened the Jewish community,[21] while in Austria–Hungary, anti-Jewish sentiments extended from the large cities to the ethnically mixed provinces.[22] In France, there was the violent and divisive Dreyfus Affair (1894–1906), and in Russia an even deadlier round of pogroms between 1903 and 1906 followed by the Beilis Affair of 1911.[23]

In respect to the Balkans, the Great Powers as a collectivity tended to overlook Turkey's violations of the religious clauses of the Treaty of Berlin. They treated outbreaks of violence against religious and national groups as isolated phenomena, especially because the invisible victims usually fled to shelter in nearby havens. In addition, the rivalry between Austria–Hungary and Russia prevented the formulation of a coherent interventionist strategy. Russia in particular remained adamant against the recognition of any

18. Hobsbawm, *Age of Empire.*
19. Lucien Wolf, "Anti-Semitism," in *Encyclopedia Britannica*, 11th ed. (Cambridge: University Press, 1910–11), Vol. 2, pp. 134–46.
20. Although recent research suggests that the tsarist regime neither planned nor encouraged the pogroms, which followed no specific pattern, it is also clear that the local authorities did little to stop the anti-Jewish violence. See the essays by Michael Aronson, Moshe Mishkinsky, and Erich Haberer, in Klier and Lambroza, *Pogroms*, pp. 39–134; Klier, "Pogrom Tradition."
21. Pulzer, *Jews and the German State*, pp. 96–194; other forms of anti-Semitism are described in Judd, "Kosher Butchering Debates in Germany."
22. McCagg, *Habsburg Jews*, pp. 161–222; Lohrmann, *Zwischen Finanz und Toleranz*, pp. 212–16.
23. Sternhell, "Popular Anti-Semitism"; Bredin, *Alfred Dreyfus*. For different views, see Lindemann, *The Jew Accused*; Linke, *Blood and Nation*.

"national" groups claiming special rights. Only after the murderous struggles unleashed by the Ilinden Uprising of 1903 did the Great Powers turn their attention to the conflict among Turks, Slavs, and Greeks in Macedonia; but at the end of five fruitless years of negotiation, there was a new wave of band warfare that further inflamed the region.[24]

The world community could not as easily ignore the exodus of some 2.5 million Jews from Eastern Europe. These immigrants, comprising not only victims of physical violence but also sufferers of economic, political, social, and personal restrictions, sought refuge and opportunity in Western Europe, Southern Africa, South America, and, especially, the United States. By stealth or official countenance, singly or in families and organized groups, this "greatest population movement of post biblical Jewish history" formed the major part of Eastern and Southern European population movement that forcibly focused world attention on the problem of minorities.[25]

Ironically, the impulse of voluntary, as opposed to coerced, emigration had been one of the basic premises of European Zionism.[26] Theodor Herzl's response to the acceleration of European anti-Semitism was to insist that a minority without a territory remained perpetually vulnerable to exclusion, persecution, and expulsion.[27] Herzl's followers recognized the limits of Great-Power support for minority rights; for example, despite periodic expressions of sympathy for the sufferings of the Armenians, the West had done virtually nothing for an endangered people who lacked a homeland and a powerful protector.[28] In their annual conferences after 1897, the Zionists challenged Jewish assimilationists, their own governments, and the prevailing international system by insisting that the Jewish people constituted a national entity with the same historical right as Greeks, Romanians, Serbs, and Bulgarians to occupy their ancient homeland.[29]

The consequences of the unforeseen mass Jewish emigration to the already teeming cities of Central and Western Europe and the United States were politically and socially explosive. Immigrants, once welcomed in menial trades, sweatshops, and factories, came to be regarded with disdain and fear. Because of their distinctive language, dress, and customs, the Jews were branded as dangerous outsiders, threatening to destabilize whole communities with their diseases and crime. Trade unions agitated against unfair competition. Teachers and social workers deplored their charges' degraded minds

24. Danford, *The Macedonian Conflict*, pp. 38–9.
25. Marrus, *The Unwanted*, pp. 27–39.
26. Vital, *Origins of Zionism*, pp. 4, 10–12.
27. Herzl, *A Jewish State*; also Herzl, *The Diaries of Theodore Herzl*.
28. Detailed in Trotsky, *The Balkan Wars*, pp. 235–47.
29. Vital, *Origins of Zionism*, pp. 354–75.

and morals. Politicians campaigned against the threat to democracy posed by these former inhabitants of feudal monarchies who had also brought anarchism, Socialism, and Communism to their new places of abode.[30]

The traditional Jewish organizations in Central and Western Europe, still nominally led by the AIU, proved powerless to contain the flood of migrants that threatened the security of existing Jewish communities. Working through the Jewish Colonization Association as well as their own national organizations, Austrian, German, French, Belgian, and British Jews sought to make the emigration a more orderly process and ministered generously to the needs of the new arrivals; but they also tried to redirect the Jewish masses' itineraries overseas, particularly to North and South America. Working privately and publicly, they sought their governments' support for their welfare work, combated the growing anti-immigration sentiment, and disseminated information on the sufferings of their fellow Jews in Eastern Europe.[31]

The mounting divisions within almost every Jewish community, particularly between the establishment and the newer arrivals, blunted these self-protective, humanitarian efforts. The debates over aid to the *Ostjuden* between Jewish assimilationists and the Nationalists, Zionists, and Radical Socialists reflected a larger power struggle. The Jewish gentry of Western Europe and the United States, who were still confronted with prejudice and exclusion,[32] faced challenges and rivals from the newcomers who disputed their elitist values and political cautiousness in dealing with the problem of mass Jewish suffering.[33]

If western Jews found themselves divided and relatively powerless to protect their eastern kindred, so too were those states, large and small, that considered themselves the defenders of their dispersed peoples. From mighty tsarist Russia, which had styled itself the protector of Balkan Christendom, to the small Balkan kingdoms of Greece, Romania, Serbia, and Bulgaria, which were officially dedicated to freeing their unredeemed relatives, there were similar debates between cautious politicians and ardent interventionists over the best means of protecting their threatened kin in the Ottoman and

30. Gainer, *Alien Invasion*; also Gartner, *Jewish Immigrant*, pp. 61–2, 114, 127, 157; Green, *The Pletzl of Paris*, pp. 172–82; Wertheimer, *Unwelcome Strangers*, pp. 23–74, 123–61.

31. Norman, *An Outstretched Arm*, pp. 7–114; Troen and Pinkus, *National Jewish Solidarity*, pp. 3–10; Wischnitzer, *To Dwell in Safety*, pp. 37–140.

32. Upper-class American Jews were particularly sensitive about their meager representation in the executive and judicial branches and in foreign embassies; Louis Marshall, a Republican stalwart who had vainly aspired to a seat on the Supreme Court, refused to join "the procession of Jewish ambassadors to Turkey," Rosenstock, *Louis Marshall*, p. 55.

33. Berman, *Attitude of American Jewry Towards Jewish Immigration*.

Habsburg empires.[34] Governments and private organizations each undertook humanitarian activities, armed militant bands, and preached irredentism, thus inserting a kindred people into domestic and foreign policy.[35]

To be sure, any intervention on behalf of minority rights by outside governments contradicted the reigning gospel of state sovereignty that had been firmly established in 1871. After a decade of "blood and iron," during which Germany and Italy had achieved national unification, the West European model of the unitary state became firmly implanted on multinational Central and Eastern Europe. Foreshadowed by the fierce Nationalist struggles of 1848, the state building that subsequently developed east of the Rhine established a framework of master and subordinate peoples who dwelt within fixed borders. In an updated version of *cujus regio ejus religio* (the ruler's religion is the region's religion), it was assumed that every new state's laws and institutions, culture, and society would reflect this national dominance: *cujus regio ejus natio*.[36] In regions inhabited by small numbers of the state-ruling nationality such as Wales and Galicia, Finland and Dalmatia, the government allowed subruling peoples to establish local control over all other populations, still a microcosm of the principle of winner-take-all.[37]

From multinational Eastern Europe also came proposals to alleviate the inequities and dangers of the exclusivist nation–state. Given the fact that assimilation, on the western model, was not practicable, some liberal thinkers believed that economic and political modernization might proceed within the framework of a decentralized or federal state in which distinctive languages, religions, and cultures survived. In 1849, the stillborn Kremsier Constitution for a reformed Austria had planted the seed by projecting not only the division of the empire into its historic units but also the creation of smaller constituencies in which every nationality would enjoy equal rights.[38] A half-century later, faced with an intense nationality conflict that had led

34. Milojković-Djurić, *Panslavism*; MacKenzie, *The Serbs*; Dakin, *Greek Struggle in Macedonia*; on Italian irredentism, see Toscano, *South Tirol*; Freiberg, *Sudtirol*.

35. Perry, *Politics of Terror*, pp. 143–212; for a historical overview, see Chazan, *Irredentism and International Politics*.

36. "In the struggle between nationalities one nation is the hammer and the other the anvil; one is the victor and the other the vanquished. It is a law of life and development in history." Bülow, *Imperial Germany*, p. 245.

After the Civil War, the United States developed the concept of an American nationality dominated by the values of its Anglo-Saxon, Christian elite that placed native Americans, Hispanics, black Americans, Asians, and the hordes of Eastern and Southern European immigrants in a culturally as well as economically and politically subordinate position. See, e.g., Strong, *Our Country*; Alfred Thayer Mahan, letter to *The* [New York] *Times*, June 13, 1913, in Seager and Maguire, *Alfred Thayer Mahan*, Vol. 3, 1902–1914, pp. 495–9.

37. Macartney, *National States and National Minorities*, pp. 133–4; on tsarist Russia's erratic policies in Finland, see Polvinen, *Imperial Borderland*.

38. Kann, *Multinational Empire*, Vol. 2, pp. 21–40.

to political paralysis, the Austrian Social Democrats revived the Kremsier program. Two of their most brilliant theorists, Otto Bauer and Karl Renner, called for the federalization of the empire into separate political units; to ensure equal rights and representation in heavily mixed areas, they developed the revolutionary idea of a personal form of national identity, enabling all citizens, wherever they lived, to join public, representative bodies that levied taxes and were responsible for their members' cultural well being.[39] Two Jewish scholars from Russia, Chaim Zhitlovsky and Simon Dubnow, and the Austrian publicist Nathan Birnbaum made similar proposals for the reconstitution of Russia and Austria–Hungary into "multinational commonwealths."[40]

Predictably, not only did the rulers of the Habsburg, Russian, and Ottoman Empires resist the idea of autonomy, but minority leaders did as well. Ardent nationalists opposed a device that thwarted their goal of full self-determination. Among the Jews, there were particularly strong misgivings. The Zionists, while affirming the importance of recognizing Jewish cultural rights, feared to divert their constituency from more ambitious ventures. On the other hand, the Socialists and assimilationists deplored the "artificial" creation of minicouncils and the local politicking that would undermine either the class struggle or the process of integration into the national community.[41]

The political upheavals of 1905 accelerated the autonomist movement. The Russian Revolution and the electoral-reform struggle in Austria induced the Zionists, Socialists, and nationalists to rethink their opposition, coordinate their strategies, and attempt to gain a larger voice in the struggle to liberalize the two empires.[42] Even the most ardent assimilationists recognized the futility of applying western formulas of integration and assimilation to the polyglot peoples in Central and Eastern Europe, which had now reached an extremely high state of national consciousness. Autonomy formulas grew increasingly popular and elaborate. Moreover, even the inhabitants of tsarist Russia looked more favorably on the maintenance of the empire in a more liberal, decentralized form in order to preserve its vast commercial, industrial, and political fabric. More and more politicians, local, national, and foreign, viewed the prospect of

39. Bauer, *Nationalities and Social Democracy*; Renner, *Selbsbestimmungsrecht der Nationen*.
40. Dubnow, *Nationalism and History*, pp. 131–42; Birnbaum, *Schriften zur jüdischen Frage*, Vol. 2, pp. 125–76.
41. Ben Sassoon, *History of the Jewish People*, pp. 902–14.
42. Janowsky, *Jews and Minority Rights*, pp. 86–142.

self-governance as a sign of a minority's maturity and its government's beneficence. If only a partial solution, autonomy began to appear as a sound, solid measure.[43]

THE JEWISH STRUGGLE FOR MINORITY RIGHTS

The outbreak of the Balkan Wars came as an unwelcome blow to the Jews of Western Europe and North America.[44] The transnational cooperation that had contributed to their brief triumph in Berlin had not entirely disappeared; but in the postliberal climate after 1878, the Jews no longer possessed a Crémieux or a Bleichröder, with their personal ties, moral leadership, and political authority over dozens of worldwide communities. As a result of the divisions among the Great Powers, each Jewish national group now more or less pursued its own foreign and domestic policies. The continental organizations, because of their smaller numbers, strong patriotism, and negligible political power, tended to focus on low-profile practical tasks. Thus the AIU devoted itself primarily to Jewish education and welfare in North Africa, Southeastern Europe, and the Middle East, which it coordinated with France's overall *mission civilisatrice*; and the *Hilfsverein der deutscher Juden* [Welfare Society of German Jews], founded in 1901, directed government and private aid to the masses who crossed German territory. It thus fell to the Jews of Great Britain and, especially, of the United States, to function as mediators between the blocs as well as the main advocates for their distant, endangered kin.[45]

The vanguard organization of Anglo–Jewish foreign policy was the Conjoint Foreign Committee of British Jews linking two rival organizations founded over a hundred years apart.[46] Established in June 1878 by businessmen–elites who had crusaded for Jewish civil rights in Britain, the Conjoint had two international goals: to lobby for the fulfillment of the minority clauses of the Treaty of Berlin and for the extension of Jewish emancipation in Russia. After 1908, under the energetic direction of the political journalist Lucien Wolf (1857–1930), the Conjoint also urged a

43. Even the refusal of the Second International in 1907 to seat "a socialist party of the Jewish nationality" did not dampen their claim to a recognized identity. Ibid., pp. 153–4.
44. "The Balkan Wars and the Jews," *American Jewish Yearbook* (Oct. 12, 1913–Sept. 20, 1914) (Philadelphia: Jewish Publication Society of America, 1913), pp. 188–206.
45. See Lucien Wolf to Otto Kahn (Hilfsverein), July 29, 1913, YIVO W/M 48.
46. The Board of Deputies of British Jews, founded in 1760, and the Anglo–Jewish Association, founded in 1871.

Photograph 2.1. Lucien Wolf (reproduced with the permission of the Jewish Historical Society of England).

humanitarian British diplomacy that would alleviate Jewish suffering and stem the threat of mass emigration.[47]

The timing was not auspicious. Not only had Grey's liberal government only recently achieved the settlement of its outstanding quarrels with tsarist Russia[48]; but the Foreign Office, with its mounting Germanophobia, was reluctant either to concert with the Berlin signatories or embark on a solo crusade for Jewish rights that might offend its highly sensitive new partner and its pugnacious Balkan clients. For all Wolf's fervent efforts to call attention to Romania's flagrant violations of the Berlin Treaty and Russia's refusal to emancipate its huge Jewish population, his main accomplishment was to gain notoriety in Whitehall as a troublesome meddler who

47. Levene, *War, Jews, and the New Europe*, pp. 2–19; Black, *Anglo-Jewry*, pp. 243–301; background in Finestein, *Anglo-Jewry in Changing Times*, pp. 140–67.

48. "Good relations with Russia meant that our old policy of closing the Straits against her, and throwing our weight against her at any conference of the Powers must be abandoned." Grey Memorandum, Mar. 15, 1907, Gooch and Temperley, *Origins of the War*, Vol. 4, No. 257. A formal agreement between the two former imperial rivals was signed on Aug. 31, 1907.

invariably received noncommittal assurances designed to propitiate his powerful patrons.[49]

The political situation of American Jewry, which was even more complex, formed the dramatic backdrop to the failed minorities diplomacy of the Balkan Wars. The American Jewish Committee (AJC), established in 1906, was also a new defense organization linking two older structures; from the start, its oligarchic leadership was contested by more populist elements of the three million strong, highly politicized American–Jewish community.[50]

The forerunners of the AJC had already acquired considerable experience in lobbying for Jewish rights abroad.[51] In 1891 three leading Jewish figures, Oscar Straus, a New York businessman and former ambassador to Turkey, and the bankers Jacob Schiff and Jesse Seligman, who were all active supporters of the Republican Party, appealed directly to President Benjamin Harrison over the dire conditions of Russian Jews. Harrison's dispatch of a mission of inquiry, his December message to Congress, and the release of the Weber report in February 1892 stating the justification for protests against foreign governments that oppressed and impoverished their people and drove hordes of them to America's shores, gave the American Jewish elite a momentary triumph.[52]

Like their European counterparts, American Jews would rapidly learn that periodic turnovers of administrations and legislatures combined with a permanently resistant State Department made it difficult to create a sustained American stance in favor of Jewish and minority rights.[53] Despite the growing anti-immigration sentiment, the American public generally failed to make the connection between foreign oppression and the domestic consequences. Thus, when dramatic episodes and statistics disappeared from the U.S. press between 1892 and 1903, public sympathy for Russian Jews also evaporated.[54]

In 1902, Schiff and Straus used their political connections to revive the issue of Romanian Jewry, which had been virtually abandoned by the European powers.[55] The immediate cause was a new Romanian law barring Jewish workers from any trade. Theodore Roosevelt, responding to the

49. See, for example, Wolf's memorials on behalf of the Conjoint dated Dec. 17, 1912, Great Britain, Foreign Office records (hereafter GB FO) 371, Turkey/1778; July 10, 1913, ibid., Romania/1742.
50. Cohen, *Not Free to Desist*, pp. 3–36; Rosenstock, *Louis Marshall*, pp. 22–4.
51. Straus, "Humanitarian Diplomacy," especially pp. 19–38.
52. Best, *To Free a People*, pp. 20–41.
53. The Grover Cleveland administration, elected in 1892, showed far less concern than did its predecessor. Ibid., pp. 37–8.
54. Ibid., p. 38.
55. Mocatta to Straus, Mar. 31, 1902, Library of Congress, Washington, DC, Manuscript Division (hereafter LC), Oscar Straus papers.

urgent pleas of his two influential collaborators, authorized his Secretary of State John Hay to protest to the Bucharest government against its violations of "international law and eternal justice."[56] The United States, although not party to the Treaty of Berlin, also conveyed the text to the seven signatories.

The Hay Note elated European and American Jews. Indeed, the Romanian government responded with a few minor concessions. But cooler heads cautioned against too much celebration over the Jews' aggressive lobbying and over raising the immigrant scare.[57] Moreover, America's initiative failed to stir the Berlin signatories to take any action. Although Britain expressed sympathy, the rest were uninterested or opposed.[58]

The next great challenge was, once more, Russia. At Easter, between April 19 and April 21, 1903, armed mobs in southern Bessarabia attacked the Jews of Kishinev (Chişinău), leaving 47 dead, over 400 injured, and an estimated 2.5 million rubles in damage.[59] Again, American Jews took the leadership, organizing petitions and mass protest meetings and raising substantial sums for the victims.[60]

The political side was more difficult. Roosevelt responded cautiously to Jewish demands for an official remonstrance, fearing an "undignified" gesture and a rebuff, particularly because the Russian government denied official responsibility for the "spontaneous" atrocities in Kishinev. He agreed only to forward to St. Petersburg the text of the B'nai B'rith petition, which, not unexpectedly, the tsar's government refused to accept.[61]

The Kishinev episode, which underscored the limits of gaining presidential support, sent American Jews in two different directions: toward expanding the techniques of mass communication and mobilization,

56. "The United States may not authoritatively appeal to the stipulations of the Treaty of Berlin, to which it was not and can not become signatory, but it does earnestly appeal to the principles consigned therein, because they are principles of international law and eternal justice, advocating the broad toleration which that solemn compact enjoins and standing ready to lend its moral support to the fulfillment thereof by its cosignatories, for the act of Roumania itself has effectively joined the United States to them as an interested party in this regard." Hay to Wilson, July 17, 1902, U.S. Department of State, *Foreign Relations of the United States*, pp. 910–14.
57. *American Israelite*, Oct. 9, 1902.
58. U.S. Department of State, *Foreign Relations of the United States*, pp. 42–5, 549–50, 702–3, 849–50; also Notes pour le ministre, Sept. 12, 17, 1902, France, Ministère des Affaires Étrangerès (hereafter FMAE) NS 4, Roumanie, 1899–1914 (Question Juive); Wolf, *Diplomatic History of the Jewish Question*, pp. 37–8.
59. Judge, *Easter in Kishinev*.
60. Schiff to Strauss, May 5, 1903, American Jewish Archives (hereafter AJA), Jacob Schiff papers (hereafter Schiff). Despite some grumbling over assuming the burden that belonged to European Jews, Schiff and others urged their compatriots to act generously toward the sufferers in Russia. *American Hebrew*, May 8, 1903; *American Jewish Yearbook, 5667* (Sept. 20, 1906–Sept. 8, 1907), ed. Henrietta Szold (Philadelphia: Jewish Publication Society of America, 1906), pp. 34–7.
61. Saul, *Concord and Conflict*, pp. 474–7; Best, *To Free a People*, pp. 64–87.

including enlisting the support of the non-Jewish population, and toward the use of their financial resources to organize boycotts to punish Russia for its cruelty.[62] When pogroms reignited in Russia in November 1905 and Roosevelt rebuffed Schiff's "hysterical" pleas for presidential action, Congress moved into the breach, passing a resolution of "hearty sympathy" with the bereaved, which the president then agreed to sign.[63]

Out of the bloodshed of Kishinev and the pogroms of 1905, as well as the Jewish leaders' repeated failures to influence U.S. foreign policy, came the impetus for the formation of the AJC in the spring of 1906.[64] A new generation of American-born jurists and scholars now joined Schiff in the battle against pogroms, the threats of immigration restriction, and the underlying threat of domestic anti-Semitism. A key figure was Louis Marshall, a prominent New York attorney, whose biography read like an American fairy tale.[65] Even before succeeding Judge Mayer Sulzberger as the AJC's second president in 1912, Marshall had become the organization's major strategist in the defense of Jewish rights at home and abroad.[66]

By the time the AJC was founded, the cause of immigration restriction had gained the support of organized labor, influential congressmen such as Henry Cabot Lodge, regional leaders from the South and the West, and President Roosevelt himself. Among the various devices of exclusion, the Immigration Restriction League proposed a literacy test that would bar adult males who could neither read nor write in some language along with the exclusion of those whose "poor physique" and "low vitality" made it impossible for them to do productive work, and those unable to pay a head tax.[67] In its first political fight, allied with Catholics and business interests, the AJC energetically lobbied Congress and succeeded in burying the literacy

62. The head of this latter movement was Jacob Schiff, who, after Kishinev, sought to close off the U.S. money market to the Russian government. During the Russo–Japanese war, he underwrote a multimillion dollar loan to the Japanese government and reportedly paid for the distribution of revolutionary literature to Russian prisoners of war in Japan. Goldstein, *The Politics of Ethnic Pressure*, pp. 25–8; also Adler to Friedenwald, Oct. 22, 1907, Adler, *Selected Letters*, Vol. I, p. 137.
   Schiff also pursued a third direction, the Galveston movement, to divert the expected flood of Russian immigrants away from the North Atlantic ports, an effort that had only limited success. Best, *To Free a People*, pp. 141–65.
63. Goldstein, *The Politics of Ethnic Pressure*, pp. 28–52.
64. American Jewish Committee Archives (hereafter AJC), Minutes of the Executive Committee, Feb. 3, 4, May 19, 1906.
65. The son of a poor German immigrant, Marshall was born in 1856 in Syracuse, studied at Columbia Law School, and, after joining one of New York's major law firms and making a splendid marriage, rapidly entered the German–Jewish aristocracy. Adler, *Louis Marshall*, pp. 4–23.
66. Reznikoff, *Louis Marshall*.
67. $25 per male immigrant, plus $10 for each member of the family under 21 years of age. U.S. *Congressional Record*, 59th Congress, first session, 1906, Vol. XL, Part 8, p. 7293.

clause, at least temporarily. Marshall called the compromise immigration bill of 1907 a "scorching victory" for the fledgling committee.[68]

It was, however, a Pyrrhic triumph. Despite its deft work on both sides of the congressional aisles, the AJC failed to obtain a humanitarian exemption for Russian refugees from the "public-charge" restriction clause. Cyrus Adler, assistant secretary of the Smithsonian Institution who also headed the AJC's Washington office, maintained that the 1907 law represented national and international considerations that exceeded the Jews' power to control.[69] Congress, now under intense pressure from the executive and the public to halt the influx of immigrants from Eastern Europe and East Asia, was moving, unrelentingly, away from vague categories of undesirables and toward establishing numerical quotas to keep the United States as white, Christian, and Northern European as possible. America would thus inevitably have to recognize the sovereign right of other nations to exclude whole categories of peoples. A major clause in the 1907 immigration law, aimed at the Japanese, authorized the president to withhold recognition of certain passports; and in May 1907, Secretary of State Elihu Root announced that the State Department, reversing its former practice, would refuse to issue passports to American Jews unless the Russian government consented to their admission.[70]

Seizing a moment of threat and opportunity, which also coincided with the elections in 1908, the AJC launched a national campaign to punish tsarist Russia for its discriminatory treatment of Jewish–American citizens.[71] Jewish leaders had long called for the abrogation of the Russo–American commercial treaty of 1832, whose first article granted the traders of both countries freedom of entry, sojourn, and movement, subject to the laws of each government.[72] Russia had interpreted this clause to deny visas to American Jews or subject them to the discriminatory laws applied to Russian

68. See Friedenwald to Adler, Feb. 18, 1907, AJC Adler Papers; also Goldstein, *The Politics of Ethnic Pressure*, pp. 131–2.
69. "The [immigration] thing has gotten too big for any of us to handle." Adler to Friedenwald, Feb. 15, 1907, AJC Adler papers. Cyrus Adler, an eminent scholar of Semitic languages who had begun his career at the Johns Hopkins University before his appointment to the Smithsonian in 1893, was also president of the American Jewish Historical Society.
70. State Department Circular, May 28, 1907, quoted in Best, *To Free a People*, p. 168.
71. Schottenstein, "Abrogation of the Treaty of 1832."
72. "There shall be between the territories of the high contracting parties a reciprocal liberty of commerce and navigation. The inhabitants of their respective states shall mutually have liberty to enter the ports, places, and rivers of the territories of each party, wherever foreign commerce is permitted. They shall be at liberty to sojourn and reside in all parts whatsoever of said territories, in order to attend to their affairs, and they shall enjoy, to that effect, the same security and protection as natives of the country wherein they reside, on condition of their submitting to the laws and ordinances there prevailing, and particularly to the regulations in force concerning commerce." Quoted in Reznikoff, *Louis Marshall*, Vol. 1, p. 61.

Jews, and, in some instances, to prosecute naturalized American Jews for desertion or violation of Russia's emigration laws.[73]

The AJC's bold foray into international diplomacy coincided with a tumultuous period in American and Jewish politics. The twenty-seventh president, William Howard Taft, a cautious, conservative Republican elected by a huge majority in 1908, who was a pale shadow of his dynamic predecessor, immediately provoked an aggressive opposition. Moreover, the AJC, at the moment of its first legislative success, found itself increasingly challenged by more radical elements of the Jewish community. The abrogation campaign, more extensive and lavish than the fight against the literacy test, was not only an intricate advocacy project but also a high-stake struggle for domestic and foreign power.[74]

At home, by leading the fight for a new, more equitable treaty with Russia, the AJC hoped to eradicate all vestiges of second-class citizenship for American Jews. The committee's leaders, who were mainly staunch Republicans, had been stung by their government's tacit acceptance of discrimination against American Jews by a foreign power. Abroad, the AJC wanted to direct United States foreign policy in a more independent, humanitarian direction, to set a bold example for those timorous West European governments that had tolerated tsarist discrimination against their Jewish citizens. The AJC's leaders also dreamed that their intervention would ultimately "break the Pale," enabling Russia's Jews to live as free citizens in their homeland and ending, once and for all, the threats of pogroms and emigration.[75]

The struggle over abrogation exploded in 1911 when Taft announced his opposition, not only because it would damage U.S. relations with Russia and conceivably add to the burdens of Russia's Jews but also because it would complicate America's restrictive policies against the Chinese and Japanese.[76] The AJC joined Taft's numerous opponents, which included Roosevelt, the Democratic majority in the House, and a growing number of Progressive Republicans, and it generously supported politicians who sought the backing of ethnic minorities in the next election. The AJC sponsored huge demonstrations, a massive press campaign, and a widespread effort to enlist

73. The 1832 treaty recognized the principle of indefeasible allegiance. Subsequently, the United States negotiated treaties with the North German Union and Belgium (1868), Norway and Sweden (1869), Great Britain (1870), Austria–Hungary (1870), and Denmark (1872), recognizing its right to naturalize its immigrant population, but had not concluded such an agreement with Russia. See Flournoy and Hudson, *Nationality Laws of Various Countries*, pp. 660–73.

74. Cohen, "Abrogation of the Russo-American Treaty."

75. Reznikoff, *Louis Marshall*, Vol. 1, pp. 88–9.

76. "This means war," declared Jacob Schiff after hearing Taft's objections on February 15, 1911. AJC, Executive Committee minutes, Feb. 19, 1911; Reznikoff, *Louis Marshall*, Vol. 1, pp. 79–89; Schiff, *Jacob H. Schiff*, Vol. 2, p. 148.

the support of immigrant Catholic and fraternal organizations, climaxing on December 6, 1911, in a massive proabrogation rally in Carnegie Hall in New York that featured several congressmen and senators and the Democratic presidential aspirant, Governor Woodrow Wilson of New Jersey.[77]

To head off a congressional challenge, Taft took action. On December 17, 1911 the U.S. ambassador informed the Russian government that the 1832 treaty had been terminated; he gave no explanation and proposed negotiations for a new agreement. The president's tactful gesture did not prevent an explosion of Russian indignation over a hypocritical, meddlesome America that itself barred Russia's Asian and Muslim citizens and mistreated its own Negro population; there were also threats of retaliation.[78] After Wilson became president, it took more than a year to reestablish ambassadorial relations with tsarist Russia and, despite the hopes of the State Department, no successor treaty was ever negotiated.[79]

The AJC nevertheless exulted in its diplomatic and political victory,[80] again without recognizing how equivocal it was. Indeed, no European country followed America's example nor did the condition of Russia's Jews improve in any way. At home, the anti-Taft alliance immediately evaporated. In the wake of the widespread "apprehension" over 6 million new arrivals between 1907 and 1913, the swell of violent labor disputes, and the sensational reports of rising crime – grimly documented in the forty-two-volume report of the Immigration Commission – an overwhelmingly restrictionist Congress crafted exclusionist legislation, and, on February 1, 1913, passed America's first literacy test.[81] Two weeks later, as his last act of office, William Howard Taft vetoed the immigration bill[82]; the veto was upheld in the House by the narrowest of margins.[83]

By the beginning of 1913, nativism and racism had spread throughout the United States. As the AJC prepared to do battle with the Sixty-Third Congress over another literacy test and further forms of immigrant

77. Wilson, "The Rights of the Jews," in Wilson, *Public Papers of Woodrow Wilson*, Vol. 2, p. 318.

78. See, e.g., *The New York Times*, Dec. 28, 1911, p. 2; also "Russia's Protest Against Us," *The Literary Digest* (Apr. 20, 1912): 804–5; "Treaty of 1832," *Review of Reviews* (Jan. 1912): 23; "Russia and America: A Poll of the Press," *Outlook* 100 (Jan. 6, 1912): 22; "Russia's Attitude on the Abrogated Treaty," *Collier's* (Jan. 27, 1912); and, especially, Egert, *The United States and Russia.*

79. Saul, *Concord and Conflict*, pp. 570–84; Brecher, *Reluctant Ally*, pp. xiv–xv.

80. Schiff called it the greatest victory for the Jews since Napoleon granted them civil rights. Schiff to Charles P. Bloom, June 22, 1916, AJA, Schiff Papers, also AJC, Minutes of Executive Committee, Dec. 25, 1911.

81. Caminetti, *Report of the Commissioner General of Immigration*, p. 4.

82. U.S. *Congressional Record*, 62nd Congress, third session, 1913, Vol. XLIX, Part 3, pp. 3269–70. See also Taft, *The Presidency*, pp. 112–14.

83. The vote to override was 213–114, five short of a two-thirds majority. U.S. *Congressional Record*, 62nd Congress, third session, 1913, Vol. XLIX, Part 4, p. 3317.

exclusion, Tom Watson and Wilbur Franklin Phelps were disseminating anti-Catholic and anti-Semitic sentiments in the South and Midwest, the California legislature adopted the Alien Land Act that restricted ownership and leases by Asians, and the new president, Woodrow Wilson, permitted the institution of segregation in the federal government.[84] Several thousand miles away, on the Balkan Peninsula, five small states were about to acquire and rule over alien, unwilling, and relatively unprotected populations.

SALONIKA

On the west side of the Chalcidic peninsula at the head of the gulf that bears its name sits the port of Salonika. Founded in 315 B.C.E. by Macedonian King Cassander near the site of a more ancient Greek settlement, Salonika under the Roman and Byzantine empires became an important military, religious, commercial center.[85] Beginning in the tenth century, the city was occupied successively by Arabs, Normans, Greeks, Catalans, Ottomans, Byzantines, and Venetians before falling under Ottoman control from 1430 until the end of 1912.[86]

From its beginning, Salonika had had Jewish inhabitants; their numbers grew in the Middle Ages with refugees from Central Europe and Italy, swelled between 1492 and 1650 with the thousands of expellees and Inquisition victims from the Iberian peninsula, and expanded again between 1648 and 1659 with escapees from the massacres in Eastern Europe. In the late seventeenth century, Salonika also became home to several thousand Dönmeh, the followers of the messianist Sabbatai Zevi, who professed Islam but preserved many Jewish customs. Like other non-Muslims in the Ottoman Empire, the Jews of Salonika enjoyed a large measure of autonomy under the watchful eyes of local administrators, creating in this bustling Balkan port "a mother city in Israel."[87]

The Jewish population of Salonika reached its peak at the end of the nineteenth century. There were approximately 90,000 Jews, who made up about two-thirds of the total population and contributed not only to the city's commerce and manufacturing but also to the arts, literature, science,

84. Dinnerstein, *The Leo Frank Case*; Higham, *Strangers in the Land*, pp. 179–81, 185–86; Woodward, *Jim Crow*.
85. It was from Salonika in the year 863 that the two Greek brothers, Cyril (b. 827) and Methodius (b. 825) launched their famous mission to Christianize the Balkan Slavs, thus linking this city historically to the Serbs and Bulgarians.
86. Darques, *Salonique au XXe siècle*, pp. 4–23; also Hassiotis, *Queen of the Worthy*; Anastassiadou, *Salonique*.
87. Lewis, *The Jews of Islam*, p. 180.

philosophy, and religion. There were vigorous Zionist, Labor, and Socialist movements in Salonika as well as a handful of Jews who became Macedonian patriots and radicals.[88] But by 1908, the Jewish exodus had begun. In this birthplace of Mustafa Kemal and the Young Turk movement, Jewish communal rights came under threat; and there was also mounting hostility from the local Greek community. Thus thousands of Salonika Jews began seeking the security and opportunities of America.[89]

From the beginning of the Balkan Wars, Salonika was an object of local and international dispute. Led by Crown Prince Constantine, the Greek army triumphantly entered the city on November 8, 1912 and accepted the Turks' surrender. The Bulgarians, who arrived shortly afterwards, refused to recognize the fait accompli and demanded Great-Power support for their claims, based on Salonika's large Slavic population and its close economic ties with its eastern hinterland.[90] Serbia, which had its own designs on the Aegean port – as well as the fanciful idea of handing it over to Great Britain[91] – announced that it would acquiesce in an internationalized Salonika under three-power control in exchange for a port on the Adriatic.[92] And the two great outside rivals, Austria–Hungary and Russia, advocated a free port in Salonika open for use by all the Balkan states, the former to protect its extensive railroad interests and the latter to propitiate Bulgaria and block Habsburg expansion in Macedonia.[93]

Greece rebuffed these proposals with its ethnic and practical objections. It insisted that without Salonika it would be cut off from the Chalcidic Peninsula, which was "purely Greek." Internationalization was impractical, and the creation of a free port would create unfair competition with Piraeus.[94] Greece claimed Salonika "by right of conquest . . . enhanced by the fact that it had been consecrated by the King's blood,"[95] and pledged to provide facilities for Bulgarian, Serbian, and even Austrian trade. Backed openly by France and tacitly by Britain and Germany, Greece refused to withdraw.[96]

The arrival of Greek troops in Salonika had raised considerable apprehension among the community's local and foreign Jews.[97] In the first days there were widespread reports of rape and pillage in the Jewish quarter as well as

88. Matkovski, *The Jews in Macedonia*, pp. 70–5; Dumont, "Communauté juive de Salonique."
89. *Éléments d'histoire de la communauté israélite de Thessaloniki.*
90. Gooch and Temperley, *Origins of the War*, Vol. 9, Nos. 186, 201.
91. Ibid., Nos. 86, 101.
92. Ibid., Nos. 259, 263.
93. Ibid., Nos. 100, 117, 134, 165, 192, 410.
94. Ibid., No. 329.
95. King George of Greece was assassinated in Salonika on Mar. 18, 1913. At first it was suggested that his murderer was a Bulgarian; but the killer was a Greek who was insane. Ibid., ed. note, p. 600.
96. Ibid., No. 616.
97. Salomon David Coumié to Mair Cohen, Salonika, Nov. 12, 1912, AJC, Balkan Wars: Salonika; Molho, "The Jewish Community of Salonika," especially pp. 391–2; Lory, "Les Hellènes."

rumors from the Greek side of poisoned brandy, poisoned wells and ritual murder.[98] The AIU and the *Hilfsverein* immediately called for massive relief for the victims.[99] The long-term repercussions were also dire. The separation of this thriving Ottoman port from its hinterland of 4 million people threatened ruin to Jewish bankers, merchants, agents, pedlars, porters, and sailors as well as to the poor.

Not unexpectedly, the Jews of Salonika had favored an international solution that would have allowed them to retain their commercial prominence and communal autonomy.[100] As a distant second choice, they strongly preferred Bulgarian to Greek rule.[101] Were Salonika to become the chief port of this undeveloped, largely peasant state, the Jews would have retained their dominance over the grain trade, facilitated by their ties with Bulgaria's Sephardic merchant community.[102]

Greek officials, trying to calm the situation, held meetings with the Grand Rabbi of Salonika and other Jewish leaders; but they also repeated the widespread rumors that the Jews had not welcomed the Greek army with "open arms."[103] Salonika's Jewish community grew increasingly alarmed. They strongly distrusted the Greek Orthodox Church, with its long record of intolerance and persecution but especially because of the blood-ritual accusations, which, since 1860, had triggered numerous violent outbursts in other parts of Greece. Jewish businessmen feared the influx of Greeks into the community and also that their port would be sacrificed to Volos and Piraeus.[104]

The AJC, emerging from its bruising battles over abrogation and the literacy test, attempted to call Washington's attention to the menacing situation in Salonika. The outgoing Taft administration, particularly Secretary of State P.C. Knox, was unsympathetic, refusing to involve the United States in matters affecting "persons other than American citizens" and deprecating the atrocity reports.[105]

98. J. L. Magnes to Louis Marshall, Dec. 27, 1912, copy in AJC, Adler papers.
99. See Hilfsverein to AJC (Vertraulich), Nov. 15, 1912, Nathan to Schiff, Berlin, Dec. 19, 1912, AJC, Louis Marshall papers (hereafter LM); also *The New York Times*, Apr. 3, 1913.
100. In this effort, they were supported by Austria–Hungary, Italy, and the Young Turk government as well as the *Alliance Israélite Universelle*, the *Hilfsverein*, and the Anglo–Jewish Association in London as well as the Zionists. Skordylès, "Réactions juives à l'annexion de Salonique"; Gelber, "Internationalize Salonika."
101. Another attempt by Salonika's Jews to avoid Greek control was to acquire foreign citizenship from Austria–Hungary, Italy, Spain, or Portugal. Molho, "The Jewish Community of Salonika," p. 395.
102. This choice was promoted by Dr. Marcus Ehrenpreis, the Chief Rabbi of Bulgaria. Gelber, "Internationalize Salonika," p. 113.
103. Molho, "Venizelos and the Jewish Community of Salonika"; Plaut, *Greek Jewry*, p. 32.
104. Lucien Wolf, "Foreign Office Bag," *Graphic*, Jan. 4, 1913; also *Jewish Chronicle*, May 30, 1913.
105. Knox to Herbert Friedenwald, Secretary, AJC, Washington, Nov. 25, 1912, Jan. 30, 1913, AJC, State Dept. Balkans.

Weighing its options, the AJC quickly decided against sending its own emissaries to the Ambassadors' Conference in London, where their lack of authority, experience, and contacts would not only cut a sorry sight but also "slight the capacity of the English and European Jews" to do the work.[106] Instead Marshall appealed directly to Taft. The AJC's new president, citing America's practical interests as well as its previous humanitarian interventions to stave the flow of coerced refugees, proposed the naming of former Ambassador Oscar Straus as a special commissioner to London where he would speak in favor of inserting a clause in the peace treaties guaranteeing freedom of religion and equality of citizenship for all inhabitants.[107]

The Taft administration refused to involve itself in the fate of Salonika's Jews. Secretary of State Knox strongly advised the president against any form of American intervention in the Balkan Wars on either humanitarian or practical grounds. He insisted it was not in the United States' interest to assume unfulfillable moral obligations in Europe's most "confused" political, racial, and religious environment and thereby assume "moral obligations" it could not discharge. Not only was it dangerous to antagonize Russia by meddling in its special sphere of influence but such intervention might "impugn our exclusive claims in Latin America," which at the moment were about to cause Washington considerable difficulties.[108] Marshall accepted the rebuff with good grace, indeed agreeing "non-interference in European affairs was . . . the safest policy for us to pursue."[109]

Unsurprisingly, the London Ambassadors' Conference awarded Salonika to Greece with no restrictions.[110] And, despite the assurances of Greek Prime Minister Eleftherios Venizelos, the city was indeed rapidly hellenized and dejudaized.[111] The Greek government, which continued to allow the Jews to control their schools and religious organizations, immediately banned Sunday trading and imposed far stricter tax measures than the Ottomans.[112] During World War I, the Jewish population drew the ire of Greek nationalists for its support of neutrality. Venizelos' return to power in 1916 not only thrust Greece into the war but also intensified governmental intrusions and restrictions as well as outbursts of local anti-Semitism.

106. Adler to Sulzberger, Jan. 10, 1913, AJC Adler papers.
107. Marshall to Taft, New York, Jan. 14, 1913, AJC, LM. Marshall met with Taft a week later.
108. Knox to Taft, Jan. 25, 1913, U.S. Department of State, National Archives and Record Service (hereafter NA USDS) 870.4016/29.
109. P. C. Knox to Marshall, Jan. 29, 1913, AJC LM; Marshall to Adler, Jan. 30, 1913, ibid., State Dept. Balkans.
110. Grey, his marginal notes to Lowther to Grey, Constantinople, Apr. 12, 1913, GB FO 371/1794, acknowledged that "The Salonika Jews are likely to get the régime they like least."
111. Molho, "Venizelos and the Jewish Community of Salonika," pp. 117–22.
112. Plaut, *Greek Jewry*, pp. 30–2.

On August 17, 1917, a devastating fire swept the city center, destroying thirty-two synagogues and fifty religious schools and leaving over 50,000 Jews homeless. Only a fourth of the damages were paid, and many owners were barred from rebuilding when the center of Salonika was entirely reconstructed.[113] In the early 1920s came a huge influx of Greek refugees from Asia Minor, spawning nationalist and anti-Semitic movements. From 1912 to the eve of World War II, a huge wave of Jewish migration to France, the United States, and Palestine left only impoverished descendants of Salonika's golden age.[114]

Salonika's Jewish leaders recognized their helplessness to stem the destruction of their community. This once-flourishing, multiethnic port, like earlier conquered imperial cities, was transformed into a remote outpost of a small, nationalist kingdom, which considered its large Jewish population a threat to national security, prosperity, and consolidation.[115]

In the lugubrious Salonika episode, European and American Jews also recognized a challenge to their western liberal values. Lucien Wolf, although a professed assimilationist, acknowledged the perils to Salonika Jewry's existence. Thus he pleaded with the Greek ambassador to London for special protection of its communal rights and for the preservation of a separate cultural, economic, religious and social life.[116] Ionnis Gennadius' response was unequivocal:

> To ask us to make special distinctions or grant special privileges would be to upset the very principle of equality which is on the other hand demanded of us . . . You cannot ask us fairly or consistently to consider our Jewish fellow citizens differently than they are considered in England, nor has any other creed or nationality thought of requesting . . . a system of capitulations in Greece.[117]

And the London Conference undoubtedly agreed.

THE TREATY OF BUCHAREST

Silistria was a stark contrast to Salonika. This small strategic river town on the right bank of the Danube, inhabited by 12,000 Turks and Bulgarians, had

113. Wolf to Bigart, Nov. 26, 1917, AIU Angleterre I/J; also Hastaoglou-Martinidis, "The Jewish Community of Salonica"; Yerolympos, "La part du feu." Suspicions remain to this day on the origins of this fire.
114. *Éléments d'histoire de la communauté israélite de Thessaloniki*, pp. 31–32.
115. Rosillo, "Communauté séfardie de Salonique."
116. See Wolf, "Desiderata of Salonika Jewry," given to the Greek ambassador in London, Ionnis Gennadius, ca. Dec. 1913, YIVO W/M 3.
117. Gennadius to Wolf, Feb. 11, 1914, YIVO W/M 3.

been coveted by Romania since 1878.[118] As recompense for Romania's neutrality in the First Balkan War, the Conference of Ambassadors on May 11, 1913, had handed it to Romania. In return, the Bucharest government had pledged to indemnify those Bulgarians who decided to emigrate within six months. Bulgaria, on its part, was required to maintain the autonomy of the Kutzo–Vlachs within its borders and to permit Romania to provide subsidies for their schools and churches.[119]

Although there were only a few thousand Jews in Silistria, this routine territorial transfer revived the Jewish question in Romania. In particular, it enabled Jewish leaders to protest the nonfulfillment of Article 44 of the Treaty of Berlin and the suffering of Romania's 270,000 Jewish inhabitants who had been denied equal rights and citizenship.[120] During the mobilization of its army in the spring of 1913, the Bucharest government had promised to naturalize Jewish recruits; but once the short campaign was over, a new wave of anti-Semitic protest movements stifled this initiative.[121]

In light of the award of Silistria, the AJC hastened to establish a connection with the incoming Democratic administration and publicize the Romanian problem in the U.S. national press.[122] The signs seemed propitious because Wilson, as a candidate, had been a supporter of the AJC's abrogation campaign.[123] Moreover, in a growing restrictionist environment, Wilson, like his predecessors, would be alarmed over an "artificially forced increase of immigration into the United States by reason of racial or religious persecution."[124]

On March 28, 1913, Cyrus Adler, now president of Dropsie College in Philadelphia, and AJC Secretary Herbert Friedenwald called on the new president. Pleading on behalf of "a quarter of a million or more of Jews,"

118. Trotsky, *The Balkan Wars*, pp. 344, 367, 371–2; Helmreich, *Diplomacy of the Balkan Wars*, pp. 272–4. After four and a half centuries of Ottoman rule, Silistria had been awarded to Bulgaria at the Congress of Berlin.
119. Romania. Ministère des Affaires Etrangères, *Documents Diplomatiques*, Nos. 95, 96, 97, 118, 119. Gooch and Temperley, *Origins of the War*, Vol. 9, No. 970.
120. Confidential interview between AIU leaders Leven and Bigart and French Foreign Minister Stefan Pichon, Apr. 13, 1913, YIVO W/M 68.
121. Trotsky, "About the Reforms" and "The Jewish Question," in *Kievskaya Mysl*, Aug. 17, 20, 21, Sept. 17, 1913, reprinted in Trotsky, *The Balkan Wars*, pp. 387–9, 412–21. Sympathetic with the plight of the Jewish masses, the Russian Socialist leader criticized the assimilationist ("bourgeois") "Union of Roumanian Jews" for fiercely resisting the initiative by Italy's former prime minister, Luigi Luzzati, to mobilize world public opinion in favor of complete Jewish emancipation in Romania.
122. Marshall to Adler, Mar. 23, 1913, Adler to Marshall, Mar. 24, Marshall to Adler, Mar. 25, 1913, AJC, State Dept. Balkans.
123. See Wilson to Adler, Oct. 21, 1912, AJC, Adler papers; Wilson's speech at the Dec. 7 Carnegie Hall rally, *The New York Times*, Dec. 7, 1912.
124. S. Solis Cohen to Wilson, Philadelphia, Mar. 31, 1913, NA USDS 870.4016/3.

they requested he dispatch a commissioner to London "to present the views of this Government on the terms of peace in the Balkan States." Wilson was "cordial" but noncommittal.[125]

The Wilson administration, beset with other foreign-policy problems, particularly with Mexico, tabled the AJC's proposal for several months.[126] On the eve of Bulgaria's trouncing, an alarmed Adler called on Secretary of State William Jennings Bryan. Although declining to appoint a special commissioner, Bryan agreed to instruct the new ambassador to Great Britain, Walter H. Page, to notify Whitehall of America's interest in a treaty clause providing civil and religious liberty.[127] Page promptly responded that the Ambassadors' Conference, a powerless body, was unlikely to deal with subjects that the Balkan nations had already proved themselves "rather truculent and defiant toward 'the will of Europe.'"[128]

Bryan, choosing not to repeat the mistake of 1902 of consulting the Berlin signatories, went directly to the Balkan states.[129] On August 1, he instructed the American ministers in Greece, Montenegro, Bulgaria, Romania, and Serbia to inform their respective host governments that the United States would welcome a clause on civil and religious liberty in any agreement they might conclude.[130]

By the time the U.S. communication was dispatched, it was too late to exert any meaningful pressure. The representatives of the five Balkan states, already assembled in Bucharest, were determined to conclude peace without the tutelage of the Great Powers.[131] On August 5, all the delegates, claiming that their constitutions already provided civil and religious liberty, haughtily dismissed the American proposal as "superfluous."[132]

The snub could not have been more obvious. Moreover, it was no secret that the State Department's abortive action had been the result of "strong Jewish pressure."[133] Nevertheless, letters poured in to Wilson and Bryan

125. Adler to Marshall, Washington, Mar. 28, 1913; memorandum left with the president signed by Adler and Friedenwald, Mar. 28, 1913, AJC, Balkan Wars.
126. See Adler to Brylawski, May 22, 1913, AJC, Adler papers; Adler to Wilson, June 27, 1913, NA USDS 870.4016/6
127. Adler to Marshall, July 17, 1913, AJC, LM. Also, Adler to Wilson, June 27, 1913, J. B. Moore (acting secretary of state) to Adler, Washington, July 24, 1913; Tel. Moore to Page, July 23, 1913, NA USDS 870.4016/6.
128. Page to Secretary of State, London, July 25, 1913, memorandum from the Division of Near Eastern Affairs, July 30, 1913; Page to Secretary of State, July 29, 1913, NA USDS 870.4016/7-8.
129. Bryan to Page, Aug. 1, 1913, NA USDS 870.4016/8.
130. Bryan to U.S. Missions, Aug. 1, 1913, Ibid., 870.4016/8.
131. Jackson to Bryan, Bucharest, Aug. 3, 1913, Ibid., 870.4016/14.
132. Jackson to Bryan, Aug. 7 (tel. and letter), Ibid., 870.4016/12, 18; also Schuman to Bryan, Athens, Aug. 6, 1913, ibid., 870.4016/16.
133. "Bryan Admits Balkan Snub," *The New York Times*, Aug. 7, 1913.

lauding America's newest intervention on behalf of all threatened Balkan people.

The AJC tried to put a good face on its defeat. It had successfully lobbied several legislatures, mobilized the press, and forced the State Department to display America's humanitarian concern to the world.[134] Privately, however, American Jewish leaders had little cause for elation. The Ambassadors' Conference in London had ended without making any gesture on behalf of minority rights.[135] The U.S. government had no intention of championing Jewish rights abroad.[136] And with the eruption of the Leo Frank case in Atlanta, American Jews suddenly had their own Dreyfus affair on their hands.[137]

The Balkan delegates at Bucharest, having avoided outside interference, mediated their own religious and ethnic as well as territorial disputes.[138] Greece and Serbia attempted to secure religious and educational rights for their people in Bulgaria, but refused to allow reciprocity for the Bulgarians within their borders. Only Romania obtained specific guarantees from all three of its neighbors, who pledged to recognize its interests in, and respect the autonomy of the Kutzo–Vlachs.[139]

Despite rumblings from Vienna, Berlin, and St. Petersburg, the Great Powers did not revise the Bucharest Treaty.[140] The British Government assured the Conjoint Committee that all the regulatory clauses of the Treaty of Berlin remained binding. Nonetheless, the British and French emissaries rejoiced in the "coming of age" of the Balkan states.[141]

134. "America Once More Espouses the Cause of Persecuted Jews," *Jewish Morning Journal*, Aug. 7, 1913; also, Marshall's remarks in "Bryan's Appeal to the Balkans Did Much Good," *The World*, Aug. 21, 1913.
135. On July 29, 1913, Sir Edward Grey proposed the adjournment of the conference *sine die*. Cambon to Pichon, London, July 29, 1913. France. Ministère des Affaires Etrangères, *Les Affaires Balkaniques*, Vol. 1, p. 277.
136. Moore to Tabatsky, May 13, 1914, NA USDS 870.4016/13.
137. Dinnerstein, *The Leo Frank Case*, pp. 74–6.
138. Indeed, Romania helped itself to additional territory in southern Dobrudja, extending from Silistria to the port of Baltchik on the Black Sea.
139. Romania. Ministère des Affaires Étrangères, *Le traité de paix de Bucarest*, pp. 83–5.
140. Grey to Bertie, Aug. 7, 1913, Gooch and Temperley. *Origins of the War*, Vol. 9, No. 1219; Cambon to Pichon, London, Aug. 7, Pichon to Cambon, Paris, Aug. 9, 1913; France. Ministère des Affaires Étrangères, *Les Affaires Balkaniques*, Vol. 1, pp. 291, 295; Mensdorff to Berchtold, Aug. 11, 1913, Austria-Hungary. Ministerium des K. u. K. Hauses und des Äussern, *Die Ereignisse am Balkan*, p. 401; also Grey, *Twenty-Five Years*, Vol. 1, pp. 261–7; Helmreich, *Diplomacy of the Balkan Wars*, pp. 399–406, 455–8.
141. "The Treaty of Bucharest opens a new chapter in the long history of South Eastern Europe. It is the beginning of a new order of things, marking, as it does, the full coming of age of the Balkan States and showing their ability to settle their quarrels without outside assistance. Although it may be an utopian expression of opinion, would it not be far better for the peace of mind of Europe if their political independence were recognised and they be left alone to work out their own salvation?"

Two of the Balkan states also proceeded to conclude bilateral treaties with Turkey containing formulaic statements guaranteeing full religious rights to the Muslims. But there was this significant innovation. The Convention of Adrianople between Bulgaria and Turkey in November 1913 was the first interstate treaty on the exchange of populations. It sanctioned the "voluntary" removal of almost 100,000 of either Muslims or Christians who had the misfortune of living within fifteen kilometers of the frontier in Thrace. The outbreak of World War I prevented a similar arrangement between Turkey and Greece.[142]

For minorities and their defenders on both sides of the Atlantic, the outcome of the Balkan Wars foretold a bleak future. Not only had the divided Great Powers renounced their responsibility enshrined in the Treaty of Berlin, and not only had the new states rejected any further encumbrances; but the events of 1912–13 had revealed the extremely small margin of influence of the splintered Jewish world and of other advocates of minority rights.

Colville Barclay to Sir Edward Grey, Bucharest, Aug. 25, 1913, Gooch and Temperley, *Origins of the War*, Vol. 9, no. 1251.

142. Macartney, *National States and National Minorities*, pp. 430–5.

3

The Great War

"For a universal war for the Freedom of the Peoples, We beseech thee, O Lord."[1]

"Thinking of Poland and her tortured Jews, Between Goth and Cossack hounded, Crucified."[2]

"I do not think it is easy to exaggerate the international power of the Jews."[3]

The outbreak of World War I opened a calamitous era for Europe's minorities. Millions of Alsatians, Croats, Italians, Jews, Poles, Romanians, Serbs, and Ukrainians were forced to fight their kindred while those who remained behind, especially in the frontier regions, faced official and popular suspicion and persecution along with threats from the invader.[4]

The four-year conflict was especially catastrophic for Poles and Jews. Almost equally divided between the belligerents and inhabiting one of the war's main military and political battlefields, one group prayed for liberation while the other lay vulnerable to the depredations of all sides.[5]

1. Adam Mickiewicz, "The Pilgrim's Litany" (1832), *Poems by Adam Mickiewicz*, "trans. by various hands," ed. by George Rapall Noyes (New York: Polish Institute of Arts and Sciences, 1944), p. 415.
2. Israel Zangwill, "For Small Mercies" (April 1915), published in *The War for the World* (London: Heinemann, 1916), p. 274.
3. Lord Robert Cecil (Under Secretary of State for Foreign Affairs, and nephew to Balfour), March 1916, quoted in Abramsky, *The Jewish Dilemma*, p. 14.
4. Panayi, "Dominant Societies and Minorities"; Schmitt and Vedeler, *World in the Crucible*, pp. 457–8.
5. There were 6 million Jews residing in the Allied countries and some 2.5 million in the Central Powers. Duker, "Jews in the World War," and Szajkowski, *Jews, Wars, and Communism*, Vol. 1, pp. 35–6. Twelve million Poles were in Russian Poland, five in Austrian Poland and three in German Poland. Machray, *Poland*, p. 27.

A REVOLUTIONARY WAR

None of the original combatants had entered the struggle to liberate the oppressed peoples of Eastern Europe. The six belligerents, all rulers of restive peoples, claimed to be fighting a traditional defensive war and hesitated to unleash a war of nations. But everything changed at the end of 1914. Having failed to achieve a quick and decisive military victory, both sides broadened the contest into a global struggle. In their search for new allies and to open new battlefields, the Great Powers offered major inducements at their enemies' expense, commitments that affected millions of lives.

Of the two camps, the Central Powers, a tense alignment of three multinational empires plus tiny Bulgaria seemed the less likely champions of oppressed peoples. Austria–Hungary and the Ottoman Empire were both threatened by internal nationalist movements and by their neighbors' territorial appetites; and Bulgaria merely sought revenge for the Balkan Wars.

Nonetheless, it was the Central Powers' senior partner, Imperial Germany, that transformed Eastern Europe in World War I. This conservative regime, with its long illiberal record toward its non-German population,[6] developed a forceful wartime program to revolutionize the East. Ignoring its allies' sensitivities and weaknesses, Berlin was bent on creating a string of tributary buffer states between the Baltic and Black Seas. Toward this end, the Reich aligned itself with nationalist and radical left-wing groups and even gave lip service to minority rights. This crusade in the East also had its propagandistic purpose: to attract Entente liberals and win neutral support, particularly in the United States.[7]

The Entente's stance toward Eastern Europe, if less radical, was also laced with inconsistency. Tsarist Russia toyed with plans to subvert Austria–Hungary by championing its Slavic and Orthodox population, while Britain and France, although fearing to destroy an ancient pillar of the European balance of power, wooed Italy and Romania with specific Habsburg territories.[8] More ambitious, and contentious, were their plans to dismember

6. Blackbourn, *The Long Nineteenth Century*, pp. 260–1, 264–5, 267–8; Hagen, *Germans, Poles, and Jews*, pp. 118–322; Pulzer, *Political Anti-Semitism*.

7. Fischer, *Germany's Aims*, pp. 120–54; Farrar, *Divide and Conquer*.

Germany's incitement of foreign revolutions harked back to Bismarck's wooing of the Hungarians in 1866. Even after unification, the Iron Chancellor had proposed that, in a future German–Russian war, Germany should ignite an uprising in Russian Poland regardless of the repercussions in Prussia's own Polish *Ostmark*.

8. Linke, *Das zarische Russland*, pp. 41–61; Rothwell, *British War Aims*, pp. 75–9; Nere, *Foreign Policy of France*, pp. 4–9.

the Ottoman Empire, with Russia, Britain, and France, their belated Italian and Greek allies, and their Armenian, Arab, and Jewish clients, all vying over the succession.[9]

Throughout the war, there was a great discrepancy between the Entente's liberationist propaganda, directed at potential allies and neutrals, and the treatment of the subject populations in the British, French, and Russian empires. Threatened by the Reich's subversion, all three maintained tight internal security and all suppressed nationalist movements. Despite the huge moral and political damage of tsarist persecution of the Jews, Russia's Western partners shrank from criticizing an ally whose military contributions were crucial to victory and were prepared to satisfy all its territorial demands.[10] Thus for four years, the shibboleth of victory obscured the complexities of national liberation and minority rights.[11]

A few brave voices warned of the present and future dangers unleashed by the war.[12] Socialist, pacifist, and women's organizations, and, especially, the Jews, issued their grim forecasts and reports of atrocities and pleaded for international intervention. During the four years that the Central Powers dominated Eastern Europe, the defenders of minority rights focused largely on Berlin; but after the Russian Revolution and America's entry into the war in the spring of 1917, everything – including the future of minority rights – changed dramatically.

POLAND AS A COMBAT ZONE FOR NATIONAL AND MINORITY RIGHTS

After colluding for 100 years to keep the Polish question off the international agenda, the three partitioning powers suddenly styled themselves as Poland's deliverers. In the opening days of the war, to spark recruitment, material support, and loyalty in their exposed border regions, each made sweeping pledges. Tsarist Russia promised to create an expanded, autonomous Congress Kingdom by adding German and Austrian territory, Austria–Hungary, to unite the Congress Kingdom and Galicia as the third pillar of the Habsburg Monarchy, and Germany, to make a liberated

9. Gottlieb, *Secret Diplomacy*; Zeman, *The Gentlemen Negotiators*; Stevenson, *The First World War.*
10. French, *British Strategy*, pp. 42–55, 167–8, 207–10, 221–2.
11. Macartney, *National States and National Minorities*, pp. 212–13.
12. The most active of all wartime organizations was the pacifist, neutral Organisation Centrale pour une Paix Durable (OCPD) based in The Hague that, under the direction of the Norwegian historian and politician, Halvdan Koht, developed visionary proposals for balancing minority rights with state sovereignty and international stability. See *Rapport presénté par M. Halvdan Koht* (The Hague, OCPD, 1917), 45 pp.; OCPD, *Recueil de rapports sur les différents points du programme-minimum*, Parts 1–4 (The Hague: Nijhoff, 1916–18); Doty, *The Central Organization for a Durable Peace*, pp. 90–4. Also, Balch, *The Great Settlement* (New York: Huebsch, 1918).

Congress Poland part of its *Mitteleuropa*.[13] Britain and France, both longtime advocates of Polish rights but bogged down on the western front, passively observed these hollow pronouncements that were clothed in grand formulas of unity, freedom, and equality.[14]

All these liberation schemes had a powerful effect on the local population. Until the outbreak of the war the inhabitants of former Poland, whether under German, Austrian, or Russian rule, had been split among collaborators, rebels, and the many shades in between.[15] Now the occupied population would be tested still further. On August 27, 1914, when the Austrian High Command announced the formation of two Polish Legions to free Congress Poland, large numbers of Galician Poles and Jews, led by the Austrophile, right-wing Socialist leader, Józef Piłsudski, flocked to the colors as the embodiment of a "fighting Poland."[16] Piłsudski's rival, the pro-Russian National Democrat (or Endek) leader Roman Dmowski, set up the Polish National Committee (the *Komitet Narodowy Polski*, or KNP) in Warsaw, where he tried futilely to recruit Polish units for the tsarist army and also castigated the pro-German Legion and the Jews.[17] Vienna raised the stakes in embattled Galicia by promising the Poles' rivals, the Ruthenians, not only to liberate their persecuted brothers and sisters in the Russian Empire but also to create a separate Ukrainian crown land by merging Eastern Galicia and the Bukovina.[18] Germany, by contrast, did little to mobilize its Polish minority.[19] Determined not to alienate Russia completely, the

13. In contrast with their public positions, the policies of the three partitioning powers were complicated by their military and political calculations. Tsarist Russia, for example, was extremely reluctant to fulfill the impetuous pledge of autonomy, issued on Aug. 14, 1914, by its commander-in-chief, Grand Duke Nicholas, and vehemently opposed by reactionary circles and by those hoping for a separate peace with Germany. The "Austro–Polish" solution had to be hidden from the Hungarians and sold to the hesitant Germans. And the Reich's pledge to the Poles of West Prussia to establish "an independent Polish state linked to us" had to be squared not only with its token support for Austria's plans and with its aim to create a Germanized buffer region stretching from East Prussia to Upper Silesia but also with its hope to conclude a quick peace with tsarist Russia. See Conze, *Polnische Nation*, pp. 48–73; Grosfeld, *Polityka państw centralnych wobec*, pp. 33–4; Lemke, *Allianz und Rivalität*, pp. 17–38; Linke, *Das zarische Russland*, pp. 41–61; Leslie et al., *History of Poland*, pp. 110–14.
14. Calder, *Britain and the Origins of the New Europe*, p. 25.
15. Wandycz, *Partitioned Poland*, pp. 193–330.
16. Lemke, *Allianz und Rivalität*, pp. 1–17; Korzec, *Juifs en Pologne*, pp. 56–7. Leslie, *History of Poland*, p. 115, claimed, "Piłsudski's alliance with Austria was always purely tactical in character." The Polish Club in the Austrian Reichsrat called on their countrymen to support Austria's crusade against the Russian oppressors. Kumaniecki, *Odbudowa Państwowosci Polskiej*, pp. 16–17.
17. Wandycz, *Partitioned Poland*, pp. 335–7.
18. Lemke, *Allianz und Rivalität*, pp. 100–13.
19. Although reduced in strength and numbers by westward emigration and German colonization, the Poles of West Prussia were a compact group, Catholic and nationalistic. Leslie, *History of Poland*, p. 113. Berlin's plans to establish a frontier strip included the deportation of Polish and Jewish inhabitants from the borderlands and the resettling of Germans from the Reich and the Volga

Reich worked to restrain the competing nationalist ambitions unleashed by its Habsburg ally.

Instead of being wooed by the combatants, the Jews of Poland, Lithuania, White Russia, and the Ukraine faced disaster. In early August 1914 German troops crossed into Congress Poland and, under the pretext of removing snipers, bombarded the Jewish quarter of Kalisz, destroying 150 houses and causing thirty-three deaths.[20] Russian policy was even more devastating. The High Command, exploiting the rumors of Jewish smuggling, espionage, and sabotage in the frontier regions, ordered mass deportations that were carried out "abruptly and with stunning brutality." At first, more than 100,000 refugees were jammed into Warsaw and Kiev; when the tsarist army retreated in 1915, up to a half million Jews were forced into the Russian interior.[21]

Russia, although halted in East Prussia and evicted from part of Congress Poland, occupied seven-eighths of Austrian Galicia for more than a half a year between December 1914 and the summer of 1915. During this bleak episode, the conquerors, and their Endek accomplices, took revenge on the pro-Habsburg population, closing Polish schools and bringing in Eastern Orthodox clergy to proselytize among the Ukrainians. By all accounts, the Jews were targeted for the worst treatment.[22] Starting in September 1914, there were allegations of Jews' firing on tsarist troops entering Lemberg, charges that would be echoed throughout the war by Russian, German, Austrian, and, finally, Polish and Ukrainian armies. Beaten and pillaged, forbidden to publish, and denied basic freedoms, the Jews of Galicia were used

region of Russia, thus cutting off the Poles in West Prussia from their kin to the east. Geiss, *Polnische Grenzstreifen*; Fischer, *Germany's Aims*, pp. 115–16.

20. Conze, *Polnische Nation*, p. 58; Geiss, *Polnische Grenzstreifen*, p. 33. Kalisz (Kalish), the most ancient Jewish community in Poland, was settled in the late twelfth century by refugees from the Rhineland; the site of numerous atrocities, it was attached to the Congress Kingdom in 1815 in the deal at Vienna that gave the Rhineland to Prussia.

21. Klier, "The Jews," p. 698, states that 600,000 Jews were deported; see also Lohr, "The Russian Army and the Jews."

Firsthand account: Dubnow, *Mein Leben*, pp. 192–4. On Mar. 30, 1915, the French ambassador wrote that "Hundreds of thousands of unfortunates have been seen wandering across the snow, driven like cattle by squads of Cossacks, abandoned in distress in railway stations, parked in the open on the outskirts of cities, dying of hunger, of exhaustion, of cold." Paléologue found the situation all the more lamentable in light of the 240,000 [sic, 400,000] Jewish soldiers doing exemplary service in the tsar's army. Paléologue, *La Russie des tsars*, Vol. 1, pp. 335–6. See also Gatrell, *A Whole Empire Walking*.

22. S. Ansky, "The Destruction of Galicia, Excerpts from a Diary," in *The Dybbuk and Other Writings*, trans. Golda Werman (New York: Schocken, 1992), pp. 171–73, 176–203.

A British relief worker report: "The Cossack advance guards, entering a town or village, would enquire the direction or disposition of the Austrian forces from the Jews.... [They] would make a mistake or be misled, fall into what they believed to be an ambush, lose some of their officers, come back furious and burn the Jewish quarter. It can hardly be doubted that on such occasions they used their weapons on the wretched inhabitants. The Cossacks also raped Jewish women and pillaged freely." John Pollock report, enclosed in Buchanan to Cecil, Aug. 17, 1915, GB FO 371/2455.

as hostages and deported to special camps beyond the Dnieper without food or baggage.[23] Fleeing Russian terror, between 200,000 and 300,000 Galician Jews escaped westward; more than 100,000 arrived in Vienna, where they strained the local welfare system, created rifts in the Jewish community, and ignited local anti-Semitism.[24]

The first protests against the Jews' harsh treatment came from Russian intellectuals and liberal members of the Duma.[25] In the West, sparked by the exposés of the distinguished Danish–Jewish journalist, Georg Brandes, who had been alerted by Zionist sources, the French, British, and U.S. press also condemned Russian and Polish outrages against the Jews.[26] Western Jewish leaders, sensing the delicacy of promoting Jewish interests "to the detriment of the united and single-minded prosecution of the war... [by] the three Allied Powers," quietly petitioned their governments to relieve the suffering.[27]

Britain and France, while regretting Russia's excesses, refused to censure their indispensable ally and to distract the world's attention from German atrocities, particularly in Belgium.[28] Moreover, conservative Entente leaders and the right-wing press were highly receptive to Russian and Polish charges of a global German–Jewish conspiracy.[29]

Thus, while German officials and intellectuals made capital of the Russian atrocities, western Jews were loath to speak out in defense of their beleaguered kindred.[30] British Jews in particular, given the mounting domestic xenophobia as well as their own history of close ties to Berlin and Vienna, feared to incur charges of russophobia, germanophilism, and a lack

23. Wolf to Oliphant, Sept. 1, 1915 and unsigned memo, "The Eastern War Zone: Ill-treatment of the Jews," GB FO 371/2455. According to Russian–Jewish sources, some 74,000 Jews were deported from Galicia. Golczewski, *Polnisch-Jüdische Beziehungen*, pp. 121–3.
24. Hoffmann-Holter, "*Abreisendmachung*," pp. 21–141. Golczewski, *Polnisch-Jüdische Beziehungen*, pp. 121–3.
25. A parliamentary investigation revealed the fraudulence of the treason charges. Greenberg, *The Jews in Russia*, pp. 99–101. Among the Jews' strongest defenders was the writer Maxim Gorki. Korzec, *Juifs en Pologne*, p. 51.
26. On the outcry in the United States, see Drozdowski, *Paderewski*, pp. 79–80.
27. See Conjoint to Sir Edward Grey, Jan. 12, 1915, YIVO W/M 57; AIU to FMAE, July 23, 1915, AIU, L/238; Wolf to FO, Sept. 1, 1915, GB FO 371/2445. Quotation is in letter from Charles Emanuel to Dr. Hertz, Nov. 12, 1914, YIVO W/M 57.
28. On Britain's anti-German propaganda, see Zeman, *The Gentlemen Negotiators*, pp. 166–9; Sanders, *British Propaganda*, and also Horne and Kramer, *German Atrocities*.
29. The British ambassador in Petrograd, reported, "There cannot be the slightest doubt that a very large number of Jews have been in German pay and have acted as spies during the campaigns in Poland." Buchanan to Grey, Mar. 10, 1915, GB FO 800/74 (Grey papers).
30. For examples of Anglo–French concern and cooperation see, e.g., report #1 (1915); confidential memorandum, Jan. 19, 1915; report, Mar. 16, 1915; Wolf to Bigart, Mar. 2, 1915; memorandum on Jews in Poland, n.d.; memorandum of the Jewish Conjoint Committee, June 3, 1915; "The Polish Question, June 30; reports, Sept. 6, 1915; Dec. 15, 1915, YIVO W/M 57–59.

of commitment to the Allied cause.[31] French Jews, who had rallied enthusiastically to the *Union sacrée* but were not spared the anti-Semites' accusations of their alleged ties across the Rhine, clung to the government as their protector.[32]

Little support came from the neutrals. Across the Atlantic, American Jews, already split by their origins, class, and Zionist sympathies and threatened by mounting prejudice and anti-immigration legislation, were also sorely divided over their stance toward the European war.[33] Russia's excesses against its Jews forced the cautious Entente supporters onto the defensive, fueling the more militant, pro-German, nationalist, and Zionist camps, and igniting conflict with Polish nationalist organizations in the United States.[34]

Germany's Jews were less reticent about championing the rights of their threatened eastern coreligionists. Proud, patriotic, and activist, the Reich's Jews sought allies in the higher reaches of government and military who favored national rights, including rights for the Jews, as a means of gaining

31. See, for example, the blistering attack on the Conjoint leader, Lucien Wolf, by Leo Maxse, "The Fight," *National Review* (Sept. 1914).

    Another complicating factor for British Jews was the presence of between 100,000 and 150,000 Jewish immigrants. The Aliens Act of 1905, effectively ending Britain's open-door immigration policy, was largely a response to their unwelcome arrival. Although comprising only one-third of 1% of Britain's total population, this foreign population occupied a conspicuous place in an otherwise homogeneous society, all the more complicated by the war, when the Home Office began distinguishing Russian–Polish Jews as "friendly aliens" and those from Austrian Galicia as "unfriendly." Moreover, the resistance of London's East End Russian Jews to military service (fewer than 400 enlisted before Oct. 1916) and subsequently to conscription stoked British anti-Semitism. Aronsfeld, "Jewish Enemy Aliens"; Cesarini, "An Embattled Minority," especially pp. 61–68.

32. Bigart to Wolf, Paris, Dec. 10, 1915, YIVO W/M 60. The royalist *Action Française* led the attacks on the Jews, and on Jan. 19, 1916, the *Libre Parole* accused eminent Jewish sociologist Émile Durkheim, who had been working since the beginning of the war as a propagandist for the French government, of being a German agent.

    French Jews had also been forced on the defensive in June 1915 when, in response to the anti-Semites' charges of shirking against the 30,000–40,000 "Russian" [Jewish] refugees in Paris, the French government summoned all eligible men to present themselves at police stations, although some 9,000 had already volunteered for service at the outbreak of the war. To stave off a propaganda disaster abroad, Durkheim joined a municipal investigatory committee that postponed the police inquiry and produced a report strongly defending the right of asylum of foreign Jews in France. Durkheim, "La situation des Russes en France."

33. "We must see to it that nothing is done by us in America, even for the purpose of helping the Jews in Poland, which would injure the Jews in America." Cyrus Adler to Louis Marshall, Philadelphia, Nov. 8, 1915, in Adler, *Selected Letters*, Vol. 1, p. 294; also, Adler to Marshall, Philadelphia, Feb. 2, 1915, to Solomon Schechter, Philadelphia, Mar. 4, June 9, Oct. 11, 1915, to Louis Brandeis, New York, Aug. 3, 1915, to Jacob Schiff, Philadelphia, Sept. 29, Oct. 21, 1915, ibid., pp. 259–61, 264–6, 273–4, 276–84, 288–94. Marshall to Zangwill, Aug. 30, 1916, Central Zionist Archives (hereafter CZA) A120/442; Goldstein, *The Politics of Ethnic Pressure*, pp. 247–87.

34. At the outbreak of World War I, the United States had some 3 million Jews. There were also approximately 3 million Poles from all three areas of partitioned Poland, a third of whom lived in four major urban centers, Philadelphia, Pittsburgh, New York, and Chicago. Zake, *The Polish American Community*, pp. 15–21.

support for *Mitteleuropa* at home and abroad.[35] Prominent Reich Jews, including the Zionists, characterized the *Ostjuden* as a potential vanguard of Germandom. In November 1914, they helped establish the innocuous-sounding, quasi-official *Komitee für den Osten*, an organization whose long-term goal was to replace the repressive tsarist order in Western Russia with a region of autonomous peoples between the Baltic and Black Seas, which coincided neatly with Germany's imperial design.[36]

On the other hand, the Reich's leaders were also cautious about the Jews' overtures. Berlin hesitated to alienate the Poles by endorsing a multinational Polish entity. It also doubted the Reich Jews' influence over their eastern kin.[37] Moreover, Germany considered the *Ostjuden* questionable allies, more inclined to negotiate directly with their neighbors than to function as the instrument of an outside, conquering power.[38]

Austria–Hungary was even more reluctant to align itself with the Jews. Vienna feared to antagonize its Poles and Ukrainians. And indeed, from the start, the Habsburg Poles refused to establish any relations with the Reich Jews.[39]

The contest over Poland was decided in the middle of 1915. The two imperial armies reconquered Galicia and also overran Russian Poland, where they established two separate military and administrative districts, a larger German sector with its capital in Warsaw and an Austrian zone controlled from Lublin.[40] Although welcoming local and international support for their antitsarist crusade, Berlin and Vienna still hoped to conclude a separate peace with Russia and thus shrank from making any irrevocable political gestures. And the West maintained its silence over Poland.

The occupation of Congress Poland by the Central Powers marked a new stage in Polish history, an important and eventful three-year period of quasi-independence. Officially, the new rulers maintained most of the tsarist laws and edicts; but by bringing peace and order into their two sectors, permitting the establishment of local schools, courts, and self-government, opening a Polish university and polytechnic institute in Warsaw, and allowing new

35. "Denkschrift betreffend die Massnahmen, welche Deutschland, unterstützt von Österreich-Ungarn und die Türkei in Sachen der Judenfrage des Ostens zu unternehmen hätte," Germany. Politisches Archiv des Auswärtigen Amtes (hereafter Germ. PA AA) Weltkrieg, K714/K190607–17; Zechlin, *Deutsche Politik*, pp. 126–38.

36. At this time, the *Auswärtiges Amt* also created a special department of "Jewish Affairs" and provided subsidies to Jewish organizations, see Germ. PA AA Weltkrieg K714/K190217–413 (Aug. 1914–Apr. 1917).

37. See, for example, Szajkowski, "The Struggle for Yiddish."

38. Zechlin, *Deutsche Politik*, p. 129. Compare Pinson, "Theories of Simon Dubnow."

39. Zechlin, *Deutsche Politik*, pp. 150–3.

40. Further east, Germany established the Eastern Supreme Command (*Oberbefehlshabers Ost*) that governed Kurland and Lithuania as well as Vilna, Grodno, and Bialystock. Strazhas, *Deutsche Ostpolitik*.

social and political movements to develop, the Central Powers inadvertently kindled national ambitions and tensions among the Poles and the other inhabitants.[41]

Despite significant political differences, Polish leaders during World War I tended to view the minority problem in fairly similar terms. To regain as large a state as possible, if not the expansive borders of 1772, both Dmowski and Piłsudski, who recognized the existence of a national consciousness among their neighbors, the Ukrainians, Lithuanians, and White Russians, had more or less accepted the inevitability of granting concessions in regions where the Poles were numerically inferior.[42] However, every Polish politician refused to accept the national claims of the Jews, estimated as high as 14% of the population of a future Poland, but also a dispersed people nowhere in a majority. To grant a nonterritorial autonomy to the Jews would mean abandoning their goal of a strong, unitary, western-style Polish state, one with a dominant language, law, and culture, for a weak, "eastern," multinational entity, once more vulnerable to inside as well as external manipulation.[43]

Polish–Jewish tensions in the Russian Empire had greatly escalated on the eve of World War I as both sides' growing cultural and national ambitions had clashed irremediably.[44] In 1912, the National Democrats had instituted a crippling anti-Jewish boycott in retaliation for the Jews' alleged role in Dmowski's electoral defeat to the Fourth Duma. Following the Russians' disaster at Tannenberg, the Endek had tarred the Jews with charges of espionage and sabotage on behalf of the Germans. After the tsarist armies were swept from Congress Poland, Dmowski, carrying a Russian diplomatic passport, moved west to promote Poland's cause with the Entente, where he not only competed with Piłsudski's emissary, August Zaleski,[45] but found

41. By observing the terms of the Hague Convention, the Germans maintained the Russian ordinances that allowed the numerically larger Poles to exclude Jews and other minorities from local government and militias. Zechlin, *Deutsche Politik*, pp. 173–4.

42. This included the possibility of concluding reciprocal agreements of autonomy with a future Ukraine, Lithuania, and/or White Russia. There is evidence that Piłsudski was more accommodating than Dmowski. Szporluk, "Polish–Ukrainian Relations," especially pp. 50–1.

43. Żbikowski, *Dzieje Żydów w Polsce*. In his pamphlet, *Die Judenfrage in Kongress-Polen. Ihre Schwierigkeiten und ihre Lösung* (Vienna: Verlag der Wochenschrift "Polen," 1915), Leon Wasilewski, a Moderate Socialist and close associate of Piłsudski, insisted on total Jewish assimilation. Also, Zechlin, *Deutsche Politik*, pp. 182–6.

44. See Opalski and Bartal, *Poles and Jews*; compare Stachura, "National Identity and the Ethnic Minorities," pp. 63–7. The number of Jews in Congress Poland, between 10% and 15% of the population, had risen significantly because of the influx of the "Litvaks" (Russified Jews), who were deeply resented by the Poles. Korzec, *Juifs en Pologne*, pp. 30–1; Horak, *Poland and Her National Minorities*, p. 92.

45. Who himself was under the cloud of his mentor's collaboration with the Central Powers. Wandycz, *August Zaleski*, pp. 9–16.

himself immediately on the defensive before several leading British officials because of his overt anti-Semitism.[46]

The Russian occupation of Galicia had left a fresh scar on Polish–Jewish relations. During the spring of 1915, in the period between the Russians' withdrawal, which was accompanied by scorched-earth tactics and mass evacuation, and the Central Powers' return, which brought a wave of reprisals in the form of mass arrests, burning, and looting, the Poles attacked the Jews and denounced them as collaborators. When the neutral press scored Polish leaders for their silence and collaboration, the Endeks condemned foreign intrusion "in Poland's internal affairs."[47]

The Central Powers ostensibly ended Russia's official anti-Semitism, but the boycott was not lifted. Indeed, many of the first encounters between the Reich's soldiers and civilian officials and the "exotic" *Ostjuden* were fraught with incomprehension, distrust, and hostility, often resulting in public humiliation for the latter.[48] Neither the Germans nor the Austrians recognized the Jews on the same political level as the Poles, Lithuanians, or Ukrainians. Although establishing a Jewish office in their administration, the Germans treated the Jews as a "religious," not a national, minority.[49] In their district, the Austrians refused to recognize a Jewish nationality or language; and by maintaining many of the discriminatory Russian laws, they placed the Russian Jews in an inferior status to their kin in the Habsburg Monarchy.[50]

In both sectors controlled by the Central Powers, the Jews were underrepresented on the citizens' committees and discriminated against in economic, social, and political affairs. The Germans, suffering the exactions of the Allied blockade, exploited their Polish zone, and their plunder fell heavily on the Jews. Reich officials systematically confiscated raw materials and industrial machinery, raided communities for laborers, imposed forced loans, services, requisitions, and heavy taxes, and deported a quarter million farm and factory workers, more than 10% of them Jews, to the Reich.[51]

46. Wolf, Confidential Memorandum, London, June 30, 1915, YIVO W/M 129. Even before he proposed it in print in 1917, Dmowski had often hinted that "large-scale" emigration was the best solution for the "Jewish problem" in a future Poland. Latawski, "Roman Dmowski, The Polish Question, and Western Opinion"; Davies, "The Poles in Great Britain."
47. Golczewski, *Polnisch-Jüdische Beziehungen*, pp. 123–31; Korzec, *Juifs en Pologne*, pp. 42–5, 50–2.
48. Zechlin, *Deutsche Politik*, p. 165. On the "distorted image" of Polish Jews, see Friedländer, "Die politischen Veränderungen der Kriegszeit," p. 35.
49. Zechlin, *Deutsche Politik*, p. 160.
50. The Habsburg rulers made this distinction because this was "Polish" territory. Golczewski, *Polnisch–Jüdische Beziehungen*, pp. 133–5.
51. Unsigned, undated memorandum, Germ. PA AA, Abt. III, Sobernheim papers, Das Komitee für den Osten, 204–2/L350493–500; Szajkowski, "East European Jewish Workers," p. 906. Zunkel, "Die ausländische Arbeiter." On Germany's acute wartime labor shortage, see Kocka, *Facing Total War*, pp. 26–8.

In an age in which language had become the key to national identity, the most explosive issue between Poles and Jews involved schools. A German edict on September 17, 1915 establishing separate German- and Polish-language schools assigned the Jews to the former. There was an immediate outcry from the local population. The Poles were furious over competition with the master tongue. Polish Jews, many of whom preferred that their children be instructed in Yiddish, Hebrew, or even Polish, resented their exploitation as tools of *Deutschtum* by the occupiers as well as by German Jews.[52]

Polish Jewry, particularly in the Congress Kingdom, was a deeply fragmented minority.[53] Although Yiddish was their primary language, some also spoke Hebrew, Polish, Russian, and German. Their religious beliefs and practices ranged from ultraorthodox to secular and even to atheism, their politics from internationalist and radical socialism, to Zionism and Jewish nationalism, to assimilation and Polish patriotism. Like the Romanian Jews, their views of minority protection varied, from favoring international guarantees to preferring local arrangements, from seeking a corporate existence to working for guaranteed individual rights. Except for its small upper-class and bourgeois elite, the Jewish population of Poland, who were primarily artisans, shopkeepers, traders, small factory owners, peddlers, and teamsters, was extremely vulnerable not only to the occupiers' taunts and physical abuse but also to their arbitrary edicts. The growing ranks of unemployed and impoverished Jews became labor conscripts or were deported to the Reich.[54] In addition, Polish Jews were under the constant threat of their neighbors' accusations of hoarding, profiteering, and "disloyalty" to the Polish cause.[55]

MINORITIES BELEAGUERED

By the spring of 1915, the fate of minority people behind the lines had become exceedingly bleak. The Young Turk government used the cover of war to settle its "Armenian question." A shocked world learned of the deportations and massacres of hundreds of thousands of Armenians. The Turks, abetted by their allies, ignored the Entente's protests of a crime against humanity.[56]

52. Zechlin, *Deutsche Politik*, pp. 186–97
53. Julius Berger, "Die polnischen Juden in Weltkrieg (streng vertraulich)," Apr. 1916. CZA A206/14.
54. In Łodz, for example, some 5,000 inhabitants, primarily Jews, were forced into labor battalions. Conze, *Polnische Nation*, p. 135; Korzec, *Juifs en Pologne*, pp. 55–6.
55. Golczewski, *Polnisch–Jüdische Beziehungen*, pp. 142–3.
56. Dadrian, *History of the Armenian Genocide*. For specific elements of this still controversial subject: idem, "The Armenian Question"; "Armenian Massacres"; Gilbert, *The First World War*, pp. 108, 135,

The next year, this menace had spread to Europe. From the Carpathians to the Balkans, tens of thousands of refugees clogged the roads in flight from foreign conquerors.[57] Even in liberal Britain, the fear of subversion reached a fever pitch. After the failed Easter Rising, which had been aided by the Germans, Britain executed fifteen Irish leaders without concern for the repercussions in still-neutral America.[58]

A stalemated war also produced rising intolerance at home. In Germany, there was a virulent wave of anti-Semitism laced with charges of Jewish shirking and profiteering on the one hand and subversion on the other. In the Reichsland Alsace-Lorraine the Jews were especially vulnerable to charges of "anti-Reich activities."[59] The War Ministry, responding to reports of popular resentment against the unending "money war" (*Geldkrieg*), ordered the notorious Reich census to determine Jewish participation at the front.[60] At the end of that somber year of huge casualties and widespread hunger, when a war-weary population began responding to Liberal and Socialist calls for peace and reform, the German Right began blaming the "Jewish poison" and "Jewish–Bolshevik subversion" for the Reich's suffering.[61] Similarly, Austrian anti-Semites accused the Jews of hoarding and profiteering as well as of treachery and defeatism and denounced the eastern refugees for flooding the cities with disease and sedition.[62]

In the Allied countries, where material misery was less intense, the Jews fared only slightly better in the public mind.[63] Despite their great patriotism, French– and British–Jewish leaders made little headway in gaining official standing.[64] They failed to convince their governments to stop Russia from persecuting its Jews.[65] And as long as Romania remained on the

142–3, on Russia's designs on Armenia; Hovannisian, "The Allies and Armenia," on the Entente's protests as well as their eventual betrayal of the Armenians; and Melson, *Armenian Genocide and the Holocaust*, which compares the two atrocities.

57. Marrus, *The Unwanted*, pp. 48–50.

58. Hartley, *The Irish Question*, pp. 50–95.

59. Caron, *The Jews of Alsace-Lorraine*, pp. 178–86. Many Alsatian Jews fled either to Switzerland or over the Vosges into France, where they joined the republican army.

60. Oppenheimer, *Die Judenstatistik*. Also, Angress, "The German Army's '*Judenzahlung*'"; Jochmann, "Die Ausbreitung des Antisemitismus," especially p. 503.

61. Mosse, "Die Krise der europäischen Bourgeoisie," especially p. 22.

62. Pauley, *From Prejudice to Persecution*, pp. 61–72.

63. For examples of local anti-Jewish sentiment, see Holmes, *Anti-Semitism in British Society*, pp. 121–40; Hyman, *From Dreyfus to Vichy*, pp. 115–43; Landau, *Les juifs de France*, pp. 67–77.

64. France, in June 1916, refused to admit Jewish representatives to the Inter-Allied Economic Conference or to consider the AIU's petition against Russia's ban on foreign Jewish merchants and manufacturers, even those involved in the war effort. Szajkowski, "Jewish Diplomacy," especially pp. 134–6.

65. Wolf to Bigart, Dec. 14, 1915, Sept. 29, 1916, AIU Angleterre, I/J. In a strictly confidential memorandum, dated Jan. 31, 1917, YIVO W/M 54, Wolf reported these remarks by Balfour a day earlier: "It was all very well to belittle the difficulty which arose out of the fact that the persecutions were a domestic affair of the Russian State, but it was a very real difficulty." Moreover, "[T]he

sidelines, Jewish leaders were constrained from any form of pressure against a sought-after Balkan ally. When the Bucharest government entered the war in August 1916 with promises of considerable territorial gain, the Entente added another questionable partner, whose dismal minorities record was now off limits to criticism.[66]

Germany, still the unofficial patron of the nationalist movements in Eastern Europe, kept a tight grip on their direction. In 1916, one of the Wilhelmstrasse's puppet organizations, the League of Russia's Foreign Peoples, issued an appeal "to the whole civilized world" against tsarist despotism and depicted the Reich as "protector of the rights of the oppressed."[67] In June, the league played a prominent role in organizing the third conference of the Union of Nationalities that was convened in Lausanne to hear the grievances of all of Europe's minority groups.[68] At this historic gathering, which generated a wide range of proposals and some stormy debates, the Reich's allies succeeded in focusing attention almost exclusively on Russia's iniquities and blocked a broader debate on the global minorities question.[69] Shortly afterwards, a gathering of neutral Socialists that met in The Hague recommended independence for Poland as well as autonomy for

persecutors had a case of their own. They were afraid of the Jews, who were an exceedingly clever people and who, in spite of their oppression achieved a certain success, which excited the jealousy and envy of the peoples among whom they lived. No one persecuted the gypsies, because no one was afraid of them . . . One could perhaps understand the desire to keep [the Jew] down and deny him the rights to which he was entitled. He did not say that this justified the persecution, but all these things had to be considered when it was proposed that foreign governments should intervene in order to obtain emancipation for the Russian Jews."

66. Beginning in August 1915, a year before Romania's entry, almost all the Jews in its border regions, including parents and relatives of the 23,000 Jews under arms, were deported and, because most had never been granted citizenship, they were interned as "aliens." After August 1916, Romanian military authorities routinely harassed and persecuted Jewish civilians as suspected German sympathizers and routinely arrested them for hoarding and espionage; Jewish soldiers, assigned to separate units, were given inferior medical treatment and were subject to capricious charges of treason and desertion. Iancu, *L'émancipation des juifs*, pp. 73–128. For Wolf's efforts on behalf of Romanian Jewry, see Wolf to Labin, Nov. 4, 1915, YIVO W/M, 60; also Board of Deputies of British Jews, London (hereafter BDBJ) C/11/3/2/1.
67. The league, originally consisting of Jews, Muslims, Georgians, Poles, Baltic Germans, Finns, and Ukrainians, later added White Russians, Lithuanians, Letts, Estonians, and Romanians. See Fischer, *Germany's Aims*, pp. 145–6, 237, as well as the memoir of Friedrich von der Ropp, a Baltic German who collaborated with the Reich's wartime program; Ropp, *Zwischen Gestern und Morgen*, pp. 85–122, 221–6.
68. Union des Nationalités. *Sommaire de la IIIième conférence des nationalités*, pp. 3–87. The union, founded by the emigré anti-Polish Lithuanian Catholic Juozas Gabrys, who moved to Lausanne in 1915 to direct its efforts (Gabrys, *Lithuania*; idem, *La question lithuanienne*; idem, *Le problème des nationalités*), was rife with internecine conflicts.
69. Three years later Baron von der Ropp admitted to a British Foreign Office official that he, on behalf of Berlin, had organized the Lausanne conference as an "anti-Russian enterprise calculated largely for American consumption" and had had no intention of embarrassing the Central Powers, the British Empire, or France. Namier memorandum, London, Feb. 26, 1919, Sir James Headlam-Morley papers, Churchill College, Cambridge (hereafter HM CC), Box 12.

its minorities.[70] Not surprisingly, the Entente ignored these enemy-inspired deliberations.[71]

Another abortive initiative emanated from the Vatican, which suddenly offered its support to the cause of minority rights. Pope Benedict XV, seeking to expand his moral authority and the papacy's claim to temporal power, and also to secure a role in the postwar peace conference, signaled his interest in joining the Jewish struggle against tsarist oppression.[72] Through an unofficial spokesman, former French diplomat and politician François Deloncle, the Vatican asked for the support of French, British, and U.S. Jews in return for a papal denunciation of anti-Semitism and approval of the Zionists' claims to Palestine along with a papal endorsement of Polish independence and his mediation between Poles and Jews.[73] After the Pope's initiative kindled a flutter of enthusiasm in Paris and New York, Lucien Wolf convinced the *Alliance* and the American Jews to reject this "dangerous" anti-Entente gesture.[74]

POLAND REBORN

On November 5, 1916, the emperors of Germany and Austria suddenly proclaimed the formation of an "independent" Poland with a hereditary monarchy and a constitutional form of government whose foreign policy and army would be controlled by Berlin. Not only had the Central Powers failed in their yearlong effort to conclude a separate peace with Russia, but

70. On the Hague meeting, held between July 31 and Aug. 2, 1916, see Kirby, *War, Peace and Revolution*, pp. 84–5; Janowsky, *Jews and Minority Rights*, pp. 194–6. Much of the groundwork for this meeting was laid by Russian Zionist Socialists, the *Poale Zion* [Workers of Zion] who, early in the war, had established offices in the Netherlands and Sweden, maintained an active presence in the International Socialist Bureau at The Hague, and lobbied energetically for autonomy.
71. At the Lausanne meeting, Berlin had taken pains to stifle all anticolonialist sentiments on its own and on Austria's behalf as much as on the Entente's behalf. D'Encausse, *The Great Challenge*, pp. 56–7.
72. Report #6, Feb. 23–May 17, 1916, YIVO W/M 16.
73. On Deloncle's suggestion, the AJC, on Dec. 30, 1915, had issued a public appeal to the pope to speak out against the anti-Jewish excesses in Poland, to which the Vatican replied noncommittally on Feb. 9, 1916. Szajkowski, "Jewish Diplomacy," pp. 136–40.

    On the proposed "Lugano Pact," outlining future relations between Poles and Jews and providing for the pope's mediation in case of a breach by either side, see Paweł Korzec, "Anti-Semitism in Poland as an Intellectual, Social, and Political Movement," in Fishman, *Polish Jewry*, pp. 30–31 and notes 14 and 15.
74. See Alexander and Montefiore to Marshall, London, Apr. 28, 1916, Marshall to Alexander and Montefiore, New York, May 13, 1918, Marshall to Deloncle and Perquel, New York, Apr. 6, 1916, YIVO W/M 62, 63; Wolf to Bigart, May 18, 1916, AIU, Angleterre I/J.

    In leading the opposition, Wolf underlined the dangers of involving Jews in their "corporate capacity" in a gambit that challenged British, French, Italian, Russian, U.S., and even Polish sensitivities. Black, *Anglo-Jewry*, pp. 340–1, especially n. 14. Similar sentiments expressed in Cyrus Adler to Louis Marshall, Philadelphia, Nov. 8; 1915; Adler, *Selected Letters*, pp. 294–5.

in June Austria had almost collapsed before the Brusilov Offensive, which had also brought Romania into the war. The German High Command, now under great pressure at Verdun and the Somme, had impetuously decided to merge the two Polish zones into a satellite state in order to draw on its manpower resources.[75] Following extremely tough bargaining between Berlin and Vienna, a new Poland was declared without fixed borders or an established government on one-sixth of its realm of 1772.[76]

This audacious gesture "internationalized" the Polish question, placing it squarely before the world.[77] For the Reich, however, the military and political results proved negligible; Poles abroad derided the new "partition" and at home failed to rally to the Reich's colors in significant numbers.[78] After the Entente sanctimoniously denounced this gross violation of international law,[79] the Poles implored Petrograd, Paris, and London to pledge their own just, international solution to the Polish problem. Russia responded with still another promise to grant autonomy within the empire.[80] The Western Allies, buttressed by the disunity of Poland's leaders and the absence of an authoritative representative, did nothing.[81] Even U.S. President Woodrow

75. Another calculation was economic, that prewar Congress Poland had taken 75% of Germany's exports to Russia; Fischer, *Germany's Aims*, p. 243.
76. The declaration specified "an independent state with a hereditary monarchy and a Constitution" whose frontiers remained "reserved." *The New York Times*, Nov. 6, 1916.

    The internationalist–Socialist Julian Marchlewski (1866–1915) issued this ironic comment: "Today's improvisation on the Vistula by Hindenburg and Ludendorff is unique, a joke, the like of which the world has neither seen nor dreamed. An 'independent' state with unknown frontiers, with an unknown government, with an unknown constitution and, oh horror, oh shame, a kingdom without a king!"; quoted in Kitchen, *The Silent Dictatorship*, p. 93. Much later however, Wandycz, *Partitioned Poland*, pp. 352–3, termed the new regime a "'school of fresh political life.' Although it was destined to be a phantom state with a phantom government it provided some scope for national activity."
77. "Ce n'est pas grand-chose, mais c'est aussi beaucoup," Rollet, *La Pologne*, p. 78. Compare Fest, *Peace or Partition*, p. 156.
78. Hindenburg, *Out of My Life*, pp. 222–4.
79. Castlebajac, "La France et la question polonaise," pp. 57–9. Article 23 of the Hague Convention of 1907 prohibited belligerents from compelling enemy nationals to take part in military action directed against their country.
80. The communiqué of Nov. 15, 1916, reiterated the tsar's intention to create a unified, autonomous Poland within the Russian Empire, its borders yet to be determined. Linke, *Das zarische Russland*, pp. 164–7. However, this concession was linked with an Entente declaration granting Constantinople and the Straits to Russia. Rothwell, *British War Aims*, pp. 56–7.
81. Indeed, there is evidence that not only did France and Britain not wish to alienate Russia but that they – particularly Britain – opposed Polish independence. In a conversation among Colonel House, Lloyd George, Sir Edward Grey, and Arthur Balfour on Feb. 14, 1916, Balfour argued presciently that in the next war France would be endangered by the existence of an independent Poland, which could block Russia from coming to Paris's aid. Gerson, *Woodrow Wilson and the Rebirth of Poland*, pp. 27–8, 73. As late as July 18, 1917, Sir George Clerk observed, "There is unfortunately no prominent authority on whom one can rely for accurate information as to political sentiments in Poland. There is no one from whom we can derive information as to the cross currents of Polish politics and the underlying aims of Polish political leaders . . . nor is there any Pole in a position in

Wilson's support for Polish independence in his "peace without victory" speech to the Senate on January 22, 1917 failed to alter Petrograd's conviction that Poland was an "internal problem."[82]

Although the Central Powers' November proclamation was silent about the future of Poland's minorities, Polish Jews rejoiced. Disillusioned by the two autocratic military governments, they hoped for better prospects under the Poles, to whom Warsaw Jewish leaders pledged the utmost support for, and cooperation with, the new regime.[83]

The results, however, were also disappointing. For the next two years, the Jews were not only denied a separate identity but they remained underrepresented in local government and discriminated against in taxes, schools, welfare programs, and medical aid as well as in the ordinary matters of daily life.[84] The more relations cooled between Warsaw and Berlin, the more openly the Poles rejected any form of Jewish nationalism, which menaced their economic, political, and cultural consolidation.[85] In December 1917, Poland's appointed Prime Minister Jan Kucharzewski announced that the "character of Polish state must be uniformly Polish."[86]

In the summer of 1918 the Polish government, with a spate of new laws and edicts, manifested its unalterable opposition to any special rights for minorities on a local or national level. Polish was established as the universal language of school instruction. Moreover, Jews continued to suffer other forms of discrimination; the boycott remained, Sunday trading was made illegal, and a quota (*numerus clausus*) was imposed on university admissions.[87] As hunger swept the land, there was a growing swell of popular anti-Semitism as well as a new wave of plunder and pogroms.[88]

any way analogous to that of Professor Masaryk among the Czechs, who can speak with recognized and impartial authority." GB FO 371/3021.

82. Text in Wilson, *Public Papers of Woodrow Wilson*, Vol. 4, pp. 407–14.
83. Samuel Hirschhorn, "Die Selbstständigkeit Polens und die Judenfrage," *Neue Jüdische Monatshefte* 1 (1916/17), 89; also, Korzec, *Juifs en Pologne*, p. 58; Zechlin, *Deutsche Politik*, pp. 202–4.
84. Of the twenty-five seats in the Polish *Staatsrat* [State Council], which was convened on Jan. 14, 1917, only one was occupied by an assimilated Jew, Edward Natanson. Golczewski, *Polnisch–Jüdische Beziehungen*, p. 159. Also, Ludwig Haas, "Das neue polnische Schulgesetz und die Juden" and S. Jonassohn, "Das Schulwesen in Polen und die Juden," *Neue Jüdische Monatshefte* 2 (Oct. 25, 1917), 27–36. Other forms of discrimination in Golczewski, *Polnisch–Jüdische Beziehungen*, pp. 163–6.
85. "If this state grants any concession to Jewish national rights, it would be an acknowledgment that this is not a Polish, but a Polish-Jewish state." Pregowski article in *Gazeta Poranna Dwa Grosze* (Warsaw), Dec. 14, 1916, p. 1, quoted in Golczewski, *Polnisch–Jüdische Beziehungen*, pp. 166–7.
86. Zechlin, *Deutsche Politik*, p. 214.
87. Ibid., pp. 215–16; Golczewski, *Polnisch–Jüdische Beziehungen*, p. 169.
88. Golczewski, *Polnisch–Jüdische Beziehungen*, p. 170. In response, Jewish communities began organizing self-defense leagues.

Germany, although still technically capable of intervening in Polish affairs, was disinclined to alienate a restive and uncertain ally.[89] Berlin's attempts to placate Poland's disgruntled Lithuanians and Ukrainians with promises for the future had provoked all sides. The Reich made no effort to censor the virulently anti-Semitic – and surreptitiously anti-German – Polish press and allowed Polish Jews to be convicted on trumped-up charges of hoarding and corruption.[90] Dismissing the pleas of German Jews, the Reich had dropped all pretense of any commitment to establishing minority rights in Poland and, after April 1917, lost all interest in wooing neutral or U.S. Jews.[91]

THE TIDE TURNS: THE COLLAPSE OF RUSSIA, THE TRIUMPH OF ZIONISM

In 1917, after the end of tsarist rule in Russia, Poland's fate shifted dramatically. Russia's new Provisional Government, prodded by the Petrograd Soviet, on March 16 declared its support for an "independent Polish state . . . united with Russia by a free military alliance."[92] One week later the United States entered the war. Believing that the tide had turned against the Central Powers, even austrophile Polish politicians now looked to the Allies to obtain a free and united Poland "with access to the sea."[93] Piłsudski, who had lost all confidence in collaboration with the Germans, resigned his commission and was subsequently imprisoned.[94] To be sure, the Entente was still unready to commit themselves formally to Polish independence. In June 1917, France and Russia agreed to raise an army of Polish émigrés and prisoners of war to serve on the western front under French command; but

89. Ten days after the proclamation of the Polish Kingdom, the German High Command finally issued a *Verordnung* [decree] governing Jewish religious communities in the Warsaw district. Opposed by the majority of Polish Jews (only the orthodox and a small portion of the assimilationists approved, but the Zionists, nationalists, and the majority of the assimilated objected to its narrow, religious-based definition of the Jewish community), its implementation depended on Polish cooperation, which was not forthcoming. Zechlin, *Deutsche Politik*, pp. 206–9.
90. Golczewski, *Polnisch–Jüdische Beziehungen*, p. 146.
91. *Jüdische Rundschau* 21 (1916), 378. Rosenberg to Bethmann Hollweg, Bern, Jan. 31, 1917, Jacobson to Brockdorff-Rantzau, Copenhagen, Feb. 15, 1917, Germ. PA AA Gesandschaft Kopenhagen/130.
92. "The Proclamation of the Provisional Government to the Poles, March 16, 1917," in Browder and Kerensky, *Russian Provisional Government*, pp. 321–3. Because German censors delayed the news of the proclamation for several days, the proclamation's date has been given as late as Mar. 30, 1917.
    On Apr. 13, the German-appointed temporary State Council in Warsaw, terming itself "the only existing Polish state organ," roundly rejected the new Russian government's "one sided decision"; ibid., pp. 326–7.
93. "Access to the sea" was the code for Poland's acquiring West Prussia and Danzig over which British policy makers remained divided because this would prolong the war and cut Prussia in two. Rothwell, *British War Aims*, pp. 2, 156–7.
94. Jedrzejewicz, *Kronika życia Józefa Piłsudskiego*, Vol. 1, pp. 351–62.

in September, Paris, in deference to its failing ally's sensibilities,[95] recognized Dmowski's newly organized KNP not as a government-in-exile but simply as an "intermediary" between French authorities and the Polish recruits.[96]

The Russian Revolution also seemed to augur improved prospects for all the subject people of Eastern Europe. Finns, Ukrainians, Latvians, and Estonians hoped to achieve the self-government promised to the Poles. On March 20, Russia's new prime minister, Prince L'vov, signed a law abolishing all legal restrictions based on religion, nationality, and class. Between July 18 and 21, the first All-Russian Jewish Conference, representing the main organization of the empire's 3.5 million Jews, called for the establishment of civil and national Jewish rights in Poland, Romania, and Palestine.[97] Foreign Jews of all political stripes were ecstatic.[98]

Again, the breakthrough was more apparent than real. Russia's Provisional Government, dominated by western-style Cadet Liberals, supported individual and not national rights. With the exception of its somewhat lame gesture toward Poland, which, in any event, was still under German rule, the new government – and its western Allies – intended to uphold the unity of the Russian Empire against Finnish, Ukrainian, and Baltic separatists. With respect to minority rights, both the L'vov government *and* its Bolshevik opponents rejected the multinational state and, particularly, the Austro–Marxist formula of extraterritorial national–cultural autonomy. Indeed, Leninism offered Russia's most vulnerable minorities, the Jews and the Armenians, the unreal choice between secession and assimilation into a unitary workers' state.[99]

The Entente continued to maintain its reserve on the Jewish question.[100] Conservative Britons, obsessed with the specter of Jewish–German

95. Zeman, *The Gentleman Negotiators*, pp. 344–7. Moreover, the secret Franco–Russian agreement concluded in Petrograd in January 1917 was still in force, granting Russia a free hand to redraw its western borders and France its eastern. Browder and Kerensky, *Russian Provisional Government*, Vol. 2, pp. 920–1.
96. Dmowski to Paderewski, Paris, Oct. 7, 1917, Poland, Archiwum Akt Nowych, Warsaw, (hereafter AAN) KNP, Akta S.G. *Korespondencja amerykański* (1917). By the end of the year, Great Britain, Italy, and the United States accorded the same limited recognition. The results were moot. Dmowski had exaggerated the threat of a large, German-sponsored Polish army, and, by Dec. 1917, only 2,000 Poles were mobilized in France. Zeman, *The Gentlemen Negotiators*, p. 347; Wandycz, *Partitioned Poland*, p. 136.
97. Frankel, *Prophecy and Politics*, pp. 548–9.
98. For examples of the euphoria, see *Jewish Chronicle*, Mar. 23, 1917, and *Jewish World*, Mar. 28, 1917. Drawing on his sources in Russia, Lucien Wolf reported to the Conjoint Committee that the Revolution "meant the end of the Jewish question in Russia." BDBJ Report, No. 10, Feb. 6–May 17, 1917.
99. Suny, "Nationality Policies," especially pp. 661–5. Also, "The Jewish Question in Poland," *Pravda*, May 15, 1918, copy in YIVO W/M 131.
100. See Wolf to Balfour, Apr. 5, 1917, Balfour to Wolf, London, Apr. 7, 1917, YIVO, W/M 54.

complicity, now conjured up a new conspiracy by Jewish radicals to destroy Russia and remove it from the war.[101] Also, the British public was inflamed by the parliamentary debate over the Aliens' Conscription Bill, during which a sensationalist press denounced foreign Jews as parasites, shirkers, and subversives, and also as swindlers and scabs.[102] Alarmed at the new Russia's growing domestic and military feebleness as well as the recrudescence of anti-Semitism among the rising nations, Conjoint leader Lucien Wolf recalled the denouement of the Revolution of 1905 and feared a counterrevolution drenched in Jewish blood.[103]

The Zionists moved into the breach – with momentous results for the cause of Jewish and minority rights.[104] At the beginning of the Great War, the combatants had given the Zionists scant encouragement.[105] The entry of the Ottoman Empire as an ally of the Central Powers had sealed the Reich's reluctance to meddle too strongly in the affairs of Palestine; but it also failed to convince the Entente to commit scarce resources to a territory outside its vital interests.[106]

Palestine soon became less remote from the combat than anticipated. Faced with the Turks' threats against the Jewish colonists, Germany tried to temper them, and Britain to capitalize on them, in an attempt to impress neutral America.[107] In 1915 the French government, imbued with an exaggerated sense of Jewish power, moved to counter German propaganda across

101. Even before the Bolshevik seizure of power, conservative British newspapers such as *The Times* and the *Morning Post* had noted the prominence of Jews among the Bolsheviks. Kadish, *Bolsheviks and British Jews*, pp. 22–9; Holmes, *Anti-Semitism in British Society*, pp. 141–2.

102. "Aliens Eating Us Out," *Daily Mail* headline, May 1917; Kadish, *Bolsheviks and British Jews*, pp. 50–4; also, Gilam, "The Leeds Anti-Jewish Riots 1917."

103. Poliakoff-Litovtzoff memorandum, n.d., YIVO W/M 79; Kadish, *Bolsheviks and British Jews*, pp. 66–9.

104. The major documents on Zionist diplomacy before and during World War I are in Friedman, *Rise of Israel*.

105. The Zionist leader, Chaim Weizmann, had nevertheless written to Israel Zangwill on Oct. 4, 1914: "We may hope that the powers, which are going to alter the map of Europe, will find time to consider the fate of thirteen millions of Jews." On Oct. 19, he hoped that "our case will be handled at the peace conference," with "Palestine falling to Great Britain as a natural continuation of Egypt" becoming "the Asiatic Belgium" in which one million Jews could be moved within the "next fifty to sixty years," creating an effective bulwark for England, removing the pressure in Russia, the United States, and Great Britain, and ending the homelessness of the Jews. CZA A120/609.

106. In Mar. 1915, Lord Kitchener reportedly told a War Council meeting that Palestine had "no value to us whatsoever." Klieman, "Britain's War Aims."

107. At the outbreak of the war, the Porte classified 50,000 of the approximately 85,000 Jews in Palestine as enemy [Russian] aliens and subjected them to persecution. Germany, pressured by its Zionist citizens and fearing the reproaches of neutral (especially U.S.) public opinion, urged the Turks to modify their harsh policies in Palestine, which was in stark contrast with their indifference toward the fate of the Armenians. Friedman, *Germany, Turkey and Zionism*, pp. 49–206; Trumpener, *Germany and the Ottoman Empire*, Chap. 7; Dadrian, *German Responsibility in the Armenian Genocide.*

the Atlantic by creating a top-level committee directed at the Jews in neutral countries (*Comité de propagande français auprès des juifs neutres*), dispatching two Jewish Sorbonne professors to America[108] and suddenly proposing that the Western Powers deflect attention from Russia's derelictions by championing Jewish immigration to Palestine.[109] This occurred at the same time that Paris and London had begun negotiating the Sykes–Picot agreement, aiming at the partition of the Middle East.[110]

Until 1917 internal divisions had plagued the world Zionist movement. At the outbreak of the war, its German leadership had shifted its headquarters to Copenhagen in the vain hope of preserving a nonpartisan facade.[111] With the breakaway pro-Allied forces ensconced in London, the neutral and the Near East offices were caught in a vise. Moreover the Zionist movement, which still represented a tiny minority of the Jewish world,[112] was itself split among cultural, political, and practical Zionists who were in fundamental disagreement over the Jews' goals in Palestine.[113]

The Zionists could nevertheless claim strong credentials. For three years, on both sides of the battle lines, they had collaborated amicably and effectively with non-Zionists and gained national and international stature. The Copenhagen office, linked to the Central Powers and the neutrals, had gathered and disseminated information on the East European war zone and helped transmit relief money to Jewish victims and refugees in Eastern Europe.[114] In Britain, the energetic advocacy of Home Secretary Sir Herbert

108. They were Nahoum Slousch (Jan.–Dec. 1915), an Odessa-born Zionist and professor of Hebrew literature and archeology, who had spent long periods in Palestine, and Victor Basch (Nov. 1915–Mar. 1916), a Budapest-born Liberal, non-Zionist, and professor of philosophy, who founded the *Ligue des droits de l'homme* during the Dreyfus Affair and was murdered at the age of 81, in Jan. 1944, by the Vichy Militia. Nicault, *La France et le sionisme*, pp. 58–61; Basch, *Victor Basch*, pp. 139–48.

109. Bigart to Wolf, Paris, Dec. 10, 1915, YIVO W/M 59. On the success of the mission, see Victor Basch report (May–June 1916), ibid., 63. The committee consisted of Jewish and non-Jewish luminaries, including Sylvain Lévi, Émile Durkheim, Victor Basch, Antoine Meillet, Eugène Sée, Lucien Lévy-Bruhl, and Salomon Reinach.

    The original suggestion came from the French ambassador in Washington. See Jusserand to FMAE, Jan. 26, 1915, FMAE Guerre 1914–1918/1197; also, Friedman, *Rise of Israel*, Vol. 5: France and Zionism, 1914–1920.

110. Kent, "Asiatic Turkey"; Nicault, *La France et le sionisme*, pp. 63–70; Friedman, *The Question of Palestine*, pp. 48–9, 97–118.

111. On the close collaboration between the Copenhagen bureau and the German government, see Germ. PA AA. Gesandschaft Kopenhagen: Zionistische Organisation [Martin] Rosenblüth.

112. Although the official membership in 1913 was approximately 130,000 (Stein, *Balfour Declaration*, p. 66), Zionism's supporters, particularly in Russia and the United States, were undoubtedly more numerous.

113. Moreover, the practical Zionists were divided between those residing in the Central Powers who assumed a continued Turkish sovereignty over Palestine and those in the West who, like Weizmann, were counting on an Allied victory.

114. On the Copenhagen organization, Motzkin Archives CZA A126/40 and A126/41/4; also Bein, *The Jewish Question*, Part I, pp. 84–5.

Samuel and of the extraordinarily well-connected chemist Chaim Weizmann had kept the issue of a Jewish Palestine before the government's eyes. In America not only had the Zionists' political influence grown among the East European immigrant masses but their key supporters, Supreme Court Justice Louis D. Brandeis and Rabbi Stephen Wise, had the ear of Woodrow Wilson.[115] The leaders of France and Italy had openly endorsed the Zionist cause.[116] And in the vibrant political atmosphere of revolutionary Russia, Zionism seemed to have sparked considerable interest among radical and nationalist Jews.[117]

In 1917 the long split between Zionists and anti-Zionists was suddenly, and temporarily, breached by a shared international cause. This was a bleak year for the Entente, with Britain's catastrophic losses at Passchendaele added to the mounting cost of Germany's submarine warfare, the near collapse of France and Italy, the failed peace initiatives with Austria–Hungary and Turkey, and, finally, the defeat and withdrawal of Romania and Russia.[118] The new British government, headed by David Lloyd George and with Arthur James Balfour as foreign secretary, which continued to observe its predecessor's extreme caution over championing national and minority rights in Eastern Europe, suddenly espoused the Zionist cause. In a coupling of geopolitics and personal politics, the combination of an imperious Lloyd George, with his expansive Near Eastern designs,[119] and a charismatic Chaim Weizmann[120] helped forge the momentous link between the Entente and Zionism that culminated in the Balfour declaration.[121]

Moses A. Leavitt, *The JDC Story* (New York: American Jewish Joint Distribution Committee, 1953), pp. 4–7, acknowledges that the $12 million sent to Eastern Europe during World War I was distributed by both sides: the Russian *Evreiskii komitet pomoshchi zhertvam voiny* (EKOPO) [Jewish Committee for the Relief of Victims of War] and the German *Hilfsverein*, and the Austrian *Israelitische Allianz zu Wien* (which operated in Vienna, Budapest, Lemberg, and Cracow as well as in other imperial cities). After the United States entered the war, a Netherlands branch of the JDC was established in Aug. 1917 and authorized by the U.S. State Department to continue relief aid in Eastern Europe.

For details on Zionist relief work in Poland, see Mendelsohn, *Zionism in Poland*, pp. 46–7.

115. Wilson's endorsement of Zionism was based not only on his faith and his personal loyalty to Brandeis and Wise but also on its advantages to the United States, ostensibly in providing an alternative destination for fleeing East Europeans and helping "as many as 100 million Jews" [*sic*] resist radicalism. Brecher, *Reluctant Ally*, pp. 10–11.
116. See "Documents on Zionism," GB FO 371/PC 140.
117. Friedman, *The Question of Palestine*, pp. 119–202; Vital, "European Jewry," especially pp. 52–6.
118. Riccardi, *Alleati non amici*, pp. 398–581.
119. Adelson, *London and the Invention of the Middle East*, pp. 134–54.
120. Abramsky, "Wolf's Efforts for the Jewish Communities," pp. 286–7, stresses the victory of Weizmann, the visionary East European Jew, over the "entrenched, powerful Anglo-Jewish establishment." Compare Friedman, *The Question of Palestine*, pp. 227–81.
121. Weizmann, *Trial and Error*, pp. 192–6, 226–31; Stein, *Balfour Declaration*, pp. 137–40. Rothwell, *British War Aims*, p. 128, stresses Lloyd George's Turkophobia, his ambition to follow up the Baghdad conquest with the capture of Jerusalem, and his "firm personal commitment . . . to seek

Zionism's first triumph was the Balfour declaration of November 2, 1917. One of the Allies' most contentious wartime pledges, the declaration not only changed the history of the Middle East but also had major repercussions for the minority question in Eastern Europe. A beleaguered Britain and France, convinced of the power of U.S. Jewry to accelerate and expand America's mobilization as well as of the threat of Jewish left-wing radicals to deplete Russia's fighting spirit, acquiesced in the Zionists' claims to a Jewish national identity.[122] By sanctioning Jewish settlement in an as yet unconquered Palestine, the Entente hoped to thwart the Germans and Bolsheviks and also curb each other's designs in the Near East.[123] One month later General Edmund Allenby's capture of Jerusalem changed everything: It thrilled the entire Jewish world and sealed the alliance between Zionism and Britain while greatly increasing the tensions within the Entente.[124]

Taken at face value, the Palestine priority postulated the solution of the Jewish minority question by the physical removal of millions of threatened East Europeans to a tiny, impoverished, disease-ridden, and already-inhabited province in the Near East to be ruled by an outside Western imperial power.[125] This both simple and immense political solution sealed the split of the world Zionist movement into Entente and anti-Entente camps.[126]

Zionism placed all Jews in turmoil. Those who lived as a comfortable minority in western, democratic countries were appalled by the threat to their hard-won assimilation and security.[127] Even those who had dedicated themselves to combating anti-Semitism and winning equal rights for Jews and other minorities wherever they resided barely concealed their misgivings over the Allies' radical gesture.[128]

short-cuts to victory on every war front other than the western." Warman, "Erosion of Foreign Office Influence," details the prime minister's bypassing of the Foreign Office.

122. "His Majesty's Government views with favor the establishment of a national home for the Jewish people." GB FO 371/3083/132082.

 The expression of Jewish nationhood in the Balfour declaration, which was endorsed by all the Entente leaders, became the basis of the national claims of the Jews of the new Czechoslovakia a year later: See Jewish National Council of Prague (Ludwig Singer, Max Brod, and Rudolf Kahn) to T. G. Masaryk, Dec. 31, 1918, Czech Republic, Military Archive, T. G. Masaryk Institute, církve, 2.

123. Friedman, *The Question of Palestine*, pp. 282–308.

124. Fleuriau to Goût, London, Dec. 25, 1917, Picot to Goût, Jerusalem, Dec. 31, 1917, FMAE, PA-AP Jean Goût, Vol. 9. Tardieu to Clemenceau and Pichon, Jan. 17, 1918, ibid., PA-AP Tardieu, Vol. 280.

125. Ben-Avram, "Das Dilemma des Zionismus." 126. Zechlin, *Deutsche Politik*, pp. 413–48.

127. Julian H. Miller, a Chattanooga, Tennessee rabbi, begged President Wilson on Sept. 9, 1918, "Please do not take America from me . . . My flag is the Red, White and Blue, how then can I have any other National Home?" quoted in Adler, "The Palestine Question," p. 312.

128. On its most persistent and outspoken opponent, see Levene, "Lucien Wolf." Unlike the Conjoint, which had published a statement on May 24, 1917, opposing Zionism, the AIU remained officially

In a stroke, the Balfour declaration had not only validated Dmowski's hopes for a Jew-free Poland and confirmed the anti-Semites' accusations of the Jews' dual loyalty. Its premise of a separate Jewish nationality tied to a specific territorial claim also added a powerful new element to the debate over the future of the international protection of minorities in a new Eastern Europe, a debate in which the moderates sought limited, western-style, legal guarantees of freedom of speech, religion, language, and property and the maximalists sought broad-scale cultural and political autonomy.

Zionism was a problematic ideology. Predicated on the permanence of anti-Semitism, the legitimacy of the Jews' national aspirations, and the desirability of their ultimate removal from their ancient abodes, it refuted the moderates' optimism without relieving the maximalists' pessimism or answering the Socialists' criticism that their Jewish nationalism was passé and reactionary. And exalting as was this message to the war-weary Jews of Eastern Europe – with its implicit recognition of Jewish nationhood by a great power[129] – the result of Zionism's first diplomatic victory was to intensify the political and class divisions of the *Ostjuden*, to split them from some of their overseas defenders, and also to distance them from potential local allies in the struggle for cultural and political autonomy.[130]

The Bolsheviks' seizure of power on November 7 eclipsed the Balfour declaration and suddenly upset every calculation. The Soviet peace declaration called for self-determination as well as guarantees of minority rights. However, Lenin, who was mainly determined to exit from the war and consolidate his power, not only left Russia's allies in the lurch but also deserted the empire's minorities who had been conquered by the Central Powers. Irate Western observers, shocked by Russia's defection, by Trotsky's publication of the "imperialist" secret treaties – including the Sykes–Picot agreement – and by the augmented military threat posed by the Central Powers, automatically termed Bolshevism a German–Jewish plot. A London *Times* editorial on November 23, 1917 described Lenin and his colleagues as "adventurers of German–Jewish blood and in German pay, whose sole object is to exploit the ignorant masses in the interest of their own employers in Berlin."[131]

The conflation of Jews and Bolshevism had fateful consequences for the history of minority rights. Already burdened with wartime suspicions

neutral. Wolf to Bigart, May 23, 1917, AIU I/G,5; Plan de discussion, May 1917, ibid., France, I/G,3.

129. *Lemberger Tageblatt*, Nov. 16, 1917.

130. See, e.g., Frankel, "Jewish National Autonomism," especially pp. 268–70.

131. Zeman, *The Gentlemen Negotiators*, p. 152. At a War Cabinet meeting on Jan. 21, 1918, Foreign Secretary Balfour termed Karl Radek "an international Jew of the same type as Trotski [*sic*]." Great Britain, Cabinet documents, Public Record Office, Kew (hereafter GB CAB) 23/5.

of their germanophilia, the Jews were now permanently linked with an insidious global conspiracy. Despite the massive Jewish enlistment in all the armies of World War I, there were echoes of the age-long charges of Jewish perfidy that had been heard from the ancient world among warring peoples, to the medieval battles between Christians and Muslims, to the sixteenth-century wars between Catholics and Protestants, and the nineteenth-century struggles among Germans, Hungarians, and Slavs.[132] In the eyes of the opponents of any form of minority protection, the events of 1917, which had established the Jews as both permanently vulnerable and ominously powerful, tainted their international crusade.[133]

GERMAN VICTORY IN THE EAST

Back in occupied Poland, on September 12, 1917, the Central Powers had finally produced their blueprint for a figurehead government that was to be headed by a three-member Regency Council to be nominated by the two emperors until a monarch was named.[134] This puppet council would technically share its limited power over "educational and judicial matters" with an appointed prime minister and cabinet and with a half-elected legislature (the Council of State) that came into existence only in June 1918.[135]

Despite the alarms raised in London that the anti-Bolshevik Poles might yet rally to the German cause,[136] Berlin had offered the Poles too little too late. Indeed, the Reich's short-term goal had always been to exploit Poland's manpower and resources, and its long-term aim, after achieving total victory, was to create puppet states in the East and enlarge its own *Lebensraum* by annexing a swath of Western Poland and expelling the Jewish *and* Polish populations.[137] After the Bolshevik Revolution accelerated the collapse of the eastern front, the Reich revealed the dismal fate of rump Poland when it arbitrarily redrew the map of Eastern Europe. In December 1917, Germany established an "independent" Lithuania with Vilna as its capital, which Major-General Hoffmann promptly declared an ally "against

132. See, for example, Sevenster, *Pagan Antisemitism*; Feldman, *Jew and Gentile*; Roth, *Jews, Visigoths, and Muslims*; Agnoletto, *La tragoedia dell'Europa cristiana*; Namier, *The Revolution of the Intellectuals*.

133. Abramsky, *The Jewish Dilemma*, pp. 24–6.

134. Conze, *Polnische Nation*, pp. 307–18.

135. Namier memoranda, Apr. 23, Sept. 16, 1918, GB FO 371/3278. Also, Benson, *The White Eagle of Poland*, pp. 243–8; Wandycz, *Partitioned Poland*, p. 357.

136. Rothwell, *British War Aims*, pp. 157–8.

137. See note 18. In this "rectification" of frontiers in a zone of 400,000 square kilometers, Ludendorff proposed to settle between 215,000 and 265,000 Germans and expel a similar number of Polish and Jewish inhabitants who constituted 73.5% and 10% of the current population, respectively. Conze, *Polnische Nation*, pp. 330–3 as well as Geiss, *Polnische Grenzstreifen*.

the Poles."[138] After barring the Warsaw government from the Brest–Litovsk negotiations, in February 1918 the Central Powers ceded the Chełm district to their new ally, the Ukraine[139] and also agreed to partition Austrian Galicia into Polish and Ukrainian crown lands. Poles everywhere, even ultraloyalist Habsburg subjects, protested this "fourth partition of Poland."[140]

The humiliated Warsaw government vented its outrage.[141] The regents protested, the prime minister resigned, and the opposition questioned Germany's capacity to rule the East and triumph in the West. Despite the grossly limited franchise, the Polish electorate in April 1918 installed an anti-German majority in the new Council of State.[142] In Lublin, General Stanisław Szeptycki deserted the Austrians, and General Józef Haller led his troops across the border to join the Polish formations in Russia.[143]

The Poles now looked to the Entente, which finally seemed ready to outbid the Central Powers as the bestower of national liberation. Lloyd George, in his address to the Trade Union Congress on January 5, 1918, had announced, "that an independent Poland, *comprising all those genuinely Polish elements who desire to form a part of it*, is an urgent necessity for the stability of Western Europe."[144] Three days later, Wilson's more expansive thirteenth point called for "an independent Polish state . . . *which should include the territories inhabited by indisputably Polish populations*, which should be assured

138. Fischer, *Germany's Aims*, pp. 459, 464–72; Wandycz, *Partitioned Poland*, pp. 359–60; but also see the critiques of the Lithuanian patriot and former German ally, Gabrys, *Ober Ost*, and *La Lithuanie sous le joug allemand*.

139. Chełm, a mixed Polish–Jewish–Ukrainian district (and a major source of Jewish jokes on "the town of fools": Francine Prose, *The Angel's Mistake: Stories of Chełm* [New York: Greenwillow, 1997]), had been one of the centers of the 1863 Polish uprising. In reprisal, the tsarist government, renaming it Kholm, had imposed an intense Russification and finally detached it from the Congress Kingdom in March 1914; a year and a half later, the Austrian occupiers had mollified the Poles by renaming it Chełm and placing it under the Lublin authority, only to barter it back temporarily to the Ukrainians at Brest-Litovsk.

140. In his *War Diaries* (Trans. Eric Sutton [London: Secker, 1929]), on Feb. 18, 1918, General Max Hoffmann observed that the Poles had "apparently gone quite mad over the question of the Chełm district." For example, the German consulate in Cracow was attacked and demolished by Polish mobs.

During the riots in Lemberg the Jews, although they had joined the protests over the cession of Chełm, were accused by Polish Nationalists of acting as Austria's and Germany's allies. *Jüdische Zeitung* (Vienna), Feb. 22, 1918; *Jüdische Rundschau*, 1918, pp. 84, 93; Golczewski, *Polnisch–Jüdische Beziehungen*, pp. 169–70.

141. Sukiennicki, *East Central Europe*, Vol. 2, pp. 732–7.

142. Of the legislature's 110 members, only 55 were directly elected; yet, despite the left's boycott, the pro-Allied Political Circle won thirty-seven seats. When it was finally convened on June 22, 1918, the Polish Council of State displayed its anti-German inclinations, met only fourteen times, and was disbanded on July 31, never to be reconvened. Machray, *Poland*, pp. 90–1; Leslie, *History of Poland*, p. 125.

143. Wandycz, *Partitioned Poland*, pp. 363–4. By July 1918, Haller had reached France, where he took command of the Polish army.

144. Lloyd George, *War Memoirs*, Vol. 5, pp. 38–40. Emphasis added.

a free and secure access to the sea, and whose political and economic independence and territorial integrity should be guaranteed by international covenant."[145]

However, the Allies continued to send disappointing signals to the Poles. While scorning the Warsaw government,[146] they delayed granting cobelligerent status to the Polish army in France and continued to withhold formal diplomatic recognition from Dmowski's KNP, which had established itself in Paris in August 1917.[147] Although the Bolshevik Revolution had removed the major obstacle to reestablishing an independent Poland, the Allies were uneasy over altering the century-old order and creating a "perpetual occasion for European strife" by forcing too many Germans and too many Ukrainians into the new state's borders.[148] Lloyd George's pointed reference to "genuinely Polish elements," and Wilson's to "an indisputably Polish population" as well as to an international guarantee of Poland's independence and territorial integrity, highlighted the West's anxiety over creating an indefensible buffer between a hostile Germany and Russia.

Then there was the issue of Poland's prospective leadership. Despite the Regency Council's attempts at independence, the Western Powers dismissed the Warsaw Poles as German puppets, but they were equally alarmed by the KNP. Notwithstanding Dmowski's fervent and consistent loyalty to the Allied cause, his expansive territorial goals, as set forth in his *Problems of Central and Eastern Europe*,[149] and his unconcealed anti-Semitism, restrained even the most pro-Polish elements in Paris, London, Rome, and Washington.[150]

The Central Powers now weighed in with their solution to the reorganization of Eastern and Southern Europe and the future of its minorities. In

145. Wilson, *Public Papers of Woodrow Wilson*, Vol. 6, pp. 177–84. Emphasis added. On the development of Wilson's vision of U.S.–European relations during World War I, see Ambrosius, *Wilsonian Statecraft*.
146. Britain in May 1918 rebuffed the Regency Council's proposal to send an emissary to London. Rothwell, *British War Aims*, p. 230.
147. On Sept. 28, 1918, France finally recognized the Polish army on its soil as a cobelligerent force, which, with Haller's arrival, included the Polish formations in Russia. Britain followed suit. On Nov. 13, France recognized the Polish National Committee as a *gouvernement de fait* in relation to this army, its foreign policy, and the care of Poles in Allied countries, but Britain and the United States refused to follow. Leslie, *History of Poland*, p. 125; Rothwell, *British War Aims*, pp. 229–33.
148. Particularly because more than 35% of the population would be minorities.
149. Privately printed in London in 1917 in English and French in some five hundred copies, *Problems of Central and Eastern Europe*, which argued for the complete reconstruction of East Central Europe on the basis of nationality, included the famous "Dmowski line" (its author was Stanisław Grabski), corresponding to Poland's borders at the time of the second partition and extending Poland's frontiers beyond its ethnographic borders to include Ukraine, Byelorussia, and Lithuania. Wandycz, *Partitioned Poland*, pp. 360–1.
150. See intercepted copy of KNP report, London, May 15, 1917, to Warsaw, YIVO W/M 119. Also, Latawski, "Roman Dmowski, the Polish Question, and Western Opinion."

the beginning of 1918, Imperial Germany, after achieving an overwhelming military victory in the East, dictated peace treaties with the Ukraine and Soviet Russia at Brest–Litovsk and subsequently concluded treaties with Finland and Romania. The Brest–Litovsk negotiations, conducted in public, pitted the Reich against the Bolsheviks over the carcass of the tsarist empire. The former, overconfident of its military and domestic might, bullied its hesitant Habsburg partner and dominated the negotiations.[151] The latter, overestimating its appeal to the toiling masses of the West, paid heavily for a breathing space for the revolution.[152]

The first peace treaty of World War I was hastily signed at 2 A.M. on February 9, 1918, between the Central Powers and the Ukrainian People's Republic.[153] Austria–Hungary, fearing domestic complications, had initially been reluctant to negotiate with a separatist regime.[154] However, the German military was determined to create a pseudoindependent Ukraine not only as a counterweight to Poland and a barrier against Bolshevism but as a source of critically needed food, coal, and iron ore. Despite Soviet and Allied protests over this "gross distortion of the principle of self-determination" – as well as the fact that, within five hours of the signing, the *Rada* fled Kiev before the advancing Red Army – the Central Powers brought a new state into being.[155]

The short-lived Ukrainian peace treaty created a brief entry in the history of minority rights. A day before the signing, Austria–Hungary and the Ukraine concluded a secret supplementary agreement ensuring cultural and national autonomy for the Polish, German, and Jewish minorities in the Ukraine and for the Ukrainians in the Dual Monarchy.[156] In return for

151. Fischer, *Germany's Aims*, pp. 375–6, 456–66, 487; Shanafelt, *Secret Enemy*, pp. 161–70.
152. "We do not doubt for one moment that this triumph of the imperialist and the militarist over the international proletarian Revolution is only a temporary and passing one." Russian Delegates Protest against the German Terms, Mar. 3, 1918, U.S. Dept. of State, reprinted in *Proceedings of the Brest-Litovsk Peace Conference*, p. 185.
153. Text of the treaty among Germany, Austria–Hungary, Bulgaria, Turkey, and the Ukrainian People's Republic, Feb. 9, 1918, in Martens, *Recueil Général de Traités*, Vol. 10, pp. 752–62. An "additional treaty" was signed that day between Germany and the Ukraine; ibid., pp. 762–72.
154. When representatives of the Central *Rada* [Council], arrived in Brest-Litovsk on Jan. 4, 1918, Austro–Hungarian Foreign Minister Count Ottokar Czernin feared that this mutilation of tsarist Russia in the name of "self-determination" would inspire similar demands from his empire's Czechs, Ruthenians, and South Slavs. Nowak, *Der Sturz der Mittelmächte*, p. 8. The Central *Rada* declared an Independent Ukrainian Republic on Jan. 22, 1918.
155. The president of the Ukrainian delegation made this announcement: "From today the Ukrainian People's Republic . . . enters as an independent State into the circle of nations and ends the war on its front." Session of 9 February – Central Powers and Ukraine, U.S. Dept. of State, *Proceedings of the Brest-Litovsk Peace Conference*, p. 158.
156. "Secret Crownland Agreement of February 8, 1918 between Austria-Hungary and Ukraine: Secret Integral Part of the Treaty of Peace of February 9, 1918," in Horak, *The First Treaty of World War I*,

the *Rada*'s promise to provide the Central Powers with a million tons of surplus grain, the Habsburg government agreed to hand over Chełm without consulting its mixed population and to prepare legislation uniting Eastern Galicia and Bukovina into a Ukrainian crown land. When these concessions provoked a storm of opposition, especially from the Poles, Vienna admitted that its magnanimity in regard to Ukrainian national rights depended entirely on the bread deliveries.[157]

The peace treaty with Soviet Russia, signed on March 3, was an even greater travesty.[158] In forcing Russia to recognize the independence of Poland and the Ukraine and withdraw from Finland and the Baltic provinces, the Reich distorted the principle of self-determination to mask its intention of dominating a vast region extending all the way to the Caucasus.[159] Russia lost 780,000 square kilometers of its territory, 56 million of its people, one-third of its railway network, almost three-quarters of its iron ore, and 89% of its coal supply; it lost nearly the entire former Pale of Settlement and a large proportion of its prewar Jewish population; and there were no formal guarantees of minority rights.[160]

Two months later, it was the turn of oil- and grain-rich Romania, which had entered the war in August 1916, lured by the Entente's promises of territorial gains at the expense of the Habsburg Monarchy, and collapsed at the end of 1917 in the wake of Russia's total defeat.[161] The Bucharest government dragged out the negotiations, fomenting considerable friction among the victors, but finally acceded to most of their demands, which included the return of the Dobrudja to Bulgaria and ceding control over its oil and grain supplies to the Central Powers.[162] Not unexpectedly, the Central

pp. 173–4. In Jan. 1918 there had been major strikes and food riots throughout Austria. Shanafelt, *Secret Enemy*, pp. 168–75.

Background in Minc, "Kiev Zionists" and Frankel, "Jewish National Autonomism."

157. Wheeler-Bennett, *The Forgotten Peace*, pp. 219–20. To be sure, not only were Austria's political concessions dependent on the grain deliveries, but, on Mar. 4, 1918, a commission consisting of the Quadruple Alliance, the Ukraine, and Poland was created in Brest to determine the future of Chełm "in accordance with the expressed wishes of its population"; ibid., p. 235.
158. Text in Martens, *Recueil Général de Traités*, Vol. 10, pp. 773–97; four additional and supplementary agreements, ibid., pp. 797–851.
159. Fischer, *Germany's Aims*, pp. 508–9. Wilson, on Apr. 6, 1918, called it a "cheap triumph," which invited conquered peoples "to be free under their dominion." quoted in Macartney, *National States and National Minorities*, pp. 188–9.
160. U.S. Dept. of State, *Proceedings of the Brest-Litovsk Peace Conference*, pp. 39–43; idem, *Texts of the Russian "Peace"*; Macartney, *National States and National Minorities*, p. 212.
161. Zeman, *The Gentlemen Negotiators*, pp. 80–2, 115–16.
162. Text of the Treaty of Bucharest, in Martens *Receuil Général des Traités*, pp. 856–70. Bornemann, *Der Frieden von Bukarest*; also Fischer, *Germany's Aims*, pp. 515–23; Shanafelt, *Secret Enemy*, pp. 177–80. The treaty, which was actually signed at Buftea (to distinguish it from the 1913 Bucharest Treaty), was never ratified; although Austria–Hungary was to receive a one-third share of the German-dominated oil monopoly, most of the booty fell to Berlin.

Powers' negotiations with Romania also became a test of their commitment to minority rights. Jewish organizations, immobilized since Romania's entry into the war, now saw an opportunity to resuscitate Article 44 of the Treaty of Berlin that the Bucharest government had ignored for forty years and the Entente had been reluctant to enforce, thus giving Berlin and Vienna an "ill-deserved opportunity" to impose justice.[163] Pressed by their co-religionists, Austrian and German Jews had appealed to their governments to intercede on behalf of the disenfranchised, and allegedly pro-German and pro-Austrian, Jews of Romania.[164]

Vienna and Berlin were predictably at odds over the inclusion of minority clauses in the Bucharest peace treaty. Austria–Hungary, with few qualms about intervening in Romania's internal affairs, ordered its foreign minister, the Bohemian aristocrat Count Ottokar Czernin, to openly support the Jewish campaign.[165] On the other hand, the triumphant Reich of 1918 cared less about the pleas of its Jewish supporters, the potential material benefits, or the international prestige attached to supporting minority rights than about the domestic and diplomatic risks of forcing complete Jewish emancipation on a recalcitrant Romania.[166]

Vienna's last victory in World War I was for the cause of minority rights. By threatening to conclude another separate arrangement, it forced minority clauses into the treaty with Romania, although the results were modest and moot. Articles 27 and 28 of the Bucharest Treaty, briefly heralded as the Central Powers' answer to the Balfour declaration, actually gave Romanian Jews less protection than had the defunct 1878 Treaty of Berlin. Article 27 granted all religions parity with the Romanian Orthodox Church and guaranteed freedom of worship and instruction. But Article 28, calling for the institution of new naturalization laws and establishing the basis of collective

163. See Wolf, "Confidential memorandum on the Jewish question in Romania," London, May 12, 1917 and "Romania and the Minority Treaties, Sept. 1, 1917, YIVO W/M 155.

164. Bornemann, *Frieden von Bukarest*, pp. 210–11; Iancu, *L'émancipation des juifs*, pp. 147–59; Zechlin, *Deutsche Politik*, pp. 238–45.

165. *Jüdische Rundschau* 23 (1918), 89.

166. Gelber, "Bucharest Peace Conference," especially pp. 226–7.

The German High Command, as part of its overall economic design, did want Romania to remove the constitutional prohibition against foreigners' (German Jews) acquiring landed property, but it preferred an amendment to forcing a specific international commitment.

Not only did the German ambassador in Bucharest oppose any concessions to Romanian Jews, but the leading Center and Conservative members of the Reichstag strongly opposed "meddling in Romania's internal affairs." The warnings of the right-wing *Deutsche Zeitung* and *Deutsche Tageszeitung* against "Judaeophilia," and of the racist *Deutschlands Erneuerung* against the dark plots of the *Alliance Israélite* carried more weight in the Wilhelmstrasse than the pleas of National Liberal and Socialist deputies and those of the *Vossische Zeitung*, the *Berliner Tageblatt*, and the *Jüdische Rundschau*, to elevate the Reich's reputation by gaining justice for Romania's Jews. Bornemann, *Frieden von Bukarest*, p. 216; Iancu, *L'émancipation des juifs*, pp. 156–7.

enfranchisement, was limited to two nebulous categories – serving military personnel and the native born or offspring of native born – leaving the way open for new forms of official chicanery.[167] Indeed, the labyrinthine, sixty-eight-article, "Marghiloman law," passed by both houses of the Romanian Parliament and promulgated by royal decree on August 27, 1918, not only placed heavy restrictions on the acquisition of citizenship but also posed new threats to the security of an estimated 200,000 Jewish "aliens."[168] Moreover, although Romania was about to annex Bessarabia, the province, with its 300,000 Jews, was excluded from any form of special protection.

Once more, Berlin had deserted the minorities' cause.[169] Yet during the Reichstag debate over the Bucharest treaty, conservative Reich politicians fiercely opposed Germany's right to interfere in Romania's domestic affairs.[170] The stunned, long-patient Jewish leaders of Germany and Austria–Hungary barely concealed their disappointment over the setback for a cause they had championed for more than four decades.[171]

The Treaty of Bucharest was neither ratified nor implemented before the Central Powers themselves collapsed in the fall of 1918. It gave the Allies an opening to attack the Reich's hypocrisy and guile and to promote the cause of "true" minority rights.[172] However, it also left Romania's right-wing politicians all the more adamant against submitting to any future imposed outside solutions.[173]

THE ALLIES, THE POLES, AND THE JEWS

After the shocks of Brest–Litovsk and Bucharest, the British, French, and Americans finally renounced a negotiated peace with the Central Powers.

167. "La question juive de Roumanie et la paix de Bucarest," in *Bulletin du bureau de correspondance juif de la Haye* (May 1918), FMAE, Levant, 1918–1939, "Palestine," Vol. 10.
168. *Jüdische Rundschau* 23 (1918), 245; *Neue Jüdische Monatshefte* 2 (1918), 523; Iancu, *Combat international pour l'émancipation des juifs de Roumanie*, pp. 142–72.
169. *Le traité de paix entre la Roumanie et les Puissances Centrales et la question des juifs roumains* (Zurich: Comité Pro Causa Judaïca, 1918).
170. Bornemann, *Frieden von Bukarest*, p. 215, n. 93.
171. *Jüdische Rundschau* 23 (1918), 254; also Iancu, *L'émancipation des juifs*, pp. 165–6; Gelber, "Bucharest Peace Conference," especially pp. 236–7.
172. "They have definitely embittered feeling over the Jewish question. . . . Their solution is no complete one of the Jewish question, but this appears to be intentional, for it is in the German interest to leave the question unsolved in order that they may play one side against the other and themselves enjoy the role of arbiters and supporters of each in turn." Unsigned memorandum on the meaning and effect of the Bucharest 'Peace Treaty,' reprinted in Bourne and Watt, *British Documents on Foreign Affairs*, Part II, Series H, Vol. 12, p. 315; Iancu, *L'émancipation des juifs*, pp. 167–8; Zechlin, *Deutsche Politik*, pp. 248–50. See Cecil's remarks to the House of Commons, May 30, 1918, printed in *Jewish Chronicle*, July 6, 1918; Pichon to AIU, Paris, July 24, 1918, copy in AJC LM, Paris Peace Conference, Box 2.
173. Zechlin, *Deutsche Politik*, p. 250; Gelber, "Bucharest Peace Conference," p. 243.

Now in pursuit of total victory and spurred by East European émigré leaders as well as their academic and journalist boosters, the Allies dropped all restraint toward the Hohenzollern and Habsburg Empires and began emitting different levels of encouragement to the national aspirations of the Poles, Czechs, Serbs, Romanians, and Greeks.[174]

The climax came on June 3, 1918, when the Inter-Allied Conference of Versailles termed the creation of a "united, independent Poland with free access to the sea" one of the conditions of "a solid and just peace, and of the rule of right in Europe."[175] However, the Allies still withheld recognition from the KNP, which had an army fighting on several fronts, and had given little serious consideration to the issue of minority rights in Poland.[176]

Western Jewish leaders, who throughout the war had assumed that reformed multinational empires would survive in Central and Eastern Europe, became greatly alarmed. They feared a reprise of 1878 and the Balkan Wars, the creation and enlargement of states with the will and the power to persecute their involuntary inhabitants.[177] Above all, they worried about the prospect of a large, independent Poland, where Jews would constitute some 40% of the population of its towns and urban areas.[178]

Jewish leaders in Britain had established amicable relations with the Warsaw government whose emissaries had made conciliatory statements on the issue of minority rights. By contrast, the newly ascendant KNP, with its active delegates and press bureaus in France, Britain, and Switzerland, with the shrewd pianist–politician Ignacy Paderewski mobilizing popular support in the United States, and with its flagrantly anti-Semitic leader Dmowski, represented a threat to the future of Jewish life in Poland, and perhaps even elsewhere.[179] In Britain and France, where the KNP had been authorized to

174. Fest, *Peace or Partition*, Chap. 6 ("The Decision for a Policy of Disruption"); Calder, *Britain and the Origins of the New Europe*, pp. 126–44, 172–213; Zeman, *The Gentlemen Negotiators*, pp. 350–60.

175. Text of Supreme War Council statement, GB FO 371/3135/101920. "Access to the sea" meant the detachment of German territory to create a secure and viable Poland. The statement of "earnest sympathy for the nationalistic aspirations towards freedom of the Czecho-Slovak and Yugo-Slav peoples" was far more ambiguous.

176. The correspondence between Archibald Cary Coolidge and Walter Lippmann, two leading members of the Inquiry, a panel of experts appointed by the Wilson administration to work out details of a future American peace plan, on Mar. 10, 19, 25, 1918, reveals this lack of preparedness. See Records of the American Commission to Negotiate Peace, NA RG 256 Box 3; confirmed in Gelfand, *The Inquiry*.

177. Lucien Wolf, "The New Bondage in the Balkans," *Graphic*, Mar. 7, 1914.

178. Zeman, *The Gentlemen Negotiators*, pp. 342–7; Calder, *Britain and the Origins of the New Europe*, pp. 145–52. Wolf, "The Jewish National Movement," *Edinburgh Review* (Apr. 1917), 303.

179. Cyrus Adler to Louis Marshall, Dec. 14, 1917, Adler, *Selected Letters*, pp. 342–3, reported that Paderewski had once performed benefit concerts in Europe for Dmowski's rabidly anti-Semitic newspaper, *Dwa Grosza*, that the Polish press in America was exhorting "every sacrifice" to help all the Jews of Poland emigrate to Palestine, that one of the speakers at a recent mass recruitment meeting had claimed that the object of the Polish Volunteer Army was "to exterminate the Germans

certify Polish nationals, it had peremptorily excluded émigré Jews, tarring them as German or Bolshevik agents, and banned even baptized Jews from the Polish army.[180]

Moderate Jewish advocates moved cautiously against the looming threats to their East European kin. The most circumspect of all was the AIU. Still tied closely to the Quai d'Orsay, Jacques Bigart and his colleagues had long abandoned Crémieux's brave, independent stance for a prudent partnership with British and American Jews.[181] The AJC, led by Louis Marshall, devoted the bulk of its wartime efforts to domestic affairs and to organizing relief to Eastern Europe.[182] The most vigorous diplomacy came from Britain, where the new Joint Foreign Committee, inaugurated in December 1917[183] and led by Lucien Wolf, planted articles in the press, sent missives to the Foreign Office, and held talks with East European politicians.

During the last year of World War I, the bonds among American, British, French, and neutral Jewish organizations that had been frayed by the triumph of Zionism were reknit. Jewish organizations collected data and prepared drafts of future codes to protect minority rights.[184] But they had become increasingly distant from the tumultuous scene in Eastern Europe.[185]

The Western Jewish leaders had also failed to gain their governments' sympathy for the minorities cause. In late 1917, Wolf had requested permission to convene a meeting between West European Jewish representatives and emissaries of the Warsaw government to discuss the future of Poland's Jews.[186] The Foreign Office, divided unequally between polonophiles and

and the Jews," and that there was a growing fear of the spread of the anti-Semitic virus to the 4 million Poles of America.

180. On the withholding of papers: KNP to all representatives ("Kwestia Żydowski" [Jewish Question]), Paris, May 23, 1918 ("Do not issue Polish passports to Jews born on Polish territory, because they do not know Polish and are in the service of Moscow."); KNP London to KNP Paris, n.d., AAN KNP/159; Wolf Memorandum, London, June 14, 1918, YIVO W/M 131; Piltz to Degrand, Paris, July 15, 1918, AAN KNP/1813; Wolf Memorandum, July 8, 1918, BDBJ C11/12/65; KNP Paris to FMAE, Oct. 15, 1918, FMAE Z (Pologne) 60; on military exclusion: Minister of War to Pichon, Oct. 9, 1918, ibid., Z (Pologne) 35. Also, Rothwell, *British War Aims*, pp. 231–2.
181. AIU to Wolf, Paris, Nov. 8, 1917, BDBJ C11/12/56; Joint Foreign Committee: Minute Book, July 15, Oct. 2, 1918, BDBJ; *Alliance Israélite Universelle, La question juive*, pp. 7–9; Chouraqui, *Cent ans d'histoire*, pp. 215–21.
182. *Louis Marshall: Champion of Liberty*: Vol. 2, Chaps. 6–8.
183. The JFC, successor to the Conjoint, linked the Board of Deputies of British Jews and the Anglo–Jewish Association. See the agreement of Dec. 19, 1917, BDBJ C11/2/12.
184. See Wolf to Marshall, Nov. 30, 1917, Oct. 3, 1918, Marshall to Bigart and Wolf, Nov. 16, 1918, AJC LM, Correspondence.
185. For example, both Wolf and Bigart dismissed the autonomy granted in the German and Austrian treaties as a "specious bribe" to the Jewish masses in Eastern Europe. Wolf to Oliphant, June 18, 1918, GB FO 371/3386/856; the AIU's response in Feinberg, *La question des minorités*, pp. 39–40.
186. Wolf, Confidential Memorandum, London, Nov. 22, 1917, BDBJ C11/12/56; Wolf to Cecil, Nov. 26, Dec. 21, 1917, ibid., C11/12/59; Wolf to Marshall, Nov. 30, 1917, AJC LM, correspondence.

polonophobes, issued an unconditional veto.[187] Balfour also refused to make any public statement on behalf of minority rights, and Cecil responded coolly to Wolf's moderate autonomy proposals.[188] Across the Channel, the Quai d'Orsay, bent on creating as large and strong a Poland as possible, spurned proposals to establish special rights for its prospective minorities.[189]

Jewish leaders were even less effective in eliciting pledges of good conduct from East European politicians. Thomas Masaryk did issue a "fine" public statement on granting minority rights in the future Czechoslovakia.[190] However, Polish and Romanian politicians, confidant that victory was near, denied any danger to their minorities and rejected the Jews' proposals for special rights and protection.[191] Disappointed by his contacts with Polish leaders and dismayed by the reports of atrocities in Poland even before the Armistice was signed at Compiègne, Louis Marshall on November 11 appealed to President Wilson to help prevent a reprise of the Jews' "unhappy experience" in Romania.[192]

The military verdicts of 1918 conveyed a bleak message to the partisans of Jewish and minority rights. The German-imposed treaties had brought little relief to the oppressed, and the victors on November 11 were manifestly unprepared for the collapse of four multinational empires.[193] A lone voice,

187. Gregory minutes, Nov. 29, Dec. 10, 29, Cecil minutes, n.d., Dec. 19, 29, GB FO 371/3019. Wolf Memorandum, Nov. 22, 1917, details the strong pro-Polish views of Sir George Clerk ("If you were a Pole, you would also be an anti-Semite"), BDBJ C11/12/56, whereas Latawski, "The Dmowski-Namier Feud" and Rothwell, *British War Aims*, pp. 228–33, discuss the impact of Lewis Namier's polonophobia.

188. Conjoint memorandum, London, Nov. 22, 1917, Wolf to Cecil, Jan. 18, 1918, GB FO 371/3277.

189. Questions qui se posent au sujet de la Pologne, n.d. (Nov.–Dec. 1918), FMAE PA-AP Tardieu, Vol. 356.

190. Mack to Marshall, Sept. 24, 1918, CZA A405/208. In private, however, the future president was far more equivocal about the rights of the vast numbers of Germans, Hungarians, and Ruthenians, not to mention the Slovaks, within the expansive borders he claimed for the new Czechoslovakia. See "The Recognition of the National Council and of the Czechoslovak Army," Aug. 31, 1918, in Mamatney, *The United States and East Central Europe*, pp. 305–7.

191. On the AJC's discussions with Paderewski and Dmowski: Marshall to Paderewski, New York, Sept. 24, 1918, AAN Paderewski/675; Paderewski to Rosenwald, New York, July 23, 1918, CZA Mack papers A405/75; Mack to Marshall, ibid., A405/208; Adler to Marshall, Nov. 1, 1918, Marshall to Wolf, Nov. 8, 1918, Marshall to Brig. Gen. Churchill, Nov. 18, 1918, AJC LM, correspondence; Brandeis to Mack, De Haas and Wise, Washington, Oct. 13, 1918, AJC, correspondence, 1918 (Poland). On Wolf's discussions with the Poles, Joint Foreign Committee minute book, Sept. 17, 1918, BDBJ; Minutes of interview, Nov. 17, 1918, BDBJ C11/12/61, Sobański to KNP, Paris, (Summer 1918) AAN KNP 159; and with the Romanians, Iancu, *L'émancipation des juifs*, pp. 178–81.

192. Marshall to Wilson, Nov. 11, 1918, American Jewish Archives (hereafter AJA) LM 1588.

193. Across the ocean, Louis Marshall, in his congratulatory letter to Lucien Wolf on Nov. 11, 1918, exulted in the fulfillment of his dream that "the Hohenzollerns, the Habsburgs, and the Romanoffs would . . . walk the plank," but he also acknowledged that serious problems lay ahead. AJA LM 1588.

Radical Socialist H. N. Brailsford, had warned of the chaos about to explode from the victory of exclusive nationalisms and called for international charters guaranteeing minority protection.[194] But given the hatreds incited all over Eastern Europe[195] as well as the shock of the Bolshevik Revolution, such a gesture faced enormous opposition.

194. *The New Republic*, Dec. 16, 1916, Aug. 31, 1918.
195. Zechlin, *Deutsche Politik*, pp. 278–84.

4

Lemberg

"Between two great powers, Germany and Russia, there is no room for a small state."[1]

"Poland has been born with bloodstains on her forehead."[2]

"It is the duty of the Powers to discipline the Poles and to prevent them from soiling the new banner of liberty which we gave to them clean."[3]

During the long two months between the Armistice ending World War I and the opening of the Paris Peace Conference, the peoples of Eastern Europe fought over the spoils of three defeated empires. Europe divided into three distinct but overlapping zones. The Allies sought to crown their sudden triumph by replacing the Reich's realm with a belt of new and enlarged states; their clients battled over specific prizes; and the defeated Germans and Bolsheviks fanned new and ancient rivalries to reduce their losses.[4] Local incidents reverberated with national and international consequences, and local minority populations were swept up in postwar *Realpolitik*.

Poland was once more at the center of the struggle.[5] Wedged between their former masters, Poland's leaders intended to acquire sufficient strategic and material gains to outweigh the risks of creating a large, multiethnic commonwealth. As posed by Piłsudski, could this Poland be "equal to the powers of the world or a small state needing the protection of the mighty"?[6]

If Poland's western frontier largely depended on the Allies' willingness to "squeeze" a recalcitrant Germany, its claims in the East hinged on its

1. Roman Dmowski, quoted in Wandycz, "Polish Foreign Policy," p. 65.
2. *Ha-tsfira*, Dec. 5, 1918, quoted in Mendelsohn, *Zionism in Poland*, p. 90.
3. *The Times* [London], Feb. 7, 1919.
4. Debo, *Survival and Consolidation*, pp. 3–33.
5. Bierzanek, "La Pologne dans les conceptions politiques," especially pp. 273–81.
6. Quoted in Wandycz, "Polish Foreign Policy," p. 65.

own ability to "force doors open and how far,"[7] to combat the claims of its neighbors, Ukraine, Lithuania, and Belorussia, to counter Berlin and Moscow's machinations, to reassure the Allies, and to quell the fears and suspicions of the Jews. The great challenge to the new Polish government was to convince world opinion that Europe's long-martyred nation was about to become an outpost of western values and practices while bridling the national aspirations of its near neighbors.[8]

After the guns were stilled on the western front, Britain, France, and the United States prepared for Europe's first major peace conference in the new century. They had not fought to free Eastern Europe, and they regarded Poland, and particularly the problem of its borders, through the distorted lens of their hesitant and conflicting policies toward Germany and Bolshevik Russia. The victors' physical distance from the local scene, combined with their ignorance, confusion, and prejudice toward the peoples of Eastern Europe, spurred their clients to create facts that no outside statesmen could overturn.

A CHAOTIC REBIRTH

On the morning of November 1, 1918, the Polish population of Lemberg was shocked to behold blue and yellow Ukrainian flags flying over the city. As the Habsburg Monarchy moved toward complete surrender, the Polish Liquidation Commission in Cracow was preparing to extend its authority to all of Galicia. However, the Ukrainians moved more quickly. Hoping to unite Eastern Galicia with an independent Ukrainian state, the Ruthenian National Council on October 19 had claimed sovereignty over the fifty-thousand-square-kilometer, oil-rich region between the Zbruch (Zbrucz) and the San Rivers, between the Carpathians and Volhynia; two weeks later, it boldly seized the Galician capital.[9] The local Poles, outraged at the disarray

7. Piłsudski, on Feb. 7, 1919, quoted in Baranowski, *Rozmowy z Piłsudskim*, p. 124. Compare Dmowski's expansive views, Sukiennicki, *East Central Europe*, Vol. 2, pp. 894–9.
8. Paderewski, Poland's most visible and popular emissary in the United States, was highly ambivalent over the national claims of the "minority nationalities." Publicly in sympathy with the Ukrainians, Lithuanians, and Jews, privately he complained to Wilson that the unscrupulousness and rapaciousness of the partitioning powers had encouraged the "separatistic, nationalistic aspirations of every small nation, of every tribe connected with the Polish people" in order to claim "things impossible." Sukiennicki, *East Central Europe*, Vol. 2, pp. 1183–4, n. 46.
9. Wandycz, *Partitioned Poland*, pp. 366–7. Based on the generally unreliable Austrian census figure of 1910, the population of Eastern Galicia, approximately 4.5 million, was 59% Ruthenian (Ukrainian), 27% Polish, and 13% Jewish. In Lemberg, with some 200,000 inhabitants, 86% declared themselves "Polish speaking" and 11% "Ukrainian speaking"; but a large number of Jews in Eastern Galicia, estimated as high as 800,000 of a total of 872,000 had been classified as "Poles," and all Catholics, including Uniates, as well. "Eastern Galicia," in Temperley, *Peace Conference of Paris*, Vol. 6, pp. 267–8; also unsigned report [Namier?] "Eastern Galicia," n.d. [1919?], GB FO 371/4532 P.I.D.

and apathy in Warsaw, Lublin, and Cracow, were determined to wrest their "Polish island" from the Ukrainians.[10]

The news from Lemberg caused considerable consternation in western capitals. The Allies, in the final moments of World War I, were unable to halt the onset of the Polish–Ukrainian struggle for Eastern Galicia, which would drag on for eight months, lead to a wider war among Poles, Ukrainians, and Bolsheviks, and ultimately shape the peace settlement in Eastern Europe.[11] The two rivals for Eastern Galicia, each already tarred as Austro–German collaborators with huge appetites for expansion, appealed to the Allies for support.[12] The responses were divided, with France favoring Poland's claims, the United States hesitating, and Britain issuing a clear warning to the KNP against any form of Polish expansion in the East.[13]

Poland was reborn in November 1918 out of collapse and turmoil. On November 7, shortly after the Austrians' withdrawal, a group of left-wing politicians and intellectuals in Lublin, led by Ignacy Daszyński, defied the Regency Council in Warsaw by declaring a republic and summoning Lithuanians, Belorussians, Ukrainians, Czechs, and Slovaks to join an association of "free and equal nations."[14] Three days later, the fifty-one-year-old Józef Piłsudski, released by the German revolutionary government from the Magdeburg fortress, arrived in Warsaw and took control over the army. On

10. Details in Mick, "Nationalisierung in einer multiethnischen Stadt." esp. pp. 138–40.

    Notwithstanding both sides' suspicions, there is no evidence that the lame-duck imperial government either promoted the Ukrainians' coup or supported a Polish one. See Skirmunt to U.S. Ambassador Page, Rome, Dec. 1, 1918, AAN KNP 2082; also Stachiw and Sztendera, *Western Ukraine at the Turning Point*, pp. 100, 106–9.

11. On Nov. 8, 1919, Piłsudski's emissary, Michał Sokolnicki, warned the French minister in Iaşi (Jassy) that this "German-inspired attack on Poland *and* the Entente would prejudice the work of the peace conference and threatened Eastern Galicia with anarchy and bolshevism and urged Saint Aulaire to send a French mission to Lemberg to halt the bloodshed. Piłsudski Institute of America (hereafter PIA), Sokolnicki papers, ffol. 29A, pp. 16–18. Saint Aulaire dispatched Captain Henri Villaine, who arranged a three-day truce, but the ensuing negotiations were fruitless. The minister's report (Saint Aulaire to FMAE, Iaşi, Nov. 13, 1918, FMAE Z [Europe/Russie] 837 [Galicie-dossier générale, 1918–19]), sent by wire over Romanian circuits, did not reach Paris until Jan. 25, 1919.

12. See KNP memorandum to the U.S. ambassador in France, Nov. 13, 1918, and message of the "Provisional Government of Halycz" to Wilson via the new Austrian government in Vienna and the Swedish minister to the United States, Nov. 26, *Foreign Relations of the United States: The Paris Peace Conference* (hereafter FRUS PPC), Vol. 2, pp. 411–12, 195–6.

13. On Nov. 8, 1918, Balfour wrote Sobański that "His Majesty's Government would view with serious displeasure any military or other action of the Polish Government in East Galicia, or elsewhere, of a nature to prejudice or forestall the decisions of the peace conference." AAN KNP 1908; also Sobański to Balfour, London, Nov. 12, 1918, ibid.

    Also see France, Comité d'Études, "Le Problème de la Galicie Orientale," *Travaux* (Paris, 1919), Vol. 2, pp. 309–10, and British War Cabinet Reports, CAB 24/145, 1918: XC (Oct. 17), XCII (Oct. 31), XCIII (Nov. 7), XCIV (Nov. 14), XCV (Nov. 21).

14. Żarnowski, *November 1918*, pp. 135–40. Daszyński, head of the "Provisional Government of the People's Republic of Poland," was a left-wing Social Democrat and former member of the Austrian Reichsrat.

November 14, the defunct Regency Council turned full powers over to the renowned military leader. When Daszyński resigned four days later, the new chief of state appointed an interim coalition cabinet of socialists, peasants, and the radical intelligentsia, led by his associate, Jędrzej Moraczewski, and he called for national elections on January 26, 1919.[15]

Resurrected Poland, a ruined land with 450,000 dead, 900,000 wounded, 700,000 deportees in Russia, and almost 300,000 forced laborers still in Germany and Austria, faced formidable international and diplomatic problems.[16] Piłsudski, far from being a dictator, controlled only the Congress Kingdom. German armies remained in the East, the Ukrainians claimed Eastern Galicia, and there were budding local authorities in Cracow, Teschen, and Poznań controlled by Roman Dmowski's right-wing National Democrats.[17] Piłsudski's major challenger was Dmowski's shadow government, the Paris-based KNP, which denounced his pro-German, Socialist record. The KNP, with its conservative base at home, its volunteer army in France led by General Józef Haller, and its steadfast defenders in the Quai d'Orsay, claimed to represent the real Poland, which throughout the war had opposed the Central Powers and the Bolsheviks and had loyally supported the Allies.[18] Another imposing contender was Poland's voice in America, Ignacy Paderewski, the pianist and composer who had established close relations with the Polish National Department in the United States, with the State Department, and with Wilson's confidant, Colonel Edward House, and who had deftly maintained his distance from both the Piłsudski and Dmowski camps.[19]

For two crucial months, Piłsudski's provisional regime, with its leftist and vaguely federalist leanings, was isolated internationally.[20] Poland, which unlike Serbia and Czechoslovakia, had no officially recognized government and was not a member of the Entente, was excluded from the pre-Armistice

15. Garlicki, *Piłsudski*, pp. 88–9. The cabinet consisted of six Socialists, five members of peasant parties, two representatives of the radical intelligentsia, and two nonparty members, with additional slots reserved for other parts of the country.
16. For details on Poland's material, economic, and financial losses, see Wandycz, *Partitioned Poland*, pp. 367–9.
17. Ajnenkiel, "National Government in Poland," especially pp. 133–4.
18. Leslie, *History of Poland*, pp. 128–9.
19. Drozdowski, *Paderewski*, pp. 75–141. During his three-and-a-half-year stay, beginning in April 1915, the fifty-five-year-old Paderewski had played 140 benefit concerts and recitals and delivered 340 speeches in Polish and English. Ibid., p. 138.
20. Komarnicki, *Polish Republic*, pp. 247–59. The Moraczewski government repeated Daszyński's call to "the democracies of Poland, Lithuania, Byelorussia, the Ukraine, Bohemia, Slovakia, Hungary and Germany [to find] a common basis for establishing the conditions of co-existence of free and equal peoples," and, on Dec. 20, 1918, the socialist organ, *Robotnik* proposed a union of "socialist nations."

negotiations at Spa.[21] Moreover, Poland was not mentioned by name in the November 11 armistice agreement, with damaging results to its stability and future.[22] And despite the KNP's pleas, the Allies had no intention of dispatching either their own or Polish soldiers to police postwar Europe.

Worse yet for Poland, the Western Powers had readily acceded to the proposals of Matthias Erzberger, the defeated Reich's emissary, concerning the terms for the withdrawal of German troops from the East. Britain, France, and the United States had not only permitted Reich soldiers to remain temporarily on former Russian territory for the ostensible purpose of protecting the local population against Bolshevism; but, over France's objections, the victors had allowed the new Berlin government to maintain control over Reich territory, including the port of Danzig and the West Prussian railway system, thus paralyzing the newborn Poland's economic and military ties with the West.[23] Most ominous of all for the Poles in Warsaw and Paris, the Allies had insisted that until "order" – a legitimate government – was established, there was no guarantee of Poland's representation at the peace conference.[24]

While the West withheld its recognition and visible signs of moral and material support, an allegedly friendly Germany – the first state to recognize Piłsudski's government – almost immediately revealed its hostile intentions. Torn between its professed Socialist fraternalism and the aversion of its imperial holdovers to ceding Reich lands, Berlin tipped decisively toward the latter in December 1918 when Danzig, Poznań, and Upper Silesia suddenly stood in the balance.[25]

21. Rudin, *Armistice 1918*, pp. 299–300, 305–12.

22. Dmowski, who was still in America, was reportedly shocked by the "premature" armistice, preferring that the Allies march to Berlin and Eastern Europe, and he was enraged by the arrangements that allowed German troops to remain on Polish territory. Dmowski, *Polityka Polska*, Vol. 1, pp. 249–55.

23. On Balfour's suggestion, Article 16 gave the Allies "free access" to the territories on Germany's eastern frontier, either through Danzig or the Vistula, to convey supplies and maintain order. Also, Western Poland, still technically part of Germany, fell under the restrictions of the Allied blockade. Komarnicki, *Polish Republic*, pp. 225–33.

    During the British Cabinet discussion of Oct. 19, 1918, after Balfour had expressed concern about deserting the Poles and other East Europeans, Lloyd George expostulated "we cannot expect the British to go on sacrificing their lives for the Poles." ibid., p. 225. The German Foreign Ministry had nevertheless expected the Entente to take the Reich's place in the East. See Kessler, *In the Twenties*, p. 14.

24. Baylor [Dmowski] to Derby [Zamoyski], New York, n.d. (received in Paris, Nov. 15, 1918), AAN KNP w Paryzu/24, Korespondencja III/1918. French transmission of Dmowski's requests for recognition, Jusserand to Lansing, Washington, Nov. 12, 1918, FRUS PPC, Vol. 1, p. 264, Nov. 26, 1918, ibid., Vol. 2, p. 412.

25. Werner Freiherr von Rheinbaben, Aufzeichnung, Dec. 9, 1918, *Akten zur Deutschen Ausärtigen Politik*, Series A (hereafter ADAP A), Vol. 1, pp. 90–2, assumed good relations with the future Czechoslovakia, despite its three-million-strong German minority, but an irreconcilable stance

Not at all unexpectedly, Poland's chaotic rebirth was accompanied by a wave of attacks on the Jews.[26] In the confused weeks between the evaporation of Austro–German power and the establishment of the new regime, there was no central government to maintain order, quell agitators and angry mobs, and restrain marauding vagrants and demobilized troops. Congress Poland erupted with anti-Semitic tracts and scattered incidents of violence, particularly in Warsaw.[27] Even worse outbreaks took place in Western Galicia, loosely governed by the Liquidation Commission in Cracow, whose authority had been accepted by both Poles and Jews. In early November 1918 there was a swell of looting assaults and killing, which were immediately termed "pogroms" by the Polish–Jewish press.[28]

The most dramatic of all these events occurred on Armistice Day in the former Congress Kingdom. Kielce was a small industrial city of about 25,000 inhabitants located more than halfway between Warsaw and

toward Poland's "immoderate" territorial demands. In Brockdorff-Rantzau, Denkschrift, "Bedingungen eines für Deutschland annehmbaren Friedensvertrages," Jan. 27, 1919, in Miller, *Die Regierung der Volksbeauftragten 1918/19*, Vol. 2, pp. 319–22, Germany's new foreign minister, still envisaging Allied–German negotiations, proposed the following: a "neutral Poland on indisputably Polish soil"; Polish access to the sea through a free port [*Freihafen*] in Danzig as well as the canalization of the Vistula; bilateral minority agreements; plebiscites in contested areas to be conducted in local districts [*Kreisen*] after the conclusion of peace and requiring 2/3 majorities; and the possibility of bilateral exchanges of enclaves.

Jewish Independent Socialist (USPD) Minister Otto Landsberg was rapidly transformed from an advocate of friendly relations with Poland (Nov. 21, 1918) to a supporter of military intervention to protect Poznań and Upper Silesia. Protokolle der Kabinettssitzungen, Alte Reichskanzlei, Nov. 21, Dec. 28–29, 1918, Germ. PA AA 8393H/E627000, E627236-37, E627305-7.

26. On Nov. 1, 1918, the *American Jewish Chronicle*, citing Poland's "hostility to the Jews," had already labeled it "a second Roumania," with an anti-Semitism "more intense than in Roumania," and vowed to keep the western press, the United States, and the Allied governments informed about the Jewish question in Poland.

27. In response to the events in Poland, Balfour warned Sobański on Nov. 14, 1918 (AAN KNP 1908), that "if any people in Central Europe manifest an appetite for disorder the Western democracies will do nothing for their restoration."

28. "Grosse Judenpogrome in Westgalizien," *Jüdische Rundschau*, Nov. 15, 1918; "Die Judenpogrome in Galizien," ibid., Nov. 22, 1918.

On Nov. 7, 1918, Cracow's Polish–Jewish newspaper, *Nowy Dziennik*, reported beatings and plunder in the industrial suburb of Chrzanów; on Nov. 9, it reported "pogroms" in Dąbrowa, Trzebinia, Rymanów, and Mielec; a day later it listed excesses in a dozen additional towns and on Nov. 13 announced that "the pogrom movement in Western Galicia has reached horrifying dimensions," spurred by the Polish intelligentsia that "has prepared the ground for years." Reports from ninety-seven towns of Western Galicia in "Protokoll," Nov. 15, 1918, CZA Z3/174, 181, and AAN KNP 149.

The word pogrom, an organized massacre, which was derived from either the Russian noun *grom* [thunder] or the verb *gromit* [to sack or destroy], entered the English language in the wake of the post-1881 assaults on the Jews of Russia. ("The pogromen riots against the Jews must be stopped," *The Times* [London], Mar. 17, 1882; J. A. H. Murray, *A New English Dictionary on Historical Principles* [Oxford: Clarendon, 1909], Vol. 7, p. 1045). During World War I, the term was widely used as a verb. ("The Jews in Galicia are being 'pogromed,'" *Boston Journal*, Feb. 2, 1915.)

Cracow.[29] Earlier, in 1915, there had been anti-Jewish riots in Kielce between the Russians' withdrawal and the Central Powers' entry; three years later, soon after the Austrians' departure, violence erupted again. On the afternoon of November 11, the Jews held an authorized meeting in the town's main theater to celebrate independence and also to claim national rights. Polish militia, ostensibly searching for weapons, suddenly entered the hall. In the ensuing melee, Polish soldiers and civilians attacked the unarmed, terrified Jews with clubs and bayonets. The next day, which was the weekly Tuesday market day, for six hours peasants and marauders robbed and beat residents of the Jewish quarter without any restraint from the local authorities, leaving 4 dead and 250 wounded.[30]

The grim news from Kielce, transmitted by German and Jewish sources, immediately reached Western Europe and North America.[31] The Zionists warned of a "veritable war of extermination,"[32] comparable to the slaughter of the Armenians three years earlier. British and American Jews, long prepared for bad tidings, implored their governments to intercede.[33] The State Department launched an inquiry and queried Paderewski on the events.[34] In

29. Nestled among the Holy Cross range, Kielce, a twelfth-century Episcopal town with medieval, renaissance, and baroque buildings, had been annexed by Austria in 1795, then torn from its Galician hinterland in 1815 and incorporated into Russia's Congress Kingdom. In the nineteenth century, Kielce developed into a small industrial city, connected to Warsaw and to the west Russian iron, copper, and lead mines by narrow-gauge rail lines; it was also the scene of Polish uprisings in 1863 and 1905 and of subsequent russification. Kielce's Jews, who first arrived in the mid-nineteenth century, established banks, artisanal shops, and manufacturing firms, and, by 1914, made up about 40% of the city's population. During their occupation between 1915 and 1918, the Austrians did almost nothing to reconnect Kielce with Cracow economically or politically. Pazdur, *Dzieje Kielc do 1863*, and idem., *Dzieje Kielc, 1864–1939.*

30. Eyewitness account of Dr. Adolf Rothfeld, Nov. 19, 1918, to the Jewish National Council of Austria, CZA Z3/178.

31. See reports of the Zionist Organization in Copenhagen to the German Minister in Copenhagen, Nov. 19, 20, 1918, Germ. PA AA Gesandschaft Kopenhagen, Zionistische Organisation Rosenblüth.

32. Quoted in reports from French ministers in Berne, Copenhagen, The Hague, Stockholm, Nov. 22, 23, 27, 29, 30, 1918, FMAE Z (Pologne) 60. Also British Zionist headquarters to Cecil, Nov. 21, 1918, CZA Z4/364. The Central Zionist Committee meeting in Warsaw, Oct. 23, 1918, and Sokolow and Weizmann to De Haas, Nov. 4, 1918, had predicted the attacks. CZA A18/31.

33. Marshall and Mack to Lansing, New York, Nov. 11, 1918, NA USDS 860c, reel 16, Marshall to Wilson, Nov. 11, 1918, AJA LM 1588; Comité Française d'Information et d'Action auprès des Juifs des Pays neutres to FMAE, n.d. [Nov. 1918], Blanchet note (conversation with Bigart), Paris, Nov. 14, 1918, FMAE Z (Pologne) 60; Wolf to Bigart, London, Nov. 15, 1918, BDBJ; Marshall to Bigart and Wolf, Nov. 16, 1918, Bigart to Marshall, n.d. [Nov. 1918], AJA LM 1611.

34. Alerted by the reports of Alexander Kahn, the European delegate of the American Joint Distribution Committee, the U.S. minister in The Hague cabled the State Department on Nov. 13 that "pogroms" were taking place all over Western Galicia and "the worst can be expected." Responding to Secretary of State Lansing's Nov. 13 request for clarification, General Tasker Bliss' sent a cable on Nov. 20 minimizing the events and blaming "Austrian deserters"; but on Nov. 29, he reported that "Polish Jews are being persecuted . . . and many [have been] killed or wounded." NA USDS 860c, reel 16. See Philipps (U.S. Assistant Secretary of State) to Paderewski, Washington, Nov. 16, 1918 (enclosing Marshall and Mack to Lansing, Nov. 11, 1918), ibid.

his response, Paderewski chided the Jews for their "extravagant ambition" to achieve separate national rights; the suave pianist–politician reminded the State Department of the Jews' central role in the Russian revolutionary movement, and he deplored the "virulent propaganda" that had been launched against the land of Kościuszko and Pułaski.[35]

The KNP's emissaries throughout Europe denied that pogroms had occurred in Kielce and Western Galicia, blaming German and Zionist sources for the false reports.[36] In Paris, Jan Modzelewski termed the charges "tendentious lies"[37] and in London, Count Władysław Sobański accused Austrian deserters of assaulting Poles as well as Jews. In a litany that would soon become routine, Sobański questioned why the Poles – and not the Czechs, Hungarians, or Romanians – were being singled out for censure over the spread of "spontaneous" acts of violence throughout Eastern Europe.[38]

Exaggerated or not, the events in Kielce became the prototype for the anti-Jewish riots during the closing days of the Great War.[39] On the Polish side, there was the preemptive disarming of Jewish soldiers, the impassioned anti-Communist and anti-Jewish sermons from the pulpit the day before, and the spread of rumors of the Jews' hatred of the new Polish state and of their loyalty to Moscow. On the Jewish side, there was the risky blend of lukewarm patriotism with the assertion of a separate identity and separate national aspirations and the appeals for assistance to the outside world rather

35. Paderewski to Philipps, New York, Nov. 20, 1918, AAN Paderewski 675/4. Paderewski prudently deleted the following message from his reply: "The whole affair . . . seems . . . very much like some of the well-advertised South American revolutions: on the morning following the night of continuous . . . shooting, after order has been established a dead dog was found in the street. The learned people, in spite of a careful postmortem examination, were unable to determine whether man's best friend had died of a bullet or of fright."
36. In its official statement of Dec. 8, 1918 (AAN KNP 159/74), the KNP charged that 300 Jewish teenagers in Kielce, shouting "Long live Lenin, long live Trotsky, down with Poland!" had been attacked by an outraged population and that the victims had perished not as Jews "but as Bolsheviks who had offended Polish national sentiment and provoked anarchy in the country."
37. Modzelewski to FMAE, Paris, Nov. 23, 1918, FMAE Z (Pologne) 60.
38. Sobański statement, London, Nov. 17, 1918, Wolf minutes of interview, Nov. 17, 1918, BDBJ C11/12/61; Sobański to Swaythling, London, Nov. 30, 1918, YIVO W/M 80.

    The attacks on the Jews in Hungary, Bohemia, Moravia, and Slovakia in Nov.–Dec. 1918 are detailed in Sobernheim, "Überblick über die Pogromvorgänge im Osten," Dec. 10, 1918, Germ. PA AA L1287/L348875; and in Bukovina, Turczynski, *Bukowina in der Neuzeit*, pp. 216–17.
39. After World War II Kielce was once more a scene of violence. On July 4, 1946, the remnants of the former Jewish community who had returned from the concentration camps and been disarmed by the local police were attacked by Poles; forty-two Jews were murdered and scores wounded, providing the impetus for a mass exodus of Jews from Poland. For the Polish side, see *Kielce – July 4, 1946: Background, Context and Events: A Collective Work* (Toronto and Chicago: The Polish Educational Foundation in North America, 1996).

than to Warsaw along with the inflated casualty figures.[40] Because there was no official inquiry, both sides embellished the Kielce incident, the Poles depicting a spontaneous expression of outrage over Jewish speculation in food supplies, the Jews charging the local authorities with complicity, and each underscoring the irreconcilable attitudes and behavior on the part of the other.[41]

Within less than two weeks between Kielce and Lemberg, there was a significant escalation of anti-Jewish violence.[42] To be sure, conditions in Eastern Galicia were markedly different than in Northern and Western Poland. Not only were there more Jews and fewer Poles in the region, but also a civil war was raging between Poles and Ukrainians. The Jewish declaration of neutrality on November 2, 1918 had shocked the Poles.[43] Under the Empire, the Jews of Eastern Galicia had generally supported the Poles, much as they had reinforced the numerically inferior Germans and Hungarians in other ethnically mixed Habsburg borderlands.[44] However, by November 1918, the Jewish leadership of Eastern Galicia, which included avid nationalists and Zionists, preferred the Ukrainians' offer of national autonomy to the Poles' stubborn refusal to recognize any form of national rights.[45] Although this political shift created the potential for future benefits, it also created risks for a large, but isolated minority, particularly in a chaotic urban war zone.

Undoubtedly political alignments between unequal forces contain no guarantee to protect the weaker, either in victory or defeat.[46] However, by proclaiming their neutrality, the Jews of Eastern Galicia exposed themselves to the Poles' charges of opportunism and perfidy and also distanced themselves from their "loyal" coreligionists elsewhere in Poland. By tacitly joining forces with the Ukrainians, the Jews of Eastern Galicia forced the Poles at a desperate moment to confront the inconstancy of one of their least-favored subject people.[47] By becoming hostage to the vagaries of the

40. The original reports listed fifteen dead and five hundred wounded. Golczewski, *Polnisch–Jüdische Beziehungen*, p. 184.
41. Korzec, *Juifs en Pologne*, pp. 75–7.
42. During their three-week control over Lemberg, the Ukrainians committed no violent acts against the Jews. Korzec, *Juifs en Pologne*, p. 77.
43. Josef Bendow (pseudonym Joseph Tenenbaum), *Lemberger Judenpogrom*, pp. 13–29.
44. McCagg, *Habsburg Jews*; Markovits and Sysyn, *Nationbuilding*.
45. Natan M. Gelber, "Die nationale Autonomie des Juden in Ostgalizien während des Westukrainischen Republik," Central Archives for the History of the Jewish People (hereafter CAHJP) P 83/G304; Mendelsohn, *Zionism in Poland*, pp. 96–8.
46. Opalski and Bartal, *Poles and Jews*, pp. 98–147, details the unraveling of the almost legendary Jewish–Polish collaboration between 1863 and 1914.
47. Chojnowski, *Koncepcje polityki*, p. 5.

bitter Polish–Ukrainian struggle, the Jews of Eastern Galicia forced themselves and their kin people both within and outside of Poland to confront the price of separateness.[48]

POGROM

Lemberg, Austria's fourth largest city after Vienna, Prague, and Trieste, was located in a valley of the Sarmatian plateau surrounded by high wooded hills and traversed by a small tributary of the Bug.[49] One of the handsomest of Habsburg towns, the capital of the crown land Galicia possessed three cathedrals (Roman Catholic, Greek Catholic [Uniate], and Armenian), numerous old churches and synagogues, lavish residences, and spacious parks, as well as a major university. Lemberg, also the manufacturing center of Galicia, was a historic crossroads of east–west and north–south exchange and communication. Founded in 1256 by the warrior prince Danilo (Daniel) Romanovich, annexed by the Polish kingdom in 1340,[50] and by Austria in 1772, Lemberg was also a battleground that had been attacked by Cossacks, Turks, and Swedes, bombarded by the Austrians in 1848, captured by the Russians in August 1914, and recaptured by the Habsburg army nine months later.

Lemberg's Jewish community, dating back to the fourteenth century, by World War I comprised about 30% of a population of some 200,000, but it was also divided in its religious and political beliefs.[51] With the destruction of their prewar trade, financial, and commercial networks with Russia, followed by the plunder and violence of the tsarist occupation and the subsequent influx of impoverished refugees, Lemberg's Jews were unprepared for the brutal events to follow.[52]

The Polish counterattack in Eastern Galicia began immediately on November 1 with street fighting in Lemberg. Despite desultory attempts at negotiations, neither side was prepared to accept the other's political terms. The truce between November 10 and 18 created a brief, misleading impression that the combatants might yet submit their claims to the Allies. But with the arrival of reinforcements from Cracow, the Poles resumed their attack in order to create facts instead of waiting for outside decisions. On the

48. Golczewski, *Polnisch–Jüdische Beziehungen*, pp. 213–17.
49. *Encyclopedia Britannica*, 11th ed. (New York: Encyclopedia Britannica, 1911), pp. 409–10.
50. In 1349, the Polish monarchy extended the Magdeburg law to Lemberg's Ukrainians, Armenians, Jews, and Tatars, allowing them each to live according to their own communal regulations.
51. Caro, *Juden in Lemberg*.
52. Mick, "Nationalisierung in einer multiethnischen Stadt," pp. 128–38, on Lemberg in World War I.

night of November 21–22, they finally drove the outnumbered Ukrainians from Lemberg.[53]

The Jews' neutrality had been highly inconvenient and indeed threatening to the initially outnumbered Polish forces.[54] The 300-man-strong Jewish militia, formed on November 2, had spared the Ukrainians from defending the Jewish quarter and freed them to attack the Poles. On November 5, *Pobudka* [Reveille], the organ of the Polish commandos, began issuing a stream of complaints against Jewish violations of "neutral" behavior, such as hoarding weapons and shooting at Polish soldiers, not to mention the ubiquitous charge of pouring boiling water on the soldiers' heads. Although obviously exaggerated, these accusations reinforced the Poles' resentment over the Jews' political maneuvers and offset their shock and humiliation over the Ukrainians' November 1 coup. As fighting raged on the streets of Lemberg, there were threats of retaliation.[55] After the Poles' victory, they followed their practice in Western and Eastern Galicia of disbanding the Jewish militia and detaining their leaders, whereupon riots broke out almost at once.[56]

The postliberation attack on the Jewish quarter of Lemberg between November 22 and 24, 1918, was the most prolonged and extensive carnage against civilians in Eastern Europe since 1906.[57] There is little disagreement over what happened: There were two full days of looting and burning, beating, rape, and murder by Poles in uniform and civilian clothes without any restraint from the authorities.[58] The antecedents are a little less exact. If no written pronouncement sanctioning the forty-eight-hour vendetta has ever been recovered, witnesses confirmed the widespread belief that it existed and that it gave the liberators of Lemberg permission to plunder the ("enemy") Jewish quarter as their reward.[59]

53. Roos, *Polnische Nation,* pp. 54–5; for the other side, see Nahayewski, *Modern Ukrainian State,* pp. 115–31; Zaklynski, "November Overthrow."
54. Polish political and military officials did not formally acknowledge Jewish neutrality until Nov. 10; Bendow, *Lemberger Judenpogrom*, pp. 18–19. On strong Polish suspicions of the Jews' pro-Ukrainian actions, see Mrocza, "Kwestii żydowskiej w Galicji."
55. Golczewski, *Polnisch–Jüdische Beziehungen*, pp. 187–9.
56. Ibid., p. 189, n. 36, cites similar patterns in Brzozów (Nov. 4), Chrzanów (Nov. 6), Brzesko (Nov. 12), Trzebinia (Nov. 7), Rozwadów (Nov. 5), Przemyśl (Nov. 10), Cracow (Nov. 13), Jarosław (Nov. 13), and Szczakowa (Nov. 6).

    Rosa Bailey, *A City Fights for Freedom: The Rising of Lwów in 1918–1919*, trans. Samuel S. B. Taylor (London: Leopolis, 1956), which details the struggle, pp. 76–316, omits the Jews entirely.
57. Tomaszewski, "Lwów, 22 listopada 1918," pp. 279–81, reviews the historiography by Polish and Jewish scholars.
58. See French intelligence report, "Pogrom de Galicie," Dec. 20, 1918 (by Agent Nr. 524A), FMAE Z (Pologne) 20.
59. Telegram report of the Jewish National Council of Vienna, Nov. 26, 1918, CZA Z3/179; also, *Berliner Tageblatt*, Nov. 27, 1918; Bendow, *Lemberger Judenpogrom*, p. 69.

All the rest remains murky. Although the Polish military blamed the incidents on "bandits," at least one officer described the incident as a "military action," despite the fact that the last Ukrainian troops had departed Lemberg and the Jewish quarter offered no armed resistance.[60] On November 22, Brigadier General Bolesław Roja issued an order for martial law, but the city commandant, Czesław Mączyński, delayed its implementation for a day and a half.[61] In the meantime, Mączyński made an inflammatory proclamation detailing, in almost medieval terminology, the Jews' acts of treachery in ambushing harried Polish soldiers, attacking patrols with axes, and pouring hot water. For forty-eight hours, Polish fire officials cordoned off the Jewish quarter and withheld water from burning buildings. By the time Mączyński finally sent out armed patrols, there were some 72 dead, 443 wounded, 38 burned houses, and 3 burned synagogues in the Jewish quarter of Lemberg.[62]

The first reports of the "Lemberg pogrom," with their graphic details and enormous casualty figures, were transmitted from local witnesses and Jewish organizations through German officials to the Zionists in Berlin and neutral capitals and also over German press wires to the world.[63] As the Polish offensive spread through Eastern Galicia, the new Jewish councils in Cracow, Vienna, and Lemberg, and the Zionist offices in the neutral countries conveyed even bleaker reports of marauding Polish legionnaires and

Lieutenant Colonel Michał Tokarzewski reported on Nov. 25 that his soldiers had told him General Roja had allowed them to "do what they wanted" for twenty-four hours. Golczewski, *Polnisch–Jüdische Beziehungen*, p. 191, n. 49.

60. The Jewish side reported no resistance to giving up arms or the internment, whereas Mączyński (who, contrary to Roja's orders, kept the Jews in prison for six days) reported "systematic resistance." Golczewski, *Polnisch–Jüdische Beziehungen*, p. 189.

61. Mączyński, a former gymnasium professor and Austrian officer, was elected to the Polish *Sejm* in 1927 as a member of the right-wing Christian Front. Golczewski, *Polnisch–Jüdische Beziehungen*, p. 186, n. 23.

62. Bendow, *Lemberger Judenpogrom*, pp. 161–65; Chasanowich, *Les pogromes anti-juifs en Pologne et en Galicie* (a work subsidized by the German Foreign Ministry), pp. 47–74; Cohen, *Pogroms in Poland*, pp. 20–32.

63. See CZA Z3, 173–74, 179, "Pogrome: Nachkriegszeit" and ibid., L6/114 "Ostjudenfrage."

Many of the pogrom reports came by diplomatic pouch to Berlin from the German legation in Warsaw. The Wilhelmstrasse dispatched materials to Zionist headquarters in Berlin, which distributed them to various neutral capitals and also to local and foreign journalists in the German capital; another important conduit was the semiofficial Wolff Telegraph Agency. See, e.g., Otto Warburg to Copenhagen, Berlin, n.d. [Nov. 29, 1918], ibid., Z3/666; Hermann to Stockholm, The Hague, and Copenhagen, Berlin, Nov. 29, 1918, ibid., Z3/667. Also, Brockdorff Rantzau to AA, Copenhagen, Nov. 25, 1918, Germ. PA AA Österreich/94: Galizien und Bukowina/28; Sobernheim files (Pogrom 1918–1921), ibid., L1287/L348815-89; Grant Smith to State Dept., Copenhagen, Dec. 9, 20, 1918, NA USDS 860c, reel 16.

The first casualty figures from Lemberg were 3,000 dead. GB FO 371/4373/197821; the Zionist bureau in Copenhagen estimated 1,100 killed, *The New York Times*, Nov. 30, 1918; the *Berliner Tageblatt*, Nov. 28, reported 900; and "Der Judenpogrom in Lemberg," *Neue Freie Presse* (Vienna), Nov. 28, gave a figure of 300.

disarmed Jewish militias, and of more looting, burning, rape, and murder, to which the western press gave ample coverage.[64]

The new Berlin government avidly distributed the bad news from Western and Eastern Galicia.[65] Acting in the expectation that the Jews would play a "very important" role at the peace conference, the Wilhelmstrasse in November 1918 had established a special news bureau for "Jewish-Political" intelligence reports that it disseminated to neutral capitals and, especially, to the United States.[66] Germany's first republic, hoping to dissuade the Allies from ceding Reich lands to Poland, moved to reestablish a tacit alliance with the Jews by helping to expose its neighbor's "anarchy" and "unfitness" to rule non-Poles. It thus depicted the pogroms not as spontaneous episodes but the result of a "long political campaign."[67]

German Jews were alarmed by the new threat to the *Ostjuden* and also to themselves. If some, particularly the German Zionists, saw their separatist eastern kin as proof positive of their nationhood, others at this time of domestic political upheaval were frightened of anything that raised the Jews' visibility and vulnerability.[68] Reich anti-Semites, seeking scapegoats for defeat and revolution, were lambasting the "Jewish-Bolshevik conspiracies" of Kurt Eisner and Rosa Luxemburg.[69] The right-wing press, clamoring for the expulsion of foreign Jews whose numbers had almost doubled in wartime, sounded the alarm against the influx of "six million inferior, mongolized" *Ostjuden*, who would steal jobs and housing and bring disease, vagrants, and criminals into Germany.[70]

64. Chasanovitch to Weizmann, Stockholm, n.d. (received Dec. 5), 1918, CZA Z4/1702. *Der Abend* (Vienna), on Nov. 26, termed Lemberg "der grösste Pogrom der Weltgeschichte." See also "Judenmord in Galizien," *Basler Nationalzeitung*, Nov. 28, 1918; "The Polish Horrors" and "Jews Massacred," *Jewish Chronicle* [London], Dec. 6, 1918.
65. Rosen to AA, Nov. 18, 1918, Germ. PA AA Österreich/94: Galizien und Bukowina/28.
66. Jüdisch-politisch Nachrichten, #s 1–6 (Nov.–Dec. 1918), Germ. AA T-120 L1284/L338525-69. Also, Jusserand to FMAE, Washington, Nov. 15, 1918, De Billy to Tardieu, New York, Nov. 18, FMAE A Paix 214.
67. Bulletin #4, Dec. 10, 1919, Germ. AA T-120 L1284/4915/L338551.

    On Dec.18, 1918, Count Ulrich Brockdorff-Rantzau, the former imperial minister in Copenhagen who had had close ties with the Zionists, became the republic's second foreign minister. Wengst, *Graf Brockdorff-Rantzau*, pp. 9–17.
68. While assimilationists fretted over the large numbers of Jews in leadership positions in the new republic (*Deutsche Israelitische Zeitung* [Munich], Dec. 12, 1918), others were attempting to establish a distinctive German–Jewish "identity"; see Reichmann, "Der Bewusstseinswandel der deutschen Juden," especially pp. 600–2.
69. Friedländer, "Die politischen Veränderungen der Kriegszeit," especially pp. 54–5 Angress, "Juden im politischen Leben der Revolutionszeit," especially pp. 160–2, 226–308, and Jochmann, "Die Ausbreitung des Antisemitismus," especially pp. 450–1.
70. Jochmann, "Die Ausbreitung des Antisemitismus," especially pp. 413–15, 505–6. Also, Treue, "Der wirtschaftlichen Motive in deutschen Antisemitismus," pp. 400–1.

    There were already 160,000 foreign Jews in Germany, 35,000 of whom had come as forced laborers during World War I and another 35,000 as internees and prisoners of war.

Reich Jewish leaders were not sanguine about restoring Germany's reputation abroad; nor were they confident of ameliorating Poland's treatment of its minorities or diminishing Warsaw's allegedly favored status with the Entente. They nevertheless dutifully countenanced Berlin's anti-Polish campaign, urging Germany's first emissary to Warsaw, Count Harry Kessler, to establish the firmest possible link between Poland's Jewish question and "the political interests of the German republic."[71]

In Paris, the KNP, struggling for international recognition, insisted that "pogroms" were foreign to the Polish language and character and stated that the Jews of Lemberg had been accidental victims of brutal street fighting.[72] The committee's emissaries complained of a "German-Jewish" plot against Poland.[73] As foreign outrage mounted, the KNP's offices in Paris, London, Washington, and the neutral capitals scaled down the casualty figures, cited Christian as well as Jewish victims, and accused bandits, deserters, and prisoners released by the Ukrainians of stirring the disorders.[74] In Rome, the KNP representative, the great landowner Konstanty Skirmunt, denounced the "denigration and calumny of agents of the former Central Powers" and complained of the menace of Jewish-led Bolshevism. Skirmunt warned the Allies that if Berlin succeeded in reducing Poland's size, the new Central Europe would become "a great Macedonia . . . the germ of disorders, irredentism, and inevitable wars."[75]

71. Julius Berger memorandum, Berlin, Nov. 17, 1918, CZA Z3/179; but Kessler had already been warned by the Wilhelmstrasse against alienating Piłsudski by "establishing any links with Zionist or other Jewish political tendencies"; Kessler, *Tagebücher,* p. 31.
72. "Poles Deny Pogroms," *The New York Times*, Nov. 29, 1918. Communiqué du Comité National Polonais, Paris, Dec. 8, 1918, AAN KNP 159/74. Włodek to Sobański, The Hague, Nov. 29, 1918, asked the KNP's emissary to take steps to "protest and repudiate the outrageous lies spread by pro-German and Zionist organizations, whose interest is to represent Poland as in a state of anarchy, to prevent its securing Allied aid, and to make it an object of exploitation." ibid., KNP 149.
73. An intercepted letter from A. de Pomian, the KNP's delegate in Stockholm, to Sobański, Nov. 30, 1918, also alleged a "German-Swedish-Jewish plot." GB FO 371/4373.
74. See cables from the KNP's office in Lausanne to Sobański, Nov. 25, 27, 1918, AAN KNP 1911; Sobański to Lord Swaythling, London, Nov. 30, 1918, ibid., KNP 2066. Modzelewski to FMAE on the "soi-disant pogroms," Nov. 29, 1918, and "Le chantage au pogrom," *Gazette de Lausanne*, Dec. 4, 1918, "La troisième intrigue," *Tribune de Genève*, Dec. 4, 1918, and KNP statement, "Les prétendus pogroms," Dec. 4, 1918, published in *Gazette de Lausanne*, Dec. 16, 1918, all in FMAE Z (Pologne) 60. Press releases from Stockholm (Dec. 5, 1918) and The Hague (Jan. 11, 1919), AAN KNP 2066. Also, Bujak, *The Jewish Question*, p. 37.
75. Skirmunt to Page, Rome, Dec. 1, 1918, AAN KNP 2082. The U.S. ambassador informed the State Department that the KNP termed the riots "small affairs due to Bolsheviks' influence, [which] were between Poles and Ukrainians, [the] Jews having sided with Ukrainians, who are controlled and directed by Austrian generals." Page to Phillips, Rome, Dec. 5, 1918, FRUS PPC Vol. 2, p. 414. In Skirmunt to Sonnino, Jan. 27, 1919, the KNP delegate branded Polish–Jewish nationalists as a small, disruptive minority, unlike anything existing in Italy, who threatened "peaceful" Jews and Poles alike. AAN KNP 2103.

Piłsudski tried to assert his authority by taking credit for restoring "order" in Lemberg.[76] He sent signals to Berlin that he had no intention of oppressing national minorities and hinted at an investigation of the events in Eastern Galicia.[77] But his weak interim regime refused to condemn the events in Kielce and Lemberg.[78] Poles of all political stripes deplored the violence in these two places; but they were also shocked and resentful at the instantaneous censure of their entire people. Not only did the nationalist-dominated Liquidation Commission in Cracow castigate the Jews' "slanderous" campaign[79]; the Polish left attacked Jewish "chauvinists" and derided the "dreamers and noisemakers" who wished to enlist outside support to turn Poland into a bilingual Polish–Yiddish state.[80]

Polish Jews were in despair. After several inconclusive meetings with Piłsudski and Moraczewski, during which both sides simply traded recriminations, Polish Zionists concluded that help would come only from outside.[81] This fact was driven home when the military authorities in Lemberg proceeded to arrest more Ukrainians and Jews than Poles for causing the disorders and when, on December 11, the Poles took four prominent local Zionists as hostages, imprisoning them for almost two months until Allied pressure forced their release.[82]

THE RESPONSE

Not unexpectedly, the world Zionist movement led the protests over Lemberg. Its reports from the East warned of panic sales and predicted a huge exodus of Galician Jews to Palestine, Western Europe, and the United States.[83]

76. Zaleski to Lucien Wolf, Berne, n.d. (received Nov. 26), copy in GB FO 371/W33/3281.
77. Report by the Polish legation, Berlin, Dec. 1, 1918, AAN KNP 2066. According to the *Jüdische Rundschau*, Dec. 1, 1918, and the *Vossische Zeitung*, Dec. 3, 1918, a meeting was held in the Reich Chancellery on Nov. 29 among Germany's Justice and Interior ministers, a Reichstag deputy, and three Polish politicians.
78. The foreign ministry ordered an investigation of Lemberg, and there was a report dated Dec. 17, 1918 prepared by a Jewish journalist, Józef Wasercuz, and a Polish jurist, Leon Chrzanowski, detailing the violence; AAN KNP 159. Published by Jerzy Tomaszewski in "Lwów, 22 listopada 1918," pp. 181–5. The report's authenticity has been challenged in Leszek Tomaszewski, "Lwów–Listopad 1918," which contains strong pro-Polish and anti-Jewish remarks.
79. Hermann to Zionist offices in Copenhagen, Stockholm, The Hague, Berlin, Nov. 29, 1918, CZA Z3/667, to Copenhagen, Dec. 8, 1918, ibid., A405/174.
80. *Naprzód* [Forward], Nov. 29, 1918.
81. See communiques #40 (Nov. 25), #42 (Nov. 29), #44 (Dec. 4), CZA Z4/413.
82. Hermann to Zionist offices in Copenhagen, Stockholm, The Hague, Berlin, Nov. 29, 1918, CZA Z3/667. Also Weizmann to Sokolow, Dec. 17, 1918, ibid., Z4/62; Sokolow to Curzon, Jan. 30, 1919, requesting Britain's aid in the release of the prisoners, ibid., Z4/9; also GB FO 608/131/1/1. On their release, "made possible by the altered military situation in Lemberg," Howard to Dmowski, London, Feb. 6, 1919, AAN KNP 149.
83. Garrett to State Dept., The Hague, Jan. 7, 1919, NA USDS 860c, reel 16.

Chaim Weizmann, now in the midst of "delicate" negotiations with British officials, decided that Lemberg had added precious evidence of the need for a "big Palestine."[84] Rebuffing a British official's request to tone down the Zionists' "public agitation" over Lemberg, Weizmann warned "the world will never have peace until the Jewish problem is solved in a satisfactory manner."[85]

The Zionists also mobilized their comrades to rebut the KNP's charges and to stem the Western public's apathy.[86] Impatient and irate with Dmowski's minions, they demanded a halt to the anti-Jewish boycott and even threatened financial retaliation.[87] Detailing the "monstrous massacres" in Lemberg, they urged France to dispatch an Allied army to Poland.[88] Jacob de Haas, head of the Zionist organization of America, warned Washington of a "war of extermination" in Eastern Galicia and pleaded for American intervention.[89] By December, the Zionists had helped organize mass protests in Berlin, London, Paris, The Hague, Vienna, and Zurich. Non-Zionists joined the clamor. On December 11, 1918, 8,000 people gathered in New York's Madison Square Garden to "weep in sympathy with the persecuted Jews of Galicia and Poland" and to demand that the U.S. government halt the pogroms and place Poland under international supervision.[90]

The Allies were disconcerted by the public outcry, which forced them to focus on the obscure and embattled region between Germany and Russia. The putative parents of the new Poland[91] wished neither to negotiate with the ostracized Warsaw government nor take any definitive political action before the opening of the peace conference. The impassioned debates during

84. Weizmann to David Eder, London, Nov. 26, 1918. CZA A18/3/22.
85. Undated memorandum, CZA Z4/75. Also, Weizmann to Drummond, London, Nov. 25, 1918, CZA A18/32/2; interview with Balfour, Dec. 4, 1918, ibid., A18/21/3; Weizmann to Brandeis, Dec. 20, 1918, ibid., Z4/1593.
86. Sokolow and Weizmann to De Haas (New York), London, Nov. 21, 1918 ("Please take energetic action on your end"). Hermann to Zionist headquarters Copenhagen, Berlin, Dec. 3, 1918, CZA Z3/667.
87. Sobański–Swaythling exchange, London, Nov. 30, Dec. 5, 1918, AAN KNP 2066. On Dec. 6, 1918, the *Jewish Chronicle* [London] stated that "measures were being taken" in Vienna's financial circles to convince the Poles to reduce the violence.
88. See various telegrams, especially Conty to Pichon, Copenhagen, Nov. 23, 30, Delavaud to Pichon, Stockholm, Nov. 30, 1918, in FMAE Z (Pologne) 60.
89. De Haas to Lansing, Nov. 30, 1918, NA USDS 860c, reel 16.
90. *The New York Times*, Dec. 12, 1918. One of the main speakers, the leading anti-Zionist Jacob Schiff, who denounced Dmowski's anti-Semitism, admitted that although he did not share "some of the audience's doctrines . . . the Jewish heart rebels whenever injustice is done." In a display of nonpartisanship, the banker Schiff shared the platform with two Socialists, Justice Jacob Panken and Congressman Meyer Landon.
91. Evoking their parental status became habitual. Thus, two years later: "In the case of Poland (as of other new States) the Council found itself somewhat in the position of parents *vis-à-vis* a child. It can fairly be said that the child was generally obedient and docile but the young Poland, perhaps because of her extreme youth [*sic*], proved occasionally refractory." Temperley, *Peace Conference of Paris*, Vol. 1, p. 335.

the U.S. and British election campaigns had been largely over the terms of peace with Germany; but the manifestations of a tough nationalism in both countries provided no guideposts for dealing with their headstrong East European progeny, or indeed with each other.[92]

On December 3, 1918, the U.S. ambassador in Paris issued a mild admonition to Dmowski, expressing "grave concern" over the pogrom reports and warning, "if these reports are true, the sympathy of the American people for Poland's national aspirations will undoubtedly be affected."[93] One day later, Woodrow Wilson boarded the *George Washington* on his historic eight-day voyage to Europe. The president, despite the counsel of the Inquiry, the advice of Colonel House, and the appeals of the AJC, had chosen not to speak out on the issue of minority rights.[94] With only the vaguest notion of East European politics and territorial rivalries, the U.S. president counted on the new League of Nations to oversee the region's transformation from multinational empires to new democratic states.[95]

London was less detached. The British public was well aware of the Reich's machinations in the East.[96] *The Times* deprecated the atrocity reports as "greatly exaggerated,"[97] and the *Pall Mall Gazette* scolded,

> Whenever a hungry crowd in some small town loots the shops of profiteers taking advantage of human misery, the servile German telegraphic agency spreads to the whole world the news of Jewish pogroms, which have never existed in Poland and very likely will never happen.[98]

Several Whitehall officials were openly unsympathetic to Poland's Jews, who appeared "determined to do everything in their power to prevent the foundation of a great and independent Poland."[99]

92. Mayer, *Politics and Diplomacy of Peacemaking,* pp. 119–66.
93. Sharp to Dmowski, Paris, Dec. 3, 1918, AAN KNP 149. When they met three days later, Dmowski dismissed the reports as "exaggerated," promising an "authoritative report" shortly. Sharp to State Dept., Dec. 6, 1918, NA USDS 860c, reel 16.
94. "It would embarrass me to do this" Wilson to Tumulty, Nov. 30, 1918, Woodrow Wilson papers, Library of Congress (hereafter WWP) 289. See Marshall to Wilson, Nov. 7, 14, 16, 22, 1918, Wilson to Marshall, Nov. 16, 1918, AJA LM 1588; Wilson to Marshall, Nov. 20, 1918, WWP 157, termed any public statement "unwise," although the president promised to "exercise such influence as I can at the peace conference." On the Inquiry's recommendation on the need for minorities protection in Poland, FRUS PPC, Vol. 1, pp. 51–2, 66; House, in Oct. 1918, Seymour, *Papers of Colonel House*, Vol. 4, pp. 152–3, 198–200.
95. Biskupski, "The Wilsonian View of Poland." On Dec. 29, 1918, the U.S. president told a gathering in Manchester that outside powers should not impose a government on any country. Wilson, *Papers of Woodrow Wilson*, ed. Arthur Link (hereafter *PWW*), Vol. 53, p. 9.
96. See intercepted telegram of German Minister Tattenbach to AA, Berne, Dec. 5, 1918, detailing the Reich's "information" campaign. GB FO 371/3903/171819.
97. *The Times* [London], Dec. 2, 4, 1918.
98. *Pall Mall Magazine*, Nov. 28, 1918.
99. Kidston minute, Dec. 5, 1918, GB FO 371/3419; also unsigned memorandum, Jan. 7, 1919 ("There is I fear some justification to the suggestion that the Jews are the backbone of Bolshevism."), ibid., 3903. Balfour to Rothschild, Dec. 4, 1918, declined the latter's plea for British military intervention. YIVO W/M 36.

Nonetheless, the Lloyd George government, in the midst of a heavily contested election, could not ignore the Jewish outcry over the events in Lemberg. Balfour had already expressed his disapproval of Poland's expansion beyond its ethnographic limits.[100] Britain's concern about the imperiled Jews in Eastern Europe was undoubtedly linked to its still-controversial commitment to the Zionists and to the looming negotiations over Palestine. These had now become clouded by the growing opposition in the Muslim world and also by the refractoriness of its allies.[101] Consequently Britain, less than a week after the Lemberg violence, was the first to propose collective action, asking the United States and France to issue a strong warning to the KNP. If the pogroms were not stopped, Poland's prospects at the peace conference would be "materially affected."[102]

Paris, like Washington, declined to join London's démarche. The French were not simply retaliating against Britain's refusal to recognize the KNP.[103] Nor were they blindly accepting Dmowski's assurances that no attacks on Jews had occurred. France was clearly acting according to its own beliefs and interests. The Quai d'Orsay was convinced of the Reich's chicanery and also of Piłsudski's ineptitude and his Bolshevik tendencies.[104] Its leading officials considered Polish Jewry a hotbed of German collaborators and Soviet agents, predatory "strangers" who spoke an alien tongue and had

100. See protests by the Jewish Bakers' Union, Nov. 21, the Jewish Socialist Labor Party, Nov. 30, 1918, the Council of Young Judeans of London, Dec. 8, the Glasgow Jewish Council, Dec. 9, and the Bath British–Israel Association, Dec. 9, as well as Mond to Balfour, Nov. 25, 1918, in GB FO 371 W55/529.

    Degrand, note, Dec. 2, 1918, FMAE Z (Pologne) 60, passed on Count Sobański's opinion that the Foreign Office's position on Polish Jewry was "motivated by internal British politics."

101. Piltz memorandum to FMAE, Paris, Nov. 30, 1918, AAN KNP 1869. On the first anniversary of the Balfour declaration there were Arab riots in Jerusalem as well as protests by the Muslim League in India against Britain's occupation of Jerusalem and a slew of petitions against the Balfour declaration. See GB FO371/4153; FMAE PA-AP Tardieu 166.

    Britain's mideast dilemma noted in Sokolow to Weizmann, Paris, Dec. 14, 17, 1918, CZA Z4/62; Weizmann to Brandeis, London, Dec. 20, 1918, ibid., Z4/1593.

102. Derby to Pichon (urgent), Paris, Nov. 28, 1918, FMAE Z (Pologne) 60; also GB CAB XCVII, Dec. 5, 1918.

103. Balfour's refusal was based officially on the assertion that it would be "premature" to grant the KNP the status of a recognized government until the Polish people's voice was heard and privately on Britain's suspicion of Dmowski's ties to the Polish right and his expansionist designs. P. Cambon to FO, London, Nov. 15, 1918, Balfour to P. Cambon, Nov. 30, 1918, GB FO 371/3277.

    When the French inquired about the question of Polish representation at the peace conference, Balfour commented "Poland will have to be represented but *we* alone cannot decide who is to represent her – or has any of the allied Powers sufficient knowledge of Poland to say out of hand who the People of Poland would regard as a satisfactory representation." Undated minute, ibid. The United States was similarly unready to grant the KNP a place at the peace conference. Phillips to Chambrun, Washington, Dec. 24, 1918, FRUS PPC, Vol. 1, p. 264.

104. Degrand note, Oct. 28, 1918, describing Piłsudski as a "Personnage un peu légendaire, sans grande valeur, ni sécurité." FMAE Z (Pologne) 46.

abused the powerless Poles during World War I.[105] But above all, France's incipient plans to construct a *barrière de l'est* against Germany and a *cordon sanitaire* against Bolshevism were virtually identical with the large and strong anti-German, anti-Bolshevik Poland espoused by the KNP.[106]

Nevertheless, the Clemenceau government, although freed for a year from the pressure of a parliamentary election, could not ignore the events in Lemberg.[107] World War I had cost 1,350,000 French lives and caused immense physical damage to the occupied frontier regions. Victorious but exhausted, France could not disregard the pleas of its loyalist Jews,[108] the protests of its mainstream and leftist press,[109] and the remonstrances of the neutral states, whose resources would be essential for postwar reconstruction.[110] The motherland of liberty had to assure world public opinion that the Allied powers would at least investigate the alleged massacres.[111]

Like Washington, Paris sent a stiff-worded but toothless reproach to the KNP. France asked its client to do its utmost to guarantee "order and freedom" throughout a land it did not yet govern, and it received a prompt denial that any pogroms had occurred.[112] With neither the will nor the

105. Note pour l'Ambassade de l'Angleterre, Paris, Dec. 2, 1918, Pichon to Jusserand, Paris, Nov. [Dec.] 3, 1918, FMAE Z (Pologne) 60. Note, "La question juive en Pologne," Dec. 3, 1918," ibid., Z (Pologne) 61.

    On Nov. 26, 1918, the nationalist *Victoire* had characterized Polish Jews as either internationalist Marxists who hated Poland or Zionist nationalists who wished to create a Jewish state on Polish soil. Allizé to FMAE, The Hague, Dec. 21, accused the Jews of "working for our enemies" and to gain U.S. support for the German cause at the peace conference. FMAE Z (Pologne) 60.

106. "Une méthode d'action en Pologne," Paris, Dec. 20, 1918, FMAE PA-AP Tardieu 81; Wandycz, "The French barrière." Placing the Haller army under Allied command was part of Foch's grand scheme. Komarnicki, *Polish Republic*, p. 256.

    French officials who hoped to restore a friendly Russia were concerned over Poland's eastern expansion; others worried over regional repercussions of Polish imperialism. Piltz report of conversation with Pichon, Nov. 8, 1918, AAN KNP 1944.

107. Although the Chamber (elected in 1914) on Dec. 29, 1918, gave Clemenceau, the *père de la victoire*, a resounding 398–93 vote of confidence to conduct the peace negotiations, every party distrusted the elderly premier: the left his authoritarian tendencies, the right his anticlericalism, the center his contempt for parliamentary combinations, and everyone his brusque demeanor. Jackson, *Clemenceau*, pp. 209–10; Duroselle, *Clemenceau*, pp. 724–6.

108. See especially Comité française d'information et d'action auprès des Juifs des pays neutres (a group which, "throughout the war has fought for France's prestige") to FMAE, Paris, Nov. 27, 1918, FMAE Z (Pologne) 60; Bigart to Pichon, Dec. 2, (detailing the "atrocious situation" in Galicia), and Ligue des "Amis du Zionisme" to FMAE, Dec. 2, 1918, ibid. Also, *Alliance Israélite Universelle*, Pogromes de Lemberg, Nov. 1918, AIU I/8.

109. Strong criticism of France's pro-Polish policies in *Le Figaro*, Nov. 20, 1918, *Le Temps*, Nov. 25, 1918, *Le Matin*, Nov. 30, *La France Libre*, Dec. 2, 1918, *L'Humanité*, Dec. 3, 1918.

110. Allizé to FMAE, Berne, Nov. 22, 27. 1918, Conty to Pichon, Copenhagen, Nov. 23, Dec. 7, 1918, French ambassador to The Hague, Nov. 29, 1918, Delavaud to FMAE, Stockholm, Nov. 30, Dec. 5, 1918, FMAE Z (Pologne) 60.

111. See, e.g., unsigned cable on Dec. 5, 1918, to the French minister in Buenos Aires for the local Zionist organization, FMAE Z (Pologne) 60.

112. Pichon to Zamoyski, Paris, Dec. 7, AAN KNP 149, cited "hundreds of victims" in Poland and Galicia, "including women and children," and enjoined the KNP to use every means at its disposal

troops to bring order to Poland,[113] France proposed a "prudent" solution to its partner across the Channel, to dispatch a small Allied commission to conduct an inquiry and recommend "further action."[114]

Thus, less than a month after the Armistice, the Allies, stymied by their unfamiliarity with the actual conditions in Poland and their reluctance to make political and military commitments, devised a temporary machinery to assert their power and obtain information without binding themselves to any future course.[115] Instead of the substantial Allied military force to curb the violence in Eastern Galicia solicited by Poles and Jews alike, they adopted a lesser alternative, which was welcomed by the Warsaw government but inevitably deepened their involvement in Polish politics.[116] This also began the yearlong procession of foreign missions to Poland, whose political and military tasks soon outweighed their humanitarian responsibilities and whose reports, passed-on, post hoc "eyewitness" accounts and official explanations, added more obscurity than clarification to the November pogroms and their aftermath.[117]

to ensure order and freedom in a Poland "resurrected by the Allies' victory." The KNP's denial was based on "precise information." Zamoyski to Pichon, Paris, Dec. 8, 1918, ibid.

113. Despite the warning of Minister of War General Alby to Pichon, Paris, Dec. 5, 1918, on the overextension of the Eastern Army in the Adriatic and the Balkans (FMAE Z [Pologne] 60), the French government on Dec. 15 decided on an intervention against the Bolsheviks in southern Russia, and three days later its troops landed in Odessa. Thus any French military aid to Poland was conceived primarily in terms of dispatching the Haller army to the East. See Pichon to Clemenceau, Dec. 7, Pichon to P. Cambon, Dec. 13, FMAE Z (Pologne) 67.

114. Note pour l'ambassade de l'Angleterre, Paris, Dec. 2, FMAE Z (Pologne) 60. Italy also refused to raise a protest in Warsaw. Sereni (president of the Italian–Jewish Community) to Sonnino, Dec. 5, 1918, Sonnino to Orlando, Dec. 8, 1918, Italy, Ministero degli Affari Esteri (hereafter IMAE) (Polonia) 165.

115. Balfour minute, n.d., attached to Rumbold to FO, Berne, Nov. 18, 1918, GB FO 800/385.

116. Dutasta to Pichon, Berne, Dec. 28, 1918, FMAE Z (Pologne) 60, conveyed Zaleski's message of his government's "great satisfaction" in the dispatch of an interallied commission to inquire on the pogroms or "on any other subject" and promised to provide all facilities to help its investigation.

Earlier suggestions had come from the KNP (Sobański to Drummond, London, Nov. 16, 1918, AAN KNP 1909) and from Paderewski (Paderewski to Philipps, New York, Nov. 20, 1918, AAN Paderewski 765/4), who had recommended to the State Department a commission consisting of "three Americans, three American Jews, and three American Poles" to investigate the pogrom charges. After Paderewski's departure for Poland, the effort seems to have failed. See Smulski and Marshall to Paderewski, Mar. 3, 1919, AAN KNP 26.

117. In his first report from Poznań, Britain's emissary, Colonel Wade, blamed the Germans for the pogrom propaganda, whose "object is to convince the Entente that the Poles are uncontrolled and intolerant people"; GB FO 371/3896. In his second, Jan. 2, 1919, he repeated the "boiling water" charges; twenty-eight Polish soldiers had been "badly scalded" in Lemberg; GB FO 371/3896. On Jan. 23, 1919, Wade acknowledged that many "arbitrary" acts had taken place in Nov. 1918, but claimed there had been "no organized violence" and considerable "exaggerations" by the Jews, whose "immense unpopularity" was "caused by their profiteering and subserviency under the German occupation, their having escaped combat service, their part in bolshevik agitation, and the Zionist claims for national autonomy." GB CAB 24/145 #CV (Jan. 30, 1919). Howard to Balfour, Feb. 22, 1919 and Rowland Kenney report, Warsaw, Feb. 14, forwarded in Howard to Balfour, Warsaw, Feb. 22, 1919, GB FO 608/66, stressed the rift between Poles and Jews.

Britain's was the first Allied mission, a three-member group headed by its attaché in Denmark, Colonel H. H. Wade, whose vague mandate, much to the annoyance of the KNP, included the establishment of "informal relations" with the Warsaw authorities.[118] France rapidly followed, sending General M.-J. Berthelémy from the Eastern Army.[119] From the United States came a food supplies mission under Herbert Hoover's authority as well as the political mission of Lieutenant R. C. Foster.[120] The absence of inter-Allied coordination clearly indicated that each of the victors intended to acquire its own sources of information while carving out its own niche in the East. Cooperation on the spot nonetheless developed on its own.[121]

ENTER PADEREWSKI

As these foreign teams were taking shape, Piłsudski's Poland appeared increasingly volatile and vulnerable. Like Kerensky a year earlier, this brave but indecisive leader was besieged by the left and right,[122] as well as by foreign enemies. On December 26, 1918, Piłsudski watched helplessly as nationalist Poles seized power in Poznań, triggering angry protests from London

In the same vein, Colonel William Grove of the Hoover Mission wrote on Jan. 9, 1919, "The Jews in Warsaw are supposed to have large quantities of ammunition, as well as rifles, hidden away, and there are daily combats of a very local character between the soldiers searching the Jewish quarter for hoarded supplies of food, etc., and the Jewish merchants, shots being fired by the soldiers, presumably more to frighten the people than to do actual harm." FRUS PPC, Vol. 2, p. 428.

118. Draft instructions, Dec. 17, 1918, GB FO 371/3282; Sobański to KNP, n.d., AAN KNP 31. Wade, although the military attaché in Denmark, was not traveling in a military capacity but under the authorization of the Foreign Office. The other members were R. E. Kimens, the prewar British consul-general in Warsaw, who knew Polish and had extensive contacts in the capital, and Rowland Kenney, who was charged with the task of establishing contact with the Polish left. Leaving in late December, they were to travel in two groups (Wade from Copenhagen and Danzig, Kimens and Kenney via Berne, Vienna, and Cracow) and proceed together to Warsaw.

On the origins of the mission, see Esme Howard memorandum, Nov. 28, 1918, Gregory minute, Dec. 28, 1918, GB FO 371/3282. Derby to FMAE, Paris, Dec. 14, FMAE Z (Pologne) 60, described it as an "unofficial" mission to inquire into the "alleged" pogroms, and promised cooperation with a French mission.

119. Note pour le ministre, Dec. 12, 1918, FMAE Z (Pologne) 226; Pichon to Alby and Clemenceau, Dec. 23, 1918, Alby to Pichon, Dec. 27, 1918, ibid. Z (Pologne) 60. Because of Clemenceau's insistence on an "interallied mission," Barthélemy, accompanied by the British Colonel Smyth, traveled to Poland from Salonika via Fiume and Budapest.

120. Hoover to Lansing, Paris, Dec. 18, 1918, Hoover to Kellogg, Paris, Dec. 23, Herbert Hoover papers, West Branch, IA (hereafter Hoover) American Relief Administration (hereafter ARA) 18. On Foster, FRUS PPC, Vol. 12, pp. 365–7.

121. By mid-January Wade and Barthelemy were informally cooperating in Eastern Galicia as mediators between the Poles and Ukrainians. Wade to FO, Jan. 20, 1919, GB FO 371/3897.

122. Despite the brief alarm over the attempted Communist coups in Lublin, Zamość, and Warsaw, Dec. 28–29, 1918, and over the histrionic rightist coup led by Prince Eustachy Sapieha and Colonel Marian Januszatis, which was supported by the National Democrats, on Jan. 4–5, 1919, Piłsudski evidently faced neither a Polish Lenin nor a Kornilov.

and Berlin.[123] This blow was followed, in early January, by the Ukrainian counterattack in Eastern Galicia and by the Soviet incursions into Lithuania and Belorussia.[124]

Piłsudski and Dmowski, threatened with the ruin of their respective dreams, attempted to forge a coalition. The two rivals, faced with the opening of the Paris Peace Conference and some prodding by the Allies, suddenly reached out to each other. First it was the KNP that tried to convince Warsaw of the need for a national government.[125] Then Piłsudski averred his "patriotic" sentiments by renouncing a federal arrangement with Poland's neighbors, evicting the German minister,[126] and sending a spokesman to Paris. These half-hearted unity efforts were halted by a dramatic breakthrough from outside.[127]

Once France had accepted the inevitability of a coalition government, the United States and Britain furnished the indispensable mediator.[128] Paderewski, having finished his political work, departed America on November 23.[129] His first stop was London, where Balfour and the Foreign Office ostensibly urged him to form a coalition government.[130] After a brief trip to Paris, to confer with Dmowski and Colonel House, Paderewski returned to England and boarded a British cruiser heading for Poland.[131] After

123. Vogt, *Der grosspolnische Aufstand*, pp. 1–68.
Although there is no evidence of Piłsudski's direct hand in the Poznań events (as alleged in Roos, *Polnische Nation*, p. 56), recent scholarship has shown that the Polish leader "was very much interested in the drawing of the western borders" as a way of "promoting his eastern design." Wandycz, *Polish Diplomacy*, pp. 12–13.
124. In a not unrelated development, Czechoslovakia on Jan. 23, 1919, seized Teschen; see next chapter.
125. Piłsudski's deputy foreign minister, Tytus Filipowicz, had urged a direct understanding with the Entente. Pro Memoria, Dec. 1, 1918, PIA Akta Adjutantury Generalnej Naczelnego Dowództwa (hereafter AGND) IV/215.
126. But not before Kessler had organized the withdrawal of 400,000 Reich troops from Polish and Ukrainian territories and had arranged arms purchases by the Poles as well as the transport of 50,000 Russian prisoners of war, which included numerous Poles. Hausmann, "Piłsudski und die Mission des Grafen Kessler."
127. On the negotiations in Warsaw and Paris, see Leslie, *History of Poland*, pp. 128–9; Rollet, *La Pologne*.
128. "Une méthode d'action en Pologne," FMAE PA-AP Tardieu 81; also *Le Temps*, Dec. 28, 1918.
129. From a letter to the U.S. secretary of state referring to "the sudden call for my presence on the other side" (Paderewski to Lansing, New York, Nov. 23, 1918, NA USDS 860c, reel 16), some historians have inferred a British invitation (see Barclay to Drummond, Nov. 16, 1918, GB FO 371/3282), others a personal response to the Armistice; but almost all acknowledge Paderewski's considerable political ambitions and his rivalry with Dmowski and T. G. Masaryk. Drozdowski, *Paderewski*, p. 134; Komarnicki, *Polish Republic*, pp. 259–60.
130. Foster to Coolidge, Warsaw, Jan. 9, 1919, FRUS PPC, Vol. 12, p. 365. Also Gregory minute, Jan. 2, 1919, GB FO 371/3896.
131. Paderewski to Smulski, London, Dec. 12, 1918, AAN KNP 2009. In Paris, Paderewski conferred with General Archinard, chief of the Franco–Polish military mission, but not with Pichon. Archinard report, Dec. 23, 1918, FMAE Z (Pologne) 17, suspected that Britain anticipated "financial and industrial advantages" from Paderewski's mission to Poland.

picking up the waiting Colonel Wade in Copenhagen, the HMS *Condor* arrived in Danzig on December 25 to cheering crowds and a glum German reception. A day later, Paderewski arrived in Poznań on the eve of the uprising that wrested the province from German control. Exultant crowds also greeted him in Warsaw and Cracow.[132]

Piłsudski, convinced of Paderewski's indispensability in obtaining vital raw materials and recognition from the West as well as in providing a precious ally against Dmowski, agreed to drop Moraczewski.[133] According to their agreement on January 14, 1919, Paderewski created a nonpolitical government of experts, and Piłsudski, who remained chief of state, added ten of his own men to the KNP. Piłsudski also denied Dmowski control over the foreign ministry and insisted on a three-member delegation to the Paris Peace Conference consisting of Dmowski, Paderewski, and outgoing Foreign Minister Leon Wasilewski.[134]

The "Paderewski solution" was an outwardly happy compromise. The national elections held ten days later, Poland's first universal, secret ballot – and also the first elections to take place anywhere in the new Eastern Europe – revealed a profoundly divided country with uncertain boundaries as well.[135] Paderewski was widely acclaimed for bringing harmony to Poland's rival factions, bridging Dmowski's chauvinist extremism and Piłsudski's leftist populism.[136] A relieved France and Britain each believed its cause had been served.[137] The Allies nonetheless waited almost a month, until the new

132. On the tumultuous arrival, FRUS PPC, Vol. 2, 422–4; Drozdowski, *Paderewski*, pp. 142–6.

133. See Piłsudski to Dłuski, Warsaw, Jan. 17, 1919, quoted in Komarnicki, *Polish Republic*, pp. 261–2 (original in PIA).

Gerson, *Woodrow Wilson and the Rebirth of Poland*, pp. 109–10, overstates the importance of Hoover and his mission in Piłsudski's decision; nevertheless, after Fronczak to Smulski, Paris, Jan. 17, 1919, corroborated Paderewski's appointment, Smulski to Wilowieyski, New York, Jan. 27, 1919 (AAN KNP 26), confirmed the joint purchase by the American Jewish Committee and the Polish National Department of $2 million in food and $500,00 in clothing to be to sent to Danzig "through Hoover's Commission." Also Marshall to Weil, Jan. 9, 1919, Marshall to Smulski, Jan. 11, 1919, AJA LM 1589.

134. Drummond to Balfour, London, Jan. 15, 1919, GB FO 800/215.

135. In the elections for the unicameral Constituent Assembly, limited to the Congress Kingdom and Western Galicia, no party achieved a majority of the 296 seats; 44 places were reserved for the nonvoting areas of Eastern Galicia, Silesia, Poznań, and Pomorze. The KNP received approximately 34%, the peasant-dominated center 30%, the left 30%, and the minority (Jewish and German) bloc 4%. The Communists boycotted the vote. Rollet, *La Pologne*, p. 99.

136. "The New Poland," *The New York Times Magazine*, Sunday, Feb. 2, 1919, pp. 1–5; Garlicki, *Piłsudski*, pp. 89–90.

137. Whereas Pichon considered Paderewski a member in good standing of the KNP and called it a "National Government" (Pichon to Clemenceau, Jan. 22, 1919, FMAE Z [Pologne] 18), the FO recognized, and appreciated, Piłsudski's victory over Dmowski (Howard minute, Jan. 22, 1919, GB FO 608/61; Headlam-Morley to Namier, Jan. 24, 1919; Headlam-Morley, *A Memoir of the Paris Peace Conference* (hereafter Headlam-Morley, *Memoir*), p. 13.

parliament voted to retain the Paderewski cabinet, before granting official recognition.[138]

There was a less positive side to this fragile, hurried compromise, which left a bitter taste on both sides of the political spectrum. The Piłsudskiites resented their leader's surrender to the right, and the National Democrats reviled Paderewski as an agent of Anglo-Saxon and Jewish interests who had blocked Dmowski from power. Paderewski, despite his three powerful offices of premier, foreign minister, and peace conference delegate, was simply a figurehead leader. A novice politician without his own power base, he spent his less than a year in office struggling to maintain foreign support for his beleaguered homeland under the battering criticism of the left and the right.[139] From his émigré experience, Paderewski was thoroughly convinced of Jewish influence on the Great Powers and thus prepared to issue the necessary accommodating signals; but he was also deeply uninformed about the Jews' actual situation in Poland.[140]

On the eve of the peace conference, Poland's international stature remained anomalous. Although the Allies had gained a three-headed negotiating partner, they themselves were far from agreement over Warsaw's expansionist designs or over the threat to its prospective minorities. Balfour continued to harp on the Poles' need "to show, by self control and orderliness, their fitness for independence."[141] But when the Foreign Office warned the KNP against provoking the Germans or preempting the peace conference by expanding Poland's eastern or western borders, Sobański retorted that the French were emitting the opposite signal.[142]

The gulf between Warsaw and the West widened after Paderewski issued an appeal for 50,000 American troops and for a French and English division to protect Poland against a Soviet invasion.[143] Colonel Wade, Paderewski's travel companion and advocate, bombarded London with reports of German–Soviet–Ukrainian collusion and of Poland's "desperate" situation.[144] Predictably, Paris and London were at odds over the seriousness

138. And only after the Council of Ten dispatched an Inter-Allied Commission headed by Ambassador Joseph Noulens to Poland at the end of Jan. 1919. France, on Feb. 23, 1919, was the first country to recognize the Paderewski government, followed ten days later by Britain, Italy, and the United States. FMAE Z (Pologne) 79.

139. Drozdowski, *Paderewski*, pp. 161–70.

140. See discussion in the Protocol of Council of Ministers, Vol. 5, Jan. 28, 30, 1919, AAN PRM.

141. Balfour to Wade, Jan. 5, 1919, GB FO 608/68.

142. Howard memorandum, London, Jan. 4, 1919, GB FO 371/3896.

143. Osborne to Commission to Negotiate Peace, Copenhagen, Jan. 4, 1919, forwarding Paderewski to House, FRUS PPC, Vol. 2, pp. 424–5.

144. Wade reports, Jan. 8, 15, 12, 25, 1919, GB FO 608/68. Also War Office to FO, Jan. 7, 1919, Wade to War Office, Jan. 13, 1919, Rumbold to FO, Berne, Jan. 13, 1919, GB FO 371/3896.

of the Soviet danger and over designating Warsaw as their bastion against Bolshevism, with Paris magnifying the menace from the East and London skeptical of Poland's *Drang nach Osten.*[145] Lacking a coherent anti-Soviet policy, and with their restive forces tied down at the edges of Russia, the Allies recognized that the dispatch of even a token contingent to Poland would be both ineffectual and highly unpopular. Publicly, they reiterated their unwillingness to send troops to aid the new Paderewski government.[146] And, notwithstanding Dmowski's pleas and Foch's urging, the Haller army remained in France.[147]

THE JEWS MOBILIZE

Western Jewish leaders observed the Allies' piecemeal gestures towards Poland with a mixture of expectancy and caution. Weizmann succeeded in convincing the Foreign Office to give unofficial support to a fact-finding mission to Poland by the pro-Zionist journalist, Israel Cohen, who had been commissioned by *The Times* of London to investigate the November pogroms. Two months later, at the beginning of the peace conference, Cohen documented a concerted wave of anti-Semitic violence in Poland.[148] Weizmann's colleague, Nahum Sokolow, used his connection with T. G. Masaryk to stem the threat of Czechoslovakia's announced deportation of thousands of Jewish refugees from Eastern Galicia.[149] German Zionists, on

145. Compare Degrand memorandum, Situation en Pologne, Paris, Jan. 13, 1919, FMAE Z (Pologne) 98 with Namier and Leeper minutes, London, Jan. 14, 1919, GB FO 608/68.

146. Cecil to FO, Paris, Jan. 7, 1919, Curzon to Cecil, London, Jan. 10, 1919, GB FO 371/4383, and announcement in the *New York Herald*, Jan. 14, 1919.

147. France hesitated to dispatch the Haller army until a stable government was established in Warsaw. Cecil to FO, Paris, Jan. 7, 1919, GB FO 371/4383. Dmowski was also responsible for delaying Haller's departure by insisting on additional French cadres and equipment and that the Allies seize control of Danzig and the railways; Gower to Gregory, Paris, Jan. 13, 1919, GB FO 371/3896; Balfour to Wade, Jan. 21, 1919, GB FO 608/68.

There was also the threat of German opposition to the transport of the Haller army through Danzig, technically not covered by Article 16 of the Armistice agreement, which was about to be renewed, with some other difficult issues at hand, on Jan. 16, 1919. FRUS PPC, Vol. 2, pp. 11–15. Wengst, *Brockdorff-Rantzau*, pp. 21–5.

On Jan. 21, 1919, Balfour assured Wade that he was "pressing French authorities" to fulfill Poland's arms requirements but also strongly recommended that Warsaw obtain arms from the departing Germans in return for their safe conduct home, GB FO 608/68.

148. Clerk memorandum, Nov. 29, 1918, on conversations with Weizmann and Cohen; Balfour to Weizmann, Dec. 2, 1918, authorizing the mission, GB FO 371/3281.

Cohen, a British Zionist and journalist, who between 1914 and 1916 was interned by the Germans in Ruhleben, wrote on Lemberg in the *Manchester Guardian*, Nov. 30, 1918, and in the *Jewish Chronicle*, Dec. 6. See *The Times*, [London], Feb. 8, 1919, and Cohen, *Pogroms in Poland*.

149. Hermann to Weizmann, Berlin, Dec. 1, 1918, and to Zionist office in Copenhagen, Dec. 11, 12, CZA Z3/667; Sokolow to Masaryk, Paris, Dec. 14, 1918 (with text of Weizmann to Sokolow, Dec. 13), Czech Republic, Military Historical Archive, T. G. Masaryk Institute, Cifkve 2, Sokolow

the other hand, maintained an extremely low profile, cautioning their Polish compatriots to deal prudently with Colonel Wade.[150]

Between the Armistice and the Paris Peace Conference, Jewish nationalism had grown stronger. Spurred by the manifesto issued by the Zionist office in Copenhagen on October 25, 1918, which detailed "The Demands of the Jewish People," Jewish national councils sprang up in all the major cities of Eastern Europe and voted their support for Jewish settlement in Palestine, autonomy for the Jews in Eastern Europe, and Jewish representation in the new League of Nations.[151] Between December 15 and December 18, the first American Jewish Congress meeting in Philadelphia voted its support for a Jewish homeland within a British trusteeship in Palestine.[152] It also issued an appeal for the "civil, religious, and national rights" of the Jews of Romania; the use of the word national was indeed a breakthrough, clearly denoting the special status of East European Jewry.[153]

The shadow of Lemberg hung over the American Jewish Congress.[154] Under the direction of Louis Marshall, four committees, consisting of fifty-two delegates, debated more than thirty hours over the wording of a "Bill of Rights" for the new Eastern Europe, which they presented at the very last session. Consisting of seven articles to be inserted in the peace treaty as the condition for the recognition of all the new and enlarged states, the bill included not only equal access to citizenship and the principle of nondiscrimination against racial, national, religious, and linguistic minorities; it also called for the "autonomous management of communal institutions" and the protection of the Sabbath and Sunday trading as well as the highly controversial item number four: "The principle of minority representation

to Weizmann, Paris, Dec. 24, 1918: "Mes représentations auprès de M. Masaryk ont porté leur fruits. . . . Je suis heureux de constater que le décret d'expulsion des réfugies a été annulé en conséquence." CZA A18/21/3; Hantke to Zionist offices in Stockholm, Zurich, and The Hague, Copenhagen, n.d. (Jan. 1919), CZA Z3/135a; Beneš to Pergler, Prague, Jan. 13, 1919, Czech Republic, Archiv Ministerstva Zahrančních večí (hereafter AMZV) PA 17.

150. Hantke to Hermann, Copenhagen, Dec. 20, 1918, on his talks with Wade; Hermann to Warsaw Zionist organization, Berlin, Dec. 24, 1918 (*streng vertraulich* [strictly confidential]), CZA Z3/668. Weizmann rejoiced in the prospect of German Jewry's replacing the leadership of the assimilated "Ballins and Rathenaus" with committed nationalists. Weizmann to Eder, London, Nov. 16, 1918, ibid., A18/32/2.

151. Text of the "Copenhagen Manifesto," CZA Z3/665. Also see *Report on the Work of the Zionist Organization*; Chasanowich and Motzkin, *Die Judenfrage der Gegenwart. Dokumentensammlung.*
    On the spread of the Jewish councils, see *The Times* [London], Jan. 17, 1919.

152. *The New York Times*, Dec. 17, 1918. Stephen Wise to De Haas, London, Dec. 22, 1918, CZA A404/108, conveyed Balfour's satisfaction with the Congress's support, CZA A404/108.

153. Marshall to Mayer Sulzberger, New York, Dec. 21, 1918, AJA LM, Box 1588. Acknowledging the explosiveness of the term "national" to American ears, Marshall always added "in the Eastern sense." Marshall to Brandeis, Feb. 27, 1919, ibid., LM 1589.

154. At the close of the first session all the members stood in silence for two minutes in memory of the "Jewish victims of pogroms in Eastern Europe."

shall be provided for by the law."[155] The Bill of Rights was adopted "without a single word of debate," and the congress appointed a nine-member delegation to present it to the peace conference.[156]

The Jewish world, facing the century's first peace conference, was more than ever divided nationally and internationally, by geography, ideology, and national loyalties as well as by religious practices.[157] These rifts intensified the split between the two seemingly joined causes of Zionism and national rights. With Weizmann's and Sokolow's offices in London and Paris focusing on the Palestine negotiations, the Zionists in Berlin and Copenhagen still hoped to direct the national program of East European Jewry. Western Zionists, with their sterling pro-Allied credentials, spoke in practically a single voice. However, the national-rights advocates, many tainted by their German and Bolshevik connections, emitted a variety of inconsistent and even conflicting demands in a cacophony of tongues.

Indeed, the two sides were potential competitors. Whereas most East European Jewish nationalists ardently supported Zionism, the Zionist leaders hesitated to commit themselves wholeheartedly to a blanket endorsement of Jewish national rights. Sokolow, aware of the Quai d'Orsay's prejudices, on November 18, 1918, deplored the "agitation" and "exaggerations" in the pogrom reports that had alienated potential supporters.[158]

At the core of the rift was not simply disagreement over which cause would go first in Paris, but also the inherent rivalry between two kindred movements, one based on the removal of a massive number of Jews to Palestine, the other on securing a robust national life for the Jewish masses in Eastern Europe.[159] Moreover, the Zionists, bolstered by their powerful contacts with Allied leaders and by the disunity and disrepute of the rival cause, clearly intended to maintain control over the national-rights movement in all possible ways.[160]

155. Marshall to Rabbi Isaac Landmann, Dec. 19, 1918, AJA LM 1588, defended this provision, already included in several U.S. state constitutions and local charters, for setting aside a fixed number of electoral offices specifically for minority representation and preventing the "tyranny of the majority." Marshall to Lansing, Nov. 15, 1918, ibid., stated, "The justice [of this proposition] is self evident."
156. *The New York Times*, Dec. 18, 1918; Marshall to Benjamin Stolz, New York, Dec. 20, 1918, AJA LM 1588.
157. Angelo Sereni to Weizmann, Rome, Dec. 23, 1918, CZA A18/32/1, describes the rift in Italy.
158. Sokolow to Jacobson, Paris, Nov. 18, 1918, CZA L6/529.
159. During his talk with Balfour on Dec. 4, Weizmann lamented the bleakness of the Jewish situation – "falling between the wheels of the new political machine being set up in the East of Europe." He predicted a "formidable emigration," but because the traditional host countries were about to close their doors, he now proposed the emigration of some "four to five million settlers" to Palestine who could also "radiate out into the Near East and contribute mightily to countries which were once flourishing." CZA A18/21/3.
160. Unsigned telegram to Zionist organization in Copenhagen, Paris, Dec. 30, 1918, CZA L8/1023.

In a separate but prominent position stood the Jews in the democracies of Western Europe and North America. While the Zionist masses lined up behind Weizmann, the native-born non-Zionists contested the diversion of the Jews' diplomatic and material resources into the struggle for a Palestine where, among other things, "the medieval Ghetto ideas of Judaism may be revived and where agnostics and anarchists and the Russian poison may find a home."[161]

On practical as well as ideological grounds, the non-Zionists, such as Louis Marshall and Lucien Wolf, made the cause of defending their endangered brethren in Eastern Europe their main assignment.[162] Although startled by Lemberg, they still preferred discreet negotiations to mass demonstrations, concentrating on working to end the crippling boycott instead of launching global accusations against the Polish people.[163] The new Poland, now supplanting Russia and Romania as the major site of Jewish suffering, threatened to unleash a torrent of refugees and prolong the already-high wartime levels of anti-Semitism in Britain, France, and the United States.[164] Louis Marshall, leader of the world's second largest Jewish community, who was a staunchly conservative Republican and patriot as well as a Jewish advocate, well recognized the connection between establishing minority rights in distant Poland and maintaining them in America.[165]

161. Simon Wolf to Jacob Schiff, Feb. 10, 1919, AJA Felix Warburg papers (hereafter Warburg) 184. Cyrus Adler to Marshall, Jan. 27, 1919, ibid., LM 52, identified "American-born Jews" as primarily non-Zionist.
162. "It is my duty to go [to Paris] in order that the welfare of the six million Jews of Eastern Europe shall not be lost sight of in the effort to emphasize the Palestinian question"; Marshall to A. Leo Weil, New York, Dec. 21, 1918, AJA LM 1588.
163. Marshall to Guttman, Dec. 13, 1918, AJA LM 1588, Marshall to Schiff, Dec. 14, 1918, ibid., questioned the reliability of German-inspired pogrom propaganda.
164. On French and British wartime anti-Semitism, exacerbated by the issue of foreign Jews, see Black, *Anglo-Jewry,* pp. 372–7.
165. Marshall to Simon Wolf, Feb. 15, 1919, AJA LM 1589, acknowledged "a widespread and deliberate anti-Semitic movement" in the United States, "to some extent fomented by Paderewski and his followers." A month earlier he was alarmed over reports of American–Polish priests' inveighing against Jews from the pulpit and of American Poles being recruited "to exterminate the Jews of Poland." Marshall to Weil, Jan. 21, 1919, Marshall to Smulski, Jan. 21, 1919, ibid. On Jan. 24, 1919, Marshall implored the director of the American Committee for Relief in the Near East to modify the organization's sermons, which contained negative images of ancient Jews: "In these days, when racial feeling runs high, when national antagonisms are artificially stimulated, when a train of gunpowder may be exploded by an inadvertent reference and lasting hatred and prejudice created, it would seem that those who are advocating a work of mercy, humanity and benevolence should exercise extreme care . . . If in describing the pogroms of which the Jews have been the victims in Eastern Europe one were to describe the mob as Christian, if in giving an account of the notorious lynching of Leo M. Frank one were to say that the mob was Presbyterian or Methodist or Baptist or Catholic, if the Jewish pulpit were to characterize unlawful acts by referring to the creed or nationality of those perpetrating the acts, it would give rise to just criticism. Why then,

A huge task awaited western Jewish leaders at the peace conference. Given Germany's exclusion, they were about to become practically the sole spokesmen for the rights of minorities in Eastern Europe, a cause whose parameters were not yet well defined.[166] Both Wolf and Marshall were discomfited by the political risks of espousing the claim for national rights. The victor governments had expressed only lukewarm interest in the model charters they had drafted for Poland.[167] Even more ominous, after having established harmonious wartime relations with moderate Poles, western Jewish leaders now faced an obdurate KNP.[168] Neither Dmowski nor Paderewski was prepared to accept outside dictates over Poland's political future or to promise special rights for Poland's Jewish population.[169] The crusade for national rights, however discreetly and patiently pursued, pitted Jews against Poles in a public, zero-sum competition.

Lemberg – later renamed Lwów and then Lviv – represented both a defining and deforming moment in the international history of minority rights.[170] By unleashing an explosion of sensationalist reportage, charges and countercharges, investigations and retribution, the violence in Lemberg in November 1918 resounded far beyond Eastern Galicia, shattering Poland's already precarious reputation,[171] encouraging its enemies, promoting radical

this constant reference in the Christian pulpits of various denominations in an offensive way to the Jews?" Ibid.

Marshall at the time was also dealing with the problems of immigration restriction, anti-Semitic statements in public gatherings, books, and in the press, the inclusion of ritual wine in the impending Prohibition Amendment, a pending bill in South Dakota prohibiting the teaching of religion in a language other than English as well as employment discrimination based on religion; ibid.

166. Janowsky, *Jews and Minority Rights*, p. 261.

167. Marshall to Wilson, Nov. 14, 1918, to Lansing, Nov. 25, 1918, AJA LM 1588; Wolf to Balfour, London, Dec. 2, 1918, GB FO 371/3419. Bigart to Pichon, Dec. 9, 1918, FMAE Z (Pologne) 60.

168. Sobański to KNP Paris, [July 23] 1918, AAN KNP 159; Dmowski to Zamoyski (via Quai d'Orsay), Oct. 15, 1918, ibid., KNP 24/3 (1918); Sobański to Swaythling, Nov. 30, 1918 [copy], GB FO 371/3281.

169. Marshall to Adler, Nov. 14, 1918, to Brigadier General M. Churchill [director of Intelligence Division, War Dept.], Nov. 18, 1918, to Senator Henry Cabot Lodge, Nov. 19, 1918, to James White, director, Associated Polish Press, Dec. 10, 1918; AJA LM 1588.

170. On the afterlife of Lemberg, see Ther, "Chancen und Untergang einer multinationalen Stadt," and Engel, "Lwów, 1918: The Transmutation of a Symbol."

171. The charges of Polish "fanaticism and quarrelsomeness" detailed in unsigned note, n.d, AAN Paderewski papers 675/1.

The allegations of the Poles' inability to govern, based either on their three unsuccessful nineteenth-century revolts or their craven collaboration with the partitioning powers, were embellished after Versailles, when Britons such as John Maynard Keynes, David Lloyd George, E. H. Carr, and Lewis Namier left scathing portraits of an inept and/or bloodthirsty Poland. Davies, *God's Playground*, Vol. 2, p. 393.

solutions, and obliging the victors to focus on the threat to Europe's new minorities. The resurrected Poland, neither as strong and unified as its southern neighbors nor as weak and dependent as the lands to the East, became a test case less of an alleged Jewish power and influence than of the Allies' desire and commitment to shape the new Eastern Europe they had neither liberated nor knew very well.

In "Great Britain and the Polish Jews, 1918–1920," Norman Davies critiques "the basic British misconception of Poland as 'the country with a perennial Jewish problem'" as does Peter D. Stachura, "National Identity and the Ethnic Minorities," which contests "the comprehensive disparagement of Poland's attitude towards minorities" by two generations of historians.

Another Poland in 1918–19, remote from its leaders' nationalistic clamor and the violence in the East, a rural society that longed for the return of its soldiers and prisoners of war and for normal social and economic conditions, is detailed in Wapiński, "Postawy i Oczekiwania."

PART TWO

The Minority Treaties

5

Paris

"The great men of the conference – Lloyd George, Wilson & Co. – have no idea of the magnitude of the questions with which they are dealing."[1]

"The day of the Grand Dukes [has] passed away, in Jewry as everywhere else."[2]

On Saturday, January 18, 1919, history's largest and most controversial peace conference formally opened in the foreign ministry of France's capital.[3] Unlike previous congresses in Vienna (1814–15), Paris (1856), and Berlin (1878) – which junior officials had dutifully examined for historical precedents – the Paris Peace Conference had a truly global reach.

Moreover, the victors in their pronouncements during the last year of the war had kindled the world's hopes for a new form of diplomacy in which justice would prevail over power. Writing from Paris, W. E. B. DuBois stated that "thirty-two nations, peoples, and races" had assembled, expecting to be included in a new world system.[4] Wilson's Fourteen Points had created seemingly clear guidelines for a liberal peace with new boundaries based on solid ethnographic principles. And, although the Allies had made no specific commitment, there was also a widespread belief in their support for the protection of minority rights.

1. Sir William Tyrrell, quoted in Lucien Wolf, Diary, Mocatta Library, University College, London (hereafter Wolf, Diary), Jan. 18, 1919.
2. Nahum Sokolow, quoted in Wolf, Diary, Feb. 11, 1919.
3. In his opening remarks, French President Raymond Poincaré reminded the delegates that forty-eight years earlier the German Empire, "born in injustice," had been proclaimed at Versailles. Holding in their hands "the future of the world," they were assembled "to repair the evil." FRUS PPC, Vol. 3, p. 164.
4. W. E. B. Dubois, "Opinion," *The Crisis* 18 (May 1919), 7. Compare Dillon, *Peace Conference*, p. 6: "Chinamen, Japanese, Koreans, Hindus, Kirghizes, Lesghiens, Circassians, Mingrelians, Buryats, Malays, and Negroes and Negroids from Africa and America were among the tribes forgathered in Paris to watch the rebuilding of the political world system and to see where they 'came in.'"

The victors, however, were moving in a different direction. Not only had the "Big Three," France, Great Britain, and the United States, delayed convening the peace conference for more than two months after the Armistice, but their differences over priorities and procedures had left them little flexibility in dealing with the problems they were about to face. The British and French, prepared to make quick decisions on territorial *and* minority issues, had yielded reluctantly to Woodrow Wilson's desire to give priority to the establishment of the League of Nations, whose principles would ostensibly guide all the individual elements of the peace settlement.[5] Although bound by the U.S. president's promise of democratic deliberations ("open covenants openly arrived at"), the Big Three were nevertheless determined to maintain control over every major decision.[6]

The victors' improvised solutions had momentous consequences. During its first two months, under Paris's wintry skies and beset with local shortages, press leaks, and growing popular disgruntlement, the peace conference moved at a snail's pace on two separate tracks.[7] While the larger "democratic" commissions grappled with creating the League as well as with labor, transport, and reparations problems, the wartime Supreme Council, transformed into a private conclave, functioned as the "steering committee" of the entire conference, "controlling and supervising the business, taking important decisions for approval," holding audiences with a procession of supplicants, and appointing experts to guide their deliberations.[8]

RESHAPING EASTERN EUROPE

No peace had been established in the volatile borderlands of Eastern Europe. Defeated Germany and an embattled Soviet Russia were excluded from the Paris deliberations. Because many of the region's actors were prepared to use force, facts were created in the winter of 1918–19 over which the Great Powers had little control.[9]

On this remote frontier, vulnerable minority populations, no longer ruled by the German, Austro–Hungarian, Russian, or Ottoman Empires, looked to the Allies for protection; but as long as the peacemakers delayed making specific territorial decisions, the minorities' fate remained in

5. Eduard Beneš, Rapport sur la situation générale, Paris, Dec. 24, 1918, Czech Republic, Military Historical Archive, Masaryk Institute, c. 2. The huge scope of the Paris program was outlined succinctly in Lugan, *Les problèmes internationaux et le congrès de la paix*.
6. Marston, *Peace Conference*, p. 104.
7. Marston, *Peace Conference*, p. 69.
8. Hankey, *The Supreme Control*, p. 29.
9. Macartney and Palmer, *Independent Eastern Europe*, pp. 103–5.

a limbo, and their spokesmen would make little headway in defending their cause.[10]

To the victors, who had neither liberated Eastern Europe nor formed their new regimes, fell the burdens of policing, feeding, and certifying thousands of miles of new borders. Their tasks were increased by four major factors: the looming peace with Germany, the dilemma over dealing with Soviet Russia, the huge territorial appetites of their client states, and the fundamental disagreements within and among the Allied delegations.

Following the precedent of the Balkan Wars, the new rulers of Eastern Europe expected to solve their territorial and minority issues without outside interference. The most notorious example was Romania, which on November 10, 1918, had reentered the war against Germany for the express purpose of benefiting from the Allies' victory. During the chaotic two-month post-Armistice period, the Bucharest government, using force and rigged assemblies, arranged "unions" with Bukovina, Transylvania, and Bessarabia without consulting the non-Romanian populations. On December 28, 1918, it announced the settlement of its Jewish problem, a decree–law regulating the acquisition of Romanian citizenship that scarcely mitigated the plight of native Jews and menaced those in the newly annexed provinces.[11] The Allies, with only meager forces in the region, issued disapproving statements; but they also admitted Romania to the peace conference as a full partner in arms.[12]

POLAND AND THE PEACEMAKERS

Except for their treatment of Germany, nowhere were the peacemakers' discord and inconsistency more apparent than in their dealings with Poland. The resurrected republic, wedged between Germany and Soviet Russia and at odds with its other neighbors, embodied the collapse of the old, imperial order in Eastern Europe and the appearance of militant, quasi nation–states. Poland in January 1919, led by an unstable right–left coalition, was in combat on three of its borders and still not recognized by the major powers[13] (see Map 5.1).

The victors were not unprepared. During the last months of the war, a broad range of Allied experts had studied Eastern Europe, and Poland in

10. Lucien Wolf to FO, Dec. 2, 1918, GB FO 371/3419.
11. Wolf, confidential memoranda, Dec. 5, 24, 1918, Wolf to Marshall, Dec. 29, 1918, YIVO W/M 154; Marshall to Schneiderman, Jan. 30, 1919, AJA LM 1589; Iancu, *L'émancipation des juifs* pp. 191–7.
12. Spector, *Rumania at the Paris Peace Conference*, pp. 74–9.
13. Latawski, *The Reconstruction of Poland, 1914–1923*, pp. xvii, 164.

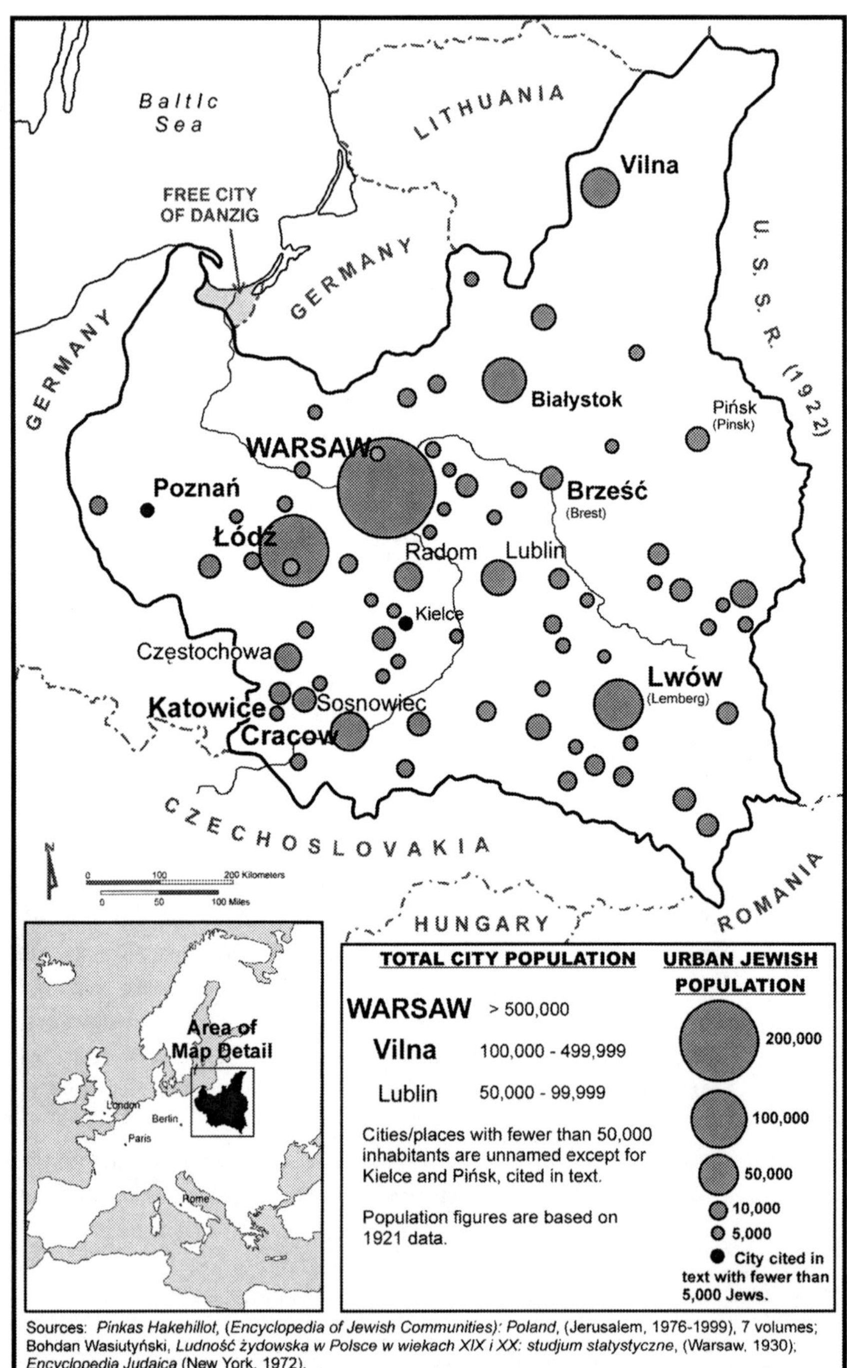

Map 5.1. The Rebirth of Poland, 1919–23.

particular. Like the other claimants, Roman Dmowski's KNP had conducted major press and public campaigns in the West to promote its maximum territorial aims, and its adversaries had spoken too. Faced with conflicting opinions, and with the wave of violence following the Armistice, France, Great Britain, and the United States had reached a rough consensus over the new Poland. All agreed on the fragility of Paderewski's coalition government, the hostility of its neighbors, the threats of famine and disease, and the risks of creating large Ukrainian, Jewish, and German minorities.

The Allies had nevertheless devised different solutions. France, having barely survived the Reich's onslaught in 1918, endorsed a large Poland that would seal Germany's defeat and ensure a lasting enmity with its new eastern neighbor. Still shocked by Russia's desertion, France also hoped that Poland would provide a shield against the currently "sick and contagious" Bolshevik state. For the long term, the French envisaged a vigorous Polish ally tied to Czechoslovakia and Romania (and someday to a restored Russia) that would ensure France's security on the Rhine.[14]

Nonetheless, France's actual plans for Poland's frontiers were neither fixed nor rigid. Paris's preparations had been hasty and its officials divided between Clemenceau's deputy André Tardieu's moderate position and Foreign Minister Stephen Pichon's pro-KNP stance. For Poland's western borders, Paris approved Warsaw's maximum demands (Danzig, Poznań, West and East Prussia, and most of Upper Silesia), despite the large number of German inhabitants involved; but French officials also foresaw the creation of German–Polish commissions to draw borders in heavily ethnically mixed frontier regions.[15] In the East, France wholeheartedly supported Warsaw's claim to all of Eastern Galicia; but it hesitated over its demand for Vilna, preferring a Polish–Lithuanian union for the present and future border adjustments with a non-Soviet Russia.[16]

French policy makers revealed considerable doubts over Poland's capacity for independence. Although publicly labeling Warsaw an indispensable ally, Paris officials viewed Poland as a dependent client whose future depended on France's ability to dominate the Big Three, reduce Germany, and destroy

14. Unsigned memorandum [Tardieu?] "Une méthode d'action en Pologne," Dec. 20, 1918, FMAE PA-AP Tardieu 81 (Pologne)
15. "Une méthode," pp. 10–11.
16. "Une méthode," pp. 7–8. The same principles applied to White Russia, where France proposed a temporary expansion of Polish territory up to the Bug River, a mixed commission to establish definitive frontiers, an autonomy statute for the annexed territory, but also a future transfer to a non-Soviet Russia. See also "Les limites au point de vue ethnographique et la politique de l'État Polonaise", Paris, Dec. 24, 1918, FMAE A Paix (Conditions de la Paix) Pologne, Dossier général, 331.

Soviet power. Moreover, contrary to the Anglo–German caricatures of an obdurately pro-Polish partisan, the Clemenceau government was prepared to make concessions, provided they benefited France.[17]

Britain's standpoint, although ostensibly more dispassionate, was not without dissension and contradictions.[18] The Lloyd George government, while acknowledging the historical justice of Poland's resurrection, recognized that the large state promoted by Paris and Warsaw posed serious problems for Britain's European policy, which was neither as anti-German nor as anti-Soviet as the French. It also decried the Quai d'Orsay's sponsorship of Dmowski's vision as evidence of France's hegemonic designs over the continent.[19] Fully expecting Germany to be restored almost immediately to its Great-Power status and also hoping for an agreement with the current rulers in Moscow, London viewed Poland's expansionist goals as at best an inconvenience, at worst a menace to European peace. Also, London was dismayed by the threat to Poland's Jews.[20]

The Lloyd George government, which shared France's lack of confidence in Poland's leadership and its capacity to serve as a buffer state, opted for a small, "democratic" state inhabited primarily by Poles that would be placed under the protection of the League of Nations. Britain's prime minister arrived in Paris not only opposing Polish control over Danzig, Lemberg, and Vilna and any increase in its troop strength, but also prepared to issue military and economic threats to force the Poles to stay within their ethnic frontiers.[21] Lloyd George, whom the Poles accused of fronting for Britain's Jews, became their *bête noire*, the Allied leader who most fervently denounced their claims, belabored their shortcomings, and predicted their enemies' resurrection.[22]

Most Britons lined up behind the prime minister. In government circles there were a few ardent polonophiles who argued Warsaw's value to the Entente as an anti-Soviet bastion.[23] But they were outweighed by Whitehall's East European specialist, Lewis Namier, who penned barbed critiques

17. Even to the point of creating a "free city" of Danzig. "Une méthode d'action en Pologne," Dec. 20, 1918, FMAE PA-AP Tardieu, 81 (Pologne). In *Grandeur and Misery of Victory*, pp. 190–2, Clemenceau recalled the recentness of France's transformation from Russia's ally to Poland's.
18. See discussions in Imperial War Cabinet, Aug. 13, 1918, GB CAB 23/43.
19. Sprawozdanie z Londynu [Report from London], Feb. 15–18, 1919, PIA AGND IV/256. Lundgreen-Nielsen, *Polish Problem*, pp. 58–70.
20. FO to Sobański, Nov. 8, 1918, AAN KNP 1908, Nov. 14, 1918, ibid., KNP 159.
21. FRUS PPC, Vol. 3, p. 642.
22. Sprawozdanie z Londynu [Report from London], Feb. 15–18, 1919, PIA IV/256.
23. Particularly Colonel H. H. Wade, who led the British mission to Poland, and Esmé Howard and Eric Drummond in the Foreign Office; see, e.g., Wade to FO (via Berne), Warsaw, Jan. 9, 1919, GB FO 371/3896, #7719; Wade to Howard, Warsaw, Jan. 8, 1919, Howard minute, nd., GB FO 608/68, #354, #292; Wade to Department of Military Intelligence (DMI), Jan. 13, 1919, GB FO 371/3896, #7131; Drummond to Kerr, Jan. 18, 1919, GB FO 800/215.

of Poland's chaotic politics, intolerance toward minorities, "White Bolshevism," and reckless *Drang nach Osten*,[24] and also by a group of Central European experts trained in traditional balance-of-power concepts, who deprecated the Bolshevik threat and insisted on a Poland "within her proper ethnographic limits."[25] Even more influential was Britain's Conservative, seventy-one-year-old Foreign Secretary Sir Arthur Balfour, who distrusted the new regime in Warsaw.[26] While reiterating Britain's support for Poland's legitimate aspirations, Balfour warned against further territorial grabs and strongly opposed bolstering its military forces.[27] Nevertheless, given the volatility in Eastern Europe and the absence of an Allied military presence, British leaders had little control over the local decision-making that would affect Poland's future. Thus their "objective" stance, marked by unceasing demands for restraint, was undermined by their powerlessness and frustration over Poland's weakness and aggressiveness.

The United States, the only power to commit to Polish independence before joining the war, held the decisive voice at the peace conference. Wilson in the beginning of 1917 had been the first western statesman to endorse a "united independent Poland."[28] A year later, this pledge was repeated in his thirteenth point, although it was now hedged with the qualification of "indisputably Polish" territory.[29] Although recognizing the

24. Namier, whose original name was Ludwik Bernsztajn vel Niermirowski, was born in 1888 in a wealthy polonized Jewish family in Russian Poland but raised on estates in Eastern Galicia where, at an early age, he embraced Socialism and Jewish nationalism. Fluent in Polish, Ukrainian, German, and English, Namier studied in Lemberg, Lausanne, the London School of Economics, and Oxford, and served in the Royal Fusiliers before entering the Foreign Office's intelligence bureau (DIIB) in 1917, transformed in 1918 into the Political Intelligence Department (PID), where he quickly became known for his anti-Polish stance. See, e.g., Namier minute, Jan. 14, 1919, GB FO 608/68; Namier to Headlam-Morley, June 22, 28, 1919, Sir James Headlam-Morley papers, Churchill College, Cambridge (hereafter HM CC), Box 12; Headlam-Morley to Kerr, Jan. 25, 1919, ibid.; also Hunczak, "Sir Lewis Namier."
25. This group's leading figure was James Headlam-Morley, a historian and assistant director of the PID, who was supported by George Prothero from the Foreign Office's Historical Section and by H. J. Paton, the Admiralty Intelligence Department's Polish expert.
26. Balfour memorandum, Oct. 18, 1918, GB CAB 24/70.
27. Balfour to Wade, cipher telegram #600, London, Jan. 5, 1919, GB FO 608/68; Balfour to Lloyd George, Paris, Jan. 20, 1919, Lloyd George Papers, House of Lords (hereafter LGP) F3/4/9.
28. In his speech to the Senate, Jan. 22, 1917, shortly after the German declaration of an independent Poland and the Allied announcement of their war aims but also after the U.S. presidential election of 1916.
29. Point 13, "An independent Polish state should be erected which should include the territories inhabited by indisputably Polish populations, which should be assured a free and secure access to the sea, and whose political and economic independence and territorial integrity should be guaranteed by international covenant," contained several ambiguities: (1) Wilson's "shoulds," instead of the "must" in his Belgian and French articles, suggested more of a moral than a practical political goal; (2) a Poland "erected" rather than resurrected implied the rejection of historical criteria; (3) "access to the sea" did not necessarily entail the acquisition of Danzig and possibly the internationalization of the Vistula; (4) "indisputably Polish populations" connoted a limit to Polish expansion; and (5)

slim prospects of a democratic Poland, Wilson was less personally engaged in its politics than were his French or British partners,[30] and simply repeated his two mantras: self-determination and the League.[31]

The White House had largely controlled U.S. peace planning. The "Inquiry," appointed by the president to bypass the State Department, had, like the British experts, advocated a small democratic, "Polish" Poland without Danzig, Lemberg, or Vilna that included substantial guarantees of minority rights.[32] The main dissenter was Robert Lansing, who argued for Poland's possession of Danzig but not of Eastern Galicia. The secretary of state, with his traditional balance-of-power perspective, counted on a revived Russian Empire to check any future German threat.[33]

Wilson, characteristically, kept his options open. Although the United States had no vital interest in Poland's frontiers, he recognized the connection between Poland's dreams, its vulnerability, and America's need to create a stable order in the new Eastern Europe. Even more than the French and British, Wilson deprecated the Poles' abilities and magnified the Allies' power. It is questionable whether the president's views were dominated by domestic political considerations[34] or by his anti-Bolshevik convictions.[35] More likely, this "conservative revolutionary," who was reluctant to make radical territorial changes, favored a small, weak Poland dependent for its security on the League of Nations as a test case for his vision of bringing justice and security to the new Eastern Europe.[36]

THE SUPREME COUNCIL

After ten days of focusing on procedural issues, the Supreme Council turned its attention to the volatile region between Germany and Russia. On January 22, France formally introduced the Polish problem.[37] Alarmed by reports of

"international guarantees" suggested a Poland dependent on outside powers. Wandycz, "The Polish Question," especially p. 321.

30. On board the *George Washington*, Wilson reportedly told Bowman he favored the Poles' "having any government they damned pleased." Quoted in Lundgreen-Nielsen, "Woodrow Wilson and the Rebirth of Poland," p. 109.
31. Biskupski, "War and the Diplomacy of Polish Independence."
32. Biskupski, "Re-Creating Central Europe."
33. Lansing, *The Peace Negotiations*, p. 195; also Lansing memorandum, May 1, 1917, Seeley G. Mudd Manuscript Library, Princeton University, Lansing papers, Box 2. Compare Gelfand, *The Inquiry*, pp. 190–1; Mamatey, *The U.S. and East Central Europe*, p. 225.
34. Alleged in Dmowski to Zamoyski, Oct. 27, 1918, AAN KNP 139; also in O'Grady, *Immigrants' Influence on Wilson's Peace Policies*; and Gerson, *Woodrow Wilson*, but contested in Mamatey, *East Central Europe*, p. 131, Komarnicki, *Polish Republic*, p. 146, and Link, *Wilson*, Vol. 5, pp. 124–64.
35. Mayer, *Political Origins of the New Diplomacy*, p. 365 and passim; Schwabe, *Woodrow Wilson*, pp. 397–9 and passim.
36. Biskupski, "The Wilsonian View of Poland," p. 139.
37. There are two versions of this crucial meeting: The British (FRUS PPC, Vol. 3, pp. 670–5) and the American (ibid., pp. 684–6).

the Red Army's threat to Warsaw, Marshal Foch revived his earlier proposal to dispatch the Haller army from France via Danzig, using Allied troops to guard the port and rail lines.[38] The Allied commander in chief, who castigated the "divergent and eccentric actions" of Poland's current leadership – "facing the Bolsheviks on the east, and invading Posen on the west and Galicia in the south" – also warned the statesmen that, without outside intervention, "Poland might be suffocated before its birth."[39]

The British and Americans were loath to launch the rescue operation Foch proposed or make any specific political commitments to Poland.[40] The Supreme Council was about to offer mediation to the warring parties in Soviet Russia, engage in tough negotiations with Germany over the terms of its disarmament, and begin deliberations over creating the League and apportioning the Reich's former colonies.[41]

Poland added an unwelcome distraction. The council shared Foch's doubts over Warsaw's political and military prowess and his disapproval of its aggressiveness; but they were also less convinced of the Bolshevik danger. All had refused to commit their own troops to Poland's defense; all were reluctant to provide a new and feeble government with arms that might fall into the opposition's hands; and all were unwilling to endorse the Haller scheme, which threatened to provoke the Germans, bolster the KNP, and add little to Poland's defense against Bolshevism.[42]

Moreover, this early in their deliberations the Supreme Council was reluctant to "isolate" the Polish question from the frontier problems of the entire region where the principle of self-determination was bound to create intractable problems. Wilson had hoped to designate the League as the successor to the entire Habsburg monarchy, to draw the new frontiers and compose the differences among its various peoples.[43] The council, however, adopted Jan Smuts' earlier recommendation, that Poland, along with Czechoslovakia and Yugoslavia, would "probably be found sufficiently capable of statehood and . . . recognized as independent states of the usual type."[44]

38. "The disturbances that exist [on the Eastern frontiers of Germany] are a danger for the whole of Europe." Foch, Note on the Situation in Poland, Jan. 11, 1919, FRUS PPC, Vol. 3, pp. 477–8.
39. FRUS PPC, Vol. 3, pp. 670–4.
40. See especially, comments by Balfour and Wilson, FRUS PPC, Vol. 3, pp. 672–3.
41. Hankey, *The Supreme Control*, pp. 42–66.
42. General Józef Haller, an ardent Dmowski supporter, commanded a brigade of some 50,000 troops. 80% had been recruited in America (Gibson to Grew, Warsaw, May 10, 1919, Yale University Library, Bliss Lane Papers, 1/4); the rest consisted of French citizens of Polish extraction, Poles from the Russian Auxiliary Army in France, and Polish prisoners of war from the armies of the Central Powers. No Jews were admitted. Lundgreen-Nielsen, *Polish Problem*, pp. 125, 136–61.
43. Wilson's "Second Paris Draft," Jan. 20, 1919, in Miller, *Covenant* Vol. 2, p. 90.
44. Smuts, *The League of Nations*, reprinted in Miller, *Covenant*, Vol. 2, p. 29. Wilson nevertheless reserved the more "unformed, less developed" parts of the monarchy for potential League mandates. Miller, "Mandates System," p. 282. Compare DDI, Ser. 6, Vol. 2, pp. 142–3. Specific candidates

The victors' policies toward the successor states were already highly inconsistent. While fretting over Warsaw's military adventures, they had adopted a hands-off strategy elsewhere, tacitly countenancing the entry of Czech and Serb as well as Romanian troops into former Habsburg territories as a way of bolstering their respective territorial claims.[45] Once the peace conference began, however, the victors were confronted not only with their clients' rivalries but also with the threat that further armed coups would stiffen resistance in Berlin, Budapest, and Moscow and make their work even more difficult.

The peacemakers recognized that their handling of the borders of Eastern Europe would create precedents and sow dissension among themselves. Two Supreme Council members, Italy and Japan, insisted on the annexations stipulated in their secret treaties with the Entente; Italy and France laid claims to territories in violation of the principle of self-determination; and several of Britain's imperial partners demanded outright annexation of Germany's former colonies instead of mandates supervised by the League. The hurriedly assembled victors, barred by Wilson from any secret meetings or arrangements, hesitated to plunge into a foreign terrain of obscure political figures, ethnic groups, and historical and economic details, while facing a barrage of bad news from other fronts.

The Supreme Council decided to buy time. On January 22 it grasped Foch's suggestion to "reorganize" their scattered missions in Poland and dispatch the Inter-Allied Commission (IAC) to obtain "precise information" and "compose all disturbances."[46] Aware of the public's concern over Europe's eastern borderlands,[47] the council decided to dispatch neither military nor material aid to Poland but to send emissaries with an impossible mandate.[48]

Events in Teschen[49] lent urgency to the situation. On January 23, the government of Czechoslovakia, capitalizing on Poland's distraction, sent troops across the demarcation line established on November 5, 1918, by the two national councils, a frontier that largely conformed to the province's ethnic composition. Prague's leaders, disputing the population statistics, staked a

for mandates, according to the U.S. delegation's legal advisor, were German Austria and Eastern Galicia, Miller, *Covenant*, Vol. 2, p. 87.

45. Wilson to House, Washington, Nov. 1, 1918, reprinted in Weinberg, ed., *Transformation of a Continent*, p. 110.

46. FRUS PPC, Vol. 3, pp. 684–6.

47. Ibid.

48. See instructions, Ibid., pp. 779, 839–40; critique in Headlam–Morley to John Bailey, Feb. 3, 1919, HM CC, Box 12; Polish discontent in Major Douglas Johnson to House, Jan. 30, 1919, Yale University Library, House Papers, 206.

49. In Polish, Cieszyn; in Czech, Těšín.

historical claim to the entire coal-rich and heavily industrialized duchy.[50] Irritated and divided,[51] the Supreme Council created another investigatory commission. Thus the question of Teschen, with its 430,000 inhabitants, 881 square miles, and almost 400 years of peaceful Habsburg rule, became a harbinger of the victors' "confused and dilatory" treatment of complex East European issues.[52]

The next day, January 24, 1919, the Great Powers issued a "solemn warning" against further *coups de main.* Echoing their earlier empty admonitions to Romania and to Poland,[53] the council proclaimed its collective moral and political authority over the entire region of Eastern Europe. It is likely that Wilson provided the text,[54] which stated that acts of force "will seriously prejudice the claims of those who use such means," creating "the presumption that those who employ force doubt the justice and validity of their claim" and imply that their purpose was to "set up sovereignty by coercion rather than by racial or national preference and natural historical association. . . . If they expect justice, they must refrain from force and place their claims in unclouded good faith in the hands of the Conference of Peace."[55]

Clemenceau, impatient to tackle Europe's problems, pressed further. On January 29, during a break in the council's deliberations over the League and mandates, he suddenly introduced the parties to the Teschen issue.[56] The results were discouraging. Summoned on short notice, Dmowski irritated his audience with two perorations, delivered in French and in English, repeating the KNP's claims and warning of a Poland "crushed and submerged by bolshevism."[57] After Wilson discouraged one Czech delegate, Eduard Beneš, from voicing his territorial desires, his more volatile partner, Karel

50. Teschen, which became part of the Bohemian crown in 1335 and passed to the Habsburgs in 1526, had, according to the Austrian census of 1910, a population that was 55% Polish, 27% Czech, and 18% German. Kusielewicz, "The Teschen Question," pp. 1–9.

51. France and Great Britain supported Czechoslovakia's historic and economic claims; Italy and the United States backed Poland on ethnographic grounds.

52. Sharp, *The Versailles Settlement*, p. 150.

The Teschen issue was settled eighteen months later, in the midst of the Polish–Soviet War, at the Spa Conference of July 1920; Czechoslovakia's gains were slightly reduced, but 139,000 Poles remained under Prague's rule along with a legacy of bitterness between the two neighbors. *Documents on British Foreign Policy* (hereafter DBFP), 1st Ser., Vol. 8, pp. 548–51.

53. FRUS PPC, Vol. 2, pp. 404–7; DDI, Ser. 6, Vol. 1, pp. 430–1.

54. Seymour, *Papers of Colonel House*, Vol. 4, pp. 233–4, n. 1.

55. The statement, transmitted by telegraph throughout the world, in FRUS PPC, Vol. 3, p. 715.

56. Much to the surprise of the Americans (Miller, *Diary*, Vol. 1, p. 96) and annoyance of Lloyd George (FRUS PPC, Vol. 3, p. 813). Dmowski acknowledged France's initiative in *Polityka Polska*, p. 373.

57. FRUS PPC, Vol. 3, pp. 773–9, 780–2; Wandycz, "Dmowski's Policy."

Kramář, raised the "Bolshevist" danger threatening his northern neighbor to justify Czechoslovakia's seizure of Polish Teschen.[58]

Although the council hesitated to proceed further, Clemenceau goaded his colleagues to "courageously deal with European questions."[59] On February 1, Ian I. C. [Ionel] Brătianu, the eldest son of the former Romanian prime minister, now representing an "exhausted" Romania (Europe's main "rallying point... against bolshevism"), laid claims far exceeding the terms of the secret treaty of 1916 that had brought his country into the war. Queried by Orlando and Lloyd George, Brătianu pledged "the greatest possible freedom" for minorities.[60]

More was to come. The Czech, Greek, and Serb leaders also presented their expansive claims. Although all three alluded to the mixed populations about to come under their control, only Beneš gave specific assurances of the equitable treatment to be given Czechoslovakia's huge German minority population.[61]

With the fires now lit, Lloyd George set an old Franco–British project in motion. After Brătianu's presentation, the British premier proposed the appointment of an "expert" committee to "reduce the questions for decision within the narrowest possible limits, and... make recommendations for a just settlement."[62] A dubious Wilson distanced himself from any prior territorial arrangements or future commitments; he also insisted that the council sought only "advice" on "territorial and racial questions" but had not relinquished its power to decide all the major political questions, including "the protection of minorities."[63]

The establishment of these ad hoc "expert" committees, with their vague mandates and authority, became one of the hallmarks of the Paris Peace Conference. This was an ominous development for dealing with the separate fragments of Eastern Europe.[64] Not only was there little coordination among these committees,[65] but each inevitably breached the porous boundary between purely technical and political issues. Although the leaders expressed confidence in their analysts,[66] there was a vast amount of contradictory

58. FRUS PPC, Vol. 3, p. 783. Beneš to Pichon, Paris, Jan. 10, 1919, raised the "Bolshevik" charge against Poland; AMZV PA 4.
59. FRUS PPC, Vol. 3, p. 814.
60. Brătianu spoke twice, on Jan. 31 (together with the Serbian claimants to the Banat) and on Feb. 1. FRUS PPC, Vol. 3, pp. 824–30, 841–51.
61. Ibid., Vol. 3, p. 881.
62. Ibid., Vol. 3, p. 852. Each commission contained two representatives from the Supreme Council.
63. Ibid., Vol. 3, p. 852. For the opposite reason, Orlando reluctantly agreed, so long as "it did not create a precedent" regarding the clauses of previous treaties; ibid., p. 855.
64. On Feb. 27, 1919, the Supreme Council set up a ten-member central committee, chaired by Tardieu, to oversee all territorial questions; GB FO 608/148. Critiques in Marston, *Peace Conference*, pp. 54–68, 115; Perman, *Shaping of the Czechoslovak State*, p. 72.
65. Except for some overlapping personnel.

evidence and short time limits set for the experts' recommendations. Moreover, their sources of information were severely circumscribed; the council's refusal to invite spokesmen for potential minorities to meet with the experts[67] weighted the scales heavily toward their new governments.

In less than a month the victors were headed on an uncharted path. Despite fundamental disagreements over the shape of the new Eastern Europe, they had launched several initiatives that allowed them to temporize while awaiting clarification over the situation in Soviet Russia[68] and Germany[69] and gaining intelligence over the actual conditions in the lands between them. But they lacked a coherent policy for handling all three.[70] Neither their anti-Bolshevism[71] nor their anti-Germanism[72] was consistently applied; nor were they capable of coordinating their efforts to restrain the appetites of their East European clients, which were all prepared to challenge the principle of self-determination with a welter of historical, economic, and strategic arguments, offering themselves as anti-Bolshevik or anti-German shields and producing more unpleasant surprises.

The Allies' policies toward Poland were particularly erratic. Britain and the United States generally upheld the January 24 warning against the use of force[73]; France concurred, but implicitly preferred a case-by-case approach.[74] Britain was prepared to assert Allied authority and force good behavior on the Poles through the use of the "food lever" and threats to withhold arms deliveries to the Poles, but was stopped by Clemenceau's veto.[75] With British officials fuming over the delay, the IAC finally left Paris on February 9 and arrived in Warsaw on February 12. That day, an impatient Balfour urged the appointment of a Polish experts committee to sift the commission's dispatches and report the "big questions" up to the council.[76] Two weeks passed, however, before the council formally

66. FRUS PPC, Vol. 3, p. 852.
67. Ibid., Vol. 3, p. 854.
68. Ibid., Vol. 3, p. 692.
69. Ibid., Vol. 3, pp. 694–6.
70. Balfour to Lloyd George, Paris, Jan. 19, 1919, LGP F3/4/7.
71. Unwilling to follow Foch's formula for overthrowing Lenin by force or Lloyd George's inclination to meet with the Bolsheviks, Allied leaders wavered between mediating the Russian conflict and using surrogates to build a quarantine against Moscow. Thompson, *Russia,* pp. 33–130; Mayer, *Politics and Diplomacy of Peacemaking,* pp. 334–43.
72. Schwabe, *Woodrow Wilson,* pp. 161–243.
73. "The Polish government should be warned against adopting a policy of an aggressive character. Any appearance of attempting to prejudge the decisions of the Conference will have the worst possible effect." Draft of Instructions for the Delegates of the Allied Governments in Poland, Paris, Jan. 29, 1919, FRUS PPC, Vol. 3, p. 779.

This was nevertheless contradicted by the Allied-brokered armistice of Feb. 17 that sanctioned the Poles' use of force in Poznań.
74. Clemenceau statement, Jan. 23, 1919, FRUS PPC, Vol. 3, p. 695.
75. Meetings on Jan. 24, 29, FRUS PPC, Vol. 3, pp. 716, 722.
76. Ibid., Vol. 3, p. 1007.

requested that this committee produce a recommendation on Poland's borders with Germany.[77]

Balfour's rash suggestion, plus the extended absences of Wilson and Lloyd George,[78] momentarily tipped the balance to the Franco–Polish side. The experts committee, chaired by veteran French diplomat Jules Cambon,[79] worked swiftly and harmoniously. Dmowski spoke twice, no non-Pole gave testimony, and the committee's frontier proposals included the award of Danzig to Poland as well as a corridor separating Germany from East Prussia.[80]

In the meantime, the Big Three had granted unconditional recognition to the new Warsaw government, although the latter had issued no public statement granting religious and national equality to non-Poles.[81] In Poznań, after the Allied-brokered armistice of February 17 sanctioned the Poles' seizure of almost the entire province, the new rulers immediately launched retaliatory measures against local Jews as well as Germans.[82] Gravest of all, Poland, in the expectation of gaining its territorial claims against Germany, had defied the January 24 declaration and launched offensives in Lithuania and Eastern Galicia.

Not unexpectedly, the pendulum swung back in mid-March after Lloyd George and Wilson returned to Paris. Both leaders, operating on tight political schedules, were intent on concluding peace with Germany and halting the spread of Communism but also on curbing their small partners'

77. Commission des Affaires Polonaises, Formation, mandat et rappel des séances, n.d. [Feb. 1919] (Très Secret), FMAE PA-AP Tardieu 81.

78. Lloyd George departed for London on Feb. 8 and returned on Mar. 6; Wilson left for the United States on Feb. 15 and returned on Mar. 17. Also, Clemenceau was absent for ten days after an assassination attempt on Feb. 19.

79. The other members included Italy's former ambassador to Russia, the Marquis Pietro Della Torretta, Sir William Tyrrell from the British Foreign Office, the American geographer and Inquiry member Isaiah Bowman, and the Japanese representative Otchiai. FRUS PPC, Vol. 3, p. 1014; Note, Feb. 12, 1919, FMAE PA-AP Tardieu 356. Cambon also chaired the Czechoslovak and Romanian commissions.

80. "Danzig yes." *Dokoła konferencji* [Concerning the (peace) conference], Paris, Mar. 4, 1919, AAN Ministerstwo Spraw Zagranicznych (hereafter MSZ) 1480 (33–34); unsigned telegram ("We believe that the solution to our Western frontier is going in a good direction"), Paris, March 6, 1919, ibid., KNP 368; Laroche [Dmowski] to MSZ, Paris, Mar. 7, FMAE A Paix 332, reporting that the western frontier question "est en bonne voie." Compare Headlam-Morley to John Bailey, Paris, Mar. 8, 1919, Sir James Headlam-Morley papers, University of Ulster at Coleraine (hereafter HM UU Col) 4.

81. Paderewski at the Jan. 28 cabinet meeting had stressed the Jews' "great influence" over the victors but had failed to elicit support for a grand statement or gesture on behalf of minority rights. Protocol, Jan. 28, 1919, AAN, Protocol of the Council of Ministers (hereafter PRM), Vol. 5. On the consequences of unconditional recognition, see Wolf, Diary, Mar. 3, 1919.

82. Reports on the Poznań incidents, which included house searches, hostage taking, and forced contributions, July 1, 1919, CZA Z3/185; Kollenscher, *Aus der deutsch-polnischen Übergangszeit*, pp. 64–74, 160–2. Also, Hagen, "Murder in the East," especially pp. 23–4.

overweening territorial claims. On March 25, Lloyd George, in his Fontainebleau memorandum, urged a moderate peace based on self-determination.

A bloated and aggressive Poland, based on the Cambon committee's recommendations, became a prime target of Anglo–American censure. The British prime minister decried the assignment of 2 million Germans to Poland[83]; and his complaint was widely aired in the French press.[84] Wilson, disowning Colonel House and his experts, linked the award of Danzig with the violation of self-determination elsewhere, particularly in Fiume and the Saar.[85]

The crisis over Poland, plus the jarring news of the Communist coup in Hungary, spawned another major structural alteration. Wilson on March 24 warned his colleagues of the "race between peace and anarchy" and of the public's "impatience" with the slowness of their proceedings.[86] To speed things up, plug embarrassing press leaks, and establish a common policy to guide their experts' labors, Clemenceau, Lloyd George, Orlando, and Wilson agreed to supplant the Supreme Council with a Council of Four and to hold daily meetings to discuss "the most important and difficult questions."[87]

Near the top of the council's list, challenging all their authority, ingenuity, and cohesiveness, was their problematic client, Poland. Each border decision placed the spotlight not only on Warsaw's three-headed regime but also on the inconsistency of the Allies' responses.[88] Balfour, normally one of Warsaw's severest critics, identified the victors' moral and political predicament: While ostensibly defending ethnographic principles over Poland's economic, strategic, and historical claims, they were applying the opposite arguments in support of Czechoslovakia's.[89]

Forthwith, Poland's Premier and Foreign Minister Ignacy Paderewski embarked on his long-postponed journey to Paris.[90] Hoping to repair the damage and supplant the problematic Dmowski, Paderewski joined the dozens of claimants clamoring for the distracted victors' attention.[91]

83. FRUS PPC, Vol. 4, pp. 414–15, 417.
84. Ibid., p. 444.
85. Schwabe, *Woodrow Wilson*, p. 255.
86. Link, ed., *Deliberations of the Council of Four* (hereafter *Council of Four*), Vol. 1, p. 3. A day earlier, during his brief first visit to the battlefields in northern France, Wilson was approached by a woman demanding, "When will you give us peace?"
87. *Council of Four*, Vol. 1, p. 3; see Marston, *Peace Conference*, pp. 161ff; Hankey, *The Supreme Control*, pp. 107–8. The Council of Foreign Ministers was established to handle details.
88. Compare Dmowski's report, Feb. 23, 1919, to the KNP, PIA AGND I/50 and unsigned letter to Minister of Foreign Affairs, Paris, Mar. 31, 1919, ibid. I/97.
89. Balfour memorandum, Apr. 1, 1919, pointing out the dangers of inconsistent policies in delimiting the frontiers of the new states, GB FO 608/5; this was also the case with Romania.
90. Polish Council of Ministers, AAN PRM, Vol. 5, pp. 1071–4.
91. Bonsal, *Suitors and Suppliants*, pp. 118–34 and passim provides colorful, if often inaccurate, details.

JEWISH DIPLOMACY

On the minority side, the prospects were even less promising. Despite the powers' protests, violence had continued throughout Eastern Europe. New minorities were about to be created under governments determined to resist any form of outside control.[92]

The burden of promoting minority rights in Eastern Europe fell on a handful of West European Jews. During the first two months of the peace conference, because of the exclusion of the defeated states and the absence of spokesmen for other potential minorities, Jewish leaders from France and Great Britain constituted the sole advocates for those groups about to be transferred involuntarily from one regime to another and denied self-determination.

These emissaries were not without assets. Israel Cohen's graphic reports of the events in Lemberg, published in *The Times* of London in February 1919 and widely reprinted, had revived public concern over guaranteeing minority rights in Poland and all over Eastern Europe.[93] The minorities' cause was promoted by groups such as the Women's International League for Peace and Freedom and the Socialist International.[94]

The Jewish communities of Germany and Austria stayed discreetly silent.[95] But the new German republic, facing large and indeterminate territorial losses, recognized the importance of its old ally.[96] The Foreign Ministry (*Auswärtiges Amt*) consulted Jewish leaders, and it provided generous subventions, visas, and transit facilities for Jewish emissaries as well as publicity for anti-Jewish incidents in Eastern Europe.[97] The new foreign minister, Count Ulrich von Brockdorff-Ranztau, the former ambassador to Copenhagen with a strong pro-Zionist record, reinforced the partnership.[98]

Berlin, however, was a questionable ally for the Jewish cause. Not only was the republic an equivocal minorities champion that was proposing extensive rights for Germans abroad but unready to grant concessions to its own

92. FRUS PPC, Vol. 4, pp. 417, 409.

93. Posner to Namier, Feb. 11, 1919, CZA A312/56; "Kwestiia żydowska w opinii zagranicznej" ["The Jewish question in Foreign Opinion"], Paris, Feb. 24, 1919, PIA AGND VI/475.

94. Warburg to Zionist Office in Copenhagen, Berlin, Feb. 13, 1919, CZA Z3/670.

95. "Der Judenfrieden," *Wiener Morgenzeitung*, Jan. 3, 1919, denied a "Jewish program" for the conference and called for a peace of equality and fraternity for all peoples.

96. "Schutz der nationalen Minderheiten," in Richtlinien für die deutschen Friedensunterhändler, Berlin, Jan. 27, 1919, Präsidialkanzlei, Deutsches Zentralarchiv (hereafter DZA) microfilm roll 19787, reprinted in Schwabe, *Friedenschluss von Versailles*, p. 105.

"Die Judenfrage auf der Friedenskonferenz," *Deutsche Allgemeine Zeitung*, Jan. 30, 1919, characterized the Jews' peace aims as "desirable" for Germany.

97. Detailed in Germ. PA AA Abt. III, Sobernheim Nachlass, L1288/L350158-393.

98. Rosenblüth to Brockdorff-Rantzau, Copenhagen, Dec. 24, 1919, CZA Z3/21; Warburg to Brockdorff-Rantzau, Berlin, Jan. 2, 1919, ibid., Z3/23.

minority groups[99]; it was also clear to Jewish leaders that any manifestation of the Reich's support would raise the Allies' suspicions and bolster their resistance to the cause of minority rights.[100]

Because of the conference's location, the AIU, with its long, distinguished diplomatic record, expected to play a prominent role at the peace conference.[101] It still enjoyed close relations with the Quai d'Orsay, parliament, and press, and it counted leading French Jews among its members. However, in recent times, with growing foreign rivals and a more timid leadership, the organization's power and prestige in the Jewish world had diminished. At home, confronted by France's small, but vocal, Zionist movement, the *Alliance*, under its staunchly anti-Zionist President Eugène Sée, upheld the "spirit of 1789" of full national integration.[102] Although it had joined the protests against the Lemberg pogrom, the *Alliance* opposed granting special rights to Polish Jews and "erecting walls" against the majority people.[103] Still a proud partner in disseminating France's *mission civilisatrise* in the Balkans, the Levant, and North Africa, the *Alliance* was extremely reluctant to dispute its government's pro-Polish orientation or to follow Britain's line over Poland, Greece, or Palestine.[104]

British Jewry was represented by Lucien Wolf, the secretary of the Joint Foreign Committee. Wolf, a highly experienced, if not always successful, advocate for Jewish questions, had made extensive preparations for the peace conference.[105] Considered even by his critics a "wise" and "prudent" diplomat,[106] Wolf had close ties with members of the British delegation in Paris as well as access to emissaries from Eastern Europe.[107]

Wolf, rejecting the role of a junior partner to his French colleagues, opted to create a new Entente Cordiale. He convinced the *Alliance*'s secretary,

99. Gaus to Simon, Jan. 9, 1919, Germ. AA T-120 4069H/2026/ D918553-4; also Cabinet discussion, Mar. 21, 1919, ibid., 4080H/2040/D924434.
100. See, for example, Clemenceau to Pichon, Paris, Mar. 23, 1919, and Cambon memorandum, Apr. 3, 1919, FMAE Z (Pologne) 61.
101. On behalf of the AIU, Sylvain Lévi to Goût, Dec. 2, 1918, had proposed a meeting of Jews of all Allied countries, giving France a "magnificent occasion to take the leading role in international Jewish affairs." FMAE E (Levant) Sionisme, 1.
102. Chouraqui, *Cent ans d'histoire.*
103. *Alliance Israélite Universelle, La question juive*, p. 38.
104. AIU, Conférence de la paix, dossiers généraux, AIU Fr. II/D7; cf. Wolf, Diary, Jan. 15, 16, 1919.
105. Wolf, *Diplomatic History of the Jewish Question*; Black, "Lucien Wolf."
106. Lévi to FMAE, Jan. 20, 1919, FMAE A Paix 31.
107. See Wolf to Montefiore, Jan. 18, 1919, YIVO W/M 210; Wolf, Diary, Jan. 18, 1919, Wolf to Tyrrell, Jan. 21, 1919, GB FO 608/66; also Wolf, Diary, Mar. 5, 1919, E. H. Carr minute, Mar. 6, 1919, GB FO 608/151.

Wolf's extensive circle of contacts included the PID members Sir William Tyrrell, James Headlam-Morley, Alexander Leeper, and E. H. Carr as well as George Prothero of the Historical Section and Sir William Ormsby-Gore, a member of Lloyd George's Secretariat. Levene, *War, Jews, and the New Europe*, pp. 237–8.

Jacques Bigart, to form a central bureau to handle Jewish questions at the conference.[108] Anglo–French relations were immediately strained, however, because of their divergent views over language rights and over granting any form of autonomy to the Jews of Eastern Europe.[109]

Wolf's bureau was born under other serious impediments. France's strict censorship and its ban on large gatherings confined the scope of its public activities.[110] The bureau's membership was diminished by the absence of the largest Jewish communities in Russia, Ukraine, Germany, Austria, and Hungary, as well as those in the neutral countries.

Most damaging was the two-month delay of the most influential group of all, the delegation of the American Jewish Congress, whose leaders, Judge Julian Mack and Louis Marshall, awaited Wilson's return to Washington.[111] Marshall, dreading the long sea voyage and an extended stay in Paris, had accepted the president's directive in order to win Wilson's favor.[112] The activist president of the AJC, who had developed his own program for minority rights in Eastern Europe, assumed that all the major Jewish questions would be handled late in the peace conference, well after the League had been established. He therefore stayed home, more or less patiently, and attended to his own weighty political and personal obligations.[113]

While the American Jewish Congress's leaders tarried, the balance tipped to the Zionist side. On the urging of Weizmann, U.S. Zionists headed for Europe.[114] First came the bold and outspoken Rabbi Stephen Wise, who presented their Zionist program to Balfour, Tardieu, and Wilson,[115] followed by the Harvard law professor, Felix Frankfurter, who engaged intensely in the Palestine question.[116]

108. Wolf, Diary, Jan. 14, 1919.

109. Wolf, Diary, Jan. 17, 18, 1919.

110. Wolf, Diary, Jan. 15, 1919. It is nevertheless doubtful that either Wolf or the AIU had contemplated large, public demonstrations.

111. According to the cable from Rabbi Stephen Wise, "The president much prefers to see American Jewish Congress delegation in Washington end of February before it leaves for Paris," conveyed in De Haas to Marshall, Jan. 7, 1919, AJA LM 54. Later, Wise to Wilson, Feb. 24, 1919, Wise 74-74, reminded the president of "the engagement made with you in Paris" that delayed the departure of the American Jewish Congress leaders.

112. Marshall to Adler, Jan. 23, 1919, AJA LM 1589.

113. A widower with two young sons at home, Marshall had a full agenda of political chores in the winter of 1919, including Jewish war relief, antidefamation and antilynching cases, fighting the impending immigration-restriction legislation, and defending the Jews against charges of Bolshevism. Marshall to Weingarten, Feb. 20, 1919, AJA LM 1589. Marshall also feared "a widespread and deliberate anti-Semitic movement in this country, . . . to some extent fomented by Paderewski and his followers . . . also due in some degree to the jealousy of pinheaded politicians and petty military officers." Marshall to Simon Wolf, Feb. 15, 1919, ibid.

114. Weizmann to Brandeis, London, Nov. 26, 1918, CZA A18/32/2.

115. Wise to De Haas, Dec. 22, 1918, CZA A404/77, memorandum, Jan. 4, 1919, ibid., A404/78, and report to the National Executive Committee, Feb. 9, 1919, ibid., A404/80.

116. Brandeis to de Haas, Feb. 10, 1919, Frankfurter to Brandeis, Mar. 7, 23, 1919, CZA A404/106. Justice Louis Brandeis did not arrive until June and then sailed at once to Palestine.

The Zionists threatened to overshadow the traditional proponents of minority rights. In late February 1919, Weizmann convened an international conference in London. His purpose was not only to assume formal leadership over the world Zionist movement and move its central office to the British capital; it was also to challenge the claims of *Alliance* and the Joint Foreign Committee as spokesmen for national rights.[117]

In Paris, the veteran Zionist deputy, Nahum Sokolow, who enjoyed good relations with the Quai d'Orsay, had established his own office.[118] In return for his collaboration with their bureau, Sokolow convinced Wolf and Bigart to delay any joint minority proposals to the peace conference until the arrival of "democratically elected" representatives of the masses of Eastern Europe.[119]

Thus a month passed in almost virtual inactivity,[120] with growing irritation and suspicions, and with French and British Jews going their separate ways.[121] By mid-February, Wolf was suddenly aroused not only by the Zionists' growing prominence but by also by the realization that Jewish rights were being ignored by the territorial commissions. On learning of another major setback in the League of Nations Commission, Wolf hastened to repair the damage.[122]

THE LEAGUE OF NATIONS AND MINORITY RIGHTS

Coinciding with the Supreme Council's preliminary deliberations over Eastern Europe, the minorities question entered the peace conference through another portal, where it was roughly handled. The debate in the League of Nations Commission revealed still another discrepancy between Wilsonian expectations and peace conference realities.

117. Background in Weizmann to Eder, London, Nov. 16, 1918, CZA A18/32/2; Jacobson to Berlin Zionist office, Copenhagen, n.d., Hantke to Berger, Berlin, Nov. 24, 1918, Warburg to Jacobson, Nov. 26, 1918, ibid., Z3/667; Sereni to Weizmann, Rome, Dec. 23, 1918, ibid., A18/32/1; unofficial reports of the heated, secret (Feb. 24–26) and public (Mar. 3–12) Zionist meetings in *Jewish Chronicle* [London], Feb. 28, Mar. 7, 14, 1919.

    Two members of Zionists' Commission on National Rights, Leo Motzkin and M. I. Rosoff, were dispatched to Paris.
118. Sokolow to Zionist office in Copenhagen, Paris, Jan. 9, 1919, CZA Z3/103; ties to the Quai d'Orsay: Jean Goût to Sokolow, Paris, Feb. 13, 1919, ibid., L8/236 and "France, 1917–20," ibid., A18/24.
119. Wolf report, London, Jan. 27, 1919, YIVO W/M 51; Wolf, Diary, Feb. 10, 11, 15, 18, 20, 1919; Zionist organization to Bigart, Feb. 19, 1919, AIU II/D6.
120. By late February, Wolf complained that "[The Zionists'] object is clearly to prevent us from doing anything, or at any rate to hold us back while they complete their own preparations for action." Wolf, Diary, Feb. 18, 1919.
121. Wolf sent two memorials to his government on Poland and Romania, Wolf, Diary, Feb. 21; the AIU sent proposals on Greece and Romania, Sée and Bigart to FMAE, Feb. 12, 1919, AIU France II/D6.
122. Wolf, Diary, Feb. 28, Mar. 1, 3, 1919.

The League of Nations Commission was one of the most remarkable entities of the peace conference. The Council of Ten had intended to limit its membership to the five Great Powers plus Brazil, China, Portugal, and Serbia; but at the second plenary meeting on January 25, a small-power revolt, led by Belgium, brought in the representatives of Czechoslovakia, Poland, Greece, and Romania, four states whose borders had not yet been set and whose minority obligations not yet established, as founders of the League of Nations.[123]

The bulk of the League Commission's work had been prepared in advance. American and British officials, working separately, had blended old prescriptions for collective state action to preserve peace with modern democratic and humanitarian terminology.[124] To gain Britain's support, Wilson at the last minute had reluctantly accepted the "Hurst–Miller" draft, a compromise document of twenty-two articles laying out a new world organization that combined international arbitration, collective security, and respect for national sovereignty.[125]

The League of Nations Commission, chaired personally by Wilson, was convened on February 3, 1919. Conforming to the president's tight schedule, it met hurriedly – ten times within eleven days, on an average of three hours per session. Wilson, despite his preference for informal and secret proceedings, bowed to French demands to record the deliberations.[126] Although the delegates made few major changes to the Anglo–American draft, there was heated debate over the League's structure and membership as well as over arbitration, disarmament, and, especially, the implementation of collective security.[127]

At the League Commission's sixth meeting on February 8 the minorities question entered the Paris Peace Conference.[128] Wilson introduced his Article 19, which had survived the last-minute drafting process:

"The High Contracting Parties agree that they will make no law prohibiting or interfering with the free exercise of religion, and that they will in no way discriminate,

123. Debate in FRUS PPC, Vol. 2, pp. 188–201; also Miller, *Covenant*, Vol. 1, pp. 83–5; Vol. 2, pp. 255–60. The final commission membership comprised nineteen members, two representatives of France, Great Britain, Italy, Japan, and the United States and one from Belgium, Brazil, China, Czechoslovakia, Greece, Poland, Portugal, Romania, and Serbia.

124. Egerton, *Great Britain*, pp. 57–62.

125. Miller, *Covenant*, Vol. 2, pp. 231–7; Bonsal, *Unfinished Business*, p. 61.

126. Miller, *Covenant*, Vol. 2, pp. 229–33, 395–500, contains the sketchy, often inconsistent, English and French minutes.

127. Hankey, *The Supreme Control*, pp. 62–3; Knock, *To End All Wars*, pp. 214–23.

128. Miller, *Covenant*, Vol. 1, p. 191.

either in law or in fact, against those who practice any particular creed, religion, or belief whose practices are not inconsistent with public order or public morals."[129]

Lord Robert Cecil, the League's most ardent partisan, offered an amendment authorizing the council to respond to acts of "religious persecution and intolerance" that "endangered the peace of the world."[130] This renegade initiative, opposed by the entire British delegation as well as by most members of the commission, had little chance of success.[131] After a barrage of criticism by the Belgian, Portuguese, Italian, French, and Greek delegates, the commission sent Article 19 and Cecil's amendment back to the drafting committee.[132]

Wilson's religious-freedom article was a recent development. The U.S. president had originally conceived of the League as a flexible instrument that would guarantee peace by enabling nations to strive for self-determination, even at the cost of regular border changes. Indeed, Wilson's August 1918 draft had contained no provision for the international protection of minority rights.[133]

By the time the U.S. president arrived in Paris, much had changed. The collapse of the Habsburg Monarchy and the fierce struggle among the Allies' clients forced Wilson to recognize the limits of self-determination in Eastern Europe, the threat of unbridled territorial revisionism, and the dangers to peace if the new and existing minorities, whose national claims could never be fulfilled, were to suffer persecution.[134]

129. Miller, *Covenant*, Vol. 2, p. 237.

130. "Recognising religious persecution and intolerance as fertile sources of war, the High Contracting Parties agree that political unrest arising therefrom is a matter of concern to the League, and authorise the Executive Council, wherever it is of [the] opinion that the peace of the world is threatened by the illiberal action of the Government of any State towards the adherents of any particular creed, religion, or belief, to make such representations or take such other steps as will put an end to the evil in question." Quoted in Miller, *Covenant*, Vol. 2, p. 276.

131. Headlam-Morley, "The Minorities Treaties," May 17, 1929. GB FO 371/14125.

132. Miller, *Covenant*, Vol. 1, p. 191, Vol. 2, pp. 273–4, 441.

133. Text in Miller, *Covenant*, Vol. 2, pp. 12–15. Article 3 of that document contained this remarkable clause: "The Contracting powers unite in guaranteeing to each other political independence and territorial integrity; but it is understood between them that such territorial readjustments, if any, as may in the future become necessary by reason of changes in present racial conditions and aspirations or present social relationships, pursuant to the principle of self-determination, and also such territorial readjustments as may in the judgment of three fourths of the Delegates be demanded by the welfare and manifest interest of the peoples concerned, may be effected, if agreeable to those peoples. . . . The Contracting Powers accept without reservation the principle that *the peace of the world is superior in importance to every question of political jurisdiction or boundary.*" (Emphasis added)

134. The reports of the Inquiry had already made these dangers clear. See FRUS PPC, Vol. 1, pp. 18, 20, 51–2, 66. Viefhaus, *Die Minderheitenfrage*, pp. 110–11 stresses the "Jewish influence" on Wilson's change of emphasis, citing his conversations with Rabbi Stephen Wise in Washington and in London in Nov. and Dec. 1918, and his assurances to a B'nai B'rith delegation on the eve of his departure "that every race shall have justice," Wilson, *Public Papers of Woodrow Wilson*, Vol. 5, p. 306.

Wilson's desire for a global solution to the minorities question through the new League of Nations had elicited skepticism from his advisors who asked for more specifics.[135] British officials were generally negative, fearing to incite ambitious and irredentist minorities, to burden the new organization,[136] and to assail the holy principle of "full internal sovereignty."[137] London preferred to handle the minorities question in the traditional manner, by writing specific provisions in the territorial treaties and setting up local enforcement procedures.[138] At the commission meeting of February 10, Wilson's article survived, but Cecil's disappeared.[139] Now, however, the president faced an even greater challenge from Japan.

For Japan, the Paris Peace Conference represented a giant step from its earlier meetings at Shimonoseki and Portsmouth that had capped its triumphs over China and Russia in 1895 and 1905.[140] Now, for the first time, it joined a group of victors; but it was a middle, not a great, power, and one that viewed world politics largely through the lens of its Asian interests.[141]

The risks were considerable. Japan, which had sustained minimal losses and greatly profited from the war, now confronted the West's puissant power and ideology. During the war, the Tokyo government had frequently been excluded from Allied decision-making; it now feared that the United States

135. "The purpose . . . is beneficent, but . . . general treatment is impossible. Doubtless equal religious and cultural privileges should be accorded in all cases, but it is impossible to suppose that all racial minorities can be entitled, for example, to have their languages used in official records. In the case of several small minorities in one country, this would be impracticable even locally." Miller, *Covenant*, Vol. 2, p. 91.

136. "It would clearly be inadvisable to go even the smallest distance in the direction of admitting the claim of the American negroes or the southern Irish, or the Flemings or Catalans to appeal to an interstate conference over the head of their own government. Yet if a right of appeal is granted to the Macedonians or the German Bohemians it will be difficult to refuse it in the case of other nationalist movements." Alfred Zimmern, Paper on the League of Nations, GB FO 371/4353 (PC 29/29). "Some general clause giving the League of Nations the right to protect minorities in all countries which were members . . . would give [it] the right to protect the Chinese in Liverpool, the Roman Catholics in France, the French in Canada, quite apart from more serious problems such as the Irish. . . . Any right given to the League . . . must be quite definite and specific and based on special treaties. . . . Even if the denial of such right elsewhere might lead to injustice and oppression that was better than to allow anything which means the negation of the sovereignty of every state in the world." Sir James Headlam-Morley, Extract from Diary [undated], in Headlam-Morley, *Memoir*, p. 113.

137. James Headlam-Morley, minute, Nov. 20, 1918, GB FO 371/4353 (PC 29/29).

138. See commentary by Lord Eustace Percy, in Miller, *Covenant*, Vol. 2, pp. 129–30, urging that international minority questions be handled by a "regional commission . . . under an impartial chairman" instead of involving either the League or the Great Powers.

139. Miller, *Covenant*, Vol. 2, p. 282, resumé of the discussion in English and in French, Vol. 2, pp. 449–50; also FMAE SdN (1919) 10.

140. The Japanese government and public nevertheless resented the restraints that the Western powers had placed on both triumphs. Rich, *Great Power Diplomacy*, pp. 316–20, 327.

141. Dickinson, "Japan's Asia in the Politics of a New World Order."

and Britain, freed from the European struggle, intended to limit its expansion in China and the Pacific. Moreover, the prospect of a western-sponsored League of Nations, promoting collective security, international arbitration, disarmament, mandates, and the rights of labor were all threatening to Japan's traditional diplomacy and politics. Wilson's call for democracy challenged the underlying basis of the modern Japanese state; the president's sponsorship of self-determination and freedom had not only stirred liberation movements in Korea and China but had also inspired anti-militarist, anti-imperialist criticism among a small group of Japanese politicians and sparked demonstrations by Japanese students and workers demanding universal suffrage.[142]

Japan's apprehensive Prime Minister Hara Takashi had stayed home to "moderate the impact of an undesirable peace."[143] He instructed the delegation, whose main spokesman was the western-educated former foreign minister, Baron Nobuaki Makino, to defend Japan's interests with vigor.[144] Wilson's prized League, a potential instrument of western domination, would be a useful target.[145]

On the eve of the discussion of Wilson's and Cecil's minority proposals, Makino launched his bombshell by introducing a new draft clause for the League Covenant:

> The equality of nations being a basic principle of the League of Nations, the High Contracting Parties agree to accord, as soon as possible, to all alien nationals of State members of the League equal and just treatment in every respect, making no distinction, either in law or in fact, on account of their race or nationality.[146]

The underlying issues of this famous "racial-equality" clause were the severe restrictions placed on Asian immigration in North America, Australia, and New Zealand as well as the discriminatory legislation in the western United States against overseas Japanese workers and businessmen,

142. Dickinson, *War and National Reinvention*, pp. 207–31.
143. Ibid., pp. 237, 226–7. Morris to Lansing, Tokyo, Mar. 20, 1919, warned of a "political crisis" if the nation's expectations were not met. NA USDS 894.00/150.
144. Dickinson, *War and National Reinvention*, pp. 111–18; also Burkman, "Japan, the League of Nations, and the New World Order." The titular head of the Japanese delegation was Saionji Kinmochi, a former prime minister.
145. A crucial source for Japanese policy in Paris is "Pari kowa kaigi ni okeru jinshu sabetsu teppai mondai ikken" ["On the issue of the elimination of racial discrimination at the Paris Peace Conference"] in *Nihon Gaiko bunsho [Japanese Diplomatic Documents] 1919*. Vol. 3, Part 1 (Tokyo: Gaimusho, 1971), pp. 436–515, containing most of the major documents in the Japanese Foreign Ministry archives on this subject. My thanks to Sumiko Otsubo for her excellent translations of this as well as the additional handwritten documents I brought back from the Foreign Ministry and National Diet Library in Tokyo.
146. Text in Miller, *Covenant*, Vol. 1, p. 183.

particularly in regard to schools and property ownership,[147] which diminished Japan's stature as a major power. Unlike western governments, which had routinely overlooked Russia's and Romania's slights against their Jewish citizens, an overpopulated, export-driven Japan could not ignore the widespread prejudice against hundreds of thousands of its people without defying its aroused public and relegating itself to permanent second-class status vis-à-vis its western partners.[148] However, Japan was not seeking *universal equality* but simply to overcome racial prejudice against its people.[149]

Makino's proposal was actually no surprise. He had already exhibited an independent streak during the mandate discussions in the Council of Ten meetings.[150] Also, he had notified U.S. and British leaders of his intention to raise the race issue and had gained House's sympathy.[151] Whether Makino was acting under orders or on his own,[152] here was an excellent opportunity for Japan to gain diplomatic leverage on the eve of the expected, tough negotiations over the future of the former German concessions in Shantung (Shandong).

Japan's initiative coincided with other appeals for a just peace by labor leaders and women suffragists.[153] Despite France's restrictions, Paris in the winter of 1919 had become a magnet for the world's supplicants. Between February 19 and February 21, the Pan-African Congress met at the Grand Hotel. Operating under tight surveillance, its fifty-seven delegates demanded that the League establish rules and enforcement procedures to protect the native populations of Africa.[154]

Japan's ostensible attempt to assume leadership over the world's aliens, immigrants, and colonized peoples as well as the "colored races who form sixty-two per cent of the whole of mankind" raised a diplomatic storm.[155] While Italy, China, and France offered mild diplomatic support, imperial Britain was strongly opposed.

Foremost among the opponents was Australia's abrasive fifty-seven-year-old Prime Minister William Hughes, a passionate social imperialist and

147. Daniels, *Politics of Prejudice*. Prewar tsarist officials had responded to U.S. protests by pointing out the similarities between America's race laws and Russia's restrictions on foreign Jews.
148. Lauren, "Human Rights in History," especially pp. 257–62. Opposition leaders used this issue: *Japan Weekly Chronicle*, Apr. 3, 1919.
149. Shimazu, *Japan, Race and Equality*, is an extremely thorough, well-documented analysis.
150. FRUS PPC, Vol. 3, p. 5.
151. Yale University, Edward M. House Diary (hereafter House, Diary), Feb. 4, 6, 9, 12, 1919.
152. Fifield, *Woodrow Wilson*, pp. 158–61, supports the first conclusion; Burkman, "Japan, the League of Nations, and the New World Order," pp. 254–5, the second.
153. FRUS PPC, Vol. 3, pp. 1022–3.
154. W. E. B. DuBois, "The Pan-African Congress," *The Crisis* 17 (Mar. 1919), 271–4; Contee, "Du Bois, the NAACP, and the Pan-African Congress."
155. Baker, *Woodrow Wilson*, Vol. 2, p. 235. Quote is from "What Japan Should Demand at Paris," *Japan Times*, Jan. 15, 1919.

champion of "White Australia," whose scorn for Wilson's League and the new diplomacy exceeded even that of Japan's most extreme nationalists.[156] Fearing pressure to open his country's gates to hordes of Asian immigrants, Hughes insisted on the suppression of the racial-equality clause as compensation for Australia's wartime sacrifices and in recognition of its exposed position in the Pacific.[157] Wilson and Lloyd George who, because of their own domestic constraints had given only tepid support to Makino's initiative, were disconcerted but also rescued by the "little digger's" obstreperousness.[158]

At the League Commission's tenth and last meeting on February 13, the minorities question came to a boil. Wilson, about to return to the United States, insisted on completing the Covenant before his departure, but was detained that afternoon by a crucial council session on Palestine. Cecil, the replacement chair, read the amended minority article,[159] which drew disapproval from the French and Portuguese delegates. Cecil disclosed the drafting committee's misgivings, but twice reminded the group of Wilson's strong personal desire to include an article on minority rights.[160]

Makino, in a lengthy, passionate speech pleading for a joining of racial and religious equality, delivered the *coup de grâce*. Collective security, he insisted, now depended on the contributions of all the world's peoples; thus the principle of equality must be established among all the League's members. But Japan's actual proposal, presumably on House's advice, had been considerably diluted, simply calling for "equal treatment and rights, in law and in fact... as soon and as far as practicable."[161]

Japan's amendment, scored by Cecil for raising "extremely serious problems within the British Empire" and supported only by the Chinese

156. The London-born Hughes, an elementary school teacher of Welsh descent, migrated to Australia in 1884 where, with his powerful oratorical style, he became active in union and labor politics. Named prime minister in 1915 as a "win-the-war" leader, he went to Britain a year later, where he contributed to Lloyd George's victory. Fitzhardinge, *William Morris Hughes.*

Wilson had already sparred with Hughes on Jan. 30 over the mandates issue: FRUS PPC, Vol. 3, pp. 786–8, 793–4, 799–800.

157. Hughes, forced to retreat on his reparations and colonial demands, impervious to the mediating efforts of his Dominion colleagues Jan Smuts, Robert Borden, and William Massey, and unafraid of infuriating Wilson and Lloyd George, wielded this clause as his talisman. Fitzhardinge, "W. M. Hughes." Background in Andrews, *The Anzac Illusion*, pp. 206–12.

158. Miller, *Diary*, Feb. 9, Vol. 1, p. 116; notes dictated by Balfour, Feb. 10, 1919, GB FO 608/240.

159. "The High Contracting Parties agree that they will not prohibit or interfere with the free exercise of any creed, religion or belief whose practices are not inconsistent with public order or public morals, and that no person within their respective jurisdictions shall be molested in life, liberty, or the pursuit of happiness by reason of his adherence to any such creed or belief." Miller, *Covenant*, Vol. 2, p. 315.

160. Miller, *Covenant*, Vol. 1, pp. 267–8, Vol. 2, pp. 323, 486; Miller, *Diary*, Vol. 5, p. 452.

161. Miller, *Covenant*, Vol. 2, pp. 323–5, 486–9; also *procès verbaux*, Feb. 13, 1919, FMAE SdN 10.

delegate, Wellington Koo,[162] threatened at the last minute to block passage of the Covenant. The Greek delegate, Eleutherios Venizelos, produced the solution by suggesting they omit Wilson's "delicate" article from the Covenant and also leave the treatment of racial and religious issues to future consideration by the League of Nations.[163] To halt further debate and meet the president's deadline, House agreed, pending Wilson's assent.[164]

On the next day, February 14, 1919, Wilson read the text of the Covenant's now twenty-six articles to a hurriedly assembled plenary session.[165] The chorus of support for the new principles of international diplomacy was jarred by the French delegate, Léon Bourgeois, who insisted the League provide a "military means" to prevent future aggression, and also by Makino, who made clear his intention to revive "a certain project."[166] That night Wilson headed home.

More than three months after the signing of the Armistice, the public reception of the peacemakers' first accomplishment, a draft League Covenant, was decidedly mixed. The French, feeling more vulnerable than ever against a still large, unrepentant Reich as well as a menacing Bolshevik Russia, blamed Wilson for wasting time.[167] The British were dismayed by the president's inconsistency on such key issues as mandates, disarmament, and collective security, distrusted his grasp of economic questions, and resented his taking major credit for the Covenant.[168] Although the U.S. public generally greeted the birth of a new international order, Wilson's political opponents prepared to defend the Monroe doctrine and America's freedom from entangling Old World engagements.[169]

When details of the Covenant leaked out, partisans of minority rights were sorely disappointed. Although Makino had pleaded for national, not minority, rights, Japanese politicians and journalists stressed the universality

162. Who nevertheless admitted he had no instructions on the issue.

163. Greece, with its own vast territorial claims in Thrace, Epirus, the eastern Mediterranean Islands, and Asia Minor, was particularly vulnerable to claims of racial and religious equality. (See Venizelos's statement to the Council of Ten on Feb. 3: "After the experience gained in this war, neither race, nor language, nor skull, could be taken by itself as determining nationality: national conscience alone must decide." FRUS PPC, Vol. 3, p. 860.)

164. "With this reservation [the article] was dropped from the covenant." Miller, *Diary*, Vol. 5, p. 455; Miller, *Covenant*, Vol. 2, pp. 325, 488–9.

165. FRUS PPC, Vol. 3, pp. 208–15; also House, Diary, Feb. 14, 1919.

166. FRUS PPC, Vol. 3, pp. 219–25.

167. Cambon, "La paix," especially pp. 12–14.

168. Headlam-Morley to John Bailey, Feb. 15, 1919, HM CC Box 12; also, Egerton, *Great Britain*, pp. 141–7.

169. *Harvey's Weekly*, on Feb. 15, 1919, suggested that the League "must be either a strenuous body so transcending nationality as to be impossible of American approval, or a futile thing of pious aspirations and impotent achievement." Quoted in Walworth, *Wilson and His Peacemakers*, p. 124.

of their crusade and the importance of their defeat.[170] On March 14, Ambassador Ishii Kikujiro, addressing the Japan Society in New York, pleaded for an end to "race humiliation."[171]

U.S. Jews were shocked by the "blanks" in the Covenant. To be sure, they had failed to foresee the connection between the Allies' inflexibility toward Japan and their own looming struggle for Jewish rights.[172] Some blamed the Zionists for having drowned the cause of minority protection with their noisy propaganda.[173] Some accused Wilson of abandoning a great principle out of "politics and expediency."[174] During the president's long-delayed interview with four members of the American Jewish Congress delegation on March 2, 1919, he acknowledged the setback, but he also pledged to defend "the right of the Jewish people everywhere to equality of status," and deemed himself a champion of minority rights: "Racial minorities must be taken care of everywhere, not only Poland. There will be hell to pay if they are not."[175] Back in Paris, Lucien Wolf also recognized that the burial of Wilson's religious-freedom clause "prejudices our cause," encouraging more radical elements and impeding any future negotiations with Poland, Romania, and Czechoslovakia on the Jewish question.[176]

Wilson's grand project had failed not only because of Britain's lukewarm support, Japan's démarche, Hughes's obduracy, Dmowski's opposition, and

170. *New York Herald*, Feb. 17, 1919; also *Japan Times*, Mar. 13, 15, 1919. Japan's right-wing Union for the Abolition of Racial Discrimination held mass rallies in Feb. and Mar. 1919.

171. *The New York Times*, Mar. 15, 1919.

172. Earlier, in Marshall to Lansing, Nov. 25, 1918, AJA LM 1588, Louis Marshall had stressed the *difference* between Jewish claims for citizenship in Poland and Romania and Japan's demand for equal rights for its citizens in Western countries.

173. Rabbi Isaac Landman to Louis Marshall, Mar. 6, 1919, AJA LM 1588; *Morning Journal*, Mar. 5, 1919.

174. Landman to Adler, Aug. 15, 1919, AJC Adler papers. Based on his interviews with most of the League Commission's members, who had all expressed "surprise" at Wilson's withdrawal of his proposal, the Rabbi insisted, "If Wilson had stood his ground the Japanese amendment could have been defeated and the religious liberty clause included in the Covenant. Mr. Wilson, however, was afraid of our Western politicians and Japan. Instead of winning out, he played into her hands."

175. According to Stephen Wise's notes, the president alluded to an alignment between "men like Dmowski" – "to get rid of their own difficulty" – and the Japanese over the racial-equality clause and explained America's withdrawal as follows: "To include racial discrimination terms would have meant throwing open our doors and the doors of Canada to Japanese immigration, and the whole problem of mandatories would have been complicated. The Japanese question haunted all round the peace table. Colonel House explained to me that it was impossible to have the religious discrimination or test included in the covenant without having a row, and the covenant was finished that day." Memorandum of the interview of the American Jewish Congress delegation consisting of Mack, Marshall, Wise, and Richards with the president at the White House, Mar. 2, 1919. Wise 74–60; Wise to Nathan and Lena Straus, Mar. 6, 1919, *Stephen S. Wise*, pp. 86–7. Also, two memorials, by the American Jewish Congress in Wise to Wilson, Mar. 1, 1919, WWP 394.

176. Wolf, Diary, Feb. 26, 1919. In his report to the British Empire delegation, GB CAB 29/28, Cecil emphasized Polish opposition to the amendment.

the president's inability and unwillingness to forge a compromise[177]; it failed because all the victors of 1919, large and small, were reluctant to assume even the most abstract collective burdens. The minority clause, limiting every League member's power over its citizens, was potentially as grave an encroachment on national sovereignty as the collective security obligation in Article 10. Cecil's effort to specify terms of enforcement had solidified the opposition. Even the League's most ardent supporters envisaged a compact among sovereign governments, not a peoples' court of justice or an instrument of outside humanitarian intervention.[178]

The main result of Wilson's retreat was to diminish the international status of minority rights and bolster Britain's position. The League Commission's refusal to issue a global statement meant that any form of minority protection devised after World War I would, as in the past, be framed as part of each separate territorial arrangement and, under the conditions operating in Paris, in secretive, noncoordinated bodies. At the same time, the Allies' retreat served to encourage more radical proposals by minority advocates and reinforce the resistance of the new and enlarged states.

PALESTINE

Among the peace conference's other initial challenges was the establishment of a new form of rule over the non-Turkish territories of the Ottoman Empire. This onerous task involved reconciling several, often contradictory, wartime secret agreements with Wilson's twelfth point and with the Franco-British declaration of November 7, 1918, promising self-determination to the peoples they had liberated.

Britain stood at the forefront of the deliberations over Palestine. After an arduous campaign its troops had occupied the entire province over which it had established a military administration. In December 1918, after extensive internal debate, the British government grasped a novel solution. Seeking

177. At the last League Commission meeting on the night of Apr. 11, 1919, Japan reintroduced its proposal in the form of a watered-down addition to the preamble of the Covenant endorsing "the principle of the equality of Nations and the just treatment of their nationals." The delegates of Italy, France, Greece, Czechoslovakia, and China supported Japan, and there was an 11–6 vote; but Wilson, backed by Sir Robert Cecil (representing Australia's interests) as well as an obdurate Roman Dmowski, applied the unanimity rule to bury a clause that "would raise objections in the United States." Miller, *Covenant*, Vol. 2, pp. 391–2 (which does not mention Dmowski's opposition), Robert Cecil Diary, British Library London (hereafter Cecil, Diary), Apr. 11, 1919 (which does).

Jewish leaders made several last-minute efforts to save the civil- and religious-liberty clause in the Covenant: See Morgenthau to Cecil, Apr. 9, 1919, LC Henry Morgenthau papers on microfilm (hereafter Morgenthau), cont. 9; Oscar Straus's appeal to the president, in Wolf, Diary, Apr. 18, 1919. Wise to Tumulty, May 16, 1919, WWP 289.

178. Wolf, Diary, Mar. 1, 1919.

to avoid outright annexation, override its wartime agreements, and assuage U.S. sensibilities, the Lloyd George government elected to seek a League mandate over the Holy Land's mixed population of Arabs and Jews.[179]

There were clouds on London's horizon. Although Clemenceau, in return for Britain's support against Germany, had relinquished France's claims to Palestine under the Sykes–Picot agreement of 1916,[180] officials at the Quai d'Orsay continued to assert the totality of France's rights in order to keep pressure on its partner. Moreover, the Arabs, whom Britain had courted with pledges of independence, were reluctant to omit Palestine from their map of "Greater Syria." Finally, militant Arabs in Palestine, in their slogans, public rallies, and terrorist acts, had begun to express their strong opposition to both a British mandate and a Jewish national home.[181]

The question of Palestine loomed large behind the issue of minority rights in Eastern Europe. The Zionist movement, spurred by the Balfour declaration and a nationalist ideology that merged biblical texts with contemporary civic, material, and personal ideals, championed an at least partial solution to "the Jewish problem" through voluntary emigration to the Middle East. The object of the Zionists' longing, however, was a small, poor, sparsely settled region of coastal plain, northern swampland, and southern desert, 150 miles long and 80 miles wide, which in 1919 contained some 700,000 inhabitants: 568,000 Muslim Arabs, 74,000 Christian Arabs, and 58,000 Jews.[182]

Throughout the Jewish world, a vocal, ardent, and influential minority upheld the Zionist doctrine. Like the Back to Africa programs of the nineteenth century, Zionism postulated a rightful, if distant, claim to a homeland against which all others, however comfortable and long established, were impermanent and insecure. Few of the leading western Zionists, however, intended to migrate. Prominent Jewish leaders, such as Louis Brandeis in America and Herbert Samuel in Great Britain, had built a strong political program and redemptive project from the search for a refuge for the endangered masses of Eastern Europe.[183] Their opponents raised the dangerous question of dual loyalty and chided the western Zionists' efforts to control lands they were unwilling to inhabit.

179. Dockrill and Goold, *Peace without Promise*, pp. 145–50.

180. There is only one piece of written evidence of this conversation in London on Dec. 1, 1918 (Lloyd George, *Peace Treaties*, Vol. 2, p. 1038). Balfour to FO, Paris, Aug. 11, 1919, DBFP, Ser. 1, Vol. 4, pp. 340–1, asserted that Clemenceau recognized the agreement; and neither side ever renounced it.

181. Cohen, *Israel and the Arab World*, pp. 146–51.

182. These figures are approximate. According to the 1922 British census, of a total of 757,182 inhabitants, there were 590,890 Arab Muslims, 73,024 Arab Christians, 7,028 Druze, and 83,794 Jews in Palestine. Luke and Keith-Roach, *Palestine and Trans-Jordan*, p. 37.

183. Berkowitz, *Western Jewry*, pp. 26–55.

Britain, in stark contrast with its critical stance toward Poland, was in an awkward position over Palestine. Paralleling Lloyd George's ardent support for Armenian statehood and for the Greeks' claim to Thrace, Britain's endorsement of the Zionists' claims refuted both old-fashioned *Realpolitik* and the new principle of self-determination. London's assorted list of justifications – the existence of an ethnically mixed Palestine, the special consideration that was due to its Jewish minority, the defense of Christian sites in the Holy Land, and Britain's own strategic interests, which took precedence over the political aspirations of the local inhabitants – all made Britain vulnerable to internal opposition as well as to its partners' obstruction.[184]

Wilson too was in a difficult situation. Much like his plight over Eastern Europe, the U.S. president was faced with military *faits accomplis* and brawling allies and clients as well as a Britain insistent on rapidly easing its military burdens and creating an internationally sanctioned regime in Palestine. Despite its vague wording,[185] Wilson's January 1918 declaration had signaled America's interest in the Middle East and kindled hopes that it would champion local self-determination over the imperialist schemes of the European powers. Just one year later the United States, although a noncombatant, held a major, if undefined, role in the partition of the Ottoman Empire.[186]

The Zionist issue was especially troublesome to the president, pitting Wilson's political and humanitarian inclinations against the precepts of democracy and the need for stability in the region.[187] The United States had both the power and prestige to replace Britain in Palestine; but Britain had cooled to this prospect. In any event, Wilson resolutely opposed an appeal to the American public to assume a "military responsibility in Asia."[188]

Britain easily won its first victory on January 30, 1919, when the Supreme Council agreed that Armenia, Syria, Mesopotamia, Palestine, and Arabia were to be "completely severed" from the Turkish Empire. Instead of an

184. PID Memorandum, Nov. 21, 1918, GB CAB 24/72; statement of British policy, Feb. 18, 1919, GB FO 608/83. But see the important exchange between a wavering Lloyd George and an insistent Philip Kerr, Feb. 15, n.d., 1919, LGP F89/2/15, F89/2/22. Also Curzon to Balfour, Jan. 16, 1919, urging the government to "go slow," ibid., F3/4/4, lest the government provoke "an Arab rising... by 9/10 of the population [that] would make short shrift of the Hebrews."

Only Italy, urged on by Italian Zionists and also seeking concessions for its non-Jewish citizens to migrate to Palestine, was prepared to support London, although it too feared an Arab backlash. Sonnino to IMAE, Rome, Jan. 17, 1919, Comitato "Pro Israele," to Salvago Raggi, Florence, Feb. 4, 1919, Manzoni to Sonnino, Mar. 19, 22, 1919, Federazione Sionistica Italiana to Sonnino, Mar. 29, 1919, Comitato delle Comunità Israelitiche Italiane, Memoriale, n.d. included in Angelo Sereni to Sonnino, May 7, 1919, IMAE Conf. Pace, Sionismo.

185. Wilson's Point 12 called for "an absolutely unmolested opportunity of autonomous development" for the nationalities under Turkish rule.

186. Evans, *United States Policy*, pp. 77–85.

187. Howard, *The Partition of Turkey*, p. 226.

188. FRUS PPC, Vol. 3, pp. 788, 807.

outright annexation of conquered lands, these territories, "inhabited by peoples not yet able to stand by themselves under the strenuous conditions of the modern world," were to be placed under the tutelage of "advanced nations" acting as mandatories on behalf of the League of Nations as a "sacred trust of civilization."[189] To sweeten the pill, the council recognized that the character of these mandates would vary according to the inhabitants' preparation for independence. Finally, it agreed that the "wishes of the communities [formerly belonging to the Turkish Empire] must be a principal consideration in the selection of a mandatory power."[190]

Having opened this door, the Supreme Council became the forum for claims and counterclaims over the fate of the Middle East.[191] First to speak on February 6 in the famous clock room of the Quai d'Orsay was the dazzling leader of Arab revolt, Emir Faisal, who had led his troops into Damascus on October 1 and then departed for Europe to lobby for his cause. Although fluent in French, Faisal spoke in Arabic, translated by his wartime comrade, Colonel T. E. Lawrence, stressing his people's long suffering and their substantial contribution to the Allied victory. Basing his claims on the Allies' pledges, Faisal called for the unity and independence of all Arabs and their right to choose their own mandatory.[192]

The Arab leader, who openly challenged France's dreams to rule Syria,[193] was ostensibly backed by Britain and the Zionists. On January 1, he had envisaged "a great trustee" for Palestine to "hold level the scales in the clash of [its] races and religions that have . . . so often involved the world in difficulties." On January 3, after a meeting with Chaim Weizmann in Paris, he had pledged mutual friendship and toleration of the Jewish community in Palestine.[194] In his speech on February 6, Faisal had expressly excluded Palestine, with its "universal character," from an independent Arab realm.[195]

189. "Because of the historical mis-government by the Turks of subject peoples and the terrible massacres of the Armenians and others in recent years the Allied and Associated Powers are agreed that Armenia, Syria, Mesopotamia, Palestine and Arabia must be completely severed from the Turkish Empire." This did not include other parts of the Ottoman Empire not under Allied military control. FRUS PPC, Vol. 3, p. 795.

190. FRUS PPC, Vol. 3, p. 796. Turkey, like the other defeated powers, had no voice in these deliberations.

191. The victors, on Dec. 24, 1918, had agreed to invite "nations in the making" along with those like the Poles and Czechs who had already declared independence to state their cases before the peace conference. FMAE Y 15.

192. FRUS PPC, Vol. 3, pp. 888–94.

193. Clemenceau, on March 20, described Faisal as "practically a soldier of England," FRUS PPC, Vol. 5, p. 13; Compare Cloarec, *La question de Syrie*.

194. Faisal's agreement with Weizmann had been based on the Arabs' obtaining their independence. Weizmann, *Trial and Error*, pp. 308–9. Long ago, George Antonius, *The Arab Awakening* (Philadelphia: Lippincott, 1939), pp. 283–6, questioned Faisal's authority to assume a binding obligation.

195. FRUS PPC, Vol. 3, p. 891.

But even had Faisal obtained the improbable – unconditional U.S. and British support for his vast territorial and political claims, from Alexandretta to Persia and then south to the Indian Ocean – it was unlikely that any Arab leader could forswear Palestine.

Wilson, who was indispensable to British, Zionist, and Arab hopes, was determined to avoid a rash commitment over Palestine; and he had France on his side.[196] On February 13, he missed the final League Commission meeting to direct the Palestine debate. That afternoon, he introduced the Reverend Howard S. Bliss, president of the American University of Beirut, who urged the Supreme Council to dispatch an Inter-Allied Commission to Syria and the Near East to "ascertain . . . the desires of the people" toward political independence and the choice of a mandatory power. Clemenceau then ushered in the "Syrian Commission," led by Faisal's political rival Shukri Ghanim, who attacked Faisal's pan-Arab claims and demanded that a Greater Syria, including Palestine, be placed under a French mandate.[197]

Tensions over the Middle East did not abate during Wilson's month-long absence from Paris. Britain continued to usher its clients before the council.[198] At 3:30 P.M. on February 27, 1919, a hurriedly assembled Zionist delegation received their first hearing before representatives of the world's leaders.[199] There were five speakers, all in different voices, and no American Jews appeared.[200] On behalf of the Zionist Association, Nahum Sokolow called for an "autonomous Commonwealth" from Haifa to Akaba; Chaim Weizmann provided the details; Menahem Ussishkin delivered Russian Jewry's endorsement in Hebrew; and André Spire spoke for French Zionism.[201]

Last was Sylvain Lévi, a professor of ancient languages at the Collège de France with close ties to the Quai d'Orsay and the AIU, who introduced himself as non-Zionist, "a Jew by origin and of French sentiment above all."[202] Lévi roused the drowsing council with the longest speech of the afternoon, a prepared address that sharply criticized Weizmann's proposal

196. At Wise's urging, Wilson had received Faisal and T. E. Lawrence on Jan. 23, Wise to Wilson, Jan. 15, 1919, WWP 390; but the president's advisors implored him to restrain the Zionists. Shotwell, *Paris Peace Conference*, pp. 129–32, 169–70.

197. FRUS PPC, Vol. 3, pp.1024–38. Ghanim, who had lived outside Syria for thirty-five years, was reportedly a French citizen; Helmreich, *From Paris to Sèvres*, p. 55.

198. On Feb. 26, Armenian representatives appeared: FRUS PPC, Vol. 4, pp. 147–57.

199. Clemenceau, Lloyd George, and Wilson were all absent. Sylvain Lévi to AIU, Mar. 1, 1919, AIU France II/D.

200. Frankfurter to Brandeis, London, Mar. 7, 1919, CZA A404/106, claimed he was unable to reach Paris; Weizmann's choice, Jacob DeHaas, was delayed in London. *Jewish Chronicle*, Mar. 7, 1919. Some considered the exclusion deliberate: Manual, *American–Palestine Relations*, p. 231.

201. André Spire, "Le sionisme devant la Conférence de la Paix," n.d., CZA A93/1.

202. FMAE A Paix, Procès verbaux. 46 Séance [Secret], Feb. 27, 1919; AIU France II D/8; FRUS PPC, Vol. 4, p. 166, renders Lévi's statement differently.

to resettle "at least four to five million" East European Jews in the "empty spaces" of Palestine, and warned against introducing "explosive passions" into a barren, destitute land inhabited primarily by Arabs.[203]

A "profoundly embarrassed" Weizmann was rescued by Lansing, who asked for a definition of a Jewish commonwealth. Weizmann defended his immigration figures and refuted Lévi's allegations of any double allegiance, but also made the audacious announcement that Zionism's ultimate goal was

> to build up gradually a nationality which would be as Jewish as the French nation was French and the British nation British. Later on, when the Jews formed the large majority, they would be ripe to establish such a government as would answer to the state of the development of the country and to their ideals.[204]

On returning to London, an exultant Weizmann claimed a victory for the Jewish national home and the endorsements of Lansing, Balfour, and Tardieu.[205] Three days later Wilson buoyed the Zionists' hopes. During his long-delayed interview with Jewish leaders in Washington, the president reassured the delegation of the American Jewish Congress that "the allied nations, with the fullest concurrence of our own Government and people, are agreed that in Palestine shall be laid the foundations of a Jewish Commonwealth."[206] Germany also gave public support to a Jewish homeland in Palestine.[207]

The expected backlash occurred. Lord Curzon who was in charge of the Foreign Office during the peace conference, decried a Holy Land dominated by the Jews "living off the fat of the land" [*sic*] and dominating Arab Muslims and Christians "under the shelter of British trusteeship."[208] The French, unready to accept their exclusion from Palestine, publicized Lévi's critical

203. FRUS PPC, Vol. 4, pp. 466–9. Compte rendu de M. Sylvain Lévi sur la question sioniste à la Conférence de la paix, Mar. 1, 1919, AIU France II/D. Political analysis of Lévi's remarks, A.M., Nota per il Ministro, n.d. [Feb. 28, 1919], IMAE Conf. Pace, Sionismo.
204. FRUS PPC, Vol. 4, pp. 169–70.
205. *Manchester Guardian*, Feb. 28, 1919; *Daily Mail*, Mar. 1, Weizmann report in *Jewish Chronicle*, Mar. 7, 1919, and GB FO 608/152, 503/2/2.
206. Memorandum of the interview of the American Jewish Congress delegation with the president, Mar. 2, 1919, Wise 74-60; "President Gives Hope to Zionists," *The New York Times*, Mar. 3, 1919.
207. *Deutsche Allgemeine Zeitung*, Mar. 14, 1919.
208. "While Weizmann may say one thing to you, or while you may mean one thing by a National Home, he is out for something quite different. He contemplates a Jewish State, a Jewish Nation, a subordinate population of Arabs, etc., ruled by Jews, the Jews in possession of the fat of the land, and directing the Administration . . . behind the screen and under the shelter of British trusteeship." Curzon to Balfour, London, Jan. 26, 1919, British Library, Curzon papers, Box 65 F112/208. See also Kerr to Balfour, Feb. 18, 1919, FO 800/215; Balfour to Lloyd George, Feb. 19, 1919, LGP F3/4/12, Curzon minute, Mar. 7, 1919, GB FO 371 W44/1051/4170; Curzon memorandum, Apr. 22, 1919, GB FO 371 4180/60671; also *Le Momento* (Turin), Mar. 16, 1919.

statements.[209] Non-Zionist Jews were appalled by Weizmann's exorbitant claims.[210] A group of prominent American Jews termed the Zionist project "reactionary in tendency, undemocratic in spirit, and totally contrary to the practices of free government."[211] Moreover, Weizmann's statement to the council diminished Faisal's already lukewarm commitment to a Jewish homeland in Palestine.[212]

On March 20, the first order of business of the newly constituted Council of Four was the "Syrian question."[213] Faced with a fundamental clash between Britain and France plus America's refusal to assume any mandates, the council bowed to Wilson's proposal to dispatch an interallied commission composed of "men with no previous contact with Syria . . . to elucidate the state of opinion and the soil to be worked on by any mandatory."[214] Balfour alone objected to postponing the peace with Turkey.[215] But Clemenceau, Lloyd George, and Orlando could not refuse the president's sensible, if risky, proposal without contesting the "basic principles under which the peace conference purported to operate."[216]

Wilson's victory for self-determination on March 20 elated the Arabs and disheartened the Zionists.[217] The delay in a decision over Palestine vexed Balfour and stirred fears among British Jews over an eruption of Arab violence to "create facts" for the peacemakers.[218] It also brought the French and British together. Faced with the threat of America's power to determine the fate of the Middle East, France and Britain patched up their differences over Syria, but failed to halt Wilson's initiative. On May 29, 1919, an American

209. *Le Temps*, Feb. 28, Mar. 1, 1919, *Journal des Débats*, Mar. 1, 2, 1919, *Le Petit Parisien*, Feb. 28, Mar. 3, 4, 1919.
210. Montague to Balfour, Feb. 20, 26, 1919, GB FO 800/215.
211. *The New York Times*, Mar. 5, 1919.
212. In an interview in *Le Matin*, Mar. 1, 1919, Faisal was quoted as saying "if the Jews desire to establish a state and claim sovereign rights in the country, I foresee and fear very serious dangers and conflicts between them and the other races." There was no great outcry among the Zionists who, except for Weizmann, had neither counted on Faisal's support nor overestimated his influence among the Arabs. Sicker, *Reshaping Palestine*, pp. 149–50.
213. Underscoring the novelty of the new proceedings, the four leaders met in Lloyd George's Paris flat on the rue Nitot.
214. FRUS PPC, Vol. 5, pp. 1–14; quotation p. 12.
215. PPC FRUS, Vol. 5, p. 13; Lansing was also skeptical, FRUS PPC, Vol. 11, p. 66.
216. Helmreich, *From Paris to Sèvres*, p. 66; background to Wilson's "bombshell" in Brecher, *Reluctant Ally*, pp. 16–23.
217. Frankfurter to Wilson, May 8, 1919, Wise 74–47.
218. Samuel to Balfour, Mar. 27, 1919, Balfour to Samuel, Mar. 31, Apr. 12, Mond to Balfour, n.d. [ca. Apr. 7], Balfour to Mond, Apr. 11, British Library, Balfour papers 49745. In his Mar. 31 letter to Samuel, Balfour, quoting "objective" sources, expressed concern over the aggressive behavior of the Zionists in Palestine, where they were interfering in the local administration and antagonizing the Arabs.

commission, headed by the Chicago businessman, Charles Crane, and the president of Oberlin College, Henry King, departed, and with them the hopes and fears for a quick settlement of the future of Palestine.[219]

Much like the dispatch of the IAC to Poland, which ultimately failed to check Warsaw's expansion, the King–Crane Commission kindled Arab hopes of a Wilsonian settlement; but it only postponed for sixteen months the implementation of the Entente's December 1918 agreement. In the meantime, the important issues in Palestine, immigration, land purchases, and borders as well as the nature of its future government, remained in suspense.[220]

The Zionists, after their brief audience before the victors, suffered a major setback on March 20, 1919.[221] Wielding their charter, the Balfour Declaration, relying on Anglo–American support to offset French hostility, and counting on the mercurial Faisal to contain Arab nationalism, the Zionists had ignored their own weak flank, their denial of the Wilsonian principles of democracy and self-determination.[222] Like other Jewish emissaries in the international arena, the Zionists had chosen to deal with western statesmen and not with the local population of Palestinian Arabs. Despite their considerable assets – their powerful political connections, the looming danger to millions of East European Jews, and the Allies' fears of revolution in Eastern Europe – and the likely prospect of an eventual British mandate, they had failed to convince the Supreme Council of the urgency of a Jewish commonwealth under Britain's protection and to obtain a clause in the peace treaty establishing their goal.[223]

219. After visiting Palestine (June 10–25) and Syria (June 26–July 21), the commission on Aug. 30 rejected the separation of Palestine from Syria and recommended a "greatly reduced Zionist program" and a U.S. mandate. However, as a result of America's withdrawal from the peace with Turkey, the King–Crane report vanished. Howard, *The King–Crane Commission*, pp. 87–154, 220–7, 249–81.

220. Britain's mandate over Palestine and France's in Syria and Lebanon were established at the Supreme Council conference at San Remo in April 1920, at which the United States was not present. Helmreich, *From Paris to Sèvres*, pp. 302–3.

221. On March 26, Frankfurter reportedly complained that the "Inter-Allied Commission which is to be sent to Syria is about to cheat Jewry of Palestine." House, Diary, Mar. 26, 1919. Compare Lord [Frankfurter] to Brandeis, Paris, Apr. 11, 1919, Frankfurter to House, Apr. 14, 1919, Frankfurter to Brandeis, Apr. 17, 1919, CZA A404/106.

222. The Zionist program drawn up London in Feb. 1919 included the following terms for Palestine: absolute control of immigration, official sanction for all Jewish holidays, control of water rights and the adjacent land, Jewish nationalization of public land and control of public works and educational institutions, as well as the use of Hebrew as a main language in the schools. GB FO 608/99.

223. Frankfurter to Wilson, Paris, May 8, 1919, CZA A404/107. In his letter to Brandeis, May 25, 1919, ibid., Frankfurter termed the commission "a study of ignorance, intrigue, ineptitude, and the haphazardness of government." Despite Wilson's assurances of the U.S. commitment to the Balfour declaration, Frankfurter was "fully aware of the potentialities for mischief."

This treatment of the Palestine question, first privileged, then postponed, unnerved the protagonists of Jewish rights in Eastern Europe.[224] However questionable, this "safety valve" for the Jewish masses – and this lethal weapon for the anti-Semites – was placed in suspense just as the United States was heading toward a restrictive immigration policy. On an operational level, Western Jewish leaders, who had uneasily deferred to the Zionists, were now forced to move into the spotlight just as the situation in Paris and in Eastern Europe grew graver.

From the bright hopes of January, to the first criticisms in February,[225] to the growing cynicism in March,[226] the opening two months of the Paris Peace Conference were an agitated and abnormal period. Even before Wilson left, his stock in the French capital had plummeted "almost to zero."[227]

In Vienna a century earlier, the victors assembled *after* concluding peace with France, which had freed them to compose their differences and dispose of the rest of Europe. In Paris, the peacemakers, having delayed a treaty with Germany and a decision on Russia, immediately plunged into a host of arcane, divisive issues that paralyzed their deliberations.[228]

The protection of minority rights lay tantalizingly close to the surface of the Allies' deliberations, but it failed to take root. Not only were its partisans limited in their resources, divided, and sorely inexperienced in the ways of the new diplomacy; their potential patrons were remote and harried and their enemies resolute and unified. Moreover, Wolf and company shrank from seeking allies, from linking their cause with the Germans or Bolsheviks, the Irish or Blacks, the women or the Socialists. To be sure, Japan shunned a role as leader of the cause of minority rights and never solicited Jewish support. What remained to the Jews were their traditional devices, beseeching the world's statesmen or appealing to the new rulers of Eastern Europe.

The opening of the Paris Peace Conference revealed the great changes since the Congress of Berlin, at which Bismarck had induced his colleagues

224. Wolf, Diary, Feb. 28, 1919, recorded Baron Edmond de Rothschild's observation that, by granting a hearing to the Zionists, the peacemakers thought "they had done quite enough for the Jews."

225. "There has been a lamentable waste of time, and even now there is no organization and matters are not being handled the way they should." House, Diary, Feb. 6; Bailey to Headlam-Morley, London, Feb. 15, HM CC, Box 12.

226. "It is now evident that the peace will not be such a peace as I had hoped or one which this terrible upheaval should have brought about," House, Diary, Mar. 3, 1919.

227. John Marley to Headlam-Morley, London, Feb. 13, 1919, HM UU Col. 85.

228. Major critiques by participants include Keynes, *Economic Consequences of the Peace*; Lansing, *The Big Four*; Clemenceau, *Grandeur and Misery of Victory*; Hardinge, *Old Diplomacy*; Hankey, *The Supreme Control*; and Nicholson, *Peacemaking*.

to write minority provisions in the peace treaties with the newly recognized states.[229] Thirty-five years later, the Balkan Wars had stiffened the small powers' resistance to outside control. Moreover, the peace conference of 1919 was a *global* gathering. Even if minority protection were restricted to Eastern Europe, it was clear that its implications affected the world's mightiest empires.[230]

The League of Nations, the dream of past generations, was created in February 1919, but it was burdened by its peculiar birth. Dominated by a distracted and divided Big Three, it had barred the defeated and admitted regimes that were battling over the spoils of war and revolution. The protection of Europe's minorities still depended on the whims of the Great Powers. Would they be willing in Paris to breach the barrier of national sovereignty, and, if so, to what extent?

229. Wolf, Diary, Feb. 28, 1919.

230. Cecil, *A Great Experiment*, pp. 120–1.

6

Pinsk

"The Jews don't want a strong Poland at any price; they want a strong Germany."[1]

"Our work is now making some progress."[2]

"The atmosphere here is very pessimistic. The peace delegations seem to have little sympathy for our cause."[3]

"Good Friday we spent about the Jews, seeing how much of their claims ought to be secured to them. In the old days I believe the right method of spending Good Friday was to massacre the Jews . . . so the world progresses!"[4]

"Everything now is on the knees of the Olympians."[5]

By April 1919, there was a heightened sense of urgency among the diplomats in Paris. With the arrival of spring, the Allied public was expressing impatience over their prolonged deliberations and clamoring for the fruits of victory.[6] Veiled by their new, streamlined deliberative apparatus, the Council of Four began evaluating the commissions' reports and now faced the most difficult decisions of the peace conference.

The portents were not favorable. First, the problems in the East had not abated. After two failed diplomatic initiatives, the Western Powers, split over the danger and durability of Lenin's regime, had broken off all contact with Moscow; the Soviet government, on its part, had created the Comintern to

1. Handwritten, unsigned note, Apr. 5, 1919, AAN Paderewski 978 (*Stosunki z Wielką Brytanią*, II).
2. Louis Marshall to his children, Apr. 7, 1919, AJA LM 82.
3. Levite to Grynbaum, Paris, Apr. 19, 1919, CZA A127/315.
4. Headlam-Morley to Koppel, Paris, Apr. 21, 1919, in Headlam-Morley, *Memoir,* p. 85.
5. Cyrus Adler to Racie Adler, Paris, Apr. 23, 1919, in Adler, *Selected Letters*, p. 368.
6. See the Apr. 21, 1919, reports of the Intelligence Division of the U.S. delegation on the anger, cynicism, and despair of almost all segments of the U.S. and French press; LC Henry White papers (hereafter White) 42.

promote its revolutionary mission abroad. The appearance of radical left-wing governments in Budapest and Munich raised alarm in Paris but also encouraged several East European states to launch new anti-Bolshevik crusades against their Hungarian, Ukrainian, Lithuanian, and Soviet neighbors. The news from Germany, the indispensable signatory, was also grim. The fledgling Weimar government, an uneasy coalition of moderate Socialists and old-guard imperialists that complained loudly of the long-delayed summons to Paris and of the Allies' "hunger blockade," was preparing Germany's first republican constitution but also a defiant peace program.

As the Big Three struggled to formulate their final terms with Germany, each championed their special interests. Faced with a threatening situation in the Far East, the United States hoped to pacify Europe by creating a liberal political and economic order; Great Britain fought for its imperial requirements as well as its share of reparations; and France insisted on its versions of security and territorial guarantees. At the last minute, their two smaller partners tested their unity, consistency, and patience. Italy, facing opposition to its claims to Fiume and the Eastern Adriatic, made a dramatic exit from Paris on the eve of Germany's arrival. Japan, by threatening to revive its campaign for racial equality and torpedo the League, received a grudging acknowledgment of its claims in Shantung.

The three key decision-makers, all vulnerable to political criticism, drew further apart. Wilson, weakened by his arduous schedule and the fierce attacks of the Paris press, fell seriously ill on April 3 and afterward threatened to leave; with each concession to secure "his" League and finish the treaty, the president grew more irritable and suspicious. The seventy-seven-year-old Clemenceau, recovering from an assassination attempt, was an exigent host and a pragmatic supplicant; conducting his last political battle, the "tiger" often reminded his partners of the *longue durée* of German aggressiveness. Lloyd George was by far the most assertive of all. Backed by his loyal entourage and effectively wielding the "demands of British public opinion," the "Welsh wizard" assumed the role of pilot and prophet, who prodded his colleagues for speed and concessions.

On Wilson's insistence,[7] the drawing of borders in Central and Eastern Europe could no longer be postponed. With each difficult decision requiring a trade-off, the peacemakers risked adding charges of "inconsistency and hypocrisy" to the accusations of "sluggishness and disarray" already hurled at them. In their labors to delineate frontiers, the Allies bared their ignorance of

7. "The only way to kill Bolshevism is to establish boundaries and open all doors to trade." *Council of Four* (Mar. 27, 1919), Vol. 1, p. 47.

local conditions, of the hunger, disease, poverty, fear, and hatred in this war-ravaged region, and also their powerlessness to shape the religious, ethnic, and ideological rivalries that had suddenly erupted. Moreover, by raising the issue of the millions of people about to be "denied self-determination," they stirred the putative defenders of minority rights to action.

THE SHOOTINGS IN PINSK

Despite the peacemakers' warnings, Poland in February 1919 had suddenly launched an offensive against the month-old Soviet Socialist Republic of Lithuania–Belorussia ("Lit–Bel") as well as against the Ukrainians in Eastern Galicia.[8] Warsaw's lone struggle against the Red Army would last two years. Both sides, using World War I soldiers, uniforms, and equipment, combined open assaults with guerrilla tactics in the fierce contest over the regions of the former tsarist empire that lay between them.[9]

On March 5, the Poles captured Pinsk, a strategic river town in the western lowlands of Polesie, after the ragtag Bolshevik forces had either fled or deserted. Polish and Soviet records agree on the ease of Pinsk's capture by the 34th Infantry Regiment of the Ninth Polesie Division, commanded by a former tsarist officer, General Antoni Listowski.[10] Within a week, however, the Polish offensive, checked by spring rains and the need for fresh troops and supplies, halted just beyond this ruined outpost. Pinsk was swollen with refugees, stripped of doctors, and suffering inflation, unemployment, and food shortages. The Germans before their departure had destroyed most of the factories, the Bolsheviks had requisitioned the meager food stores, and the Poles, on their arrival, had unleashed a wave of plunder.[11]

8. The sense of a "northeastern side-show" was evident to outsiders, based on the Soviets' reluctance to engage the Poles. See Chicherin to Paderewski, n.d. [early Mar. 1919] asking for an "amicable adjustment of frontiers," in Howard to Balfour, Mar. 4, 1919, GB FO 608/68, and Carr minute, Mar. 11, 1919, ibid.: ("Contrary to general opinion, the Bolsheviks are not contemplating armed hostilities with Poland, but have their hands full in the Ukraine") on the Poles' obsession with capturing Eastern Galicia.

   Carr also warned that "The Poles are trying to use the menace of bolshevism as an excuse for annexing large areas which do not belong to them." Minute, Mar. 11, 1919, GB FO 608/206.

9. Davies, *White Eagle, Red Star*, pp. 33–9, depicts the conflict from a Polish perspective; Isaak Babel's fictionalized memoir, *Red Cavalry*, trans. Nadia Helstein (New York: Knopf, 1929), gives a searing view from the Soviet side.

10. With Trotsky's main strength concentrated against the armies of Yudenich, Denikin, and Kolchak, the Bolshevik forces in the Pinsk region consisted of "marauding bands, poorly armed, badly disciplined and actuated by motives of loot and aggrandizement." Col. Mason memorandum, Apr. 1919, American Expeditionary Force (AEF) reports on Poland, NA Record Group (RG) 120 1620–21/5887; also Lewandowski, "History and Myth."

11. By mid-March the fields surrounding Pinsk were untilled, the hospitals, orphanage, and almshouse without bread, and the cooperative stores empty; Pinsk's two public kitchens had to be closed for lack of food. Reports on Pinsk's "deplorable state" in Major Wade Wright, [director of the

The local atmosphere was exceedingly tense. On April 1, as part of the "struggle with the Bolshevik enemy," Poland's Interior Minister Stanisław Wojciechowski had announced a state of emergency in the eastern war zone, making all public meetings subject to special authorization. There were widespread reports of riotous behavior by Polish troops and of anti-Semitic incidents.[12] The Soviet government protested against Polish atrocities in various captured towns.[13] Western observers feared more bloody incidents along the trail of Polish conquest.[14]

Pinsk's inhabitants were particularly vulnerable. Over half of its population of 26,000 – perhaps as high as 80% – were Jews.[15] One of the oldest cities in Russia, first mentioned in 1097, Pinsk had played an important role in Jewish history since the arrival of a dozen families from Lithuania in 1506.[16] Formerly known as a "Jewish Hansa town," this inland port was once the home of Jewish steamboat owners, timber, fur, and salt traders, manufacturers of domestic goods, and skilled artisans and laborers as well as of notable rabbis, scholars, and writers; but Pinsk's economic fortunes declined sharply before World War I. When Russia's main north–south

American Red Cross Commission's Department of Medical and General Research] to Lt. Col. Walter C. Bailey, [Commissioner for Poland, Mar. 13–May 31, 1919], n.d. [mid-March 1919], National Archives, American Red Cross (hereafter NA ARC) 947.11/08, Bass to Ammission Paris [American Commission to Negotiate Peace], Warsaw, Mar. 18, 1919, LC White 41.

On Mar. 21, 1919, British journalist H. N. Brailsford wrote to the Supreme Economic Council: "I saw at Pinsk the body of a middle-aged Jew, who had just fallen dead in the street. It was so emaciated that it might have served for a demonstration in anatomy." Grove, *War's Aftermath*, p. 74.

12. First reports of atrocities, quoting notices on Feb. 26, 1919 in the Warsaw Jewish Press, in Marconi House, London, #3501, Mar. 5, 1919, GB FO 608/63.

    Based on articles in the Socialist press ("*Zbrodnicza agitacja w wojsku*" [Criminal agitation in the army], *Robotnik*, Mar. 12, Apr. 4, 1919), on the eve of the murders in Pinsk there was a heated exchange in the *Sejm* between Socialist Deputy Ignacy Daszyński and Minister of War General Józef Lesniewski over "hooligans in uniform." *Sprawozdania Stenograficzne Sejmu Ustawodawczego*, Apr. 4, 5, 1919; also, cabinet discussions in AAN *Kancelaria Cywilna Naczelnika Państwa*, Vol. 145, pp. 49–51.

    Korzec, *Juifs en Pologne*, p. 78, cites the unpublished papers of Michał Kossakowski, adjutant to the commissioner-general of the civil administration of the eastern lands, who witnessed numerous instances of abuse, pillage, and crime by officers and men.
13. Telegram, "Aux gouvernements de l'Entente comme puissances protectrices de la Pologne," Zarskoiescelo, Mar. 28, 1919 (intercepted at Towyn by Marconi Wireless Company), GB FO 371/3903.
14. Namier to Tilley, London, Mar. 22, 1919 (quoting *Robotnik*, Mar. 12), GB FO 608/66; L. B. Namier, memorandum, Apr. 7, 1919, GB FO 371 3903/50097.
15. Tomaszewski, "Pińsk," p. 234.
16. The seat of an early Russian princedom, Pinsk between the thirteenth and the sixteenth centuries was ruled by Lithuania, then joined to Poland in the Union of Lublin where, in the mid- and late-seventeenth century, it was in the bloody path of the Chmielnicki uprising and the Swedish wars and, after 1760, became a religious battleground between the Hassidic Jews and traditionalists. Assigned to Russia in the Second Partition of 1793, Pinsk in the nineteenth century was a center of the Haskalah movement and Zionism, where Chaim Weizmann did his gymnasium studies between 1885 and 1892. Weizmann, *Trial and Error*, pp. 22–43; *Jewish Encyclopedia* (New York and London: Funk and Wagnall's, 1905), Vol. 10, pp. 48–51.

railway was assigned to Brest, people and capital began leaving for Odessa and Siberia, Palestine and the United States, leaving a poor community behind.[17]

Ruling this population was a Polish army, hurriedly assembled by Piłsudski in early 1919, which included numerous tsarist officers and recruits imbued with old religious prejudices and more recent forms of judaeophobia. The average Pole, ignorant of Yiddish, regarded this language as an alien, germanic tongue written in a sinister, indecipherable script. Drenched in right-wing, nationalist propaganda, these Polish soldiers linked the Jews with three new demons: the Elders of Zion, Trotsky, and the clamor for minority rights. Convinced of Jewish collaboration with the Bolsheviks, Pinsk's newest occupiers had reported shots from windows on their entry into the town and suspected the Jews of harboring arms, sending signals to the enemy, and committing acts of sabotage.[18]

When the Polish Command, awaiting the next offensive, stripped the forces in Pinsk to some fifty to sixty nervous soldiers, an explosive situation threatened. On April 5, word circulated of an ambushed patrol and of broken telephone and power lines. The local preparations for the Jewish Passover plus the rumors of a Bolshevik assault before Easter may have increased the anxiety of the undermanned and exposed Polish garrison.[19]

The events in Pinsk on April 5, 1919, can be pieced together from several conflicting reports.[20] At 72 Kupiecka Street stood the *Bet Am* [People's House], the headquarters of the city's thirty-seven-year-old Zionist organization. At approximately 4 P.M. on Saturday April 5, there was a meeting, authorized by the local commandant, of some 150 members of the Zionist cooperative to organize the distribution of the matzo flour provided by the American–Jewish Joint Distribution Committee.[21] After two hours the meeting ended, but the building remained filled. Some of the

17. During the interwar period, Pinsk nevertheless retained one of the highest percentages of Jews of any city in Poland. *Jüdisches Lexikon* (Berlin: Jüdischer Verlag, 1930), Vol. 4, pp. 949–50; *Encyclopedia Judaica* (New York: Macmillan, 1971), Vol. 13, pp. 538–46; Rabinowitch, *Pinsk Jewry*.
18. Pinsk Military Commission Report, in Tomaszewski, "Pińsk," pp. 242–4; also, Frank Golczewski, *Polnisch–Jüdische Beziehungen*, p. 218.
19. *Robotnik*, Apr. 9, 1919; Golczewski, *Polnisch–Jüdische Beziehungen*, p. 218.
20. These include the report of the Pinsk Military Commission, summarized in Tomaszewski, "Pińsk," pp. 242–4; the parliamentary investigation detailed in the Grynbaum papers, CZA A127/75; the "Pinsk" file of the American Joint Distribution Committee (JDC); the KNP file "Sprawa egzekucji bolszewików w Pińsku dnia 5 kwietnia," AAN KNP 149; and the account of Szymon Rykwert, who was in Pinsk on April 5 to deliver money on behalf of the Polish Zionist organization, *Robotnik*, Apr. 9, 1919.
21. The Zionists, one of Pinsk's six (five Jewish and one Christian) cooperative societies, were to elect delegates to the general meeting to be held on Monday, Apr. 7, 1919. Permission to hold both meetings had been granted to a Christian, Konstanty Trofimowicz. "Jewish Testimony," in Lieutenant Foster report to Coolidge, Warsaw, Apr. 13, 1919, Hoover ARA 18.

participants stayed, and there were also visitors reading newspapers and checking the lists of funds sent from America.[22]

After nightfall, some time before 6:30 P.M., a troop of fifteen Polish soldiers, led by Corporal Stanisław Cichosz, burst into the building. Two Jewish informers had warned the local garrison of an impending uprising.[23] As the armed men approached the *Bet Am*, there were unconfirmed reports of shots fired from the building and of the wounding of a Polish soldier. After a hurried search of the premises for weapons and Bolshevik literature,[24] Cichosz's small troop marched the 80–100 terrified occupants to the local military headquarters. There, without any formal investigation, the district commander, Major Alexander Luczyński, ordered a selection.[25] At around 7 P.M., thirty-four Jewish men were shot in the market square before the whitewashed walls of the Russian Orthodox church.[26] Twenty-six people were thrown into prison, the rest were released, and a fine of 100,000 marks was levied on the Jewish population of Pinsk for causing a disturbance. The local commandant, Colonel Konrad Landsberg, was not summoned.[27]

The impact of this seemingly minor event in a remote war sector was magnified by the presence of foreign nationals in the region. In January 1919 the new Polish government, threatened with mass starvation and disease as well as a flood of refugees, had opened the entire country, including the

Although it was the Sabbath, minutes were taken and later "found to be in order" by the commanding officer in "Pinsk, Military Testimony," Foster report, ibid.

22. Statement by Judel Auzenberg, chair of the Zionist cooperative, in CZA A127/75. According to one Jewish female witness, some people were hiding in the *Bet Am* to escape compulsory work. Foster Report, Apr. 13, 1919, Hoover ARA 18.

    The size of the remaining crowd was crucial to subsequent events; although the commandant had apparently set no time limit, authorized meetings were expected to end at sundown.

23. The night before in a Pinsk synagogue, two Jewish soldiers, Daniel Kozak, an illiterate recruit from Brest who had formerly worked for the Germans, and Motel Kolkier, a young vagrant from a village in Lithuania, had allegedly been offered a bribe to join the Red conspiracy. JDC "Pinsk," Vol. 224.

24. There is no proof that they found any weapons in the *Bet Am* ("These circumstances could not be satisfactorily verified during the investigation." Military Commission Report, in Tomaszewski, "Pińsk," p. 244) or any Bolshevik insignia or literature; all the records and memorabilia in the building, written or printed in Hebrew or Yiddish, would have been incomprehensible to the Poles and their two Jewish informants (K. Staromiejski statement, Apr. 28, 1919, CZA A127/75).

25. No names were taken. Luczyński ordered the captives to stand in a row and forced every other one to come forward; after women, children, and the aged were removed, thirty-four remained. Staromiejski statement, Apr. 17, 1919, CZA A157/75.

    In his memoir (Narbut-Luczyński, *U kresu wędrówki*, p. 269) the commander described the capture of Pinsk but was silent over the shootings; he told the military inquiry that on Apr. 5 he had countered a threat to the Polish Army.

26. Szymon Rykwert, who was marched with the group from the *Bet Am* but released by a Polish officer, later heard the shots and learned of the executions from eyewitnesses. *Robotnik*, Apr. 9, 1919.

27. Official communique by Gen. Litowski, Brest–Litovsk, Apr. 7, 1919, AAN KNP 149; statements by Staromiejski and Landsberg, Apr. 9, 1919, CZA A127/175.

eastern zone, to foreign philanthropic organizations.[28] The most prominent was the American Relief Administration (ARA), a department of the U.S. Food Administration, led by Paderewski's friend, Herbert Hoover, who had deftly directed the emergency relief operations in occupied Belgium. On January 4, 1919 the ARA, headed by Colonel W. R. Grove, established its headquarters in the "Blue Palace," the Warsaw residence of the richest man in Poland, Count Maurycy Zamoyski.[29] During the next six months the ARA, which became the dominant partner of the inter-Allied relief effort in Poland, brought massive amounts of surplus food and supplies by rail and by sea, led a children's relief campaign, and also attempted to rebuild Poland's economic infrastructure while the new and inexperienced government went into battle in the east.[30]

Under the ARA's auspices, two private U.S. organizations also arrived in Poland. First was the Joint Distribution Committee (JDC), whose commissioner, Dr. Boris Bogen, was attached to the ARA.[31] During the war the JDC, with the State Department's approval, had conducted massive as well as politically delicate aid operations for Jews behind enemy lines. In January 1919, the JDC entered another precarious terrain to distribute food, funds, and medical assistance to local Polish–Jewish groups, most of them isolated, destitute, faction ridden, and threatened by the battles in the East.[32] Second was the American Red Cross (ARC), which in late February 1919, in response to pleas by the JDC and the overwhelmed Polish relief organizations, reluctantly dispatched a commission to combat the threats of typhus, smallpox, and cholera carried by refugees and returning soldiers from the

28. "Amerykańska pomoc charytatywna dla Polski, 1919–1921," AAN Paderewski 993.
29. Zamoyski, who was vice chairman of the KNP, was named Poland's ambassador to France in Apr. 1919.
30. The ARA brought some 253,000 metric tons of foodstuffs to Poland. Grove to Hoover, Warsaw, July 3, 1919, "Report of the ARA Mission to Poland (covering operations up to June 30, 1919)," Hoover ARA 18.

    Also, Grove, *War's Aftermath*, pp. 61–87; Surface and Bland, *American Food in the World War*, pp. 222–31, 750–91; Lerski, *Herbert Hoover and Poland*.
31. Its full title was the "Joint Distribution Committee of the American Funds for Jewish War Sufferers" (abbreviated as the Joint or the JDC). Chaired by banker Felix Warburg, it managed the relief work of three disparate welfare organizations (the American Jewish Relief Committee representing the German–Jewish oligarchy, the Central Relief Committee organized by East European Jews, and the People's Relief Committee formed by the Socialists), distributing more than $15 million in wartime aid to the Jews of Europe, Turkey, North Africa and Palestine.
32. Bogen, a social worker, was responsible for the distribution of cargo from the *Westward Ho* (a joint gift of the combined U.S. Jewish organizations and the Polish National Department of America, purchased and shipped by the U.S. Food Administration that supervised the ARA), cash for relief purposes, and food and clothing for Polish children. JDC Bulletin #12, AJA Warburg 183; also, Report, Dec. 3, 1919, ibid., 182; Kahn and Rosen, *Activities of the Joint Distribution Committee*, pp. 6–15.

east.[33] The JDC and the ARC, ostensibly working collaboratively under the ARA's umbrella,[34] had entirely different personnel as well as approaches to their humanitarian tasks. Whereas the JDC sought to reinvigorate Jewish life in Poland, the ARC, staffed exclusively by Christians, was bound totally to the political authorities in Warsaw and to the military leaders in the field.[35]

Although forbidden to engage in "political work," these wide-ranging, well-heeled outsiders, clothed in exotic foreign uniforms, were immediately swept up by local issues. Not only did the massive infusion of goods and supplies force down prices and flood eastern Poland with foreign currency[36]; it also raised highly delicate political questions of distribution.[37] The outsiders were drawn into the Polish–Soviet conflict and the fate of their collateral victims. Immediately after the Poles captured Pinsk, aid workers noted the lack of local organization and initiative as well as the mistrust between Poles

33. Taft (ARA) to Col. Olds (ARC), Paris, Apr. 5, 1919, "Typhus Relief in Eastern Europe," Hoover ARA 19.

In early March, the ARC Commission for Poland, led by Lieutenant Colonel John Bailey, a close friend of Paderewski's, arrived in Warsaw with forty-five workers and fifty carloads of medical supplies transported by Hoover's ARA, with $2 million allocated for its headquarters and salaries. ARA, *Annual Report* (June 30, 1919), pp. 199–200; Bicknell, *Red Cross in Europe*, pp. 344–51; Bykofsky, *History of the American National Red Cross*, Vol. 29 (*Foreign Relief in the Post-Armistice Period, 1918–1923*), pp. 44–50.

Originally conceived as a four-month operation, the ARC's mission remained until the end of the Polish–Soviet War in 1921 and was its largest single postwar campaign in Europe.

34. Adler to Warburg, Paris, Apr. 9, 1919, AJA Warburg 183, expressed enthusiasm over this collaboration.

35. Operating in a region inhabited primarily by non-Poles and already served by the JDC, the ARC's personnel were unlikely to sympathize with local Jews. In Maciejow, for example, which Major Wright described as a "dingy settlement of 3,000 Jews," the ARC set up the headquarters of its first two mobile units on the commodious estate of Count Józef Rzyszczewski, who had accompanied the mission. In Pruzana, where headquarters were established on Apr. 16 in a local palace, the ARC set up separate canteens for Jews and Christians. Wright to Bailey, NA ARC 947.11/08.

Earlier, Marshall to Billikopf, Dec. 5, 1918, AJA LM 1588, had deprecated the ARC's capacity to render aid to Polish Jews. Not only was there no Jew in any position of authority (the ARC, despite massive Jewish contributions, rejected any applicant whose ancestors had migrated from Germany), but Marshall insisted that its personnel neither understood nor appreciated "the unique status" of Poland's Jews.

In an interview with the journalist Hermann Bernstein, n.d. [after Aug. 1919], Bernstein papers 766, YIVO, the deputy ARC Commissioner Colonel Taylor deplored Polish political "interference" in the organization and noted its pronounced anti-Jewish attitudes.

36. "How Poland Fights Profiteering," ARA *Bulletin* I (Mar. 17–June 6, 1919) (Paris, 1919), p. 11.

The ARA reported that the arrival of its supplies "brought out from storage considerable quantities of material which had been withheld by speculators for high prices on the assumption that the Allies would not make good their promise to deliver relief supplies." Grove to Hoover, July 3, 1919, p. 10, Hoover ARA 18.

37. According to the agreement between the KNP and the JDC, the *Westward Ho*'s cargo was to have been distributed without distinction of nationality or religion. Initially, the Polish government insisted on assigning "one-half to the Poles and half to the Jews," but later ordered the Jewish half to be given out on a "non-sectarian basis, under the auspices of the ARA and the ARC." Bogen to U.S. Ambassador Hugh Gibson, May 15, 1919, ARA *Bulletin* I (Mar. 17–June 6, 1919), p. 10.

and Jews.[38] It is thus not surprising that the two Americans who happened to be in Pinsk on April 5 issued diametrically opposite reports.

The first, Barnet Zuckerman, one of four representatives of the JDC, was reportedly an ardent Jewish nationalist from the lower East Side of New York City.[39] The first Jewish worker to visit Pinsk, Zuckerman between April 1 and the morning of April 5 met with local leaders to organize the distribution of goods and cash from America.[40] On the night of the 5th, after his arrival in Brest some 170 kilometers away, Zuckerman learned of the shootings from those who had fled. Instead of returning to Pinsk, he raced to Warsaw and alerted his Allied colleagues[41]; Zuckerman also reportedly obtained Grove's permission to inform the Jewish *Sejm* deputies and the Central Zionist organization, which immediately publicized his account of the massacre of innocent civilians.[42]

The second American in Pinsk was Dr. Francis Fronczak, the former health commissioner of the city of Buffalo, New York, who identified himself as a Lieutenant Colonel and medical counselor of the ARC Commission for Poland on an official mission to inspect local hospital and sanitary conditions.[43] More to the point, Fronczak was one of the leaders of the National Polish Department of America, the political organization of 3 million Polish-Americans that had raised enormous relief funds as well as 22,000 soldiers to fight for the liberation of their homeland. Between June 1918 and

38. "At Pinsk alone it required 6 days of continual effort for Col. Wojewodzki, Civil Governor of the Brest Area, Mr. Frankowski, representing the Minister of Approvisation and Mr. Puzyna, representing the American Mission to get the organization underway." Report by Second Lieutenant Maurice Pate, Mar. 26, 1919, Hoover ARA 18; Compare Pate report, Mar. 12, 1919, ibid.; Pate and Col. Nowak reports in ARA *Bulletin* I, pp. 26–9; also note 10.

39. Polk to Ammission Paris, Washington, n.d. [rec'd Apr. 6] 1919, LC White 41, termed Zuckerman a Jewish nationalist and "radical socialist," who was also "honest and reliable . . . pro-Ally and anti-pacifist."

    In his "Report to the Ober Ost," Apr. 25, 1919, JDC "Pinsk," Vol. 224, Zuckerman referred to permission from the "civil authorities to organize relief work in Pinsk" but did not specify *which* civil authorities had allowed him to do so. Compare Foster to Hoover, Apr. 14, 1919, Hoover ARA 18: "He went in and out of town without the Polish authorities knowing of his coming and going."

40. During his four hurried days in Pinsk, Zuckerman had set up a local flour-distribution committee, devised registration forms for all inhabitants, allocated 100,000 marks to Pinsk's charitable organizations, and arranged for a representative to go to Warsaw to retrieve the money. Details in JDC "Pinsk," Vol. 224. Zuckerman to Bogen, Warsaw, Apr. 7, 1919, ibid.; Harriet Lowenstein to JDC, Paris, Apr. 18, ibid.; Rabbi Hurwicz testimony, CZA A127/75.

41. Kimens to Balfour, Warsaw, Apr. 8, 1919, GB FO 608/66; Grove to Hoover, Apr. 10, 1919, Hoover ARA 18.

42. Zuckerman to Warsaw Zionist organization, n.d., CZA Z3/136, to Bogen, Warsaw, Apr. 7, 1919, JDC "Pinsk," Vol. 224. See *Hajnt*, April 8, 1919; *Nowy Dziennik*, Apr. 11, 1919.

43. Several months later, Deputy ARC Commissioner Colonel Taylor accused Fronczak of wearing a bogus officer's insignia, criticized his "political work," and faulted his fabricated report of the events of Apr. 5; Bernstein interview, n.d. [after Aug. 1919], YIVO Bernstein papers 766.

    The ARC's personnel records for Poland do not include Fronczak's name; NA ARC 943.3.

February 1919, Fronczak had occupied a seat on the KNP in Paris and directed the KNP's Department of Public Welfare, ministering to the thousands of Polish soldiers, prisoners of war, and refugees in Allied countries.[44] In March 1919, with the U.S. government's approval, Fronczak had joined the ARC's relief effort in Poland but also continued his political work "under an American cover" and was labeled "very anti-Semitic" by several of his colleagues.[45]

Although not an eyewitness, Fronczak claimed to have heard shots fired at Polish soldiers from the *Bet Am* and heard a confession from a Jewish conspirator. At the military inquiry he swore under oath that "thirty-three [*sic*] communists" had been executed on the night of April 5 "for plotting to seize, disarm, and kill a small outpost . . . on the most Eastern frontier of Poland."[46] From Warsaw, the testimony of this prominent U.S. aid worker went out over the wires as the official story of Pinsk.[47]

44. Fronczak had sailed to Europe in May 1918 with the permission of the State Department; Lansing to Fronczak, Mar. 18, 1918; State Dept. to Fronczak, May 1, 1918; Fronczak to Paderewski, June 10, 1918. AAN KNP Paryż 24.

Although designated a major in the Medical Corps of the AEF, Fronczak's 14-page report to the AEF commander in chief, NA RG 120/260, Box 5886, describing his close relationship with the Red Cross organizations as well as the French and KNP War Ministries, noted a lack of contact with, and supervision by, the U.S. military. He also complained that the report of his battle injury – on June 18, 1918, during an inspection tour of the trenches occupied by the First Regiment of Polish Chasseurs in Champagne, he was hit by an exploding piece of shrapnel – had gone unanswered; ibid.

Despite Jewish protests in the allied countries, after World War I the Polish armed forces continued to exclude Polish Jews.

45. Foster to Coolidge, Apr. 14, 1919, Hoover ARA 18; also Fronczak to Dmowski, Warsaw, Apr. 1, 1919, AAN KNP 27.

After the United States recognized the new Warsaw government, the National Polish Department in the United States and the KNP in Paris urged Hoover to reassign Fronczak to the ARC mission to Poland. Smulski to Wielowieyck, Jan. [?], 1919; Fronczak to Smulski, Jan. 17, 1919; Zamoyski to Sharp, Feb. 6, 1919, AAN KNP 24; KNP to Paderewski, Feb. 19, 1919, AAN KNP 114.

46. In his Apr. 8 report to the military commission, Fronczak claimed that at least one Polish soldier had been shot from the *Bet Am* and that he had watched the Jewish captives marched to the town hall. On hearing more shots, he had raced to the market square, where he found the bodies of thirty-three men, one of whom had cried "plainly" in a "poor Polish," which Fronczak nevertheless claimed to have understood perfectly: "Officer, how foolish we were – I am still living . . . put a bullet into my head." The man was killed with a revolver shot, as were the others who were still alive.

Fronczak made no effort to speak with the victims or to elicit their names. Based on the remarks of a Jew, spoken also in Polish – "Serves them right . . . to try to make an insurrection . . . and kill the Polish soldiers" as well as Luczyński's assurances about the "conspiracy" – he went calmly about his business. The next morning, Fronczak observed the dead bodies still in the same place, awaiting a common burial that afternoon in the Jewish cemetery. He then left for Kobryń, where he discussed the incident with General Listowski, who assured him that everything was "quiet" in Pinsk. Original, undated statement in AAN Paderewski 773; another copy in AAN KNP 161, reprinted in Tomaszewski, "Pińsk," pp. 236–40.

47. Radio transmission from Warsaw, Apr. 8, 1919, recorded in JDC "Pinsk," Vol. 244; *Kurjer Polski*, Apr. 9, 1919.

Fronczak to [Dmowski?], Apr. 9, 1919, AAN KNP 156 (62), denounced Zuckerman's report.

The Polish government treated the news as a major security, political, *and* diplomatic threat and trumpeted the Bolshevik menace behind the lines in the East.[48] However, to stave off domestic and foreign criticism, Piłsudski had ordered the military inquiry. Luczyński, who took responsibility for the incident, acknowledged that he had forgone certain "formalities" in order to avert a Red insurrection.[49] The Polish military's report, based almost entirely on Fronczak's testimony, completely vindicated the local authorities and denounced the victims.[50] Alerted by Polish officials, a sympathetic U.S. journalist assured the U.S. Peace Delegation in Paris that nothing untoward had occurred in Pinsk: "There was no destruction of property or attacking of homes or people, but an orderly execution following upon disregard of military orders by Bolsheviks in the city and their firing upon soldiers."[51]

Zuckermann's charges could not, however, be suppressed.[52] On April 10, Jewish and Socialist *Sejm* deputies, quoting the JDC emissary's account, rejected the war minister's version of an "armed rebellion" in Pinsk and demanded a more thorough investigation.[53] A ten-member parliamentary commission, which included two Jews, went twice to Pinsk.[54] However, because of harassment by the military, factional divisions, and other impediments, the lawmakers' inquiry was buried until the end of the Russo–Polish War, in March 1921.[55]

The ARA, a temporary guest in a beleaguered allied country, was embarrassed by these two conflicting reports.[56] Not only had it failed to muzzle

48. KNP to American Commission to Negotiate Peace, Paris, Apr. 8, 1919, AAN KNP 149.
49. Luczyński claimed that, because the local prison and personnel were inadequate to guard the arrested, he had chosen the "elimination principle." Testimony, Apr. 9, 1919, CZA A127/75.
50. Piłsudski to Listowski, Warsaw, April 7, 1919, in Switalski, "Listy Józefa Piłsudskiego."

    On Apr. 8–9, 1919, Colonel Stefan Strzemieński interrogated Luczyński, Landsberg, and Fronczak as well as a handful of frightened Jews; his report supported Luczyński's "emergency measures" and censured Pinsk's Jewish population for its sympathy with Bolshevism and hostility toward the Polish army and state. CZA A127/75.
51. Bass [Czarnecki] to Ammission Paris, Warsaw, Apr. 9, 1919, LC White 43. However, Grove [Foster] to Ammission Paris, Warsaw, Apr. 9, 1919, ibid., White 41, warned of a "pogrom" announcement based on Zuckerman's report.
52. In Poland there had virtually been no public debate over the Jewish question after Mar. 18, 1919, when the *Sejm* established a fourteen-member study commission to "calm domestic and foreign opinion." Korzec, *Juifs en Pologne*, pp. 99–103.
53. "Texte de l'interpellation adressée le 8 avril 1919 par des députés juifs et la fraction du parti socialiste polonais de la diète polonaise au Ministre-président et au Ministre de la guerre relativement aux événements de Pinsk," AIU France II/D.

    Although War Minister Józef Leśniewski announced that "a special investigating commission" would conduct an inquiry, no report was filed. Tomaszewski, "Pińsk," pp. 229, 231.
54. The commission took testimony from a number of inhabitants, including released prisoners; the second time it was accompanied by journalists.
55. Documentation in the papers of the Zionist deputy, Isaak Grynbaum, CZA A127/75.
56. Foster to Ammission Paris [for Grew], Warsaw, Apr. 9, 1919, LC White 41.

two of its politically ambitious auxiliaries; but the political tensions underlying its aid work had been painfully exposed.[57]

Warsaw's strategy of highlighting the testimony of a U.S. citizen nevertheless forced the Allies into the picture.[58] The British and American members of the IAC sped to Pinsk, where for three full days, April 10–12, 1919, they interrogated civilians but spoke mainly with the commander of the Ninth Polesie Division. No one questioned the fact that only a handful of soldiers had managed to arrest more than a hundred, possibly armed, conspirators. In their reports, the two envoys denied that a pogrom had occurred. They assured their governments that the commanding officer's action had been justified by the "the critical military situation" and that the town was now quiet after the suppression of a Bolshevik uprising.[59]

But the Pinsk episode would not evaporate. After a four-month lull since Lemberg, the news of anti-Jewish violence struck a nerve. The German press challenged their neighbor's capacity to rule non-Poles.[60] British officials were agitated over the shootings, which were reminiscent of German atrocities in Belgium, and contradicted Paderewski's assurances of "exemplary" Polish conduct in the East.[61] Even the U.S. envoy who had journeyed to Pinsk questioned Fronczak's report, admitting that a "contrary opinion based on the same evidence [was] possible," and urged his superiors to

57. Grove to Hoover, Warsaw, Apr. 10, 1919, Hoover ARA 18. Although acknowledging the inadequacies of Poland's relief facilities, Hoover to Grove, Apr. 14, 1919, ibid., urged a "retire[ment] from this entire relief business at the forthcoming harvest."

    Fronczak and Zuckerman, who had met in Warsaw on Mar. 30, 1919 (Bogen to Lucas, Warsaw, May 6, 1919, AJA Warburg 182), both left Poland almost immediately after the Pinsk incident, Adler, Diary, Apr. 27, 1919; MSZ to KNP Paris, Apr. 28, 1919, AAN KNP 156 (23). Fronczak later became Health Commissioner for Erie County, NY.

58. General Grove to American Mission in Paris, Apr. 10, 1919, NA USDS 860c.4016; Bogen to JDC, Apr. 9, 14, 1919, JDC "Pinsk," Vol. 244. Although Fronczak had told Major Taylor of the ARC that he had been a target of the Pinsk conspirators, the ARC apparently shrugged off his warning to depart Poland at once.

59. Kimens to Balfour, Apr. 14, 1919, enclosing report from Major Paris (GB) and Lieutenant Foster (U.S.), GB FO 608 66/447–58; A. C. Coolidge to American Commission to Negotiate Peace (containing Foster reports), NA USDS 184.01102/365.

    In his report, Pralon to FMAE, Warsaw, Apr. 12, 1919, FMAE Z (Pologne: Israélites) 61, the first allied minister to Poland characterized Luczyński as an amiable man ("homme doux") and added two gallic embellishments to the official version of Pinsk, that one of the Jewish victims had sung a "revolutionary hymn" before dying, and another had written "Died for freedom" (*Mort pour la liberté*) on the wall.

    Polish satisfaction with the visit in KNP news bulletins, Warsaw, Apr. 11, 28, AAN KNP 115; MSZ to KNP, Apr. 26, 1919, ibid., MSZ 156/23.

60. "Judenverfolgungen in Pinsk," *Vossische Zeitung*, Apr. 17, 1919.

61. Balfour to Kimens, Paris, Apr. 18, 1919, GB FO 608/66; also Paton minutes, Paris, Apr. 19, 25, GB FO 608/66/502-4; Namier to Headlam-Morley, London, Apr. 17, 23, 25, HM CC 12.

    H. L. Brailsford, a prominent British left-wing journalist who, two weeks before Apr. 5, had been in Pinsk on an aid mission and returned to interview eyewitnesses, wrote, "Polish intolerance is incurable." *The Times* (London), May 23, 1919.

calm the tension between Jews and Poles by issuing an "official American statement."[62] Washington asked for a fuller investigation.[63]

Along came the new Polish offensive in Lithuania and with it more grisly reports over the German and Zionist news wires.[64] On April 17, 1919, Polish troops captured Lida, and on the 19th they reached the outskirts of Vilna. These relatively easy victories were accompanied by Polish attacks on the local, largely Jewish, population, once more suspected as Bolshevik sympathizers acting as spies, snipers, and saboteurs. After three days of street fighting in Vilna, some fifty-four Jews were killed, hundreds taken prisoner and hostage, and numerous homes and synagogues were plundered.[65]

For the western Jews in Paris, whose numbers were suddenly augmented by the arrival of the Americans, the Zionists, and the representatives of the Jewish councils of Eastern Europe, the news from Pinsk, Lida, and Vilna represented a major setback. It not only confirmed the vulnerability of their kin but it also intensified the burden of defending them against Polish charges of treachery and Bolshevism. Moreover, Pinsk underscored the failure of their traditional strategies. Despite months of negotiations, threats, financial cajolery, and negative publicity, the Warsaw government had not yet granted equal rights and protection to the Jews; and the victors had yet to support their cause.[66]

62. Foster to Ammission Paris, Warsaw, Apr. 16, 1919, LC White 41.
63. Phillips to Gibson, Washington, Apr. 25, 1919, NA USDS 860c (Poland), reel 14.
64. The path of transmission went from the German stations in Grodno and Kovno via Königsberg to Berlin, where either the AA released the news over the Wolff Telegraph Bureau (see Bericht von Augenzeugen über die jungsten Geschehnisse in Wilna, Germ. PA AA Abt. III L1287/L348921-23), or the Zionist offices in Berlin alerted their colleagues in Stockholm and Copenhagen. (See, e.g., Zionist Bureau Berlin to Copenhagen, May 4, 7, 14, 16, 1919, CZA Z3/674; Zionist Bureau Berlin to Martin Cohn, Kovno, May 21, 1919, CZA Z3/136; the collection of telegrams regarding Vilna in ibid., Z3/181; Jewish Press Bureau Stockholm to AIU Paris, May 14, 1919, and to Zionist Office London, May 30, 31. AIU France Z/17).

On these "German–Jewish" reports: Grant Smith to State Dept., Copenhagen, May 14, 1919 NA USDS 862.20221/1592, Marling to FO, Copenhagen, May 14, 1919, GB FO 371/3903; Gibson to Ammission Paris, Warsaw, May 18, 1919, NA USDS 860c (Poland), reel 16; Delavaud to FMAE, Stockholm, May 23, 1919, FMAE Z (Pologne) 61.
65. Piłsudski to Paderewski, n.d. [late Apr. 1919], AAN Paderewski 777, insisted that he had "tried to curb the anti-Semitic excesses" but that the civilian Jewish population, which had enjoyed many privileges under the Bolsheviks, had "shot Polish soldiers from windows and roofs and thrown hand grenades."

The Zionists' original casualty figures, emanating from Stockholm, were as high as 2,220 dead, but these were rapidly corrected. Report of the Jewish Press Bureau in Stockholm, May 8, 1919, CAHJP P83/G297. Marling to FO, Copenhagen, May 14, 1919, GB FO 371/3903, transmitted an "amended" report from Zionist headquarters in Berlin reducing the number of casualties; "The Vilna Pogrom," May 28, 1919, GB FO 371/3903, gives fairly accurate detail. Compare Cohen, *Vilna*, pp. 377–8.
66. Wolf, Diary, Apr. 3, 22, 1919.

The expanding trail of Polish violence, which spread to the interior of the country, offered the Jews an opportunity to revive the campaign for minority rights.[67] In a well-orchestrated operation, Jewish leaders and their political allies flooded the peacemakers with telegrams and letters urging them to protect Polish Jews against Polish atrocities.[68] The western press came alive with details of the murders in Pinsk as well as with often-exaggerated reports from Lida and Vilna.[69] And Berlin provided ample publicity as well.[70]

Predictably, the clamor over Pinsk, Lida, and Vilna provoked antagonism in the Allied camp. The right-wing press deprecated the atrocity reports and stood firmly behind Poland's anti-Bolshevik crusade.[71] Western military observers in Poland insisted that these alleged pogroms were "acts of military necessity, not religious hatred."[72] The Allied emissaries in Poland, whose sympathies lay more with the fledgling Piłsudski–Paderewski government than with the endangered Jewish masses, dismissed the inflated atrocity figures.[73]

Most outspoken was U.S. Minister Hugh Gibson, a friend of Hoover's and former ARC worker, who blamed the current uproar on the unsavory link between the Zionists and Berlin.[74] By denying a racial or religious basis

67. Kaplan to Berlin Action Committee, Grodno, Apr. 22, 1919, CZA Z3/136; Motzkin to Sokolow, Paris, Apr. 25, 1919, ibid., A18/32/3.

    Namier memorandum, London, May 28, 1919, GB FO 371/3903, detailed the anti-Jewish incidents in Warsaw and Western Galicia.

68. Motzkin to Sokolow, Paris, Apr. 25, 1919, CZA A18/32/3, urged an appeal to French Foreign Minister Stephen Pichon over Pinsk.

    Central Zionist Organization to FO, London, May 2, 12, 1919, GB FO 371/3903; Edmond de Rothschild to MAE, Paris, May 16, 1919, FMAE Z (Pologne) 61; Bigart and Sée (AIU) to Clemenceau, May 22, 1919, AIU France II D/8; United Washington Jewry, to State Dept, May 5, Zionist Organization of America to State Dept., May 5, 1919, NA USDS 860c (Poland), reel 14.

69. *Manchester Guardian*, May 1, 1919; *New York Tribune*, May 25, *New York Herald*, May 26, 27, 28; *Le Temps*, May 15.

70. *Berliner Tageblatt*, May 7, 1919.

71. "Apocryphal Pogroms," *Morning Post* (London), Apr. 11, 1919; Israel Cohen's rejoinder, Apr. 15, unsigned Polish rejoinder, Apr. 24. On the KNP's ties with this newspaper and also with the *Chicago Tribune*, see memorandum, July 25, 1919, AAN KNP 301 (3).

72. Report by Captain B. Crewdson, Chief British Mission Warsaw, GB FO 371/3903; French intelligence summary, "L'enquête anglo-americaine faite à Pinsk le 11 avril 1919," FMAE Z (Pologne) 61.

73. Howard (Britain's representative on the IAC) to Lloyd George, Apr. 19, 1919, LGP F57/6/1, denied that any pogroms had taken place. Pralon to FMAE, Warsaw, Apr. 12, 1919, FMAE Z (Pologne) 61, termed the Warsaw Jews' protests over Pinsk a "calibrated assault on the Polish government"; the newly named British Minister Percy Wyndham to FO, May 18, 1919, GB FO 371/3903, denied a pogrom in Vilna; and French Consul Duchesne to FMAE, Warsaw, n.d. [June], FMAE Z (Pologne) 61, scored the Jews' "flagrant distortions and exaggerations" about Lida and Vilna.

74. Gibson to State Dept., May 30, 31, 1919, NA USDS 860c (Poland), reel 14; Gibson to Ammission Paris, Warsaw, May 31, LC White 41.

    Colonel House took credit for the president's appointment of Gibson (House, Diary, Apr. 12, 1919), who had originally hoped to be assigned to Prague (Gibson to Lane, Mar. 16, 1919, Yale University, Bliss Lane papers, I/1/4).

for the Poles' behavior and emphasizing the Jews' social, economic, and ideological transgressions, Gibson turned the victims of Pinsk, Lida, and Vilna into an exploitive "other," whose plight could be rectified only by the Jews themselves.[75]

There were also practical reasons for western statesmen to deplore the controversy over Pinsk. Unable either to halt the Polish advance or remove the Bolshevik threat – and still divided over Poland's future – the Allies hesitated to issue more empty protests and threats, to create additional commissions, or to place more pressure on a weak government.[76] Hoover, charged with rescuing millions of needy people in the East, implored Jewish leaders to remove "politics" from their relief work and tone down their campaign against the "existing government" in Poland.[77]

Why did the summary shooting of thirty-four Jews in an obscure town of Belorussia reverberate in Paris and outside? The event was scarcely unanticipated, and the loss of life was small compared with the 31,000 Jews killed in all the pogroms during and after World War I.[78] What happened in Pinsk on April 5, 1919 was not literally a "pogrom" – an organized, officially tolerated or inspired massacre of a minority such as had occurred in Lemberg – but rather a military execution of a small, suspect group of civilians. To be sure, *all* these civilians were Jewish. The entry into the *Bet Am*, the capture of its occupants, and the order to shoot were done precisely because they were Jews, giving the incident its macabre slant.

The misnamed "Pinsk pogrom," a plain, powerful, alliterative phrase, entered history in April 1919.[79] Its importance lay not only in its timing, during the tensest moments of the Paris Peace Conference and the most crucial deliberations over Poland's political future: The reports of Pinsk once more demonstrated the swift transmission of local violence to world notice and the disfiguring process of rumor and prejudice on every level.

75. Gibson to his mother, Mary Gibson, Warsaw, May 29, 1919: "The Jews all over the world have been excited about [Pinsk]. I have never seen a matter concerning which so many versions were issued.... There is no doubt that the Jews were killed; there is also no doubt that their behavior was such as to invite trouble. It was in no sense a religious matter. However, official reports are powerless to quiet the propaganda artists and they are growing stronger and stronger every day. Now they are manufacturing massacres of Jews at all sorts of places, sending cables about the needs of saving the lives of all sorts of Jews who are very much surprised when we ask about them to know that they have been considered in danger." Hoover Institute, Stanford. CA. Hugh Gibson Papers (hereafter Gibson) 36.

76. H. J. Paton minute, May 29, 1919, GB FO 608/67.

77. Conversation with Mr. Herbert Hoover in Paris, Apr. 19, 1919, AJA Schiff 161; also, memorandum of interview with Hoover, May 26, 1919, AJA LM 131.

78. Or, indeed, the Nazi slaughter in Pinsk in 1942.

79. Lewandowski, "History and Myth." During the Communist era, Polish historians treated Pinsk as a minor episode in the war against the Bolsheviks, whereas Jewish and Israeli scholars considered it an important episode of post-World War I Polish anti-Semitism.

The contradictory testimonies by Zuckerman and Fronczak reinforced two powerful myths, of the Poles' incurable anti-Semitism and of the Jews' sympathy with Bolshevism.[80] On a broader level, this murky incident in a distant place, signaling the danger to captive populations, raised the stakes in the debates over borders and placed more pressure on the Poles, the Jews, and the peacemakers.

PADEREWSKI IN PARIS

On the morning of April 6, 1919, immediately after the events in Pinsk, Ignacy Paderewski made his long-delayed appearance in Paris.[81] The two main goals of Poland's premier and foreign minister were to reverse the powers' decision over Danzig and to raise foreign loans.[82] In addition, his assignments included unifying the fractious Polish delegation, gaining political support for Warsaw's ventures in the East, and repairing his country's tarnished image among the peacemakers and the Allied public. During his month-long stay, despite his elegant demeanor, personal connections with Allied leaders, and hard-working entourage of moderate envoys, Paderewski largely failed to achieve these goals.[83]

His first chore was to calm the furor over Pinsk.[84] Facing concerned British and American officials, Paderewski dismissed charges of Polish anti-Semitism and stressed the Jews' culpability. In his meeting with Lloyd George on April 9, the day of a major anti-pogrom demonstration in London, Paderewski defended his countrymen's behavior by recalling the Jews' devious wartime record, "by turns for the Germans, for the Russians,

80. In "Bolshevism and the Jews," *Daily Express*, June 18, 1919, Israel Cohen tried to puncture this "popular, pernicious delusion," promoted by anti-Semites and accepted by those "ignorant of Jewish life," by drawing the connection between the "Bolshevik" accusations and the old blood-ritual libel and also insisting that not only had few Jews turned to Bolshevism but that the Communist movement menaced Jewish survival in Eastern Europe, remarks that drew immediate rebuttals and a major letter-writing debate in the British press.

81. To avoid crossing Germany, the Polish leader had traveled to Paris via Cracow, Vienna, and Zurich, lengthening his journey by several days.

82. Kimens report, Warsaw, Apr. 5, 1919, GB FO 608/71. Also, Paderewski to Piłsudski, Apr. 14, 1919, PIA AGND 55/636.

One of the strongest partisans of a Polish Danzig, Paderewski, on his arrival, learned that the Allies, bowing to German objections, had decided not to assert their rights to the port and transported General Haller's army to Poland by train.

83. Detailed description of the mission, punctuated by an Easter weekend (ca. Apr. 17–21) in Switzerland, in Lundgreen-Nielsen, *Polish Problem*, pp. 267–313.

Zamoyski, *Paderewski*, pp. 186–93, misdates the arrival and departure, describes meetings with Dmowski, Clemenceau, Wilson, Lloyd George, and Balfour, and praises Paderewski for overcoming Poland's material weakness by his political savvy.

84. *Raporty polityczne* (Apr. 9, 1919), AAN Paderewski 776; Piłsudski to Paderewski, Warsaw, Apr. 10, 1919, ibid., KNP 149.

for the Austrians, and very little for Poland herself."[85] In his reply to Hoover, Paderewski termed the Pinsk incident the "just sequel of a most dangerous bolshevist plot" and assured his friend that, although "no difference is being made between the various peoples who form the Polish population," . . .

> It is the duty of the government to safeguard the Nation to the best of its power as well as to see that justice is applied when it becomes necessary.[86]

In dealing with the Jews, the Polish leader deftly widened the rift among their forces in Paris.[87] He won over the anti-nationalists Lucien Wolf and Henry Morgenthau by deploring the events in Pinsk and vowing to lead in the establishment of equal rights and protection for Poland's minorities.[88] On the other hand, he enraged the nationalist group, led by Louis Marshall, by minimizing the atrocities, resisting financial blandishments, and denouncing Jewish claims for special rights.[89]

Paderewski also wielded his political contacts skillfully. In a brilliant ploy, he urged that the Galician-born Lewis Namier, one of Poland's severest critics in London, who had been excluded from the British peace delegation, meet him in Paris to discuss the pogroms and facilitate negotiations with the Jewish delegations.[90] Paderewski's major coup was to propose that the United States appoint an "impartial" commission to investigate the alleged pogroms, a proposal that split the Allies *and* the Jewish leadership and,

85. Lloyd George statement, May 1, 1919, *Council of Four*, Vol. 1, p. 440. Also, Headlam-Morley to Namier, Apr. 9, 1919, Headlam-Morley, *Memoir*, p. 70; Kerr to Zaleski, Apr. 14, 1919, AAN Paderewski 547.
86. Paderewski to Hoover, Paris, Apr. 16, 1919, Hoover ARA 18; earlier, Hoover to Paderewski, Paris, Apr. 12, 1919, ibid.
87. At the same time, his rival Dmowski urged Warsaw to dispatch to Paris a delegation of assimilated and Orthodox Polish Jews to offset the "newest wave of Zionist propaganda." KNP report #30, Warsaw, Apr. 28, 1919, AAN KNP 115.
88. Wolf to presidents of the Joint Foreign Committee, Apr. 23, 1919, YIVO W/M 82; Wolf, Diary, Apr. 23, 1919; LC Morgenthau, Diary, May 6, 1919.
89. Wolf, Diary, Apr. 23, 1919. Paderewski, although declaring his personal opposition to pogroms, admitted that he was powerless to end the strife between Jews and Poles; he also warned that the effort to improve the Jews' lot in Poland "through influence in foreign countries . . [was] foolish and naïve." *American Jewish Yearbook* 21 (1919–1920), 273.
90. The proposal, conveyed by August Zaleski, was kept secret; Headlam-Morley memorandum, Paris, Apr. 22, 1919, GB FO 371/4379, Headlam-Morley to Zaleski, Apr. 25, 1919 HM CC, Box 1, Balfour [Headlam-Morley] to FO, Paris, Apr. 30, 1919, GB FO 371/4379.

    Namier to Headlam-Morley, Apr. 11, 1919, HM CC, Box 12, had called Paderewski a "fantastic liar, if anything worse than Dmowski." Namier to Headlam-Morley, Apr. 14, 1919, ibid., agreed to meet the Polish leader. Account of Namier's Paris mission, May 22, 1919, GB FO 371/3903 and Headlam-Morley, *Memoir*, p. 99, which praised his work as an intermediary, "buzzing about between Poles and Jews."

although it failed to quiet the immediate clamor for minority protection, ultimately produced a split report.[91]

By showing the face of a moderate, liberal Pole, opposed both to Dmowski's anti-Semitism and the Zionists' immoderate demands, Paderewski hoped to still the clamor over Pinsk and block any threats to curtail Poland's independence.[92] However, by placing himself squarely in the western tradition of constitutional guarantees for religious freedom and equal rights, Paderewski also revealed himself a fierce enemy of any form of foreign interference in Poland's internal affairs, almost indistinguishable from his KNP rivals. With no progress in the direct Polish–Jewish negotiations,[93] Paderewski's obduracy against any externally imposed minority arrangement greatly diminished his political effectiveness, particularly because his principal role in Paris was to plead for Poland's territorial demands before the Council of Four.

This task was neither easy nor comfortable for the novice politician. On April 9, before facing Lloyd George over lunch, Paderewski answered a last-minute summons to appear before the Council of Four on the question of Poland's boundaries.[94] Speaking emotionally in the name of Poland's "democratically-elected *Sejm*," comprising "peasants, workers, and a small number of petite bourgeoisie" – a body, in fact, dominated by the right-wing KNP – Paderewski asked for a "complete alliance with the Entente"[95]

91. Paderewski to Hoover, Paris, Apr. 16, 1919, Hoover ARA 18; Lansing to Paderewski, July 2, 1919, AAN Paderewski 774.

    Between July 12 and Sept. 13, 1919, the three-member U.S. commission, personally appointed by Wilson and led by his close political friend, the ardently anti-Zionist Ambassador Henry Morgenthau, visited Pinsk and other places in Poland where atrocities had allegedly taken place. Morgenthau's report found no premeditated plan in Pinsk or elsewhere but noted "widespread anti-Semitic prejudice aggravated by the belief that the Jewish inhabitants were politically hostile to the Polish State." The two other members blamed both sides for the excesses but absolved the government and military authorities from direct responsibility. LC Morgenthau, cont. 29, and ibid., Morgenthau Diary; full text of the reports in *Foreign Relations of the United States, 1919* (Washington, DC: Government Printing Offices, 1920), Vol. 2, pp. 774–800.

    Over Paderewski's strong objections (Wyndham to FO, Warsaw, Aug. 19, 20, Curzon to Samuel, Aug. 30, GB FO 371/3904; "Misja Samuels," Sept. 26, 1919 [Secret], AAN Paderewski 774), Britain sent its own two-member commission, led by Sir Stuart Samuel who was accompanied by Captain Peter Wright. Samuel, who was attacked by the Polish right-wing press (Namier minute, Nov. 20, 1919, GB FO 371/3904), departed on Dec. 6 and Wright on Dec. 18. Their reports, containing different conclusions over the causes and remedies of Polish violence against the Jews, were never published but were turned over to the League: Wright report, Jan. 1920, Samuel report, Mar. 1920, GB FO 371/3904, minutes by Gregory, Apr. 18, 29, 1920, Harmsworth, Apr. 20, 1920, Curzon, May 1, 1920, ibid., 3905.
92. Dmowski had joined Cecil in voting against the Japanese proposal to amend the covenant. Cecil, Diary, Apr. 11, 1919. Compare "The Situation," AAN Paderewski 774.
93. Conducted by Wolf, Marshall, Sokolow, and Polish Jews.
94. Once more, Clemenceau overcame his partners' reluctance to hold more hearings. *Council of Four*, Vol. 1, p. 187.
95. This "alliance," voted unanimously by the Diet, drew immediate protests from the Ukrainians fighting the Poles in Eastern Galicia. Sydorenko to Allies, Paris, Apr. 4, 1919, FMAE PA-AP

as well as for the "territorial guarantees necessary for our existence": Danzig, Lemberg, and Lithuania.[96] Answering objections over his claims to Danzig, he pledged to "treat the Germans well who will reside on Polish territory" without imitating the Reich's heinous practices.[97]

Despite the histrionics and eloquence,[98] the Four were unconvinced. To be sure, Paderewski offered a genteel counterpart to his intractable rival, Roman Dmowski. Also, the council recognized that it held the pianist's political future in its hands. Nevertheless, the prime minister failed to overcome the growing impression of a chaotic Poland, led by militarists and expansionists as well as by last-minute converts to the Entente cause, who daily increased its vulnerability by provoking its neighbors, crying "Bolshevik" or "germanophile" at every turn, and requiring outside intervention to reduce its number of enemies.[99] The Four not only maintained their decisions to establish a free city of Danzig and hold a plebiscite in Marienwerder but also assumed a hard line over Poland's eastern expansion.[100]

The Allies' almost-solid resistance to Paderewski's blandishments and sudden firmness toward Poland derived from a number of external factors.[101] These included Britain's mounting fears of German recalcitrance and its suspicions of French policy in Eastern Europe along with the general burst of optimism that month over Kolchak's advances, which kindled hopes of a restored Russian Empire.[102] The Council of Four, locked in paralyzing disputes over the Saar, Fiume, and Shantung, seized on Poland's high-profile territorial demands as a way of proclaiming its commitment to self-determination.

Of course, the Allies were inconsistent in applying this principle.[103] They violated it egregiously in Europe, transferring territories to friends and

Tardieu 399; also, Howard to Balfour, Mar. 28, Kimens to Balfour, Apr. 3, Paton minute, Apr. 10, GB FO 608/63.

96. Howard to Lloyd George, Apr. 10, 1919, LGP F57/6/1, warned of an "explosive" situation in Poland if Danzig were lost.
97. *Council of Four*, Vol. 1, pp. 200–3.
98. Paderewski had allegedly wept in the course of his presentation; *Council of Four*, Vol. 1, p. 233.
99. Three days later Paderewski made a similar impression on the Polish Commission, where he denied any form of Polish imperialism. France. Ministère des Affaires Étrangères Conférence de la Paix, 1919–20, *Receuil des actes de la conférence* (hereafter *Receuil*), Part I, Vol. 4, pp. 109–13.
100. The only concession Paderewski obtained was the delay of the Allies' formal decision awarding Teschen to Czechoslovakia. Unsigned letter to Ministry of Foreign Affairs, Paris, May 2, 1919, PIA AGND 11/721.
101. Among them were the arrivals of vocal Jews, Lithuanians, and Ukrainians in Paris to plead their cause.
102. Namier to Headlam-Morley, London, Apr. 24, 1919, HM CC, Box 12.
103. Coolidge to Allen Dulles, Mar. 10, 1919, recommended strict ethnic boundaries for the territories of former Austria–Hungary, including Eastern Galicia; but Dulles to Coolidge, Mar. 14 ("strictly confidential") justified breaching self-determination "to favor the friend over the enemy." Seeley Mudd Manuscript Library, Princeton University, Allen W. Dulles papers (hereafter Dulles) 6.

punishing former enemies, for example by prohibiting *Anschluss* between Germany and Austria, establishing nonethnic borders in Czechoslovakia,[104] awarding Memel to Lithuania,[105] and equivocating over such "secondary" regions as Teschen and the Banat.[106] Further afield, Britain, now the reluctant sponsor of the Zionists' national aspirations in Palestine, was prepared to use force to suppress the Arab majority's protests against the Jews and the mandate.[107] But faced with Poland's egregious use of force to bolster its territorial demands, its attacks on pro-Allied (or at least anti-Bolshevik) peoples, and its threats to the integrity of a future Russia, the peacemakers fell back piously on Wilson's frayed principle.

The hardening of the Allies' attitudes toward Poland also revealed some fundamental changes since the opening of the peace conference. Clemenceau, for example, famously reduced his support for the award of Danzig and Marienwerder to Poland in return for the Anglo–American guarantee; also, in accordance with France's traditional policy toward Russia, he was lukewarm toward Warsaw's claims to Lithuania; but the French leader continued to stand firm over Polish control over all of Eastern Galicia.[108] Lloyd George, the fervent opponent of non-Polish annexations, suddenly

104. On Apr. 4, the Council of Four, unanimously refusing any alterations in the Cambon Commission's report, briskly voted to retain the "historic border of Bohemia." House, substituting for the ailing president, ignored the warnings of the major U.S. experts and the protests of the Sudeten Germans as well as Lansing's last-minute appeal to the spirit and letter of Wilson's Fourteen Points (Council of Foreign Ministers, Apr. 1, 1919, FRUS PPC, Vol. 4, pp. 543–7). Lloyd George, despite his recent qualms over an unfair peace, readily accepted a gross violation of self-determination in an area of secondary importance to Great Britain.

    To be sure, the transfer of an additional 330,000 Germans – who had neither been part of the Wilhelmian Reich nor were included among Berlin's current interests – to Czech rule represented a far less explosive compromise than the concessions Warsaw demanded. Beneš had already pledged publicly to respect minority rights; and Clemenceau cleverly sweetened the pill by anticipating future "territorial exchanges" between Bohemia and Germany. *Council of Four*, Vol. 1, pp. 144–5.

    Background in Perman, *Shaping of the Czechoslovak State*, pp. 121–82. Goldstein, *Winning the Peace*, pp. 257–9.

105. On Apr. 18, after a pause for Lloyd George to consult his associates over Memel's ethnic composition, the council voted to assign this German city to the Allied and Associated Powers to be turned over to Lithuania as its "only outlet to the sea." *Council of Four*, Vol. 1, p. 272.

106. *Council of Four*, Vol. 1, pp. 145, 234.

107. See Balfour to Weizmann, Apr. 3, 1919, Weizmann to Balfour, Apr. 9, Balfour to Weizmann, Apr. 21, CZA A264/5.

    Henry Richards and Robert Szold, strictly confidential report from Palestine (via London), May 2, 1919, reported the suppression in Apr. 1919 of two armed, anti-Jewish riots by Palestinian Arabs that was due to "prompt and visible British action," CZA A264/7; Robert Szold to Frankfurter, Apr. 1919, Friedenwald to Frankfurter, May 2, 1919, paint a gloomier picture, ibid., A204/5.

108. "To divide Galicia would benefit the German game," note, Apr. 12, 1919, FMAE Z (Russie) 612; also Mar. 18, Apr. 4, ibid.

    An unsigned memorandum, May 1, 1919, alleged German and Austrian recruits in the Ukrainian army as well as arms supplied by the "Hungarian bolsheviks." FMAE Z (Pologne) 254.

warned his colleagues that putting "too many screws" on the Poles might lead them toward Bolshevism.[109] Wilson, on the other hand, impatient with France and Italy's delusions over "strategic frontiers," bore down on the Poles, whom he termed "our troublesome friends."[110] Threatening to end all American aid to Warsaw, the president demanded the removal of the recently arrived Haller army from Eastern Galicia and a cease-fire with the Ukrainians as well as an immediate armistice conference in Paris.[111] Moreover, after dragging its feet for almost a month, the Polish Commission, almost immediately after Paderewski's arrival, began serious deliberations over Poland's eastern borders.[112]

Piłsudski's Easter-week campaign against Lithuania further weakened Paderewski's position in Paris.[113] Once more, the Poles had violated the Allies' January 24 declaration, and again they had attacked Jews in the battle zone. From Warsaw, Britain's emissary reported threats against the capital's Jews for "not celebrating the liberation of the East."[114] British observers termed the new Polish assault "another Eastern Galicia" disguised as an anti-Bolshevik, anti-German crusade and designed to force the peacemakers' hand.[115]

In fact, the capture of Vilna had merged Poland's internal power struggle with its foreign ambitions. Piłsudski had not only struck a blow at his KNP rivals and compensated the Polish public for the loss of Danzig, but had warned Paris of Warsaw's intention to block the establishment of tiny Baltic succession states.[116] Although the West considered him a "moderate," Piłsudski, with his cloudy wartime record, had now lent his name to his country's expansionist ambitions.[117]

109. On the Vilna question, however, Britain's prime minister was more pro-Polish than his colleagues, considering Lithuania too small to be viable and likely to fall under German influence. Paton minute, Mar. 31, 1919, GB FO 608/68.

110. *Council of Four*, Vol. 1, p. 118.

111. *Council of Four*, Apr. 18, 1919, Vol. 1, p. 271, Apr. 21, 1919, Vol. 1, p. 309. Compare notes, n.d. [Apr. 17–18, 1919, Apr. 28 or 29, 1919], FMAE Z (Pologne) 83.

Haller, who arrived in Poland on Apr. 18, sent out shock waves by announcing his aim to "liberate" Danzig, Teschen, Lithuania, and White Russia as well as Lemberg. *Daily Express*, Apr. 23, 1919; Carr minute, May 4, 1919, GB FO 608/71.

It is likely that Piłsudski welcomed Wilson's restrictions on his KNP military rival. Note, n.d. [early May, 1919], FMAE Z (Pologne) 83.

112. Note sur les frontières orientales de la Pologne, Apr. 24, 1919, FMAE Z (Pologne) 137.

113. Paderewski to Piłsudski, Paris, May 2, 1919, PIA AGND 1/27, offered congratulations on the "recent victories," which made a "great impression here."

114. Kimens report, Warsaw, Apr. 27, 1919, GB FO 608/71.

115. On April 28, Polish troops entered Grodno, chasing out the Germans and alarming British officials. Campbell to Hardinge, Warsaw, Apr. 29, 1919, FO 608/197, Bourdillon, Carr, and Kisch minutes, Paris, May 5, 1919, ibid.

116. Kimens report, Apr. 27, 1919, GB FO 608/71.

117. Born in 1867 in the Vilna province to an impoverished Polish noble family, Piłsudski had studied in Vilna and there began his political career as a Polish Socialist.

On April 22, Piłsudski stirred the pot further. Embracing the idea of a "Polish Austria–Hungary," more modern and liberal, and also evoking the old commonwealth from the fourteenth to the eighteenth century, the general issued a ringing proclamation in Vilna calling for a federal union between Poland and Lithuania[118]; and, in a bow to self-determination, Piłsudski offered national rights to Lithuania's minorities.[119] This rash initiative, designed to impress the peacemakers, infuriated the Polish military, the KNP, and the Polish landowners in the East, threatening to bring down the government and hastening Paderewski's departure from Paris.[120]

Piłsudski's elective war against Lithuania – while Danzig, Teschen, and Lemberg hung in the balance – dismayed Poland's critics and friends alike.[121] The Jews and Lithuanians issued joint protests over Polish atrocities,[122] the French press reprimanded Warsaw, and the normally sympathetic Polish Commission suddenly began examining the Ukrainians' claims to Eastern Galicia with greater attentiveness.[123]

The Council of Four, unready to make final decisions on Russia's future boundaries, rejected Warsaw's efforts to dictate the new frontiers and political order of Eastern Europe. Detecting only minuscule differences among the expansionist programs of Piłsudski, Paderewski, and Dmowski, the council reserved its right to establish Poland's northeastern frontiers and endorsed "minimum" borders based on strict ethnographic criteria.[124] But, as in the

118. Text in Piłsudski, *Pisma zbiorowe*, Vol. 5, pp. 75–6. Internal debate over his federal plan, Romer, *Pamiętnik paryski*, pp. 298–9; diplomatic implications in Piltz to Berthelot, May 3, 1919, FMAE (Lithuanie) 13, Pralon to Pichon, May 4, 1919, ibid.

A critique of Piłsudski's "federalism" in Lewandowski, *Federalizm*, pp. 76–9, 125–8; more positive appraisals in Komarnicki, *Polish Republic*, pp. 450–60; Wandycz, *Soviet–Polish Relations*, pp. 97–100, 118–20.

119. Namier minute, Apr. 17, 1919, GB FO 371/3903, deprecated Piłsudski's politically motivated gesture, giving Jews and Poles extensive privileges in the Grand Duchy that the Jews were denied in Poland.

Earlier, Howard to Balfour, Apr. 2, 1919, GB FO 608/66, had noted Piłsudski's hope that "at least 150,000 Lithuanian Jews," whom he deemed irrevocably anti-Polish, "would return to Russia."

120. On the *Sejm* debate over Piłsudski's unilateral declaration, Lossoski, *Stosunki polsko–litewskie w latach*, p. 79.

121. Gibson to Ammission Paris and State Dept., Warsaw, May 9, 1919, LC White 42, quoting Piłsudski's defense of his Lithuanian campaign as well as his depiction of the Poles as "children, playing with a toy republic, a toy army, a toy Diet; like children they carry the play to extremes while the novelty lasts." NA USDS 860c, reel 16.

122. See remarks by Lithuanian representative Woldemaras to Polish subcommission, Apr. 23, 1919, FMAE PA-AP Tardieu 361.

123. Unsigned [Michał Moscicki] to Piłsudski, Paris, May 6, 1919, PIA AGND 1/751, warned that a *Sejm* resolution to annex Vilna "might cost us Lwów."

124. Report on Lithuania, Apr. 18, 1919, minutes by Carr, Apr. 29, Hardinge, Crowe, Apr. 30, Bourdillon, May 6, GB FO 608/198.

Article 87 of the Versailles Treaty stipulated that the Allied and Associated Powers would establish Poland's eastern boundaries with the former Russian Empire.

tangled case of Eastern Galicia, the peacemakers lacked the political and military power to enforce their will.

Paderewski, after joining Dmowski at the ceremonial presentation of the peace terms to the German delegation,[125] departed Paris on May 9 and arrived in Warsaw two days later. During his arduous mission, he had produced a mixed impression among Poland's Anglo–American critics and the Jewish leaders.[126] Almost everyone acknowledged Paderewski's sincerity, eloquence, and patriotism, but almost everyone recognized his political inexperience and vulnerability. After failing to enlist political and military support for Poland's ventures in the East or quash the efforts to establish written guarantees of minority rights in Poland, Paderewski achieved a few gains: the dispatch of a British ambassador as a first step in establishing a more amicable relationship,[127] words of personal praise from the Council of Four,[128] and, conditional on his remaining in office, pledges of support from influential British Jews[129] and of renewed U.S. civilian aid for his embattled homeland.[130]

THE JEWISH DELEGATIONS

On the nights of April 5 and 6, 1919, coinciding with the events in Pinsk and Paderewski's arrival, the Jewish representatives in Paris conducted a heated debate over the shape of their program before the peace conference. With the arrival of the Zionists and the Americans, enormous political and

125. *Council of Four* (Apr. 28, 1919), Vol. 1, p. 395, on the last-minute decision to admit Poland and Czechoslovakia to the proceedings. House, Diary, May 7, noted Paderewski's "prima donna" late arrival at the plenary session.
126. From the accounts of his local Zionist informants, the German consul general in Zurich claimed that during the prime minister's stay Poland's stature had greatly diminished. Plehn to AA, May 21, 1919, Germ. PA AA K695/K181914.
127. Lloyd George to Piłsudski, Paris, May 2, 1919, LGP F57/5/1.
128. Miller, *Diary* 1, Apr. 23, 1919.
129. Wasilewski note, Paris, May 22, 1919, AAN Papers of Leon Wasilewski (hereafter ALW) 30, recording his conversation with Sir Stuart Samuel, a prominent Jewish anti-nationalist, who was president of the Board of Deputies of British Jews and cohead of the Joint Foreign Committee as well as an influential MP and partner in the powerful banking firm of Samuel, Montague and Company and who later led an investigatory mission to Poland.
130. In Gibson to House, Warsaw, Apr. 29, 1919, Yale University, House Papers, 8/37, the new ambassador wrote, "There seems to be a great deal of apprehension that unless Paderewski brings back something definite to show that he has been successful in his mission, there will be an attempt to oust him and his government either by the radicals or by the Dmowski group, or possibly by both" and urged a considerable loan; similar advice in Dolbeare to Lord, Warsaw, Apr. 29, 1919, NA USDS 186.3111/153.

    Wilson on May 17 told the Council of Four, "Paderewski had a letter in his possession from Mr. Hoover, informing him that aid would only be extended to Poland so long as he was in charge." FRUS PPC, Vol. 5, p. 676.

personal gaps were fully exposed. Meeting in the shadows of the suspended Palestine decision, the exclusion of an equal-rights clause from the League Covenant, and the impending treaties with Germany and Austria, the Jewish delegations brought their separate hopes and fears as well as their conflicting definitions of the term "minority rights."

Unlike Zionism, which, despite partisan variations, had the shared goal of a Jewish homeland in Palestine, the cause of minority rights in Eastern Europe was split into nationalists and anti-nationalists. The former, drawn largely from the ranks of the Zionist movement, claimed that the Jews were not merely a religious group but one of the many successor nations of the former German, Russian, Austro–Hungarian, and Turkish Empires, entitled not only to their religion, language, and communal facilities but also to political and even international representation.[131] The latter, championed by assimilated Jews throughout the world, denied a special Jewish peoplehood, except in Palestine, and restricted their program to religious freedom and equal rights and protection for all citizens.[132]

This ideological split was reflected in the two groups' organization and tactics. After the collapse of the Central Powers, Zionist groups in the United States and Eastern Europe had held elections and convened congresses that had drawn up pro-Palestine and nationalist resolutions and chosen delegations to represent the Jewish masses before the peace conference. On the other hand, the elite-led, anti-nationalist groups from the three principal victor powers, the AIU, the Joint Foreign Committee, and the AJC, with no popular mandate, expected to play the role of their forbears at the Congress of Berlin, when politically well-connected westerners had represented the entire Jewish world and the East Europeans had bowed to their leadership. War and revolutions, however, had irretrievably transformed this relationship.

Trouble began at once. Nahum Sokolow, the Zionists' designated representative of Polish Jewry, had protested the *Alliance*'s efforts to accredit and control all foreign delegations. Sokolow demanded equal representation for East European Jews and denounced any démarche to the peace conference until his colleagues arrived from London.[133] Wolf and the *Alliance*'s leaders,

131. Memorandum of the Zionist Organization on the Jewish question in Poland, Jan. 19, 1919, CZA A405/75; on Mar. 30, Dr. Osias Thon, a newly elected *Sejm* deputy, claimed this program represented the will of 400,000 Polish-Jewish voters; ibid., A405/77/IB.

132. There was a significant range in this group, with the French the strictest in opposing any form of national rights, the Americans accepting proportional representation, and the British willing to endorse a modified form of national autonomy.

133. Sokolow to Wolf, Paris, Feb. 14, 1919, Réunion, 18 Feb. 1919, Marks to Bigart, Feb. 19, 1919, AIU France II/D; Bigart to Sokolow, Paris, Mar. 3, 1919, CZA A405/75; Sokolow to Bigart, Mar. 4, 1919, AIU France II/D.

bristling over Sokolow's pretensions and delaying tactics, had proceeded on their own, conducting talks with East European leaders.[134] Without consulting the populations involved, they had dispatched a protest against Romania's latest naturalization formula[135]; and the *Alliance* had urged its government to promote an autonomous regime for the Jews of Salonika.[136]

Most important, on February 21, 1919, the Joint Foreign Committee (JFC) and the *Alliance*, alarmed over the appointment of the territorial commissions, had sent separate memorials to the peace conference secretariat. Calling for a special commission to take up the question of Jewish rights in each of the new states, the leaders of British and French Jewry listed the essentials of minority protection, including a novel clause promoted by the *Alliance* that enabled aggrieved individuals or groups to appeal to the new League of Nations.[137]

Wolf, sharing credit with the AIU, boasted of being "the first to champion before the Peace Conference of 1919 the cause of Civil and Religious Liberty."[138] However, his grand gesture proved politically barren, buried in the papers of the secretariat. Even had Wolf found a patron among the delegations, no plenary session was held between February 14 and April 28 in which to propose a special minority commission. Once the Council of Four took charge of the peace conference, there was even less likelihood that any serious consideration would be given to the problem of Jewish and minority rights. Given the strained debates in the League Commission and the huge agenda before them, Allied statesman had dropped this taboo subject.

Things changed suddenly in mid-March. Arriving in large numbers from London, the Zionists came armed with their ambitious resolutions, which included extensive autonomy as well as national and international representation.[139] The leader of this campaign, its ideologue and organizer, was the feisty, fifty-two-year-old Zionist from Kiev, Dr. Leo Motzkin.[140] Motzkin, who had served in the Copenhagen office during World War I, had also

134. Astruc note, Feb. 6, 1919, AIU Romania VII/C52; Wolf, Diary, Feb. 26, Mar. 5, 1919; "Report on the Polish Negotiations in Paris, Mar. 10, 1919," BDBJ, Joint Foreign Committee of British Jews (hereafter JFC) minute book, Mar. 11, 1919.

135. Wolf, Report, Mar. 10, 1919, YIVO W/M 82; text of the AIU and JFC notes on the draft law, CZA A405/75.

136. Sée to Pichon, Paris, Feb. 12, 1919, AIU France II/D7. Critical summary of Wolf and the *Alliance*'s separate actions in De Haas to Brandeis, Feb. 17, 21, 1919, CZA A404/93.

137. Wolf, Diary, Feb. 15, 21, 1919; Texts, *Alliance Israélite Universelle, La question juive*, p. 44; *Report of the Delegation of Jews of the British Empire*, pp. 77–80.

138. Wolf, Report, London, Mar. 10, 1919, BDBJ, JFC minute book. Wolf gave copies of his memorial to *The Times* (London) and the *Daily Mail*.

139. Communique of the Zionist Bureau, London, Mar. 4, 1919, GB FO 371 W44/1051; De Haas to political committee, Paris, Mar. 4, 11, 1919, CZA A404/94.

140. Motzkin, "Les revendications nationaux des juifs," pp. 7–25.

Photograph 6.1. *Comité des délégations juives* at the Paris Peace Conference (reproduced with the permission of the American Jewish Archives, Cincinnati, OH).

spent two years in the United States on a futile mission of uniting American Jewry behind the claim for national rights in Eastern Europe.[141]

Leading the delegation of the American Jewish Congress was the distinguished arbitrator, Judge Julian Mack, whom the East Europeans immediately recognized as their leader.[142] Between March 20 and 25, 1919, Jewish nationalists from a dozen countries founded the *Comité des délégations juives auprès de la Conférence de la Paix*, set up their headquarters in the Zionist offices in Paris, and prepared to represent the interests of "nine million Jews" before the Great Powers[143]; they also invited the French and British Jewish leaders to join them.[144]

141. On Motzkin, see Zionist Office Copenhagen to Zionist Office Berlin, Feb. 9, 1919, CZA Z3/670; also Motzkin, "Leo Motzkin and Minority Rights," with thanks to the author.

142. The fifty-three-year-old Mack, who served on the U.S. Circuit Court of Appeals, had mediated issues during the war ranging from labor disputes to judgments over conscientious objectors. Barnard, *The Forging of an American Jew*, pp. 244–54; also Mack, *Americanism and Zionism*, pp. 3–15.

143. Motzkin to Stephen Wise, Paris, Mar. 21, 1919, CZA A243/6/85; minutes of meeting, Mar. 25, 1919, ibid., A405/77; Thon to Grynbaum, Paris, Apr. 1, 1919, ibid., A27/315; Sokolow, Diary, Mar. 18–30, 1919, ibid., A16/556.

The *Comité*'s records are in CZA Z6; its founding members included representatives from the United States (Mack, Marshall, Syrkin, Barondess, Richards,) Canada, and Great Britain (Bentwich), France (Braunstein), Ukraine (Motzkin, Ussischkin) Italy (Colombo), Czechoslovakia (Rosoff, Bergmann), Poland (Sokolow, Levite, Thon, Braude), Eastern Galicia (Reich, Tenenbaum, Ringel), Palestine (Jellin, Wilkansky, Eisenberg), Soviet Russia (Schechter, Rossoff), Romania (Filderman, Niemirower, Rosenstein), and the Zionist movement (Weizmann).

144. Mack to Wolf, Mar. 24, 1919, CZA A405/75; Richards to Wise, Mar. 22, 1919, Wise 74–60.

The prospect of an international, and possibly permanent, Jewish organization raised hopes and alarms. The Jewish press cheered the new group[145]; and Berlin trumpeted it as a major challenge to the peace conference.[146] On the other hand, the traditionalists raged over the coup of the "extremists." The *Alliance*'s leaders fumed over their deliberate exclusion. Wolf, deploring the "choice between ostracism and helpless association in the making of which we had not even been consulted,"[147] tried to overshadow the *Comité* by organizing the "Moderates."[148]

The man Wolf most counted on was Louis Marshall, the vice chair of the American Jewish Congress's delegation, who finally reached Paris on March 27, 1919. Accompanied by Cyrus Adler, one of American Jewry's intellectual luminaries who represented the conservative AJC, Marshall brought his substantial legal skills, vigor, and ambition as well as his considerable financial resources.[149] Irritated with Mack, suspicious of Wolf, deferential toward the French, but also sympathetic toward the East Europeans, Louis Marshall, a veteran "champion of justice," was determined to bring the minorities' case before the peace conference.[150]

Marshall's first task was to convince the two sides to meet together. At the Zionist headquarters, before a distrustful throng, Marshall warned that only the Jewish citizens of the victor powers could hope to exert influence at the

145. See, e.g., *Jüdische Rundschau*, Apr. 25, 1919; *Jewish Chronicle*, May 2, 1919.

146. See Jüdische-Politisches Nachrichten, Apr. 4, 12, 1919, Germ. PA AA L1284/L330699, L330708-10. The *Berliner Tageblatt*, Apr. 16, 1919, reported the German peace delegation's support of the *Comité*'s program; also *Hamburger Fremdenblatt*, Apr. 19, 1919.

147. Wolf, Diary, Mar. 24, 1919: "When it is borne in mind that this impertinent document has been addressed to the leading Franco-Jewish Society in the city where it is at home, by an improvised assembly of foreign Jews who have only been in the country for a few weeks, it will be realised with what feeling it [the invitation] has been received."

148. Wolf, Diary, Mar. 25, 1919. Wolf's strategy included mobilizing a small group of East European anti-nationalists, who had formed the *Comité d'israélites originaires de l'Europe orientale*. See Haffkine to Sokolow, Mar. 20, 1919, CZA A18/38.

Critique of the Zionists' "disorganization and inaction" by a Lithuanian Jew, Dr. S. Rosenbaum, quoted in Berger to Jacobson, Berlin, Mar. 26, 1919, CZA L6/610.

149. Marshall not only paid his own expenses but added $5,000 from his own funds to the *Comité*'s treasury to keep "a roof over their heads" and "pay for [their] incompetent clerical forces" and also secured a "further contribution" from the AJC; Marshall to Zuckerman, New York, June 6, 1923, AJC LM [Peace Conference], 1919–23.

On Adler, the president of Dropsie College in Philadelphia, who was also an ardent Wilsonian and supporter of the League, see Naomi W. Cohen, "Introduction," in Adler, *Selected Letters*, pp. xxv–xlii; Adler to Warburg, Jan. 3, to Louis Marshall, Jan. 20, 27, 1919, ibid., 356–60. Also, Adler and Marshall to Warburg, Apr. 9, 1919, AJA Warburg 183, on their other function in Paris as emissaries of the JDC helping to organize relief to Eastern Europe.

150. Adler, Diary, Mar. 26, describes his and Marshall's briefing by the anti-nationalists in London; ibid., Mar. 27, 28, on their initial reception in Paris. Compare De Haas to Frankfurter, London, Mar. 26, 1919, CZA A405/76; Wolf, Diary, Mar. 30, 1919.

Four years later, Marshall insisted that "None of our European friends had the slightest idea of what to do or how to do anything." Marshall to Zuckerman, June 6, 1923, AJC LM PC 1919–1923.

Photograph 6.2. Louis Marshall and Cyrus Adler (from the Photograph Collection of the American Jewish Committee and reproduced with the permission of the American Jewish Committee, New York).

peace conference and also that their opposition could prove dangerous.[151] In the hall of the Paris *Consistoire*, he advised the outraged anti-nationalists to bolster their political influence by forming a union with their beleaguered East European brethren.[152] Neither side, however, was prepared to compromise. In fiery rhetoric, Sokolow, Thon, and Ussischkin rejected the right of Crémieux's moribund successors to issue their feeble memorials

151. Meeting, Mar. 28, 1919, CZA A405/77.

152. Minutes of meetings in the Salle du Consistoire, Mar. 30, 31, 1919, CZA A405/77/IB; réunion du 29 mars, AIU France II/D; réunion du 30 mars, ibid.; Adler, Diary, Mar. 29, 31; Wolf, Diary, Mar. 30.

in the name of the entire Jewish people.[153] Eugène Sée, refusing to bury the *Alliance* in a morass of hotheads, insisted that "the business of the peace conference is to create a sovereign state for Poland, not for the Jews."[154]

After sundown on April 5, on the very night of the Pinsk shootings, all the major Jewish representatives to the Paris Peace Conference convened at the *Consistoire* under the chairmanship of Louis Marshall, who stressed the urgency of their mission and pleaded for unity.[155] Neither side appeared anxious to bury their grievances. Behind the struggle over national rights lay the battle for control over the destiny of the Jewish people. Sée's glorification of his *patrie-liberateur* and Wolf's endorsement of the conference's "great cause" of reviving Poland were pitted against Ussischkin and Thon's claims that the Jews were one people of whom they represented the greatest number. Close to midnight on the second day, Sokolow, who had opened on a conciliatory note, suddenly demanded a rupture ("*divorçons! divorçons! divorçons!*"). Chairman Marshall, still hoping to keep union alive, appointed a Committee of Seven.[156]

As expected, this committee, chaired by Marshall and comprising the leading nationalists and anti-nationalists, failed to find a common formula on which to unite.[157] In an ironic reversal of their political histories as well as their positions on Palestine, the western Jews insisted on exclusive privileges and the East European Zionists clamored for "democracy." When the inevitable break occurred, Marshall elicited their pledges to act cooperatively where possible and where not, to abstain from obstructing the other side's initiatives. Although neither side fully complied, Marshall had paved the way for an at least more superficially harmonious Jewish diplomacy.[158]

Following the April 5–6 debacle, the *Comité*, with its peripatetic membership ranging between thirty to fifty delegates, redoubled its efforts to assert its authority.[159] The *Comité*'s small staff churned out press reports and

153. Minutes of meeting, Mar. 28, 1919, CZA A405/77/IB.

154. Minutes of meeting, Mar. 31, 1919, CZA A405/77/IB; Adler, Diary, Mar. 31.

155. Forty-five delegates attended the session, which lasted from 8:30 P.M. until midnight and continued on Sunday, Apr. 6, from 8:00 P.M. to 1 A.M. Minutes, Apr. 5–6, 1919, CZA A405/77/1B; also Adler, Diary, Apr. 5, 6; Report of [British] Delegation on its visit to Paris, Apr. 3–13, YIVO W/M 82.

156. Minutes, Apr. 5,6, CZA A405/77/1B; Marshall to Warburg, n.d. [Apr. 9] 1919, AJA Warburg 183, described the tempestuous proceedings, conducted in English, French, Hebrew, and "camouflaged Yiddish," and thus requiring tedious translation.

157. The members were three main anti-nationalists, Wolf, Bigart and Adler on the one side and three nationalists, Sokolow, Ussischkin, and Thon on the other.

See Marshall to his children, Paris, Apr. 7, 1919, AJA LM 82; Marshall to Warburg, Apr. 9, 1919, ibid., Warburg 183; Adler to Gracie Adler, Apr. 8, 1919; Adler, *Selected Letters*, Vol. 1, p. 365.

158. Richards to Edlin, Paris, Apr. 12, 1919, AJA Schiff 161.

159. Motzkin to Hermann, Paris, Apr. 18, 1919, CZA Z4/1791/I, Levite to Grynbaum, Apr. 19, 1919, ibid., A127/315.

pamphlets,[160] and its emissaries met with Czech and Polish leaders.[161] On April 13, despite the local prohibition on demonstrations, it invited sympathetic French lawmakers, intellectuals, and human-rights advocates to a mass meeting endorsing the Jews' demands for Palestine and national rights.[162]

Moreover, a large and unwieldy subcommittee, chaired by Leo Motzkin, had already begun drafting the *Comité*'s official memorandum to the peace conference. In addition to claiming national rights, this document also surpassed the two western memorials by including *all* the minorities of Eastern Europe, including ex-enemies. Marshall, the group's most influential member, convinced his colleagues to drop their most radical proposal, that the world's 15 million Jews be granted representation in the new League of Nations.[163]

The *Comité* continued in its dilatory, argumentative ways.[164] Although the memorandum was virtually completed by the end of April and adopted by the membership two weeks later, it was not officially submitted until May 10 or published until early July.[165] In the meantime, the dominant trio of Sokolow, Mack, and, especially, Marshall, the men with the official connections, who spoke the languages of the Big Three, slipped briskly into the role of the *Comité*'s spokesmen.[166] Watching their numbers, resources, and influence diminish, the hard-core nationalists challenged Marshall by

160. At an executive committee meeting, Marshall opposed the establishment of a press office, insisting, "the less the press knows, the better for us," Minutes, Apr. 25, 1919, CZA A126/52/2.
161. Negotiations with the Czech delegation, memorandum, Apr. 7, 1919, CZA A405/77/IB; and with the KNP and more moderate Poles: Levite to Grynbaum, Apr. 19, 1919, ibid., A127/315 (Grabski "not unfriendly with our national demands"), Sokolow, Diary, Apr. 27, 29, 30, ibid., A18/556; Thon to Grynbaum, Apr. 29, 1919, ibid., A127/315 ("negotiations with Polish delegation in full swing.").
162. Janowsky, *Jews and Minority Rights*, p. 330.
163. It also dropped the claim for a Jewish share of war indemnities, but retained damages for pogrom victims, dropped the demand for a department of Jewish affairs, a minority legislature and administrative organs, and Jewish control of emigration, but retained minority management of educational, religious, and social institutions, and proportional representation in local and national elections. Thon to Grynbaum, Paris, Apr. 1, 1919, CZA A127/315; Janowsky, *Jews and Minority Rights*, pp. 311–14.
164. And grew increasingly distant from its "anxious" colleagues in London and Copenhagen; see Hermann to Motzkin, London, May 1, 1919, CZA Z4/2077; also Richards to Wise, Apr. 10, 12, 1919, Wise, 74–60.

    Accusation of the *Comité*'s "ineptitude" in Adler to Marshall, June 20, 1919, AJC LM PC 1919–1923.
165. *Comité des délégations juives* to their Excellencies, the President and the Members of the Peace Conference, May 10, 1919, Miller, *Diary*, Doc. 889; *L'Univers Israélite*, July 4, 1919.

    From these dates, Marshall later claimed that the minority treaty was essentially drafted *before* the *Comité*'s document was submitted. Marshall to Zuckermann, June 6, 1923, AJC LM PC, 1919–1923; the nationalists' version, supported by Janowsky, *Jews and Minority Rights*, p. 314, termed the delay "of no consequence."
166. Janowsky, *Jews and Minority Rights*, p. 319.

calling for a permanent bureau of the *Comité* at the seat of the League of Nations to protect Jewish rights.[167]

The "oligarchs" also refused to quit. Wolf continued to negotiate with the East European delegations, only to discover that their sole aim was to enlist the Jews' support in their territorial disputes.[168] Wolf maintained his links with the *Alliance* and also with Henry Morgenthau, a prominent anti-Zionist close to Wilson.[169] In his meetings with British officials Wolf took every opportunity to deprecate the *Comité* and reinforce Whitehall's anti-nationalist bias.[170] Playing a double game, the JFC secretary went along with Marshall's "union" efforts but also leaked tales to his government contacts of the disarray within the Committee of Seven.[171] Once the rift occurred, Wolf maintained contact with Sokolow and Marshall,[172] but also used his role as the emissary of well-connected British Jews and his government's unofficial counselor on Jewish questions to enshrine his proposals in the peace treaty.[173]

The news from Pinsk, which arrived in Paris by mid-April, widened the chasm between the Jewish delegations. One side used the image of victimization to bolster its claims for national rights; the other, denying the permanence of Polish anti-Semitism, warned against creating a permanent wedge between Poles and Jews.[174] Behind their rhetoric, both sides were responding to their different fears. The nationalists sought protection against a palpable threat to Jewish life in Eastern Europe, the anti-nationalists against a threat to their hard-won status and influence in the western democracies.

The stakes for both sides were extremely high. On April 25, the KNP's *Kurjer Poznański* denounced the "28th" state represented in Paris, world

167. Minutes of Executive Committee meeting, Apr. 25, 1919, CZA A126/52/2.

168. This included the moderate Count Władysław Skrzyński, Poland's deputy foreign minister, who asked for an endorsement of Poland's claims to Danzig, Teschen, and Lemberg and its "conservative treatment" of Poland's agrarian question and doubted Wolf's denial of the western Jews' power to shape international questions or their inclination to interfere in Poland's internal affairs. Wolf, Diary, Apr. 14; also Apr. 10, 11, 17, 1919.

Compare Wolf's Note on The Polish-Jewish Question for Paderewski, Apr. 23, 1919, (copy in AIU France II/D; Wolf, Diary, Apr. 25, 1919), outlining specific constitutional clauses.

169. Record of conversation, Paris, Apr. 24, 1919, LC Morgenthau, cont. 44.

170. Wolf, Diary, Apr. 3, 1919.

171. Speaking with Headlam-Morley, Wolf reportedly said "There was nothing to choose between Dmovski and Ussishkin [*sic*]." Wolf, Diary, Apr. 14, 1919.

172. "When can we meet? I have a great deal to tell you." Wolf to Marshall, Apr. 21, 1919, AJA LM 52; Wolf, Diary, Apr. 25, 1919.

173. Wolf, Diary, Apr. 19, 1919. In his May 1, 1919 report in London, Wolf assured the JFC that "no damage" had resulted from the split with the nationalists and that he was still confident that "the demands in his Feb. 21 memorial would be granted." BDBJ, JFC minute book.

174. Wolf, record of conversation [with Morgenthau, Bigart, and Isaac Landman], Apr. 24, 1919, YIVO W/M 82.

Jewry, with its elaborate network of finance and politics, that was demanding its own state in Poland. But earlier, Cyrus Adler had cautioned the Eastern Jews that "Whatever they did would affect 3,300,000 Jews in America, 3/4 of whom had come in the last 40 years."[175]

SEEKING A SOLUTION

Amid April's tumult, and with only a few cards to play, Louis Marshall developed a careful strategy for promoting the program of the American Jewish Congress. Contrary to the *Comité*'s aspirations, he had accepted, and perhaps even welcomed, the fact that the Jews were unlikely to receive a second hearing before the peacemakers. None of the harried Council of Four seemed inclined to introduce them publicly and thereby antagonize the Poles and Romanians as well as their own more moderate Jewish groups.[176]

Second, Marshall recognized that only his government had the power and impetus to insert minority guarantees into the peace treaty. To achieve this goal, he was prepared to deploy his renowned persistence as well as political assets. Although lacking the warm ties of a Wise or a Morgenthau to the president, Marshall – unlike his rivals Wolf and Sokolow, who had no direct access to the chief British and French policy makers – was able to meet with four of the five members of the U.S. peace delegation: Lansing, House, Tasker Bliss, and Henry White.[177]

Fresh from the battle among the Europeans, the disparate trio of Marshall, Mack, and Adler proceeded to seek a formula that united Wilsonianism and minority protection. Buoyed by "two remarkable Seders" for the Jewish Passover conducted at the Hotel Crillon under the auspices of the AEF, Marshall termed this "a critical moment in Jewish history."[178] Brandishing the *Comité*'s name and numbers, the seeming rout of the traditionalists, and the mounting press campaign over Pinsk, the Americans began their campaign.

175. Minutes, Apr. 6, 1919, CZA A405/77/1B.
176. Executive Committee Meeting, Apr. 25, 1919, CZA A126/52/2.
177. Marshall also conducted talks with Kazimierz Dłuski, Piłsudski's brother-in-law and chief emissary in Paris, Ciechanowski report, Apr. 10, 1919, AAN Paderewski 452, as well as with Émile Vandervelde, the Belgian Socialist leader, letter to children, Apr. 18, 1919, AJA LM 82.

On Feb. 12 Lucien Wolf had appealed for Balfour's endorsement of his memorial and was rebuffed two days later; GB FO 800/215. Nahum Sokolow later claimed to have "appealed, at various times, to Clemenceau, Pichon, Lloyd George, Balfour, Sonnino, Nitti, and others" on behalf of the *Comité*'s program, but there is no record of any meetings with these statesmen; Janowsky, *Jews and Minority Rights*, p. 348.

178. Adler, Diary, Apr. 14–16, 1919; Marshall to his children, Paris, Apr. 18, 1919, AJA LM 82; Rosenthal, "Louis Marshall."

Indeed, Marshall's operation came at a highly propitious time and reached a receptive audience. The long-deferred minorities issue, raised several times during the deliberations of the Council of Ten, the territorial commissions, and the Council of Four, was now ripe for serious consideration. Jules Cambon, who headed the Polish, Czech, and Romanian Commissions, had recently advised his government to take steps to secure minority protection in order to deflect German chicanery.[179] British officials, who had always expected to include minority-protection clauses in the territorial treaties,[180] also called for specific material obligations to be imposed on all the new and enlarged states.[181]

For the Americans, the most influential argument came from A. C. Coolidge, the Vienna-based head of an Allied fact-finding mission, who recognized the strong link between minority rights and a durable peace in Eastern Europe. In a special memorandum for Wilson, the Harvard historian urged the president to go beyond the "vaguely benevolent assurances" of the interested governments, issue a binding declaration to the "new national minorities . . . which now seem so gravely menaced," and assign to the new League of Nations the task of elaborating "the details."[182]

Several outside sources reinforced the groundswell for international minority protection. The German delegation, which was due to arrive at the end of April, was expected to exploit Pinsk to plead against large territorial cessions to Poland.[183] Western liberal opinion, aroused by the pogrom reports, was urging its leaders to "do something." In late April the Socialist International, meeting in Amsterdam, declared its support for equal rights

179. Cambon letter, Apr. 3, 1919, FMAE Z (Pologne) 61. In his earlier reports, however, to the Council of Four concerning Poland's western border, Cambon had minimized the problem of German minorities, stressing the "recentness" of their arrival and likelihood of their migration. FRUS PPC, Vol. 4, pp. 413, 415, 452, 454.

180. Unsigned minute, Apr. 16, 1919, GB FO 608/66, indicates a conference between Mack and Major Webster; Headlam-Morley to Koppel, Apr. 21, 1919, described the "Good Friday" deliberations, Headlam-Morley, *Memoir*, p. 85; Hurst memo, Apr. 25, 1919, GB FO 608/61, noted that Malkin was drafting a treaty "between the five Allied and Associate Powers and Poland."

181. Smith (Permanent Secretary of the British Board of Trade) note, Apr. 28, 1919, FRUS PPC, Vol. 5, pp. 399–401, made the important distinction between the treatment of Germany's cessions in the West and the East, proposing the inclusion of Alsace-Lorraine and Schleswig in the treaty's transit and insurance clauses but imposing a long list of other provisions only on the New States.

182. "Rights of National Minorities," Apr. 1, 1919, conveyed by Grew to all six members of the U.S. delegation. Copies in LC White 41; Miller, *Diary*, Vol. 7, pp. 366–7.

183. Item III, ("The Protection of National Minorities,") in "Instructions given to the German Plenipotentiaries of Peace," Apr. 1919, in Luckau, *The German Delegation*, p. 202.

On Apr. 3, 1919, the Zionist artist and wartime activist for Jewish rights in Poland, Hermann Struck, was named a member of the German delegation. Germ. PA AA L1288/L351457; *Deutsche Allgemeine Zeitung*, Apr. 3, 1919. The French noted the "large" number of Jews in the German delegation: "Délégation allemande," n.d. [May 1919], FMAE PA-AP Tardieu 28.

and protection for the Jews and for all minorities.[184] And that month America's most distinguished female peace activists stopped in Paris to plead for the rights of all people to justice and self-determination.[185]

At first Marshall's efforts to enlist the U.S. delegation's support fell on deaf ears. Although White was sympathetic, Lansing firmly rejected a special minorities commission and suggested another memorial to the secretariat.[186] Even after the events in Pinsk, Marshall's friend Hoover adamantly opposed the Jews' claim to national rights in Poland.[187]

Mack and Marshall found their patron in the person of Edward M. House. Formerly the president's closest advisor, House had filled in for his chief on the Council of Four and the League Commission, but had suddenly alienated the president and other U.S. officials with his pretensions and political misjudgment.[188] House, who had already involved himself in the question of Palestine,[189] received Mack and Marshall on April 15, 1919 and was apparently receptive to their project. His backstairs approach matched Marshall's proclivities. Counseling against an audience with the busy president or seeking publicity for their program, the Texas "colonel" urged the Jews to devise a definite plan that he would present to Wilson.[190]

184. Text in *Vorwärts*, Apr. 30, 1919; background in CZA A307/7/261.

185. Among them were Jane Addams, Emily Balch, Alice Hamilton, Florence Kelley, Lucia Ames Mead, Rose Nichols, Leslie Post, and Jeanette Rankin. Church Terrell, Memorandum, Apr. 22, 1919, Harvard University Law School Library, Manley O. Hudson papers (hereafter Hudson).

Addams returned to Paris in late May after the founding of the Women's International League for Peace and Freedom in Zurich. (Of the league's 200 original members, 27 were Germans who could not travel to Paris. Alonso, *Peace as a Women's Issue*, pp. 81–2). Addams to Hudson, Paris, May 31, 1919, Hudson.

186. Mack to Lansing, Mar. 28, 1919, requesting a meeting with Lansing, House, Bliss, and White, CZA A405/195; Richards to Schiff, Paris, Apr. 3, 1919, AJA Schiff 161, describing it. Adler, Diary, Apr. 3, 4, 9, 10, 11, 1919, reflects a growing sense of crisis.

187. Hoover was on friendly terms with Adler and Marshall because of the close ties between the ARA and the JDC. See "Conference [Marshall and Adler] with Mr. Hoover in Paris," Apr. 19, 1919, AJA Schiff 161; Adler to Racie Adler, Apr. 18, 1919, Adler, *Selected Letters*, Vol. 1, pp. 367–8; Adler, Diary, Apr. 19, 1919; also, Wentling, "The Engineer and the *Shtadlanim*."

188. A recent study, Esposito, "Imagined Power," termed House a "vain, self-deluding personality" with a shallow knowledge of world affairs who exaggerated his importance and misled Wilson.

Floto, "Colonel House in Paris: The Fate of a Presidential Adviser," reviews the literature; Walworth, "Woodrow Wilson and Edward M. House," introduces new documentation; Rossini, "'Alleati per caso,'" analyzes one of the primary causes of the dispute. Neither George and George, *Woodrow Wilson and Colonel House*, nor Floto, *Colonel House in Paris: A Study of American Foreign Policy*, discusses House's role in the Jewish question.

189. House, Diary, Jan. 3, 6 [agreeing to present Weizmann to the president, but warning against "discussing Zionism"], Feb. 4 [talks with Flexner and de Haas, and also with Faisal]; de Haas to Brandeis [n.d.], CZA A404/93.

190. House, Diary, Apr. 15, 1919: "I advised how to proceed and promised when they had done their part I would try to do the rest." Marshall to House, Aide-Mémoire, Paris, Apr. 15, 1919, AJA LM 52, written on *Comité* letterhead.

The Intimate Papers of Colonel House, ed. Charles Seymour, Vol. 4, Apr. 15, 1919, omits the Jews' visit; on that day House also met Orlando in a futile effort to mediate the Fiume question.

In a move of considerable importance, House placed two of his protégés, Manley Hudson and David Hunter Miller, at Mack's and Marshall's disposal. This disparate team, both lawyers, had worked together on the Inquiry and now represented their government on one of the peace conference commissions.[191] The junior, thirty-three-year-old Hudson, a Missouri-born peace activist and ardent internationalist, was sympathetic to the Jewish cause.[192] Currently awaiting an appointment to the Harvard Law School with the endorsements of Felix Frankfurter and Judge Mack, Hudson was also a close friend of Jacob Billikopf, the Vilna-born social worker who had brilliantly directed the American Jewish Relief Committee's fundraising campaign, was a champion of Jewish rights in Poland and was about to become Louis Marshall's son-in-law.[193]

The more senior Miller, a New York attorney whose partner, Gordon Auchincloss, happened to be House's son-in-law and secretary, was less supportive of the Jews' agenda. Appointed by House as one of the Inquiry's five officers and recognized mainly for his skills in drafting and critiquing legal briefs, Miller had accompanied House's mission to the Supreme War Council in Paris.[194] At the peace conference, serving as the U.S. delegation's chief legal advisor, Miller had played a major role in drafting the League Covenant and was now consumed with its final details.[195] Although he was on cordial terms with Frankfurter and Mack,[196] Miller favored a highly restrictive warrant for minority rights. Like Coolidge and Wilson, he maintained that the function of international protection was not to promote special privileges

191. Miller was the U.S. delegate on the Commission on International Regime of Ports, Waterways, and Railways, with Hudson as his alternate and, in late May, his replacement. Gelfand, *The Inquiry*, p. 320.

192. Hudson (1886–1960), who later had a distinguished career as a Harvard professor, member of the Permanent Court of International Justice, and editor of the statutes of international law (*Biographical Dictionary of Internationalists*, ed. Warren F. Kuehl [Westport, CT: Greenwood, 1983], pp. 361–4) had written papers for the Inquiry advocating League protection of minority rights; Gelfand, *The Inquiry*, pp. 308–10.

193. On Hudson's anxious wait for the Harvard appointment (Hudson was on leave from his position at the University of Missouri Law School), Hudson, Diary, entries #332, May 3, 1919, #336, May 5 #352, May 10, #353, May 11, #354, #363, May 15, #421, June 6, Frankfurter to Hudson, June 6, 1919, Hudson.

On Billikopf, #388, May 23, 1918, #392, May 24, #398, May 27, #462, June 17, #465, June 18, #466, June 19, #467, June 20, also Billikopf to Hudson, Warsaw, May 20, 1919, "Billi" to Hudson, Paris, undated [June 1919], ibid.

Hudson, who was also acquainted with the U.S. peace leaders Jane Addams, Emily Balch, and Lucia Ames Mead, attempted to provide introductions for them in Paris; e.g., memorandum, Apr. 22, 1919; Gannett to Hudson, Apr. 24, Addams to Hudson, May 31, ibid.

194. Gelfand, "David Hunter Miller."

195. Miller, *Diary*, Apr. 22, 1919, recorded House's order to work exclusively on the League and "not be bothered with anything else."

196. Miller, *Diary*, Vol. 1 (Apr. 2, 1919), p. 217, records his discussion with Mack over the failed League amendment and the Coolidge memorandum.

but to break the chain of local violence, threats of irredentism, and calls for outside interference – revived by the events in Pinsk– that would destabilize the entire peace settlement.[197]

Following a pause for their observance of the Jewish Passover, Mack and Marshall met the two U.S. legal counselors.[198] On April 20 they presented draft treaty clauses that combined the American Jewish Congress's "Bill of Rights," the *Comité*'s call for specific national rights, and the *Alliance* and JFC proposals for League protection.[199] Miller made major changes. He diluted the Jewish articles on citizenship, rewrote the language-rights, equal-protection, and nondiscrimination clauses, proposed an alternative to proportional representation, deleted all references to "national" rights, dropped the Sabbath clause, and removed any minority appeal to the League of Nations.[200]

Mack and Marshall also maintained a vigorous diplomatic schedule. On House's advice, they communicated their draft to the French and British delegations, which gave encouraging replies.[201] They also kept the *Comité* apprised of the outlines of their work[202] and were able to convince the leading anti-nationalists, Bigart and Rothschild, Wolf and Samuel, Morgenthau and Straus, to refrain from any "hostile actions."[203]

Just under the deadline, on the eve of the Germans' arrival, Miller sent his draft to House for the president to submit to the Council of Four. Although

197. Miller, *Covenant*, Vol. 1, pp. 52–3; Miller, *Diary*, Vol. 7, p. 368.

On Miller's activities at the Paris Peace Conference, see Posey, "David Hunter Miller as an Informal Diplomat,"; idem, "David Hunter Miller and the Far Eastern Question"; idem, "David Hunter Miller and the Polish Minorities Treaty."

198. Miller, *Diary*, Vol. 1 (Apr. 19, 1919).

199. Miller, *Diary*, Doc. 888; also, Adler, Diary, Apr. 20, 1919.

200. Memorandum, Apr. 25, 1919, Miller, *Diary*, Document 916; Vol. 1, pp. 264–5, 267, 270, 281; Vol. 9, pp. 7–8, 182–5.

201. Memorandum remis par le juge Mack, Apr. 25, 1919, FMAE PA-AP Tardieu 166. Cambon to Mack, n.d. [Apr. 26? 1919], CZA A405/75, indicated the Quai d'Orsay's "contacts" with *Comité* delegates Reich and Lemberg, and authorized the "confidential mission" of its Jewish expert, Sylvain Lévi, to "acquaint himself with your work."

Mack to Hurst, n.d. [Apr. 21?], GB FO 608/61; Hurst to Mack, Paris, Apr. 25, 1919, CZA A405/77/1B, assured Mack that he had passed the papers on to the British delegation, which was "fully alive of the necessity of securing protection for the rights of minorities in Poland."

On the other hand, E. H. Carr memorandum, Apr. 25, 1919, GB FO 608/61, complained, "Everyone is working in the dark on this question, and no one knows how far the Americans who are having strong Jewish influences brought to bear on them may press the question of Jewish rights."

202. Executive Committee Meeting (Mack, Marshall, Sokolow, Ussischkin, Thon, Reich, Ringel, Motzkin), Apr. 25, 1919, CZA A126/52/2.

203. Adler, Diary, Apr. 22, 23, 24, 26, 27, 29, 1919. Wolf's return to London (Wolf, Diary, Apr. 27–May 3) undoubtedly eased the Americans' task during the crucial last days.

much watered down, it included a bold statement recognizing the Jewish population of Poland as a "national minority."[204]

On a raw, snowy, late-April day in Paris, Marshall's démarche reached its critical moment; his was now the primary Jewish initiative on the peace conference's agenda. The anti-nationalist American Jews had failed to settle things by reinstating a clause in the League Covenant [205]; and the Zionists had been stymied by the delayed departure of the commission to investigate conditions in Palestine.[206]

Marshall was both apprehensive and hopeful.[207] He had dissuaded Mack from enlisting the support of Clemenceau and Lloyd George.[208] And thus the initiative to place the fate of millions of Jews and other minorities in Eastern Europe into the peace treaty rested with the leader who had dominated the council in April but had been silent over their concerns.

April 1919 was a momentous month. In Eastern Europe new wars had erupted, producing more material destruction and thousands of civilian and military casualties as well as adding to the region's hunger, poverty, and disease. In Paris the peacemakers, hastening to conclude their labors, grew testy and slipshod, provoking their weaker partners, encouraging German resistance, and alarming the world's liberal opinion.[209]

204. Miller to House, Apr. 29, 1919, Yale University, House papers, 81/2721. That day, House wrote to the president (ibid., Box 121a/4298): "The Jews and some other nationalities [?] have been working on this question for several weeks, and under the direction and advice of Miller they have formulated the clauses which I herewith enclose and which they are counting upon your assistance to get into the Treaty."

    Miller's text, in FRUS PPC, Vol. 5, pp. 397–8, recommended similar clauses in the Austrian treaty for Czechoslovakia and Romania.

205. See Morgenthau to Cecil, Apr. 9, 16, 1919, LC Morgenthau, cont. 9; Morgenthau, Report on Reintroduction of Religious Liberty Clause in the Constitution of the League of Nations, Apr. 18, 1919, ibid., roll 44; Adler, Diary, Apr. 19, 1919.

    Japan, which had never intended to tie its racial-equality proposal with, or to block, a religious-liberty clause, at the plenary meeting on Apr. 28, 1919, withheld another appeal in return for concessions over Shantung. *Council of Four*, Vol. 1, pp. 396–7, 399–408.

206. On Apr. 30, 1919, Felix Frankfurter pleaded futilely to House to remove Palestine (where Arab unrest was now rampant) from the purview of the King–Crane Commission, CZA A264/30.

207. Marshall to his children, #13, Apr. 28, 1919 ("We are staking all on one card – a rather risky proceeding, but then what is one to do when there are no others?"); also #14, May 1, #15, May 3, AJA LM 82.

208. Mack, despite House's assurances, remained anxious over their strategy; Miller, *Diary*, Vol. 1, Apr. 30, 1919. House, Diary, Apr. 30, 1919. Adler, Diary, Apr. 30, 1919, recorded White's complaint of the tendency to throw everything on the president.

209. On Apr. 26, 1919, Oswald G. Villard wrote in *The Nation*, "The struggle is ending in Paris with bitterness and hatred as well as with colossal hypocrisy"; in *The Nation*, May 24, 1919, Witter Bynner's poem, "Shantung," chided the peacemakers' ethnocentrism: "In the west you free Jerusalem/But in the east you sell/T'ai Shan, the Holy Mountain."

The news of the shootings in Pinsk on April 5 had exposed the dark side of state building in Eastern Europe. Poland's denial of a pogrom clashed with the widespread publicity and with the Jews' fervent appeals for the Allies' protection. The peacemakers, swayed less by anti-Germanism and anti-Bolshevism than by practical concerns, moved slowly and reluctantly toward accepting responsibility for those about to be denied self-determination.

Also that month, a major event occurred in the history of minority rights, when the cautious leadership of western Jewish intercessors was challenged by the radical voices of the affected. The East European nationalist delegates, appearing for the first time at an international peace conference, created a new organization, held public meetings, and drafted a radical document demanding group rights and protection for *all* minorities in Eastern Europe.

In the historiography of the Paris Peace Conference, the influence of the "American Jews" has invariably been cited as the essential ingredient in the origin of the minority treaties after World War I.[210] Like all simple explanations, this one overlooks the multiple personal, political, and diplomatic factors that brought Mack's and Marshall's enterprise to fruition. The *Comité*'s coup over western Jewry plus Marshall's assumption of its leadership, combined with the Pinsk controversy and the Allies' foreboding over Poland and their other clients' behavior, plus the broader questions of minority persecution and outside intervention left unsolved by the League's founding and revived by Coolidge's memorandum – all worked together to thrust the protection of minority rights onto the peacemakers' brimming agenda in May 1919. The results were not at all what Marshall anticipated.

210. In a Feb. 1921 speech, Manley Hudson credited the American Jews and Wilson for rescuing the minority question from oblivion; House and Seymour, *What Really Happened at Paris*, p. 473. Neither of the older works devoted to minority treaties discusses the importance of Pinsk: Janowsky, *The Jews and Minority Rights*, stresses the role of the *Comité*; and Viefhaus, *Die Minderheitenfrage*, credits the *Comité*, Mack and Marshall, Coolidge, and Wilson. Among more recent works, Levene, *War, Jews, and the New Europe*, pp. 292–4, does mention Pinsk but without evaluating its international significance, whereas Sharp, "Britain and the Protection of Minorities," omits the pogroms. The assertion that a "powerful, well-organized 'Jewish Lobby'" at the Paris Peace Conference was behind Poland's minority treaty has been revived in Stachura, "National Identity and the Ethnic Minorities," pp. 68–70, which also misidentifies the committee of Jewish delegations as "representing American, British, and French Jewry" and continues ". . . personalities such as Lucien Wolf (1857–1930) and Leon Reich (1875–1929) made known in no uncertain terms their opposition to the establishment of an independent Poland, arguing essentially that the Poles were incorrigibly anti-Semitic and incapable, therefore, of treating the Jewish minority with fairness and respect," an inaccurate assessment of both.

7

May

"America is supplying us food, clothes, shoes, linen-ware and other materials on long credit."[1]

"Straight orders should be given to Paderewski telling Polish commanders to prevent the pogroms. If this were honestly done, pogroms would cease."[2]

"I was a good deal pestered by the Jews who, however, turned out to be quite reasonable."[3]

"We felt satisfied that the president is fully informed not only in general but in the conditions of the Jews in Eastern Europe; that he is giving ample consideration to the subject; that it has his profound sympathy and . . . his fullest support."[4]

May 1919 was a month of realism and difficult decisions. The arrival of the Germans altered the character of the Paris Peace Conference. Facing the victors were the proud and feared representatives of the German Reich on whom they intended to impose major territorial cessions, economic burdens, and military reductions, whose signature was required for bringing the long deliberations to a close and allowing the weary and exasperated British and American leaders to go home.

Not unexpectedly, German Foreign Minister Count Brockdorff-Rantzau, in his May 7 response to the Allied terms, presented the face of a defiant Reich.[5] A day later in Berlin, President Friedrich Ebert and

1. Summary of Paderewski's May 22 speech to the *Sejm*, in Gibson to Ammission, Warsaw, May 23, 1919, LC White 42.
2. Unsigned minute, to #10923, May 25, 1919, GB FO 608/66.
3. Headlam-Morley, *Memoir*, p. 117.
4. Adler, Diary, May 26, 1919.
5. Text of his speech, delivered seated, and translated sentence by sentence into French and English, in Luckau, *German Delegation*, pp. 220–3; also Scheidemann, *Ulrich Graf Brockdorff-Rantzau*, pp. 462–73. Clemenceau, "red with anger," restrained himself from interruptions and "Lloyd George laughed." Simons to his wife, Versailles, May 10, 1919; Luckau, *German Delegation*, p. 119; also, Wilson was

the cabinet declared the peace conditions "unbearable," "unrealizable," and contrary to the armistice agreement six months earlier.[6] Before the National Assembly in Weimar on May 12, Socialist Chancellor Philipp Scheidemann singled out Wilson for betraying his own Fourteen Points.[7] Mass protests, many of them government sponsored, spread throughout Germany, with only the Communists opposing a rejection of the treaty.[8]

The Allies were in a quandary. Unwilling to negotiate with their former foe, they demanded written responses from the Germans. This cumbersome procedure, which lasted until the end of May, not only raised tempers, workloads, and expense, but also poisoned the political atmosphere. Germany's well-prepared assault on the treaty terms intensified the Allies' fears of a Reich attack on Poland, of its collusion with the Bolsheviks, or of a major revisionist campaign linked to the mounting atrocity reports from the East. The peacemakers also recognized the risk of driving the Scheidemann government to resign and of its replacement with even more intransigent leaders.

Under pressure from their own irate and impatient public opinion, the Big Three responded strongly to the German presence in Paris. Lloyd George, underscoring Scheidemann's "contempt for the Poles,"[9] launched his own critique of the proposed eastern boundaries of Germany. Wilson, although resentful of the German attacks on himself, acknowledged the clamor against an "unjust peace."[10] Clemenceau, scolded daily by the left- and the right-wing press, resisted surrendering any fruit of France's hard-won victory except the Entente itself.[11]

After May 1, 1919 the minority question became a part of the Allies' deliberations. The council appointed a new committee, adopted its recommendations, and agreed to impose supplementary treaties on all the new and enlarged states of Eastern Europe. After three months of delay, these important decisions were made rapidly and erratically against the backdrop of tumultuous events in Eastern Europe: the continuation of pogroms, a new Polish offensive in Eastern Galicia, and the looming struggle for control over

greatly annoyed. Walworth, *Wilson and His Peacemakers*, pp. 392–3, provides a colorful description of the May 7 "ceremony."

6. Schulze *Akten der Reichskanzlei*, pp. 303–6; *Deutscher Geschichtskalender*, pp. 489–90.
7. Germany, *Verhandlungen des Reichstags, Stenographische Berichte*, Vol. 327, p. 1084.
8. Schwabe, *Woodrow Wilson*, pp. 333–7.
9. *Council of Four*, May 13, 1919, Vol. 2, pp. 49–50.
10. For example, Walter Lippmann, "Mr. Wilson and His Promises," *The New Republic* (May 24, 1919), 104–5, and, privately, "I can't see peace in this document." Lippmann to R. S. Baker, May 15, 1919, LC R.S. Baker papers (hereafter Baker).
11. See statements to *Council of Four* (June 2, 1919), Vol. 2, pp. 272–4; also, Duroselle, *Clemenceau*, pp. 758–66.

Upper Silesia. At the same time, the Jewish emissaries in Paris, partaking in their first experience of twentieth-century Great-Power politics, dimly perceived their roles.

THE COMMITTEE ON NEW STATES

On the afternoon of the first of May, the center of Paris exploded in violence. With stores, restaurants, and hotels closed and all public transportation shut down, a huge throng attempting to hold a mass demonstration in the Place de la Concorde was halted by French police, firemen, soldiers, and cavalry, and there were numerous casualties.[12]

That morning, with the deadline for the final treaty terms with Germany two days off, Wilson dropped his own small bombshell at a meeting of the Big Three.[13] After expressing his concern over the Jews' condition in Eastern Europe, the president revived his League proposal, recommending the insertion of two brief clauses in the German and Austrian treaties guaranteeing religious tolerance to the populations of the new states of Poland and Czechoslovakia:

1. The State of... covenants and agrees that it will accord to all racial or national minorities within its jurisdiction exactly the same treatment and security, alike in law and in fact, that is accorded the racial or national majority of its people.
2. The State of... covenants and agrees that it will not prohibit or interfere with the free exercise of any creed, religion, or belief whose practices are not inconsistent with public order or public morals, and that no person within its jurisdiction shall be molested in life, liberty or the pursuit of happiness by reason of his adherence to any such creed, religion, or belief.[14]

Lloyd George, chiming in, proposed similar articles for all the mandates.[15]

Wilson also disclosed the existence of the Miller document, "drafted after consultation with the representatives of the minorities"; but he immediately criticized the proposal for a "sort of autonomy." Lloyd George termed as "dangerous" the "claim of the Jews" for "a kind of state within a state." And when the president announced that his draft "would probably be sufficient," Clemenceau readily agreed.[16]

12. Report, #324, May 1, 1919, Hudson; Louis Marshall to his children, #14, described it as a "most peculiar day." AJA LM 82.
13. Italy did not return to the council until May 7; and the Japanese were only occasionally invited to participate.
14. FRUS PPC, Vol. 5, p. 393. Wilson himself drafted the text.
15. FRUS PPC, Vol. 5, p. 393; *Council of Four*, Vol. 1, p. 439. Lloyd George's response indicates that Wilson's initiative probably came as no surprise; it was also an acknowledgment of Britain's sensitivity over its role in the League Commission debate.
16. *Council of Four*, Vol. 1, pp. 439–40.

Photograph 7.1. Sir James Headlam-Morley (from Headlam-Morley, *Memoir*, p. ii)

Wilson's hope for a quick, simple solution stumbled when Lloyd George added more conditions. The British premier insisted that Poland and Czechoslovakia, before their formal recognition in the treaties, not only assume international obligations to protect their racial and religious minorities but also adhere to existing transit, postal, telegraph, industrial, property, and copyright conventions. The council adopted Wilson's proposal that a committee composed of Miller, Headlam-Morley, and a French representative meet "immediately" to frame the appropriate articles for the German treaty.[17]

This slapdash assignment produced unforeseen results. Instead of being an advocate, Wilson had revealed his inclination to bury minority rights in two anodyne, unenforceable treaty clauses. Clemenceau had concurred. But Lloyd George's initiative had rescued the minorities of Poland, Czechoslovakia, and ultimately the rest of Eastern Europe from the perfunctory treatment meted out by the Congress of Berlin.[18]

17. FRUS PPC, Vol. 5, p. 395.
18. Sharp, "Britain and the Protection of Minorities."

The next day, when the committee assembled, the Britons easily buried Wilson's project. Miller, unpleasantly surprised by his appointment,[19] was no match for his more numerous and better-prepared British colleagues.[20] Before a French representative could even appear, Headlam-Morley and company had overwhelmed Miller with the enormity of their task. After long deliberations, the Briton and the American agreed to propose "separate treaties negotiated [*sic*] between the Five Allied and Associated Powers on the one hand and the New States . . . on the other" that would cover not only economic and other obligations but also the protection of minorities. They also recommended the insertion of a clause in the German treaty establishing the binding nature of these supplementary agreements.[21]

Even without French and British legal advisors or adequate documentation, the committee also drew up several momentous proposals. The first was to have a special Polish treaty ready for signature at the same time as the German treaty, which granted official recognition and bound the new state "against her Allies." The second was to impose similar conditions on Czechoslovakia. And the third was to include in each treaty specific conditions of citizenship and public law pertaining to the rights and protection of minorities.[22]

On May 3, 1919 the Big Three, beset with the Italian crisis as well as last-minute details for the presentation to the Germans four days hence, deliberated hurriedly over the committee's recommendations. Without much debate, the council adopted the clause, drafted largely by Headlam-Morley, which linked the German with the new Polish treaty.[23]

The peacemakers undoubtedly recognized the extraordinary path they had embarked upon. However narrow their definition of minority rights,[24]

19. As was House who, when briefed on May 2, warned his protégé that "he did not want to offend the Poles as he thought more of the Poles than he did of the Jews." Miller, *Diary*, Vol. 1, May 2, 1919.

    Miller, expecting an imminent departure to Washington to brief the U.S. Senate on the German treaty and the League of Nations, that day had to cancel his trip to Verdun and the western front; ibid., May 2, 1919.
20. Headlam-Morley to Hankey, May 2, 1919, disparaged Miller for "tak[ing] in their crude form certain Jewish suggestions which we have had before us here for several days and have been trying to persuade the Jews to withdraw"; Headlam-Morley, *Memoir*, p. 92; Miller, *Diary*, Vol. 1, May 2, 1919; Hudson, #330, #331, May 2, 3, 1919. Miller came alone to the first meeting; Headlam-Morley was accompanied by E. H. Carr and several economic experts.
21. FRUS PPC, Vol. 5, pp. 440–4; also in Miller, *Diary*, Document #915.
22. Committee meeting, May 2, 1919, GB FO 604/50.
23. The text of what, ultimately became Article 93 of the peace treaty; FRUS PPC, Vol. 5, p. 440.

    Different details of the brief, fifteen-minute, council discussion reported in FRUS PPC, Vol. 5, pp. 439–40, *Council of Four*, Vol. 1, p. 472, Miller, *Diary*, Vol. 1, May 3, 1919, and Headlam-Morley, *Memoir*, pp. 114–15.
24. Although there is nothing specific in the records, Miller stated "that the sentiment was entirely against creating any communities such as the Jews want." Miller, *Diary*, Vol. 1, May 3, 1919.

both Wilson and Lloyd George understood that they were about to demand far more from Poland than the Powers had extracted from Romania in 1878, and that Clemenceau had acquiesced. Lloyd George, ever ready to exert pressure on the Poles, flaunted the Allies' power to gain their signature: "So long as we have not told them that we are resolved to hold out against the protests of the Germans concerning Danzig and Silesia, the Poles are in our hands."[25] Consciously or not, the Powers had also embarked on the unprecedented procedure of removing minority protection from the territorial treaties, thereby highlighting the burdens to be imposed upon their clients.[26]

Thus charged, and given a tight deadline, the newly anointed "Committee on New States" was born.[27] Chaired by Philippe Berthelot, the director of political and commercial affairs at the Quai d'Orsay, the committee's almost-daily deliberations in the French Foreign Ministry took place briskly between its members' other committee assignments.[28] Like the other expert commissions, the Committee on New States applied the rule of secrecy inconsistently, keeping the press and Allied delegations ignorant of its existence while allowing discreet soundings of interested parties.[29]

At its first formal meeting on May 5 the committee flexed its muscle. It voted to proceed first with a model Polish treaty but also to extend its purview beyond Czechoslovakia to the other East European states receiving substantial minorities, including the "new" Serb–Croat–Slovene state as well as the established governments of Greece and Romania, which were about to receive vast territories. Moreover, unlike the territorial commissions, the committee expected to hear testimony from both Jews *and* Poles but decided to defer this prospect until reaching "its own conclusions."[30]

25. *Council of Four*, Vol. 1, p. 473. This statement is absent from the record in FRUS PPC, Vol. 5, pp. 439–40.
26. A decade later, Headlam-Morley rued this decision to replace a traditional diplomatic transaction attached to territorial transfers with what the Poles and other minority states would mistakenly label an "invidious and unfair" form of discrimination. "Memorandum respecting the Minorities Treaties," May 17, 1929, GB FO 371/14125.
27. The name was, of course, significant; it was not a "minorities" but a new states committee.
28. The main sources of its secret deliberations are in France, Ministère des Affaires Étrangères, Conférence de la paix, 1919–1920, *Receuil des actes de la conférence*, Part VII, Procès Verbaux des Commissions, Section B, Commission des Nouveaux États (hereafter *Receuil* PV), Headlam-Morley's minutes, and the notes of the Italian member, De Martino, who joined on May 12, supplemented by the diaries of Headlam-Morley, Miller, and Hudson.
29. Around May 18, Headlam-Morley (Headlam-Morley, *Memoir*, p. 117) boasted that the Allies' foreign secretaries were unaware of the committee's existence and that even the Poles – who had enjoyed exceptional access to the Cambon Commission – "have not found out who are the members." Hudson #410, June 2, 1919, confirmed that Lansing was uninformed of committee's existence.
30. *Receuil*, PV No. 2, May 5, 1919; second meeting, May 5, GB FO 604/150; also Miller, *Diary*, Vol. 1, May 5, 1919; FRUS PPC, Vol. 5, p. 483.

Like the council's, the committee's decisions were laced with inconsistency. There were no discussions of binding Germany, still considered a great power and one about to be stripped of almost all its non-German population, with minority clauses[31]; but on May 13, with virtually no debate, the committee voted to insert minority articles in the peace treaties with Austria, Hungary, and Bulgaria, states with only small minority populations but considerable numbers of kin people outside.[32] Much later, in discussing Italy's acquisition of former Habsburg territory that contained numerous Slavs and Germans, the committee used Rome's status as a great power as well as their colleague's personal assurances to justify Italy's exemption from the new minorities system.[33]

From the outset, Headlam-Morley, with his bevy of trained assistants, took command. Backed by the generally silent and preoccupied Berthelot and, belatedly, by the obliging Italian spokesman Giacomo De Martino, the British member easily supplanted Miller's unpolished drafts (which Headlam-Morley had erroneously labeled "the President's proposals") with his more modest and specific minority program.[34] Headlam-Morley consulted Wolf, Marshall, and the Romanian–Jewish representative, Wilhelm Filderman, but at this stage omitted the Poles.[35] Using Namier as an intermediary, Headlam-Morley offered this consolation to the excluded *Comité* members, that the "really stringent clauses assuring them of citizenship," legal protection, and educational rights outweighed their futile claims for national rights.[36]

By May 13 the committee's work on the Polish treaty was complete, except for two significant items.[37] Appearing before the council on May 17, Headlam-Morley explained his solitary defense of the Jewish Sabbath against

31. Headlam-Morley, memorandum, May 17, 1929, GB FO 371/14125. In the original terms presented to the Germans on May 7, all of Upper Silesia had been assigned to Poland.
32. *Receuil*, PV No. 7, May 13, 1919; seventh meeting, May 13, 1919, GB FO 604/150; a day earlier they were joined by an Italian representative, De Martino, who was briefed on all the earlier sessions; IMAE Conferenza della Pace 1919. Segretario, Commissione dei nuovi Staati (hereafter CDPS/CNS) 209/24, May 7, 8, 9, 12, 13, 1919.
33. De Martino to Orlando, May 31, 1919, IMAE CDPS/CNS 84/61; *Receuil*, PV No. 42, Aug. 5, 1919.
34. Headlam-Morley, *Memoir*, pp. 92, 99, 105–6, 117.
35. Headlam-Morley, *Memoir*, pp. 107, 111; *Council of Four*, Vol. 2, p. 89; Wolf, Diary, May 6, 7, 8, 1919.
36. Headlam-Morley to Koppel, May 8, 1919, May 8, 1919, Headlam-Morley, *Memoir*, p. 99; also Diary (ca. May 18), ibid., p. 117.
37. Second Report of the Committee on New States, May 13, 1919, *PWW*, Vol. 59, pp. 180–3; also Headlam-Morley to Hankey, May 13, 1919, Headlam-Morley, *Memoir*, pp. 105–6; Miller, *Diary*, Vol. 1, May 12, 1919.

It was at the fifth meeting, May 9, 1919, that the U.S. proposal for proportional minority representation was formally voted down, to be replaced by an exchange of notes between Poland and the Allied and Associated Powers; *Receuil*, PV No. 5, May 9, 1919; GB FO 604/150 (489/4/2).

Miller and Berthelot's resistance[38]; Headlam-Morley's compromise formula was not only to grant protection against any forcible violations by the state authorities but also to forbid Poland from holding elections on Saturday.[39] Wilson, alerted by a vexed Miller of an Anglo–Jewish conspiracy as well as a serious abridgement of Polish sovereignty,[40] and seconded by Clemenceau, called for immediate negotiations with Dmowski and Paderewski.[41]

Headlam-Morley also informed the council that the committee had made no decision on the League's role in enforcing the new treaty.[42] During this crucial discussion, it became clear that no council member wished to give aggrieved minorities direct access to the new world organization. Wilson insisted that the Covenant already provided a mechanism for its members to call attention to threats to world peace.[43] Lloyd George refused to allow "propagandistic associations and societies from all over the world" the possibility of "flooding the League with their complaints."[44]

After a final editing, copies of the draft treaty were conveyed on May 22 to Dmowski in Paris and Paderewski in Warsaw.[45] Because of time constraints, the text omitted the economic clauses, which the French were attempting

38. Miller was also an outspoken opponent of legalizing Sunday trading for Polish Jews (Wolf, Diary, June 1, 1919), a privilege not granted by any state in America, including Miller's and Marshall's home state of New York.
39. Committee meetings, May 8, 9, 12, 13, 1919, GB FO 604/150 (489/4/2); on the Sabbath clause, see Annex B to the Committee report, *PWW*, Vol. 59, p. 179, n. 4. Headlam-Morley to Namier, May 17, 1919, Headlam-Morley, *Memoir*, p. 111.
40. Miller, memoranda to president, Miller, *Diary*, Document #945 (May 13, 1919), #954 (May 15, 1919), scoring the British proposal as "contrary to the law of many of the States of the American union." Lord's critique in Hudson, #350 (May 10, 1919).

    Miller, who had just been assigned to mediate the Fiume dispute, was annoyed by Headlam-Morley's *volte face*, agreeing with House that "Lloyd George had sold out to the Jews." Miller, *Diary*, Vol. 1, May 19, 1919.
41. Headlam-Morley, *Memoir*, p. 117; FRUS PPC, Vol. 5 (May 17, 1919), pp. 678–9; *Council of Four*, Vol. 2, pp. 89–90.

    Miller, in his memorandum for the president, May 13, 1919, *Diary*, Document #945, noted that the committee had not yet heard any representatives of Poland or of the Jews in Poland but had consulted with American, British, and Romanian Jews.
42. Headlam-Morley, memorandum on the Right of Appeal of Minorities to the League of Nations, May 16, 1919, WWP 406.
43. FRUS PPC, Vol. 5, pp. 680–1, and not recorded in *Council of Four* minutes. Wilson's restrictive position was clear: The League Covenant reserved to its member states the right to "call attention to matters affecting the peace of the world" and this was "not to be regarded as an unfriendly act." He expected the Jews of Poland to "introduce [induce] their friends in other countries, such as the United States of America, Great Britain, or France, to draw the attention of the League to their position." To be sure, "the League of Nations could not change the minds of the people. Dislike of the Jews of Poland would continue in spite of everything."
44. "The Jews, in particular, are very litigious." *Council of Four*, Vol. 2, p. 91; not reported in the FRUS account.
45. *Receuil*, PV No. 11, May 21, 1919; eighth meeting, May 21, 1919, GB FO 604/150 (489/4/2); discussion in Polish delegation, Paris, meeting May 24, 1919, AAN KNP 169/17,15; copy of the text in ibid., Paderewski 846.

to expand and the Americans to limit[46]; and it still contained no specific statement on the League's guarantee.[47] The document, a model of British realism, recognized the minorities' need for protection but eliminated the Jews' most radical demands; it attempted to avoid offending Poland's sensibilities but also demanded its signature.[48] Nonetheless, the Polish press grumbled over a "vexing and humiliating arrangement."[49]

On May 29, 1919, David Hunter Miller joined the crowd departing from Paris, leaving his assistant Hudson with the burden of facing the Jewish, Polish, and Allied responses.[50]

"WE ARE RAISING A ROW"[51]

Lucien Wolf, returning to Paris on May 2 from a six-day trip to London, was delighted to learn of the appointment of the Committee on New States.[52] "Instead of more or less banal Clauses in the Peace Treaty," there would be something "safer and solid," a "detailed Statute of Minorities."[53] With almost daily access to Headlam-Morley and to the committee's secretary, E.H. Carr, Wolf exulted that his influence far surpassed that of the dilatory *Alliance*, the arrogant Americans, and the radical East European nationalists.[54] He nevertheless continued his crusade against the *Comité*.[55]

Louis Marshall was less sanguine. While the *Comité* debated over "semicolons," he was gathering scraps of mixed information. From Miller he learned of the council's dismissal of the Jews' national claims[56] and from

46. Hudson #368, May 16, 1919, records his efforts to reduce the economic clauses as much as possible against Britain's demands and the French efforts to force the Poles to accept their portion of the German debt (which France would not).
47. Hudson #379, May 21, 1919.
48. Balfour to Wyndham, May 24, 1919, GB FO 608/70: "While their observations on questions of detail will be welcomed, their assent to the principles involved is, under Article 93 of the German treaty, definitely required."
49. Reports on the Polish press by the Zionist office in Copenhagen; CZA A126/46/1, A126/52/6.
50. Memorandum for the president, May 21, 1919, Miller, *Diary*, Document #980; Marshall to Hudson, May 24, 1919, Adler, Diary, May 24; entry, June 12, 1919, Yale University, Frank Lyon Polk Diaries 19.

    On the political damage of the growing list of departures, Headlam-Morley to Namier, June 11, 1919, Headlam-Morley, *Memoir*, p. 142.
51. Marshall to his children, #13, Apr. 28, 1919, AJA LM 82.
52. "The new Committee is just what we asked for in our Memorial," Wolf, Diary, May 3, 1919; Carr confirmed this, ibid., May 6, 1919.
53. Wolf, Diary, May 6, 1919.
54. Wolf, Diary, May 8, 9, 1919.
55. See, e.g., copy of the "Haffkine committee's" proposals to the peace conference, pronouncing the Jews a distinct "ethnic group" and claiming the right to proportional representation, Paris, May 15, 1919, copy in Adler, Diary.

    Wolf also welcomed the arrival of a delegation of non-nationalist Orthodox Polish Jews, sponsored by the Polish government and endorsed by the *Alliance*. Wolf, Diary, May 9, 11, 12, 1919.
56. Marshall to his children, May 3, 1919, to Ruth Marshall [his daughter], May 7, AJA LM 82; Miller, *Diary*, Vol. 1, May 3, 1919; Adler, Diary, May 4, 1919. Adler to Racie Adler, May 8, 1919, Adler,

the British that a minorities committee had been appointed.[57] On their daily calls, Mack and Marshall found Tardieu friendly,[58] Headlam-Morley guarded,[59] and Miller uncommunicative, refusing to divulge any information on the committee's deliberations and counseling against further audiences with House or the president.[60] Wolf, Marshall, and Sylvain Lévi, each in his own way, attempted to sway the committee's three members.[61]

The Americans were the first to see the committee's draft minority treaty.[62] On May 15 Miller, breaching confidentiality and political prudence, suddenly disclosed the text, which shocked almost all the Jewish leaders.[63] Not only were their national claims dismissed and their cultural, linguistic, educational, and political aims denied, but the treaty's citizenship clauses were extremely weak.[64] There were no special provisions for the Jewish Sabbath and no protection for Sunday trading, which both Wolf and Marshall considered indispensable to the survival of Polish Jewry.[65] Wolf

Selected Letters, p. 369, exulted at the prospect of "now bring[ing] the Alliance and the English into relations with the other delegates here."

57. Miller, *Diary*, Vol. 1, May 4; Wolf, Diary, May 4, 1919.
58. Marshall to Ruth Marshall, May 7, 1919, AJA LM 82; Marshall to Tardieu, May 14, 1919, copy in Adler, Diary.

 The contact with André Tardieu who, unlike the Quai d'Orsay's Jewish expert, Jean Goût, was sympathetic with Zionism and Jewish rights (De Haas to Brandeis, London, Feb. 21, 1919 CZA A404/93), was made by Stephen Wise; see Wise to Edmond de Billy, Paris, Mar. 4, 1919, ibid., A93/5.
59. "Our conversations with you have been of the greatest value, and I think that now we are fully advised of all the points that you wish to lay before us." Headlam-Morley to Mack, May 7, 1919, HM CC, Box 1; Headlam-Morley, *Memoir*, p. 117.
60. House, absorbed by the negotiations with Italy, warned Miller against "discuss[ing] with the Jews any details of what had happened"; Miller, *Diary*, May 3, 1919.
61. Adler, Diary, May 8, 1919. "Prospect hopeful." Telegram, Marshall and Adler to AJC, Paris, May 12, 1919, AJA Schiff 161; Richards to Wise, May 5, 9, 1919, Wise 74–60.
62. Adler, Diary, May 10, 1919, reported a meeting with House; and on May 12 Miller suddenly broke his silence. Miller, *Diary*, Vol. 1, May 12, 13, 14, 1919.
63. And irritated Headlam-Morley, (see Wolf to Headlam-Morley, May 16, 1919, HM UU Col. 127), who had withheld specific information from Wolf and the Poles.

 Having complained privately of Miller's "dullness," Headlam-Morley lamented the political consequences (Headlam-Morley, *Memoir*, pp. 106, 111, 111–2) and protested before the committee (*Receuil*, PV No. 8, May 18, 1919); eighth meeting, May 16, 1919, GB FO 604/50 (689/4/2); May 16, IMAE CDPS/CNS 209/24; also, Miller, *Diary*, May 15, 1919. Wolf, Diary, May 15, 16, 1919.

 Cyrus Adler called the "supplemental treaty" a "great triumph" (Adler, Diary, May 15, 1919) and registered his satisfaction with the American delegation (ibid., May 17); but he still believed the text was "open to change" (ibid., May 19).
64. On Mack's protests over Jewish control over their schools, Hudson #363, May 15, 1919; Namier to Headlam-Morley, May 19, 1919, HM CC, Box 12, pointed out the lack of protection for the Yiddish language as well as for Jewish hospitals and citizenship,
65. Marshall and Mack to Miller, May 15, 1919, Adler, Diary; Marshall and Mack to Wilson, Paris, May 16, 1919, WWP 406.

 Also, Wolf, Diary, May 15, 16, 20, 1919. Poland's Orthodox Jewish delegation had warned Wolf of the danger of a national *repos dominical*, which would extend the boycott and ruin the Jews economically; ibid., May 18, 1919.

envisaged an uphill struggle to secure the minority's right of appeal to the League of Nations.[66]

Had they had access to the council records, Wolf and Marshall would have been even more chagrined. In their glib remarks on May 17, the Big Three had clearly differentiated their upstanding Jewish fellow citizens from their eastern brethren, the shrewd traders and despised neighbors, the potential victims and potential Bolsheviks. The world's leaders were not only prepared to refuse the bulk of Polish Jewry's claims[67]; they also considered them unwelcome supplicants before their new League of Nations.[68]

In mid-May, the worried Wolf and Marshall formed a temporary alliance to revise the draft treaty with Poland.[69] Their brief collaboration was facilitated not only by Mack's departure on May 18[70] and Marshall's disgruntlement with the nationalists,[71] but also by Wolfs disappointment with Paderewski, who had declined to issue a straightforward condemnation of the shootings in Pinsk.[72] Nonetheless the two rivals continued to pursue their separate paths, with Marshall working to broaden the treaty's stipulations[73] and Wolf prepared to defend an admittedly imperfect document against radical Jewish proposals.[74]

The Jewish proponents of minority rights still had considerable resources. Their cause was undoubtedly bolstered by the presence of the German delegation in Versailles who spoke in the name of millions of people about

German Zionists were also convinced of the urgency of Sunday trading for the Jews of Eastern Europe. Hantke to Zionist office Copenhagen, Berlin, May 13, 1919, CZA Z3/674.

66. Wolf, Diary, May 14, 16, 20, 1919.
67. Wilson had remarked that banning elections on the Jewish Sabbath would make "Saturday rather more sacred than Sunday," and Lloyd George condemned Sunday trading as "an unfair advantage against the Christians" that was prohibited in Great Britain, FRUS PPC, Vol. 5, p. 679.
68. FRUS PPC, Vol. 5, pp. 394, 679–81.
69. Wolf, Diary, May 16, 1919; Adler, Diary, May 16, 17, 19, 20, 1919.
70. Although the judge pronounced the "outlook good" (Jacobson to DeHaas, London, May 19, 1919, CZA A404/97), he confided to Namier his disappointment with Miller and the draft treaty (Namier to Headlam-Morley, London, May 20, 1919, HM CC, Box 12).
71. Marshall to his children, #15, May 12, 1919, AJA LM 82.
72. Through August Zaleski, Wolf had requested a "satisfactory letter," Wolf, Diary, May 7, 8, 1919; but Paderewski, adhering to Warsaw's line, continued to label the victims as "Bolsheviks" and declined to excise this phrase for publication (ibid., May 17, 19, 23, 1919; Wolf to Paderewski, May 21, 1919, AAN Paderewski 774).

    Sir Stuart Samuel also asked for a statement by Paderewski that the Polish army had been ordered to end the pogroms and that the perpetrators would be punished; Sobański to KNP, London, May 30, 1919, AAN KNP 35.
73. See Mack and Marshall to Wilson, May 16, 1919, AJC Marshall, PC 1919–1923; Marshall to Tardieu, May 14, 1919, ibid.; also, Mack and Marshall to Miller, May 15, 1919, Miller, *Diary*.

    Belief that "genuine guarantees" were still possible, Marshall to Mack (on the *Carmania*), Paris, May 22, 1919, CZA A264/5.
74. Incensed by Israel Cohen's May 22 article in *The Times* [London] threatening to revive the *Comité*'s proposals, Wolf joined forces with Headlam-Morley to "correct its mischievous effects," offering to publicly praise the committee's accomplishments, Wolf, Diary, May 23, 25, 1919.

to be torn from their homeland and placed under alien rule.[75] In their first written response to the Allies' peace terms, the Germans had called for guarantees of the "national individuality" of all minorities in regard to their languages, education, culture, science, and press as well as a "separate agreement... to determine the manner in which the right of the minorities can be asserted before the official bodies of the League of Nations."[76] The Reich delegation, split between defiance and negotiation, was prepared to link its protests over Germany's territorial losses with a campaign for generous minority protection.[77]

An even more powerful asset was the massive antipogrom campaign organized in America. Jewish communities from all over the country wired protests against the events in Pinsk and Vilna to the State Department and Congress. Moreover, a self-appointed "Committee for the Defense of the Jews of Poland"[78] won over the workers, Zionists, and even the AJC; with extraordinary speed, cooperation, and publicity it mounted a huge demonstration in New York City on May 21, 1919.[79] That day every Jewish establishment was closed, and at noon 300,000 workers, joined by Jewish veterans of the European, Spanish, and Civil Wars, marched in silent protest. In the evening, a huge throng gathered in Madison Square Garden, where Supreme Court Justice Charles Evans Hughes accused Poland of "betray[ing] the cause for which we have fought" and Jacob Schiff threatened that "Poland cannot be free until it gives good guarantees that it will give protection for Jew and gentile alike."[80] Five days later, the U.S. Senate

75. French intelligence noted that among the German delegation's book purchases was *Le juif errant*, Bulletin de renseignements #11, May 18, 1919, FMAE PA-AP Tardieu 28.
76. German note of May 9, 1919, on the Covenant of the League of Nations, in Luckau, *German Delegation*, p. 232.
77. Bulletin de renseignements, May 22, 1919, FMAE PA-AP Tardieu 28.
78. Made up of "Yiddish newspapermen, actors, and radical agitators"; Schneiderman to Schiff, May 12, 1919, AJA Schiff 161.
79. DeHaas to Zionist office London, Apr. 29, 1919, CZA A126/46/1; Schneiderman to Schiff, May 12, 19, 1919, AJA Schiff 161; Blanche Jacobson to DeHaas, May 20, 1919, announcing the "monster mass meeting" at Madison Square Garden, CZA A404/97.

    Compare DeHaas to Zionist Office London, May 13, 1919, complaining, "We receive from London and Copenhagen only Polish pogrom material, which are not money raisers." CZA Z4/4131.
80. Schiff to Nippert, May 26, 1919, AJA Schiff 161; Schiff to Richards, May 27, 1919, AJA Warburg 182.

    The lengthy May 24 cable, signed by Schiff, Elkus, Wise, and others, which Marshall presented to Wilson (WWP 407), was intercepted by French intelligence; it gave extensive details of the meeting as well as the text of its resolutions, FMAE Z (Pologne) 61/2.

    See coverage in *The New York Times*, *New York Sun*, *New York Globe*, *New York Evening Post*, and *New York Herald*, May 22, 1919.

    Also Smulski to KNP Paris, Washington, May 21, 1919, AAN KNP 26; Barclay to Curzon, Washington, May 23, 1919, GB FO 371/3903.

passed a resolution deploring acts of violence against racial and religious minorities.

The "monster indignation campaign" to pressure the peacemakers resonated strongly in Paris.[81] On May 26 Louis Marshall and Cyrus Adler, in a brief but well-publicized interview with Wilson, summarized the text of a 2,000-word cable from New York and conveyed the gathering's demands for guarantees of protection for the Jews of Poland and Eastern Europe.[82]

Berlin, encouraged by the New York rally, stepped up its own efforts. German authorities generated more reports from the East[83] and intensified the prominority campaign in neutral countries. In Amsterdam, the German consul general, who delivered an impassioned speech against the pogroms, claimed to have stirred the Grand Rabbi of the Netherlands to dispatch appeals to western Jewish leaders as well as telegrams to Clemenceau, Lloyd George, Orlando and Wilson.[84]

British Jewry, less numerous and still operating under wartime restrictions, responded more slowly. The conservative Jewish establishment preferred diplomatic carrots and financial sticks to the risks of provoking its government with mass demonstrations.[85] But the less restrained Zionists, acting independently, flooded Whitehall with protests,[86] inundated the press with pogrom reports that were widely reprinted abroad,[87] and enlisted

81. Wolf, Diary, May 27, 1919.

82. Meeting, May 26, 1919, Adler, Diary; Richards to Schiff, Paris, May 31, 1919, AJA Schiff 161.

83. Prof. Sobernheim (the *Auswärtiges Amt*'s Jewish expert) to Humboldt, Berlin May 31, 1919, citing Wilson's "strong response" to the New York mass demonstration, urged Germany's consul general to insert more pogrom material in the Dutch press. Germ. PA AA L1266/L350245–46.

Recognizing the delicacy of its actions, Berlin orchestrated its publicity campaign cautiously, staying at least one step behind Jewish information sources. See, e.g., Bericht über die Ereignisse in Wilna, den die Wilnaer Gemeinde der polnischen Regierung als Protest einzureichen beabsichtigt, dated May [?] 1919, 18 pp., but marked "June 1, 1919" and "not to be released beforehand," Germ. PA AA Abt. III Prof. Sobernheim, L1287/ "Pogrom."

Germany's efforts did not go unnoticed; Namier memorandum (confidential), London, May 15, 1919, HM CC, Box 12, described the Reich's propaganda work in Copenhagen as well as its intention to link up with the "American Jewish press."

84. Humboldt to AA, Amsterdam, June 5, 1919, Germ. PA AA K695/K181915. On Berlin's subsidies to the Jewish Press Offices in Denmark, the Netherlands, Sweden, and Switzerland as well as Austria, see, e.g., ibid., K695/K181776–80; L1288/L350315, L350350–51.

85. See minutes of meeting, London, May 23, 1919, CZA Z4/69, led by Sir Stuart Samuel.

Wolf also counseled against public protests: "Any ill-considered action in London in regard to the pogroms may easily jeopardize the final triumph of our work." Wolf to Mowschowitch, Paris, May 21, 1919, YIVO W/M 37.

86. See, e.g., Zionist Office to Harmsworth, Under Secretary of State for Foreign Affairs, May 21, 1919, CZA Z4/58. Namier memorandum, May 28, 1919, GB FO 371/3903.

87. See articles on the pogroms in the *Manchester Guardian*, May 1, 10; *The Times*, May 21, 23; *Westminister Gazette* on May 27, 1919; *Daily Herald*, June 12, 1919.

On the press campaign, Israel Cohen to Hyamson, London, May 2, 1919, CZA L8/400; Cohen, "Polish Jewry," *The Times*, May 22, 1919; also Sobański to KNP Paris, London, May 26, 30, 1919, AAN KNP 35.

sympathetic members of parliament to question London's response to Pinsk and Vilna.[88] Roused to action, Britain's Jewish elite, stung by foreign criticism of its "supineness," appealed against Whitehall's ban on demonstrations[89]; ultimately the leaders of the JFC joined the Zionists and brought in prominent non-Jews for London's own massive antipogrom protest on June 26.[90]

Paris remained quiet. Nevertheless, French Jews, joined by artists, professors, Socialists, and human-rights activists, composed written protests against the pogroms that were reported in the left-wing press.[91] Elsewhere in Europe, particularly in the neutral countries and among the Socialists, there were strong expressions of support.[92]

Wolf and Marshall, suddenly abandoning their conservative garb, had decided to use the public outcry to force the peacemakers' hands.[93] Struck by the first, inflated reports of the Vilna casualties issuing from the Jewish Press Bureau in Copenhagen, even Wolf became convinced of "a deliberate attempt to thin out the Jewish population of Poland by massacre . . . [W]e cannot stand still."[94] Two days before the New York demonstration Marshall, the newly elected *Comité* president, was quoted on the atrocities in Pinsk and Vilna on the front page of *The New York Times*.[95] And on Saturday night, May 21, addressing a meeting of the *Ligue des droits de l'homme*, he demanded "full protection for minorities."[96]

88. Namier to Headlam-Morley, May 20, 1919, described a "whole flood of questions" in parliament answered by the official reports from Paris and Warsaw; HM CC, Box 12. Compare extracts of parliamentary debates, May 19, 20, 1919, GB FO 371/3903.
89. In their interview in the Foreign Office, the Jewish leaders complained of pressure "from all over the world to take action," whereupon Lord Nathaniel Rothschild produced a telegram from the Grand Rabbi of the Netherlands. Harmsworth to Curzon, June 10, 1919, GB FO 371/3903, recommended lifting the ban.
90. Jacobson to Sokolow, London, May 28, 1919, to Brailsford, June 13, 1919, CZA A126/46; Jacobson to Samuel, June 17, 1919, ibid., Z4/69; additional documentation in ibid., Z3/674 and "Jewish matters," June 11, 1919, GB FO 371/3903.
91. E. Fleg and Rabbi Back to Pichon, June 1, 1919, FMAE Z (Pologne) 61/2; that day, French intellectuals launched a signature campaign, "An Appeal to Humanity," against the pogroms in Poland.
92. Intercepted telegram from Huysmanns to Frossard, Amsterdam, May 30, 1919, FMAE Z (Pologne) 61, calling for the mobilization of French Socialists; the Jewish Press Bureau in Stockholm also dispatched Huysmanns' appeal to French and British labor groups, AIU France Z/17.
93. Wolf, Diary, May 18, 19, 20, 1919; Wolf to Lloyd George [on behalf of the Jews of the British Empire], May 20, 1919, YIVO W/M 81; Wolf to FO, May 21, 1919, GB FO 608/67; Marshall to Wilson (in the name of the *Comité des délégations juives*), May 23, 25, 26, 1919, AJC LM PC 1919–23.
94. Wolf, Diary, May 22, 1919.
95. Charles A. Selden in *The New York Times*, May 23, 1919.
96. Marshall to his children, #19, May 27, 1919, AJA LM 82; French intelligence report, May 28, 1919, FMAE Z (Pologne) 61/2.

In a well-coordinated operation, Wolf and Marshall gathered influential Jewish allies. They convinced the cautious *Alliance* leaders to join.[97] They induced America's premier Zionist emissary, Felix Frankfurter, who was also functioning as an informal advisor to the U.S. delegation, to break his long silence.[98] And Sokolow readily took part.[99]

The Big Three were affected by the Jews' publicity campaign. The French, in particular, feared that Wilson would "crack" and the Germans profit.[100] At once, Britain, France, and the United States ordered its emissaries in Warsaw to investigate the events in Vilna.[101] Predictably, all three western diplomats continued to deny that any pogrom had occurred, corrected the inflated casualty figures, and underlined Germany's treacherous role.[102]

Still, the echoes of Pinsk and Vilna could not be silenced. Even the Quai d'Orsay, for obvious political reasons, hesitated to publicly demolish the Zionists' inflated casualty figures.[103] Whitehall's experts, increasingly skeptical of the British minister's tranquilizing reports from Warsaw, feared the long-term impact of Vilna on Polish–Jewish relations.[104]

There were obvious risks in the Jews' public strategy. Although the Poles and their neighbors had not yet been heard, Wolf incautiously believed that the treaty was now "safe enough" to launch an aggressive demarche and to "set an example of the Poles in good time."[105]

97. Edmond de Rothschild to FMAE, "Les pogromes anti-Juifs en Pologne," May 16, 1919 and Pichon minute, May 18, 1919, FMAE Z (Pologne) 61; Sée and Bigart to Clemenceau, May 22, 1919, AIU France II/D8.

98. Frankfurter to Lloyd George, Wilson, Clemenceau, Paris, May 22, 1919, enclosing copy of Alsberg report, Warsaw, May 12, GB FO 608/67; DeHaas to Zionist Office London, New York, May 13, 1919, had urged Frankfurter to "speak out," CZA Z4/4131.

Frankfurter, standing in for the delayed Louis Brandeis, had intended to proceed to Palestine immediately after the London Zionists' meeting; but "the Big Four, who rule the world for the moment, will it otherwise"; Frankfurter to Robert Szold, Paris, Apr. 7, 1919, CZA A264/30.

99. "We have this matter well in hand here." Sokolow to Jacobson, Paris, June 2, 1919, CZA Z4/2080.

100. Libert to FMAE, New York, n.d. [received May 22] 1919, FMAE Z (Pologne) 61, remarked on the synchrony between the New York demonstration and the Germans' refusal to sign the treaty. Also, unsigned memoranda, for Tardieu, May 27, 1919 "L'Amérique et les pogromes contre les Juifs en Pologne et en Russie," May 28, 1919, ibid., Z (Pologne) 61/2.

101. FMAE to Warsaw, May 31, 1919, FMAE Z (Pologne) 61/2.

102. Pralon to FMAE, Warsaw, June 1, 3, 14, 19, 1919, FMAE Z (Pologne) 61/2; also Wyndham to FO, May 27, 1919, GB FO 371/3903, Gibson to State Dept. and Ammission Paris, Warsaw, May 30 (three messages), 31, 1919, LC White 43.

103. Unsigned note for Pichon, Paris, June 5, 1919, FMAE Z (Pologne) 61/2; Ringel to Grynbaum, Paris, June 5, 1919, CZA A127/315.

104. Minutes, by Carr, May 24, 1919, and Paton, June 11, 1919, GB FO 608/67.

On May 31 Namier complained to Headlam-Morley, "I would prefer people who would openly say that anti-Semitic pogroms are no concern of ours or even that it is quite a good thing if a number of Jews get massacred . . . but this deliberate doubting in the face of overwhelming evidence strikes me as too revolting for words." HM CC, Box 12.

105. Wolf, Diary, May 22, 1919.

This clamor also exposed a new element of Jewish vulnerability further to the east.[106] Wolf and Marshall's public demands for the strongest possible minority protection were clearly aimed as deterrence against the ascendant anti-Bolshevik forces in Russia and the Ukraine, widely suspected of plotting bloody forms of retaliation against the Jews.[107] The impending triumphs of the White generals, combined with Romania's conquests of Bessarabia and Transylvania and the violence in Pinsk, Lida, and Vilna all threatened a "new round of Jewish troubles" in Eastern Europe, while the routes of emigration were fast closing and the future of Palestine still hung in the balance.[108]

It is not surprising that the political impact of the Jews' publicity campaign was largely negative. It produced the predictable backlash by a political and diplomatic establishment that resented the Jews' assault on a new and weak allied government.[109] Hoover, in particular, expressed "impatience" with the unending reports of pogroms and massacres, preferring to concentrate on "feeding a starving population."[110] There was also mounting sentiment in favor of honoring Paderewski's proposal to send an impartial investigatory commission to Poland.[111]

The campaign also failed to move the principal object of their efforts, Woodrow Wilson.[112] The president, during his half-hour meeting with Marshall and Adler on May 26, expressed his confidence in the proposed treaty.[113] He reassured his Jewish visitors that the Allies had communicated

106. "Great Pogrom Feared as Vent for Wrath against Bolsheviks," *The New York Times*, May 25, 1919.
107. Zuckerman was first to raise the alarm; Adler, Diary, May 6, 1919; also Wolf, Diary, May 22, 1919; Barclay to FO, Washington, May 23, 1919, GB FO 371/3903, June 2, 1919, ibid., FO 371/4371, and Marshall report to the American Jewish Congress, May 30, 1920, AJA LM 131.
108. Discussion of Arab opposition to Jewish emigration, and the need to enlist British support, in Fifth Meeting of Advisory Committee to Palestine Office, Herbert Samuel residence, May 10, 1919, CZA Z4/16045.
109. Phillips to Gibson, Washington, June 6, 1919, Gibson 56, commented on the "appalling . . . amount of antagonism against the Poles which has been deliberately created during the last month by the Jews in this country" and boasted of blocking an anti-pogrom resolution in the House "by reading some of [Gibson's] cables which fortunately came in the nick of time."

Lord to Herter, Paris, June 3, 1919, LC White 43, protested the Jews' "agitation from all parts of the U.S." based on "wholly unfounded or exaggerated" information; Leland Harrison to W. L. Winslow, Paris, July 24, LC Leland Harrison papers (hereafter Harrison) 105, scored Zuckerman and Billikopf, praised Gibson, and asked his State Department colleague to "see what you can do, in a quiet way," to counter the "scandalously untruthful articles" in the U.S. press.
110. Memorandum of interview with Mr. Hoover, Monday, May 26, 1919, AJA LM 131.
111. Paton minutes, May 24, 26, 29, 1919, GB FO 608/67.
112. See Wilson's noncommittal responses to Marshall, May 19, 24, 1919, WWP 406.
113. Memorandum of interview . . . with President Wilson, Monday, May 26, 1919 by Louis Marshall and Cyrus Adler, AJA LM 131; Adler, Diary, May 26, 1919; Richards to Schiff, May 31, 1919, AJA Schiff 161.

their concerns to Kolchak.[114] However, he also adhered to his earlier statement to the council, opposing minority appeals to the League. Confident that American and West European Jews would continue to "keep a sharp eye" on conditions in Eastern Europe, he dismissed the *Ostjuden*'s objections to "being beholden to their brethren." The president had made up his mind to avoid the political risks of either admitting all minority complaints to the League, including those involving the millions of Germans in Bohemia and Poland, or singling out the Jews of Eastern Europe for special privileges.[115]

Paradoxically, an important result of this discouraging interview with Wilson was to accelerate the break between Marshall and Wolf.[116] Wolf, acting on his own, had endorsed the scheme proposed by Lord Cecil's aide, Philip Baker, in which the minorities could take their grievances first to Polish courts and then to the International Court of Justice. Headlam-Morley, although still favoring minority access to the League, had enlarged the Baker Plan with a clause providing for emergency appeals in cases such as pogroms.[117] Wolf, haunted by the "Berlin precedent," had grasped this concrete alternative to another dreary round of protests on behalf of a distant, difficult kin, to force the Great Powers to fulfill another empty guarantee.[118]

114. Wilson was somewhat deceptive. Three days earlier, the council's dispatch to Kolchak (*Council of Four*, May 23, 1919, Vol. 2, pp. 193–5), stating its terms of recognition contained no specific reference to the Jews but only the phrase "civil and religious liberty of all Russian citizens."

On mounting fears of wholesale pogroms after the victory of Kolchak and Denikin, see Wolf, Diary, May 28, 1919, recounting E. H. Carr's concerns; Harvard University Archives, Samuel Elliot Morrison, Diary, June 3, 1919 (courtesy of David S. Foglesong) ("Russian refugees boast openly that 6 million Jews will be killed when Kolchak conquers Russia. The Russian church is circulating a pamphlet giving what purports to be a procès-verbal of a Zionist Congress in 1902 that drew up the whole bolshevist program in order to get Jewish revenge on Russia"); Adler, Diary, June 13, 1919.

Wolf, however, remained optimistic, claiming credit ("the persistency with which we have kept the Jewish Case before the Conference") not only for the Allies' initiative but also for Kolchak's "satisfactory" response (*Council of Four*, June 6, 1919, Vol. 2, p. 33), Wolf, Diary, June 11, 1919.

115. A day later, Wilson assured Rabbi Wise: "The safeguards against religious discrimination which we all have so much at heart will be embodied in the arrangements by which the new states are to be set up." Tumulty to Wise, Washington, May 27, 1919, Wise 74–77.

Taft (who was barnstorming the country with Wise to gather support for the covenant) to Tumulty, May 9, 1919, CZA A404/115, had warned that the Jews might desert the League and impede the uphill struggle for treaty ratification in the Senate. Wise to Tumulty, May 16, 1919, WWP 289, had pleaded for a presidential statement on Jewish rights.

116. R. S. Baker conveyed to Wilson Marshall's "pleasure" with the interview. Notebook, May 29, 1919, LC Baker, Ser. II, Cont. 125.

117. Headlam-Morley to Baker, May 20, 1919, HM UU Col 49. In his memorandum, May 16, 1919 (Headlam-Morley, *Memoir*, pp. 108–11), Headlam-Morley had favored an unrestricted right of appeal to all the Jews of Eastern Europe and a restricted grant to the Germans, Ruthenians, White Russians, and Ukrainians of Poland.

118. Wolf, Diary, May 23, 1919. Text, Wolf, Diary, pp. 293–4.

Marshall vehemently opposed the Baker plan.[119] Invoking his and Miller's legal credentials, he termed it a "destructive" and "dangerous" proposal ("a Greek gift of so fatal a character") that shifted the treaty's enforcement from the signatories to the questionable judicial systems of Eastern Europe.[120] Wolf, on his part, argued against "humiliating" Poland by abridging its sovereign rights. The *Comité*'s arch-opponent also hoped to empower Polish Jews who, he insisted, would be far safer without "an exterritoriality [*sic*]" separating them from the Polish nation and placing them "permanently under some mandate of the League of Nations."[121]

Behind the fracas were two different temperaments, professions, and national traditions, as well as a decade of Anglo–American competition in defending Jewish rights in Eastern Europe and several months of non-cooperation at the peace conference.[122] A bitter Wolf, blaming "the Americans" for the failed League article and Sunday trading clause, railed against Marshall's threat to "all the guarantees" that would make the new treaties "of any practical use."[123] Marshall, flattered by the president's courtesy and attentiveness, believed that his government intended to honor its commitment to minority rights.[124] And he had millions of anxious East Europeans behind him.[125]

WARSAW / PARIS

On May 3, 1919, the very day the Council of Three voted to establish minority treaties, Poland celebrated its first national holiday since 1791. On a huge field at the edge of Warsaw, the head of state, the cabinet, and a throng of 40,000 proud Poles viewed a parade of Haller's army and other troops as well as of students, workers, and school children. Proceeding to the city center, the marchers stopped at the Hotel Bristol, the residence of

119. Adler, Diary, May 27, 1919; Wolf, Diary, May 27, 28, 1919.

120. Adler, Diary, May 27, 1919; Hudson #400, #403, May 28, 29, 1919; Marshall to Wolf, Paris, May 29, 1919, Wolf, Diary, pp. 309–17.

Marshall's alternative formula, in Wolf, Diary, p. 295, was to maintain the enforcement power of the signatories and also – "upon such conditions as the League of Nations may prescribe" – of "the authorised representatives of any racial, linguistic, or religious minority whose rights . . . shall in any manner be infringed."

According to Wolf, Headlam-Morley termed this proposal "contrary to everything we had been asking for . . . and the very things that we had hitherto been anxious to avoid." Wolf, Diary, May 28, 1919.

121. Wolf to Marshall, June 1, 1919, in Wolf, Diary, pp. 318–24, Mack to Frankfurter, July 26, 1919, CZA A404/107.

122. Wolf to Adler, Paris, May 26, 1919, AJC LM, PC 1919–23, complained that the Americans were "springing documents and asking for parallel action."

123. Wolf, Diary, May 28, 1919.

124. Marshall to his children #19, May 27, 1919, AJA LM 82, described the May 26 interview as the "turning point in my work."

125. Marshall to Wolf, May 29, 1919, Wolf to Marshall, June 1, in Wolf, Diary, pp. 317, 318.

the U.S. ambassador, where they cheered President Wilson and America.[126] Except as members of workers' and Communist organizations, Poland's Jews were "conspicuously absent."[127]

Nine days later, on the morning after his return from Paris, Paderewski warned the cabinet that the atrocity stories emanating from Poland were producing "adverse consequences for Poland's international policy." Troubled by reports of a new wave of violence unleashed by Haller's troops against the Jewish population in Galicia, the prime minister announced an "immediate investigation."[128]

The antipogrom campaign had struck an alarm in Warsaw.[129] Paderewski was deluged with telegrams from Jewish and Allied leaders. Ignoring all the practical impediments and political consequences, Paderewski's foreign friends urged him to condemn the violence publicly and order stiff reprisals.[130] Instead, the Polish government took the offensive, castigating the sensationalist German press reports of "new" pogroms.[131] With France's support, Poland scored the Reich's "transparent" attempts to disgrace its eastern neighbor in order to bolster its assault on the peace treaty.[132] Even before the council's minority clauses arrived in Warsaw, Poland sent a delegation of "patriotic Jews" to Paris to plead against any minority treaty at all.[133]

126. Gibson to U.S. Embassy Paris and Ammission, Warsaw, May 3, 1919, LC White 42.

127. Kimens Report #5, May 4, 1919, Howard minute, May 13, GB FO 608/71.

128. AAN PRM Council of Ministers, May 12, 1919.

129. FMAE to Pralon ("urgent") with documentation on the New York manifestation for immediate communication to the Polish government, Paris, May 26, 1919, FMAE Z (Pologne) 61/2.

Sobański to KNP Paris, May 26, AAN KNP 35: "As soon as the Polish cause rises against the Germans, there is immediately a Jewish pogrom campaign . . . always coming from Stockholm or Copenhagen" also attacking "Poland's imperialistic policies against the Ukraine, Lithuania, etc."; also Dłuski to Piłsudski, Paris, May 27, 1919, PIA AGND 56/905; Ciechanowski Report #1, AAN MSZ 1480.

130. Smulski to KNP, Washington, May 21, 1919, AAN KNP 26, pleaded with Warsaw to end its "embarrassing silence."

131. *Moniteur Polonais*, May 17, 1919.

132. On May 1, 1919, a French intelligence source in Copenhagen warned that the Germans were writing anti-Semitic tracts that were to be attributed to Haller's army, FMAE Z (Pologne) 61/2; unsigned memorandum, AAN Paderewski 774, identified Tattenbach, the German consul in Berne, as advocating the increased use of anti-Jewish pogroms in Poland and Galicia to counter Polish claims.

See also MSZ to Polish delegation Paris, Warsaw, May 22, 1919, AAN KNP 161; Polish Army headquarters to MSZ, Warsaw, May 30, 1919, ibid., KNP 869 (39); Ciechanowski report #1, Paris, May 30, 1919, ibid., MSZ 1480 as well as Conty to FMAE, Copenhagen, May 17, 1919, Delavaud to FMAE, Stockholm, May 23, 1919, Casenave to Tardieu, New York, June 11, FMAE Z (Pologne) 61/2, on the German propaganda campaign.

133. Dmowski to MSZ, Paris, May 27, 1919, AAN KNP 161. Despite the ideological differences between the Socialist deputy, Herman Lieberman and the assimilationist Edward Natanson over recognizing Polish Jews as an "independent nation"(Biuro Kongresowe, May 26. 27, 1919, PIA AGND II/97) and their demands that Warsaw condemn the pogroms (KNP delegation meetings, May 26, 27, 29, 1919, AAN KNP 169), both Lieberman and Natanson opposed the treaty.

Suddenly, and at the worst possible moment – just as the Germans were threatening not to sign and influential Britons were assailing the treaty's territorial provisions – Poland placed itself at serious odds with the peacemakers.[134] Piłsudski, yielding to Haller's charges of the Ukrainians' "plunder, violence, and bolshevism," defied the council, their ministers' restraining efforts, and Paderewski's pledges, and unleashed a brief, bloody offensive in Eastern Galicia.[135] Breaking the armistice brokered in Paris, Haller's troops recaptured Lemberg, swept through the oil fields, and on May 27 reached the Romanian border.

Once more the Poles were forced to defend themselves against charges of imperialism. A discomfited Paderewski, his honor impaired, termed the battle for Eastern Galicia a struggle for "law and order" and blamed the Ukrainians for breaking the armistice.[136] Nevertheless, on the eve of his second trip to Paris, the prime minister persuaded the *Sejm* to pass an anodyne resolution favoring autonomy for Eastern Galicia and a Polish–Ukrainian agreement.[137] The KNP's news service chimed in, trumpeting the Jews' and White Russians' expressions of "gratitude" for their "liberation" from the Ukrainian "bandits."[138] Piłsudski, alert to the diplomatic repercussions, ordered an end to the offensive on May 30, the removal of Haller's troops from Eastern Galicia, and the placing of Foch in command of the Polish army.[139]

The harried Council of Four dealt reluctantly with Poland's newest assault. Dmowski had already shown the face of a defiant Poland before the Armistice Commission for Eastern Galicia; and the Ukrainians, who

See Piltz to Pichon, June 2, 1919, FMAE Z (Pologne) 61/2, requesting an audience for the two before the Committee on New States.

134. Namier, "The Present Crisis in Poland," HM CC, Box 12. The timing was propitious in the sense that the council was about to complete the Austrian treaty under which the settlement of Eastern Galicia would fall.
135. Lord to Herter, "Weekly Summary," May 25, 1919, LC White 42; "Great Britain: Weekly Report," May 25, 1919, ibid.; also Gibson to Ammission, May 14, 16, 1919, ibid.
136. Wyndham to Curzon, Warsaw, May 14, 1919, GB FO 608/71. Ever alert to Poland's turbulent politics, Namier interpreted the Eastern Galician operation as a coup by Dmowski against Paderewski ("who had grown too big for him in Paris") backed by the French who had been offered concessions in the oil fields. Namier to Headlam-Morley, May 20, 1919, HM CC, Box 12.
137. "We nowhere pursue criminal war of conquests; we sacrifice our lives and property in defense of the life and property of our compatriots." Gibson to Ammission, Warsaw, May 23, 1919, LC White 42; Compare Pralon to Pichon, Warsaw, May 25, 28, 1919, FMAE Z (Pologne) 69.
138. KNP bulletin, May 28, 1919, FMAE Z (Pologne) 61/2; British Commission in Warsaw to FO, May 27, 1919, GB FO 608/67, confirmed that everything was "quiet" in Eastern Galicia, that the Poles had behaved "well since arrival & had made no reprisals."
139. In response to Allied criticisms, Piłsudski stressed his resistance to Haller and the KNP's pressure as well as the strategic importance of Poland's linking up with Romania. Pralon to FMAE, Warsaw, May 31, 1919, FMAE Z (Pologne) 69.

were also battling the Bolsheviks, were garnering considerable sympathy in Paris.[140] The peacemakers, having dispatched an unprecedented minority treaty to Warsaw, now had to grapple with the fate of an additional 700,000 Jews and 4 million Ukrainians.[141] At that moment, however, the Great Powers viewed the fate of Eastern Galicia as a sensitive, but not urgent, issue, linked not to the German but to the Austrian treaty, and, more specifically, to the fortunes of Kolchak.[142]

Even more important, the issue of Eastern Galicia divided the council, with Lloyd George loudly fulminating over Warsaw's latest mischief, Wilson more restrained, and Clemenceau clearly siding with Poland.[143] On May 21, as Haller's troops swept eastward, Britain alone insisted on punishing Warsaw for seizing the oil fields and an unwilling population. Lloyd George, rejecting the old anti-Bolshevik excuses – "They are doing everything required to revive Bolshevism, just at the very time when it is about to die" – urged the council to apply economic pressure and once more hinted at repercussions for Poland's claim to Silesia.[144]

Would these harsh measures topple the fragile government in Warsaw? The British premier shrugged off the danger, deriding Paderewski's probity and competence; but Wilson, evoking the Russian and Hungarian experiences, termed Paderewski's government "a dike against disorder, and perhaps the only one possible."[145] Even discounting Warsaw's anti-Bolshevik rhetoric, a viable Poland remained the sole barrier to a German–Russian rapprochement. France, in any event, had the final word. By delaying the council's rebuke until after Piłsudski had met his goals and Paderewski was back in Paris, it alerted Warsaw once more to the feebleness of the Allies' threats.[146]

Nevertheless, Paderewski returned on May 27 to a charged atmosphere of Anglo–American mistrust.[147] Wilson had not only threatened an arms

140. Paton minute, May 20, 1919, GB FO 608/71; FRUS PPC, Vol. 5, pp. 775–8.
141. Figures by General Botha, *Council of Four* (May 21, 1919), Vol. 2, p. 148.
142. *Council of Four* (May 23, 1919), Vol. 2, pp. 189–91. The White leader claimed all of the Baltic and the Ukraine, including Eastern Galicia.
143. FRUS PPC, Vol. 5, pp. 754–5, 778–82.
144. *Council of Four* (May 21, 1919), Vol. 2, pp.151–3.
145. Ibid., p. 150; more abbreviated statement in FRUS PPC, Vol. 5, p. 780.
146. Text of the telegram in FRUS PPC, Vol. 5, p. 859. The British general, Adrian Carton de Wiart, pointed out on May 28, 1919 (GB FO 608/71) that because the Ukrainians and Czechs had already "taken the law into their own hands," it would be difficult for the peacemakers to "enforce restraint on Poland," still facing a threat from a Germany that could easily capture Warsaw. Compare Pralon to FMAE, Warsaw, May 31, 1919, FMAE Z (Pologne) 61; Wyndham to Howard, Warsaw, June 3, 1919, GB FO 608/71.
147. Clemenceau to Paderewski (copy), May 27, 1919, GB FO 608/71. Despite all Clemenceau's efforts, the Polish premier was not invited before the council until June 5.

embargo but had insisted "that the existence of Poland and the determination of her borders depends on us."[148] Lloyd George and his entourage, repelled by Warsaw's chauvinism and militarism,[149] sought to reshape Poland into an ethnically compact, democratic state under the tutelage of the League of Nations, a land of small-landholdings, at peace with its neighbors, and, above all, disarmed.[150]

Paderewski's arrival was also spoiled by new anti-Jewish violence, this time in the heart of Poland at one of its most celebrated pilgrimage sites.[151] In Częstochowa, on May 27, after an unknown assailant wounded one of their comrades, Haller's troops joined a furious local crowd in a three-hour rampage through the Jewish quarter, leaving five dead and forty-five wounded.[152] The Poles, who accused a German *agent provocateur* of inciting the crowd, again challenged the Jews' casualty figures; terming the events a "food riot" and not a pogrom, Warsaw insisted that the military and civil authorities as well as the local priests had done "their utmost" to prevent bloodshed and restore order.[153] Nonetheless, the mounting reports of anti-Jewish excesses by the Haller army – including the widespread shaving of the beards of orthodox men – plus Piłsudski's prediction that his rival, whom the Allies had armed and transported to Poland, would "make life miserable for the Jews," added to Britain's disquiet.[154]

148. *Council of Four* (May 21, 1919), Vol. 2, p. 152. This statement is not in the FRUS account.
149. In the May 21 debate, General Louis Botha, head of the Armistice Commission, termed the Bolshevik danger a "bogey" and accused Poland of "crush[ing] a smaller nation in order to procure a so-called strategic advantage" just as Germany had done in Belgium. *Council of Four*, Vol. 2, p. 150.
150. On disarmament, Headlam-Morley, *Memoir*, pp. 106–8 and Lloyd George's remarks to the Council of Four, FRUS PPC, Vol. 5, pp. 628, 635, and, especially, 904–5; British disappointment over the Polish government's postponement of any major land reform, Reports from Warsaw, May 25, 31, 1919, GB FO 608/71.
151. Częstochowa, on the Warta River, was 130 miles southwest of Warsaw on the rail line to Cracow. Before World War I, 400,000 Poles from Austrian, Russian, and Prussian Poland annually visited its monastery, which stood atop the Jasna Gora [Shining Mountain] and housed a beloved national as well as religious symbol, the "Black Madonna," traditionally believed to have been painted by St. Luke and brought to Poland in the fourteenth century.
152. Joint report on Częstochowa by Allied emissaries, Bevan, Dolbeare, Duchêne, May 31, 1919, FMAE Z (Pologne) 61/3; Wyndham to Curzon, Warsaw, May 31, June 1, 2, 1919, GB FO 371/3903; MSZ to Polish delegation Paris, June 4, 1919, AAN KNP 161; also Namier to Tyrrell, May 28, 1919, GB FO 371/3903.
153. Wróblewski to Polish delegation Paris, Warsaw, June 4, 1919, AAN KNP 869, admitted brief "anti-Semitic excesses" in Częstochowa and Eastern Galicia, "provoked by German agents." Also, Report on Częstochowa by Polish Commissioner, June 11, 1919, Captain Crewdson's report, June 11, 1919, repeating the widespread rumor that the Jews, the only food sellers of Częstochowa, were charging "exorbitant" food prices; GB FO 371/3903.
154. Wyndham to Howard, Warsaw, June 3, 1919, GB FO 608/71; Namier to Headlam-Morley, London, June 3, HM CC, Box 12, termed the current violence "one of the worst series of pogroms now passing over Poland. It means a lot if Piłsudski himself admits it and ascribes the guilt to Haller . . . a man we trained and helped get back to Poland."

Another challenge facing Paderewski was the threat to Poland's possession of Upper Silesia, which the Allies had earlier approved.[155] With Danzig and Marienwerder already lost, Poland now risked the surrender of one of Europe's richest sources of coal as well as lignite, zinc, lead, and iron. Dmowski, blaming "the Jews" for all of Poland's territorial losses, linked the pogrom reports as well as the row over Eastern Galicia with Lloyd George's *volte face* over Upper Silesia.[156]

Lloyd George's shift was undoubtedly caused more by practical concerns than by the protests of Upper Silesian Jews against the "conquerors of Posen, Pinsk, and Vilna."[157] Stirred by Germany's loud protests over the cession of this province, Britain's premier and his advisers feared armed resistance and, especially, the diminution of Berlin's ability to pay reparations.[158] By May 21, Lloyd George had succeeded in persuading Wilson to endorse a plebiscite in Upper Silesia to ascertain "not what the race and the language of the people are, but under which regime they prefer to live."[159] Thus a county-by-county plebiscite in Upper Silesia suddenly became the banner of British and American skeptics of the treaty's wisdom and practicality, appearing to reward German intransigence and to punish Polish misdeeds.[160]

155. Lying in the basin of the upper and middle Oder River, Silesia, seized from Austria by Frederick the Great in the mid-eighteenth century, was Prussia's largest, and one of its richest, provinces, with 15,576 square miles and a population in 1905 of 5 million inhabitants.

 "Upper" Silesia, the region south of the Malapane River, contained the major mineral wealth and largest landholdings. According to the 1905 Reich census, Upper Silesia had a Polish majority, predominantly in the mining and agricultural districts, but most of the towns were German.

156. Dmowski to St. Grabski, n.d. and May 27, 1919, in Kułakowski, *Roman Dmowski*, Vol. 2, pp. 162–3.

 According to the French Mission in Berlin, May 20, 1919, FMAE Z (Pologne) 61, the Jews constituted approximately 4% of the population of Upper Silesia, but held important industrial holdings as well as municipal offices and judgeships.

157. Rabbi D. Braunschweiger, "Bericht über meine Reise nach Kopenhagen im Interesse Oberschlesiens, 24 April bis 4. Mai 1919," Oppeln, May 11, 1919, Germ. PA AA K695/K181866–69 and Beilage, K181870–75.

158. Headlam-Morley may have been the first to anticipate that Upper Silesia, a "considerable district with a very mixed population . . . which has not been Polish for over five hundred years . . . will turn out to be the real crux of the signing." Letter to Saunders, May 12, 1919, Headlam-Morley, *Memoir*, p. 104. One day later, Lloyd George called his colleagues' attention to Chancellor Scheidemann's protests over the cession of Upper Silesia. *Council of Four*, Vol. 2, pp. 49–50. Headlam-Morley to Kerr, May 30, 1919, HM UU Col 76/12, on the threat of a local uprising. Compare Ciechanowski report #1, Paris, May 30, 1919 AAN MSZ 1480(95).

159. *Council of Four*, Vol. 2, p. 131.

160. "Of course, the report of the Polish Committee on this is quite indefensible. . . . It is particularly unfortunate that this decision should have been made in a district which is of such great economic importance, for the Germans will be able to make it appear that our real object has been to deprive Germany of coal mines, which are essential to her existence," Headlam-Morley, Diary extract, June 1, 1919, in Headlam-Morley, *Memoir*, p. 135. Compare Biuro Kongresowe, Meetings, May 29, 31, AAN KNP 169.

"THE REVOLT"

The draft treaty with Austria, delayed by the squabble with Italy as well as by confusion over Austria's identity as an "old" versus a "new" state, was finally completed at the end of May.[161] Germany's "voluminous" response had just arrived, blasting its entire treaty. Now came the turn of the Allies' client states to voice their objections.[162] Poland and Romania, the two main targets of the Jews' efforts, joined together to oppose the minority treaties.[163]

At 3 P.M. on May 31, 1919, a secret plenary meeting was convened in the dining room of the Quai d'Orsay to discuss the still-unfinished Austrian treaty.[164] With Clemenceau in the chair, flanked by Wilson on one side and Lloyd George on the other, the delegates of seventeen states were seated in alphabetical order around the table with their secretaries behind them. The youthful Hudson found the atmosphere "strained"[165]; but the veteran Headlam-Morley found the proceedings both "interesting and amusing."[166]

During the intense debate over the fate of East–Central Europe, two worlds faced one another, one claiming the power to shape new borders and police the settlement, the other the zone of war and pogroms, lying between Germany and Russia. Indeed, this was one of the rare peace conference sessions in which a "real issue was discussed."[167]

Brătianu, as rabid a nationalist as his father, led the attack on the proposed minorities treaties.[168] The Romanian leader assailed their weakest political component, the singling out of small states for imposed obligations. Shrewdly, he recalled how the Great Powers had avoided a minority-protection clause in the League covenant. He also complained of an assault

161. "The Austrian treaty is in a most awful mess." Headlam-Morley to Koppel, May 30, 1919, Headlam-Morley, *Memoir*, p. 131.
162. FRUS PPC, Vol. 3, pp. 424–30.
163. On their collaboration, see Congress Bureau session [*Sesja Biura Kongresowego*], May 26, 1919, report by Grabski, n.d., PIA AGND II/97; Romania, which on May 30 had threatened to withhold its signature to the Austrian treaty if a minority clause was attached, had recently issued its third decree–law on citizenship and enlisted its Jewish inhabitants' support. Headlam-Morley, *Memoir*, p. 134.
164. Among the most significant omissions were the political clauses relating to Italy and the military and reparations clauses.

    Two days earlier, in a brief, secret plenary meeting, Brătianu, as spokesman for Greece, Poland, Czechoslovakia, Yugoslavia, and Romania, had requested more time to examine the text, and Clemenceau had agreed to a forty-eight-hour adjournment. FRUS PPC, Vol. 3, pp. 391–3; Headlam-Morley, *Memoir*, p. 134.
165. Hudson #408, May 31, 1919; also reports in *Le Matin*, June 1, *New York Herald*, June 1.
166. Headlam-Morley, Diary, June 1, 1919, in Headlam-Morley, *Memoir*, p. 135.
167. Manley O. Hudson, "The Protection of Minorities," in House and Seymour, *What Really Happened at Paris*, p. 213.
168. Eight days earlier, the Committee on New States had sent him a draft copy of the proposed minority treaty with Romania and asked for his "comments and suggestions." *Receuil*, PV No. 12, May 23, 1919.

on Romania's honor and sovereignty, warning that the threat of foreign interference would neither pacify the region nor ensure national consolidation.[169] In the "new world about to be established," states must "find in the persons of their citizens devoted sons [*sic*] and a life of brotherly concord":

> If minorities are conscious of the fact that the liberties which they enjoy are guaranteed to them not by the solicitude for their welfare of the State to which they belong but by the protection of a foreign State . . . the basis of that State will be undermined . . . the seed . . . sown of unrest.

Paderewski, although in briefer, less fiery terms, added to the Powers' discomfort. Announcing that the *Sejm* would accept the treaty and invoking his people's long tradition of religious tolerance, he cannily declared Poland's readiness to accord to all its citizens "all the liberties which have already been or may be granted to them by the Great Nations and States of the West" and would "amplify" them "to the same degree" as all members of the League of Nations.[170]

Two more voices joined the chorus of complaint. Karel Kramař, representing Czechoslovakia, protested against the humiliation of a dictated treaty.[171] The Serb leader, Ante Trumbić, who seconded Kramař's objection, also insisted that minority clauses be restricted to newly acquired territories and demanded equal protection for the South Slav minorities to be assigned to Italy.[172]

Wilson assumed the burden of defending the minority treaties.[173] In a long and imposing speech, he credited the Great Powers with winning the independence of Poland and Czechoslovakia and of expanding the others' territories. Bearing the responsibility for defending the new order, these powers were obliged not only to ensure a just settlement but also to remove all causes of future disorder and conflict, specifically "the treatment . . . meted out to minorities."[174] Without referring specifically to the Jews, the

169. "History is there to prove that the protection of minorities . . . has done more to disintegrate States than to consolidate them." FRUS PPC, Vol. 3, pp. 395–401 (quotation on p. 397); Brătianu also criticized the draft treaty's financial clauses; ibid., pp. 398–99.
170. FRUS PPC, Vol. 3, p. 401; KNP delegation Paris to Wróblewski, June 1, 1919, AAN MSZ 1480/99, and report #2, Paris, June 3, 1919, AAN Paderewski 777, described the speech as a "success."
171. FRUS PPC, Vol. 3, pp. 401–3. Beneš, like Dmowski, remained silent, cleverly allowing his nationalist rival, whose star was waning at home (R. W. Seton-Watson to Headlam-Morley, Prague, May 18, 1919, HM UU Col. 97), to bear the onus of challenging the Great Powers.
172. FRUS PPC, Vol. 3, pp. 403–5; the latter demand was submitted in writing on May 30, 1919: De Martino to Sonnino, May 31, 1919, IMAE Conferenza della Pace, Segretario, Minoranze, 84/61.
173. Clemenceau issued a short, sharp rebuttal to Brătianu's tirade. FRUS PPC, Vol. 3, pp. 399–400.
174. Wilson's expansive engagement to protect European peace, reported in *The New York Times*, June 3, 1919, came back to haunt him in the 1920 election.

president alluded to the dismal historical precedents and also insisted on the "impossibility" of separating old Romanian or Serbian territory from the new states they were about to become.[175] Lloyd George, who remained silent, nodded in approval.[176]

The small states refused to be silenced.[177] Brătianu, protesting the application of "dangerous principles," pleaded for an "undiminished" sovereignty for small states as well as large.[178] Eleutherios Venizelos, who had earlier calmed the League debate and was the spokesman for Europe's oldest "new" state, suggested "negotiations" between the Great Powers and the interested parties.[179]

Several important results emerged from this historic session. The council was obliged to draft formal replies to the Romanian and Serbian reservations.[180] But it also rejected Kramář and Venizelos's proposals to conduct negotiations. Treating them identically with the Germans, the council invited the states on which minority treaties were to be imposed to submit written observations.

Jewish leaders, banned from the May 31 meeting, pored over the details in the Parisian press.[181] Marshall, initially frightened, was reassured by Baker, House, and especially by Hudson that the minority treaty had survived.[182] Wolf, briefed thoroughly by Headlam-Morley, was unruffled by the East Europeans' complaints; indeed, he calmed the panicked *Alliance* leaders, who were prepared to demand an audience before the council and to launch a public protest.[183]

It is difficult to overestimate the impact of the May 31 plenary. Faced with the Small Powers' protests, the Great Powers fell back on bullying tactics and moot historical arguments; but they also recognized they would have to appease their outraged clients. The excluded Jewish emissaries understood the limits of their influence, their dependency on western statesmen, and the intransigence of the opposition. Even the seasoned Wolf saw an uphill struggle to maintain, if not to expand, the treaties.

Brătianu's fiery rhetoric, combined with Germany's written display of obstreperousness two days earlier, influenced the fate of international minority protection at the Paris Peace Conference. Forced back to the drafting table

175. FRUS PPC, Vol. 3, pp. 405–8.
176. Headlam-Morley, *Memoir*, p. 136.
177. When Brătianu took the floor once more, Lloyd George muttered audibly, "This damned fellow; he cannot even get coats for his soldiers without us." Headlam-Morley, *Memoir*, p. 136.
178. FRUS PPC, Vol. 3, pp. 408–9.
179. Ibid., Vol. 3, pp. 409–10.
180. Ibid., Vol. 4, p. 181.
181. Adler, Diary, June 1, 1919.
182. Adler, Diary, June 2, 3, 1919. Marshall to House (aide mémoire, June 3, 1919), ibid.
183. Wolf, Diary, June 2, 1919; Adler, Diary, June 2, 1919.

at the eleventh hour, the council was now prepared to offer concessions to its friends as well as to its former enemy.

Wilson had insisted that minority obligations would be imposed on all the new and enlarged states. Nevertheless the peacemakers, aware of the resentments they had stirred, now faced their clients' demands for equal treatment as well as for strict limits on the treaties' incursions on their new, or expanded, sovereignty.[184]

Tired and exasperated, the peacemakers were entirely aware of the inconsistency of their position. They were making demands on the new states that they themselves were unwilling to accept, exacting rights for minorities that they did not extend within their own borders and establishing an international framework to which they would never submit.[185] Not only would the West European recipients of enemy territories, Belgium, Denmark, France, and Italy, not be forced to assume any onerous minority or financial obligations, but defeated Germany, still considered a "western" state, would not be obliged to give guarantees for the rights and safety of its minority population.

Wilson's rationale on May 31 failed to satisfy his irate audience; and it also placed a heavy burden on the emerging, and supposedly improved, international minority system. By embedding the protection of vulnerable individuals within the framework of old-fashioned *Realpolitik*, the president had opened the broad gate of interventionism without having committed himself to the establishment of strong and effective rules.

184. After the May 31 plenary, Headlam-Morley, anticipating demands by the East European governments for the identical treatment of all minorities, reversed his position on direct appeals to the League or the International Court of Justice; see memorandum, June 5, 1919, Headlam-Morley, *Memoir*, p. 139,

185. See Duff, "The Versailles Treaty and the Irish-Americans," p. 596, on a major issue of embarrassment.

8

The "Little Versailles"

"Should the new Poland be formed . . . without the necessary guarantees for the minority peoples . . . it would mean the advancement of the pogrom limit far towards the west."[1]

"The Polish imperialists are winning all along the line and flouting us successfully."[2]

"This has been a great day for us as for the rest of the world."[3]

"I am afraid we shall not really have pleased either the Jews or the Poles."[4]

"To create new boundaries is always to create new troubles."[5]

Five years after the shots were fired at Sarajevo, on June 28, 1919, the peace treaty with Germany was finally signed in the Hall of Mirrors in Versailles. Shortly afterwards, in a far more modest ceremony virtually unnoticed by the press, Dmowski and Paderewski placed their signatures on the "little Versailles," the world's first separate minority treaty between Poland and the Allied and Associated Powers.

Uncertainty had reigned during the first three weeks of June as to whether either treaty would be accepted. The council, its weary and irritable Anglo–American members bristling to return home, tried to appease both parties and drove their overburdened experts to draft more conciliatory texts. With the Austrian treaty left in abeyance, but the Eastern Galician question looming importantly in the background, Central Europe's two belligerent

1. German Counterproposals of May 29, 1919, in Luckau, *German Delegation*, p. 338.
2. Namier to Headlam-Morley, London, June 26, 1919, HM CC, Box 15.
3. Wolf, Diary, June 28, 1919.
4. Headlam-Morley to Koppel, June 30, 1919, Headlam-Morley, *Memoir*, p. 179.
5. House, Diary, June 29, 1919.

neighbors moved into the spotlight as the world awaited the conditions of Germany's defeat and Poland's surrender to the dictates of the Great Powers.

GERMANY AND THE MINORITY TREATY

Germany, whose main aim in Paris was to reduce its territorial and financial losses, played a complex and ambiguous role in the minorities question. Claiming rights for lost Germans was but a small part of the Reich's program, one that could also be turned against Berlin.[6]

Although the Reich on November 9, 1918, had become a republic under a moderate Socialist leadership, conservative monarchists, whose core beliefs were largely unchanged, retained almost all the major political, diplomatic, and military offices. Saturated with four years of unremitting war propaganda, the nation's sense of superiority vis-à-vis non-Germans had left it unprepared for defeat and resentful of the consequences. Thus the new Weimar Republic, which had seized every opportunity since the Armistice to denounce Poland's misdeeds, was also unready to promote a generous "new deal" for its own non-German population.[7]

Germany's Jewish community, with its high, but not total, degree of assimilation, occupied a unique status as a minority people. Its elite, regardless of their religious and political differences, rallied to the new regime, even to the point of selfless disregard for their own religious and cultural interests. Fifteen professing Jews were elected to the Weimar national assembly; Hugo Preuss wrote the first draft of the Weimar Constitution; and Max Warburg, Carl Melchior, and Moritz Julius Bonn were prominent members of the Reich delegation to Versailles. Moreover, Jewish leaders in the disputed eastern territories of Poznań (Posen), West Prussia, and Upper Silesia offered verbal and even physical support to keep their lands German.[8]

6. "In general, it is not advisable to intercede too forcefully for the German minorities abroad." Cabinet meeting, Apr. 17, 1919, Schulze, *Akten der Reichskanzlei*, p. 181, n. 7.

7. According to the Reich census of 1925, there were approximately 1,235,000 German citizens (or slightly more than 1.5% of a total population of 62,400,000) who reported their mother tongue as other than German. These included 886,000 Poles in East and West Prussia, Upper Silesia, Berlin, and the Rhineland; 120,000 Masurians (Polish Protestants in East Prussia who spoke a Polish-related dialect but were largely assimilated), 120,000 Wends (a Slavic people distantly related to the Czechs who inhabited Central Prussia and Saxon Lusatia), 30,000 Czechs in Upper Silesia, 12,000 Danes in Schleswig, and 8,000 Lithuanians in East Prussia. *Statistisches Jahrbuch für das deutsche Reich*, Vol. 49, p. 8.

8. *Jüdische Rundschau*, May 16, 1919, protested the Allied peace terms and criticized Polish anti-Semitism; an unsigned, undated memorandum by the Berlin Zionist office feared the fate of 60,000 Jews in Poznań and West Prussia who, because of their high level of German assimilation, would be hated by their Polish masters; CZA 23/103. On the government's side, Langwerth to Warburg, Berlin, May 15, 1919, Germ. AA Deutsche Friedensdelegation Versailles (R22513), Polen/Pol 8a, supported the proposed appeal to Wilson by the Jews of West Prussia, Poznań, and Silesia against

Nonetheless, German Jewry was politically weaker than its western kindred. Abroad, it had not only surrendered its leadership over world Zionism but also sundered its ties with Entente Jewry and lost its commanding position vis-à-vis the *Ostjuden*. At home, despite its patriotism and its economic and cultural prominence, this small group exerted far less political influence on the government than did its American and British cousins.[9] Moreover, faced with the vast wave of postwar public anti-Semitism clothed in anti-Bolshevik, anti-Republican rhetoric that blamed them for the Reich's defeat and for the left-wing uprisings in Berlin and in Munich, German Jewry was even more on the defensive than during the previous years.[10]

The new republic, hoping to express the Reich's "new spirit" and gain sympathy abroad, intended to expand its uneven wartime partnership with the Jews. In November 1918, the Foreign Ministry appointed Professor Moritz Sobernheim as its "Jewish specialist."[11] A gifted Jewish scholar of Near Eastern studies who had never attained an academic post, Sobernheim had taken part in the wartime Komitee für den Osten, where he had gained expertise in national and international Jewish questions. The new government official, who established close ties with all elements of German Jewry, supported the Zionist cause, and endorsed the *Ostjuden*'s autonomy demands.[12] Sobernheim's office facilitated the financial transactions between German Jews and Palestine and between western and eastern Zionists[13]; it

their transfer to Poland despite the risks of Polish retaliation. ("Eine geschickt abgefasste Erklärung könnte nach meiner Meinung doch vielleicht nützlich wirken.") See also Niewyk, *Jews in Weimar Germany*, pp. 105–9; Pulzer, *Jews and the German State*, pp. 208–14.

9. Because the Reich census was based solely on religious affiliation, it is difficult to ascertain the exact number of German Jews; in 1910, there were 539,000 professing Jews; in 1925, augmented by the influx of *Ostjuden*, there were 568,000, or less than 1% of the population, a figure counterbalanced by the concentration of Jews in bourgeois occupations and urban areas. Niewk, *Jews in Weimar Germany*, pp. 12–15.

10. The right-wing *Deutsche Zeitung*, Mar. 12, 1919, led the attack on the "Jewish republic" as well as on the Spartacists and Bavarian Bolsheviks; major anti-Semitic publications included *Das Geheimnis der jüdischen Weltherrschaft* (Berlin: "Deutsches Wochenblatt," 1919) and Arnim [Alfred Roth], *Die Juden im Heere: Eine statistische Untersuchung nach amtlichen Quellen* (Munich: Deutscher Volks-Verlag, 1919).

    See also Jochmann, *Gesellschaftskrise und Judenfeindschaft*, pp. 128–70.

11. Sobernheim to Warburg, Dec. 4, 1918, Germ. PA AA L1288/ L350393, to Zionist Central Bureau, Berlin, Dec. 12, 1918, CZA Z3/23, to Warburg, Dec. 20, 1919, Germ. PA AA L1288/L350370.

    On Sobernheim's wartime career as a Palestine specialist and liaison between Reich and East European Jews, see Zechlin, *Deutsche Politik*, pp. 133, 144, 154, 426, 432, 556.

    A dissenting voice: Rosenblüth to Zionist Office Berlin (cc to Brockdorff-Rantzau), Copenhagen, Dec. 24, 1918, termed Sobernheim "a radical, dangerous anti-Zionist," CZA Z3/21.

12. Sobernheim to Zionist Central Bureau, Berlin, Dec. 12, 1919, CZA Z3/23; Sobernheim to Walther Schotte, Feb. 17, 1919, Germ. PA AA L1288/L350423–28. Sobernheim to Rosen, Berlin, Mar. 14, 1919, ibid., L1288/L350310; Aufzeichnungen (undated) on meetings with Jewish organizations, ibid., L1288/L350365, L350367.

13. Sobernheim to Zionist Bureau, Jan. 23, 1919, Goebel to Zionist Bureau, Mar. 8, 1919, Zionist Bureau to AA, May 1, 1919, May 2, 1919, CZA Z3/23.

eased the travel restrictions on German Zionists, enabling them to travel to neutral capitals and reestablish ties with their former comrades.[14] And, beginning with Lemberg, it was also Sobernheim who disseminated news of the pogroms in Eastern Europe, drawing information from German, Jewish, and Austrian sources, transporting witnesses, and subsidizing the Jewish Press Bureaus in neutral countries that kept the atrocity reports flowing rapidly from east to west.[15]

Sobernheim's other important function was as the Jews' liaison with the Reich's peace delegation. On February 28, 1919, he met the two principal leaders of German Jewry, Eugen Fuchs, who headed the large, assimilationist *Centralverein*, and his rival, Richard Lichtheim, the spokesman for Germany's politically activist Zionists.[16] Together, they formulated a five-point program for the peace conference that included support for a Jewish homeland in Palestine; equal treatment for Jews throughout the world; the removal of all anti-Jewish ordinances and laws, especially those curtailing immigration and emigration; the establishment of national and cultural autonomy for Jews in all the new states of Eastern Europe; and the creation of an international commission by the League of Nations to administer all the clauses adopted by the peace conference pertaining to the Jews.[17]

Three of these aims immediately clashed with the Jews' and the Reich's interests.[18] Palestine was the easiest to resolve.[19] On the Jewish side, certain wordings were changed to appease the anti-Zionists' objections; and Berlin, which accepted the idea of a British mandate, nevertheless insisted on equal treatment for *all* German citizens in the Holy Land.[20]

14. Zionist Bureau Copenhagen, Mar. 6, 1919, reporting the loud applause at Motzkin's statement of regret that "not all Zionist groups" were represented at the London meeting (with a copy to Sobernheim); Handtke to Sobernheim, Apr. 7, 1919; and Warburg to Sobernheim, July 14, 1919, requesting a passport to Switzerland to hold his first meeting with Weizmann since 1914, all in CZA Z3/23.
15. Warburg to Zionist Bureau, Copenhagen, Feb. 2, 7, 13, 14, 16, 1919, CZA Z3/670; Sobernheim to Walther Schotte, Feb. 17, 1919, Germ. PA AA L1288/L350423–28, to Lieutenant Wollstein, Kovno, Feb. 27, 1919, ibid., L350333; memoranda, n.d., ibid., L350315, L350333, L350350–51, L350368, L350371; K695/K181776–80; reports in the Copenhagen office, CZA L6/110, 114, 119. A French Intelligence officer in Berne, Apr. 16, 1919, reported an active German campaign to recruit agents to stir up strife in Poland. FMAE Z (Allemagne) 403.
16. With its 45,000 members, the *Centralverein* was Germany's major Jewish institution; however, the Zionists, with 20,000 members, were far more politically active.
17. Lichtheim, Protokoll der Sitzung mit Geheimrat Fuchs bei Prof. Sobernheim, Feb. 28, 1919, Berlin, Mar. 2, 1919, CZA Z3/102. A month later a sixth demand, compensation to pogrom victims, was added. Aufzeichnung (Vertraulich), ibid., Z3/21.
18. Sobernheim, Aufzeichnung, Berlin, Mar. 1919, Germ. PA AA K695/K181838–41.
19. On wartime collaboration between Berlin and the Zionists, see Warburg to AA, Oct. 24, 1917, Jacobson to AA, Nov. 21, 28, 1917, CZA Z3/22; Warburg to Brockdorff-Rantzau, Jan. 2, 1919, ibid., Z3/23.
20. AA to Zionist Bureau, Berlin, Mar. 3, 1919, reporting on the council session, CZA Z3/23; Lichtheim, Aufzeichnung, Mar. 5, 1919, ibid, Z3/102; Sobernheim to Zionist Central Bureau Berlin, May 5, 1919, ibid., Z3/23.

More problematic was the ban on discriminatory laws and actions against Jews.[21] In the spring of 1919, Prussian and Reich officials suddenly began mass expulsions of foreign Jews born in Russian Poland and the Ukraine, who were either wartime forced laborers or postwar refugees, based ostensibly on the dangers of typhus, black-marketeering, and Bolshevism. Jewish protests, combined with Sobernheim's pleas against tarnishing Germany's case before the peace conference, brought a temporary halt.[22] Nevertheless, Reich and Prussian officials, evoking the danger of "eight million" *Ostjuden* crossing Germany's frontiers, refused to yield their right to close borders and to expel unwanted foreigners.[23]

Most difficult of all was the issue of cultural or national autonomy in Eastern Europe, which equated the Jews' claims with the German communities of Poland, Hungary, and Czechoslovakia. Sobernheim was enthusiastic about Karl Renner's autonomy proposals as, expectedly, were the German communities about to be severed from their former homeland.[24]

German Jews, however, were clearly divided over identifying themselves as part of a separate people.[25] Despite the warnings of the industrialist and wartime patriot, Walther Rathenau, against the potentially "undesirable" consequences for the Reich and its Jews, both Zionist and anti-Zionist leaders initially supported the *Ostjuden*'s national claims.[26] Sobered, however, by the news from Pinsk, Lida, and Vilna and by the rising tide of Reich anti-Semitism, German Jews quickly retreated, suggesting that autonomy questions be handled on a "case-by-case" basis.[27] They expected "others" – the *Comité*, Wilson, and "world public opinion" – to provide

21. Prussia, on Apr. 24, 1918, had issued an ordinance specifically barring the entry of foreign Jewish workers. Aufzeichnungen, undated, Germ. PA AA L1288/L350331; Dec. 20, 1918, ibid., L350339; Naumann to Zionist Bureau, Berlin, Apr. 6, 1919, CZA Z3/23.
22. Berger to AA, Apr. 8, 1919, "Forderungen bezüglich der Behandlung ausländischer Juden," CZA Z3/23. Protokollauszug der Sitzung über die jüdische Ausweisungen im Auswärtigen Amt am 10 April, 1919, Germ. PA AA L1287/L348710–13.

    In Mar. 1919, Sobernheim pleaded for a halt in the expulsion of *Ostjuden* from Upper Silesia, which would adversely affect Germany's peace program and its reputation abroad. Sobernheim to R. M. des Innern, Mar. 1919, ibid., L1288/L350329.
23. Statements by Lenz and Hering, Protokoll, Mar. 31, 1919, CZA Z3/102; also Protokoll, May 2, 1919, ibid, Z3/23; Sobernheim Aufzeichnung, Berlin, n.d. [June 1919], Germ. PA AA L1288/L350234–38.

    On the continued expulsions (in June 1920, Walther Rathenau's cousin, Fritz Rathenau drafted the Prussian edict sealing the eastern border and dealing harshly with illegal immigrants), and the increasing tension between German Jews and the *Ostjuden*, see Niewyk, *Jews in Weimar Germany*, pp. 115–20.
24. E. Schmid, "Vorschläge für die Regelung des Rechts der nationalen Minderheiten in den Friedensverträgen, 1919–1920," Mar. 11, 1919, CZA Z3/103.
25. Protokoll der Sitzung über jüdische Fragen in der Friedensstelle des Auswärtigen Amtes am 31 März (Vertraulich), CZA Z3/102.
26. Reported in *Deutsche Allgemeine Zeitung*, Apr. 1, 1919.
27. Protokoll, June 3, 1919, CZA A306/7.

relief for their threatened kin in Eastern Europe; they were also too divided to claim any form of special rights and protection for themselves in the new Germany.[28]

The Weimar government was similarly restrained. In its written counterproposals of May 29, 1919, the Reich delegation made only the most general statements, demanding basic rights for Germans passing under "alien sovereignty," deeming further cultural autonomy "desirable," and pledging vaguely to treat Germany's minorities "according to the same principles."[29] A future alliance between the *Auslandsdeutschen* and the *Ostjuden* would benefit Berlin's long-term interests; but the defeated, divided Reich in June 1919 was unready to risk the domestic or international consequences of openly championing generous minority rights.[30]

Indeed, the text of Germany's new constitution revealed the republic's liabilities as a potential minority defender abroad. Behind the liberal clauses adopted in Weimar in July 1919, was a compromise document, uneasily balancing a unitary versus a decentralized, a secular versus a Christian, a capitalist versus a Socialist, and, especially, a powerful versus a pariah state.[31] Article 114, for example, granting non-German speakers an unhindered use of their language in the schools, courts, and internal administration, was aimed originally at the mixed regions the Reich had failed to retain at the peace conference, the Sudetenland and Poznań[32]; but the new German government was unready to accept the Zionists' pleas for the recognition of either Hebrew or Yiddish.[33]

Even more equivocal was Article 137, inserted to win Catholic and Protestant support for the republic, that allowed religious communities to form state-recognized national associations and receive public subsidies.[34] German Jewry, hindered by its ambivalence over a religious versus a national identity, but also intimidated by the huge political risks and local administrative obstacles, would fail during the Weimar years to achieve the

28. On "others," see Lichtheim statement, Protokoll, Mar. 31, 1919, CZA Z3/102. Fuchs to Sobernheim, June 4, 1919, Germ. PA AA Sobernheim Handakten, L1288/L351399–400.
29. German counterproposals, May 29, 1919, Luckau, *German Delegation*, pp. 324–5.
30. On Sobernheim's persistence on this issue, Aufzeichnung, n.d. [June 1919], CZA Z3/125.
31. Vermeil, *La constitution de Weimar*, Brunet, *New German Constitution*.
32. Apelt, *Weimarer Verfassung*, pp. 58, 79.
33. Berger to Preuss, Apr. 7, 1919, CZA Z3/21, Warburg to Sobernheim, July 16, 1919, ibid., Z3/23. Sobernheim to Jacobson, Aug. 1, 1919, ibid., Z3/23, justified the omission, insisting, "the overwhelming majority of German Jews would oppose your suggestion," which would also attract "negative attention abroad."
34. Apelt, *Weimarer Verfassung*, p. 326, considered this an indication of Weimar's sham separation between church and state.

promise of this article to obtain any measure of official autonomy.[35] Moreover, the Poles of Germany, despite the generous provision of Article 73 of the Prussian constitution and the support of the *Auswärtiges Amt* and the *Auslandsdeutschen*, waited almost a decade before obtaining their own state-supported minority schools.[36]

THE LEAGUE GUARANTEE

While the council prepared its response to Germany's counterproposals and awaited Poland's written reply, the Committee on New States tackled its most controversial chore: determining the role of the League of Nations in enforcing the minority treaties, a decision that lay at the heart of the Jews' aspirations and their governments' fears.

The Cecil–Baker plan, enabling minorities to appeal the rulings of Polish courts before the Permanent Court of International Justice, was still on the table.[37] On May 29, Lord Cecil defended it forcefully.[38] Berthelot tried to water it down.[39] And two days later, Headlam-Morley, struck by the East Europeans' loud protests, withdrew his own tepid support for the plan. Falling back on the text of the Covenant, Headlam-Morley ruled against permitting minorities direct access to *any* international body.[40]

June 3 marked the first of several contentious committee meetings, pitting the seasoned British official against the very persistent American.[41] Manley Hudson, an aspiring international jurist,[42] sought to enlarge the basis of the League's minority protection, even against Wilson's well-known

35. Details in Hildesheimer, "Die Versuche zur Schaffung einer jüdischen Gesamtorganisation," and Niewk, *Jews in Weimar Germany*, pp. 178–94, which also describes the Jews' failure to maintain the separate schools approved by the new constitution that, for the majority, threatened "the German–Jewish synthesis"; ibid., pp. 110–14.

36. "Die Rechtsverhältnisse der nationalen Minderheiten in Deutschland," Jan. 15, 1929, Germ. AA T-120 K1764/5448/K432544–45.

    Questioned by the Big Four on June 23, 1919 over the treatment of Poles in German schools, Headlam-Morley had admitted "the use of Polish is forbidden, even for prayers." *Council of Four*, Vol. 2, p. 527.

37. Hudson #400, #402, #403, May 28, 29, 1919.

38. *Receuil*, PV No. 14, May 29, 1919; Hudson, #404, May 29, 1919. Jules Cambon to Paul Cambon, June 12, 1919, labeled the internationalist Cecil a large and "dangerous" spirit. FMAE PA-AP Cambon 100.

39. Berthelot to Cecil, June 1, 1919, GB FO 608/156.

40. "The League of Nations [is] a compact between states and . . . only states should have immediate access," Headlam-Morley to Namier, June 11, 1919, Headlam-Morley *Memoir*, p. 141; also Headlam-Morley to Namier, June 2, 1919, memorandum, June 5, 1919, ibid., pp. 137, 139.

41. Hudson #414, #415, June 3, 4, 1919, recording his irritation with Headlam-Morley and attempts at collaboration with De Martino; cf. IMAE CDPS/CNS, June 3, 1919; Wolf, Diary, June 3, 1919.

42. On the morning of June 3, Auchincloss had told Hudson that House was "planning for me to enter the Legal Department of the League of Nations," Hudson #412, June 3, 1919.

convictions.[43] Reversing his predecessor's narrow stance, and with House's ostensible blessing, Hudson strongly endorsed Cecil's proposals; and he also suggested a role for *all* League members in enforcing the minority treaties.[44] Headlam-Morley, who disparaged his new colleague as a novice controlled by American Jews, nevertheless felt compelled to counter Hudson's unexpected initiative.[45] Both sides courted the Italian and Japanese committee members, and both sides compromised, but not enough.[46] On June 5, the Committee on New States, forced to admit its failure to devise an enforcement formula, sent the two rival proposals up to the council.[47]

Hudson's dispute with Headlam-Morley reflected the lopsided debate emerging within the victors over the League's future, between the handful of partisans of an activist world organization and the dominant proponents of unfettered state sovereignty. While the peacemakers were assigning responsibilities to the new League, and Allied officials began assembling in London to create the structure of the world's first international organization, U.S. senators in Washington, DC, were voicing loud objections to any incursion on America's independence.[48]

The terms of enforcement of the minority treaties struck a nerve among the great powers as well as the small.[49] In its debates over the right of direct minority appeal, the Committee on New States had raised the specter of an extensive League involvement in the internal affairs of *all* its members, including their newly acquired overseas possessions.[50] Thus, over the next

43. As reported by Marshall, following his interview with the president, Hudson #398, May 27, 1919.
44. Hudson #406, #410, #411, #412, #414, #418, May 30, June 2, 3, 4, 1919.
45. "We have only Hudson, who is very young and inexperienced and frightened of coming to any decision on his own responsibility"; Headlam-Morley to Namier, June 2, 1919, Headlam-Morley, *Memoir*, p. 137; even stronger criticism, Headlam-Morley to Namier, June 30, 1919, ibid., p. 176.
46. Hudson accepted a vaguely worded formula that would involve the court even without a state-sponsored initiative. Although indicating he might agree to all League members' participating in the treaty's enforcement (Hudson #419, #420, June 5, 1919), Headlam-Morley voted with France and Japan to preserve the Council's sole role, *Receuil*, PV No. 17, June 5, 1919.
47. On the two contested issues, the Court and the role of League members, Hudson, supported only by the Italian De Martino, was outvoted by Headlam-Morley, Berthelot, and Adatci. *Receuil*, PV No. 17, June 5, 1919; copies of June 5 report to the council in Committee on New States, June 5, 1919, GB FO 604/50; IMAE CDPS/CNS 209/24; Frankfurter files, CZA A264/5; see also Hudson #420, June 5, 1919; Headlam-Morley to Namier, June 11, 1919, Headlam-Morley, *Memoir*, pp. 141–2.
48. Miller, *Diary*, Vol. 20, p. 440; Miller was now in Washington to brief the Senate Foreign Affairs Committee on the League Covenant and the peace negotiations.
49. Headlam-Morley memorandum, June 5, 1919, Headlam-Morley, *Memoir*, p. 139: "If we once let it be supposed that anyone but states can appear before the Court, we should be opening the way to a very dangerous agitation for allowing minorities in other countries the same privilege."
50. George Louis Beer, who was drafting the mandate agreements and was widely expected to head the League's mandates section, viewed the minority-appeal procedure as a possible model for

twelve days, Hudson and Headlam-Morley were each pleading for a council resolution that would affect the entire postwar order.[51]

Lucien Wolf, who had long hoped for a direct-appeal procedure, watched this debate helplessly and in great dismay.[52] Recognizing the deficiencies in both Hudson's and Headlam-Morley's amended proposals and missing Cecil, who had departed for the League negotiations in London, Wolf predicted that the Jews might end up with "nothing at all."[53] Wolf blamed Marshall for sabotaging the Cecil–Baker plan and feared that Wilson, yielding to the East Europeans' protests and Marshall's assurances, would countenance a worthless treaty.[54] Above all, the Briton dreaded the burden of defending millions of fractious East Europeans under even less propitious conditions than in the past; he also credited the rumors that the Poles, backed by France, would refuse to sign.[55]

It was at the height of the mid-June heat wave, and just as the alarming news of Senator Knox's anti-League resolution reached Paris,[56] when the council finally responded to the Reich's extensive counterproposals. Following two-and-a-half weeks of frantic meetings and drafting sessions, the Four on June 16, 1919, rendered their decisions and also dealt a serious setback to Poland. Despite Paderewski's eloquent pleas for Upper Silesia, backed firmly by France, Lloyd George had convinced the council to hold a plebiscite within two years. Scarcely a "victory for self-determination," this reversal over Upper Silesia represented a deft act of appeasement. It was a gesture to allay the Allied public's growing unease over the wisdom and justice of the treaty; it was a prod to the German government to withstand internal opposition, sign, and accept reparations; and it was also a punishment to the Poles for their misdeeds in the East.[57]

"persons who are denied their rights in a mandated country." Hudson #435, June 11, 1919; others immediately saw the parallel between minority and mandate supervision.

51. Hudson, #421, #422, June 5, 6, 1919; memo for the president, June 6, 1919, WWP 412; Headlam-Morley to Hankey, June 11, 15, 16, 1919, Headlam-Morley, *Memoir*, pp. 141, 145–47.
52. "Without a clearly defined and effective Right of Appeal to the League, the Polish and other Treaties will be quite useless – more sword-thrusts in the water, like the similar Treaty of Berlin," Wolf, Diary, May 28, 1919.
53. Wolf, Diary, June 7, 1919; Wolf found Headlam-Morley's proposals "too political," Hudson's "too vague and indefinite." Wolf, Diary, June 10, 1919.
54. "I should not be surprised if in the end Wilson yielded and agreed to relinquish the right of appeal altogether, more especially as Marshall is there to tell him on behalf of American Jews that a right of intervention by the Signatory Powers will do just as well. In that case, the Treaties will not be worth the paper they are written on. The whole outlook to-day is bad." Wolf, Diary, June 1, 1919.
55. Wolf, Diary, June 16, 1919.
56. On June 10, 1919, Philander Chase Knox, the senator from Pennsylvania, former secretary of state under William Howard Taft, and a vehement opponent of the League, proposed to separate the treaty with Germany from the United States' adherence to the League. See "Paris is Shocked by Knox Proposal," *The New York Times*, June 15, 1919; Hudson, #450, June 14, 1919.
57. The linkage between Upper Silesia and Eastern Galicia in Lloyd George's diatribe on June 5, FRUS PPC, Vol. 6, pp. 197–201; "punishment" alleged by the two bitter opponents, Dmowski (Simson to

Paderewski had more success with his claim for all of Eastern Galicia, a remote region involving no immediate Great-Power interests. Notwithstanding Lloyd George's vicious harangue on June 5, contrasting the Allies' huge human sacrifices for Polish independence with Warsaw's "imperialism" against its small neighbors, the Allies recognized their helplessness to impose a plebiscite, restrain further Polish military action, or dictate the future borders or political order in Eastern Galicia.[58] With Kolchak faltering, the Ukrainian forces in disarray, and the Austrian treaty still contested, the Four decided to pass the problem to the largely idle Council of Foreign Ministers, which immediately turned the matter over to Cambon's pro-Polish Territorial Commission.[59]

It was within this context that the Council of Four, on June 17, 1919, issued its long-delayed ruling on the nature of the League guarantee of history's first minority treaty.[60] Earlier, the Four had already expressed their unwillingness to grant minorities a direct hearing before the new international organization.[61] On June 6, they had censured the amended Cecil–Baker–Hudson proposals to allow any form of access to the court[62]; and on June 17, they buried them for good.[63]

The council's negative decision over including all League members as treaty guarantors was also predictable. Although Wilson had initially endorsed the idea, he and his colleagues had recognized the risks; by reducing the Great Powers' burden and expanding the minority states' international exposure, this offered the irate East European leaders a fine excuse not to sign.[64] After personal consultations to ascertain their clients' preferences,[65] the council on June 17 assigned sole responsibility for the treaty's enforcement to the members of League of Nations Council.[66]

Tyrrell, June 7, 1919, GB FO 371/4380) and Namier (Namier to Headlam-Morley, June 7, 1919, HM CC, Box 12).

58. *Council of Four*, June 5, 1919, Vol. 2, pp. 307–14; FRUS PPC, Vol. 4, pp. 191–201; Lloyd George's speech, p. 197.
59. *Council of Four*, June 12, 1919, Vol. 2, p. 420; FRUS PPC, Vol. 6, pp. 352–3.
60. Hudson, #458, June 16, 1919, Hudson to Wilson, June 16, 1919, WWP 412.
61. *Council of Four*, May 17, 1919, Vol. 2, pp. 88–91; FRUS PPC, Vol. 5, pp. 680–1.
62. Details of discussion in *Council of Four*, June 6, 1919, Vol. 2, pp. 331–2; notification by Berthelot, Hudson, #436, June 10, 1919.
63. *Council of Four*, June 17, 1919, Vol. 2, pp. 481-82; FRUS PPC, Vol. 6, p. 530.
64. *Council of Four*, June 6, 1919, Vol. 2, pp. 331-2; FRUS PPC, Vol. 6, pp. 221–2.
65. Overcoming Clemenceau's disinclination to consult these irate East European leaders, Lloyd George had spoken with Paderewski and Venizelos, Wilson with Beneš, Orlando with Brătianu, and Clemenceau with Vesnić. Headlam-Morley, Council of Four and New States, June 6, 7, 8. 16, 1919, HM CC, Box 11.
66. FRUS PPC, Vol. 6, p. 530; *Council of Four*, June 17, 1919, Vol. 2, pp. 481–3, omits this decision.

Far less of a blow than the defeat of the Cecil–Baker plan, this was nonetheless a setback for the minorities cause.[67] By restricting the burden of minority protection to individual Great Powers, in a forum within which any of its members could veto a resolution, the Council of Four had salved the East Europeans' *amour propre*. They had redesigned the old system in a new League garb without establishing an automatic process for handling another Pinsk; and they had not removed the still-prevailing reluctance to intervene in other states' internal affairs.[68]

The council's decisions on June 17 were undoubtedly affected by the arrival of Paderewski's long-overdue written response to the proposed minority treaty.[69] Dispatched the day after he had learned of the council's decision to hold the plebiscite in Upper Silesia, the Polish premier, emulating the Germans' assertive tactics, objected to almost every clause in the treaty and threatened not to sign.[70]

ANSWERING POLAND'S CHALLENGE

Paderewski, at the midpoint of his second arduous sojourn in Paris, had so far failed to quash Germany's threats, the Jews' antipogrom campaign, or the Four's growing skepticism of his leadership.[71] He and his colleagues had also failed to raise the substantial foreign funds Poland required for its war effort and its acute civilian needs.[72] His letter of June 15, drafted with Dmowski

67. Wolf, who mistakenly labeled the restriction to council members the "British formula" (Wolf, Diary, June 18, 1919), tried to see the bright side in "the novelty . . . [of giving] the right of intervention to any one of the Signatory Powers instead of to all of them in a body"; ibid., June 19, 1919.
68. "I very much regret this decision." Hudson #18, June 18, 1919. Except for De Martino, no member of the Committee on New States attended the crucial June 17 meeting.
69. Headlam-Morley to Hankey, June 15, 1919, Headlam-Morley, *Memoir*, pp. 145–6, suspecting that someone [Pichon?] in the French Foreign Ministry was encouraging the Poles to delay and assuring them they would not have to sign; Hankey to Paderewski, June 15, 1919, AAN Paderewski 629, urging the premier to respond. Also, Hudson to Wilson, June 16, 1919, WWP 412.
70. The twelve-page memorandum, June 15, 1919, AAN Paderewski 846; also in FRUS PPC, Vol. 6, pp. 535–40; covering letter: Paderewski to Lloyd George, June 15, 1919, LGP F57/5/2.
71. Biuro Kongresowe meetings, June 2, 7, 14, 1919, AAN KNP 169; Jan Ciechanowski reports to MSZ, Paris, June 10, 18 (secret), 1919, ibid., MSZ 1480; Report #7, Paris, June 13, 1919, ibid., Paderewski 777; also Lipski to Sobański, Paris, June 7, 1919, ibid., KNP 1959, alleging the "deliberate" timing of British Jewry's huge anti-Polish campaign in order to influence the territorial decisions in Paris.
72. See, e.g., Lamont to Paderewski, June 2, 1919, AAN Paderewski 989; Monfries, British Food Mission Paris, to Cresom, Warsaw, June 19, 1919, ibid., MSZ 1480 (urging the Poles to sign a bond), Tyrrell to Sobański, London, June 27, 1919, ibid., KNP 114 (refusing £13 million in credits for military materiel, accepting £1 million for civilian credits on condition that £5 million be provided by banks).

 Britain did approve Poland's request for an Interior Ministry official, Zygmunt Jedrzewiowski, to study its police system. MSZ to Paris, May 20, 1919, ibid., KNP 35; Sobański to Vereker, June 12, 1919, Spicer to Sobański, London, June 17, 1919, ibid., KNP 1909.

several days earlier and, in all likelihood, given covert French assistance, came in response to the Allies' veiled threat simply to impose a minority treaty on Poland.[73]

In his lengthy missive Paderewski raised a series of fundamental and specific objections to the minority treaty. Recalling Poland's destruction by its intrusive neighbors and quoting the *Sejm*'s refusal to submit to any new form of external control, Paderewski protested the treatment of his people "as a nation of inferior standards of civilization . . . ignorant of the conception of the duties of a modern State." Promising to grant full rights to all Polish subjects, he also insisted that "all citizens should develop a consciousness of their duties towards the State." And, echoing Brătianu, he denounced an imposed agreement and a procedure that encouraged Poland's minorities to lodge complaints with outsiders, which would "fatally provoke excitement against the minorities and . . . become the cause of incessant unrest."[74]

Paderewski also objected to the treaty's arbitrary constitutional stipulations that mixed inalienable rights with administrative details.[75] Appealing to equity and to the venerable principles of international law, he demanded reciprocal treatment for the Polish population remaining in Germany and insisted that citizenship questions be regulated in the territorial treaties.[76] In his most emphatic general complaint, Paderewski expressed Poland's "ardent desire that the principles of freedom should be *universally* applied," vowing "to realise the stipulations . . . which the League of Nations will recognize as being obligatory for all States belonging to the League, in the same way as with regard to the protection of labour."[77]

On the Jewish question Paderewski assumed a completely inflexible stance. Evoking Poland's history as a tolerant haven for a persecuted people, and citing the "good understanding" that had prevailed between Poles and Jews in the nineteenth century, he blamed the recent "strained" relations solely on the Jews' "hostility" toward the new state. Only an internal solution would ensure the resumption of "normal" relations; the internationalization of the Jewish question would "create difficulties," and not, he warned, for Poland alone.[78]

73. Report by Grabski, Biuro Kongresowe meeting, June 16, 1919, AAN KNP 169.
74. FRUS PPC, Vol. 6, p. 535.
75. Ibid., p. 540.
76. Ibid., p. 540.
77. Ibid., p. 537, emphasis added.
78. Ibid., pp. 535–39. "It is to be feared that the Great Powers may be preparing for themselves unwelcome surprises, for taking into consideration the migratory capacities of the Jewish population, which so readily transports itself from one state to another, it is certain that the Jews, basing themselves on the precedent thus established, will claim elsewhere the national principles which they would enjoy in Poland," ibid., p. 539.

Getting down to specifics, Paderewski flailed the clauses pertaining to the Jews. Underscoring this large community's religious and political differences, the premier attacked each of the committee's carefully crafted provisions. Invoking western liberal values, he objected to the maintenance at state expense of separate minority schools as well as cultural and charitable institutions. Appealing to the Allies' prejudices, he dismissed the elevation of Yiddish as a language of instruction and its use in the courts as the privileging of "a corrupted German . . . spoken in the middle ages, . . . inadequate to modern intellectual requirements, and merely adaptable to the germanisation of the Jews." Attacking the much-diluted Sabbath clause, Paderewski insisted on the duty of all citizens in a democracy not to refuse to perform public and military service.[79]

Stunned by this sweeping critique of "the entire order of things we had wanted to establish,"[80] the Council of Four took stock on June 17. Questioning neither their right nor determination to impose the minority treaties, both Wilson and Lloyd George acknowledged that they might have gone "a bit far" in their concessions to the Jews, thereby threatening Poland's national consolidation and also opening the way for "German intrigues."[81] Before taking a three-day break, the council ordered the Committee on New States to draft a prompt response, fully recognizing, at this late hour in their deliberations, that the time for dictating terms to Poland was over.[82]

Headlam-Morley drove the Committee on New States to defend its model treaty upon which the whole new edifice of minority rights was to be built. Backed by his Italian and Japanese colleagues, the Briton rebuffed Berthelot's proposal to abandon the document and merely ask the Poles for a declaration of good intentions.[83] In record time, the committee produced a new draft that bolstered the council's position but appeased Paderewski with five, not inconsiderable, modifications. These included the removal of the Jewish clauses from the category of "fundamental" Polish laws, long the centerpiece of the American Jews' program; the removal of military service from

79. Ibid., pp. 536–9.
80. Quotation, ascribed to Lloyd George, in *Council of Four* (June 17, 1919), Vol. 2, p. 481.
81. *Council of Four*, Vol. 2, pp. 481–3; FRUS PPC, Vol. 6, pp. 529–30.
82. Lloyd George to Paderewski, Paris, June 18, 1919, AAN Paderewski 429. Following this meeting, Wilson traveled to Belgium, and Lloyd George to Verdun. Paderewski also left Paris, traveling privately to London to receive an honorary degree. Clerk to Sobański, London, June 13, 1919, ibid., KNP 1909, Ciechanowski report (secret), June 18, 1919, ibid., MSZ 1480.
83. Meetings June 18, 19, 1919, GB FO 608/156; IMAE CDPS/CNS; *Receuil*, PV No. 23, June 18, No. 24, June 19, 1919; also Hudson #463, #465, June 18, 1919; Hudson, memorandum for the president, n.d., WWP 5B 37/27121.

The main basis of French opposition to the treaty in Pralon to Pichon, Warsaw, June 30, 1919, FMAE Z (Pologne) 61.

the Sabbath-protection clause; limiting state-supported minority-language instruction to the primary schools; restricting German minority rights to territories belonging to the former Reich; and allowing amendments to the treaty by a majority decision of the League of Nations Council.[84]

Headlam-Morley, overburdened and weary, doubted the Anglo-Saxons' ability to "stand firm" in the face of French chicanery, Polish obstinacy, and the uncertainty still prevailing over Germany's final decision.[85] Turning to Wolf, he ostensibly asked the Jewish leader to enlist his friends in bringing "some immediate pressure to bear" on Lloyd George and Wilson to defend the treaty.[86]

At this crucial moment, however, in stark contrast with the well-coordinated antipogrom campaigns that were sweeping the major Allied countries, the Jewish forces in Paris were in utter disarray.[87] Wolf and Marshall blocked a bid by the *Alliance* to establish an international bureau.[88] But they could not suppress the *Comité des délégations juives*, which suddenly circulated its radical memorandum (containing Marshall's signature), issued a "Bulletin" infused with nationalist rhetoric, and proclaimed itself a permanent body to uphold Jewish national and minority rights.[89]

Marshall was also embroiled in two major political squabbles, both resulting from the Jews' antipogrom campaign which had caused a great stir in America. One involved the new U.S. minister to Warsaw, Hugh Gibson, who, vexed by the torrent of State Department inquiries over the pogrom reports, not only contested their authenticity but also made highly critical comments, leaked to the press, about the character of Polish Jewry.[90]

84. Berthelot to Hankey, June 19, 1919, FRUS PPC, Vol. 6, pp. 570–3. Wolf, Diary, June 19, 1919; Hudson #470, June 21, 1919, Hudson to Wilson, June 21, 1919, WWP 412.

85. His work burdens: Headlam-Morley, Diary, June 19, 1919, Headlam-Morley, *Memoir*, pp. 154–5; suspicions of Dmowski's collusion with the Quai d'Orsay to sabotage the treaty, ibid., p. 175; Headlam-Morley's fears that a "nearly overwhelmed" council might not "appreciate the gravity of the situation and . . . consent to a postponement of the Polish Treaty," Wolf, Diary, June 19, 1919.

86. Wolf, Diary, June 19, 1919.

87. Adler, Diary, June 20, 1919.

88. Adler, Diary, June 11, 1919.

89. Adler, Diary, June 11, 1919; Wolf, Diary, June 22, 30, 1919; Marshall's protest to Motzkin, June 23, 1919, in Adler, Diary.

The *Comité*'s first *Bulletin*, appearing on June 17 and produced once or twice a month for the remainder of 1919, was sent to 400 journals and periodicals as well as major political leaders and peace-conference officials. Janowsky, *Jews and Minority Rights*, p. 357, n. 19.

90. *The New York Times*, June 8, 11, 12, 1919; among the most critical reports were Gibson to Ammission, June 16, 18, 19, 1919, LC White 52, and, especially, Gibson to Ammission, June 2, 1919, Hoover ARA 18, which, in describing Poland's Jewish communities, contained the references to a Jewish "criminal class" and to Jewish "spies and provocateurs" that infuriated Marshall.

Gibson was, indeed, more favorably impressed by the new Poland than were his Jewish critics (see especially Gibson to Phillips, Warsaw, June 6, 1919, Gibson 56); he strongly believed in the Bolshevik danger and in a German–Jewish conspiracy, and he urged the assignment of all of Eastern Galicia to unconditional Polish rule. See, e.g., Gibson, memorandum for the Secretary of State, Paris, June 25, 1919, Gibson 100; Gibson to Phillips, July 6, 1919, Gibson 56.

An infuriated Marshall struck back. Publicly, in articles in *The New York Times* and dozens of other American newspapers, he castigated the envoy for his errors and bias.[91] Privately, he and his associates issued veiled, if risky, threats to oppose Gibson's Senate confirmation.[92] Gibson's appearance in Paris on June 24 produced no reconciliation between the envoy and his accusers.[93] Not only did Gibson's nomination sail through the Senate,[94] but the Jews also suffered a backlash of resentment in Foggy Bottom as well as in Warsaw.[95]

Marshall's second, and related, struggle, involving the long-delayed U.S. Commission to Poland, was even more acrimonious and less successful. Wilson, urged by Hoover, House, and Gibson, had finally accepted Paderewski's proposal that the United States conduct an "independent investigation" of the events between November 1918 and May 1919 in order to dampen the Zionists' propaganda and calm American public opinion.[96] On his advisors' suggestion, endorsed by Paderewski, the president had asked the staunchly anti-Zionist Ambassador Henry Morgenthau to head the commission.[97]

Marshall, appalled by this prospect, had urged the president to reconsider the appointment or postpone the mission.[98] Leading American Jews of all persuasions tried to dissuade Morgenthau from undertaking this explosive

For a pro-Gibson presentation of the imbroglio, Kapiszewski, *Hugh Gibson . . . A Documentary History*.

91. *The New York Times*, June 10, 16, 17, 1919; also Marshall to Lansing, June 20, 1919, LC Robert Lansing papers 43; Wolf, Diary, June 14, 19, 1919.
92. "You know how the President stands by his nominees." Adler to Schiff, Paris, June 20, 1919 AJA Schiff 34; next to Marshall, Adler was Gibson's severest critic (Adler, Diary, June 10, 1919) joined by Oscar Straus, Lewis Strauss, and Felix Frankfurter, all of whom had originally supported the minister's appointment.

    Wolf shared their outrage (Wolf, Diary, June 16, 1919): "[Gibson] has adopted all the legends of Jewish pro-Germanism, treachery, espionage, profiteering and bolshevism . . . the pogroms . . . do not exist for him. [His] report . . . is a most mischievous document, and fully entitles the Jews of America to demand Gibson's recall."
93. On House's initiative, Gibson met Louis Brandeis and Felix Frankfurter as well as Marshall; House, Diary, undated, June 25; Lansing to Polk, June 26, 1919, NA USDS 860c 4016/101. Compare Gibson to Mary Gibson, Paris, June 24, 1919, Gibson 36; Gibson to Dolbeare (Warsaw), Paris, June 26, 1919, Gibson 21; Gibson to Mary Gibson, Paris, June 29, 1919, Gibson to Phillips, Warsaw, July 6, 1919, Gibson 56.
94. Polk to Ammission, June 27, 1919, WWP 5B, Box 49/28059.
95. Gibson to Mary Gibson, June 24, 1919, Gibson 36; Gibson to Dolbeare, Paris, June 26, 1919, Gibson 21; Gibson to Phillips, Warsaw, July 6, 1919, Gibson 56; cf. Hudson, #479, June 24, 1919; Adler, Diary, June 29, 1919.

    A disturbed State Department: Polk to Ammission Paris, June 11, 1919, LC White 52; Leland Harrison to Winslow, Paris, June 24, 1919, LC Harrison 105, accusing Jews such as Zuckermann, Billikopf, and Loewenstein of spreading "inflammatory propaganda."
96. Hoover to Wilson, Paris, June 2, 1919, Hoover ARA 19; Wilson to Hoover, June 3, 1919, ibid.; Ciechanowski report #2, Paris, June 3, 1919, AAN Paderewski 777, Adler, Diary, June 3, 4, 1919.
97. Grew to Morgenthau, Paris, June 17, 1919, LC Morgenthau, cont. 9.
98. Marshall to House, June 3, 5, 1919, in Adler, Diary; also, Lansing to State Department, Paris, June 19, 1919, NA USDS Poland 860C, reel 14.

task.[99] Marshall's efforts were foiled, however, not only by Wolf's support of the mission[100] but, especially, by Wilson, who removed all of Morgenthau's doubts and kindled his zeal to serve his country.[101]

Marshall and Wolf were indeed pursuing opposite goals in their last-minute efforts to rescue the minority treaty. The feisty Marshall, who was challenging the U.S. administration and was also caught uncomfortably between the East and West European Jews, still sought a clear-cut victory over the intransigent new leaders of Eastern Europe; while the less powerful, more cautious Wolf aspired only to maintain Europe's tradition of minority protection under even less auspicious circumstances than earlier.

Both held strong convictions about the future of Jewish life in Eastern Europe. The American, believing in the permanence of Polish anti-Semitism, desired ironclad protection for a safe and independent Jewish existence, whereas the realist Briton sought to defend Poland's sovereignty and restrict Jewish separateness. The isolationist Marshall, who opposed the League, placed his faith in Washington's ability to enforce the Powers' decisions, whereas Wolf, the seasoned intercessor, recognized that no system of external control would work without the interested parties' cooperation.[102]

On June 21, 1919, the council, sensitive to the public outcry and belying Headlam-Morley's fears, refused to back down over the minority treaty.[103] The Four ordered the Committee on New States to prepare a final draft as well as an official answer to Paderewski's protest.[104] Nonetheless, to compel both the Germans and the Poles to sign, the victors stood firm over essentials but were prepared to retreat, even over significant details, such as Germany's audacious scuttling of its fleet at Scapa Flow.[105]

The Powers were also prepared to offer major concessions to Poland. These were already hinted at on June 18 when the Council of Foreign

99. Adler to Schiff, Paris, June 20, 1919, AJA Schiff 34; Adler, Diary, June 12, 19, 20, 22, 1919; Mack to Frankfurter and Marshall, June 23, 1919, NA USDS Poland 860C, reel 14.
100. Wolf, Diary, June 20, 21, 27, 1919; Wolf to Marshall, June 26, 1919, YIVO W/M 209.
101. Morgenthau, Diary, June 26, 1919; House, Diary, June 26, 27, 1919; Morgenthau to Schiff, July 4, 1919, LC Morgenthau, cont. 9; Mack to Frankfurter, July 26, 1919, CZA A404/107.
102. [Marshall] "really detests the League of Nations which he regards as a danger to American interests, and it is with great reluctance that he supports the association of the League with our Minority Treaties. This is really why he has been trying all along to vest the guarantees of the Treaties more in the Signatory Powers than in the League"; Wolf, Diary, June 16, 1919; also June 19, 20, 21, 23, 1919; earlier, Marshall to Wolf, Paris, May 29, 1919, Wolf to Marshall, June 1, 1919, in Wolf, Diary.
103. Among the last minute pleas to uphold the Polish treaty, Samuel and Montefiore to Balfour, June 18, 1919, YIVO W/M 36; Morgenthau to Wilson, June 20, 1919, in Adler, Diary; Marshall to Wilson, June 21, 1919, WWP 412.
104. FRUS PPC, Vol. 6, pp. 569–70; Hudson #470, June 21, 1919.
105. The Scapa Flow discussions, June 25, 1919, FRUS PPC, Vol. 6, pp. 656–7, 671, 679, found Wilson and Clemenceau preaching moderation to a furious and vindictive Lloyd George.

Ministers had sanctioned the movement of Polish troops in Eastern Galicia up to the River Zbrucz without, however, reaching agreement over the region's future political status.[106] Another indication was Wilson's refusal to back down over Morgenthau's appointment and the dispatch of the investigatory commission, despite the obvious discomfiture of American Jews[107]; indeed, pleading the pressure of work, the president declined another interview with Marshall, but sent assurances that the treaty would survive.[108]

The last political battle over the Polish minority treaty centered on Yiddish, the mother tongue of millions of Ashkenazic Jews and one of their two religious, literary, and political languages. Jewish nationalists had demanded a separate, publicly supported Yiddish school system to preserve their people's freedom and identity[109]; their opponents, Jewish as well as non-Jewish, termed Yiddish a "dying," minor tongue but also a tool of Jewish nationalism and an instrument of germanization.[110]

Transformed into another Anglo-American contest, the Yiddish debate pitted an implacable Headlam-Morley against a stubborn Hudson,[111] with the Quai d'Orsay supporting the British. Seeking to discredit Yiddish as one of the national languages of Poland, Headlam-Morley labeled it a medium for teaching very young children as distinguished from German, a language

106. FRUS PPC, Vol. 4, pp. 827–32. Balfour, citing the Ukrainians' objections to Polish overlordship, had resisted Cambon's and Sonnino's proposals to assign the region immediately to Poland with provisions for local autonomy. Significantly, no speaker mentioned the Jewish population of Eastern Galicia, whom the Polish Commission had added to the *Polish* side of its demographic statistics. Balfour memorandum, June 18, 1919, FRUS PPC, Vol. 6, pp. 687–8; Ciechanowski to MSZ, June 18, 1919, AAN MSZ 1480.

107. See Chapter 6, n. 91. Polk to Wilson, Washington, June 23, 1919 (conveying the pleas of Schiff, Mack, Rosenwald, Straus, Wise, Elkus), NA USDS Poland 860C, reel 14; Ammission [Wilson] to State Dept., Paris, June 27, 1919, ibid., reel 15, explaining that the telegram had arrived "too late" to recall the appointment or the commission.

Much to Paderewski's chagrin, the Morgenthau mission did not leave Paris until July 10 (Lansing to Paderewski, July 2, 1919, Paderewski to Lansing, July 4, 1919, AAN Paderewski 774) almost two weeks after the Minority Treaty was signed. Shortly afterwards, Felix Frankfurter paid an independent visit to Poland (Adler, Diary, July 2, 1919, Grew to Warsaw, Paris, July 17, 1919, LC Morgenthau, cont. 9; Gibson to Grew, Warsaw, July 31, 1919, Gibson 42; Gibson to Phillips, Aug. 29, Gibson 56). To quell the Jewish clamor in Great Britain, the Lloyd George government insisted on sending its own mission; Balfour to Wyndham, Aug. 9, Sept. 4, 1919, GB FO 371/3904; Misja Samuels a Polsce, Sept. 26, 1919, AAN Paderewski 774. France's *Ligue des droits de l'homme* sent one as well. Memorandum, Sept. 12, 1919, AAN Paderewski, 774.

108. G. F. Close to Marshall, June 23, 1919, WWP 413.

109. Voicing the objections of Jewish nationalists, Lewis Namier to Headlam-Morley, July 2, 1919, HM CC, Box 12, deemed Yiddish indispensable for the intellectual and cultural life of the Jewish masses: "The Polish language and Polish culture is strange to us and hostile. It is permeated by a spirit of Roman Catholicism and by the most rampant, aggressive, intolerant anti-Semitism. To make the Jew feed on it is the same as to make men eat straw or wood."

110. Headlam-Morley statements to council, June 23, 1919, FRUS PPC, Vol. 4, p. 627.

111. *Receuil*, PV No. 26, No. 27, June 21, 23, 1919; Hudson, #471, #472, #473, June 21, 22, 1919; Wolf, Diary, June 23, 1919; IMAE CDPS/CNS, June 24, 1919.

worthy of state-supported instruction. The ardent assimilationist Sylvain Lévi, seeking to remove all barriers between Poles and Jews and to promote Jewish integration into Poland's cultural and intellectual life, quietly proposed a total ban on Yiddish.[112]

On June 23 the leaders of the world's mightiest powers debated the issue of Yiddish instruction, to the British a threat to national cohesiveness, to the Americans the shield of a threatened people living in "medieval conditions."[113] Balfour and Lloyd George strongly backed Headlam-Morley's allegations of an "aggressive" Jewish nationalism.[114] Wilson thwarted their efforts to suppress Yiddish entirely[115]; but the president nonetheless made two significant concessions. The first was to accept the obligatory teaching of Polish and restrict Yiddish as a language of instruction to the state's primary schools. The second was to authorize local committees, and not a central Jewish bureau in Warsaw, to administer Jewish schools, thus dismissing, once and for all, the Jews' hopes for any form of national cultural autonomy.[116]

That evening, at around 6 P.M., Paris learned of the new German Cabinet's decision to sign the peace treaty.[117] The next day Headlam-Morley, after settling his disputes with Hudson, dispatched the two finished documents to a council too busy to review them.[118] At once Clemenceau transmitted to Paderewski the heavily diluted minority treaty along with the covering letter he had signed that explicitly repudiated the Jewish claim to national rights.[119]

112. Wolf, Diary, June 27, 1919.

113. Headlam-Morley to Carnegie, June 23, 1919, HM UU Col. 18/6; Headlam-Morley to Hankey, June 23, 1919, Headlam-Morley, *Memoir*, p. 157–9. Both Headlam-Morley and Hudson were present for part of the council meeting.

114. *Council of Four* (June 23, 1919), Vol. 2, pp. 526–7; FRUS PPC, Vol. 6, pp. 624–7.

115. FRUS PPC, Vol. 6, p. 627, reading Hudson's memorandum, endorsed by American Jews, Hudson #475, June 23, 1919.

116. FRUS PPC, Vol. 6, pp. 625, 628; Headlam-Morley explained the committee's purpose in "prevent[ing] the establishment of a central administration of Jewish schools"; *Council of Four* (June 23, 1919), Vol. 2, p. 526; his disgruntlement over the council's "reversal" over Yiddish in Headlam-Morley to Carnegie, June 23, 1919, HM UU Col. 18/6.

One important question was left open: While Balfour pressed for a religious definition of Jewish identity (FRUS PPC, Vol. 6, p. 628), Wilson apparently demurred (*Council of Four* [June 23, 1919], Vol. 2, p. 527).

117. Wolf, Diary, June 23, 1919. "This news immediately created a different feeling on the part of everybody around Paris and a very noticeable buoyancy could be seen on every hand." Hudson #477, June 23, 1919.

118. Committee on New States, June 23, 1919, GB FO 608/156; Headlam-Morley to Hankey, June 24, 1919, Headlam-Morley, *Memoir*, pp. 159–60; Wolf, Diary, June 25, 1919, Headlam-Morley to Berthelot, June 25, 1919, HM CC, Box 1.

119. See Clemenceau to Paderewski, June 24, 1919, AAN Paderewski 629 also FRUS PPC, Vol. 6, pp. 629–34. Hudson, #475, #477, #478, June 23, 24, 1919.

Much relieved, Lucien Wolf and Marshall each thanked their countrymen, Headlam-Morley and Hudson, for rescuing the treaty.[120]

It was still possible that the Poles would refuse to sign.[121] At the last minute, an officially sponsored deputation representing a tiny segment of assimilationist Polish Jews pleaded against the minority treaty and proposed that Yiddish be relegated to an "auxiliary" language.[122] From Warsaw came strong warnings against signing the treaty from the *Sejm* Foreign Affairs Committee.[123] In Paris, Paderewski and company, desperately short of money and battered by the Jews' press campaign,[124] used all their resources to enhance Warsaw's tarnished image; and up to the last minute, they resisted a surrender to Great-Power dictates.[125]

This set the stage for the peacemakers' most dramatic group of concessions. On June 25, 1919, after hostilities had again erupted in Eastern Galicia, the Council of Four unanimously sanctioned Poland's "temporary" military occupation of the entire province. Although they delayed ruling on Eastern Galicia's political future, the victors had virtually sealed the province's fate under a permanent Polish control.[126] Officially, they claimed a belated

120. Wolf, Diary, June 25, 1919; Hudson #480, #481, June 24, 25, 1919.
121. Biuro Kongresowe, June 24, 25, 1919, AAN KNP 169.
122. Biuro Kongresowe, June 13, 1919 AAN KNP 169, on the first arrivals; MSZ to KNP, June 14, 1919, on the rest, ibid., MSZ 1480; Wolf, Diary, June 25, 27, 1919; Wolf to Marshall, June 27, 1919, AJA LM 52; Headlam-Morley, note of interview, June 26, 1919, Paderewski statement to Council of Four, June 27, 1919, FRUS PPC, Vol. 6, p. 725; Headlam-Morley to Namier, June 30, 1919, Headlam-Morley, *Memoir*, pp. 173–4, 175. On an earlier delegation, led by M. P. Lieberman, which had denied the pogroms and denounced the minority treaty, Ringel to Grynbaum, Paris, June 7, 1919, CZA A127/315.
123. Skrzyński to KNP, Warsaw, June 26, 1919, AAN KNP 169.
124. On June 25, on the eve of the giant Hyde Park demonstration, Balfour reprimanded Paderewski over the "strong feeling aroused in England and parts of the British Empire in consequence of the reports in the press respecting the treatment of the Jews in Poland and in the districts recently freed from the Bolsheviks." GB FO 608/70.

    On June 30, 1919, Paderewski offered a British writer, William Walter, the sum of $6,000 plus expenses and interpreters to gather material for a book "rebutting the reports and stories of Jewish persecutions since the armistice on November 11, 1918." AAN Paderewski 774.
125. KNP Delegation Paris to Skrzyński, June 25, 1919, AAN MSZ 1480, admitted, "we must sign this treaty, but we intend to make changes that benefit us." Paderewski's final, eight-page protest, June 26, 1919, ibid., Paderewski 846, reprinted in Paderewski, *Archiwum Polityczne Ignacego Paderewskiego*, Vol. 2, pp. 220–3.
126. At the foreign ministers' meeting immediately preceding the Council of Four's fateful decision, the victors remained deeply divided over Eastern Galicia's political future, with Balfour insisting on a League high commissioner and eventual plebiscite, Lansing a mandate administered by Poland, and Imperiali and Pichon endorsing unrestricted Polish control; FRUS PPC, Vol. 4, pp. 847–56.

    Headlam-Morley to Namier, June 30, 1919, Headlam-Morley, *Memoir*, p. 177, again blamed the Americans for "let[ting] us down on the most important points"; within six months, the United States formally endorsed the Franco–Italian position. Allen Dulles memoir, Nov. 21, 1919, Dulles 8.

acceptance of Poland's role as the West's proxy against Bolshevism[127]; but this reversal of months of Anglo–American resistance to Warsaw's expansion beyond its ethnic borders and their abandonment of the Ukrainians' claims was undoubtedly a conciliatory gesture toward Paderewski as well as toward his nationalist rivals.[128] Moreover, the Allies now made it clear that they had no intention of pursuing autonomy for the non-Poles of Eastern Galicia.[129]

Two days later, the council allowed Paderewski to express his grievances against the minority treaty and the accompanying economic clauses.[130] No member of the Committee of New States was present. While dismissing the premier's final assault on Yiddish and his protests against internationalizing the Vistula,[131] Wilson and Lloyd George assuaged one of Poland's major complaints; much to Headlam-Morley's chagrin, both leaders suggested that Germany might not escape a minority obligation when it sought entry into the League of Nations, thus undermining the carefully limited basis of Europe's new minorities arrangements.[132] In still another striking reversal,

127. Crediting rumors of a Bolshevik move into Eastern Galicia to link up with Béla Kun's beleaguered forces and the ragtag Ukrainians' inability to resist, (Paderewski to Pichon, Paris, June 25, 1919, FMAE Z [Pologne] 83), the council's message to Warsaw began: "In view of protecting the persons and property of the peaceful population of Eastern Galicia against the dangers to which they are exposed by the Bolshevist bands." FRUS PPC, Vol. 6, p. 677; also Balfour statement, June 18, 1919, FRUS PPC, Vol. 4, p. 828; Headlam-Morley, *Memoir*, p. 177, n. 2; Temperley, ed., *Peace Conference of Paris*, Vol. 6, pp. 272–3; Wandycz, "The Polish Question," p. 331.

    For a dissenting voice: Namier to Headlam-Morley, June 26, 1919, HM CC, Box 15: "The Bolshevik danger has proved a bogey. Thirty-two Polish soldiers were able to advance for scores of miles into White Russia and occupy Pinsk. . . . A small Polish army was able, even before Haller's arrival, to occupy Vilna and invade White Russia and Lithuania. Haller's arrival enabled them absolutely to crush the Ukrainians of East-Galicia. . . . From one end of Poland to the other national minorities, and in the first place the Jews . . . are being ill-treated in the most infamous manner. And we keep silent and help the Poles."

128. Clemenceau [Pichon] to Pralon, Warsaw, June 25, 1919, FMAE Z (Pologne) 83; French legation Warsaw to MSZ, n.d., French Military Mission to Piłsudski, Aug. 13, 1919, AAN MSZ 92. Piłsudski, who was at the front in Eastern Galicia, did not learn of the Allies' decision until June 28.

    The Ukrainians protested to Clemenceau on July 2, 1919; another disgruntled party was Czechoslovakia, which had considerable interests in the oil refineries of Eastern Galicia. See Beneš to Paderewski, June 5, 1919, AMZV PA 9.

    On Sept. 10, 1919, in the Treaty of St. Germain, Austria ceded Eastern Galicia to the Allied and Associated Powers, which did not assign it officially to Poland until 1923.

129. See n. 171.

130. *Council of Four* (June 27, 1919), Vol. 2, pp. 578–82; FRUS PPC, Vol. 6, pp. 723–6; Polish account of meeting, AAN Paderewski 848.

131. Paderewski also objected privately to Poland's assuming its portion of tsarist Russia's state debt, inserted by the French.

132. FRUS PPC, Vol. 6, pp. 723–5. Headlam-Morley, in his minute of Aug. 5, 1919, GB FO 608/70, deplored Lloyd George's and Wilson's "complete surrender" of the principle of limiting the League's prerogatives to guaranteeing the existing minority treaties in order to prevent the risk of the new world organization's claiming to supervise other states, including France and Italy.

the council that day agreed to the reentry of Haller's army into Eastern Galicia; and it also promised military aid for the new Polish campaign in the East.[133]

Cajoled and trapped, Paderewski promised to sign the minority treaty and also assured the council that the Diet would ratify it.[134] On the next afternoon, at precisely the moment when the guns began firing to mark the Germans' signing, Paderewski and Dmowski, in a separate wing of the castle, signed the detested "little Versailles."[135]

THE TREATY

In its final form, Poland's minority treaty contained three major elements, the basic minority rights proposed by Wilson and the Jewish organizations, the special minority rights advanced by the *Comité* and the American Jews, and the enforcement procedures originally championed by French and British Jewry.[136] All had been considerably modified to conform to the Allies' desiderata and Poland's objections.[137]

At the core of the treaty resided Articles 2–8, deemed fundamental laws that overrode any legislation, decree, or official action. Wilson's signal contribution was in Article 2, compelling Poland to ensure "full and complete protection of life and liberty to all inhabitants . . . without distinction of birth, nationality, language, race, or religion." Echoing the U.S. Constitution, it also stated that "all inhabitants . . . [were to] be entitled to the free exercise, whether public or private, of any creed, religion, or belief whose practices are not inconsistent with public order or public morals."

This broad guarantee of religious freedom, fiercely debated in the League Commission, was a blatant infringement on Poland's sovereignty. It also effaced the distinction between citizens and foreigners.[138] Based on the

133. FRUS PPC, Vol. 6, pp. 726–7.

134. Ibid., p. 727; Notes of June 27, 1919, meeting in AAN Paderewski 848. Before Paderewski conceded, Mantoux had conveyed the jurists' opinion that if Poland signed the German treaty but refused to sign the minority treaty it would still not escape an international obligation under Article 93.

135. Headlam-Morley to Koppel, June 30, 1919, Headlam-Morley, *Memoir*, p. 179; Hudson, #495, June 28, 1919.

Headlam-Morley had hoped that Czechoslovakia would also sign that day; but complications raised by Prague delayed this second treaty until September. Wolf, Diary, June 28, 1919; Hudson, #481, June 25, 1919; #483, #486, June 26, 1919.

136. Fink, "The Minorities Question," especially pp. 269–72.

137. Full text in FRUS PPC, Vol. 13, pp. 791–808.

138. Including the large number of Jews whom the Poles were in the process of classifying as aliens. The wording of Article 2 was also considered a response to previous tsarist and Romanian discrimination against western Jews, which the Poles resented as a new form of extraterritoriality.

Allies' response to Japan's demands as well as on their own internal ethnic, racial, and religious problems, Article 2, a declaration without teeth, would be impossible to enforce.

Articles 3–6 were devoted to the acquisition of Polish citizenship. In determining the qualifying date of residency, the Jews had pleaded for August 1914, the Poles for the latest possible date in order to exclude as many non-Poles as possible.[139] The result, an awkward compromise, set the qualifying date at the time of the treaty's ratification but also established generous terms for claiming Polish nationality.[140] Minority advocates were disappointed.[141] The Jews deplored the vagueness of the terms, which failed to address the thousands of wartime expellees and refugees likely to fall into the unprotected category of statelessness. The treaty's omission of specific guidelines for naturalization exposed Poland's minorities to official chicanery, particularly against the recent German colonists and Russian–Jewish settlers whose claims would fill the court dockets for many years. Finally, in conformity with the gender and family beliefs of the time, husbands were to decide their wives' citizenship and parents that of their children under eighteen years of age.

Article 7 established the basic civil, political, and cultural rights agreed on by virtually everyone: All Polish citizens were to be equal before the law and were to enjoy equal rights as citizens and workers. Notwithstanding the establishment of Polish as the official language, minority languages could be used freely in private intercourse, public meetings, commerce, and religious practice.

Article 8 also seemed unobjectionable, guaranteeing equal legal protection to minorities and to all other Polish nationals, allowing them to establish, manage, and control at their own expense charitable, religious, educational, and social institutions, and permitting them to use their language and practice their religion therein.

Nevertheless, this final "fundamental" article represented a clear Polish victory.[142] Not only did it define minority status in individual rather than

139. Headlam-Morley to Namier, June 2, 1919, Namier to Headlam-Morley, London, June 5, 1919, HM CC, Box 12.

140. Poland was to give automatic citizenship to all former nationals of the German, Austro–Hungarian, and Russian Empires "habitually resident" within Poland's new boundaries on the date the treaty came into force (Article 3) as well as to persons born of habitually resident parents (Article 4) and to those born on Polish territory who were not nationals of another state (Article 6). Articles 3, 4, and 5 also contained provisions for renouncing Polish citizenship and opting for another nationality without penalty to property rights.

141. Headlam-Morley to Namier, June 30, 1919, Namier to Headlam-Morley, July 1, 1919, HM CC, Box 12

142. Paderewski to Skrzyński, July 1, 1919, AAN MSZ 1480.

group terms – instead of the earlier American reference to a "national minority," it referred specifically to "Polish nationals who belong to racial, religious or linguistic minorities" – but it also granted rights to minorities without guaranteeing any state support whatsoever.[143] The reduced German community in Poland would undoubtedly obtain subventions from the Reich; but the far larger Polish Jewry, threatened by its poverty, dispersion, and divisions, had gained but an empty gesture.

The next three "nonfundamental" articles contained the remnants of the Jewish nationalists' proposals without the legal and moral force of the preceding eight. In the awkwardly worded Article 9, applicable only to areas inhabited by "a considerable proportion of Polish nationals of other than Polish speech," the state was obliged to establish primary schools with instruction in the minority tongue and also to fund local religious and charitable institutions.[144] The restrictions, however, demanded by Paderewski, were significant.[145]

The watered-down Articles 10 and 11, dealing specifically with the Jews and representing Marshall's victory over Wolf and the *Alliance*, had been obtained through hard bargaining among the committee members over Poland's bitter opposition. Article 10 provided for the establishment of local Jewish committees, "subject to the general control of the State," to disburse public funds to religious schools and other institutions. In Article 11, Jewish Sabbath observance was protected except during state emergencies and the performance of military service. Poland also agreed to refrain from elections on Saturday.

Despite these small victories, the partisans of Jewish rights had suffered several major setbacks. To be sure, Yiddish had not been banned, but it would receive no governmental support to survive and flourish as an officially-recognized language. There would be no national curiae, proportional representation, or administrative offices for minorities.[146] Instead of a central Jewish Bureau dreaded by the Allies and the Poles, there would be only powerless local associations. Above all, the controversial Sabbath

143. Ironically, among mainstream Jews and non-Jews, the pseudoscientific term "racial" was considered a far more neutral, and far less politically objectionable, designation than "national."

144. Headlam-Morley termed the wording a clumsy substitute for the U.S. reference to collective minority groups, minute, Sept. 1, 1919, GB FO 608/54; one of the League's administrators later admitted "We were never able to discover [the article's] real meaning nor the value of its practical application"; Azcárate, *The League of Nations*, pp. 60–1.

145. Polish-language instruction was obligatory in all schools; no public funds would be available above the primary level; and state subsidies for German schools and institutions were restricted to "that part of Poland which was German territory on August 1, 1914."

146. The possibility of proportional representation had been reduced to a private exchange of notes; Wolf, Diary, Apr. 23, 1919, Miller, *Diary* (May 9, 1919), 13, 76.

clause – disputed by the British, Americans, and Poles – was silent on the most crucial issue of all, Sunday trading.[147]

Article 12 dealt with enforcement. Breaches in any of the treaty's clauses were placed under the responsibility of the Council of the League of Nations. Any differences of opinion between Poland and the Council were to be adjudicated by the Permanent Court of International Justice, whose decisions were to be final.

This last and longest article was the most extraordinary and contested part of the minority treaty. From it sprang the seed of a new form of international regulation but also the denial of the minorities' hopes to gain access to a world audience. Moreover, it was highly unlikely that an individual council member would undertake the onerous chore of accusing a fellow government of mistreating its minority population, even if such intervention could no longer be construed as constituting unwarranted or unfriendly interference.[148]

AFTER ALL

Overshadowed by the German treaty signed that day, Poland's little Versailles remained in obscurity for several months.[149] It nevertheless represented one of the peace conference's notable innovations. The free and independent Poland envisaged in Wilson's Point 13, carved out between defeated Germany and Bolshevik Russia, had been encumbered by an unprecedented international obligation.[150] The minority treaty, dictated by Great Powers that had refused to accept, even theoretically, similar obligations, had been imposed on behalf of largely anonymous minorities who had not been consulted and would play no role in the enforcement process.

Why was a special *treaty* necessary? The victors, who had all experienced the repercussions of Romania and tsarist Russia's mistreatment of the Jews, expressed their determination to bind Poland and its neighbors to better behavior. Even had they wavered, the public clamor stirred by Jews' anti-pogrom campaign undoubtedly forced their hands.

147. Which Wolf, up to the end, continued to work for; Wolf to Carr, June 16, 1919, Carr, Howard minutes, June 23, 1919, GB FO 608/67; Wolf, Diary, June 17, 18, 1919.

148. Lloyd George statement, May 17, 1919, *Council of Four*, Vol. 2, p. 90.

149. The treaty was officially released for publication on July 14, 1919, with a brief summary published in *The Times* and *The New York Times*, July 1, 1919. Headlam-Morley to Seton Watson, July 21, 1919, HM UU Col. 8, deplored the absence of explanatory material in the press.

150. "This creates not peace but internal conflict, because a measure of this importance imposed on the Polish state and affecting its sovereignty and the unity of its administration, will create a rancor slow to dissipate," Note sur le projet de convention entre la Pologne et des puissances concernant les droits des minorités, Aug. 12, 1919, AAN KNP 1259.

Moreover, there were important political calculations embedded in the minority treaty. The brilliant covering letter to Paderewski, drafted by Headlam-Morley, not only flattered the premier and met his key objections but hinted at something more. Besides asserting its right and obligation to protect minority rights, the council was attempting to shape the new Poland, using the treaty to bolster the moderate Paderewski's position and diminish the obdurately anti-Semitic Dmowski.[151]

There were two other aims as well. By providing specific, if limited, assurances of the survival of *Deutschtum*, the victors hoped both to ensure the Reich's acceptance of its treaty and to relieve the pressure on Poland's western border. Finally, this first treaty was necessary to convince the recalcitrant Romania as well as the more pliant Czechoslovakia, Greece, and Yugoslavia to sign similar accords.

In a broader sense, the Polish Minority Treaty represented the culmination of almost six months of equivocation over the widespread nonfulfillment of self-determination in Eastern Europe and the political dangers resulting therefrom. With this treaty the victors – caught in the contradictions of their economic, strategic, and ideological decisions, constrained by the limits of their knowledge of, and power in, the region, and limited by their own domestic politics – had constructed a new, but also a *conservative* solution to an explosive issue, a treaty solidly grounded in past precedent with the liberal patina of the new League of Nations and the World Court.[152]

Given the divisions among the Big Three, this solution was also the only one available. France, which throughout the negotiations had sought to protect its new clients and stiffen their will against foreign interference, would accept only a limited control instrument. Britain, the most alert to the international dangers of the East Europeans' chauvinism and expansion, but also the most ambivalent over excessive international control, aimed at eliciting the minimum number of concessions from Warsaw to create a stable state and loyal minority citizens. The United States, which also recognized the political dangers posed by Poland's "unmeltable" population, exceeded Britain with some of its demands but also possessed less will or capacity to enforce the new international minorities regime.[153] Not unexpectedly, the

151. Headlam-Morley to Namier, June 30, 1919, Headlam-Morley, *Memoir*, pp. 175–7; rebuttal in Namier memorandum, June 30, 1919, GB FO 608/67.

152. Headlam-Morley to Seton Watson, July 21, 1919, HM UU Col. 8, stresses the aim of reducing "absolute sovereignty" without going "too far in the other direction" and giving the League "an unlimited right to interfere in the internal affairs of States."

153. Indeed, Wilson's incautious statement to the plenary meeting on May 31, 1919 (FRUS PPC, Vol. 3, p. 406), "We cannot afford to guarantee territorial settlements which we do not believe to

Polish treaty, blending three different perspectives, left more questions open than it solved.

Jewish leaders exulted in their accomplishment.[154] The usually restrained Marshall and Wolf welcomed the culmination of their long labor and a new era of minority protection.[155] The Zionists and nationalists were jubilant over the "bitter pill" Poland had been forced to swallow[156]; and Wise praised Wilson as a "friend of the Jewish people."[157] Even German Jews were cautiously optimistic over the fate of their eastern kindred.[158]

Nonetheless, the Polish Minority Treaty fell far short of their goals. In the course of his final interview with Paderewski on July 7, Marshall recognized not only that Polish Jewry remained vulnerable to the ongoing boycott, mob violence, and other forms of persecution, but that their government remained suspicious and resentful, unregenerate in its desire for national uniformity and opposed to outside control.[159]

Far from winning a brilliant victory, the Jews had revealed their many weaknesses in the international arena, among them, their personal and political divisions as well as their tactical naiveté.[160] The groups they had represented had not only been denied official status and collective rights but now risked the resentment and backlash against their meddling as well as the declining international interest in their suffering.

be right, and we cannot agree to leave elements of disturbance unremoved . . . " became a rallying point for his opponents in the presidential election of 1920.

154. For example, Wolf, Diary, June 28, 1919; also Marshall to his children, June 28, 1919, AJA LM 82; Adler, Diary, June 29, 1919; Richards to Wise, July 4, 1919, Wise 74–60; Marshall, Adler, and Sokolow to Bogen, Paris, July 11, 1919, AJA LM 82; Julius Rosenwald to Schiff, July 17, 1919, ibid.

155. "We have gained all we had the right to expect." Marshall to Schiff, June 30, 1919, AJA Schiff 161, Wolf, Diary, June 28, 1919.

156. Mack to Filderman, July 26, 1919, CZA A405/75; also Motzkin to Zionist Office Copenhagen, July 18, 31, ibid., CZA A4/2077.

157. Wise to Wilson, July, 1919, Wise 74–47; also Wise to House, July 11, 1919, *Stephen S. Wise*, p. 88.

158. *Jüdische Rundschau*, Aug. 1, 1919, commenting, "Although this treaty contains no clear formulation on the Jewish nation, it recognizes a Jewish organism in Poland as a minority entitled to specific national rights." The rest would depend on the efforts of Polish Jews themselves. See also German Zionist Office to Copenhagen, July 7, 1919, CZA Z3/673.

159. Adler, Diary, July 7, 1919; Wise to Mack, July 9, 1919, Wise 74–73; Marshall and Sokolow to Paderewski, Paris, July 11, 1919, AJA LM 131; also Wolf, Diary, July 11, 1919; Marshall to Prince Lubomirski, New York, July 26, 1919, AJA LM 1533.

Namier to Headlam-Morley, July 2, 1919, HM CC, Box 12, again denied any great difference between Paderewski's and Dmowski's anti-Semitism; Smulski to Paderewski, July 12, 1919, AAN Paderewski 773, proposed issuing an official statement on Poland's future policy toward the Jews to calm world public opinion.

160. For example, Adler to Isaac Landman, Aug. 19, 1919, AJA LM 52, scored the rabbi's "independent" diplomacy in Paris. Landman, editor of the *American Hebrew* and head of the liberal Union of American Hebrew Congregations, had shunned the American Jewish Congress delegation, interviewed scores of foreign emissaries, and criticized Wilson vigorously.

The Jewish leadership remained as divided as ever.[161] Moreover, their labors in Paris had contributed to "a great swell of anti-Semitism" in the United States and Great Britain, fueled by accusations of Bolshevism and Germanophilism.[162] They soon discovered that many Americans and Britons were uncomfortable over forcing Poland to accept controls that the western democracies had specifically rejected and that threatened to "wreck" the new republic.[163] On the heels of their ostensible triumph in Paris, arduous domestic struggles against discrimination, immigration restriction, and the dissemination of the Protocols of the Elders of Zion lay before them.[164]

Weary and piqued, Paderewski stressed the essentials. In his final words to the Great Powers, he expressed the "joy" and the "pain" of the minority treaty, which had simultaneously recognized Poland's independence and cast a stigma of humiliation and servitude.[165] Gratefully acknowledging France's support, he deftly underscored the Allies' retreat over Eastern Galicia.[166]

With Dmowski publicly renouncing all responsibility for the treaty, the prime minister faced an infuriated Poland alone.[167] A day after his return, Paderewski reminded the *Sejm* Foreign Affairs Committee of Poland's culpability for its humiliating obligation[168]; but he mainly blamed others, the Jews, the Americans, and the British, for imposing an "unnecessary" treaty.[169] On July 30, after a heated debate, the *Sejm*, by an overwhelming

161. For example, Wise to Mack, July 23, 1919, Wise 74–73, Wise to DeHaas, Aug. 15, 1919, CZA A404/116, on the bitter falling out between Wise and Marshall; Hermann to Motzkin, July 31, 1919, CZA Z24/2077, on the "self-glorification" of Wolf and Marshall.
162. Adler to Marshall, Aug. 15, 1919, AJA LM 52. In June and July, the Poles in Brooklyn, N.Y. boycotted Jewish shopkeepers; ibid., 82.
163. Adler to Marshall, Aug. 19, 1919, AJA LM 52. Also, "The Plot against Poland," *Morning Post* (London), June 18, 1919.
164. Lebzelter, "Political Anti-Semitism in England, 1918–1939" in Strauss, *Hostages of Modernization*, Vol. 1, pp. 385–424; see also Bronner, *A Rumor About the Jews.*
165. Even the Morgenthau mission, considered a coup by Paderewski, provoked resentment and dark humor: "It was a standing joke in the Polish press that at the head of the mission on the question of the lynching of negroes in America should be a colored gentleman from Haiti and a full blooded delegate from Central Africa." "The Situation," AAN Paderewski 774.
166. Paderewski to Dutasta, June 30, 1919, AAN Paderewski 841; also Piltz to Pichon, Paris, July 7, 1919, ibid., Erazm Piltz papers 16.
167. *Nowy Dziennik*, July 24, 1919. Posner to Namier, Paris, July 8, 1919, CZA A312/56; MSZ to Paderewski, July 10, 1919, AAN MSZ 1480. On the widespread press and political opposition to the Allies' interference in Polish affairs, their treating the new republic as a "savage tribe in Africa," and their thirst for the oil of Eastern Galicia, see "Review of the Polish Press," July 1919, CZA A126/52/6; also Jüdische–Politische Nachrichten, #35, Germ. PA AA L1284/L338862–73.
168. "We ourselves are to blame for this result"; Paderewski speech to the Sejm Peace Commission, July 24, 1919, *Moment*, July 24, 1919.
169. Wyndham to Balfour, Warsaw, July 28, 1919, GB FO 608/70; *Jüdische Rundschau*, Aug. 12, 1919. Significantly, the premier emphasized the Anglo–American assurances that the rights withheld from the Poles in the Reich might yet be protected.

vote, ratified both the large and the little Versailles treaties, and the next day was proclaimed an official day of rejoicing throughout Poland.[170] By then, Poland's armies had reached the river Zbrucz.[171]

Contrary to the assertions of several historians,[172] the little Versailles represented neither a Jewish victory nor a Polish defeat, neither a triumph for self-determination nor a totally realist solution, but a hybrid experiment, balancing the Anglo-American vision of protection against Jewish demands and Franco–Polish opposition. The Great Powers, in their attempt to remove minorities as pawns in world politics, tried to have it both ways, both by internationalizing the problem and also containing it as best they could, leaving to the unborn League the thankless task of turning confusing words into purposeful action.[173]

To be sure, the Polish minority treaty was an undoubtedly *temporary* arrangement, aimed primarily at easing the transition from the old imperial order in Eastern Europe to a new realm of polyglot "nation–states" lodged between a potentially resurgent Germany and Soviet Russia. After expending enormous effort to create the "big Versailles," all three Great Powers were reluctant to make binding political or military commitments to Poland's new borders.[174] Out of the peacemakers' stopgap measure, whatever international regulation emerged from the little Versailles would thus be built on a fragile foundation of erratic Allied pressure and fierce Polish resistance, and of a lingering threat to Poland's minorities as well as the menace of its neighbors' irredentism.

170. Wyndham to Balfour, Warsaw, Aug. 2, 1919, GB FO 608/70.
171. Louis Marshall to Wilson, Aug. 6, 18, 1919, pleaded for a special autonomous regime for the Jews of Eastern Galicia, WWP 289; but Wilson to Marshall, Aug. 14, 1919, reiterated the president's opposition to "creating separate Jewish bodies," and the British and French concurred. Marshall to Eastern Galician National Council (Vienna), Aug. 29, 1919, CZA A18/20.
172. Janowsky, *Jews and Minority Rights*; Macartney, *National States and National Minorities*; Viefhaus, *Die Minderheitenfrage*.
173. "The New Poland," *The Times* [London], July 16, 1919.
174. Indeed, Article 19 of the League Covenant foresaw "the reconsideration by Members of the League of treaties which have become inapplicable and the consideration of international conditions whose continuance might endanger the peace of the world."

PART THREE

A New Era of Minority Rights?

9

Geneva

"The role of individual powers to protect minorities has disappeared."[1]

"I recognize that all the countries concerned are more or less sore about the Treaties . . . [but] by raising no protest . . . will it not be said that we have abandoned the important principle of international control and acquiesced in the principle of the sovereign right of every state to deal with its minorities as it pleases?"[2]

"There is in the League's glass palace a dark room in which the light never enters and no sound emerges. This is the place where the protection of minorities is implemented."[3]

Within fourteen months of the signing of the Polish Minority Treaty, the victors compelled seven additional states to accept similar obligations. Article 12 was replicated in all these treaties. Thus the victors, who had excluded the League of Nations from almost all the major military and economic issues between themselves and the vanquished, assigned to this organization several of the most delicate political questions of the interwar period, including the Saar and Danzig, mandates, and disarmament as well as the protection of minority rights in Eastern Europe.

The League's burden as minorities' protector was formidable. America's absence removed one of the organization's principal creators and the minority treaties' main authors; and its restrictive immigration legislation blocked the minorities' most important place of refuge. With defeated Germany and Bolshevik Russia excluded, and behaving as hostile outsiders, the League faced the radically transformed political and social landscape in Eastern Europe. A brand new international civil service sought to create procedures that balanced treaty enforcement with state sovereignty and also balanced

1. Van Hamel Memorandum, Oct. 1, 1920, League of Nations Archives (hereafter LNA) S336.
2. Wolf to Colban, Jan. 30, 1923, LNA R1684.
3. W. Pagen, "Das Minderheitenproblem in Genf," *Deutsche Stimmen* (Mar. 20, 1929).

individual protection with the goals of national integration and regional peace and security.

As could be anticipated, the League's work was hampered by the inconsistencies and gaps in the peacemakers' design. Having rejected a universal commitment to minority rights, the victors had imposed a degrading and detested form of international control over a disparate group of new, expanded, and defeated East European states. In a dramatic break with the "Berlin precedent," the peacemakers had set down fundamental laws as well as special conditions and assigned the responsibility for their enforcement to an unborn organization, but given no clear guidelines as to the actual goals or duration of the minority treaties.

And also, not unexpectedly, the League's new minorities system became engulfed in the debate over the peace settlement itself. Neither embedded in the Covenant nor elaborated in the territorial treaties, the League's procedures became a target both for the critics *and* beneficiaries of the Paris Peace Settlement. Whereas the revisionists, using Wilsonian rhetoric, clamored for a substantial expansion of minority rights, the states bound by the treaties sought to minimize their obligations or to replace them with a universal minorities regime. In the midst of this international debate, all the conditions emerged that Wilson and his colleagues had sought to avert: aggressive state building throughout Eastern Europe that endangered minority rights, the persistence of German irredentism, and a fundamental reluctance among those responsible for enforcing this volatile element of the "Versailles system."

THE "MINORITY STATES"

Once the ceremonies on June 28, 1919 were over, almost all the main overseas participants left Paris; but the Committee on New States functioned for another six months. In this "duller but more orderly" atmosphere,[4] an expanded committee, guided by a less forceful council and subject to fewer outside pressures, drafted the treaties that were signed by Czechoslovakia (September 10, 1919), Yugoslavia (December 5, 1919), Romania (December 9, 1919), and Greece (August 10, 1920) as well as the articles inserted in the peace treaties with Austria (September 10, 1919), Bulgaria (November 27, 1919), and Hungary (June 4, 1920).

Using the Polish negotiations as their model, the committee and council maintained their cautious, conciliatory manner in dealing with the other

4. Headlam-Morley to Koppel June 30, 1919, Headlam-Morley, *Memoir*, p. 180.

minority states. Their treatment of Czechoslovakia was exceptionally lenient.[5] Based on Beneš' written vow to create a "little Switzerland" and establish secondary schools for minorities, combined with his astute propaganda campaign portraying the Prague government as a paragon of western liberalism, Czechoslovakia's treaty contained no recognition of its 3 million German citizens and no provision for its 650,000 Magyars. Despite the fervent pleas of Jewish leaders, there was no mention of special Jewish rights.[6]

Even in dealing with one of the peace conference's most egregious violations of self-determination for strategic purposes, the assignment of Sub-Carpathian Ruthenia to Czechoslovakia, the Committee on New States meekly bowed to Beneš.[7] Undoubtedly with an eye on Eastern Galicia, the committee adopted four vaguely worded clauses for an eventual autonomous regime.[8] In dealing with the new Germany, however, Beneš reached too far. He famously failed to gain special rights and privileges in southeastern Germany for the Lusatian Sorbs, a western Slavic people distantly related to the Czechs.[9] Joining Paderewski, Beneš urged the Allies to compel Germany to issue a minority-protection declaration as a condition for its entry into the League of Nations.[10]

5. Important background in R. W. Seton Watson to Headlam-Morley, Prague, May 18, 1919, Headlam-Morley to Seton Watson, Paris, May 27, 1919, HM UU Col. 76; Allen Dulles to Miller, May 20, 1919, to Hudson, May 30, 1919, Dulles 6, 7.

   In accordance with Beneš' wishes, the Allies in the preface to Czechoslovakia's minority treaty made no claims to have liberated his nation but simply confirmed the cessation of its historic bonds with Austria and acknowledged the "voluntary" union of the peoples of Bohemia, Moravia, a part of Silesia, and Slovakia, as well as the "adherence" of the Ruthenians south of the Carpathian mountains.

   D. Perman's solid and objective *The Shaping of the Czechoslovak State* omits any mention of the minority treaty.

6. Beneš to Committee on New States, Paris, May 20, 1919, AMZV MK 50; Beneš to Kammerer, Paris, June 26, 1919, ibid., PA 4. On the omission of special Jewish rights, based on the Jews' small numbers but particularly on the difficulties this might create in Slovakia: LC LH, Committee on New States, Aug. 12, 1919, p. 195; Beneš to Max Brod, Aug. 25, 1919; Max Brod to President T. G. Masaryk, Sept. 19, Dec. 28, 1919, Czech Republic, Military Historical Archive, Records of the T. G. Masaryk Institute, C. 2; also Wolf interviews with Beneš, Paris, Apr. 10, Aug. 22, 1919, YIVO W/M 159; Marshall to Wilson, Aug. 18, 1919, AJA LM 1589.

   On Czechoslovakia's propaganda campaign between Jan. 1 and July 31, 1919, stressing the "German menace" and the new republic's probity and stability, see Beneš to Pergler, Paris, Apr. 15, 1919, AMZV PA 17, Beneš report, n.d. (ca. Aug. 1919), ibid., PA 71.

7. LH, Committee on New States, 11th, 13th, 14th, 22nd, 30th meetings, pp. 33–4, 38–41, 43, 73–5, 114–19. Full text of the minority treaty and economic clauses in FRUS PPC, Vol. 13, pp. 808–22.

8. But one that would apply to only two-thirds of the 600,000 Ruthenians of Czechoslovakia within the gerrymandered frontier recommended by Prague. Moreover, the Ruthenians were now separated by the new borders from their kin in Eastern Galicia and the Bukovina. Background in Magocsi, *The Rusyn–Ukrainians of Czechoslovakia*.

9. Beneš to Clemenceau, Mar. 15, Apr. 17, 1919, AMZV PA 5.

10. Beneš to Clemenceau, Paris, Aug. 29, 1919, AMZV PA 5.

The negotiations with "Yugoslavia"[11] and Romania proved far more difficult. As expected, these "old" states, still bound technically by the long-ignored Treaty of Berlin, resisted any international commitments affecting their pre-1914 acquisitions or their new territories. On September 11, 1919, neither joined Czechoslovakia at the signing ceremony in the chateau of St. Germain. Both offered compelling dissents, the Belgrade government protesting Italy's exemption and the rulers in Bucharest insisting on a *universal* minorities system for all League members.[12]

Failing to intimidate their pugnacious Balkan clients, the committee and council retreated on several significant issues. Yugoslavia, backed firmly by France, successfully resisted the British, Italian, and American efforts to establish autonomous regimes for Macedonia and for its Albanian districts or to grant special rights to its Romanian, Italian, and Jewish citizens, although it did accept minor concessions toward its Muslim population.[13] Romania, although lacking a foreign backer, used the threat not to sign to remove the special Jewish clauses from its treaty[14]; but when the Allies stood firm, Romania agreed to grant local autonomy to the Germans and Hungarians in Transylvania in the matter of their schools and religious institutions subject to the government's control.[15] In a piquant symbolic as well as legal gesture, the victors annulled the minority clauses of the Treaty of Berlin, thereby transferring their authority over Greater Serbia and Greater Romania to the unborn League of Nations.[16]

11. Officially, its title was SHS (the Serb–Croat–Slovene state) but, for convenience's sake, it is labeled Yugoslavia, even though this name was not in official use until 1929.

    In its discussions in May 1919 the Committee on New States treated Yugoslavia as a "new" state with a breach in Serbia's identity; on June 30, it discussed the issue once more without coming to any decision.
12. Pašić to Clemenceau, Nov. 23, 1919, Misu to Cambon, Bucharest, Nov. 9, 1919, LH, Committee on New States, pp. 272–5.
13. LH, Committee on New States, July 15, 16, Aug. 1, 4, 9, 28, Sept. 8, 9, Nov. 8. 9, 1919, pp. 122–5, 126, 165–6, 168, 170–1, 186–90, 201, 206, 219–24, 230–2, 234–6, 247–53, 260–2; Pašić to Clemenceau, July 24, 1919, to Berthelot, Aug. 1, 1919, to Clemenceau, Sept. 4, Nov. 23, 1919, ibid., pp. 161–4, 172–4, 217–20, 266–7, 274–5.

    The Muslim clause in Yugoslavia's Minority Treaty was far weaker than that signed by Serbia with Turkey in 1913; and the treaty's education clauses applied to only the newly acquired territories.
14. LH, Committee on New States, July 16, 1919, pp. 126–36 and especially Nov. 29, Dec. 9, 1919, pp. 270, 272–83.

    Only the U.S. delegation, pressed by Louis Marshall and by peace activists (Addams and Hamilton to Hudson, n.d. [July 1919], Hudson to Addams and Hamilton, Paris, July 31, 1919, Hudson) supported special rights for Romanian Jews.

    Lucien Wolf had opposed any "special privileges" for Romanian Jews (Wolf to Carr, Dec. 1, 1919, YIVO W/M 154), but had demanded a binding treaty ensuring citizenship rights. Wolf, Diary, Aug. 15, Sept. 8, 16, 1919, and "Diplomaticus" [Wolf], "Romania and the Minority Treaties," Sept. 1, 1919, ibid.
15. Wolf to Mitrany, Oct. 13, 1919, YIVO W/M 82.
16. This represented a British victory over France, which preferred to maintain the lighter Berlin obligations for its clients. Headlam-Morley, memorandum respecting the Minority Treaties, May 17, 1929, GB FO 371/14125.

Greece, another great gainer, joined the Balkan chorus of opposition, protesting control over "old Greece"[17] as well as any grants of autonomy in its most recent acquisitions from Bulgaria and Turkey.[18] The Greek Minority Treaty, whose signature was delayed until the sultan acquiesced in the harsh Treaty of Sèvres, was, at best, an equivocal document. Underlying the mélange of formal obligations that Athens had already accepted in 1913 toward the Kutzo–Vlachs and the monks of Mount Athos with the few new minor cultural and religious concessions to the Jews and Muslims was the expectancy among the Greeks and Allies alike that vast numbers of its Bulgarian, Albanian, and Turkish population would relocate and that the Jews of Salonika would either do so or submit to hellenization.[19]

Even more peculiar were the minority obligations imposed on Austria, Hungary, and Bulgaria.[20] Despite their treatment as ex-enemies, with almost identical war-guilt, reparation, and disarmament clauses as Germany's, the new governments in Vienna and Budapest failed to escape the stipulations forced on their neighbors, although they were spared the special Jewish clauses. After some grumbling, all three defeated states, which had lost huge numbers of their prewar population,[21] became absorbed into the new system.

This initial grouping, a belt of eight contiguous states from the Baltic to the Aegean and Adriatic Seas, included some 25 million minorities.[22] Almost two-thirds were peoples with putative state defenders across their borders; others, particularly the Jews, had private group spokesmen abroad. Uniform neither in their size and power nor in their politics and history, all these minority states were committed to a nationalist program and to dominating their religious and ethnic minorities.[23] On the other hand, all eight governments, now linked by a common encumbrance, were at odds with their immediate neighbors. Almost all held irredentist designs and brooded over their "lost" populations (see Map 9.1).

17. Greece, which acquired no territory in the 1878 Treaty of Berlin, was not bound by its minority clauses.
18. Venizelos to Berthelot, July 31, n.d., Sept. 15, 1919, Clemenceau to Venizelos, Sept. 18, 1919, LH, Committee on New States, meetings, Aug. 5, 9, 12, 25, 28, Sept. 5, 1919, Oct. 22, 1919, pp. 176–9, 186, 190–2, 194, 198, 202, 204, 206–9 210, 213, 215–16, 219, 229, 237–40, 242–3.
19. Wolf, in his interview with Venizelos, Aug. 23, 1919 (YIVO W/M 82), failed to convince the Greek premier to accept either a Sunday-trading clause or a prohibition against elections on the Jewish Sabbath.
20. This committee decision (*Receuil*, PV 6–7, May 12, 13, 1919), which "deviated from . . . general principle," originated with David Hunter Miller; Headlam-Morley Memorandum, May 17, 1929, GB FO 371/14125.
21. Austria did acquire the Burgenland from Hungary.
22. Fouques Duparc, *La protection des minorités;* Winkler, *Statistisches Handbuch der europäischen Nationalitäten.*
23. Macartney, *National States and National Minorities*, pp. 208–11, quotes the various constitutions: For example, "The Kingdom of Roumania is a national, unitary, and indivisible state"; also pp. 370–423.

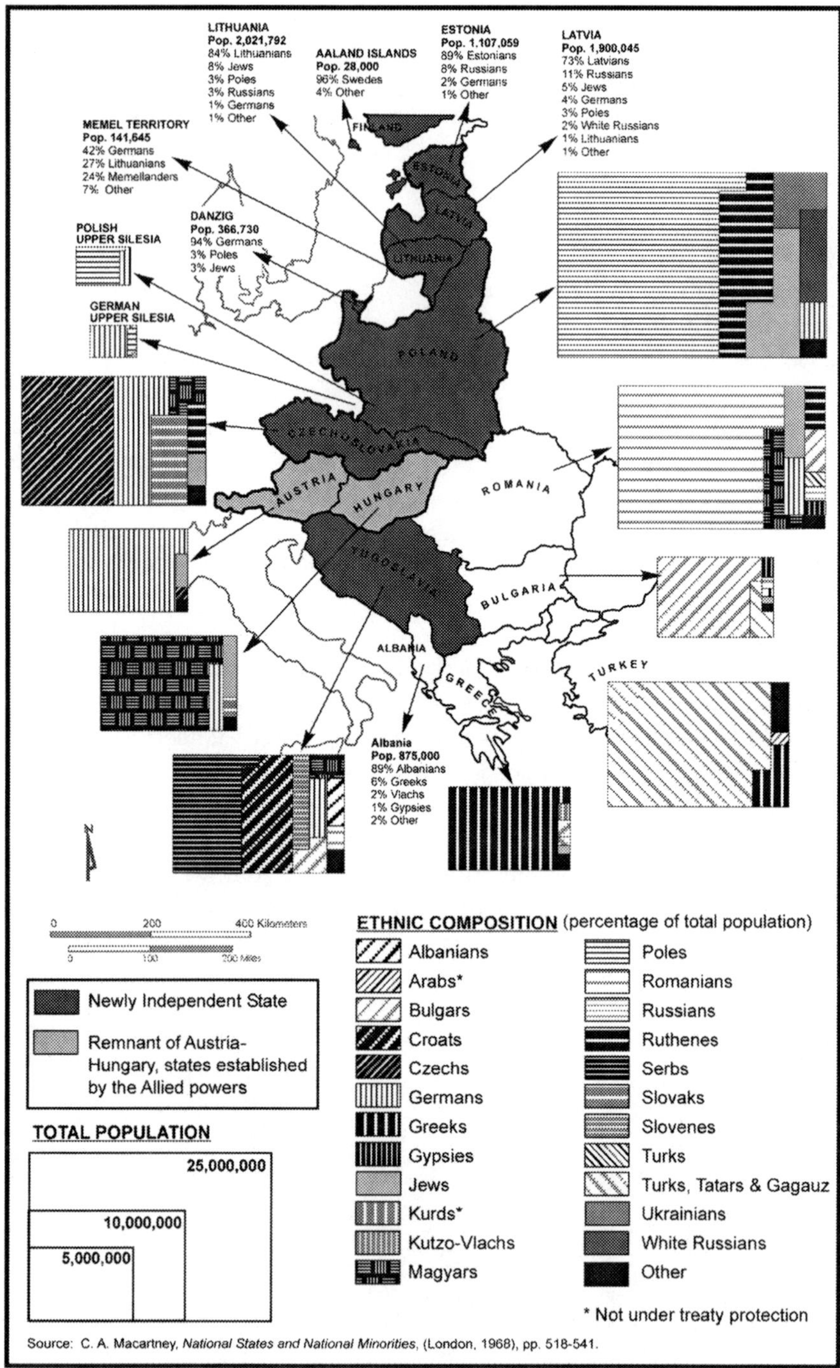

Map 9.1. Eastern Europe after the Paris Peace Conference, 1919–24.

The peacemakers had justified the new, semisovereign status of the minority states with forceful, if inconsistent, arguments.[24] In establishing a protective mantle over Eastern Europe, Wilson and Lloyd George, updating the old Berlin terminology, had staked a dubious claim as the liberators of Poland and Czechoslovakia as well as the sponsors of Romania, Yugoslavia, and Greece's expansion. Wilson, on May 31, had gone further, holding out the improbable lure of Great-Power protection of their borders in return for the new states' submission to their separate minority treaties.

But it was Clemenceau's June 24 letter to Paderewski, carefully drafted by Headlam-Morley, that provided the most sensible and enduring rationale for the minority treaties. Drawing on a century of diplomatic precedents, the Great Powers claimed the right and obligation to impose minority regulations in return for recognizing the new borders in Eastern Europe. Moreover, between an unrepentant Germany and a revolutionary Russia lay a volatile region of mixed populations that required special treatment to alleviate the threats of irredentism by their neighbors.[25] Notwithstanding the novelty of their language and format, Europe's first minority treaties, neither excessive in their demands nor unlimited in their duration, were essentially transitional measures, to reassure minorities, restrain their governments, and help things settle down.

Indeed, despite the widespread anguish over the Armenian tragedy during the war and over the postwar violence against the Jews throughout Eastern Europe, the peacemakers had deliberately omitted any specific means of punishing governments that transgressed against the new treaties. The League Commission, led by Wilson, had roundly rejected Cecil's proposal to treat violations as a threat to world peace. The Council of Four deemed their initiative more of a deterrent than a vital element of the peace settlement. Thus the minority treaties set an international surveillance system in process, whose ultimate purpose was its own obsolescence.

Nonetheless, the stipulations drafted in Paris, much like the new mandates system, introduced new rules of governance and new categories of citizens as well as new transnational distinctions between named and unnamed minorities, "protected" and "unprotected" peoples. For example, Polish Jews had Sabbath protection, Greek and Romanian Jews did not; the Germans of Transylvania had some autonomy, those of Czechoslovakia and Yugoslavia did not. The treaties not only created resentment among

24. Including their own surrender of sovereignty to the new League of Nations as well as the obligations to be assumed by the new mandatory powers.
25. Headlam-Morley, memorandum, May 17, 1929, GB FO 371/14125.

the minority states but also stirred high expectations among the presumed beneficiaries of a "new order" of international intervention.

As could be expected, some minority states immediately sought means to escape their international servitude. The first such move, proposed by Greece and concluded with the Allies' blessing at the peace conference itself, was the Greco–Bulgarian treaty governing the "voluntary emigration" of their respective minority populations.[26] Less radical were the twenty-five bilateral agreements signed over the next decade, including several negotiated under the League's auspices, which regulated the conditions of their respective minorities. Far less specific than the minority treaties, each of these agreements asserted a few general principles and established interstate machinery for handling minority disputes.[27]

These reciprocal instruments offered an alternative to the peacemakers' design in the form of a more direct, expeditious, and practical solution to the minority question. Fundamentally, however, these agreements undermined the entire basis of the minority treaties. Not only did they favor the strong over the weak, but they also eliminated the Great Powers' role in minority protection and threatened peoples without a state patron. Thus Lucien Wolf, who in his last decade remained East European Jewry's foremost spokesman, directed all his hopes and efforts toward the new League of Nations to breathe life into the minority treaties.[28]

CREATING THE "LEAGUE SYSTEM," 1920–1925[29]

On January 16, 1920, one long year after the convocation of the Paris Peace Conference and six days after the Versailles Treaty came into force, a far more modest gathering assembled in the famous Clock Room of the Quai d'Orsay for the ceremonial opening meeting of the Council of the League

26. Welcomed by the Committee on New States (July 25, 1919), LH, p. 146, Greece's initiative was considered a model for the entire Balkan area; Yugoslavia, however, fearing complications with its neighbors, declined to participate. See Berthelot to Venizelos, Sept. 10, 1919, ibid., Committee on New States, Nov. 3, 15, 17, 24, 1919, pp. 227–8, 252–5, 265–70, 275–7.

    Because the United States refused to participate, there was no collective guarantee of this bilateral treaty, ibid., Committee on New States, Nov. 15, 17, 1919, p. 257–61.
27. Detailed in Bagley, *General Principles and Problems in the International Protection of Minorities.*
28. Colban memorandum, Aug. 17, 1920, LNA R1613.
29. League of Nations, Secretariat, Information Section, *League of Nations and the Protection of Minorities*, and Azcárate (the League's third Minorities Director), *League of Nations and National Minorities* outline the procedure.

    Among the older scholarly studies: Macartney; *National States and National Minorities*; Claude, *National Minorities*; and Bagley, *General Principles and Problems in the International Protection of Minorities* remain useful; newer works, based on archival sources, include Gütermann, *Das Minderheitenschutzverfahren* and Frentz, *A Lesson Forgotten.*

of Nations. One month later, at its first working session in London presided over by Balfour, the eight-member council[30] formally accepted three of the League's most onerous obligations, Danzig, the Saar, and the protection of minorities.[31]

As the Polish–Soviet war heated up and violence spread throughout Eastern Europe, threatened minorities looked to their new protector.[32] At once the League was forced into action by an event unforeseen in the treaties, the arrival of two petitions from the German minority in Poland, which the secretariat dutifully distributed to all members.[33] The council, however, which held its meetings at irregular intervals in various European capitals, was manifestly unready to meet this new challenge.[34]

Thus the League secretariat assumed control over the international minorities problem. The main credit belongs to one individual, Erik Andreas Colban, who in 1919, at the age of forty-three, had been named the director of the secretariat's new Minorities Section. For eight years this ambitious and vigorous Norwegian diplomat, supported by a small youthful staff, was the League's chief interpreter of the minority treaties as well as the principal architect of its system.[35]

Colban, backed by Secretary General Sir Eric Drummond, took energetic steps to establish the League's authority and gain the cooperation of all the minority states while neither ignoring nor exaggerating the treaties.[36] Given the inhibition of individual council members to accuse a fellow government

30. Consisting, according to the prearranged bloc system in the Covenant, of the four Great Powers (Britain, France, Italy, and Japan) together with three European members (Belgium, Greece, Spain) and one from Latin America (Brazil).
31. League of Nations, *Official Journal* (hereafter LNOJ) (Feb. 13, 1920), pp. 45–59.
32. Colban memorandum, Feb. 4, 1920, on discussions with Headlam-Morley, LNA 336; also memorandum on the protection of minorities submitted by Emily Balch on behalf of the Women's International League for Peace and Freedom (WILPF), Dec. 15, 1920, ibid, 1647.
33. Dated June 10 and Aug. 4, 1920 and emanating from the *Vereinigung des deutschen Volkstums in Polen* and the *Unierte evangelische Kirche*, their circulation caused a Foreign Office official to protest, "[The League] may next print Sinn Fein apologia on the same analogy." Crankshaw memorandum, London, Dec. 9, 1920, GB FO 371/5415, and Headlam-Morley to recall that the committee had "deliberately intended to prevent individuals or corporations . . . from having direct access to the Council," Headlam-Morley to Malkin, London, Dec. 18, 1920, ibid.
34. Between January 1920 and December 1923, a period encompassing the *coups de main* in Vilna, Memel, and Corfu as well as the Franco–Belgian invasion of the Ruhr, the council met twenty-seven times in six different capitals.
35. LNA, Colban personnel file. After postings in Paris, The Hague, and Stockholm, Colban entered League service on June 12, 1919, as director of Administrative Commissions and the Minorities Section; he left this position on Dec. 17, 1927 to become director of the Disarmament Section until July 9, 1930 when he became Norway's minister to Paris.

    During World War II, while in exile in England, Colban briefly recounted his work: "The Minorities Problem," *The Norseman* 1 (Sept.–Oct. 1944), 309–17.
36. Van Hamel, Rosting memoranda, Oct. 1, 1920, LNA S336.

Photograph 9.1. Erik Colban (reproduced with the permission of the League of Nations Section of the United Nations Library, Geneva, Switzerland).

of mistreating its own citizens as well as the council's unanimity rule,[37] it was unlikely that a minority case would ever be raised in an international forum. On the other hand, the League could neither reject nor bury petitions without raising a public uproar, or accept and distribute them without antagonizing the accused governments. Colban and his colleagues, seeking to translate the unworkable terms of Article 12 into a coherent international system, created an ingenious, durable, but also provocative solution.[38]

At its meeting in Brussels in October 1920 the League Council launched its career as defender of minorities. After Balfour's lament over their "hard and thankless task," followed by an impractical proposal by the Belgian delegate, Paul Hymans, the council adopted the secretariat's two

37. Despite Headlam-Morley's repeated insistence that the peacemakers had *not* intended to give a vote to accused states (Van Asch Van Wijck memorandum, Apr. 22, 1922, LNA R2156), the secretariat construed Article 4, Paragraph 5 of the Covenant ("Any Member not represented on the Council shall be invited to send a Representative to sit as a Member at any meeting . . . during the consideration of matters specifically affecting the interests of that Member of the League") as giving minority states a veto over any resolution, which Poland exercised in 1923 and 1934. Gütermann, *Das Minderheitenschutzverfahren*, pp. 154–5.

38. Memoranda by Van Hamel and Rosting, Oct. 1, 1920; Colban to Tittoni, Brussels, Oct. 21, 1920, LNA S336.

innovations.[39] The first was to establish a formal procedure for receiving and distributing minority petitions; these, however, were to be treated merely as sources of information unless taken up by an individual council member. The second was to create the committee-of-three system, whereby *every* petition deemed receivable by the secretariat was examined by an ad hoc group of council members (the acting president and two selected governments) to determine whether a treaty violation had occurred and should be reported to the council.[40]

The world's first international minorities system was based on two blatantly contradictory principles and practices. The petition procedure combined a relatively permissive sanction for minority complaints with an underlying denial of their legal status. The committee of three, despite its mandate to investigate every authentic petition, was always dependent on the cooperation of the accused state. Both inconsistencies served the same League purpose, which was to supplant the Great Powers' burden with a centralized administrative system for handling minority grievances that fulfilled the minority treaties efficiently and without great fanfare.[41] It also served the Great Powers' need to create a politically feasible solution.[42]

The secretariat's adroit remedy for the "responsibility gap" in Article 12 went neither unnoticed nor uncontested. The minority states were suspicious and council members wary of their new investigative responsibilities.[43] Minority advocates fretted over their exclusion from every stage of the procedure.[44] Britain's influential League of Nations Union (LNU) went one step further. Suspecting that the Geneva bureaucracy would bury most petitions, it offered to examine them and to advise the council on minority conditions throughout Central and Eastern Europe in the hope that the League would hold periodic, public inquiries into treaty violations.[45] Such

39. Colban to Tittoni, Brussels, Oct. 21, 1920, LNA S336. Hymans' proposal, that three council members examine *every* petition, ignored the individual responsibility written into the minority treaties and would have been rejected by the minority states. Colban to Drummond, Feb. 16, 1923, ibid., R1664.

40. Texts of the two meetings, Oct. 22, 25, 1919, LNA S336.

41. Colban memorandum, Feb. 4, 1920, LNA S336, warned that Britain "overrun with zealous humanitarians . . . , interpellations in parliament, and all sorts of stories in the press," might take separate action through its minister in Warsaw instead of routing minority issues through its member on the council; three years later Colban observed that that danger had been averted by the League's becoming "the only proper channel through which minority questions are handled." Memorandum to secretary general, Feb. 16, 1923, ibid., R1664.

42. Colban to Drummond, Feb. 16, 1923, LNA R1664. "The system ha[s] the enormous advantage that questions come before the Council only after having been thrashed out by the experts of the secretariat and by three council members."

43. Colban to Rosting, Feb. 20, 1921, LNA S336.

44. Colban to Drummond, n.d. [Oct. 1920], copy in YIVO W/M 83.

45. Colban memorandum, Apr. 13, 1921, LNA S336.

radical proposals were precisely what the secretariat, and the Great Powers, wished to avoid.[46]

The peacemakers had expressly excluded the assembly from any role in minority protection. Nevertheless, the annual, five-week-long meetings in Geneva's crowded, austere halls gave every League member an opportunity to evaluate the council's performance in this sensitive political domain.[47] Discussed by a special commission of the whole and debated in the plenary session, the emerging minorities system became one of the indicators of the League's commitment to replace the old order with something new.[48]

Not unexpectedly, it was in the assembly that the two most daring reform proposals were introduced. In September 1921, the Oxford classicist and LNU activist Gilbert Murray called for the creation of a permanent minorities commission on the order of the permanent mandates commission; one year later he called for the generalization of the minority treaties to all members of the League.[49]

The secretariat did its utmost to squelch Murray's recommendations, whose effect would have been both to tighten and extend the League's supervisory activities. Behind the scenes, Geneva officials, arguing political as well as financial constraints, easily blocked a permanent minorities commission.[50] However, in 1922, the assembly flexed its muscle[51] by passing a famous resolution underlining the League's obligation to protect minority rights, specifying the duties of states and their minorities, and exhorting *all* League members to "treat their populations with at least as high a standard of justice and toleration as is required by any of the Treaties."[52]

Spurred by the new internationalism of the early 1920s, the League's responsibilities expanded. Following highly delicate negotiations, new members Albania, Finland, Estonia, Latvia, and Lithuania were all required to accept various minority obligations.[53] After the council's controversial

46. Memoranda by Colban, Apr. 3, 1921, LNA R1661, Apr. 13, July 2, 1921, Drummond, July 2, 1921, Hudson, Aug. 6, 1921 ibid., S336.
47. Article 3, Paragraph 3, of the Covenant specified that "The Assembly may deal at its meetings with any matter within the sphere of action of the League or affecting the peace of the world."
48. Beginning in 1922, minority questions were discussed annually in the Assembly's Sixth (Political) Commission.
49. Between 1920 and 1924, Murray, representing South Africa, was part of Great Britain's assembly delegation. Wilson, *Gilbert Murray*, pp. 283–94.
50. Memoranda by Colban and Drummond, July 2, 1921, Manley Hudson, Aug. 6, 1921, LNA S336. The secretariat easily convinced the assembly in September 1921 to allow the committee-of-three system to go forward before introducing innovations.
51. Unsigned, confidential memorandum, n.d. [June 30, 1922], Colban memorandum, Aug. 7, 1922, LNA S336.
52. LNOJ, Records of the Third Assembly (Geneva, 1922), p. 186.
53. Wolf, Report, London, Jan. 12, 1921, YIVO W/M 8.

decision to partition Upper Silesia, Colban brokered the May 1922 Geneva Convention between Germany and Poland.[54] Far exceeding the minority treaties, this convention created an elaborate, fifteen-year transitional regime that combined an apparatus for local appeals with direct minority access to Geneva, and it also established Germany's first official link with the League.[55] Fourteen months later, the League assumed responsibility for implementing the minority clauses in the Treaty of Lausanne, not only for the protection of Turkey's non-Muslim population but also for supervising the compulsory Greco–Turkish population exchange involving more than a half million people.[56] Finally, after the conclusion of the Memel Convention in May 1924, the League was charged with protecting the autonomy of the former German seaport that had been placed under the "sovereignty of Lithuania."[57] By 1924, the number of states under the League's supervision had swelled to fifteen; fifty different minorities, and a total of 30 million people, had come under the League's protection.[58]

The League's Minorities Section rose to the challenge.[59] Once the assembly increased its budget in 1922, Colban created an extensive intelligence network, dividing his staff of Spaniards and Scandinavians into regional specialists who pored over treaties, constitutions, and laws, sifted newspapers and journals, and examined minority petitions.[60] Optimizing his modest travel funds, Colban in 1922 began his annual round of visits to Central and Eastern Europe to cement the League's ties with government leaders.[61] Colban also maintained a discreet contact with minority representatives as well as with foreign spokesmen such as Lucien Wolf.[62]

54. League of Nations, *Treaty Series*, Vol. 9, pp. 466–98.
55. Colban to Mair, May 22, 1922 termed the convention "one of League's finest achievements," LNA S336.
56. League of Nations, *Treaty Series*, Vol. 28, pp. 12–116.
57. League of Nations, *Treaty Series*, Vol. 29, pp. 86–110.
58. Colban, "The League of Nations and the Minorities Problem," Aug. 18, 1926, LNA S336.
    The League's last minority treaty was negotiated in 1932 with Iraq, whose minority population of Assyrians, Jews, Kurds, and Turks numbered 700,000 out of a total of 3.2 million.
59. Colban memorandum, May 9, 1922, LNA S336. The Minority Section's annual budget in the 1920s ranged between 200,000 and 300,000 Swiss francs, of which 90% went to salaries for its staff of between ten and thirteen persons.
60. Except for a Greek member, Thanassis Aghnides, at the very beginning, citizens of minority states were excluded; also, there were no members from the principal Allied and Associated powers.
61. Colban to Drummond, Feb. 19, 1923 and memorandum, Mar. 25, 1923, LNA S337, outline the section's work. The travel budget between 1922 and 1931 ranged between 15,000 and 30,000 Swiss francs; Gütermann, *Das Minderheitenschutzverfahren*, p. 349. In 1924, Colban visited eight countries, and in 1926, he spent six months abroad. Ibid., p. 322.
62. Colban memorandum, Dec. 2, 1920, LNA S336; Colban also established a formal, if cool, relationship with the German consul general in Geneva, one of his severest critics: Aschmann to AA, Geneva, May 20, 1922, Germ. AA T-120 L683/4801/L215870–74.

To be sure, under its patina of neutrality and expertise, the League's Minorities Section was engaged in a highly sensitive political enterprise.[63] Colban's staff ruled on the receivability of *all* minority petitions and assembled *all* the documentation, including background material on the petitioners.[64] Colban nominated and briefed committee-of-three members, attended all their meetings, and implemented their decisions.[65] Indeed, it was well known in Paris and London that Colban had devised special procedures for Romania, next to Poland the League's foremost accused state, involving frequent on-site visits to advise the government and local officials on settling a host of religious, school, and agrarian-reform petitions.[66]

On a larger scale Colban was the League's exclusive minorities spokesman. In addition to preparing the annual minorities report, he advised the secretary general on every reform proposal emanating from the council, assembly, and general public.[67]

Before long the Minorities Section, along with other parts of the League's bureaucracy, developed a self-protective shell.[68] Like the handling of petitions from the mandates, minority complaints required extreme political prudence; but because of the explicit obligation of Article 12, plus the high public interest in Europe's minorities, the latter could not be buried as easily as the former.[69] Colban welcomed the frequent, brief council meetings during which he worked amicably with the minorities rapporteur, generally a nonwestern council member, with the Great Powers, and with

63. Colban to Attolico, May 29, 1922, confidential memorandum, June 31 [*sic*], 1922, LNA S336. In a secretariat dominated by Allied nationals, the Minorities Section, during its twenty years of existence, was run by six neutral chiefs: two Norwegians, two Spaniards, and two Danes. Gütermann, *Das Minderheitenschutzverfahren*, p. 57.
64. For example, at its meeting on Mar. 26, 1922, a committee of three consisting of Spain, China, and Belgium dismissed three petitions regarding Czech minorities in Austria, option rights for Eastern Galician Jews, and citizenship rights for the Jews of Bessarabia. LNA S336.

    On Dec. 11, 1923, a blue-ribbon committee consisting of Britain, France, and Japan in one session dropped two of the eight petitions it examined (Ruthenians of Czechoslovakia, Bulgarians in Yugoslavia), deferred three others involving Romania, Albania, and Poland for further information, dispatched an Upper Silesian complaint to Warsaw for referral to the council, and summed up a complex German petition. Étude du comité des trois, Dec. 11, 1923, FMAE (Société des Nations, hereafter SDN) 1934.
65. If a case reached the council, either Colban or one of his deputies always attended the meeting.
66. Mutius to AA, Nov. 10, 1926, Germ. AA T-120 L1769/5453/L434810–11, Note, Jan. 18, 1927, FMAE SDN 433.
67. Colban to Drummond, Feb. 19, 1923, LNA S337; also, Gütermann, *Das Minderheitenschutzverfahren*, pp. 325–6.
68. This did not quash an occasional reform proposal emanating from the section itself. See Helmer Rosting, confidential memorandum to secretary general, Aug. 16, 1921, LNA S336.
69. Rappard note, Jan. 5, 1923, LNA R1664; also Catastini remarks, directors' meeting, Jan. 16, 1929, ibid.

representatives of the minority states; but he dreaded the annual assembly meetings with their long speeches and public scrutiny of the League's accomplishments.[70]

By far, the greatest danger to the League's authority came from the minority states whose patience, by 1923, had snapped.[71] Poland and Czechoslovakia, vexed by a flood of "propagandistic petitions" and accusing committees of three of multiplying minority complaints, attempted to wreck Colban's system by means of obstruction as well as their "reform" proposals.[72]

Deftly, the secretariat recalibrated the system. In September 1923, the council adopted a series of resolutions that tightened the rules of receivability,[73] granted generous extensions to accused governments to prepare their observations,[74] and restricted the distribution of all materials to council members alone.[75] These changes satisfied the minority states and the

70. Colban memorandum, Oct. 4, 1923, LNA S337, lamented the "difficult, even dangerous work" required by the assembly; at the directors' meeting, June 25, 1924, ibid., he promised to "make every effort to prevent extravagant and exciting proposals on minorities questions [from] being submitted to the Assembly."

Colban's staff occasionally strained his renowned prudence; for example, despite the chief's insistence on the peacemakers' tactful formula of "*persons* belonging to racial, religious, and linguistic minorities," they were known to slip the "dangerous" collective abbreviation *minoritaires* into their internal discussions and documents. Colban to Rosting, Jan. 2, 1923, LNA S337.

71. Rosting memorandum, Dec. 28, 1922, LNA S336; also Fouques Duparc, "L'état de la protection des minorités" [1923], FMAE SDN 1934. Panafieu to FMAE, Warsaw, Mar. 3, 1923, FMAE Z (Pologne) 128; Rosting memoranda, Apr. 26, 1923, June 1, 1923, Colban memorandum, June 6, 1923, LNA R1664.

72. See copies of Poland's (Apr. 23 1923) and Czechoslovakia's (Apr. 5, 1923) protests in FMAE SDN 1934; Arcizewski to Rosting, July 13, 1923, Drummond memorandum, Aug. 23, 1923, LNA S337; Rappard note, Jan. 5, 1923, Colban to Drummond, Feb. 16, 1923, Rosting memorandum, Apr. 26, 1923, Colban, Record of Negotiations in Warsaw and Prague, Mar. 25, 1923, ibid., R1664.

Among their proposals were to restrict the receivability of petitions, limit the circulation of materials, and, following the practice of the League's mandates procedure, compel petitioners to submit their complaints first to the accused government.

In a typical example of obstruction, Beneš to Colban, Jan. 7, 1925, FMAE SDN 1934, refused to provide "statistics" of Czechoslovakia's agrarian reform, because of a lack of information over the "donors," many of whom were now outside the country or of uncertain nationality.

73. Petitions had to be consistent with the terms of the minority treaties, make no separatist demands, not emanate from an anonymous or unauthenticated source, abstain from violent language, and not repeat the allegations of an earlier appeal.

74. And allowed an accused government to contest the secretariat's decision on the receivability of a petition, whereupon a committee of three was to decide.

75. Council resolution, Sept. 9, 1923, LNOJ 4 (1923), Vol. 2, min. 1048, p. 1292. Dismissing concerns over the assembly's exclusion, Colban assured the council that "Cases might also arise in which the Government concerned would be less inclined to give the Council its whole hearted assistance if certain petitions were distributed to fifty-two governments . . . [and] published or commented on by the Press."

Background in memoranda by Rosting, Dec. 28, 1922, LNA S336, Apr. 26, 1923, June 1, 1923, and Colban, June 6, 1923, ibid., R1664.

Great Powers, but also increased the disgruntlement of the minorities and their defenders.[76]

To be sure, the establishment of the League's control over the minorities question emerged during a brief and anomalous period of postwar history between 1920 and 1925. The "Paris group" had been sundered by America's defection, Italy's turn to Fascism, and Japan's focus on its Asian interests. This had left Britain and France, still with their vast global interests but also with their mutual mistrust and disagreement over Europe's future, the sole enforcers of the Paris Peace Treaties; and it had given Colban a virtually free hand to develop the League's system.[77]

The opponents were weak, but not silent. Weimar Germany and Soviet Russia were still too diplomatically and physically feeble to challenge the peace settlement. However, liberal and left-wing activists, grouped in organizations such as the World Federation of League of Nations Societies, the Inter-Parliamentary Union, and the International Law Association all criticized the treaties and prodded the League to create a peace of justice; and within these groups, Jewish and German activists found considerable support for strengthening the League's commitment to minority rights.[78]

Between October 24 and 26, 1925, at the height of the euphoria over the Locarno meetings, the League's most direct challenge appeared in the form of a "European Minorities Congress."[79] Covertly subsidized by Berlin, this congress invited delegates of all minority groups to convene in Geneva, raising the specter of an annual gathering in the League capital.[80]

To be sure, League officials, in their handling of the minorities problem were scarcely evenhanded. Bound by the principle of state sovereignty, they not only guarded the minority states' interests and dismissed all but the most politically explosive complaints; they also blocked outside improvement proposals, shrouded their work in secrecy, and excluded petitioners from every stage of the investigations.[81] Colban, who defined his task as transforming 30 million individuals into "loyal citizens," was unmoved by

76. AIU to FMAE, Paris, Aug. 31, 1925, FMAE SDN 433.
77. Colban, in the directors' meeting, Oct. 7, 1924, LNA, boasted of his section's many successes.
78. Note, La Société des Nations et la question des minorités, June 17, 1925, FMAE SDN 433.
79. *Sitzungsbericht der ersten Konferenz des Kongresses der organisierten nationalen Gruppen in den Staaten Europas im Jahre 1925 zu Genf* (Geneva: no publisher, n.d).
80. See Junghann to AA, Geneva, Oct. 22, 1925, Germ. AA T-120 K1764/5448/K431884–89, Aschmann to AA, Oct. 16, 1925, Podewils, Aufzeichnung, Berlin, Oct. 26, 1925, ibid., 4555H/2298/E147299–304, Gündisch to AA, Budapest, Nov. 4, 1925, ibid., K1766/5450/K433179–90.

Compare Colban to Clauzel, Geneva, Aug. 15, 1925, FMAE SDN 443.
81. See Marshall's reasoned protest to Colban, Geneva, Aug. 17, 1925, AJC LM, General Correspondence, Minority Rights, 1919–27, over this issue.

criticism.[82] Until 1926, the Minorities Section had little fear of German or Soviet irredentism and also scant enthusiasm for the ardent internationalists. The pragmatism of an Eduard Beneš was far more congenial in the halls of Geneva[83] than Gilbert Murray's vision of a world organization that meted out perfect justice to minorities.

DEFENDING JEWISH RIGHTS IN EASTERN EUROPE

Flushed by their heady experience at the Paris Peace Conference, western Jewish leaders braced for the task of ensuring that the minority treaties would be enforced. They recognized the minority states' bitterness and threats of defiance.[84] Building on their existing political and press contacts, they now sought links with international humanitarian organizations and other minority groups, but they remained extremely cautious toward the new government in Berlin. Despite the republic's professed pro-Jewish and pro-Zionist orientation,[85] Germany's internal chaos and underlying irredentist goals appeared threatening to the foreign Jews' mission and to their political loyalties.

In 1920, the sixty-three-year old Lucien Wolf, still aligned with the AIU, assumed almost complete control over the Jews' minority diplomacy.[86] His nemesis was the *Comité des délégations juives*, the nationalist group now claiming to speak for 12 million Jews including the American Jewish Congress. Still intent on seeking representation in the League, the *Comité*

82. Colban, "The League of Nations and the Minorities Problem," Aug. 18, 1926, LNA R2156.
83. Even President Masaryk's conciliatory attitude toward the Germans of Czechoslovakia was tempered by his refusal to recognize their political "pretensions." Couget to FMAE, Dec. 29, 1920, FMAE SDN 527; also, Nolte, "The New Central Europe."
84. Compare Wolfs euphoria (Diary, Sept. 16, 1919) with a KNP internal note, Aug. 12, 1919 (AAN KNP 1259) denouncing the treaty as well as the Polish mass protests against it (*The New York Times*, Nov. 11, 1919).

    Moreover, Jewish spokesmen continued to emit mixed signals to the world. Morgenthau, after his return from Poland, urged the League to establish a special "Jewish commission," but Wolf denounced this proposal. Drummond, Colban memoranda, Sept. 25, Oct. 23, 1919, LNA R1620.
85. Germ. PA AA (AA III Akten, betr. Jüdisch–politische Angelegenheiten, Nov. 1921–Jan. 1922), L1279/L329550–601, describes the links between the foreign ministry and German Zionists; Sobernheim, Aufzeichnung, Feb. 13, 1922, L1287/L349197–99, details his work, which included gathering and disseminating information on Jewish questions in Eastern Europe and Palestine and working with the *Comité des délégations juives* in Paris; functioning as specialist on Jewish questions with other Reich ministries; and promoting Jewish interests abroad, particularly in the United States, as a way of gaining sympathy for the Reich.

    However, on Jan. 22, 1921, the anti-Semitic *Deutsche Zeitung* ridiculed the government's effort to spread the mantle of international Jewish protection over the "new Germany."
86. *L'Univers Israélite*, Oct. 10, 1919, expressed some resentment for its ally's slighting of its "discreet, if extremely effective role" at the peace conference. During the 1920s, the Joint and the *Alliance* employed a permanent agent in Geneva.

threatened to move its headquarters to Geneva; but its new leader, Leo Motzkin, lacked Sokolow's political connections, Wolf's experience, and, above all, the resources to pursue an assertive minorities diplomacy without the support of U.S. Zionists, who were leery of following his lead.[87]

Across the Atlantic was Wolf's archrival, Louis Marshall, who immediately claimed the major credit for the Polish treaty.[88] Relieved to be back home, Marshall now had a full agenda of his own, staving off mass Jewish protests against Poland[89] and organizing relief for the thousands of postwar Jewish victims in Eastern Europe,[90] refuting Minister Gibson's "distortions" to the State Department,[91] and adding his support to the controversial Versailles Treaty.[92] Before him lay still another arduous public and congressional debate over immigration restriction, now tinged by the precarious fate of 3.5 million Polish Jews, and millions more in Romania, Hungary, the Ukraine and Russia, most of whom, Marshall recognized, would never find a home either in the vast spaces of America or in the tiny and still contested Palestine.[93]

Marshall also recognized the limits of his influence in Washington along with his government's unwillingness to protect the *Ostjuden* from further violence.[94] Still, the AJC leader intended to monitor conditions in Poland,[95] and his colleagues to exert a certain amount of financial pressure to induce

87. See Sokolow to Board of Deputies of British Jews, Feb. 9, 1920; *Comité des délégations juives, Bulletin*, Feb. 19, 1920; Wolf, Report, Dec. 1920–Mar. 21, 1921, YIVO W/M 19; Wise to Motzkin, May 25, 1922, Wise 74–56. In his memoranda, Aug. 13, 1920, n.d. [Nov. 1920], and Apr. 13, 1921, Wolf railed against the *Comité*, labeling it "obnoxious" and dangerous, risking the safety of all Jews by provoking anti-Semitism, and lacking access to the western governments "on whose good will the defense of minorities depends"; ibid.

    Nonetheless, Wolf and the *Comité* sent a joint petition to the League Assembly in 1920 protesting the persecution of Jews during the Russo–Polish War, LNA R1613.

88. *Jewish Chronicle*, Aug. 22, 1919. Report on the July 28, 1919 banquet (at which Stephen Wise was not present) and the public celebration, Sept. 11, 1919, AJA LM 82.
89. For example, Marshall to Chaloff, Sept. 9, 1919, to Rosenthal, Oct. 31, 1919, AJA LM 1589.
90. Marshall to Warburg, Aug. 7, 8, 1919, AJA LM 1589, which contained detailed proposals for a thorough reform of the JDC.
91. Marshall to Elkus, Aug. 19, 1919 to Schiff, Aug. 22, 1919, to Mack, Aug. 25, 1919, AJA LM 1589.
92. But with, as Marshall underlined to Motzkin, a necessary amendment regarding the League that would not "plung[e] the United States into war without action by Congress." Marshall to Motzkin, Aug. 6, 1919, AJA LM 1589.
93. Aside from the political considerations preventing a mass Jewish exodus to the United States, Marshall acknowledged the *practical* impediments of resettling millions of aged, impoverished *Ostjuden* in America, particularly because "it took nearly forty years to absorb the two and a half million who came since 1880." Marshall to R. Fink (a journalist for the *American Hebrew*, who had proposed this mass resettlement), Sept. 9, 1919, AJA LM 1589.
94. On Dec. 10, 1919, he and Stephen Wise pleaded futilely for U.S. intervention to stop the pogroms in the Ukraine; Lansing to Marshall, Dec. 11, 1919, LC Robert Lansing papers, 50, Marshall to Warburg, Dec. 13, 1919, AJA LM 1589.
95. Exchange of letters with Polish Minister Casimir Lubomirski, Oct. 20, 30, 1920, AJA LM 154.

Warsaw to comply with the treaty.[96] But once America renounced Wilson's League, Louis Marshall was relieved of the burden of more trans-Atlantic journeys and of having to vie again with his British competitor in an even more complicated international forum.[97]

Thus, in Lucien Wolf's hands lay the fate of any Jewish diplomacy in Geneva, and his task was enormous. Immediately after the war there were the pogroms in the Ukraine, the White Terror in Hungary, and the continuing atrocities against the Jews of Poland[98]; and at home, he faced a rising wave of popular and official anti-Semitism.[99] Finding Whitehall's doors closed to his entreaties,[100] Wolf applied to the League.[101] He also resumed his ties with Robert Cecil[102] and with his old Polish contacts.[103]

In the League's new headquarters in Geneva, a small, remote city nestled between the Alps and Lac Léman that had suddenly become a world capital, the seasoned British supplicant encountered an entirely new milieu. Here Wolf, with his legendary discretion and persistence,[104] born of almost twenty years of international advocacy, confronted not only a new and ambitious bureaucracy but also the annual fall procession of world statesmen through Geneva. Assisted by his dedicated staff, Wolf issued a steady stream of suggestions to improve the League's procedures. And, virtually following

96. See Namier minute, Jan. 23, 1920 (PID 803), GB FO 371/ 4384; also Pease, *Poland, the United States, and the Stabilization of Europe,* pp. 12, 45–6.

97. In the summer of 1925 Marshall paid his only trip to Geneva to discuss the dire situation of the Jews of Romania and the League system in general (Marshall to Schneiderman, Geneva, July 24, 1925, AJA LM 154); Reznikoff, *Louis Marshall,* Vol. 2, p. 657, during which he also boasted to the League's minorities director of his central role at the peace conference. Colban memorandum, Aug. 18, 1925, LNA S339, Colban to Wolf, Nov. 5, 1925, YIVO W/M 8.

98. Churchill to Lloyd George, Oct. 10, 1919, LGP F9/1/35; also *La Tribune Juive,* Dec. 13, 1919; *Jewish Chronicle,* Feb. 6, 1920.

99. Holmes, *Anti-Semitism in British Society,* pp. 141–60, details the campaign of Wolf's foremost antagonist, the right-wing, anti-Jewish, and pro-Polish *Morning Post,* against "Jewish treason and bolshevism" and against the Jews' overwhelming influence at the Paris Peace Conference and in the League of Nations.

Wolf, on Nov. 28, 1924, protested Curzon's Oct. 25 speech in Leicester that had referred to the Bolsheviks as a "small gang . . . [of] mostly Jews who are preying like vultures on that unhappy [Russian] people," but received no reply, YIVO W/M 12.

100. Palairet to Wolf, July 17, 1920, YIVO W/M 8, advised Wolf to direct all his minority complaints to the League secretariat.

101. Wolf to Drummond, Sept. 2, 1920, LNA S336; Oct. 15, 1919, ibid., R1620, Colban memorandum, Aug. 17, 1920 ibid., R1613.

102. Wolf to Cecil, Dec. 6, 1920, YIVO W/M 8.

103. Wolf to Polish Delegation, Nov. 29, 1920, Paderewski and Ashkenasy to Wolf, Dec. 5, 1920, YIVO W/M 8, copies in LNA R1613.

104. As well as his sense of humor. Commenting on the "Matsui report," named after the council's first minorities rapporteur, Wolf wrote thus to G. H. Mair on Feb. 12, 1920: "to get a Japanese to report on a Judeo–Polish question is worthy of 'The Mikado,'" YIVO W/M 8.

in Colban's footsteps, Wolf visited the minority states, including Austria, Hungary, Poland, and Romania.[105]

Wolf's first démarches in the summer of 1920 brought mixed results. Stunned by the extreme violence wracking Eastern Europe, he was able to convince the secretariat to set up emergency procedures for distributing urgent petitions.[106] On the other hand, Wolf failed to impose a strong judicial component within the new minority-protection system. Reviving Cecil's defunct proposal to the Committee on New States, he urged that the new Permanent Court of International Justice be given compulsory jurisdiction over *all* minority cases and that any council member could apply for its decision[107]; but neither Balfour, the League's Jurists' Committee, nor the council wished to handle minority cases in court. Wolf, who long rued this setback, continued to strive for judicial rulings in politically sensitive cases.[108]

Wolf also failed to secure a prominent role for minorities and their defenders in the Council's procedures.[109] Except for a formal acknowledgment, the petitioner was given neither the government's response nor the committee of three's decision and was thereby barred from providing additional data or seeking a council member's intervention.[110]

Wolf claimed credit for other accomplishments, for inspiring the creation of the committee of three in 1920 and also for Cecil's proposal to impose minority obligations on all new League members.[111] Neither, however, represented a clear-cut triumph. Wolf, who considered the committee a poor substitute for an active involvement by individual council members, would have preferred a permanent minorities commission but feared to press this delicate cause too energetically.[112]

105. Wolf to Colban, June 25, 1924, YIVO W/M 8, pointed out that the minority director had gained "false" impressions during his visit to Romania.

106. Colban memorandum, Geneva, Aug. 17, 1920, LNA R1613; Wolf to Drummond, Sept. 2, 1920, ibid., S336.

107. Colban to Anzilotti, July 2, Aug. 3, 1920, Anzilotti to Colban, July 6, YIVO W/M 8; Colban to Drummond, Aug. 17, 1920, LNA S336; Wolf, report to the presidents, Geneva, Dec. 1, 1920, YIVO W/M 8, Wolf note, London, 20, 1920, ibid.

108. Anzilotti (chair of the League's ten-member jurists' committee) to Wolf, Geneva, Nov. 11, 1920, LNA S336.

109. Wolf to Cecil, Aug. 11, 1923, YIVO W/M 8.

110. Wolf to Drummond, June 15, 1922, YIVO W/M 8. "Strictly speaking, the minorities have no right under the treaties." Colban memorandum, May 31, 1923, LNA S337; also AIU to FMAE, Paris, Aug. 31, 1925, FMAE SDN 433.

111. Wolf to the president of the Fifth Commission, Nov. 26, 1920, LNOJ, First Assembly, Séances des Commissions, p. 241; Mantoux to Wolf, Geneva, Dec. 24, 1920, YIVO W/M 8.

112. One of Wolf's initiatives seriously backfired. His protest that the publication of negative committee-of-three decisions could inhibit council members from raising a minority case led the secretariat in 1922 to discontinue sending any committee reports to the council. See Wolf to Rosting, Apr. 7,

Cecil's initiative in the assembly, adding sensitive conditions for all applicants, went against the majority sentiment for a rapid League expansion and provoked resentment against Wolf's meddling.[113] After a long and acrimonious commission debate, the assembly, in December 1920, voted to confine these minority obligations to Eastern Europe; even so, Jewish advocates were disappointed in the results. Despite their blatantly discriminatory legislation and practices, Finland entered the League with only an obligation to the Aaland Islands, Latvia and Estonia with only formal declarations, and Hungary only after a two-year delay.[114]

In 1922, Wolf passed up an opportunity to associate Jewish interests with the assembly's populist impulses but also to risk a clash with his government and the secretariat. Despite his close ties with the LNU, he openly rejected Murray's generalization proposal, thereby forswearing an alignment with the neutrals and the minority states.[115] Uppermost in this decision were Wolf's political realism and his loyalty as a British subject, but, above all, was his fear of diluting, or destroying, the existing minority system centered on Eastern Europe where the greatest threats to Jewish existence remained.[116]

Indeed, what Wolf had most dreaded in 1919 came to pass. With many new governments adopting blatantly restrictive legislation, Jewish minorities too frightened to petition the League, and individual council members content to let Geneva discharge their obligations, the burden fell on him to protest the most significant discriminatory acts.[117] Fearing damaging precedents, Wolf hesitated to ignore any but the most minor treaty violations,[118] a practice that tended to magnify individual cases and limit his room for maneuver. On the other hand, Wolf's realism frequently tempered his zeal and anxiety.

Also, as he had anticipated, the main requirement for Jewish survival in Eastern Europe lay not in achieving national goals but in obtaining the basic rights of citizenship and equal protection under the law. Indeed, one of Wolf's first and most difficult chores as head of the Jewish Colonisation

1922, Rosting to Wolf, Apr. 14, 1922, Wolf to Rosting Apr. 21, 1922, Rosting to Wolf, May 1, 1922, Wolf to Rosting, May 5, 1922, Rosting to Colban, Apr. 22, 1922, LNA 41/20350/7727.

113. Wolf, Report, Nov. 8, 1921, YIVO W/M 8.

114. Wolf to Colban, Sept. 28, Nov. 29, 1921, YIVO W/M 8.

115. Wolf to Colban, Sept. 11, 1922, YIVO W/M 8.

116. Wolf to Colban, Sept. 9, 1924, Colban, record of discussions during the assembly period, Aug. 28–Oct. 4, 1924, LNA S337.

117. Of the nineteen petitions sent to the League involving the Jews of seven countries (Austria, Greece, Hungary, Latvia, Lithuania, Poland, and Romania), all were submitted by external organizations, and all but two by the JFC acting on its own or in conjunction with the AIU.

118. For example, Wolf to Colban, Jan. 30, 1923, YIVO W/M 8, pointed out that any concessions to Romania would be exploited by Latvia and Estonia.

Association was to resettle the tens of thousands of displaced persons from the wars raging in Eastern Europe.[119] Working closely with the famed Norwegian explorer Fridtjof Nansen, the League's great champion of displaced persons, Wolf fiercely resisted proposals to deport the Jewish refugees to Soviet Russia and attempted to find them permanent homes in Poland and Romania as well as abroad.[120] With America virtually closed, he also tried, with only minor success, to open the gates of the British Dominions to Jewish refugees.[121]

In undertaking his minority advocacy in Geneva, Wolf soon discovered serious gaps in the system. The first alarm came from Austria. In a case fraught with future menace, in late 1921 a virulently anti-Semitic government in Vienna denied the citizenship applications of more than a half million German-speaking Galician Jews on purely racial grounds.[122] Wolf's protests were to no avail. Not only did this case fall outside Austria's international minority obligations[123]; but Britain and the League refused to challenge Austria's exclusive definition of germanism, which barred the Jews of Galicia.[124]

Another setback involved the Jews of Salonika. Trusting Venizelos's pledges in 1919 to protect Jewish rights, the peacemakers had omitted any special provisions for Sunday trading in Greece's minority treaty.[125] But in August 1924, after Greece's revolutionary–republican government, pressured by thousands of exiled businessmen from Asia Minor, announced

119. Marrus, *The Unwanted,* pp. 68–121.

120. Wolf worked on the League's Advisory Committee to the High Commissioner for Refugees, becoming head of the committee in 1929. See Wolf to Viscount Cave, May 6, 1921, LNA R1663.

121. Wolf to Grynbaum, London, May 21, 1921, to Eduard Frick, Oct. 14, 1921, Nov. 11, 1921, YIVO W/M 8; also report of Jewish World Relief Conference, n.d. [Nov. 1924], ibid., W/M 12; Wolf to Viscount Cave, May 6, 1921, LNA R1663; Wolf, report on the second meeting of the Assembly of the League of Nations, Nov. 8, 1921, YIVO W/M 8; Report, Nov. 20, 1924, ibid.; Sobernheim Bericht, July 1924, Germ PA AA L1279/L330173–86.

122. Wolf memorandum, Nov. 9, 1921, petitions, Nov. 1921, Jan. 1922, Austrian observations, n.d. [Jan. 23, 1922], YIVO W/M 8.

123. In "Observations du gouvernement autrichien," YIVO W/M 8, the Vienna government based its decision on the option clauses of the Treaty of St. Germain in which Article 80 specified that "Persons possessing rights of citizenship in territory forming part of the former Austro-Hungarian Monarchy and differing in race and language from the majority of the population of such territory shall, within six months . . . be entitled to opt for Austria, Italy, Poland, Roumania, the Serb-Croat-Slovene State or the Czecho-Slovak State, *if the majority of the population of the State selected is of the same race* and language *as the person exercising the right to opt*" (emphasis added).

124. Wolf to Curzon, May 19, 1922; Lampson to Wolf, June 23, 1922, YIVO W/M 8.

Protesting Balfour's endorsement of Austria's position, Wolf exclaimed, "For the first time in the history of the Jews in Europe it creates a racial disability to their prejudice at a moment when a whole series of Treaties have been negotiated with the object of clearing away the last vestiges of legal discrimination." Wolf to Lampson, July 17, 1922, ibid.

125. Like the Romanians, the Greek premier had threatened not to sign unless the Jewish provisions were removed. Wolf, Diary, Aug. 23, 27, 1919.

a universal Rest Day on Sunday, the JFC and the AIU petitioned the League.[126]

Wolf recognized the weakness of his position. Sunday trading, a purely domestic issue, was covered neither by the minority treaty nor by the Covenant. To launch a major press campaign would endanger Athens's efforts to raise loans abroad and cause widespread suffering among the Greek refugees without altering the plight of Salonika's Jews. Combining forces with his old ally Morgenthau, who was promoting the loans, Wolf met with the Greek delegates during the 1924 assembly and simply hoped for the best.[127]

Even in dealing with the most blatant treaty violations, Wolf was constrained by political realities, as would become evident in his *numerus clausus* petitions against Poland and Hungary. Wolf's struggle against the quotas on Jewish access to higher education, a tsarist practice adopted immediately by several East European states – and that also existed in the western democracies[128] – demanded extraordinary patience and persistence in the face of official obfuscation, the minorities' anxiety, and the lassitude of the League and the Powers.

Poland in the beginning of 1923 had been vastly expanded with the capture of Eastern Galicia, Vilna, and the territory seized from Soviet Russia; but it also faced acute political, economic, and ethnic problems within its lengthened borders. After a brief period of national reconciliation, a new National Democrat–Peasant coalition government turned aggressively against minority groups, thereby precipitating a spate of petitions to the League. When, in June 1923, the Minister of Public Worship and Education announced legislation allowing universities to limit their admissions, the JFC, the *Alliance*, and the *Ligue des droits de l'homme* petitioned the League against a threatened violation of Article 7 of Poland's Minority Treaty.[129]

Poland fought back. Already facing a major case before the Hague Court involving its German minority, Warsaw denounced these "outside"

126. Wolf, report, n.d. [end 1924], YIVO W/M 8.

127. Wolf, report, Nov. 20, 1924, YIVO W/M 8; on Germany's interest in this case, Fabricius to AA, Salonika, Mar. 20, July 10, 21, 1924, Weber to AA, Salonika, Aug. 12, 1925, Germ. PA AA L1279/L330117–18, L330141–42, L330154, L330490–91.

128. Reacting to the mass immigration of Jews after 1881, America's medical schools and elite undergraduate institutions such as Harvard, Yale, and Columbia, had established quotas on Jewish admissions, which remained in place until after World War II. Wise to Ismar Elbogen, Apr. 18, 1923, *Stephen S. Wise*, pp. 122–3.

129. AIU to League Secretary General, June 16, 1923, *Ligue française des droits de l'homme* to Secretary General, Aug. 27, 1923, FMAE Z (Pologne) 128; Wolf to Drummond, London, July 6, 1923, YIVO W/M 8.

petitioners[130] and pressured Colban's blue-ribbon committee of three, consisting of France, Great Britain, and Japan, to drop this high-profile petition.[131]

France, already embroiled with the Germans, British, and Americans over the Ruhr invasion to collect reparations, tried to rescue its errant ally from League censure.[132] Poincaré quietly convinced Warsaw to postpone any national legislation on the universities' rights and privileges.[133] However, French and Polish nationalists were outraged when the elated *Ligue* published Poincaré's reassuring communication that the case had been settled. Stung by Warsaw's rebuke, the French government rued its one brief foray into the realm of international minority politics.[134]

Wolf declared himself satisfied. On Colban's recommendation, the committee of three had not dropped his petition and had required Poland to furnish statistics for the next academic year.[135] Nevertheless, there was no improvement in the Jews' condition. Polish institutions, possessing considerable autonomy over their own admissions, continued to discriminate against Jewish applicants without interference from the central authorities.

After a new flood of complaints, Wolf tried direct diplomacy. In the summer of 1925 he paid a well-publicized visit to Warsaw, where he brokered a controversial political agreement that included promises of redress from a government desperate for foreign loans, but also about to collapse.[136] Wolf's

130. Modzelewski to secretary general, July 30, 1923, LNA 41/29289/1153.
131. Arcizewski to Rosting, July 13, 1923, LNA July 13, 1923: "No self-respecting state can engage in polemics, even indirectly, with any sort of international organization on the subject of its internal affairs," LNA S337; also, unsigned note, Paris, July 20, 1923, Panafieu to FMAE, Aug. 6, 1923, FMAE Z (Pologne) 128.
132. Keiger, "Raymond Poincaré."
133. Panafieu to FMAE, Aug. 3, 27, 1923, Bigart to FMAE, Paris, Aug. 28, 1923, FMAE Z (Pologne)128; Committee of Three, Sept. 29, 1923, LNA 41/30601/402.
134. Appearing first in the *Cahier des Droits de l'Homme* and the *Tribune Juive*, Poincaré's Sept. 12 letter to the *Ligue* was reprinted in the right wing and anti-Semitic *Echo de Paris, Echo Nationale*, and *Libre Parole*, provoking fury in Warsaw. Lacroix note, Paris, Oct. 10, 1923, FMAE to Warsaw, Oct. 14, 1923, Panafieu to FMAE, Warsaw, Oct. 14, 1923, note, Paris, Oct. 25, 1923, FMAE Z (Pologne) 128; Panafieu to FMAE, Warsaw, Jan. 31, 1924, ibid., 129.
135. Memoranda by Rosting, Sept. 12, 1923, Colban, Sept. 28, Azcárate, Oct. 8, LNA 1613; Wolf memorandum, Sept. 1, 1923, Wolf to Rosting, Sept. 30, 1923, Rosting to Wolf, Oct. 3, 1923, ibid., S337; Panafieu to FMAE, Warsaw, Jan. 31, 1924, FMAE Z (Pologne)129.
136. Wolf to Colban, May 27, 1925, LNA S339; Skrzyński to MSZ, London, May 14, 1925, AAN MSZ 205, on Wolf's "importance;" ibid., MSZ 101, and Pease, *Poland, the United States, and the Stabilization of Europe*, pp. 40–58, on Skrzyński's unsuccessful U.S. mission.

The short-lived accord between Władysław Grabski's KNP-dominated government and the Jewish Club in Parliament (*The New York Times*, June 28, July 19, 1925) trading the lifting of the *numerus clausus* and other economic restrictions for "a more cooperative relationship [between the Jews and] the republic," was strongly opposed by the Zionist deputies as well as by Poland's other minority groups; and it also failed to overcome U.S. reservations against providing political and financial support for Poland in the wake of the Locarno treaties.

The new Locarno partners followed these negotiations closely, with France noting the breach in the Minorities bloc in parliament (Panafieu to FMAE, Warsaw, June 7, 24, 1925, FMAE SDN

last political effort took place in September 1926, when he appealed to Piłsudski's foreign minister, his old friend August Zaleski, who was about to occupy Poland's semipermanent council seat, to renounce the *numerus clausus* once and for all[137]; but it was too late.[138]

The Hungarian case, even more protracted and politically delicate, began in November 1920, with the issuance of "Law 25." A reactionary Whitist government, aiming to protect the interests of Hungarians returning from the lost territories, had barred from the universities those deemed not "loyal from the national and moral standpoint" and set admission quotas based on the proportion of ethnic and national groups within the entire population. A year later, Wolf petitioned the League. The Budapest government flooded Geneva with bogus statistics, using the names of baptized individuals to swell the number of Jewish admissions. Wolf urged the secretariat to request an advisory opinion by the World Court.[139]

Again, Wolf was politically vulnerable. Finding virtually no support for his case in Geneva[140] and renounced by a terrified Jewish leadership in Budapest, Wolf played the supplicant with various Hungarian emissaries, who responded with empty promises.[141] The secretariat, while granting Budapest generous extensions, kept Wolf increasingly in the dark[142]; and the council refused to ask for a judgment by the Permanent Court of International Justice. Unwilling to defy the League or to antagonize one of the few states that championed minority rights in the assembly, Wolf refrained from an anti-Hungarian press campaign.[143] In December 1925 the council

508), and Germany exulting in their ultimate failure. Sobernheim, "Die jüdische Frage in Polen," June 6, 1925; Sobernheim to German Consul General Cracow, June 30, 1925, Pannwitz to AA, Warsaw, June 25, July 3, 10, 1925, Wallroth to German Embassy Washington, Berlin, July 17, 1925, Rauscher to AA, Warsaw, Oct. 9, 1925, Germ. PA AA L1392/L360493–532, L360509–19, L360521, L360526–27.

137. Wolf to Zaleski, Sept. 29, 1926, in *Report of the Secretary and Special Delegate of the Joint Foreign Committee*, p. 31; Zaleski to Wolf, Warsaw, Oct. 31, 1926, in Joint Foreign Committee, *The Jews of Poland*, pp. 5–6.

138. According to Polish statistics, the proportion of Jewish university students dropped from 24.6% in the 1921–2 academic year, to 20% in 1928–9, to 14.9% in 1934–5, and to 9.9% in 1937–8; Marcus, *History of the Jews in Poland*, p. 160; Beyrau, "Antisemitismus und Judentum in Polen," p. 225.

Poland in 1927 finally issued a statute, based on Article 10 of its minority treaty, giving local Jewish communities the right to establish schools and providing modest subsidies.

139. Wolf, Report, n.d. [end 1924], YIVO W/M 8; also "Numerus clausus," n.d., Germ. PA AA L1279/L330629–35.

140. Wolf to Bellot, Aug. 15, 1924, and Rosting, Aug. 15, 1924, YIVO W/M 8.

141. See, e.g., Wolf to Hungarian Minister Racz, London, May 3, 1923, YIVO W/M 8; also "The Hungarian 'Numerus Clausus,'" in *Report of the Secretary and Special Delegate of the Joint Foreign Committee*, pp. 13–14.

142. Wolf to Colban, May 7, 1925, YIVO W/M 8, Wolf to Colban, Aug. 7, 1925, LNA S339; but through a friendly contact in the Foreign Office, Wolf was kept apprised of the case; see Wolf to Bigart, Nov. 10, 1925, YIVO W/M 51.

143. Wolf, Minorities and the League, May 16, 1925, YIVO W/M 8.

closed the case, based on Hungary's assurance that Law 25 had been temporary and its pledge to modify it forthwith.[144]

The denouement was appalling. Two years later, with scant improvement in the situation of Hungarian Jews, Wolf and the *Alliance* sent a follow-up petition; but in March 1928, the committee of three dismissed the petition even before the Hungarian Parliament had passed a minor amendment to Law 25.[145]

By far, Wolf's greatest, but least successful, efforts involved the problem of statelessness. Almost a half-million East European Jews, buffeted by revolutions and wars and victimized by the new borders, had been denied passports enabling them either to return to their newly annexed birthplaces or to emigrate abroad. Poland and Romania, the two chief offenders, aimed at reducing their Jewish populations by evading the citizenship clauses in their minority treaties; emulating Austria, they claimed that, under the treaties of Riga and St. Germain, these people were "foreigners."[146]

Except for pleading with Warsaw and Bucharest and working with international relief agencies, Wolf could do little for the stateless, particularly because the secretariat and the council sided with the new states.[147] Wolf's last chance to raise this delicate issue was in 1926, when Poland and Romania both became candidates for council seats; but he failed to convince the League of its urgency.[148]

Even during the League's so-called "golden" years, Lucien Wolf was not alone in his disappointment over its performance. German, Hungarian, Lithuanian, and Albanian petitioners were equally, if not more, frustrated over Geneva's slowness and secrecy, its partiality toward the minority states, and its tendency to shun court rulings and ignore all but the most egregious violations.[149] However deft the minorities' spokesmen, however well grounded their petitions, their cause was weakened not only by America's

144. Wolf to Colban, Mar. 16, May 27, Aug. 5, 1925, LNA S339; LNOJ (1926), 47–8, 145–6, 148–53, 171; Wolf, Report, Oct. 15, 1926, YIVO W/M 8.

145. Wolf to Drummond, Apr. 10, 1928, YIVO W/M 9. The Budapest government no longer added baptized Jews to its lists of Jewish students and used the percentage of Jews in the total population, not the university population, to establish the quotas.

146. Wolf to Colban, Jan. 30, 1923, YIVO W/M 8.

147. Wolf, "Minorities and the League of Nations," May 16, 1925, YIVO W/M 8; "Questions of 'Staatenlosigkeit,'" in *Report of the Secretary and Special Delegate of the Joint Foreign Committee*, pp. 10–11.

148. Wolf to Drummond, Mar. 29, 1926, LNA S337; *Report of the Secretary and Special Delegate of the Joint Foreign Committee* (1926), pp. 10–13, 23–30, 33–6, YIVO W/M 8.

149. In the directors' meetings on Apr. 8 and June 17, 1925, League officials reviewed the mounting press criticism of the handling of minority complaints; but Colban on Oct. 7 still boasted of all the "positive work" that had been accomplished. LNA.

vacant seat but also by the absence of Germany and Soviet Russia from the council.

Wolf's efforts to pressure the League to enforce the minority treaties were weakened by his personal handicaps as well. To the secretariat, Wolf represented an antique, meddlesome figure who tended to inflate his accomplishments.[150] Geneva officials, unimpressed by his credentials and influence, rebuffed many of Wolf's procedural suggestions, withheld information, and discouraged his "exaggerated" view of the minority treaties.[151]

Wolf also failed in his efforts at direct diplomacy. During the crucial years between 1922 and 1925, he was ostracized by the Foreign Office and by the leaders in Warsaw.[152] Moreover, aside from Poincaré's extraordinary intervention during the Ruhr crisis, Wolf and his *Alliance* partner failed to gain French sympathy for the plight of minorities in Eastern Europe.[153] The Quai d'Orsay, their main antagonist, scored Jewish "separatism and fanaticism" and viewed minorities as "instruments of dissolution and bolshevism" that menaced France and its allies.[154]

Wolf did seek alliances with the "other side." An active participant in the Minorities Committee of Britain's LNU, he helped craft some of its reform proposals but dissociated himself from its more radical ideas. Moreover, Wolf cautiously established ties with Berlin in order to promote the Jewish cause.[155]

150. Memoranda by Drummond, Oct. 17, 1919 and Colban Oct. 23, 1919, n.d. [1926], LNA R1620.

151. Memoranda by Colban, July 16, 1920, Hudson, Aug. 25, 1920, LNA 41/5543, Wolf, Sept. 2, 1920, ibid 6525/402; Colban, Dec. 2, 1920. ibid., R1647, Rosting, Feb. 4, 1921, ibid., S336; Colban to Wolf, June 1, 1922, YIVO W/M 8.

Wolf in early 1922 received copies of the observations of the Austrian and Hungarian governments (Wolf to Rosting Feb. 22, 1922, Rosting to Wolf, Feb. 24, 1922); but later that year, Colban abruptly ended the practice. Wolf to Colban, Nov. 9, 1922, LNA 41/17190/17190, 41/23393/7727; Colban to Wolf, Feb. 15, 1923, LNA S337.

152. Wolf to Chamberlain, Apr. 19, 1928, YIVO W/M 5, complaining of a lack of access and asking for closer contact between minority representatives and the Foreign Office.

Wolf's proposal in 1928, to establish a Minorities Treaty Committee under the auspices of the Royal Institute of International Affairs was vetoed by the Foreign Office; YIVO W/M 9.

153. Unsigned Note, Paris, Mar. 2, 1925, FMAE SDN 508, declining the entreaties of the Grand Rabbi of Paris and Sylvain Lévi to intervene against Jewish persecutions in Poland.

Bigart to Wolf, Nov. 29, 1922, YIVO W/M 8, confirmed that, except for those such as Paul Mantoux who had been given special assignments, no French Jew served in the regular diplomatic service.

154. Barante to FMAE, Warsaw, Jan. 22, 1921, Corbin note, Paris, Mar. 2, 1925, Panafieu to FMAE, Warsaw, June 7, 14, 1925, FMAE SDN 508. Indeed, a later French ambassador to Warsaw regarded Poland's minority treaty as an unfair imposition by an America that "lynched and murdered" its minorities. Laroche to FMAE, Warsaw, Oct. 23, 1927, ibid., Z (Pologne)129.

155. See, e.g., Friedmann, Aufzeichnung, May 9, 1921, Germ. PA AA L1279 L329449–51, on Wolf's support for Germany's case for Upper Silesia; Wolf to Sobernheim, Mar. 31, 1922, ibid., L329659, describing his meeting with Walther Rathenau; Sobernheim to Sthamer, May, 1922, ibid., L329465, forwarding materials for Wolf; Sthamer to AA, London, Jan. 18, 1923, ibid., L349631, forwarding Wolf's urgent request that Berlin take immediate steps to prevent pogroms

Lucien Wolf never ceased to plead for a better system in which the League scrutinized the behavior of the minority states and the Powers played an active role in settling minority petitions.[156] The number of petitions submitted, dismissed, or acted on cannot measure his achievements. His main contribution was to keep the hopes of a more active League alive; but his main failure was his inability to recognize the League's deficits of will and power to protect minorities.

After the great cataclysm of World War I, the Great Powers sought to establish a semblance of normality in Eastern Europe. With new governments, borders, and languages transforming every aspect of life in four former imperial realms, the League of Nations was given the responsibility for protecting millions of designated individuals.[157] Geneva's officialdom administered this burden with tact and realism; during the first five years the voices of minority defenders were largely unheeded.

By 1925, however, Germany's revival augured a whole new political direction in Central and Eastern Europe.[158] It also meant the eclipse of Lucien Wolf's almost solo efforts to defend Jewish minority rights.[159]

against German Jews; Sobernheim, Bericht über meine Reise nach London in Monat Juli 1924, ibid., L330173–86, on Wolf's work for minorities and his support for Germany's entry into the League.

156. Wolf, Memorandum, May 16, 1925 on discussions with Colban, YIVO W/M 8.

157. Including a German–Jewish writer in Prague, who was intimidated by the postwar anti-Jewish riots, eased out of his government post by the new Czech government, and prevented by the new border and currency restrictions from recuperating from his tuberculosis in an Austrian sanatorium. Fink, "Franz Kafka."

158. Mantoux memorandum, Mar. 1926, LNA Fonds Mantoux 10.

159. Wolf to Colban, Mar. 29, 1926, LNA S337; Wolf, Report, Oct. 15, 1926, YIVO W/M 8.

10

Berlin

"Germany must . . . be the protector of minorities in Europe."[1]

"There will be no peace in Europe without assurances to minorities of their national cultural rights."[2]

"Today the Jew is the greatest instigator of the complete destruction of Germany."[3]

For seven years, between 1926 and 1933, Germany occupied a unique position on the League Council as the foremost champion of minority rights.[4] After a brief, calm period of apprenticeship, the Reich led a popular but unsuccessful campaign to alter the League's procedures and expand its commitment to minority rights. This failure had dire consequences. By 1930, all the minorities of Central and Eastern Europe were threatened by the explosion of right-wing movements as well as by the ravages of the world depression that diminished their security and political rights. After the Allies ended the Rhineland occupation, Gustav Stresemann's harried successors browbeat Germany's neighbors, the Powers, and the League with barely concealed irredentist goals and the Locarno triumvirate evaporated. The Jews, who had championed minority rights in the 1920s, became divided and leaderless. The League of Nations, staffed by a new generation of officials, reeled over its greatest challenges; and after Adolf Hitler's seizure of power in 1933, the Third Reich dealt a mortal blow to the world's first international minorities system.

1. Gustav Stresemann, anonymous article in *Hamburger Fremdenblatt*, Sept. 14, 1925.
2. Speech by Ewald Ammende, May 28, 1930, to the Royal Institute of International Affairs.
3. AA to all German missions, Berlin, Feb. 28, 1934, Germ. PA AA L1279/L332849–62.
4. The secondary literature on this subject includes Fink, *Weimar Republic as the Defender of Minorities*; idem, "Defender of Minorities"; Pieper, *Die Minderheitenfrage*; Kimmich, *Germany and the League of Nations*; Schot, *Nation oder Staat?*; Frentz, *A Lesson Forgotten*.

ENTER THE MINORITIES CHAMPION

Germany's long-awaited arrival as a permanent council member suddenly brought the minorities question into the public limelight. In "selling" the Locarno treaties and League membership to a skeptical German public, Foreign Minister Gustav Stresemann had promised to defend the interests of Germans abroad (*Auslandsdeutschtum*) vigorously in Geneva.[5] In response, the League and the minority states took measures to protect the existing system against their most powerful critic.[6] In June 1925, the council voted to "reform" the committee of three, excluding from membership not only the government accused in the petition but also neighboring states and states whose majority population were related to the petitioner. Allegedly confirming a five-year practice, the council's two main restrictions were aimed at Germany, with the largest number of kin minorities and surrounded by four minority states.[7] Although Germany's right to bring minority complaints directly to the council remained unimpaired, Colban conceded to an irate Reich emissary that it would be virtually impossible to reverse a committee decision.[8]

The council's "tactless" gesture stirred the expected protests in Germany over the value of League membership; but it could have been worse.[9] Poland and Czechoslovakia, terrified over the prospect of a minorities champion examining their citizens' petitions, had demanded an even more drastic alteration.[10] During the two secret, stormy council meetings on June 9 and 10,

5. Among Stresemann's numerous statements, see speeches to the Deutsches Auslandsinstitut in Stuttgart, May 21, 1925 (Stresemann Nachlass, Germ. AA T-120 3112/H147721ff); to the Reichstag Committee on Foreign Affairs, July 17, 1925 (Stresemann, *Vermächtnis*, Vol. 2, p. 150); to DVP party leaders (Turner, "Eine Rede Stresemanns," p. 435), and to the Arbeitsgemeinschaft deutscher Landsmannschaften in Gross-Berlin (ADAP B, Vol. 1, pp. 727–53).
6. Avenol, Note confidentiel, Geneva, June 4, 1925, FMAE SDN 440.
7. The neighbor provision was as controversial as the ethnic exclusion because it prohibited the Reich from examining petitions from the Hungarians and Ruthenians of Czechoslovakia or the Jews, White Russians, Lithuanians, and Ukrainians in Poland; but the council resolution banned neither another minority state nor the ally of an accused government, such as France, from participating in a particular committee of three.
8. Aschmann to AA, June 13, 1925, Germ. AA T-120 K1764/5448/K431685–88, transmitted with Colban's assurances that with a state such as Germany on the council, committees would be "painstaking" in their investigations.
9. Bülow to all missions, Berlin, Aug. 22, 1925, Germ. AA T-120 K1764/5448/431785–91, called the resolution "not as decisive as we had feared."
10. Colban's visits to Prague and Warsaw, Colban, Drummond memoranda, May 25, 28, 1925, LNA S337; Rauscher to Köpke, Warsaw, June 4, 1925, Germ. AA T-120 K1764/5448/K431664–65.
    On June 9, Beneš presented the Polish–Czech demands to the council; in addition to the two exclusions, they included (1) forcing minorities to exhaust all domestic means before applying to the League, (2) restricting referrals to the Hague Court to unanimous council decisions, and (3) making committee-of-three decisions binding on the council. France opposed the third proposal as a violation of the minority treaties, Fromageot, Avis, n.d. [June 1925]; unsigned note, June 17, 1925, FMAE SDN 433.

Britain's Foreign Secretary Sir Austen Chamberlain, joined by Belgium and Sweden, had warned against jeopardizing Germany's adhesion to the League; by accepting the exclusion resolution, Britain had saved the essential element of Article 12.[11]

The League secretariat, responding to mounting criticisms by minority partisans, closed ranks.[12] During the December 1925 council session, Brazilian Minorities Rapporteur Alfranio de Mello Franco, coached by Colban, not only dismissed the assembly's latest proposal to create a universal minorities system; answering the partisans of cultural autonomy, Mello Franco insisted that the purpose of the minority treaties was to "prepare the way . . . for the establishment of a complete national unity."[13] Chamberlain's addendum, despite its conciliatory tone, only reinforced the impression that the League intended to "settle the minorities question once and for all before Germany's entry."[14]

Undoubtedly, the strongest repercussion of Germany's post-Locarno challenge was the reform of the council itself. In March 1926, Stresemann's ceremonial arrival in Geneva was foiled by Poland's insistence on a permanent seat as well as the identical demands by Spain and Brazil.[15] The secretariat's deft compromise was to expand the council's membership from ten to fourteen with a provision for a "semipermanent" seat for Poland and that, following a bloc system, ensured that at least one other minority state would always be represented on the council.[16]

11. Unsigned note, June 17, 1925, "La Société des Nations et la question des minorités," FMAE SDN 433.

    On Berlin's diplomatic campaign to block the Polish–Czech maneuver: Bülow to all missions, Berlin, May 25, 1925, Bülow to Aschmann, Berlin, May 25, 1925, conveying a stiffly-worded message to Colban, also, Sthamer to AA, London, May 27, 1925, Hoesch to AA, Paris, June 5, 1925, Germ. AA T-120 K1764/5449/K431641–50.
12. The protestors included the Third International (meeting, June 17–July 8, 1924, *International Press-Korrespondenz* 4, no. 16; Colban, report, n.d. [Aug. 1924], LNA S337), the World Federation of League of Nations Societies, the European Minorities Congress, which, at its second meeting assembled delegates from forty countries representing 40 million people, (*Journal de Genève*, July 10, 1926), and speakers at the Sixth League Assembly in Sept. 1925; LNOJ, Records of the 6th Assembly (Geneva, 1925). Minutes of the 6th Committee, Special Supplement #39, pp. 15–21.
13. "The object of the Minority Treaties and of the Council in discharging its duties under them . . . was to secure for minorities that measure of protection and justice which would gradually prepare them to be merged into the national community to which they belonged," Meeting, Dec. 9, 1925, LNOJ 7 (1926), Vol. 1, minute 1615, pp. 138–44; Mello Franco statement, p. 142; also, Clauzel to Briand, Dec. 10, 1925, FMAE SDN 433.
14. *The New York Times*, Dec. 10, 1925; also Aschmann to AA, Geneva, Dec. 23, 1925, Germ. AA T-120 L784/5101/L229618–28. One month earlier, Chamberlain wrote privately that the minorities treaties served "only to keep alive differences which might otherwise be healed in time." Minute, Nov. 11, 1925, GB FO 371/10701, quoted in Finney, "'An Evil for All Concerned,'" p. 537.
15. Stresemann, Runderlass, Mar. 20, 1926, ADAP B, Vol. 1, pp. 424–7.
16. According to the new configuration, there were five permanent members, Britain, France, Italy, Japan, and Germany, and two members eligible for unlimited reelection, Poland and Spain (Brazil,

Stresemann's two new partners, Chamberlain and French Foreign Minister Aristide Briand, were also disconcerted by the threat of a minorities defender in their midst. To be sure, the Locarno agreements had not barred the prospect of *peaceful* change in Eastern Europe[17]; but neither Britain nor France, each with their own domestic weak points, welcomed a raucous campaign to stir minority grievances and undermine the treaties' territorial provisions. Of the two, Briand was the more vexed by Stresemann's agitation. Not only did it provoke Poland to demand a universal minorities system, but it also threatened the emerging Franco–German detente by forcing Briand to defend Warsaw and the League against Stresemann's complaints.[18] Chamberlain, more skeptical of the League's procedures, sought improvements; but he also rejected universal schemes, separatist proposals, and irredentist goals.[19] The third Locarno partner, Benito Mussolini, who had readily manipulated minority complaints against Yugoslavia and Greece, lashed out at Stresemann for championing the Germans of South Tirol.[20]

But the Reich was not alone. Its putative minority campaign drew support not only from international humanitarian organizations but also from several governments, including a Soviet Union at least officially committed to minority rights, from revisionist Hungary, Bulgaria, and Lithuania, all clamoring for protection for their lost populations, and from the European neutrals and Belgium, who were intensely critical of the Great-Power-dominated League.[21] Had Stresemann wished to raise the minorities banner

rejecting a subordinate status, resigned from the League in June 1926; Spain resigned, but returned to the League in 1928), and seven nonpermanent members, three from Latin America, one from Asia, one representing the Little Entente, one the European wartime neutrals, and one the British Commonwealth. This bloc system excluded Austria, Hungary, and Bulgaria from the council.

Although Geneva officials welcomed an enlarged and more malleable council, German critics fretted that the simple majority needed to quash the minority treaties had become all the more obtainable. Aschmann to AA, Geneva, May 31, 1926, Germ. AA T-120 K1769/5453/K434702–8.

17. On June 30, 1925, Stresemann instructed all German missions to "launch propaganda for a revision of the eastern frontiers on a grand scale." ADAP B, Vol. 1, pp. 473–4.
18. Laboulaye to Briand, Berlin, Jan. 1, 6, 1926, Margerie to Briand, Feb. 6, 1926, Briand to all missions, Feb. 23, 1926, FMAE Y 585; Chamberlain, Memorandum, Feb. 1, 1926, DBFP, Ser. 1A, Vol. 1, pp. 383–4. France's opposition to generalization derived from its fear of Germany's exploitation of Alsatian separatism.

    Official French policy in Fouques Duparc, "Développement de la protection des minorités."
19. Chamberlain to Cecil, London, Feb. 9, 1926, DBFP, Ser. 1A, Vol. 1, pp. 412–13. Britain, still hoping for America's adhesion to the League, believed that generalization would alienate Washington. Headlam-Morley memorandum, Feb. 7, 1922, GB FO 371 W1031/48/98. Moreover, Britain still had its own "Irish problem." On Sept. 25, 1925, the *Journal de Genève*, Sept. 25, 1925, reported a petition to the League by the Irish Free State, protesting the situation of 500,000 Ulsterites "terrorized" by an occupying army of 45,000 British soldiers, which Chamberlain easily buried.
20. On the brief German–Italian flareup: Stresemann, *Vermächtnis*, Vol. 2, pp. 483–501; DBFP, Ser. 1A, Vol. 1, pp. 409, 415–18, 429, 430–2.
21. Orde memorandum on the foreign policy of the USSR, Feb. 10, 1926, DBFP, Ser. 1A, Vol. 1, p. 445; on other state supporters, Schubert, Aufzeichnungen, Feb. 23, Apr. 28, 1926, Germ. AA T-120 4555H/2298/E147351–52, E147414–17; 4569H/2339/E168681–87.

when Germany finally took its seat on the council in September 1926, he would undoubtedly have stirred up considerable trouble for the League and the minority states.

But this realist politician and Nobel-prize statesman, more akin to the prudent Bismarck than to his bombastic exiled kaiser, recognized the risks of an international minorities crusade. It was one thing for Berlin to renew its ties with Moscow and also to expand the Reich's covert subsidies to the *Auslandsdeutschen*,[22] support the European Minorities Congress,[23] and help found and subsidize Europe's most prominent minorities journal[24]; it was another to provoke Germany's new Locarno partners and the United States with demagogic rhetoric and revisionist threats while his country was still occupied and bound by reparations.

It was not only his western agenda that restrained Stresemann from unfurling the minorities banner; he also recognized that Germany's own house was not yet in order. The council, ignoring earlier Polish and Czech demands, had not considered imposing a minorities obligation as a condition of Germany's admission to the League.[25] Nevertheless, it had been seven years since the Reich delegation had vowed at Versailles that Germany would grant generous treatment to its minorities, and this promise had not been fulfilled.[26]

The obstacles to creating a model minorities regime in Germany were both structural and ideological. On one side of the Wilhelmstrasse, Stresemann and the *Auswärtiges Amt* endorsed cultural autonomy for Germany's small number of linguistic minorities to bolster the claims of Germans abroad.[27] On the other, Prussia, the giant state-guardian of the Reich's

22. Denkschrift (secret), Mar. 23, 1926, ADAP B, Vol. 1, pp. 430–2. On the subsidies to *Auslandsdeutschtum*: Krekeler, *Revisionsanspruch und geheime Ostpolitik*. Schot, *Nation oder Staat?*

23. The congress's second meeting, Aug. 25–27, 1926, dominated by German and Jewish delegates and assembling representatives from forty countries and 40 million people (*Sitzungsbericht des Kongresses der organisierten nationalen Gruppen in den Staaten Europas* [Geneva: n.p., 1927]), struck French and League observers as a "sort of minorities international battling the League." French consul general reports, July 12, Aug. 28, 1926, 1926, FMAE Y 585. Colban attended as an observer. Aschmann to AA, Geneva, Sept. 3, 1926, Germ. AA T-120 K1764/5449/K432265–79.

24. This was *Nation und Staat*, based in Vienna, that from its beginning in 1927 rapidly became Europe's most authoritative minorities periodical, read closely by League officials. Originally proposed by Prussia's Interior Ministry to counteract Polish propaganda, *Nation und Staat* was taken over by the *Auswärtiges Amt*, which selected its editors and provided funds and source materials for its articles: Freytag to R.M. Interior, Berlin, Sept. 2, 1927, Germ. AA T-120 K1770/5454/K435719–23.

25. Although there was disagreement within the secretariat over the Allies' intention to impose an obligation on Germany, Colban, because of Headlam-Morley's advice (minute, Aug. 5, 1919, LNA S336), ruled negatively.

26. Article 113 of the Weimar Constitution, permitting "free national development" of linguistic minorities, was ambiguous over the status of foreigners with rights of permanent residence, an issue of particular importance to the *Ostjuden*.

27. Stresemann, "Kultur Autonomie der Minderheiten," *Tägliche Rundschau*, Sept. 2, 1925, Aufzeichnung, n.d. [Sept. 1925], Germ. AA T-120 4555H/2298/E147365–409.

reduced frontiers, defended its "Germanizing mission" against the bogey of Polish separatism and irredentism.[28]

This fundamental clash between the Reich and Prussia had not been resolved when Germany applied to the League. On February 9, 1926, Prussia issued a very restricted Danish school ordinance, limited to three districts in Schleswig.[29] A day later, at an interministerial conference, Stresemann termed the protection of minorities "one of the great questions of the present" and called for the establishment of minority schools throughout the Reich.[30] Prussia, with its majority vote in the Reichsrat, was able to block any national legislation and then delayed a Polish ordinance for two years.[31]

Stresemann was also constrained by the world's concern over the republic's Jews, who neither considered themselves nor were officially regarded as a national minority.[32] In the immediate postwar period, anti-Semitism, fueled by the anti-Bolshevik, anti-Versailles, and racist propaganda of radical right-wing organizations as well as by foreign sources, had raged through Germany, aimed at Jewish citizens as much as the *Ostjuden*.[33] The murder of Germany's first Jewish foreign minister, Walther Rathenau, in June 1922 had shaken foreign confidence in the republic.[34] Almost immediately after Stresemann assumed office in August 1923, the *annus horribilis* of the Ruhr invasion, hyperinflation, and the Hitler–Ludendorff *putsch*, international opinion castigated the Reich over the expulsions of scores of *ostjude*

28. In his impassioned speech to the Landtag on June 9, 1923, Prussia's Social Democratic Prime Minister, Otto Braun, declared that Poland, by its persecution of minorities, had lost any right to protest the treatment of its kin abroad. Broszat, "Aspekte der preussisch-deutschen Minderheitenpolitik," pp. 399–400.

29. The ordinance, establishing state-supported public and private elementary instruction, was restricted to children of parents born in those districts or in Denmark. Prussia. Ministry of State, Erlass, Feb. 9, 1926, Germ. AA T-120 5063/2521/E291490–91; *The Times* [London], Feb. 15, 1926.

    This "ungenerous" law kindled little enthusiasm among the Danes, Poles, and *Auslandsdeutschen* (Bruns [the Reich's legal expert on minorities questions] to Chancellor Luther, Feb. 25, 1926, Germ. AA T-120 3225/1624/D699216–19; *Deutsche Allgemeine Zeitung*, Mar. 10, 1926); was ridiculed by France as a veiled effort to curry favor with the League (Margerie to Briand, Berlin, Feb. 6, 1926, FMAE Y585, Feb. 26, 1926, ibid, SDN 446; Wertheimer to AA, Paris, Feb. 15, 1926, Germ. AA T-120 4555H/2298/E147243); and produced the predictable outcry from the German right (*Deutsche Zeitung*, Feb. 25, 1926).

30. Podewils, Aufzeichnung, Feb. 10, 1926, Germ. AA T-120 K1764/5448/K432106–21.

31. Niederschrift, May 31, 1926; Dirksen, Aufzeichnung, June 6, 1926, Freytag to Schubert and Stresemann, Berlin, Dec. 8, 1927, Germ. AA T-120 5462H/2770/E368438–51, 4555H/2298/E147424–41, K1764/5449/K432383; compare Margerie to FMAE, Berlin, May 12, 1926, Nov. 24, 1927, FMAE SDN 446.

32. Silbermann, "Deutsche Juden oder jüdische Deutsche?"; Pulzer, *Jews and the German State*, especially pp. 271–86.

33. The most popular foreign works were the *Protocols of the Elders of Zion* and Henry Ford's *The International Jew*.

34. Fink, "'As Little a Surprise as a Murder Can Well Be.'"

families from Munich and Nuremberg, and for the bloody attacks on Jewish immigrants in Berlin.[35]

The Weimar Republic stood judged by foreign opinion. Now in the invidious position of its despised eastern neighbor, it used almost the same rhetoric to excuse its helplessness against local chicanery and the "blind despair" of urban mobs.[36] Berlin also exploited its weakness, urging its Jewish contacts in London to demand Whitehall's support for Germany's parliamentary government against "the Hitlerite menace."[37]

As Germany revived politically, economically, and diplomatically, the republic actively courted local and foreign Jewish support. The *Auswärtiges Amt*'s Jewish specialist, Moritz Sobernheim, worked generously and evenhandedly with Germany's rival Jewish organizations.[38] The government subsidized tiny and impoverished Jewish congregations.[39] Above all, Weimar's Jewish spokesman played an active role in international Zionist circles, where he was welcomed as a dedicated, politically neutral figure.[40]

On September 10, 1926, Stresemann's triumphal entry into the League assembly was accompanied by cheering crowds and a standing ovation by forty-eight foreign ministers and ambassadors along with the hearty endorsement of German and foreign Jews.[41] However, this occasion was somewhat tarnished by a pair of viciously anti-Semitic articles a month earlier in the *Völkischer Beobachter* and *Der Stürmer.* Stung by the widespread foreign

35. See, e.g., *Nieuwe Rotterdamsche Courant*, Nov. 12, 1923, *Het Volk*, Nov. 13, 1923, *Daily Telegraph*, Nov. 16, 1923, *American Israelite*, Nov. 22, 1923, *New Yorker Staats-Zeitung*, Dec. 3, 1923. Details in Maurer, *Ostjuden in Deutschland,* pp. 436–506.
36. Wiedfeldt to AA, Washington, Dec. 4, 1923, Germ. PA AA L1279/L330045.
37. Aufzeichnung, Nov. 20, 1923, Germ. PA AA L1279/L330040.
38. Sobernheim, Aufzeichnung, June 3, 1925, Germ. PA AA L1279/L330424–45.
39. Sobernheim, Aufzeichnungen, Nov. 11, 1924, Dec. 16, 1925, Germ. PA AA L1279/L330205–6, L330571–3, indicated the concern of U.S. Jews over the fate of declining Jewish communities in Prussia.
40. The Reich's representatives, greeted warmly by Zionist leaders who generally used German as their language of communication, aligned themselves with British and other foreign Jews against French and Vatican policies in Palestine. Aufzeichnung, Mar. 3, 1920, Germ PA AA L1287/L349347–48; Bericht über Zionistenkongress, Berlin, Aug. 25, 1923, ibid., L1279/L329927–30; Der XIV Zionistenkongress in Wien, 18–31 August, 1925, ibid., L330499–505; "Die auswärtige Politik des Zionismus," *Wiener Morgenzeitung*, Nov. 30, 1925.

Sobernheim, who as a member of the advisory board of the Institute of Jewish Studies for the Hebrew University of Jerusalem attended the gala groundbreaking ceremony in Apr. 1925, took every opportunity to increase Germany's economic and cultural links with Palestine. See, e.g., Bericht (Vertraulich), n.d. [1925], Bericht über meine Reise nach Palästina in März und April 1925, Germ. PA AA L1279/L330473–75, L330499–505, L330430–39.

Signaling the Reich's neutrality in international Jewish affairs, Sobernheim also attended the non-Zionist World Congress of Liberal Judaism, where he received a warm welcome; Aufzeichnungen, June 25, 1926, July 15, 1928, ibid., L330695, L330745–47.
41. *Jüdische Rundschau*, Sept. 10, 1926, claimed a victory for "Rathenau's policies of reconciliation."

criticism,[42] the *Auswärtiges Amt* failed to convince Bavaria to muzzle the Nazi press.[43]

It is thus not surprising that Stresemann, during his first two years in Geneva, amazed supporters and antagonists alike with his moderate stance.[44] Not only did Germany eschew a leadership role in the "democratic" assembly and stake its political fortunes on the more narrow council,[45] but the Reich maintained an extremely low profile in minorities issues.[46]

Accepting Colban's offer of an "apprenticeship," Germany acquiesced in all the elements of the League's system.[47] Stresemann, unlike his Locarno partners Chamberlain and Briand, rarely attended committee of three meetings. In these private sessions, Germany's representative passed up opportunities to censure Romania, whose friendship it sought, over serious violations against its Hungarian and Jewish citizens.[48] The Reich also failed to intervene when committees of three dismissed German minority petitions from the Baltic, Czechoslovakia, and Poland.[49]

Stresemann's famous restraint met its limits in Memel and Upper Silesia, two lost German territories under special international regimes that permitted minorities to petition the League directly. Although the Memellanders had ample grievances against the Woldemaras dictatorship for threatening

42. Even from such friendly sources as the *Jewish Chronicle* and the *Manchester Guardian*, Sept. 10, 1926.

43. Sobernheim to Reichskanzlei, Reichskanzlei to Sobernheim, Sept. 8, 1926, Haniel to Sobernheim, Munich, Sept. 27, 1926, Sobernheim to Haniel, Oct. 18, 1926, Haniel to AA, Munich, Oct. 20, 1926, Germ. PA AA L1279/L330756–57, L330759, L330774, L330847–48, L330892–93.

44. Contrary to expectations, Stresemann's eloquent inaugural speech made no reference to the minorities question and was silent over referring it to the Sixth (political) Commission, thus ending a five-year practice that was not resumed until Sept. 1930.

45. Remarks to the cabinet, Sept. 24, 1926, Germ. AA T-120 3242/1591/D714207ff.

46. Colban, in the directors' meeting, Feb. 10, 1927, LNA, boasted that Germany's entry had "changed nothing"; and in his Apr. 30 speech to the Nobel Institute in Oslo called Germany a less difficult member than Italy; Fr. Min. Norway to FMAE, Oslo, May 5, 1927, FMAE Y 585.

Paris rejoiced in Colban's "political" settlements, the council's diminished activity, and Germany's quiescence. Note pour M. Cassin, May 23, 1927, FMAE SDN 433.

47. Aschmann to AA, Geneva, June 18, 1926, Germ. AA T-120 K1769/5453/K434711–14. Colban, alert to Germany's own unsolved minorities problem, traveled twice to Berlin, urging Reich officials to explore "untapped possibilities" in the existing system. Soehring, Aufzeichnung, Berlin, Oct. 14, 1926, Germ. AA T-120 4555H/2298/E147452–55; "Mitwirkung Deutschlands in Dreierkomitees," Berlin, Nov. 19, 1926, ibid., K1764/5449/K432287–92.

48. Mirroring the German minority's grievances against Poland, one was a protest against the closing of Hungarian religious schools, the other a petition by the *Comité des délégations juives* against mob attacks on the Jews of Chişinău; Germ. AA T-120 K1769/5453/K434798–809, K435111–16.

49. Berlin, with little interest in protesting land confiscations against the Baltic barons of Estonia and Latvia (Freytag to Frank, Berlin, Aug. 25, 1927, Germ. AA T-120 K1769/5453/K435029) or championing relatively minor complaints against Czechoslovakia (Margerie to Briand, Feb. 6, 1926, FMAE Y585, June 1, 1927, ibid SDN 527; Aufzeichnungen, June 9, 1927, n.d. [July 1927], Germ. AA T-120 K1769/5453/K435077–84)), also stood by while Colban deftly disposed of a major petition by two German *Sejm* deputies against Poland's agrarian reform law of Dec. 1925 (Schack to Stresemann, Dec. 1, 1927, Germ. AA T-120 5462H/2775/E372037).

their autonomy, Berlin sought good relations with Lithuania, which was Moscow's protégé, Poland's antagonist, and an otherwise staunch minority champion in the League.[50] In January 1928 Stresemann silenced this awkward quarrel by prodding Kovno to accept a bilateral arrangement that for two years regulated Memel disputes without recourse to the council.[51]

Polish Upper Silesia, with its vast mineral and industrial wealth, chauvinist local government, and militant minority, tested all of Stresemann's diplomacy, the League's resources, and the council's endurance.[52] Predictably, a deluge of German petitions accompanied the Reich's arrival in Geneva. Among these was a highly publicized protest by the local minority organization, the *Deutscher Volksbund*, against the Polish governor's language examinations, which had removed more than 7,000 children from minority schools.[53]

Underneath this "Great School petition" were complex demographic, legal, and political issues. Most Silesian children, regardless of descent, spoke the local dialect and were unfamiliar with standard German; but Articles 74 and 131 of the Geneva Convention, inserted at Poland's insistence, had prohibited any challenge to minority applicants. In essence, the school struggle pitted Poland's efforts to control its resources and stem the threat of local German domination against the *Volksbund*'s stubborn, unrealistic insistence on a purely subjective definition of minority identity: "*Minderheit ist, wer will.*"[54]

In Stresemann's first turn as council president in March 1927 his most dreaded challenge had materialized. Behind him stood an irate minority and German public as well as an impeccable legal case; but before him was the prospect of a dreary squabble with Zaleski at a low point in Germany's relations with Poland and France.[55]

50. Dirksen to Wallroth, Geneva, Sept. 23, 1926, Germ. AA T-120 5265/2575/E320511; Stresemann, *Vermächtnis*, Vol. 3, pp. 226–7.
51. Niederschrift, Jan. 28, 1928, Germ. AA T-120 5544H/2749/E387418–20; Schubert to consul general in Memel and all missions, Berlin, Jan. 30, 1928, ibid., 5265/2574/E391856–62.
52. Despite having its own regional assembly, Polish Silesia was actually ruled by its Warsaw-appointed governor, MichałGrazyński, a Piłsudski confidant and the honorary head of the paramilitary "Insurgents," which had led the uprising of 1922. Zechlin, Aufzeichnung, Sept. 3, 1926, Germ. AA T-120 5462H/2768/E366815–32.
53. Aufzeichnungen, Sept. 7, 14, 1926, Germ. AA T-120 5462H/2768/E366833, E366862–64; *Hamburger Nachrichten*, Sept. 14, 1926, raised the number to 11,000. Polish documentation in AAN MSZ 4743–44.
54. Frentz, *A Lesson Forgotten*, pp. 229–31.
55. With Poland, the breakdown of trade talks and the discovery of a German spy ring in Silesia, followed by bitter press exchanges, *The New York Times*, Feb. 19, 1927; with France, the outrage over the remarks by the Nationalist deputy, Count Westarp, over the "minorities problem" in Alsace, Germ. AA T-120 4587H/2363/E183186.

Photograph 10.1. Gustav Stresemann (reproduced with the permission of the League of Nations Section of the United Nations Library, Geneva, Switzerland).

The League came to Germany's rescue. Colban guided the council committee in drafting the "Great School compromise," which authorized one more round of examinations by a Swiss pedagogue.[56] Chastised at home for his retreat,[57] Stresemann claimed to have saved "thousands of children from languishing on the streets" and insisted that Germany's legal rights were unimpaired.[58] However, when Poland continued the tests and closed scores of minority schools, Stresemann reluctantly applied for a ruling by the Hague Court.[59]

Germany won a Pyrrhic victory on April 26, 1928. The Permanent Court of International Justice, while condemning the examinations, denied that

56. Besprechung mit Herrn Colban, Mar. 7, 1927, Germ. AA T-120 4571H/2340/E160601–2; LNOJ (1927), p. 401.
57. Questioned closely by Reich President Paul von Hindenburg over the details of this compromise, Stresemann said it was customary for the German delegate to work "from day to day." Ministerrat, Mar. 15, 1927, Germ. AA T-120 3242/1592/D714320.
58. Stresemann to all German missions, Mar. 18, 1927, Germ. AA T-120 3147/1550/D658541–46, acknowledged that his goal was to avoid an unseemly wrangle with Poland on a "secondary issue," thereby alienating France, Britain, and the secretariat.
59. Schubert to Drummond, Nov. 14, 1927, Germ. AA T-120 3147/1550/D659128–29; Schubert, Aufzeichnung, Dec. 13, 1927, ibid, K1773/5457/K437877.

Photograph 10.2. August Zaleski (reproduced with the permission of the League of Nations Section of the United Nations Library, Geneva, Switzerland).

parents in Upper Silesia had an unlimited choice of either language or school for their children.[60] Stresemann chose to downplay the court's equivocal decision. In the council session in June 1928, German State Secretary Carl von Schubert failed to challenge Zaleski's warning that "Polish children shall attend Polish schools"[61]; and three months later, Schubert passed up the opportunity to endorse seven additional *Volksbund* petitions, which the *Auswärtiges Amt* considered "minor."[62]

60. M. O. Hudson, ed., *World Court Reports* (Washington, DC: Carnegie Endowment for International Peace, 1934–43), Vol. 2, pp. 268–319; Poland's satisfaction, Notatka, Warsaw, May 1, 1928, AAN MSZ 4744.
61. Schubert to AA, Geneva, June 9, 1928, Germ. AA T-120 5462H/2770/E368578–83; Briand to all missions, Paris, June 25, 1928, FMAE SDN 433.
62. Germany, planning to raise the Rhineland and disarmament issues in the League assembly, wished to avoid another minorities squabble. Dirksen, Aufzeichnung, n.d., Germ. AA T-120 5462H/2771/E369131–35; also, Reich representatives were unfamiliar with these last-minute complaints.

    On the *Volksbund*'s disappointment, Dirksen, Aufzeichnung, Sept. 14, 1928, ibid., E169743–47; and domestic criticism, Hermann to Stresemann, n.d., ibid., 4571H/2340/E169743–47, *Deutsche Tageszeitung*, Sept. 11, 1928.

Despite Colban's move to the Disarmament Section and a less vigorous successor, the League's minorities system continued unchanged.[63] The result, not unexpectedly, was an explosion of frustration over Geneva's famous "compromises." In 1928 Lucien Wolf came forward with new proposals for League reform.[64] International organizations voiced criticism of the League's slowness and secrecy.[65] Neutral statesman urged an increased scrutiny of the minority states.[66] There was also a groundswell in the League Assembly to replace the pillar of Colban's system, the ad hoc committees of three, with a permanent minorities commission.[67]

Germany came under heavy criticism for its baffling inactivity. Minority leaders scored the foreign ministry's lack of support.[68] In an inflammatory speech in German Silesia, Reich President Paul von Hindenburg castigated Poland's persecution of minorities.[69] With German journalists and politicians demanding a more energetic *Deutschtumspolitik*, the Reichstag's Foreign Affairs Committee on October 4, 1928, called for "greater attention and concern" to the protection of minorities.[70]

63. The League's new minorities director, Spaniard Aguirre de Carcer, served until the end of 1929. In his memorandum, Aug. 12, 1928, LNA R2153, Colban strongly defended the existing system against "fanciful" reform proposals.
64. Wolf to Drummond, Apr. 10, Aug. 24, 1928, YIVO W/M 9; Wolf to Colban, Apr. 28, 1928, LNA R2153.
65. Céspedes, Rapport sur les activités des organisations privées dans le domaine des questions rélatives aux minorités, n.d. [Aug 1928], LNA R2165. In the summer of 1928, the International Peace Conference, the International Law Association, the International Union of Churches, and the Inter-Parliamentary Union all called for more effective League protection of minorities. The most far-reaching proposal came from the World Federation of League of Nations Societies, which adopted a German motion that the council create a permanent minorities commission. In its fourth annual meeting, the European Minorities Congress denounced the "hostile attitude" of some council members toward minorities. See, "26 Congrès universel de la Paix," Germ. AA T-120, K1769/5453/K435429; "Institut de Droit International," ibid., K1764/5449/K432500–1; Inter-Parliamentary Union, *Bulletin* (1928); "Vollversammlung des Weltverbandes der Völkerbundligen," Germ. AA T-120 K1771/5454/K435781–82, Volkers to AA, Geneva, Sept. 1, 1928 [on the European Minorities Congress], ibid., K1764/5449/K432473–83.
66. In Sept. 1928, Dutch Foreign Minister Belaerts van Blockland, one of the League's foremost critics, visited Slovakia and sub-Carpathian Ruthenia to investigate the situation of ethnic minorities. Charles-Roux to Briand, Prague, Sept. 23, 1928, FMAE SDN 433.
67. Berthelot to Briand, Paris, Nov. 15, 1928, FMAE SDN 444; Berthelot to all missions, Nov. 15, 1928, ibid., Y585.
68. See Bruns (legal advisor to the *Ausschuss der deutschen Minderheiten*, representing the German minorities in eight countries) to Freytag, May 14, 1927, Germ. AA T-120 K1001/4603/K261678–80, complaining of Stresemann's "aloofness"'; Krahmer-Moellenberg (Director of the *Deutsche Stiftung*, which distributed Reich subsidies) to AA, June 30, 1928, ibid., K1769/5453/K435363–64, protesting Aguirre's appointment; Weizsäcker, Aufzeichnung, Mar. 31, 1930, ibid., K1764/5449/K432628–30, reviewing this difficult period.
69. The president's remarks on Sept. 17, 1928, not cleared beforehand with the foreign ministry, provoked an irate Polish response; Rauscher to AA, Warsaw, Sept. 19, 1928, Germ. AA T-120 4569H/2339/E169171–72.
70. Loebe to Stresemann, Oct. 5, 1928, Germ. AA T-120 3147/1551/D659476–78; compare Guerlet to FMAE, Berlin, Oct. 4, 1928, FMAE Y585.

Yet Stresemann was still hesitant to challenge the League and the western powers.[71] Only fifty years old, he was in extremely poor health and exhausted by the election campaign of 1928.[72] Forced to miss two crucial council meetings, Stresemann defied his doctors in August and journeyed to Paris to press for Poincaré's agreement over an early evacuation of the Rhineland and a reduction of reparations.[73] The price was clear. In the fall assembly meeting, Briand, responding to a barrage of complaints against the council as well as Hindenburg's provocative speech, warned Germany against exploiting the minorities question and provoking a hostile atmosphere in Europe.[74]

One impediment to a future German minorities campaign was finally removed. On November 20, 1928, Prussia's long-awaited minorities laws were complete, permitting private, minority-controlled but also state-subsidized minority schools throughout the giant *Land*.[75] Although greeted with cynicism by the French and the Poles, this gesture was well received in League and neutral circles.[76]

On the other hand, foreign opinion remained anxious over Germany's Jews who, even during Weimar's golden years, remained under threat.[77] By the fall of 1928 there had been scores of desecrations of Jewish cemeteries, spreading from villages in the Rhineland and Bavaria to some of Germany's largest cities and bringing numerous expressions of concern.[78] Anti-Semitic incidents had returned to Berlin after Joseph Goebbels became the Nazi *Gauleiter* in 1926.[79] Moreover, the Reich's unqualified endorsement

71. Guerlet to FMAE, Oct. 6, 1928, FMAE Y585, speculated that the Germans were awaiting a new U.S. administration, which was expected to help Berlin on the debts and reparations question.
72. On May 7, after collapsing from kidney failure, Stresemann withdrew from the election campaign. Stresemann, *Mein Vater Gustav Stresemann*, pp. 508–12.
73. Stresemann's trip, officially for the purpose of signing the Kellogg–Briand pact, made him the first German foreign minister to visit Paris since 1871. Stresemann, *Mein Vater Gustav Stresemann* pp. 520–33; Baechler, *Gustave Stresemann*, pp. 748–51.
74. LNOJ (1928) Special Supplement No. 64, pp. 82–83; Massigli to FMAE, Geneva, Sept. 8, 10, 1928, FMAE Y585.
75. Prussia. Ministry of State. Ordnung zur Regelung des Schulwesens für die polnische Minderheit, Germ. AA T-120 K1764/5449/K432514–19; in addition, the Danish ordinance was extended to the entire province of Schleswig, and the ethnic qualifications were removed; ibid., 5063/2531/E1291476–78.
76. *Journal de Genève*, Dec. 20, 1928; Margerie to Briand, Berlin, Jan. 30, 1929, FMAE Y585; Weizsäcker to Renthe-Fink, Jan. 18, 1929, Germ. AA T-120 K1764/5449/K432510–12, Gesamtüberblick über die polnische Presse, ibid., 5462H/2771/E369627–32.
77. Blumenfeld, *Erlebte Judenfrage*, p. 183, contested the "rosy" picture of the Weimar years.
78. U.S. Congressman Dickstein to Ambassador Maltzan, Washington, Sept. 20, 1928; also Centralverein deutscher Staatsbürger jüdischer Glaubens to AA, Oct. 19, 1928, Sobernheim to Maltzan, Oct. 25, 1928, Germ. PA AA L1279/L331364, L331365–73.
79. "Nationalsozialistische Gewalttätigkeiten," *Der Schild*, Jan. 17, 1927; *Berliner Tageblatt*, Mar. 21, 22, 23, 1927.

of the Zionist project began to waver. Following the riots in Jerusalem in 1928, the *Auswärtiges Amt* was forced to acknowledge the complications of its Palestine policy, Britain's "sensitivity" to Arab opinion, and the Jews' "tactical mistakes."[80]

In December 1928 the League Council met in Lugano, Switzerland.[81] Contrary to Stresemann's hopes, there was no breakthrough on a western settlement.[82] On the final day's agenda were eight petitions by the *Deutscher Volksbund*, all settled in advance through League-brokered German–Polish negotiations.[83]

Without much warning, these petitions provoked one of the League's rare moments of high public drama. Canada's representative, Senator Raoul Dandurand, recalling the assembly's heated debate on minority protection, proposed that the council devote part of its next meeting to a discussion of its procedures.[84] Thereupon Zaleski delivered a long, prepared attack on the *Volksbund* for inundating the council with its ceaseless, trivial complaints and accused its leaders of treason.[85] Interrupting, Stresemann pounded his fists on the table and demanded the floor. In his impromptu speech, Germany's furious foreign minister not only defended the *Volksbund* and ridiculed Zaleski's paean to Polish rule over Silesia, but issued the startling announcement that he intended to raise the *entire* problem of the League's protection of minorities in March.[86] A shaken Briand used his role as council president to soothe Stresemann with the assurance that the League would never renounce its "sacred obligation to minorities."[87]

The sensational news of the *Faustschlag* forced the inconclusive Western negotiations off the front pages.[88] Stresemann was deluged with congratulatory telegrams on his brave riposte in defense of the principle of minority rights.[89] The entire Reich press exulted that Germany was "finally"

80. Nord to Sobernheim, Jerusalem, Nov. 28, Dec. 20, 1928, Germ. PA AA L331401–5, L331414–15.
81. Pleading his doctors' instructions, Stresemann had prevailed on his colleagues to meet in a more temperate climate than Geneva.
82. Schubert, Aufzeichnung, Lugano, Dec. 14, 1928, Germ. AA T-120 4587H/2365/E184637. Tempers had flared among the Big Three over Briand's insistence that a reparations settlement come first, auguring months of financial bargaining before the Rhineland could be liberated.
83. Noebel, Aufzeichnung, Berlin, Dec. 19, 1928, Germ. AA T-120 5544H/2746/E384731–32. Zaleski had warned the Japanese minorities rapporteur that he intended to make some remarks about the "tendentious character" of the *Volksbund*; Massigli, to FMAE, Lugano, Dec. 15, 1928, FMAE Y 585; and, on entering the council chamber, he had warned Schubert of his plan to speak, ignoring the state secretary's pleas to avoid a quarrel, Schubert, Aufzeichnung, Lugano, Dec. 15, 1928, Germ. AA T-120 4587H/2365/E184646.
84. LNOJ (1929), p. 68.
85. LNOJ (1929), pp. 68–70. As the Pole began speaking, Chamberlain whispered to Drummond "Now we are in for a hell of a row!" Drummond to Cadogan, Feb. 6, 1929, GB FO 371/14123.
86. LNOJ (1929), p. 70.
87. LNOJ (1929), pp. 70–1.
88. See Presse-Abteilung to delegation in Lugano, Berlin, Dec. 15, 1928, Germ. AA T-120 3147/1551/D659722–25.
89. Stresemann, Nachlass, Germ. AA T-120 7382H/3175/H168764–813.

acting like a great power.[90] French and Polish nationalists accused Stresemann of feigning surprise and preparing to launch an aggressive minorities campaign.[91]

The evidence, however, points elsewhere. Stresemann, who was indeed startled by Zaleski's diatribe, had clearly won the match and thus had little to gain from protestations of ignorance.[92] Briand, on the other hand, was furious over his ally's *gaucherie*, which was especially embarrassing after the recent heated Chamber debate over the Alsatians' demands for autonomy.[93] To be sure, Zaleski's script, drafted in Warsaw, was as much a protest over Poland's exclusion from the Locarno *tête-à-tête* as a warning against German irredentism.[94]

On December 15, 1928, Stresemann dropped his legendary sangfroid and made two bold pronouncements. The first, almost universally accepted, was the instinctive response of any shrewd political leader to defend a kin minority against brutal threats. The second, however, the impulsive challenge to the League, the minority states, and his Locarno partners, jeopardized two years of careful diplomacy to regain Germany's freedom of action. Unable to retreat, Stresemann reluctantly embarked on the long-awaited minorities campaign.

REFORM?

Europe's capitals nervously awaited a clarification of Stresemann's intentions. In Geneva, there was considerable anxiety over an assault on its

90. See, especially, Georg Bernhard in *Vossische Zeitung*, Dec. 16, 1928; also Rumbold to Chamberlain, Berlin, Dec. 19, 1928, GB FO 371/12907.

    In his Nachlass (Germ. AA T-120 7376/3174/H167702) Stresemann had kept an article by the right-wing French historian Jacques Bainville, equating his famous restraint with Bismarck's: "On ne frappe pas du poing sur la table tant qu'on n'est pas le plus fort." *Liberté*, May 3, 1928; but his son Wolfgang recalled Stresemann's chagrin ("Dies war nicht meine beste Tat") over this bombastic gesture: Stresemann, *Mein Vater Gustav Stresemann*, p. 547.

91. "Pertinax" (André Géraud, the foreign correspondent of the ultraright *Echo de Paris*) stressed the "latent violence" in the German character, recalling that Stresemann only ten years earlier had demanded the annexation of Belgium; Hoesch to AA, Paris, Dec. 16, 1928, Germ. AA T-120 4517/2340/E169788–91, on the French press. Rauscher to AA, Warsaw, Dec. 21, 1928, Germ. AA T-120 5462H/2771/E369644–46, on the Polish press.

    The *Neue Freie Presse* (Vienna), Dec. 18, 1928, published Zaleski's charges of a "calculated maneuver."

92. Chamberlain, Secret memorandum, London, Jan. 8, 1929, GB FO 371/12907.
93. Drummond to Cadogan, Geneva, Feb. 6, 1929, GB FO 371/14123.
94. Massigli to FMAE, Lugano, Dec. 15, 1928, FMAE to Warsaw, Dec. 15, 1928, FMAE Y585; Rauscher to AA, Warsaw, Dec. 21, 1928, Germ. AA T-120 5462H/2771/E369631–68.

    Following Stresemann's private talks with Poincaré and Briand, Poland's minister in Paris had scored the Allies' "betrayal" and predicted a nationalist resurgence in Germany; Frankowski to MSZ, Sept. 21, 1928, AAN MSZ 1.

minorities system.[95] From Beneš, the veteran of the Paris Peace Conference and spokesman for the minority states, came the threat to veto even the slightest change in the League's procedures.[96] While Germany's partisans proclaimed a "year of minorities," the other side sought a quick solution.[97]

Stresemann's strategy, to delay a major confrontation for several months, was both subtle and risky. Much to the minorities' dismay,[98] he intended merely to propose a "study committee" to examine improvements in the current system.[99] But much to Briand's annoyance, Berlin also unleashed a press campaign calling for a major expansion of the League's commitment to minority rights.[100]

Stresemann's Locarno partners dreaded the March council meeting, particularly because Germany was not the sole actor in the impending drama.[101] Off in Canada, there was Dandurand, trumpeting his bold effort to revamp the "old World's" minorities system. In Warsaw, there was Zaleski who, still resentful over Germany's escape from the League's control, asked the council to deliberate over a universal minorities system. Chamberlain, who was fending off the Labour Party's charges of his "hostility" toward minorities,[102] directed his efforts against Canada.[103] France applied strong pressure

95. Memoranda by Drummond, Dec. 19, 1928, Madariaga [?], Jan. 16, 1929, Drummond, Mar. 19, 1929, LNA R2153; ibid., directors' meetings, Jan. 16, Feb. 13, 1929; also Chamberlain minute, Feb. 28, 1929, GB FO 371/14123.
96. Koch to AA, Prague, Mar. 1, 1929, Germ. AA T-120 K1772/5455/K436246.
97. Max Beer (German official in the League's Information Section) to Weizsäcker, Geneva, Jan. 5, 1929, Germ. AA T-120 K2366/5778/K339397–401.
98. And to the fury of the Prussian government that Stresemann had just browbeat into major concessions; Niederschrift, Feb. 14, 1929, Aufzeichnung, Feb. 23, 1929, Germ. AA T-120 K1772/5455/K436063–65, K436015–18.
99. Stresemann to Reichstag Foreign Affairs Committee, Jan. 25, 1929, Germ. AA T-120 3147/1551/D659781–90.
100. Margerie to Briand, Berlin, Feb. 4, 1929, FMAE SDN 434. Suggestions that Stresemann "tone down" the campaign in Briand to Margerie, Paris Feb. 13, 1929, FMAE SDN 434. Hoesch to Schubert, Paris, Feb. 8, 1929, Germ. AA T-120 5544H/2746/E384707–10.

    The Reich paid 1000 marks for the journey of a Baltic journalist, von Berg, to Paris and London, where he met leading political figures and provided material for the press. Aufzeichnung, Feb. 13, 1929, Germ. AA T-120 L1673/5691/L4891048–49. Zaleski was reportedly furious over reports that German Nationalists had given Stresemann a present of a "fist carved in oak." Erskine to Chamberlin, Warsaw, Feb. 13, 1929, GB FO 371/14123.
101. Hoesch to AA, Paris, Feb. 16, 22, 28, 1929, Germ. AA T-120 4555H/2298/E147582–84. Mussolini's government called Stresemann's initiative a "virtual challenge to Fascism" and alluded to a Polish–Italian front. Neurath to AA, Rome, Feb. 22, 28, 1929, ibid., K1772/5455/K436180–90, K436235.
102. Sthamer to AA, London, Feb. 21, 1929, Germ. AA T-120 4555H/2298/E147498. *Manchester Guardian*, Feb. 20, 1929; *The Times* [London] Feb. 23, 28, Mar. 1, 1929, "Minorities," *The Economist* 108 (Mar. 9, 1929): 487–98.
103. Chamberlain to high commissioner, Feb. 18, 1929, high commissioner to Chamberlain, Feb. 22, 1929, GB FO 371/14123. Compare Kempf to AA, Montreal, Feb. 15, 1929, Germ. AA T-120 K1772/5455/K436210–11.

    Dandurand's idea was simple: to abolish the committee of three and to force minorities to submit petitions first to the government and, if not satisfied, to a committee of the entire council.

on Poland, whose retreat over generalization gave Berlin a moment of malicious glee.[104]

The Piłsudski government responded vigorously to the West's reprimand. Poland arrested the *Volksbund*'s leader, Otto Ulitz, on charges of treason, announced the resumption of liquidations of German property in the provinces of Poznań and Pomorze, and demanded from the Allies a firm guarantee of its western border.[105] Thus the world press swarmed to Geneva, anticipating a reprise of the *Faustschlag*.

Everyone had underestimated the secretariat's ingenuity in stage-managing public sessions.[106] On March 6, 1929, the main positions were stated. Dandurand offered his fanciful proposals; Stresemann introduced his study committee; and Chamberlain, while acknowledging the need for improvements, censured Germany's more expansive goals, scoring the use of minorities for irredentist purposes and demanding "clean hands" from minorities.[107]

Turning words into action, the secretariat easily buried Stresemann's study committee. Its mouthpiece was Zaleski, who proposed that a blue-ribbon *council* committee composed of Britain, Spain, and Japan examine Canada and Germany's suggestions.[108] An outnumbered Stresemann had to accept this revision, although it augured another "gentle burial" of the minorities

104. Briand to Laroche [très urgent], Feb. 6, 1929, FMAE SDN 434; note, Feb. 8, 1929, ibid.; also Drummond to Cadogan, Feb. 6, 1929, GB FO 371/14123.

Germany, for tactical reasons had publicly accepted generalization and thus enjoyed a privileged view of the Franco–Polish quarrel. Renthe-Fink and Dufour to Weizsäcker, Geneva, Feb. 7, 8, 1929, Germ. AA T-120 K2366/5778/K669573–78; Stresemann report to cabinet, Feb. 27, 1929, ibid., 3575H/1701/D779695.

London had seconded France's initiative: Chamberlain to Erskine, Feb. 16, 1929, GB FO 371/14123; although sympathizing with Warsaw's complaints over its "inequality" with Germany, Britain insisted that Poland had no means of "escaping" its minorities obligation. Broadmead, Leeper minutes, Feb. 8, 1929, Cadogan minute, Feb. 13, 1929, ibid.

105. Rauscher to AA, Warsaw, Jan. 12, 1929, Schack, Aufzeichnung, Feb. 4, 1929, Schubert to Rauscher, Feb. 27, 1929, attempting, unsuccessfully, to postpone another *Volksbund* petition, Germ. AA T-120 5551H/2607/E392050–53, E392046–48; 4555H/2298/ E147619.

Reactions to Poland's "nervousness," *Le Temps*, Feb. 4, 21, 1929, *La Suisse*, Feb. 14, 1929, *Le Matin*, Feb. 20, 1929, *Journal de Genève*, Feb. 20, 1929.

106. Beer, Aufzeichnung, Geneva, Mar. 1, 1929, Germ. AA T-120 K2366/5778/K669715–17. Chamberlain had declined Drummond's offer to "open the dance"; minute, Feb. 28, 1929, GB FO 371/14123. Before the meeting Briand had confided to Stresemann that no one knew which way the session would go, but that he hoped the German would not "rip Zaleski to pieces." Aufzeichnung, Mar. 5, 1929, ibid., 3147/1552/D660038–42.

107. LNOJ 10 (1929), 522–6. Stresemann, looking toward the future, had incautiously remarked to the council, "I am frankly not of the opinion that the century in which we live has established *a condition of affairs which is eternal*" [emphasis added], whereupon Chamberlain, that afternoon, warned: "To cite Article 19 [the Revisions Clause of the League Covenant] in connection with the Minorities Treaties can only make trouble."

108. Zaleski's cleverly worded proposal, tacitly supported by Italian Council President Vittorio Scialoja, asked that the committee examine the extent to which the German and Canadian suggestions *exceeded* the minority treaties.

issue.[109] The secretariat provided a gracious retreat; the council committee would receive observations on the minorities question from all members of the League and report to an "unprecedented," secret committee meeting of the entire council before the public session in June.[110] In addition, Drummond produced a face-saving resolution rescuing Stresemann from another squabble with Zaleski over the *Volksbund* leader's arrest.[111]

Germany's defeat in the March council was obvious.[112] Stresemann, braving howls of disappointment and ridicule at home and abroad, devoted his declining energy to firming up the Reich government and pursuing his western prize. The Wilhelmstrasse also counted on the groundswell of public opinion, fueled by disillusionment with the League, to sustain the minorities issue.[113]

The portents were good. Fifteen governments and twelve minority organizations sent observations to the council committee.[114] Lucien Wolf,

109. Schubert, Aufzeichnung, Mar. 6, 1929, Germ. AA T-120 4587H/2365/E184853–55.

110. Stresemann, Press conference, Mar. 7, 1929, Germ. AA T-120 4587H/2365/E184873–79; Schubert to Reichstag Foreign Affairs Committee, Mar. 19, 1929, ibid., 4555H/2298/E147689–92.

There *was* one bleak precedent, the council's meeting as a committee in Sept. 1924 to draft the ill-fated Geneva Protocol.

111. Stresemann, Press conference, Geneva, Mar. 8, 1929, Germ. AA T-120 L785/5103/L231304–13; *Neue Zürcher Zeitung*, Mar. 11, 1929. Also, Schubert, Aufzeichnung, Geneva, Mar. 8, 1929, Noebel to AA, Geneva, Mar. 9, 1929, Noebel, Aufzeichnung, Berlin, Mar. 12, 1929, Schubert, Aufzeichnung, Mar. 17, 1929, ibid., 4587H/2365/E184887–88, 5544H/2747/E385431–35, 4571H/2340/E169855, 4587H/2365/E184929–39.

The *Volksbund*, in its poorly drafted petition, crafted without the advice of Berlin, had demanded Poland free its leader and League observers attend his trial; Poland, backed by the secretariat, rejected outside interference in its judicial system. Stresemann, who acquiesced in a tactful council resolution, asking that the trial be conducted in such manner that the minority would not consider itself "threatened," yielded an easy propaganda victory for good relations with the League. In July 1929, Ulitz was found guilty of treason, a decision reversed nine months later by an appellate court after the issue was almost forgotten. Aufzeichung, Apr. 23, 1930, Germ. AA T-120 5551H/2606/E391728–31.

112. In "Der Paladin der Minderheiten," the *Deutsche Zeitung* complained that all Stresemann had accomplished was a "first-class burial" for the minorities question at the hands of a hostile council committee. Similar sentiments in the normally friendly *Berliner Tageblatt, Vossische Zeitung, Vorwärts*, Mar. 8, 1929; *Deutsche Allgemeine Zeitung*, Mar. 9, 10, 1929, *Germania*, Mar. 12, 13, 1929 and also in reports from Warsaw (Rauscher to AA, Mar. 8, 1929, Germ. AA T-120 3147/1552/D660056–57), Rome (Neurath to AA, Mar. 14, 1929, ibid., K1772/5455/K435329–32), Moscow (Hey to AA, Mar. 12, 1929, ibid., K1772/5455/K436253), and Budapest (Schoen to AA, Mar. 21, 1929, ibid., K1772, 5455/K436366–366/1).

113. W. Pagen, "Das Minderheitenproblem in Genf," *Deutsche Stimmen* (Mar. 20, 1929); Ewald Ammende, "Sieg oder Niederlage?," *Berliner Tageblatt* (Mar. 22, 1929); "Die Minderheitenfrage vor dem Völkerbundsrat," *Nation und Staat* (Apr. 1929), pp. 438–43; Reinebeck, "Plan für das weitere Vorgehen in der Minderheitenfrage," Germ. AA T-120 K1772/5455/K436306–11.

On growing support for minorities, coupled with disappointment over the Preliminary Disarmament Conference, *Manchester Guardian*, Mar. 18, 1929; also Zech to AA, The Hague, Feb. 20, 1929, ibid., K1772/5455/K436120–23; Prittwitz to AA, Washington, Apr. 19, 1929, ibid., K1773/5456/K436687–98; Köpke, Aufzeichnung, May 17, 1929, ibid., 3147/1552/D660177–82.

114. Among these were the Women's International League for Peace and Freedom, European Minorities Congress, Inter-Parliamentary Union, and World Federation of League of Nations Societies.

although distancing himself from the Polish and Canadian proposals, outlined a more fair and transparent system.[115] Austen Chamberlain, the committee's key member, was publicly committed to a thorough review of the League's procedures.[116] However, the secretariat, which dispatched a large delegation to London, was mobilized to guard its system and defend the *amour-propre* of the minority states.[117]

Berlin was stunned by the committee's 100-page report, which specifically rejected every important reform proposal and offered only three modifications: (1) petitioners were to be informed of the acceptance of their appeals, (2) committees of three were to report the results of their investigations to the council, and, (3) the secretariat was to publish basic, annual statistics of the League's minorities activities.[118] Leaked in the press, the London Report was termed a "minorities catastrophe."[119]

Stresemann still had a few cards to play. With a new reparations schedule almost complete, Briand had signaled his desire for an important *tête-à-tête* at the next council meeting.[120] The Tories' defeat on May 30 meant Chamberlain's replacement with a friendlier Labour foreign secretary.[121] All signs indicated the likelihood of postponing a final decision on minorities at the June council meeting in Madrid.[122]

Stresemann, who delayed his long journey because of urgent political negotiations in Berlin, gravely underestimated the League's determination

115. The JFC's Proposal for Giving Effect to the League of Nations Guarantee of the Minority Treaties, Mar. 1, 1929, GB FO 371/14124.
116. Minutes, council committee meeting, Geneva, Mar. 8, 1929 (confidential); Cadogan to Hurst, London, Mar. 25, Leeper, Cadogan memoranda, Apr. 6, 9, 1929, GB FO 371/14124. Headlam-Morley prepared the historical background: memorandum, May 17, 1929, ibid.
117. Drummond, note, Apr. 16, 1929, GB FO 371/14124; as a courtesy to Chamberlain, the committee held its main meetings in London.
118. Divided into three parts, the London Report contained a lengthy description and analysis of the minority treaties, a summary of the League's procedure, and a short discussion of the proposed procedural improvements: Germ. AA T-120 K1773/5456/K436775–95, summarized in Beer to Stresemann, Geneva, May 14, 1929, ibid., 3147/1552/D660209–17.
119. *Deutsche Allgemeine Zeitung* and *Deutsche Zeitung*, May 22, 1929, *Leipziger Neueste Nachrichten*, May 24, 1929; Stresemann, Nachlass, Germ. AA T-120 7387H/34176/H169909–10; also *The New York Times*, May 24, 1929, and editorial, May 27, 1929.
120. Hoesch to AA, Paris, May 25, 1929, Germ. AA T-120 L785/5103/L231502.
121. Margerie to FMAE, Berlin, June 4, 1929, FMAE SDN 437. His optimism was based on MacDonald's prominorities campaign remarks. MacDonald's June 16, 1929 *Times* article, reprinted as "Die Gefahren des europäischen Minderheitenproblems. Revision der Friedensverträge?" *Zeitschrift für Geopolitik* 6 (June 1929), 441–3, infuriated France and Poland and was quickly disowned by Whitehall as "campaign rhetoric."
122. Reinebeck, Aufzeichnung, Madrid, June 5, 1929, Germ. AA T-120 K1773/5456/K437065–67.
    Madrid had been selected for the council's fifty-fifth meeting to crown the festivities of the international expositions in Barcelona and Seville and also to celebrate Spain's return to the League a year earlier.

to end his campaign once and for all.[123] German political naïveté also contributed to the Madrid debacle. Stresemann's substitute, State Secretary Carl von Schubert, defied his chief's instructions and the majority's sentiment for a postponement.[124] With his vehement attack on the London Report and failure to coordinate with any other council member, Schubert played into the hands of Briand and the secretariat and foreclosed an adjournment.[125]

Stresemann reached Madrid too late to repair the damage.[126] After three hard days of debate, the council committee had produced some improvements and was unwilling to abort its labors.[127] Sweetening the pill, Briand proposed a foreign ministers' conference in August and a final settlement between Germany and the West.[128]

Although accepting Briand's hint to restrain his ardor over the minorities issue, Stresemann signaled his defiance. On June 13, before a packed chamber, he ungraciously accepted the Madrid Resolutions; but he reserved his right "to raise the issues once more" and even to ask for an opinion by

123. Renthe-Fink and Schubert, Aufzeichnungen, Madrid, June 5, 1929, Germ. AA T-120 K2366/5778/D669968–71, 4587H/2365/E184960.

124. Schubert insisted to the Finnish council member, who strongly supported postponement, that this would be a "paltry outcome" of the March debate because "the German public" expected a denunciation of the notorious London Report (Aufzeichnungen, Madrid, June 5, 7, 1929, Germ. AA T-120 4587H/2365/E184962–64, E185024–25), told German journalists he was preparing for "battle" (press conference, Madrid, June 5, 1929, ibid., E184966–69), and informed Hungary's observer that an adjournment must be achieved in a "correct manner" (Aufzeichnung, Madrid, June 6, 1929, ibid., E184976–78).

125. Renthe-Fink, Aufzeichnung, Madrid, June 5, 1929, Germ. AA T-120 K1773/5456/K437088–91; Schubert to AA, Madrid, June 7, ibid., K436987–88; Massigli to FMAE, Madrid, June 7, 1929, FMAE SDN 437. Following Schubert's remarks, Briand asked whether the committee wished to terminate its deliberations, and there was no response.

126. Stresemann–Schubert confrontation, Schubert, Aufzeichnung, Madrid, June 10, 1929, Germ. AA T-120 4587H/2365/E185049–52. After completing his political negotiations in Berlin on June 5, Stresemann had proceeded to Paris to sign the new reparations schedule and then to San Sebastian, where he had rested for an entire day after receiving assurances that Schubert was "following his instructions." *Vermächtnis*, Vol. 3, p. 420; report of telephone conversation between Redlhammer (San Sebastian) and Strohm (Madrid), June 7, 1929, Germ. AA T-120 4587H/2365/E184991.

127. Council committee meeting, June 11, 1929, containing a sharp exchange between Stresemann and Briand along with Dandurand's plea for a "partial solution." LNOJ Special Supplement #73 (1929), pp. 20–6. These were the improvements: 1) in special cases committees of three could be enlarged to five members and might meet in the intervals between council sessions; (2) with the consent of the accused government, they could publish the results of their inquiries; and (3) all their examinations that did not terminate in a referral to the council were to be reported in a letter filed with the secretariat and distributed annually to all council members. Massigli to FMAE, Madrid, June 11, 1929, FMAE SDN 437; Graham to FO, June 11, 1929, GB FO 371/14124. Ironically, the outgoing Chamberlain had just sent instructions to postpone a final vote: Chamberlain to Graham, London, June 10, 1929, ibid.; Sthamer to Stresemann, London, June 10, 1929, Germ. AA T-120 4587H/2365/E185050–57.

128. Pünder to AA, Madrid, June 11, 1929, Germ. AA T-120 4587H/2365/E185115–19, with copies to the Reich chancellor and president, noted Briand's vague promise about the return of the Saar after the evacuation of the Rhineland; also Graham to Henderson, Madrid, June 13, 1929 (private and confidential), GB FO 800/284. Briand to all stations, June 26, 1929, FMAE SDN 444, exulted over avoiding an adjournment; Briand to all missions, June 28, 1929, FMAE SDN 437, on the impending August talks.

the Hague Court.[129] One day later, breaking all precedents, Stresemann brought a minority petition directly to the council and forced Poland to enter bilateral negotiations under the League's auspices over the liquidation of German landholdings in Poznań and Pomorze.[130] Having failed to budge the council and achieve any meaningful improvements in the League's procedure, Stresemann indicated another, more menacing direction of German activity.[131]

Again, there was almost universal judgment of a major German setback and a victory for France and the League.[132] The Reich's principal proposals, a permanent minorities commission, an enlarged role for petitioners, and the revocation of the June 1925 resolution, had all been explicitly rejected. Beneš gloated over the maintenance of the status quo.[133] The Madrid Resolutions were never amended or annulled; and the council never again debated the general minorities question.

In August 1929, Stresemann's long labors bore fruit when the Young Plan was adopted and France agreed to evacuate the Rhineland five years ahead of the Versailles schedule. During Stresemann's last journey to Geneva, the assembly celebrated its tenth anniversary but again avoided a major debate over the minorities question. Neither Stresemann nor Britain's new Labour Foreign Secretary Arthur Henderson made more than general recommendations.[134]

129. Graham to FO, June 13, 1929, GB FO 371/14124, praising Stresemann and Briand's "moderation" and expressing relief that this "difficult, delicate question has been temporarily [*sic*] . . . disposed of," Graham to Henderson, Madrid, June 13 (private and confidential), ibid., on the ambassador's efforts to "promote a conciliatory frame of mind" to save the reparations settlement. Stresemann had at least won the semantic triumph of replacing the "London Report" with the "Madrid Resolutions." Weizsäcker to AA, Madrid, June 13, 1929, Germ. AA T-120 4587H/2366/E185147–49; Pünder to AA, chancellor, and president's office, Madrid, June 13, 1929, ibid., K1773/5456/K437025; Stresemann to AA, Madrid, June 15, 1929, ibid., 3147/1552/D660653. The prepared German translation of the London Report was destroyed (ibid., K1773/5456/K437003).

130. "Germany Demands a Minorities Ruling," *The New York Times*, June 11, 1929; Stresemann's text, Germ. AA T-120 3147/1552/D660516–23; Weizsäcker to AA, Madrid, June 15, 1929, ibid., 5544H/2748/E386176–78.

131. In his report to the cabinet, June 21, 1929, Stresemann insisted that this démarche was far more significant for Germany's future minority policies than were the Madrid Resolutions, Germ. AA T-120 3175H/1702/D780920–23; also Germany, Reichstag, *Verhandlungen* (Berlin: Reichsdruckerei, 1929), Vol. 425, pp. 2869, 2883.

132. "The Council did not limit itself to refusing the narrow German proposals. . . . It did not once give Germany formal satisfaction." *Izvestia*, June 15, 1929; see also *Nation und Staat* (July 1929), 662–5 and ministers' reports: Germ. AA T-120 K1773/5456/K436036–38, K437165–66, K437197–99; L437007–8; K2366/K670002–3; Schubert, Aufzeichnung, June 27, 1929, ibid., K1773/5456/K437057–58.

133. *Prager Presse*, June 23, 1929.

134. "Wo bleibt Minderheitenfrage?" *Germania*, Sept. 17, 1929; also "Vertraulicher Bericht über die Behandlung der Minderheitenfrage," Germ. AA T-120 K1773/5456/K437276–79, Stresemann, Nachlass, ibid., 7393H/3178/H171006–11, H171032–41. Speaking before the International Association of Journalists on Sept. 5, Stresemann admitted weariness over his "Sisyphean labors"

Gustav Stresemann died of a stroke on October 3, 1929, on the eve of the collapse of the New York Stock Market and the onset of the Great Depression.[135] As the first major postwar statesman to espouse the cause of minority rights, Stresemann had raised the public's consciousness over all the "victims" of the Paris Peace Settlement; but in using this explosive issue to gain leverage with his partners, Stresemann also knew when to retreat. Like Bismarck's diplomacy, Stresemann's complex policies required an adroit helmsman. When the hopes and fears of 1929 were dwarfed by the grim realities in Central and Eastern Europe after 1930, Stresemann's successors lacked his skill, subtlety, and, above all, his sense of limits.[136]

The League's victory in 1929 was questionable. In guarding a system widely perceived as slow, secretive, narrow, and unfair, it never convinced its critics that the minority treaties were essential to preserving the Paris Peace Settlement. Geneva continued to insist, according to the mantras of Colban and Beneš, that Europe's minority problems were, above all, *local* technical or political issues, amenable to settlement with the minimum of foreign intervention.[137] But the League's minorities system, only slightly improved in Madrid, depended for its survival on an extraordinary combination of elements: firm direction from Geneva, Great-Power support, docile minorities, cooperative minority states, and compliant minority champions, all of which disappeared in the more radicalized international environment after 1930.

EXCURSUS: JEWISH DIPLOMACY UNDER THREAT

Among the most disappointed witnesses to the denouement of the "year of minorities" was Lucien Wolf. In August 1929, the new Labour government declined his offer to accompany Britain's large assembly delegation.[138] Whitehall simply passed on his final reform proposal, the "fruit of his ten years of experience," to Geneva where it languished in the secretariat's

for peace; ibid., 4587H/2366/H185264–68. On Britain's inaction, Cecil memorandum, Geneva, Sept. 3, 1929, GB FO 371/14124.

135. Rumbold to Henderson, Berlin, Oct. 10, 1929, GB FO 371/13630, paid tribute to a "great leader" and "really great man." Kessler, *In the Twenties*, pp. 367–70, on the birth of the "Stresemann legend."

136. Wright, *Gustav Stresemann*, pp. 492–525; also Krüger, "Zur europäischen Dimension der Aussenpolitik Gustav Stresemanns," which underlines the visionary quality of Stresemann's foreign policies.

137. Charles Roux to FMAE, Prague, May 17, June 3, Oct. 21, 1929, Seguin to FMAE, Prague, May 18, 25, 1929, FMAE SDN 527.

138. Memorandum, n.d. [Aug. 1929], GB FO 371/14125.

files.[139] With Wolf's death one year later, Britain and the League lost one of their oldest, most persistent gadflies and the Jews their most vigorous defender.[140]

There was no successor to Lucien Wolf who in the 1920s had been the Jews' foremost spokesman at the League of Nations.[141] American Jews, with no official voice in Geneva, were a distant and divided community, their leaders focusing primarily on overcoming U.S. immigration quotas, finding places of refuge for their persecuted European coreligionists, and supporting the human and physical development of Palestine. To be sure, whenever violence erupted in Germany and Eastern Europe, American Jews had not hesitated to urge the State Department to assert their government's continuing interest in minority protection, to organize protest meetings and press campaigns, and also to place discreet as well as public pressure on the offending regimes.[142] However, the rivalry between Louis Marshall's conservative AJC and Stephen Wise's populist American Jewish Congress diluted their effectiveness at home and abroad.[143]

American Jews, still nursing the grudges born in Paris, were extremely reluctant to align themselves with their European comrades. There was a brief entente between Wise and Wolf, who coordinated their respective press and political campaigns against the anti-Jewish violence in Germany in 1923[144] and in Romania in 1926–7.[145] However, this mating of ideological opposites, which emboldened Wolf, annoyed the Americans, and drew

139. Memorandum of Suggestions for the Improvement of the Procedure of the League of Nations for Giving Effect to its Guarantee of the Minority Treaties, LNA R2156. Wolf's ten-point proposal, termed "dignified and intelligent" by the legal expert Van Asch van Wyck, was dismissed by Aguirre's successor, Pablo de Azcárate, who in Dec. 1929 became the League's new minorities director; Memoranda, Aug. 8, 9, 19, 1930, ibid., R2155.

140. Abramsky, "Lucien Wolf's Efforts for the Jewish Communities."

141. "Since the establishment of the League, the whole burden of the defense of Jewish rights... has fallen on our shoulders.... Our work has been more successful than is generally known." Wolf to Wise, Mar. 14, 1927, Wise 74–60.

142. American Jewish Congress to German Ambassador, Nov. 8, 1923, American Jewish Congress, confidential bulletin #2, Nov. 30, 1923, Wise, 74–54, Wise to Richards, Nov. 24, 1927, Wise 74–60; also, Stone, "Polish Diplomacy and the American Jewish Community."

143. Mack to Wise, July 28, 1928, Wise 74–73. In describing his and Marshall's separate campaigns against the atrocities in Romania (Wise to Victor Sloane [editor *Jewish Chronicle*], confidential, Mar. 1, 1928, Wise 74–60), Wise disparaged the AJC leader's futile "breakfasts, lunches, and dinners" with the Romanian ambassador as compared with the Congress's mobilization of U.S. public opinion, its communications with the State Department, and its public and private negotiations at the Basel Zionist Congress in 1927 that, he claimed, had markedly improved conditions for Romanian Jews; also Richards to Wise, July 21, 1928, ibid., quelling Wise's fears of an "Ausgleich" between Marshall and Wolf over the Romanian question.

144. Wise to Wolf, Nov. 14, 1923, Wolf to Richards, n.d. [Dec.] 1923, Wise 74–54.

145. Wolf to Wise, Aug. 17, 1926, Wise to Wolf, Aug. 26, 1926, Wolf to Lowenthal (after 1925, the American Jewish Congress's observer in Geneva), Sept. 10, 16, 1926, Wolf to Drummond, Sept. 13, 1926, Wolf to Wise, Jan. 17, 1927, Wise 74–57, Wise to Richards, Feb. 2, 1928, Wise 74–60.

the European Zionists' resentment, was short-lived. The death of Louis Marshall on September 11, 1929, removed another crucial veteran of the Paris Peace Conference who had not only remained vigilant over the enforcement of the minority treaties but also, in his last years, had tried to bridge the gap between non-Zionist American Jews and European Zionism with his generous support to the settlements in Palestine.[146]

On the opposite pole to Lucien Wolf and Louis Marshall's discreet, private diplomacy was the open, egalitarian ethos of the *Comité des délégations juives* to which the American Jewish Congress still technically belonged. For five years after the peace conference, the remnants of the *Comité* had struggled to survive against Wolf's ostracism, the Zionists' distrust, and the Americans' lukewarm support.[147]

In 1926, on the eve of Germany's entry into the League, the *Comité*'s executive secretary, Leo Motzkin, convinced Stephen Wise to unite Jewish forces worldwide to mount their own defense of the minority treaties. Between August 17 and 19, 1927, sixty-five Jewish leaders from thirteen countries, representing forty-nine organizations, assembled in Zurich, a meeting that was boycotted by Marshall, Wolf, the AIU, and the *Hilfsverein der deutschen Juden*. In a move fraught with political risks, the group voted to create, "The Council on the Rights of Jewish Minorities," based in Geneva, to monitor the work of the League.[148] With Motzkin at the helm, Jewish nationalists celebrated the council as a new "bridge across the Atlantic."[149]

This move to construct a unified Jewish diplomacy revived the debate almost seventy years earlier, when the AIU had threatened to replace the individual *shtadlanim* [intercessors] with a coordinated international strategy. The specter of Motzkin's council roused the seasoned, individualist French

146. Weizmann, *Trial and Error*, pp. 385–9; Stephen Wise to Nahum Goldmann, July 11, 1928, *Stephen S. Wise*, p. 156.

147. Wise to Motzkin, May 25, 1922, Wise, 74–56, Lowenthal to Wise, Oct. 4, 1926, Jan. 17, 1927, ibid., 74–61, Motzkin to Wise, Jan. 24, Aug. 2, 1927, Wise to Motzkin, Nov. 25, 1927, ibid., 74–56, Wise to Richards, Nov. 24, Dec. 6, 1927, ibid., 74–60.

148. "The Origins and Beginnings of the World Jewish Congress," n.d., [1936], Wise 74–58. The Jews from the minority states, Austria, Bulgaria, Czechoslovakia, Estonia, Latvia, and Poland, were represented, but the communities of Hungary and Turkey, which had renounced minority protection, were absent as were the beleaguered Jews of Romania. There were also delegates from France, Germany, Greece, South Africa, Switzerland, and the United States as well as a representative of the stateless, but no delegations from Belgium, Great Britain, the Netherlands, Italy, or the Soviet Union. Despite the pleas of the Vilna group for Yiddish, the language of discussion was primarily German, with a smattering of English.

149. "Motzkin Becomes Chief Director to Protect Minorities," *Jewish Morning Journal*, Apr. 24, 1928; "Council on the Rights of Jewish Minorities," n.d. [Apr. 1928), Wise 74–60.

and British spokesmen against the prospect of a strident, motley Jewish collectivity. Wolf lambasted his rival for another demonstration of diplomatic incompetence that would stiffen the minority states' resistance and kindle suspicion among the Jews' western allies.[150] Off in America, Wise, already skeptical of Motzkin's administrative skills, quickly decided against subsidizing the council, thereby dooming the enterprise.[151] American Jews still wished to breathe life into the minority treaties, but on their own terms, without surrendering their freedom of action or dispensing financial resources to foreigners.[152]

Leo Motzkin headed in another direction. As the leader of a Jewish nationalist organization, he developed its ties with international minority organizations and with the World Federation of League of Nations Societies as well as with the Zionist communities in Central and Eastern Europe and in Palestine. Most important, Motzkin played an active role in the European Minorities Congress, the German-dominated group advocating cultural and national rights, which placed the *Comité* against the League, the Western Powers, and the minority states.[153] After 1931, the impecunious *Comité* joined the *auslandsdeutsch* groups on Weimar Germany's payroll.[154]

In 1932, faced with the eruption of anti-Semitism in Central and Eastern Europe, Stephen Wise revived Motzkin's great project.[155] Between August 14 and 17, ninety-four delegates representing Jewish communal bodies and organizations in seventeen countries assembled at the First World Jewish Conference in Geneva to declare themselves "a unified people" and lay the basis for a World Jewish Congress. The ailing Motzkin grimly detailed the deterioration of Jewish life in Germany and all the minority states;

150. Wolf to Wise, Jan. 27, 1927, Wise 74–61, Mar. 27, 1927, ibid., 74–60.

151. Lowenthal to Wise, Oct. 2, 4, 1926, Wise 74–61, Mack to Wise, July 30, 1927, ibid., 74–73, Motzkin to Wise, Jan. 23, 1927, ibid., 74–75, Lowenthal to Richards, May 17, 1927, Richards to Wise, Oct. 13, 1927, ibid., 74–60, Wise to Motzkin, Nov. 25, 1927, ibid., 74–75, Mack to Wise, July 28, 1927, ibid., 74–73, Sokolow to Wise, Aug. 3, 1928, ibid., 74–56, Motzkin to Wise, Oct. 30, 1928, ibid., 74–57, Nov. 15, 1928, ibid., 74–56, Wise to Weinberg, July 11, 1929, ibid., 74–57, Wise to Sokolow, Dec. 10, 1928, Motzkin to Richards, June 26, 1929, Motzkin to Wise, Sept. 24, Oct. 3, 1929, Wise to Motzkin, Oct. 9, 1929, ibid., 74–56.

152. Minutes of Advisory Committee of the Council for the Rights of Jewish Minorities, Oct. 7, 1929, Wise 74–56.

153. Wolf to Wise, Mar. 27, 1927, Wise 74–70.

154. Sobernheim, Aufzeichnung (vertraulich), Jan. 9, 1930, Germ. PA AA L1279/L331544; Ammende to Sobernheim, Jan. 30, 1931, Motzkin to Sobernheim, Mar. 6, 1931, on the Reich's payment of the *Comité*'s dues to the European Minorities Congress, ibid., L1288/L331981–2; Sobernheim to Abraham A. Cohen, Executive Director, American Jewish Congress, Sept. 1932, ibid., R78715/L349849–51.

155. Wise to Nahum Goldmann, June 13, 1932, to Louis Brandeis, Aug. 3, 1932, *Stephen S. Wise*, pp. 173, 174; Wise to Mack, Dec. 30, 1931, warned of the Hitlerian danger to German Jews; ibid., pp. 170–1.

not only were communal rights under threat but everywhere the individual rights of Jews were being "undermined by the waves of reaction." Assimilationist groups in the United States, Great Britain, and Germany refused to attend,[156] and the Zionists were cool toward the prospect of a rival organization of Diaspora Jews. Four long years later, after the *Comité* leader had died and Hitler's threats had become reality, it would fall to others to fulfill Motzkin's dream, and Lucien Wolf's nightmare, of a "permanent address for the Jewish people."[157]

On the eve of the Great Depression the second, often competing, element of Jewish diplomacy had also run aground. The Zionists' great hopes in 1919 that their expansive claims to Palestine, sponsored by Balfour and Lloyd George, would receive the same international support as those of the Poles, Czechs, and Serbs[158] had been dampened in the 1920s by America's withdrawal from Near Eastern affairs, Britain's fear of antagonizing 700,000 Arabs, and also the indifference, if not outright opposition, in other western capitals, the Vatican, and Geneva. Palestine, the League's most complex mandate, had been relatively tranquil until 1928.[159] That year, however, the toll of a severe three-year recession plus rising Arab opposition to Jewish immigration and land purchases triggered the "Wailing Wall" incident and the bloody riots one year later.[160] Suddenly the Zionists faced powerful opposition in the Near East and in London to transplanting thousands, if not millions, of East European Jews onto a tiny, sacred, and strategic part of the British Empire.[161]

Despite heavy criticism and numerous rivals, Chaim Weizmann, with his extraordinary political acumen and access to British officialdom, had

156. *La Suisse*, Aug. 15–19, 1932; *Frankfurter Zeitung*, Aug. 23, 1932.

157. "The Origins and Beginnings of the World Jewish Congress," n.d. [1936], Wise 74–58.

158. Wise to Maximilian Heller, Feb. 4, 1919, *Stephen S. Wise*, p. 85.

159. See discussions on Palestine in the Permanent Mandates Commission (1925), pp. 101–13, 160–3, 181–3, (1926), pp. 152–70, 195–204, and in the council, LNOJ (1925), pp. 269–70, (1926), pp. 1232–3; also Royal Institute of International Affairs, *Great Britain and Palestine, 1915–1945* (London: Oxford University Press, 1946), pp. 42–3.

160. The incident, involving control over the Western Wall of Herod's Temple and the outer perimeter of the Haram al-Sharif, a place sacred both to Judaism and Islam, was not unique except for its local and international consequences. It began on Yom Kippur (the Jewish Day of Atonement), Sept. 24, 1928, after religious Jews placed a screen at the Western Wall to separate male and female worshippers, and the police, impelled by Arab protests, forcibly removed the screen. Both sides protested to London and Geneva, mob violence spread throughout Palestine, and Chaim Weizmann, in an open letter published in Nov. 1928, announced that the only feasible solution to the problem of access to the wall was to "pour Jews into Palestine" and gain control over the ancient homeland. LNOJ (1928), pp. 1448–54; Smith, *Palestine and the Arab-Israeli Conflict*, pp. 87–9.

161. The Zionists' position was worsened in the fall of 1929 by the advent of a Labour government whose Colonial Secretary, Sydney Webb, did not share the Tory and Liberal sympathies with the Zionist cause. Sykes, *Crossroads to Israel*, pp. 111–12.

remained the Zionists' principal international spokesman in the decade after World War I. Indeed, by 1930 American Zionism had become practically moribund.[162] When Britain, after another eruption of riots in Palestine in 1929, contemplated restrictions on Jewish immigration, it was Weizmann, supported by Zionist and non-Zionist U.S. and British Jews, who obtained a renewed commitment to the Balfour declaration from Ramsay MacDonald's Labour government. However this brief triumph was dampened by the realization that once more the Anglo–Zionist partnership had been badly shaken.[163]

By the mid-1920s the *Yishuv*, the Jewish population of Palestine, had split into two competing factions, with the gradualist majority, led by David Ben-Gurion, seeking short-term collaboration with Britain while establishing the political, economic, military, and demographic foundations of an independent Jewish state, and the Revisionist minority, led by Vladimir Ze'ev Jabotinsky, advocating a swifter, more aggressive process of state building, including the use of force against the Arabs *and* the British, to forge a very large Jewish Palestine, from the Litani to the Negev, and to the eastern bank of the Jordan River.[164]

Both sides worked assiduously to win the world's support,[165] and both undermined Weizmann's cautious leadership. At the Zionist Congress in Basel in June 1931, the fifty-seven-year-old leader was forced to resign, leaving Zionism – still representing only a minority in the Diaspora – politically fragmented, financially weak, and without an authoritative spokesman on the eve of the mounting threats in Central and Eastern Europe. Weizmann's parting words to his Zionist comrades in 1931 were prophetic. Dismissing the handful of Palestinian Jewish idealists who called for a binational state,[166] he also warned that regardless of the mounting threats in Central

162. Wise to Kesselman (Jerusalem), May 8, 1930, *Stephen S. Wise*, pp. 167–8.

163. Weizmann, *Trial and Error*, pp. 410–16. The first rift with Britain had occurred in 1922 over the Churchill *White Paper*, which restricted the boundaries of Palestine to the area west of the Jordan River, renounced the goal of establishing a Jewish majority, and limited Jewish immigration to the "economic capacity of the country."

164. Halpern and Reinharz, *Zionism*, pp. 254–61; on the threat of Jewish terrorism in Palestine to Jewish unity and the Zionist cause, Wise to Mack, Aug. 18, 1933, *Stephen S. Wise*, p. 192.

165. Causing Muhammad Achtar, editor of *Falastin*, the largest Arab daily in Palestine, to lament to a Jewish assemblage on Nov. 26, 1930: "So much money and time and paper and ink were wasted on propaganda to explain Zionism to the Western nations. If only even a thousandth part of this effort were expended to clarify Zionism to the Arabs." Quoted in Sachar, *History of Israel*, p. 181.

166. This was the group Brith Shalom [Covenant of Peace] founded in 1925 by academics and religious and liberal Zionists. Led by the historian Gershom Scholem, the theologian Martin Buber, and the president of the Hebrew University Judah Magnes ("Brith Shalom Statutes" in Buber, *A Land of Two Peoples*, pp. 74–5), Brith Shalom was supported by members of the kibbutz and labor movements who called for solidarity between the Arab and Jewish working classes.

and Eastern Europe, the world would not tolerate a Jewish majority that would expel the Arabs. And although keenly aware of the limitations of Great Power patronage – Britain's desertion of the Greeks and Armenians was a painful recent example – Weizmann underlined the greater risks to the Jews of going it alone.[167]

GERMANY VERSUS THE LEAGUE

After Stresemann's death, several factors contributed to the radicalization of German diplomacy: the advent of presidential government, the explosion of ultranationalism accompanying France's evacuation of the Rhineland, the Nazis' stunning electoral victory on September 14, 1930, and the deepening of the economic depression. The first effect was manifest in the League Assembly where the new Foreign Minister Julius Curtius showed the face of a blunter, less restrained Reich. Seizing Stresemann's mantle, he termed the minority treaties a special form of "servitude" over Germany's neighbors and called for a permanent minorities commission.[168] Briand, defending France's allies, scored those who raised the minorities' expectations and encouraged disorder in Eastern Europe.[169]

At once, a major German–Polish conflict erupted. Poland's national and provincial elections in November 1930 were marked by widespread violence against the opposition.[170] Piłsudski, seeking to end his stalemate with parliament, dissolved the national and Upper Silesian assemblies in August. Appealing to national unity against "the German threat," his government arrested seventy opposition deputies, imprisoning the most prominent in the fortress of Brześć (Brest). The government also targeted minorities, the Germans in Upper Silesia[171] and, especially, the Ukrainians in Eastern

167. Weizmann, *Letters and Papers*, pp. 641–2; Weizmann, *Trial and Error*, pp. 417–21.

168. Germany, for the first time in five years, proposed the referral of the minorities question to the assembly's Sixth (Political) Committee. Curtius to AA, Geneva, Sept. 22, 1931, Germ. AA T-120 K1773/5457/K437513–14. Ratliff, "Julius Curtius."

169. Massigli to FMAE, Sept. 22, 1930, FMAE Y588, pronounced Germany "vanquished once more." Curtius, less comfortable in Geneva than his predecessor, described his first experience as a "bath in a crocodile pond." Curtius, *Sechs Jahre Minister*, p. 153.

170. Santoro, *Poland During the Elections of 1930*, the testimony of a journalist–observer; pro-Polish versions in Machray, *The Poland of Pilsudski*, pp. 276–82; and Laroche, *La Pologne de Pilsudski*, pp. 76–80.

171. During the provincial campaign, Oct. 19–26 was declared "anti-German week." The Insurgents, a paramilitary organization led by Governor Grazyński, harassed the German community; five German leaders were arrested, and two German lists of candidates were disqualified. Lütgens to AA, Poznań, Oct. 29, 30, Nov. 6, 1930, Bülow to Rauscher, Berlin, Nov. 6, 1930, Germ. AA T-120 L683/4801/L216362–63, L216384–86, L21364–66.

Galicia.[172] Curtius, despite the cautions of his minister in Warsaw,[173] singled out the German victims and hauled Piłsudski's victorious regime before the League for its assault on minority rights.[174]

This was a move fraught with political risks. Despite the seriousness of the charges, Curtius declined to summon an emergency council session; without adequate preparation, he invoked a derisory procedure to intervene in his neighbor's internal affairs. He also underestimated the significance of Piłsudski's triumph and Warsaw's determination to fend off any form of outside interference.[175] Abandoning Stresemann's supple strategy, and vaguely threatening to resign over the issue, Curtius hemmed himself in between Germany's "inflamed public opinion" on one side and a well-prepared League bureaucracy on the other.[176]

Geneva's new Minorities Director Pablo de Azcárate, a protégé of Colban's, arranged the very difficult proceedings. On January 21, 1931, Curtius and Zaleski publicly traded charges over Polish terrorism and German

172. Warsaw, responding to reports of acts of terrorism and sabotage against Polish landowners, sent an army into Eastern Galicia to "pacify" the population with searches, economic repression, arrests, and physical assaults, confirmed by the British consul in Warsaw (Savary to Zaleski, Nov. 28, 1930, AAN MSZ 5095); Polish documentation, ibid., MSZ 2258. Polish depiction of Ukrainian terror, Felinski, *Ukrainians in Poland*; Ukrainian report of Polish terror, Swystun, *Ukraine*.

In all, the League received eight petitions, from Ukrainian émigrés in Prague and Paris, Britain's Union of Democratic Control (signed by 65 MPs), a group of twenty-one Ukrainian deputies and senators, and two private citizens: LNOJ (1932), Annex 1355, pp. 823–903.

173. Rauscher to Bülow, Warsaw, Aug. 13, 1930, Germ. AA T-120 2945H/1430/D575226–29, Nov. 8, 1930, ibid., 4569H/2339/ E169371–76, Nov. 22, 1931, L683/4801/L216391–95. Eight days before the election, the foreign ministry had ordered Rauscher to deliver a protest, with a threat to take the case to the League. Bülow to Rauscher, ibid., L216364–66.

Rauscher's death in Dec. 1930, removed one of the most moderate voices of the Stresemann era, who had kept Polish–German quarrels within practical limits; his successor, the Silesian *Realpolitiker*, Hans Adolf von Moltke, later negotiated the 1934 German–Polish treaty.

174. German minority representation in the *Sejm* dropped from twenty-one to five deputies, in the Senate from five to three, and in the Upper Silesian Assembly from fifteen to seven. Cabinet meetings, Nov. 24, 26, 1930, Germ. AA T-120 3575H/1708/D785339–51, D785373–76, Curtius to Drummond, Nov. 27, 1930, ibid., 5544H/2746/E384982-E385007. Details in Fink, "Germany and the Polish Elections of November 1930."

175. Władysław Józef Zaleski, "Niemiecka polityka mniejszościowa w stosunku do Polski" [German Minority Policies Toward Poland], n.d. [Jan. 1931], AAN MSZ 2354; Skirmunt to MSZ, Paris, Berlin, Jan. 13, 1931, ibid., MSZ 5095.

Before the council meeting, Paris and London failed to convince Warsaw to accept a neutral inquiry and Britain to force the resignation of Upper Silesia's governor. Azcárate, Notes, Dec. 15, 20, 22, 23, 27, 29, 30, Jan. 6, 12, 17, 1931, FMAE PA-AP Avenol 10.

176. Bülow to Rauscher, Nov. 18, 1930, Germ. AA T-120 4569H/2339/E169380–83. According to the Wilhelmstrasse, Germany required a resounding victory to convince the German public that Stresemann's legacy had survived, even if some "tricks" were necessary to overcome the League's inhibition against censuring a member. Köpke to Hoesch, n.d. [Nov. 1930], Hoesch to Bülow, Paris, Dec. 16, 1930, ibid, L1581/5646/L480122–27.

In addition to the Nazis' protests, the calls for action included students at the leading German and Austrian universities; (*The New York Times*, Nov. 29, 1930), and the Reichstag Foreign Affairs Committee, Dec. 2, 1930 (Germ. AA T-120 K238/3870/K068605–7).

irredentism. Three days later, the council handed Germany a moral victory with an unusually stiff resolution acknowledging violations of the Geneva Convention and asking Poland to report on its judicial proceedings and on measures to revive the minority's "feeling of confidence."[177] Germany and its allies exulted over Poland's "unprecedented censure"[178]; but Warsaw, which had escaped a League Commission of Inquiry as well as simultaneous deliberations over the more serious Ukrainian complaints, had clearly won the first round.[179]

With both sides under extreme pressure to demonstrate toughness, there was no easy ending.[180] Warsaw, which called the case "closed," rebuffed London and Paris's suggestions to remove the culprits and was rescued by the storm over the Austro-German Customs Union.[181] At the May 1931 council, the League's last peacetime meeting, a desperate Curtius forced his colleagues to abandon Azcárate's anodyne resolution, thus keeping pressure on Poland for four additional months.[182]

In September, the League's longest minority case was closed, with Germany achieving an implicit censure of Poland.[183] But there were also

177. LNOJ (1931), pp. 237–8. Geneva negotiations: Avenol, *Compte-rendu*, Jan. 21, 1931, FMAE PA-AP Avenol 10; Massigli to FMAE, Geneva, Jan. 24, 1931, ibid., SDN 162; Noebel to AA, Geneva, Jan. 24, 1931, Germ. AA T-120 5544H/2747/E385441–46.

178. Curtius, in the *Ostdeutsche Morgenpost*, Jan. 25, 1931, gloated of Poland's submission to the League; also Rumbold to Henderson, Berlin, Jan. 27, 1931, GB FO 371 N667/39/55; Dirksen to AA, Moscow, Jan. 26, 1931, Germ. AA T-120 K2383870/K069150; Kurt Trampler, "Politik oder Recht?" *Nation und Staat* (Feb. 1931), 302–5.

Only the Nazis and Communists dissented, with the *Völkischer Beobachter* dismissing the proceedings as a "Kühhandel" and *Die Rote Fahne* fretting over the more systematic persecution of Poland's Ukrainian minority.

179. "Zaleski was perfect!" Massigli to Laroche, Geneva, Jan. 26, 1931, also Laroche to FMAE, Warsaw, Jan. 28, 1931, FMAE SDN 162. But Paris also wondered how long it could shield its ally from gaffes that might endanger its council seat. Massigli to Laroche, Jan. 26, 1931, Laroche to Briand, Warsaw, Jan. 30, 1931, ibid.; also Skowowski to MSZ, London, Feb. 7, 1931, AAN MSZ 5095.

180. Especially in Germany, where unemployment had reached 4.9 million, and a frenzied nationalist press was railing against Poland and France. Margerie to FMAE, Berlin, Feb. 12, 1931, FMAE SDN 162; *Deutsche Allgemeine Zeitung*, Jan. 27, Feb. 14, 15, Mar. 19, Apr. 11, May 17, 1931; Curtius's appeal for Henderson's support: Aufzeichnung, Berlin, Feb. 12, 1931, Germ. AA T-120 K238/3871/K069394, Rumbold to Henderson, Berlin, Feb. 12, 1931, GB FO 371 N1096/39/55.

In Apr. 1931, the *Auswärtiges Amt* distributed a book it had subsidized, the first critical study of the League's procedures: Truhart, *Völkerbund und Minderheitenpetitionen*, Germ. AA T-120 K1773/5457/K437690.

181. Litauer to MSZ, London, Feb. 11, 1931, AAN MSZ 5095; Henderson to Erskine, London, Mar. 10, 1931, GB FO 371/N1684/39/55, Erskine to Henderson, Warsaw, Apr. 29, minutes, Baggeley, May 5, Cadogan and Dalton, May 7, 1931, ibid., N3047/39/55; Tyrrell to Berthelot, Paris, Mar. 19, 1931, Briand to Laroche, Mar. 20, Apr. 22, 1931, Laroche to Briand, Apr. 29, 1931, FMAE SDN 162.

182. LNOJ (1931), pp. 1144–50; Massigli to FMAE, Geneva, May 23, 1931, FMAE SDN 162.

183. Curtius to AA, Geneva, Sept. 20, 1931, Germ. AA T-120 3147/1564/D662627–28.

Photograph 10.3. Pablo de Azcárate (reproduced with the permission of the League of Nations Section of the United Nations Library, Geneva, Switzerland).

negative consequences. The Locarno triumvirate had been shattered.[184] Within the League, now overwhelmed by the Manchurian crisis, there was widespread resentment over the Reich's bullying tactics and resistance by the Entente and the minority states.[185] And on the home front, the German public, stung by the Customs Union fiasco, demanded an immediate exit from Geneva.[186]

Among the principal losers of Germany's new crusade were the minorities themselves. Despite the glare of public attention, the Germans of Upper Silesia had gained no solid guarantees for their future.[187] Moreover, in January 1932, the council dismissed all eight protests over the events in

184. *Deutsche Allgemeine Zeitung*, May 14, 1931, had noted the end of the "tea parties." With Henderson's removal after Labour's stunning defeat in Aug. 1931, Berlin lost its strongest ally; after Briand's death in Mar. 1932, his successors at the Quai d'Orsay wavered erratically between appeasing Germany and resisting its claims to military equality and territorial revision.

185. Sokal to Beck, Geneva, Sept. 14, 18, 1931, AAN MSZ 2229

186. *Deutsche Allgemeine Zeitung*, May 20, 1931.

187. Grazyński was not disciplined and also remained head of the Insurgents in Upper Silesia.

Eastern Galicia, despite the seriousness of the charges.[188] Poland emerged from this prolonged and painful combat more determined than ever to end its "servitude."[189]

In 1932 the Weimar Republic, paralyzed by the Nazi threat and vying desperately for the waning loyalty of the *Auslandsdeutschen*,[190] became increasingly belligerent. In July, the European Minorities Congress, dominated by the Germans, denounced the League for "failing its mission."[191] Berlin barely concealed its revisionist goals.[192] This, however, was a hollow strategy; although the Reich's neighbors had egregiously ignored their treaty obligations, neither the Powers nor Geneva were inclined to countenance Berlin's clumsy threats to the peace settlement.[193]

The outbreak of new waves of anti-Semitism in the Reich also weakened Germany's minorities crusade. Foreign Jews were startled by the Nazis' electoral victories in 1930 and little comforted by Berlin's assurances.[194] While the Wilhelmstrasse continued to maintain ties with its Jewish allies abroad,[195] the world responded to the alarming news of official restrictions on

188. LNOJ (1932), pp. 513–19. Weizsäcker, representing Germany, had gone along with the Japanese rapporteur's (that is, the League's) proposals that sided with Poland on every count: Kamphövener to AA, Jan. 30, 1932, Germ. AA T-120 3147/1564/D663016–20; expressions of outrage at this crass "settlement" in *Germania, Deutsche Tageszeitung, Vossische Zeitung*, and *Berliner Börsenzeitung*, Jan. 31, 1932.

    Cecil, who deplored the disposal of the Ukrainian petitions, was consoled by Colban (now Norway's ambassador to France and also his country's representative on the League Council), who expressed confidence in the Polish government. The Labour government had pursued this case energetically (Skirmunt to MSZ, Mar. 10, 11, 1931, AAN MSZ 5095 AAN, Raczyński, Notatka, May 5, 1931, AAN MSZ 2259); but after Henderson's fall and the eruption of the Manchurian crisis, Britain's National government was less committed to this case (Potocki to Zaleski, London, Aug. 27, 1931, ibid., MSZ 2259), or to taking up Labour's call for an autonomous regime in Eastern Galicia, (*Manchester Guardian*, May 8, 1933, Sandys memorandum, Apr. 1, 1933, unsigned minute, June 26, 1933, Savery memorandum, Aug. 22, 1933, GB FO 371/17229).

189. An unsigned memorial, n.d. [Nov. 1931], AAN MSZ 2259, on the Ukrainian petitions expressed fear of the League's "revenge" for its helplessness over Manchuria, but acknowledged that Poland, unlike Japan, "must pay attention to the League."

190. At their annual meeting, German minority leaders complained over their reduced subsidies and diplomatic support, noting that the "honeymoon between the Reich and *Auslandsdeutschtum* was over." Bericht über die Jahrestagung des Verbandes der deutschen Volksgruppen in Europa . . . 23–6 August 1931, Germ. AA T-120 K1001/4603/K261839–42.

191. Congrès de minorités, June 29–July 1, 1932, FMAE SDN 443.

192. Bülow to German missions, Dec. 30, 1931, Germ. AA T-120 L687/4803/L217465–71. It also maintained a high level of support of German minority groups; see, e.g., Graebe to Terdenge, Mar. 12, 1932, Aufzeichnung, Aug. 12, 1932, Germ. AA T-120 K1001 4603/K261862, K261870–72 K261878–79, K261882–92.

193. "The Minority Situation," Mar. 7, 1931, GB FO 371/16449.

194. Sobernheim, Aufzeichnung, Sept. 25, 1930 (on meetings between the Jewish Telegraph Agency [New York] and high German officials), Germ. PA AA L1279/L331430–35; *The New York Times*, Oct. 20, 1930, reporting the alarm raised by Rabbi Stephen Wise.

195. On subsidies for German instruction at the Hebrew University in Jerusalem, Sobernheim to Nord, Nov. 29, 1932, Germ. PA AA L1279/L332585.

Jewish religious practice and to the growing Nazi menace to Jewish lives and property.[196] Loyal Reich Jews, attempting to quell foreign protests and stave off the threat of boycotts, declared their confidence in the Fatherland.[197] In August 1932 Moritz Sobernheim, the *Auswärtiges Amt*'s Jewish specialist, attended the conference to establish a World Jewish Congress in Geneva, where he pleaded with his foreign partners to tone down their anti-Reich declarations.[198]

The combative German republic now faced a closed front led by France. The League assembly refused to alter the existing minorities system[199]; and Poland, despite its derelictions, was soundly reelected to its council seat.[200] The last German–Polish duel in Geneva had a long, dramatic course. At issue was the operation of Warsaw's agrarian reform in the provinces of Poznań and Pomorze and a weak complaint of prejudicial treatment by German landowners. On December 9, 1932, Foreign Minister Constantin von Neurath broke another tradition by vetoing a carefully crafted council resolution.[201]

Germany's challenge to the League had reached an impasse.[202] In December 1932 the Reich achieved a spectacular breakthrough at the Disarmament

196. AJC to Ambassador Prittwitz, New York, Feb. 28, 1930, Germ. PA AA L1287/L14790, protested the desecration of more than eighty Jewish cemeteries in the Reich as well as Bavaria's anti-*shechita* [ritual slaughter] legislation; *The New York Times*, Oct. 20, 1930; *Jewish Daily Bulletin* (New York), Sept. 16, 1931, reported Nazi attacks during the High Holidays; a new wave of assaults documented in *Jewish Telegraphen Agentur*, June 5, 1932, Planck to Sobernheim, June 10, 1932, Germ. PA AA L1279/L332370, L332378–79.

197. Georg Kareski in *Le Progrès* [Belgium], Sept. 3, 1932; "German Jews are Calm," *American Hebrew and Jewish Tribune*, Sept. 9, 1932; "Ausländische Befürchtungen wegen des deutschen Antisemitismus," *Central Verein Zeitung*, Oct. 7, 1932. On the boycott by U.S. Jewish travelers and businessmen, see Zweigert, Aufzeichnung, Sept. 15, 1932, Schwarz to AA, Sept. 7, 12, Oct. 19, 1932, Germ. PA AA L1279/L332504, L332511, L332522, L332572; Melchior to Sobernheim and Melchior to Warburg, Nov. 11, 1932, ibid., L332575–76.

198. Sobernheim, Bericht über die jüdische Weltkonferenz, Aug. 14–16, 1932, Germ. PA AA L1279/L332436–41; Jüdische Weltkonferenz, n.d. [1932] ibid., L332494–96.

199. Aufzeichnung, Berlin, Sept. 9, 1932, referring to the growing impatience of German minority leaders and urging a more aggressive stance, Germ. AA T-120 K1773/5457/K437783–802; Bülow to Hindenburg, Oct. 10, 1932, Germ. AA T-120 K1773/5457/K437867–69, Kamphövener to all German Missions, Berlin, Nov. 1, 1932, ibid., L785/5104/L232570–607; and "Erstarrte Front zur Minderheitenfrage," *Nation und Staat* 6 (Nov. 1932), 70–76, on the outcome; also Massigli to FMAE, Oct. 6, 1932, FMAE Y585, confirming France's "triumph."

200. Laroche to FMAE, Warsaw, Oct. 18, 1932, FMAE Z (Pologne) 371.

201. Draft report, Oct. 1932, Azcárate memoranda, Nov. 8, 12, 14, 21, 1932, LNA S349; LNOJ (1932), pp. 1978–83; Note, Dec. 9, 1932, FMAE SDN 163; Kamphövener to AA, Geneva, Dec. 19, 1932, Germ. AA T-120 L785/5104/L232651–54; applause for Neurath's "defiance" in *Deutsche Allgemeine Zeitung*, Dec. 10, 1932; "Die Agrarreformbeschwerde der Deutschen Polens vor dem Völkerbundsrat," *Der Auslandsdeutsche* 16 (Jan. 1933), 23–25.

202. See responses prepared for the Nazis' challenges in the Reichstag Foreign Affairs Committee, Jan. 1, 16, 18, 1933, Germ. AA T-120 9294H/3549/E660095–100, E660101–4, E660016–17, E660160–63.

Conference.[203] However, this not only stiffened Poland's imperviousness to foreign criticism and its determination to gain "equality" over the handling of its minorities.[204] It also bolstered the Powers' unwillingness to appease either Germany or Poland by improving the League's minorities system, accepting generalization, or relieving Warsaw of its minority treaty.[205] During the Weimar Republic's final days, the Reich's negotiators rejected a compromise formula that would have rescued German landowners from further expropriations.[206] And on February 1, 1933, in one of its first official acts, the new Germany stunned its colleagues. The Reich's first permanent representative to the League, Baron August von Keller, seized the agrarian-reform petition from the council and announced his government's intention to apply for a ruling by the World Court.[207] Another more dangerous stage of international minority problems had begun.

EXIT FROM GENEVA

Immediately after Hitler's seizure of power, anti-Semitism became the official policy of the Third Reich. Together with the physical attacks and boycotts against non-Aryans by the Nazi Storm Troops, the government issued a series of ordinances and laws removing Germany's Jews from government service, industry, the professions, and higher education.[208]

203. On Dec. 11, 1932, Britain, France, Germany, and Italy, with U.S. support, agreed on a new convention superseding Versailles that gave Germany equal rights but also provided for the security of all nations and prohibited the use of force. Erskine to Simon, Dec. 21, 1932, Leeper minute, Jan. 29, 1933, GB FO 371/16439, on the response in Poland.

204. Smith to Garnett, London, Jan. 13, 1933, Hankey minute, Mar. 30, 1933, GB FO 371/17386; Laroche to FMAE, Warsaw, Feb. 22, 1933, FMAE Z (Pologne) 371.

205. Minutes, Gregory, Cadogan, Jan. 3, 1933, E. H. Carr, Jan. 9, 1933, GB FO 371/16439, Poliakoff, Jan. 26, 1933, ibid., 17230. Pointed attacks on Poland and the League in the *Manchester Guardian*, Jan. 24, 1933 ("[Poland] owes her swollen size and bad digestion to having swallowed a larger portion of unprotected minorities than any other country in the world"), and *New Statesman and Nation*, Mar. 25, 1933 ("The quibbling travesty of justice [in Eastern Galicia] goes a long way to explain the discount at which the League's stock now stands").

206. Trendelenburg memorandum, Jan. 14, 1933, LNA S337; confidential reports, Geneva, Jan. 18, 27, 30, FMAE SDN 163. Ironically, this was the Japanese rapporteur's last mediating effort before his country left the League.

207. Keller to AA, Geneva, Feb. 1, 1931, Germ. AA T-120 L785/5104/L232687–700. Regret over this League setback, the minority's disadvantage, and the Poles' dissipation of their moral victory by squabbling over a petition from German Silesia, expressed in Massigli to FMAE, Feb. 1, 1933, FMAE Z (Pologne) 371.

After delaying its submission to the court, Berlin withdrew the petition when it left the League in Oct. 1933. Malkin memorandum, Mar. 7, 1935, GB FO 371/19673.

208. Despite Hitler's oath to uphold the Weimar Constitution, in less than a month his government issued an emergency law "For the Protection of People and State" abolishing almost all constitutional

The German Foreign Ministry, despite its alarm over the impact on the *Auslandsdeutschen*,[209] became the mouthpiece for the new policy. In symbol, and, in fact, the sudden death of Moritz Sobernheim on January 5, 1933 marked the end of almost two decades of collaboration between the Reich government and the Jews.[210] The Wilhelmstrasse, using the Nazis' rhetoric and statistics, labeled the Jews a "racial," not a national, minority,[211] decried the "*Verjudung*" of Germany since 1918,[212] and defended the Reich's new policies against foreign "Jewish propaganda."[213]

In one significant area, however, the Third Reich followed Weimar's precedent. Mixing practical politics with its racist ideology, Nazi Germany supported the Zionist cause and promoted large-scale Jewish emigration to Palestine.[214] Building on the financial arrangements of the Brüning government, the Ministry of Economics and German and Palestinian Zionist representatives concluded the *Haavara* [Transfer] Agreement in August 1933 that enabled German Jewish immigrants to transfer a portion of their blocked assets to designated banks in Palestine for the purchase of Reich goods.[215]

guarantees. The Enabling Bill, passed by a 441–84 vote in the new Reichstag, established the basis of the Nazi dictatorship as well as its racial legislation.

209. Stieve to Bülow, Berlin, Apr. 18, 1933, Germ. AA T-120 9293H/3549/E660055; Neurath to Frick, Apr. 21, 1933, reminded the Nazi interior minister of Germany's international obligation in Upper Silesia; ibid., E660058–61.

210. Sobernheim, who died at the age of sixty of a heart attack, was, of course, not replaced; his widow, who for several years received a government pension, fled with their daughter to Switzerland immediately after the *Machtergreifung*. "Moritz Sobernheim," *Vossische Zeitung*, Jan. 6, 1933; Germ. PA AA, personnel file "Moritz Sebastian Sobernheim," Vols. 1–2.

211. AA to all missions, Berlin, Apr. 24, 1933, Germ. PA AA L1279/L332642–43. The apologia concocted by the Wilhelmstrasse and German minority leaders, Roediger, Hasselblat, Loesch, and Boehm, and sent to all German missions, "Judenfrage und das neue Deutschland," *Der Ring* (Apr. 28, 1933), accused the Jews of seeking "assimilation" whereas the true mission of a minority was "autonomy" and the "differentiation" of their culture. Were the Jews to abandon their aggressive efforts to become "one hundred percent German," they would have the "sympathy of *Auslandsdeutschtum* and could conduct a meaningful dialogue with the Third Reich," Roediger to all German missions, Berlin, May 19, 1933, ibid., E660072–77.

This ignored the fact that Nazi laws against Jewish ritual practices prevented their "differentiation."

212. Bülow to all missions, Apr. 30, 1933, Germ. PA AA L1279/332647–50.

213. Prittwitz to AA, Washington, Mar. 8, 1933, Bülow to all missions, July 11, 26, 1933, Germ. PA AA L1279/L332719–26, L332729–33.

214. Marcus, "The German Foreign Office and the Palestine Question"; Yisraeli, "The Third Reich and Palestine"; on Nazi ideology and Zionism, Nicosia, *The Third Reich & the Palestine Question*, pp. 16–28.

215. Wolff to AA, Jerusalem, Nov. 22, 1933, Jan. 15, 1934, Germ. PA AA L1279/L332815–22, L332841–48; see also the handwritten letter by Alexandre Misrahi to "M. le dictateur Hittler" [*sic*], Tel Aviv, Oct. 12, 1933, thanking the *Führer* for reviving the faith of German Jews and their desire to emigrate to Palestine; ibid., L332823–25. See also Feilchenfeld, Michaelis and Pinner, *Haavara-Transfer nach Palästina*; Black, *The Transfer Agreement*; Nicosia, *The Third Reich & the Palestine Question*, pp. 29–49, which connects the Transfer Agreement with the Reich's antiboycott efforts.

Deaf to the Arabs' enthusiasm for National Socialism, the Third Reich set a removal policy in motion that would greatly complicate Arab–Jewish relations as well as Britain's rule in Palestine.[216]

Europe and the entire world reeled from the shock of a self-proclaimed defender of minorities transformed suddenly into a persecutor of its own citizens.[217] As the grim news poured out of Nazi Germany, western governments were deluged with protests, demands for action, and pleas for succor for the Reich's victims.[218]

Despite ample warning of Hitler's intentions, the Third Reich's assault on the Jews caught foreign leaders unprepared. The League, shaken by Japan's withdrawal in March 1933 after the assembly refused to recognize its conquest of Manchuria, was undergoing major personnel changes.[219] France, afraid to antagonize its powerful eastern neighbor, expected Britain to take the lead; Britain, troubled by the unrest in Palestine, contemplated no major diplomatic initiative against the Reich; and in Washington, the new Roosevelt administration was conspicuously silent.[220] Only Poland, menaced by the Reich's threat to expel 80,000 *Ostjuden*, made vague noises over a preventive war.[221]

216. Wolff to AA, Jerusalem, Jan. 15, 1934, Germ. PA AA L1279/ L332841–48; also, Nicosia, "Arab Nationalism and National Socialist Germany."
217. Fouques Duparc, "La traitement des juifs par l'Allemagne et la protection des minorités," Apr. 1, 1933, FMAE SDN 446. FMAE to all missions, Apr. 1933, noted that, by removing the Jews' citizenship, the Third Reich had "made them a minority" and thus subject to international concern; ibid.
218. François-Poncet to FMAE, Berlin Mar. 31, Apr. 5, 11, 13, 1933; Fleuriau to FMAE, London, Mar. 29, Apr. 1, 1933, Aumale to FMAE, Jerusalem, Apr. 1, 1933, French Minister in The Hague to FMAE, Apr. 18, 1933, Charles-Roux to FMAE, Rome [Vatican], Apr. 17, May 1, 1933, FMAE SDN 446. On the growing refugee question: Note pour le service française de la S.d.N., Apr. 28, 1933, ibid.
219. "La S.d.N., peut-elle s'occuper des violences antisémite en Allemagne?" *L'Oeuvre*, Apr. 1, 1933. Unsigned notes, Apr. 5, 6, 10, 1933, FMAE SDN 446; Renthe-Fink to Kamphövener, Geneva, Apr. 4, 1933, Germ. AA T-120 9294H/3549/E660132–33.

    Two key figures connected with the League's system of minority protection were now gone: With Japan's exit, the rapporteurs who, between 1928 and 1933, had negotiated the council's most contentious cases, and, with Azcárate's promotion to under secretary general, the League's last effective minorities director, leaving the position vacant for almost a year and then assigned to mediocre officials.
220. Lamented in Wise to Mack, Mar. 8, Apr. 15, June 1, Oct. 18, 1933 ("We have had nothing but indifference and unconcern up to this time."), Oct. 20, ("F.D.R. has not lifted a finger on behalf of the Jews of Germany"). *Stephen F. Wise*, pp. 180, 184–5, 189, 195–7; Wise was later told by Brandeis (Wise to Einstein, Jan. 13, 1936, ibid., p. 208), that the president had been "restrained" by the conservative Jewish banker, Max Warburg, who deprecated the atrocity reports from Germany; also Wise, *Challenging Years*, p. 238.
221. Laroche to FMAE, Warsaw, Apr. 12, 1933, FMAE SDN 446; Consul General Poznań to AA, Apr. 18, 1933, Germ. AA T-120 L683/4801/L216469–73, and especially Moltke to Bülow, Warsaw, Apr. 26, 1933, Germ. PA AA Staatssekretär von Bülow, Akten, Bd. 9, R29520.

The *Comité des délégations juives*, long scorned by Lucien Wolf for its noisy public diplomacy but now backed firmly by the American Jewish Congress, offered the first international opposition to Nazi Germany.[222] By May 1933, it had organized six petitions to the League against the application of the "Aryan" laws in Upper Silesia, where the Reich was still bound by the Geneva Convention.[223] Not only did the Jews appeal for justice against the "cleansing" of German public life, but they also protested the new Nazi laws aimed specifically against their religious practices.[224]

The League selected the urgent petition of a cashiered department-store employee, Franz Bernheim, for the council's May agenda as a test case for its authority.[225] The secretariat invoked the emergency procedures proposed long ago by Lucien Wolf. Although no major political figures would be present, the League of Nations stood before an incensed international public that expected "decisive action" on behalf of minority rights.[226] Geneva's officials strained to deal with a radically altered political atmosphere.[227] Its jurists, overriding Berlin's objections, ruled that the Jews of Upper Silesia could indeed petition the League, because Nazi law had placed them in the category of a racial minority under the terms of the Geneva Convention.[228]

222. "The awful thing is to stand utterly impotent in the presence of impending danger and disaster." Wise to Mack, Mar. 1, 1933, *Stephen S. Wise*, p. 179; "None of us is quite alive to the fact that this may be the beginning of a world-wide movement against us, a world-wide conflagration, a world-wide undertaking against the Jews," Wise to Mack, Apr. [?] 1933, ibid., p. 177. Indeed, Lucien Wolf's successors immediately called for a conference of "representatives of Jewish organizations from every country . . . to discuss the best methods of assisting the Jewish victims of German persecution." Confidential statement of Joint Foreign Committee, July 14, 1933, Wise 74–54.

223. All six, for obvious reasons, came from outside Nazi Germany, four signed by groups, the *Comité des délégations juives* in Paris, the Jewish Club of the Polish Parliament, the Jewish Community in Praszka, Polish Upper Silesia, and the Jewish Party in Czechoslovakia, and two by individuals, Franz Bernheim and Gustav Simon, who had emigrated to Prague and Polish Silesia, respectively, and whose submissions were no doubt aided by Jewish organizations. LNA C108, C314, 315, 692.1933.I; Roediger to all missions, May 19, 1933, Germ. AA T-120 9293H/3549/E660074–77.

224. Barandon, Vermerk, Berlin, Apr. 26, 1933, Germ. AA T-120 9293H/3549/E660085–90; a Reich law on Apr. 21, 1933, banned the ritual slaughter of animals.

225. The Bernheim petition, May 12, 1933, LNOJ (1933), pp. 929–33, was a peculiar document that cited five articles of the Geneva Convention, six "Aryan" laws pertaining to the civil service, the legal and medical professions, notaries, and schools, and the Apr. 1 boycott against Jewish businesses before raising the personal issue of his dismissal on Apr. 30 by the Deutsches Familien-Kaufhaus in Gleiwitz. Azcárate memoranda [2] May 18,1933, LNA R3928; Massigli notes, May 17, 18, 19, 1933, FMAE SDN 446.

226. "Position de la France dans le débat sur la question juive en allemagne," n.d. [May 20? 1933], Massigli to Lester, Geneva, May 27, 1933, FMAE SDN 446. Portions of the council debate were rebroadcast by radio in the United States; Massigli to FMAE, Geneva, May 30, 1933, ibid.

227. Massigli reports, May 27 (2), 28, 29, 30, 1933, FMAE SDN 446.

228. LNOJ (1933), pp. 934–5.

Keller, although opposing this decision, announced his government's intention to observe its international obligations.[229]

Having elicited this key concession, several council members[230] seized the opportunity to decry the persecution of Jews throughout the entire Reich. After France exalted its historical record of protecting Jewish rights abroad,[231] Poland chastised Berlin for violating its pledge to the peace conference.[232] Moreover, the Czech delegate threatened to raise the issue of generalization in the fall assembly[233]; and the Norwegian representative insisted that *all* minority questions were international questions.[234]

Not unexpectedly, the League's solution to the Bernheim petition failed to satisfy Berlin.[235] Keller, backed by Fascist Italy, abstained; and the Reich's emissary took the opportunity to chide his colleagues for their sudden fervor over the Jews after their long, dismal record of indifference to minority rights.[236] This inconclusive ending also marked the close of the "Drummond era,"[237] thirteen thorny and hectic years in which the council had generally recognized its treaty responsibilities toward minorities despite fundamental differences over how to fulfill them.

The dramatic changes inside the Reich left their mark on the international minorities movement. German minority leaders, although endorsing the Aryan laws, urged Berlin to exempt the Danes and the Poles in order to protect the *Auslandsdeutschen* against retaliation.[238] Weimar's staunchest supporter, the World Federation of League of Nations Societies, condemned the persecution of Germany's Jews. Another pillar of Germany's old *Minderheitenpolitik*, the European Minorities Congress, lost numbers and credibility after the majority condoned the Third Reich's racist policies and the Jewish delegation walked out.[239]

229. The convention would expire in 1937.
230. With the key exception of Britain's delegate, Anthony Eden.
231. LNOJ (1933), pp. 840–1.
232. LNOJ (1933), pp. 841–2.
233. Much to Paris's displeasure: LNOJ (1933), pp. 842–3, 847–8, Noël to FMAE, Prague, June 25, 1933, FMAE SDN 440, FMAE to Noël, Paris, June 24, 1933, ibid., SDN 444.
234. LNOJ (1933), p. 848.
235. Presented by Sean Lester, the council's new minorities rapporteur from Ireland, the council resolution acknowledged the Reich's vow to the Paris Peace Conference, announced a treaty violation in Upper Silesia, and recommended that damages be ascertained by local League officials; LNOJ (1933), pp. 845–6.
236. Draeger to Kirchoff, Geneva, May 17, 1933, Germ. AA T-120 9293H/3549/E660078.
237. Drummond was replaced in July 1933 with his far less able second-in-command, Joseph Avenol, a competent bureaucrat who lacked his predecessor's energy, tact, and ability to inspire his staff.
238. Hasselblatt to Roediger, Berlin, Apr. 3, 1933, Stieve, Aufzeichnung, Berlin, May 4, 1933, Germ. AA T-120 9293H/3549/E660048–49, E660083–84; Aufzeichnung, Sept. 16, 1933, on the annual meeting of the Verband der Deutschen Volksgruppen in Europa, Sept. 12–14, 1933, Germ. AA T-120 K1001/4603/K261999.
239. Draeger to Roedinger, Berlin, May 17, 1933, Germ. AA T-120 9293H/3549/E660078–82, Aufzeichnung, Berlin, Sept. 16, 1933, ibid, K1001/4603/K261999; Junghann report of meeting, Sept. 16–18, 1933, ibid., L1675/5691/L497702–8.

Off in the United States, the American Jewish Congress, led by Stephen Wise, answered Hitler forcefully. The congress gave widespread publicity to the grim news from the Third Reich, organized giant marches and protest meetings, pressured the International Committee to force Berlin to include Jewish athletes in the 1936 Olympics, and, most important, launched a major economic boycott against goods from Nazi Germany.[240] Wise also tried to establish links with his assimilationist colleagues in Paris and London and to build ties with the League.[241]

But rifts still existed between the Jews of the Old World and the New. These became painfully manifest in September 1933 at the second international preparatory conference in Geneva to organize a World Jewish Congress and concert Jewish policies toward the Third Reich.[242] Not only were the delegates divided over supporting a generalization proposal in Geneva that would bind Nazi Germany to the League system[243]; there was also significant dissent over the Jews' most powerful weapon, the boycott.[244] Moreover, the just-concluded Transfer Agreement with the Third Reich split the Zionists from the rest of the Jewish world without solving the huge refugee problem looming over Central Europe.[245] Because of these great divisions, and the Zionists' opposition, Wise's hope of convening a World Jewish Congress in March 1934 was frustrated.[246]

International attention now focused on the League assembly, which could not avoid dealing with the Jewish problem.[247] London and Paris prepared to fend off the Polish–Czech campaign for generalization, Britain by offering minor procedural improvements, and Paris by expanding the 1922 assembly resolution to cover all citizens of all League members.[248] Nazi Germany, facing a hostile gathering, revived the old call for a permanent minorities

240. Memorandum of the Activities of the American Jewish Congress, Nov. 1933; "The Anti-Nazi Boycott: The Objective and How to Attain it," n.d. [Nov.? 1933], Wise 74–57; also Wise to Ruth Mack Brunswick, Apr. 6, 1933, to Richard W. Montague, Apr. 18, 1933, to Albert Einstein, May 9, 1933, *Stephen S. Wise*, pp. 183, 185, 187–8.

241. Goldmann to Wise, Geneva, Nov. 3, 1933, Wise 74–58.

242. Convened by Wise between Sept. 5 and Sept. 8, 1933, this meeting brought together thirty Jewish organizations, but none from Switzerland, Great Britain, Hungary, or Germany, except for three German émigrés. With the exception of Wise and the French representatives, all the delegates spoke in German. Gotthardt to AA, Geneva, Sept. 10, 1933, Germ. PA AA L1279/L332788–91.

243. Feinberg to Wise, Aug. 6, 1933, Wise 74–54; Schmieden to Kamphövener to AA, Geneva, Sept. 13, 1933, Germ. AA T-120 K1764/5449/K432812.

244. Aufzeichnung, n.d. [Feb. 1934], sent to all German missions, Feb. 28, 1934, Germ. PA AA L1279/L332849–62, confirms the effectiveness of the boycott.

245. Neville Laski to FO, June 21, 1933, YIVO W/M 9.

246. "I am just sick at heart." Wise to Nahum Goldmann, Feb. 9, 1934, *Stephen S. Wise*, p. 198.

247. Indeed, the persecutions in Germany also affected the assembly's deliberations over the mandates, with several delegates expressing concern over the "absorptive capacity" of Palestine. LNOJ Special Supplement 115, Records of the Fourteenth Ordinary Session of the Assembly. Plenary Meetings. (Geneva, 1933), pp. 73–4.

248. Sergent minute, July 4, 1933, Eden minute, Aug. 12, 1933, GB FO 371/17386.

commission; but it also insisted on excluding German Jews, except for those in Upper Silesia, from the category of a protected minority.[249] During the five dramatic sessions of the assembly's sixth committee, twenty-one delegates spoke, four proposals were submitted, and a special subcommittee was appointed to draft a resolution. Keller, who defended the Reich's racial policies with energy and vehemence, was almost completely isolated.[250] The Reich not only vetoed the committee's unanimous decision to spread the League's protective mantle over the Jews[251] but had also abstained from the assembly resolution establishing a new high commissioner for German refugees.[252]

Three days after the close of the assembly, on October 14, 1933, Hitler announced Germany's withdrawal from the League. Instead of awaiting the complete collapse of the Disarmament Conference, the Führer left the League in part, no doubt, to spare the Reich another bruising stint in Geneva, which was no longer a useful forum for achieving the Reich's aims.[253]

Nazi Germany intended to settle minority questions on its own terms. Except for Upper Silesia, where Germany observed the Geneva Convention until 1937, there were no international restraints against the Reich's persecution of the Jews. Moreover, Berlin placed the German minority problem temporarily on ice by concluding unofficial arrangements with some of its neighbors and formal bilateral agreements with others. The League's frayed minorities system, long the target of German criticism, drifted further into oblivion.

Germany's prominent role in Geneva between 1926 and 1933 altered the history of European minorities diplomacy. Clothing its irredentist aims in

249. In his warning to the cabinet over the impending debate over the Jewish question, Neurath announced his intention to withdraw the delegation if the assembly threatened to make decisions "intolerable to Germany's interests." DGFP, Ser. C, Vol. 1, pp. 795–7. For the first time since 1926, the German delegate did not address the assembly but simply moved the referral of the minorities question to the Sixth Committee. LNOJ Special Supplement 115, Records of the Fourteenth Ordinary Session of the Assembly (Geneva, 1933), pp. 35, 37.

250. LNOJ Special Supplement 120, Minutes of the Sixth Committee (Political Questions), Oct. 3–10, 1933, pp. 22–57, 59–60, Massigli to FMAE, Geneva, Oct. 3, 4, 6, 12, 19, 1933, FMAE Y588; Hacking to Simon, Geneva, Oct. 11, 1933, GB FO 371/17386; unsigned note, Paris, Oct. 20, 1933, FMAE SDN 444.

251. LNOJ Records of the Fourteenth Ordinary Session of the Assembly. Special Supplement 115, Plenary Meeting, Oct. 11, 1933, p. 88.

252. Ibid., Oct. 2, 1933, p. 57; Massigli to FMAE, Geneva, Oct. 10, 1933, FMAE Y 588. On Oct. 26, the council appointed an American, James MacDonald, allocated start-up funds, and invited twelve governments to participate on the commission's governing body. Note, High Commissioner for Refugees, n.d. [Oct. 1933], YIVO W/M 15.

253. DGFP, Ser. C, Vol. 1, pp. 922–6, Vol. 2, pp. 1–2; Werner Hasselblatt, "Deutschlands Austritt aus dem Völkerbund und die Nationalitätenfrage," *Der Auslandsdeutsche* 16 (Nov. 1933), 530–1; also Arnal to FMAE, Oct. 4, 1933, FMAE Y 588.

Wilsonian garb, the Weimar Republic had challenged the League's system but failed to alter it, leaving disgruntled minorities, obdurate minority states, and rigid Western partners. The Third Reich, intent on dominating an entirely new Europe, proceeded to shock the world with its racist definition of a state and its people.

The other side was unprepared to resist. A new generation of British, French, and Geneva officials, lacking enthusiasm for treaty enforcement, failed to recognize the crucial link between international minority protection and the preservation of European peace and security; the governments of Eastern Europe were more determined than ever to shed their "servitude;" and the Jews, without a strong, unified voice and a vigorous state or international protector, stood before the greatest threat in their history.

11

Epilogue

The Road to Munich

"Pending the introduction of a general and uniform system for the protection of minorities, my government is compelled to refuse, as from today, all cooperation with the international organizations in the matter of the supervision of the application by Poland of the system of minority protection."[1]

"The intensified persecution in Germany threatens the pauperisation or exile of hundreds of thousands of German Jews."[2]

"I certainly feel that it would be a very difficult decision to plunge Europe into war now to avert what may be a worse war later on."[3]

During the fifty-seven months between January 1934 and October 1938, the remnants of the Versailles Treaty were largely destroyed by Nazi Germany, which rearmed, reoccupied the Rhineland, seized Austria, and forced the dismemberment of Czechoslovakia. The German onslaught against the Paris Peace Settlement was facilitated by the two other expansionist powers, Italy and Japan, by two of the great beneficiaries of the peace conference, Poland and Romania, seeking to unburden themselves from international supervision, and also by the world's two greatest empires, Britain and France, which feared war more than they feared the Nazi threat to Europe.

Among the diplomats' most harrowing problems were not only the fate of 600,000 German Jews but also the survival of Jewish life in Eastern Europe, threats scarcely contemplated in 1919. Almost at once, the Third Reich's anti-Semitic propaganda and policies, together with its overt goal of expelling its racial enemies, spilled over into the neighboring states of

1. Statement by Colonel Józef Beck, Sept. 13, 1934, to the Fifteenth League Assembly, LNOJ, Records of the Plenary Meeting (Geneva, 1934), p. 43.
2. James G. McDonald, High Commissioner for Refugees Coming from Germany to the Secretary General, London, Dec. 27, 1935, LNOJ (1936), Annex 1577, p. 160.
3. Cadogan, memorandum, Mar. 17, 1938, GB FO 371/21674.

Eastern Europe with their far larger, poorer, and more threatened Jewish populations. The assault on the Jews of Central and Eastern Europe shook the composure of western Jewish leaders, who themselves faced the rise of anti-Semitism in France, Great Britain, and the United States.

The decline of the League of Nations was woefully evident. In the spring of 1936, the secretariat finally moved into the Palais des Nations on the northern shore of Lac Léman. That fall, the council occupied its elegant, new chamber, and the next year, the assembly held its seventeenth session in its huge, ornate hall. But the organization, timidly led and largely ignored by the great powers, had become increasingly isolated from the world's major problems and incapable of stemming the threats to peace. The crumbling of its minorities system was but a symptom of Geneva's growing feebleness.[4]

THE BECK DECLARATION

With the advent of Adolf Hitler and the political eclipse of the ill and aging Marshal Piłsudski, Poland opted for more authoritarian rule at home and a bolder, more independent policy abroad.[5] Signaled by the ascendancy of the new Foreign Minister, Colonel Józef Beck,[6] Warsaw signed a ten-year nonaggression pact with the Third Reich in January 1934, extended its nonaggression pact with Moscow, and threatened "radical" solutions to its quarrels with its smaller neighbors.[7] In April 1934, without consulting Paris or the minority states, Beck announced his intention of once more demanding the generalization of the minority treaties, ostensibly to match Germany's claims to military equality, but, in fact, as the first step in renouncing Poland's detested obligation.[8] Beneš, a longtime if cautious supporter of generalization, decried this unilateral démarche by the Third Reich's

4. Schou, Confidential memorandum to Secretary General, Geneva, Sept. 14, 1936, LNA 3892.
5. On Jan. 26, 1934, a rump parliament passed a new constitution reducing parliament's power, establishing a strong, indirectly elected president, and allowing curtailments of civil liberties in a state of emergency.
6. The thirty-nine-year old colonel, a Piłsudski protégé, who had fought in the Polish Legion in World War I and against the Bolsheviks in 1920–1 and had a brief stint as Poland's military attaché in Paris in 1922–3, entered political life in 1926 as the marshal's *chef de cabinet* and also served a short term as deputy prime minister in 1930 before replacing the widely popular and amiable August Zaleski in Nov. 1932 at the head of the foreign ministry. Well known in Allied circles for his intelligence, arrogance, and francophobia, Beck appeared determined to enroll Poland "among the big boys" in the League; Eden to FO, Jan. 17, 1934, GB FO 371/18537; compare Thadée Schaetzel, "Éléments biographiques," in Beck, *Dernier rapport*, pp. xi–xxiii.
7. Erskine to Simon, Warsaw, Feb. 4, 1934, GB FO 371/17794, on Beck's review of foreign policy before Senate Foreign Affairs Committee. Unsigned note, n.d. [Feb. 1934] FMAE Z (Pologne) 335.
8. Laroche to FMAE, Warsaw, Feb. 6, 1934, FMAE Z (Pologne) 335; Raczyński to Avenol, Geneva, Apr. 10, 1934, to Massigli, Apr. 11, 1934, unsigned note, Apr. 12, 1934, ibid., SDN 444, Massigli to FMAE, Geneva, Apr. 12, 1934, ibid., SDN 589.

Photograph 11.1. Józef Beck (reproduced with the permission of the League of Nations Section of the United Nations Library, Geneva, Switzerland).

new partner[9]; but Czechoslovakia's restive partners, Yugoslavia and Romania, with their pro-German, anti-Soviet, and antiminority orientation, were less hostile to Beck's proposal.[10]

From the Polish perspective, all the diplomatic signs were menacing. The Locarno powers were busily attempting to lure Hitler into new agreements, and France to incorporate Stalin in an eastern pact.[11] Even with the Reich's seat vacant, the League council had stepped up its investigation of vexatious German minority petitions,[12] continued to leak private documents,[13] and meddled in Warsaw's domestic affairs.[14] Although Moscow had never

9. Noël to FMAE, Prague, Apr. 18, 1934, FMAE SDN 444; unsigned notes, Geneva, Apr. 30, May 4, 1934, ibid.
10. Note (secret), Geneva, July 18, 1934, FMAE Z (Pologne) 335; *Gazeta Polska* (semiofficial), Sept. 7, 1934.
11. Details in Wandycz, *Twilight of French Eastern Alliances*, pp. 362–7.
12. Beck declined to attend the June council session. With French backing, and over Britain's objections, Poland delayed consideration of new agrarian-reform petitions until Sept. 1934; Massigli to FMAE, May 18, 1934, FMAE SDN 589.
13. Raczyński to Avenol, June 8, 1934, FMAE SDN 441.
14. Laroche to Barthou, Warsaw, May 16, 1934, FMAE Z (Pologne) 371.

invoked Poland's minority treaty,[15] Stalin had also not restrained the Third International from lambasting Warsaw's policies in Eastern Galicia. It was indeed possible that the Soviet emissary, Maxim Litvinov, on his arrival in Geneva in September 1934, might present himself not only as a champion of collective security but also as a new minority defender.[16]

On September 13, 1934, Józef Beck delivered his sensational speech before the League of Nations assembly, proposing an international conference to create a universal minorities system and also threatening to terminate Poland's participation in the League's investigations.[17] Beck's bombastic announcement, with its echoes of Stresemann's *Faustschlag*, was greeted by a "glacial silence."[18] A day later, in a coordinated gesture of Allied solidarity, the British, French, and Italian delegates warned Poland against repudiating a treaty.[19]

The public response was immediate. With loud applause from the press and mass demonstrations largely orchestrated by the government, Poland exploded with delight over its liberation from the little Versailles. The only dissenters were the liberal and left opposition and the Ukrainian minority.[20] Jewish leaders in Poland and abroad were silent over the repudiation of "their" treaty, fearing to ignite Polish anti-Semitism and accepting Beck's assurances of full protection under Poland's new constitution.[21] The foreign reaction was mixed. While western journalists almost unanimously scored Beck's theatrical but menacing gesture,[22] Nazi writers, with

15. The Riga Treaty of 1921 governed minority questions between Poland and the Soviet Union.
16. Payart to Barthou, Moscow, June 18, 1934, FMAE Z (Pologne) 371. Litvinov had joined Beneš in strongly opposing generalization.
17. LNOJ Special Supplement 125, Records of the Fifteenth Ordinary Session of the Assembly (Geneva, 1934), pp. 42–3. Azcárate, Note, Sept. 13, 1934, GB FO 371/18542, on the ramifications of Beck's disavowal of not only the minority treaty but of Article 93 of Versailles.
18. Massigli to FMAE, Geneva, Sept. 13, 1934, FMAE SDN 440. *The New York Times*, Sept. 18, 1934. According to the French minister, only two other people had prior knowledge of Beck's text, Piłsudski and Prime Minister Leon Kozlowski, Laroche to FMAE, Warsaw, Sept. 19, 1934, FMAE SDN 589.
19. LNOJ Special Supplement 125, Fifteenth Assembly (Geneva, 1934) Sir John Simon, pp. 46–7, Louis Barthou, pp. 47–8, Baron Pompeo Aloisi, pp. 49–50; also Massigli to FMAE, Geneva, Sept. 14, 1934, FMAE SDN 440, Barthou to FMAE, Geneva, Sept. 20, 1934, ibid., SDN 444; Patteson to FO, Geneva, Sept. 14, 1934, GB FO 371/18542.
20. Erskine to Simon, Warsaw, Sept. 25, 1934, GB FO 371/18542; Bressy to FMAE, Warsaw, Oct. 3, 1934, FMAE Z (Pologne) 371.
21. Neville Laski (JFC) to Eden, Geneva, Sept. 15, 1934, GB FO 371/18542, relaying Beck's assurances to the leaders of the World Jewish Conference the day after his speech; also, Korzec, "Polen und der Minderheitenschutzvertrag."
22. Corbin to FMAE, London, Sept. 15, 1934, FMAE SDN 589; Cambrun to FMAE, Rome, Sept. 15, 1934, ibid.

Although much of the French press was negative – *Le Quotidien*, Sept. 14, 1934, wrote that the "Versailles treaty is torn to pieces," the *Petit Parisien*, Sept. 27, 1934, scored Warsaw's ingratitude, and *L'Ordre*, Sept. 21, 1934, accused Poland of working "pour le roi de Prusse" – both the French Right and the Vatican acknowledged Poland's grievance over the Soviets' entering the League without a minority treaty; French press summary, Paris, Sept. 15, 1934, in GB FO 371/18542; Truelle to

undisguised *Schadenfreude*, cheered another blow against the peace treaties and the League.[23] Only Moscow downplayed the event, labeling the minorities problem a "bilateral issue."[24]

After the opening fireworks, the League delegates faced a tense debate in the Sixth Committee.[25] Although the sides were clearly drawn on the issue of generalization, Beck's underlying threat had created divisions within each camp. Among the major opponents, Britain alone still hoped to strengthen the League's minorities system, whereas France and Italy tacitly condoned Poland's escape from Soviet harassment.[26] Beck's excluded partners, the Little Entente, were similarly divided between mild melioration and renunciation, with Czechoslovakia upholding the minority treaties as an indispensable guarantee of their existence, and Romania and Yugoslavia, despite their suspicions, inclined to follow the Polish way.[27]

The Political Committee's discussions were dominated by Great Britain. Using a club and a carrot, Anthony Eden easily buried Warsaw's demand to universalize a system it loathed; but he also assured the minority states that the treaties were not eternal.[28] Hungary then struck a jarring note with its bitter complaints over the League's indifference to the minorities' growing plight, provoking an ugly squabble with its neighbors, Czechoslovakia and Romania.[29]

FMAE, Rome Vatican Sept. 18, Oct. 3, 1934, FMAE SDN 589. Beck, *Dernier rapport*, pp. 70–2, underlined this motive.

23. "Let the wise men of Geneva find a solution!" *Deutsche Zeitung*, Sept. 14, 1934; also Phipps to FO, Berlin, Sept. 14, 1934, GB FO 371/18542; François Poncet to FMAE, Berlin, Sept. 14, 1934, FMAE SDN 589.
24. Alphand to FMAE, Moscow, Sept. 15, 1934, FMAE SDN 589.
25. LNOJ Special Supplement 130, Fifteenth Assembly, Minutes of the Sixth Committee (Geneva, 1934), pp. 38–92.
26. The Soviet Union was welcomed into the League by a unanimous assembly vote in Sept. 1934. See note, Sept. 19, 1934, FMAE SDN 444; Corbin to FMAE, London, Sept. 22, 1934, ibid., 589; unsigned memorandum, "The Polish claim regarding the generalization of the Minority Treaties," Sept. 27, 1934, GB FO 371/18542.

    Old British liberals still insisted on a fairer system. The LNU activist, Sir Willoughby Dickinson, in a letter to *The Times*, Sept. 20, 1934, questioned the League's "two-class" system; and Lord Cecil, in the first Lucien Wolf Memorial Lecture of the Jewish Historical Society of England, entitled "Minorities and Peace," on Oct. 8, 1934, called for a permanent minorities commission, *The Times*, Oct. 9, 1934.
27. Noël to FMAE, Prague, Sept. 4, 1934, FMAE SDN 440; Palairet to Simon, Bucharest, Sept. 20, 1934, GB FO 371/18542; note, Paris, Sept. 25, 1934, FMAE SDN 444. The neutrals, which supported generalization, also attacked Warsaw's attempt to demolish the system and endorsed a permanent minorities commission; *Algemeen Handelsblad*, Sept. 21, 1934.
28. "The Minority Treaties were created to deal with a special problem existing in a given area for, we hope, a limited time." LNOJ Special Supplement 130, Sixth Committee, p. 60; Massigli to FMAE, Geneva, Sept. 20, 21, 1934, FMAE 440; Strang to FO, Geneva, Sept. 21, 1934, Eden to Simon, Oct. 4, 1934, GB FO 371/18542. Poland's generalization proposal, supported by Iraq, Turkey, Albania, the Netherlands, Sweden, the Little Entente, and Switzerland, never came to a vote.
29. LNOJ Special Supplement 130, Sixth Committee, pp. 65–70, 76–86, 88–91; Massigli to FMAE, Geneva, Sept. 22, 24, 1934, FMAE Z (Pologne) 371.

After the expected rebuff in Geneva, Poland moved dauntlessly forward.[30] At home, Beck aspired to inherit Piłsudski's mantle as a new national hero.[31] Abroad, encouraged by the complaisance of its two powerful neighbors, the Allies' divisions, and the public's seeming indifference, Poland moved closer to the revisionist camp, distancing itself from the French alliance system as well as from its minority treaty.[32] In January 1935, much to Britain's fury and the Polish public's delight, Poland's delegate Titus Komarnicki removed himself from the council chamber when minority questions were discussed[33]; and by withholding information from a blue-ribbon committee of three, Warsaw threatened to disable the entire system.[34]

Faced with another blow to the Versailles Treaty, the League and the Powers drew back. Despite the scant prospect of Poland's withdrawal from Geneva, neither London nor Paris proposed a formal censure, threatened its council seat, or even suggested procedural modifications. Joseph Avenol, far less protective of the League's prestige than was his predecessor, sought merely to overcome a bad moment.[35] With Italy refusing to chastise a fellow renegade and France reluctant to push Warsaw further toward Berlin,[36] only Britain upheld the minority treaty. But at a time when London was avidly appeasing Mussolini and Hitler, its protests rang hollow.[37] Moreover, Beck, with Poland's honor and his own political future at stake, refused to budge.[38]

30. Kierski, "Die Lage der Minderheiten in Polen," not only assured Poland's neighbors that its minorities were sufficiently protected but also indicated that Warsaw was amenable to concluding bilateral minority agreements.
31. Laroche to FMAE, Warsaw, Dec. 12, 1934, FMAE Z (Pologne) 335.
32. Aveling to Simon, Warsaw, Sept. 10, 1934, Perowne minute, Sept. 18, 1934, GB FO 371/17794; Strang report, Geneva, Oct. 16, 1934, GB FO 371/18542; Hoden note (confidential), Geneva, Nov. 2, 1934, FMAE SDN 589; Drummond to Simon, Rome, Nov. 9, 1934, GB FO 371/17794.
    The *New York Times*, Oct. 4, 1934, stated that Warsaw had "queered the pitch" of European politics.
33. Massigli to FMAE, Geneva, Jan. 19, 1935, Laroche to FMAE, Warsaw, Jan. 19, 1934, FMAE SDN 589; unsigned minute, London, Jan. 24, 1935, GB FO 371/18889.
34. Note, Geneva, Feb. 26, 1935, FMAE SDN 444; FMAE to Laroche, Paris, May 16, 1935, ibid., SDN 589; Malkin memoranda, Mar. 7, Apr. 24, 1935, GB FO 371/19673. Significantly, in 1935, the Polish government, in an effort to mollify the Third Reich, had reconfigured the year's list of expropriations to include fewer Germans and more Poles. Minister of Agriculture to MSZ, Warsaw, Mar. 25, 1935, AAN MSZ 224.
35. Massigli to Avenol, Paris, Nov. 7, 1934, FMAE SDN 589, pleaded for League action.
36. France, awaiting the political fallout after Piłsudski's death on May 12, was content to let things ride; Campbell to FO, Paris, May 13, 1935, Malkin to FO, Paris, May 23, 1935, GB FO 371/19673. Moreover, some French leaders were openly sympathetic to Poland's complaint that the "two great sinners" surrounding it were free of minority obligations. Sergent minute, London, Apr. 29, 1935, ibid.
37. "We have enough trouble on our hands without inciting a row with the Poles." Stevenson minute, Aug. 14, 1935, GB FO 371/19673. In a fascinating piece of illogic, one FO member deemed Germany's treaty violations "threats to peace" but Warsaw's simply "passive refusals" to cooperate in fulfilling its treaty obligation. Makins minute, London, May 14, 1935, ibid.
38. Noël to FMAE, Warsaw, July 30, 1935, FMAE Z (Pologne) 440, Aug. 29, 1935, ibid., SDN 589.

One year after the foreign minister's audacious challenge to the assembly, Avenol arranged the finale of the League's long, onerous stewardship over Poland.[39] Once the last German minority petitions were buried, British officials comforted themselves that the awful burden had been transferred to the Third Reich.[40] But Berlin, outwardly untroubled by any immediate threat to its kin in Poland,[41] welcomed the destruction of any barrier to its eventual resurgence[42] as well as to its internal policies. It was also in September 1935 that Hitler's Reich issued the Nuremberg laws depriving German Jews of their basic rights as citizens, except in the tiny shelter of Upper Silesia.[43] Poland's repudiation coupled with the Nazis' persecution of the Jews reversed more than a half-century of international minority protection, from the Berlin clauses of 1878, to the treaties drafted in Paris, to the ringing assembly declaration of 1922, and to the council's numerous affirmations of its rights and responsibilities. These two developments cast a shadow over all of Eastern Europe, encouraging other minority states to flaunt the League. Only Czechoslovakia, formerly Warsaw's staunchest ally in the struggle against minority champions in Geneva, stood alone and isolated in its defense of an abandoned international system.[44]

THE LEAGUE, THE GREAT POWERS, AND THE THREAT TO EUROPEAN JEWRY

By the beginning of 1936, there had been an almost complete turnover of European leaders. With the exception of Beneš, no one with direct links to

39. Clerk to FMAE, Paris, May 7, 1935, unsigned note, Paris, May 13, 1935, Massigli to French Minister in Warsaw, July 17, 1935, FMAE SDN 589. To "settle" the case, Poland passed material secretly to the French and the secretariat provided its own "research" materials, enabling the committee members (Britain, France, and Mexico) to bury the last German minority petition ever officially examined by the League; Fouques Duparc to Dew, Paris, Aug. 10, 1935, minutes, Aug. 14, 1935, Makins, Aug. 18, 1935, Clerk to FO, Paris, Aug. 28, 1935, FO to Clerk, Aug. 30, 1935, GB FO 371/19673.
40. Malkin minutes, Sept. 24, Oct. 8, 1935, Crawford minute, Oct. 4, 1935, GB FO 371/18999.
41. Or to its former Ukrainian allies, who also came under increasing pressure from Warsaw; Kennard to FO, Warsaw, Jan. 26, 1935, GB FO 371/18889.
42. Malkin to Sergent, Geneva, Jan. 21, 1935, Erskine to FO, Warsaw, Apr. 5, 1935, Crawford minute, Apr. 15, 1935, GB FO 371/18889; François Poncet to FMAE, Berlin, May 9, 1935, FMAE Z (Pologne) 371. In May 1935 Warsaw and Berlin signed a school agreement for Upper Silesia, bypassing the terms of the Geneva Convention. Kennard to Simon, Warsaw, May 8, 1935, GB FO 371/18889.
43. Jonca, "Jewish Resistance to Nazi Racial Legislation."
44. Naggiar to FMAE, Prague, Nov. 18, 1935, FMAE SDN 589. In a highly ominous development, in May 1935 Konrad Henlein's party, using Nazi tactics borrowed from the Saar plebiscite, received 70% of the German vote and threatened to become a "decisive element" in Czechoslovakia's politics. François Poncet to FMAE, Berlin, Dec. 24, 1935, FMAE SDN 527; also "German Minorities and the Little Entente," *New Statesman and Nation*, Jan. 11,1936.

the Paris Peace Conference remained in power. While the clerks in the various foreign ministries dredged up the old deliberations and commitments, Allied heads of state, bereft of U.S. support and trustworthy Soviet aid and facing a deepening economic crisis, were preparing to jettison the shreds of the Paris Peace treaties.

The strongest voice in the Jewish world was Dr. Stephen S. Wise. The Hungarian-born scholar, liberal rabbi, and Zionist, who was also a devoted Democrat and crusader for social justice, had been one of the first Jewish leaders to recognize Hitler's threat to European Jewry. Taking up Leo Motzkin's crusade, Wise on the eve of the Beck declaration had journeyed again to Geneva in August 1934 for the third preparatory meeting for the World Jewish Congress.[45] Spurred by Wise's ringing words, delegates from twenty countries, including France and Great Britain, had deplored the brutal persecution of German Jews and scored the League's "narrow" efforts to solve the Jewish refugee problem.[46]

Nevertheless there were serious divisions, and not only over the boycott and the efficacy of public protests. The assimilationists remained hostile to a World Jewish Congress,[47] and the Zionists continued to oppose a rival organization.[48]

Two long years later, on August 8, 1936, the World Jewish Congress was finally convened in Geneva.[49] Before 280 delegates from thirty-two countries, its president, the sixty-two-year-old Stephen Wise, commiserated with their absent German and Soviet brethren,[50] detailed the suffering of their East European kindred,[51] and scored those living in freedom who "out of fear or other expediency ... [had] refused to meet openly with

45. Nahum Goldmann, a German–Jewish Zionist, scholar, journalist, and editor of the *Encyclopedia Judaica*, who during World War I had worked in the Jewish Section of the *Auswärtiges Amt,* replaced Motzkin as the conference president; but a year later, when Goldmann became the representative of the Jewish Agency to the League, Wise became president. Goldmann, *Autobiography*, pp. 83–4, 93, 104–5, 114, 122.

46. Geheim! Bericht über die III Jüdische Weltkonferenz in Genf vom 20 bis 23 August 1934, Germ. PA AA L1279/L332947-59.

47. Wise to Mrs. Cyrus L. Sulzberger, Jan. 31, 1935, *Stephen S. Wise*, pp. 201–2; also, "The Origins and Beginnings of the World Jewish Congress," n.d., Wise 74–58.

48. At their Nineteenth Congress in Lucerne in 1935, the Zionists finally lifted their opposition to the World Jewish Congress. Moses to Pilger, Sept. 4, 1935, Germ. PA AA L1279/L333012; Zelmanovits, *Development of the World Jewish Congress*, p. 18.

49. After a stink bomb was thrown into the hall of Geneva's cantonal electoral building the night before the opening, Stephen Wise was assigned a guard throughout the week-long meeting; Wise, *Challenging Years*, p. 315.

50. Texts of Wise's speech in Minutes of the First World Jewish Congress, pp. 9–17, Wise 74–57, extracts in ibid., p. 20.

51. On the strong impressions of Wise's pre-conference trip to Warsaw, see Wise, *Challenging Years*, pp. 268–73.

Photograph 11.2. Stephen Wise (reproduced with the permission of the American Jewish Historical Society, Newton Centre, MA, and New York, NY).

their fellow-Jews."[52] Under Wise's guidance, the newly constituted congress acquired a voice in Geneva. It protested Germany's 1935 Nuremberg laws, called for equal rights for East European Jews, and pleaded for increased League support for Jewish refugees.[53]

This first international gathering of the Jewish Diaspora had mixed results. Wise was the first to regret the heavy price extracted by Zionists for their acquiescence; the congress subordinated itself to the Zionists' goals and ethos and thereby limited its influence and independence.[54] To be sure, Wise used his new office as well as his access to the U.S. president during the 1936 campaign to gain America's support in London for continuing Jewish immigration to Palestine.[55] Nonetheless, without a state patron in

52. Ibid., p. 316; also *The World Jewish Congress: An Answer to the American Jewish Committee.* The AJC refused to endorse the Congress's Aug. 1936 petition to the League of Nations against the Nuremberg laws.
53. *The New York Times*, Aug. 14, Sept. 16, 1936; Krauel to AA, Geneva, Dec. 17, 1936, Germ. PA AA R102270.
54. Wise, *Challenging Years*, p. 319.
55. Wise to Goldmann, July 21, 1936, to Louis Brandeis, July 24, 1936, to Emanuel Neumann (Tel Aviv), Oct. 13, 1936, to Irma Lindheim (Haifa), Nov. 18, 1936, *Stephen S. Wise*, pp. 211–12,

Geneva or in the larger halls of power, the World Jewish Congress's anti-Nazi efforts were stymied. Contrary to the fears of Lucien Wolf and Louis Marshall, the congress's belated founding in 1936 neither contributed to world anti-Semitism nor endangered western Jewry. On the other hand, the dreams of Motzkin, Goldmann, and Wise of creating a unified voice for the Jews were pared down to emergency defense efforts. Over the next nine years, the World Jewish Congress's offices in Paris, and then in Geneva, London, and New York, were to become crucial conduits of information, relief, rescue, and resistance in Nazi-dominated Europe.[56]

The threat to European Jewry was intensified by events in Palestine. In 1936, a vast Arab revolt erupted, triggered by the sharp influx of German Jews that had brought prosperity to the land but also new fears of Arab displacement.[57] Spurred by the example of Mustafa Kemal's Turkey and by the waning of western control over Iraq and Egypt, Syria and Lebanon, the Arab majority in Palestine demanded Britain's withdrawal, a halt to Jewish immigration, and an independent state.[58]

Britain, facing the Axis' threats in Europe, the Mediterranean, and Asia accompanied by a wave of anticolonialism throughout its empire, continued to draw back from its already-frayed commitment to a Jewish national home, which had been written into the 1922 mandate but already amended by the Churchill *White Paper* that year.[59] Now Britain was determined to limit Jewish immigration and eventually terminate the mandate, and the League was powerless to intervene.[60]

Indeed, Geneva defined its responsibility to European Jews in an extremely narrow and cautious manner.[61] Britain and France, still hoping for the Reich's return to the League,[62] had hesitated to antagonize Berlin with condemnations or aggressive gestures. Moreover, the new Soviet delegate

217–18; report of a visit of Dr. Stephen S. Wise to President Franklin Roosevelt at Hyde Park, Oct. 5, 1936 (strictly confidential), Wise 74–47. In what was considered a very close presidential contest, Wise campaigned energetically for FDR.

56. There is as yet no scholarly history of the World Jewish Congress. *Unity in Dispersion: A History of the World Jewish Congress*; Schwarz, *25 Years in the Service of the Jewish People*, pp. 8–18; Garai, *40 Years in Action*; and Riegner, *Ne jamais désespérer*, contain useful information on the founding years.
57. Jewish immigration to Palestine had risen as follows: 4,944 (1930), 4,075 (1931), 9,553 (1932), 30,327 (1933), 42,356 (1934), and 61,458 (1935); Nicosia, *The Third Reich & the Palestine Problem*, p. 100; the Jewish population in Palestine had risen from 55,000 in 1919 to 160,000 in 1929, to almost 400,000 in 1937; ibid.
58. Porath, *The Palestinian Arab National Movement*, pp. 63–79; also Hurewitz, *The Struggle for Palestine*; Sykes, *Crossroads to Israel*, pp. 139–41.
59. Beloff, *The Role of the Palestine Mandate*, pp. 10–22.
60. See Eden's report on the Arab riots to the Council, LNOJ (1936), pp. 1357–8.
61. See AAN MSZ 1850, for extensive records on the League and the German–Jewish refugee problem.
62. Because Germany's exit did not become official until Oct. 1935, its place was not formally considered vacant.

consistently opposed the creation of a robust international machinery to aid political refugees. In December 1935, James McDonald, the League's first high commissioner for refugees fleeing Germany, had resigned in despair, publicly condemning the Nazis' barbarity, his agency's meager resources and political support, and the world's unwillingness to open its gates to fleeing Jews.[63] Pressed by Jewish organizations and by its smaller members, the League replaced McDonald, but with a less activist chief. The council, now operating under severe financial and political constraints, gave the new commissioner additional resources but also limited his scope, which was largely to aid those who had already fled Nazi Germany. Fearful that too much succor would encourage huge waves of refugees, the League treated the problem as a temporary one and refused to tackle long-term issues.[64]

Nonetheless, except for the brief respite before the 1936 Berlin Olympics, the Third Reich intended to use official and unofficial pressure to force its Jewish population to emigrate either to Palestine or elsewhere with only the barest of resources.[65] The international Jewish problem was compounded when Hitler's eastern and southern neighbors sought to emulate the Nazis' policy.[66] The right-wing governments of Poland, Hungary, and Romania, each with far larger percentages of Jews than the Third Reich, prepared their own anti-Semitic legislation. These official actions were bolstered by the spread of popular anti-Semitism in their cities and the universities that was manifested in boycotts, segregated facilities, and violence against property and individuals.[67]

For the Western Powers, the growing dangers to the *Ostjuden* – of unbridled persecution and threats of expulsion, of uncontrolled emigration and the attendant political, economic, and social chaos – posed precisely the threat the minority treaties were supposed to alleviate.[68] With Beck, Gyula Gömbös of Hungary, and King Carol II of Romania all seeking to

63. James McDonald to Secretary General, London, Dec. 27, 1935, LNOJ (1936), pp. 160–3. Between 1933 and 1935, with the aid of private Jewish organizations, McDonald's agency had resettled 80,000 German Jews, of whom 60,000 had gone to Palestine.
64. The new commissioner's term was to expire on Dec. 31, 1938, LNOJ (1936), p. 1201; see Marrus, *The Unwanted*, pp. 132–3, 161–5.
65. Schleunes, *The Twisted Road to Auschwitz*; also, Hilfsverein der Deutschen Juden, Korrespondenzblatt über Auswanderungs- und Siedlungswesen, Germ. PA AA L1279/L332920-35.
66. Raczyński to MSZ, London, Jan. 2, 9, 20, Feb. 18, Mar. 23, 1936; Notatka, June 6, 1936, AAN MSZ 5191.
67. In contrast with Germany's 525,000 Jews, constituting less than 1% of the Reich's population, Poland had over 3 million Jews, or almost 12% of its population, Hungary, 520,000 Jews, or 6% of its population, and Romania about 800,000 or 4% of its population, most of them concentrated in the larger cities where, in some places, they numbered up to half the population.
68. At the end of 1938, a British refugee worker estimated that 5 million Jews between Russia and Germany were in danger. Hope Simpson, *Refugees: A Review of the Situation*, p. 517.

export their "surplus" Jewish population, Britain and France faced the consequences of their commitment in 1919, either to open their own homelands and empires to millions of impoverished Jews or to enforce the minority treaties.[69]

A Palestine solution was ruled out. On January 17, 1937, the royal commission to investigate the disturbances, headed by Lord Peel, called for a triple partition of Palestine into a Jewish state along the coastal plain and in the Galilee, an Arab state on the remaining territory linked to Transjordan, and a continuing British mandate over the Holy Places.[70] The Peel Report, which raised a storm in Parliament, was received coolly in Geneva. The Zionists, although incensed and divided, accepted the plan,[71] but the Arabs were unanimously opposed. Among the most ardent promoters of Jewish emigration, Poland and Romania were bitterly disappointed over the *Yishuv*'s meager allotted territory.[72] In June 1937 Nazi Germany came out unequivocally against partition, denouncing the creation of a sovereign entity that "would not absorb Jewry, but would instead create for it – along the lines of the Vatican state – an additional internationally recognized power base which could have disastrous consequences for German foreign policy."[73] In December 1937, Great Britain, alert to Palestine's strategic importance for its imperial defense, communications, and oil supply as well as the dangers of Arab–Axis collusion, backed off from partition, thereby foreclosing even a tiny refuge for endangered European Jews.[74]

An imperial solution was also moot. In the case of Britain, there was fierce opposition to an influx of foreigners into its mandates and colonies as well as into the British Dominions.[75] Indeed, under German influence, racist sentiments had spread to the empire, and particularly in South Africa.[76] Nor were France's mandates and its large empire open to Jewish settlement.[77] The Madagascar option, long championed by Poland and vaguely endorsed

69. G. W. Redel, minute, Jan. 21, 1938, GB FO 371/22453: "We have assumed a number of obligations towards the Jews which, though ill defined and the subject of much controversy, are nevertheless real. We have, in fact, obtained a good deal of value for our money, but the genuineness of that money has been open to question since up till now we have always tried to fulfill our obligations towards the Jews at the expense of third parties."

70. Great Britain, *Commission Report*, Cmd. 5479; fuller details in GB FO 371/20810.

71. Goldmann to Wise, June 15, 1937, Wise 74–70; Weizmann, *Trial and Error*, pp. 473–86.

72. Noël to Delbos, Warsaw, Jan. 21, 1937, FMAE SDN 508; British Ambassador to FO, Bucharest, Aug. 27, 1937, GB FO 371/20812.

73. Neurath to all German missions, June 22, 1937, ADAP Ser. D, Vol. 5, No. 564.

74. Cohen, *Palestine, Retreat From the Mandate*, pp. 1–9, 42; Hurewitz, *The Struggle for Palestine*, pp. 25–6; Sykes, *Crossroads to Israel*, pp. 157–78.

75. In Australia, for example, the small Jewish population shared the Christian majority's concern over importing Bolsheviks, job competitors, and other carriers of social unrest. Rutland, "Australia and Refugee Migration, 1933–1945."

76. Bridgen report, Oct. 25, 1937, GB FO 371/20723.

77. Noël to Delbos, Warsaw, Jan. 15, 1938, FMAE SDN 508.

by Nazi Germany and Romania, to remove the Jews to this large tropical island in the Indian Ocean 250 miles west of Southern Africa and already populated by 2.5 million ethnically diverse, restive people, was never a realistic possibility. Aside from the hostility of the natives and colonials and the obstruction of the French Colonial Ministry and the Quai d'Orsay, there were the insuperable financial and practical impediments to resettling millions of East European Jews in this remote, harsh environment.[78]

Nor was there room for large numbers of fleeing Jews in the western democracies, all in the throes of the Great Depression and experiencing their own waves of anti-Semitism and anti-Bolshevism as well as rising fears of Axis aggression. Major political, labor, and social groups opposed even small increases in domestic immigration.[79] In July 1938, the United States made a lame attempt to solve the Jewish refugee problem by convening a weeklong international conference sixty miles east of Geneva in the French spa town of Evian. Thirty-two states and over a hundred, mostly Jewish, organizations sent representatives. The result, on the eve of the Czech–German crisis, was only a minor relaxation of U.S. and British restrictions but also a failure to solve European Jewry's desperate plight.[80] To the Zionists who boycotted the meeting, Evian underlined the indispensability of Palestine.[81] To Poland and Romania, it spelled the final frustration of their removal hopes.[82] To Hitler, who refused to attend, it confirmed the world's rejection of the Jews.[83] And to the ex-Entente remained the burden of defending the victims they could not rescue.[84]

In the League of Nations, there was only temporizing over the shreds of the minority treaties. This was easiest in the case of Poland, which, after 1935, refused all cooperation on minority questions and openly sought the removal of much of its Jewish population.[85] Despite the blatantly

78. Tonini, *Operazione Madagascar*, pp. 17–131; also Browning, *The Final Solution*, pp. 35ff; Yahil, "Madagascar."
79. "Shall All Come In?" *Daily Express*, Mar. 24, 1938.
80. Sweetser to McDonald, Geneva, May 17, 1938, copy in Wise 74–46; also Marrus, *The Unwanted*, pp. 170–2. Sherman, *Island Refuge*, pp. 94–136; Gottlieb, *Men of Vision*, pp. 60–80; Caron, *Uneasy Asylum*, pp. 182–6.
81. Sykes, *Crossroads to Israel*, pp. 184–9; Rose, *Chaim Weizmann*, pp. 336–7.
82. LNOJ (Sept. 17, 1938), p. 85; also Kennard to Halifax, Nov. 20, Dec. 9, 1938, GB FO 371/21638, Strang memorandum, Dec. 9, 1938, ibid., 22540, Halifax report of conversation with Polish ambassador, Dec. 14, 1938, ibid., 21808; Thierry to FMAE, Bucharest, Dec. 14, 1938, FMAE SDN 523.
83. Weizsäcker, Aufzeichnung, July 27, 1938, Germ. PA AA R29827.
84. Royal Commission report, Jan. 1937, GB FO 371/20810; *The New York Times*, July 18, 1937; Hoare to Eden, Nov. 5, 1937, GB FO 371/21141. Strang, Makins memoranda, London, Dec. 9, 13, 1938, ibid., 22540.
85. Raczyński to MSZ, London, Nov. 21, 1935, Jan. 2, 9, 20, 1936, Feb. 18, Mar. 4, 23, 1936, Gwiazdowski memorandum, June 6, 1936, AAN MSZ 5191; Lubienski to Min. Riga, July 1937, ibid., MSZ 1760; Korzec, *Juifs en Pologne*, pp. 232–68; Marcus, *History of the Jews in Poland*, pp. 349–86.

anti-Semitic policies of Piłsudski's successors, neither France nor Britain contemplated any direct action in Warsaw. Ignoring the appeals of French intellectuals, British Labor MPs, and Jewish leaders as well as the grim reports of their own ministers in Poland, Léon Blum and Anthony Eden withheld any public or private remonstrance,[86] giving the Reich new evidence of the Allies' indifference to the fate of European Jewry.[87]

Romania, still technically bound by its minority treaty, was a different story (see Map 11.1). In December 1937, its newly formed right-wing government briefly adopted anti-Semitism as Romania's official policy.[88] As part of a breathtaking spate of Nazi-style edicts and laws, the Cuza–Goga cabinet threatened to strip the citizenship of tens of thousands of Jews and drive them into exile.[89] At once, several Jewish organizations, including the World Jewish Congress and the JFC, tried to force the Powers' hands by sending "urgent" petitions to Geneva and giving wide publicity to their appeals.[90]

The League was hesitant to antagonize Romania, now a council member as well as a notoriously obstreperous partner in minority investigations.[91] This great beneficiary of the postwar peace settlement was also tilting toward the revisionist camp. In an effort to blunt Hungary's territorial claims, Bucharest had encouraged its Little Entente partners to abandon the "unequal" disarmament clauses in the Treaty of Trianon[92]; but Romania, facing a deluge of Hungarian petitions, refused any concessions to the landowners

86. *Manchester Guardian*, May 25, 1937; also Mallet, Makins, Malkin minutes, June 3, July 15, 16, 1937, Eden to Gallacher, July 20, 1937, on bringing a protest to the council, GB FO 371/20765; Kennard to Strang, Warsaw, Nov. 17, 1937, Kennard to Eden, Dec. 15, 1937, ibid.; and Noël to Delbos, Warsaw, Jan. 21, Dec. 22, 1937, Jan. 15, 1938, FMAE SDN 508, on the dire conditions of the Jews of Poland.
87. Moltke to AA, Feb. 21, 1936, and reports from German consuls in Katowice, Mar. 13, 1936, and Poznań, Apr. 4, 1936, Germ. PA AA R82353, described Poland's Jewish problem as "worse than the Reich's."
88. Interviews with Octavian Goga, A. C. Cuza, and the Iron Guard leader Corneliu Codreanu in *La Voce d'Italia*, Jan. 16, 1938; political background in Rothschild, *East Central Europe Between the Two World Wars*, pp. 310–11.
89. Iancu, *Juifs en Roumanie, (1919–1938)* pp. 303–14.
90. See: *Pétition du comité pour la défense des droits des israélites en Europe centrale et orientale au sujet du traitement des juifs et autres minorités en Roumanie, 23 janvier 1938* (Paris, 1938), and *La situation des juifs en Roumanie. Pétition du comité exécutif du congrès des juifs mondiale* (Geneva, 1938); documentation in LNA R3944; also Krauel to AA, Geneva, Jan. 26,1938, Germ. PA AA R102270.
91. Krauel to AA, Geneva, June 9, 1937, Germ. PA AA R102270; "Hungarian Minorities," Jan. 14, 1938, GB FO 371/22347, on the numerous Hungarian petitions from Transylvania; more details in Gütermann, *Das Minderheitenschutzverfahren des Völkerbundes*, pp. 191–2. Ironically, as the council's mandates rapporteur, Romania reported all decisions on Palestine.
92. Hungary, newly freed from League financial controls as well as armament restrictions, emulated its neighbors by introducing its own anti-Jewish laws in the spring of 1938. Erdmannsdorff to AA, Budapest, July 14, 1938, Germ. PA AA R102270.

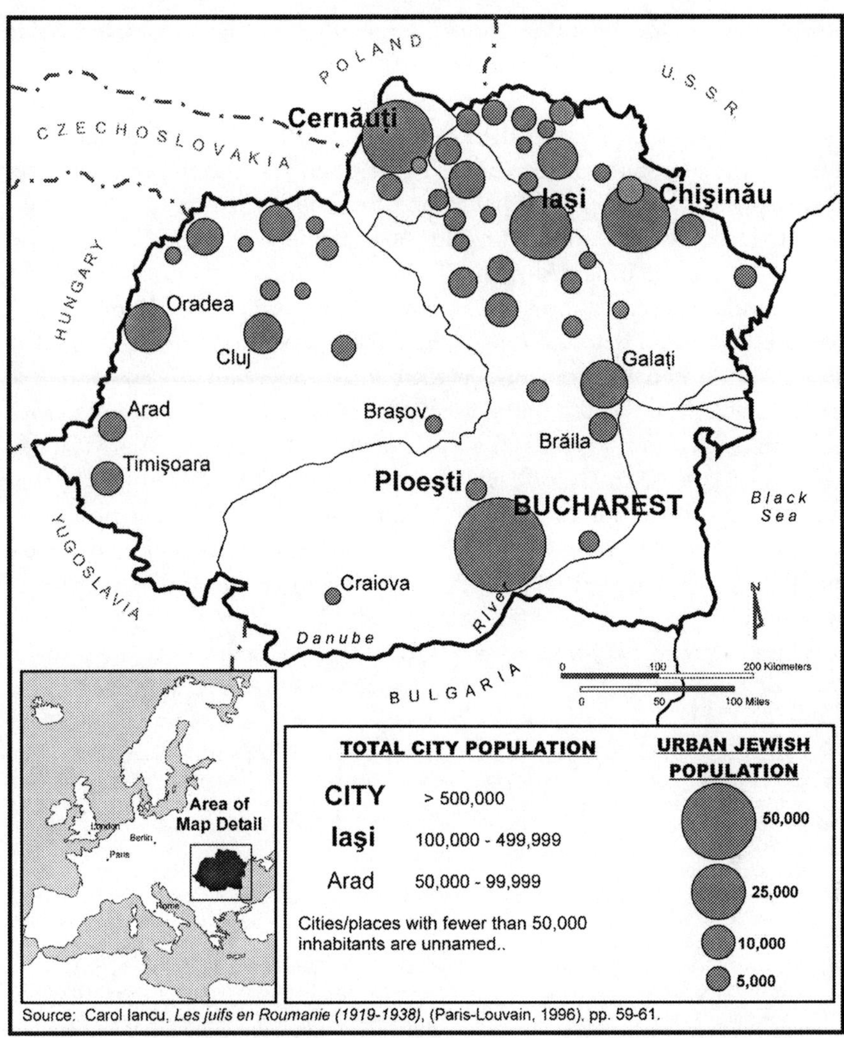

Map 11.1. Romania's urban Jewish population, 1930.

in Transylvania, periodically threatening to renounce its minority treaty and exit from the "French alliance system."[93]

Also, Geneva was ill prepared to tackle a high-profile Jewish case. Since 1937, the League council no longer had a permanent minorities

93. Newton to Eden, Prague, May 8, 1937, Knox to FO, Budapest, Sept. 30, 1937, Campbell to FO, Belgrade, Sept. 30, 1937, GB FO 371/21154; Krauel to AA, Geneva, Feb. 2, 1938, Germ. PA AA R102269.

rapporteur.[94] The newly appointed minorities director, the last in the League's history, was an undistinguished Norwegian diplomat, Rasmus Skylstad, who sympathized with the "new Germany."[95] Britain and France came to Geneva's rescue, ordering their emissaries in Bucharest to obtain assurances of the temporary nature of the legislation. Thereupon the secretariat accepted the Jewish petitions but refused to invoke the emergency procedure Lucien Wolf had pleaded for in 1920, thereby allowing Bucharest to set the pace of the League's inquiry.[96]

The only feasible solution was an internal one. King Carol II, exploiting the unprecedented British, French, and American protests, on February 10, 1938, put an end to Romania's parliamentary government, established a royal dictatorship, and also diluted the anti-Jewish laws and set up a national office for minorities.[97] Yet despite the laments of the deposed Transylvanian Nationalist, Octavian Goga[98] as well as the howls of the Nazi press,[99] this was scarcely a "triumph for Israel."[100] Not only did Carol's regime obstruct the League's investigation,[101] but the situation of the Jews rapidly deteriorated[102]; by September 1939, over a third of them had lost their Romanian citizenship.[103]

The League of Nations also failed to halt the closing of the Jews' main place of refuge. On May 17, 1939, Britain once and for all rejected the

94. Makins minute, Jan. 10, 1938, GB FO 371/22347. After a system of rotation during the first two years among various council members, the position of rapporteur had been filled by "neutral" parties: Brazil (1922–6), Colombia (1926–8), Japan (1928–33), and Spain (1933–7).
95. Neuhaus to AA, Oslo, Oct. 9, 1937, Germ. PA AA R102269; Makins memorandum, Jan. 10, 1938, characterized Skylstad as a "dim and wobbly Norwegian, who will not act vigorously." GB FO 371/22347.
96. Krauel to AA, Geneva, Feb. 2, Apr. 16, 1938, Fabricius to AA, Bucharest, May 22, 1938, Germ. PA AA R102270. In May 1938, in addition to the Jewish petition, there were nine other petitions involving Romania. GB FO 371/22547.
97. Thierry to FMAE, Bucharest, Feb. 14, Mar. 21, 1938, Spitzmuller to FMAE, Aug. 4, 1938, FMAE SDN 523; also *Foreign Relations of the United States* (1938) Vol. 1, pp. 5–6, Vol. 2, pp. 672–83. Romania's Jewish leadership had strongly opposed foreign intervention. Hitchins, *Rumania*, pp. 420–1, describes the king's coup without mentioning the Jewish issue.
98. *L'Éclair*, Feb. 15, 1938.
99. Berlin ridiculed the Entente for its ardor for the Jews after twenty years of lassitude over minority rights and its current indifference towards the Sudeten Germans: see *Deutsche Diplomatisch-Politische Korrespondenz*, Jan. 6, 1938; Forbes to FO, Berlin, Jan. 6, 1938, Henderson to FO, Berlin, Jan. 7, 1938, unsigned minute, Jan. 8, 1938 GB FO 371/22453.
100. Communiqué of the World Jewish Congress, Geneva, May 11, 1938, Wise 74–58.
101. Spitzmuller to FMAE, Bucharest, Apr. 16, 1938, Unsigned note, Geneva, May 19, 1938, FMAE SDN, 523; Fabricius to AA, Bucharest, May 22, 1938, Germ. PA AA R102270; Skylstad to Crutzesco, Geneva, Jan. 23, 1939, FMAE SDN 523.
102. Thierry to FMAE, Bucharest, Dec. 14, 1938, Thierry to Bonnet, Mar. 20, 1939. Supplementary petition, World Jewish Congress, Geneva, Jan. 15, 1939, FMAE SDN 523.
103. Starr, "Jewish Citizenship in Rumania," p. 79; World Jewish Congress to League of Nations, Geneva, Jan. 15, 1939, Skylstad to Crutzesco, Geneva, Jan. 23, 1939, Thierry to Bonnet Mar. 20, 1939, FMAE SDN 523.

Zionists' aspirations of attaining political control over any part of Palestine. In its *White Paper*, London announced the goal of replacing the mandate within ten years with an independent state that would have an overwhelming Arab majority. Until then, Jewish immigration and land purchases would be severely restricted.[104] Rejected by Jews and Arabs alike, Britain's decision was carefully examined by the Mandates Commission in June 1939. In one of Geneva's bravest acts, the majority deplored Britain's violation of its international commitment.[105] However, before the council was able to deliberate, World War II erupted. Until the British mandate ended officially in 1948, Palestine was ruled under the terms of the *White Paper*.

THE DESTRUCTION OF THE LEAGUE'S MINORITIES SYSTEM

On November 5, 1937, four months after the Geneva Convention had expired, Germany and Poland issued a joint declaration governing the future treatment of their respective minorities.[106] Despite Hitler's cordial words that day, Warsaw was clearly the loser.[107] In its last bilateral accord with the Third Reich, Poland had obtained "parity" and a declaration of non-interference as well as a demand for "loyalty" on the part of minorities; but, even ignoring the fate of the Jews in German Silesia,[108] Warsaw had sacrificed the basic civil liberties of its Polish kin for a temporary free hand against the *Auslandsdeutschen.*[109] Outraged, France issued an empty warning to other East European governments against succumbing to the lure of bilateralism[110]; but the League, its greatest minority burden lifted, breathed a sigh of relief.[111]

104. 25,000 Jewish refugees were to be admitted, and for the next five years only 15,000 per year, after which it would require the Arabs' consent. Land purchases were to be restricted to the coastal areas.
105. League of Nations, Permanent Mandates Commission, Minutes (1939), 95–8, 275–89. LNOJ (1939), pp. 107, 501; also, Walters, *History of the League of Nations*, pp. 747–8.
106. German and Polish Texts, AAN MSZ 4902; *Deutsche Rundschau in Polen*, Nov. 6, 1937.
107. Lipski to MSZ, Berlin, Nov. 5, 1937 (two telegrams), AAN MSZ 4902. Hitler had initiated the agreement to protect the German minority, and the Poles had reluctantly acquiesced only to obtain a guarantee of the status quo in Danzig; unsigned memoranda, Warsaw, June 24, 30, 1937, Lipski to Beck, Berlin, July 6, 1937, MSZ to Lipski, July 9, 1937, ibid; Weinberg, *Foreign Policy of Hitler's Germany: Starting World War II*, pp. 34–41.
108. Kennard to FO, Sept. 28, 1937, GB FO 371/20765.
109. The alarm was raised at once over how to combat the German threat inside Poland; Zberski (Interior Ministry) to MSZ, Warsaw, Nov. 24, 1927, MSZ to Interior Ministry, Nov. 24, 1937, AAN MSZ 4902. Moreover, not only had the Polish minority in German Silesia lost the protection of the League's local and Geneva machinery but they were now subject to the Nuremberg racial laws. Dalal memorandum, Geneva, Nov. 10, 1937, LNA R3950.
110. FMAE to all missions, Feb. 15, 1938, FMAE SDN 589.
111. *Journal de Genève*, Nov. 6, 1937; unsigned memorandum, Nov. 12, 1937, LNA R3950; Komarnicki to MSZ, Geneva, Nov. 16, 1937, AAN MSZ 4902.

By 1938, Geneva had lost all importance in minority affairs. The number of minority petitions had shrunk drastically, from a high of 204 in 1930–1 to 14 in 1937–8.[112] The decline of the Minorities Section, which, after Azcárate's departure, fell under a procession of mediocre directors[113] with a shrinking staff and budget,[114] clearly indicated the League's feebleness. It was even spurned by the European Minorities Congress, whose delegates, at a sparsely attended meeting in London the previous summer, had acknowledged that their fate now largely depended on their own governments.[115]

At this lowest moment in the League's history, the most spectacular minorities case of the entire interwar period was about to erupt. It centered on Hitler's despised neighbor, Czechoslovakia. Twenty years earlier Beneš and Masaryk, ending their nation's long-standing entente with Vienna against the German threat, had helped destroy the multinational Habsburg Monarchy and inherited more than 3 million involuntary German citizens.[116]

The League had long been involved with Czechoslovakia's minority problem; but until Hitler's seizure of power, Beneš had commanded sufficient influence to suppress all petitions, including those of the Germans.[117] In 1936, the newly triumphant Sudeten Party leader, Konrad Henlein, raised a trial balloon, appealing against the establishment of ethnic quotas for defense contractors.[118] After a whole year of deliberations, a committee of three, consisting of Britain, Latvia, and Sweden, dismissed the petition based on Prague's assurances that the Defense Ministry's instructions had neither been applied nor would be in the future.[119]

112. According to the statistics in LNOJ (1930–9): 1930–1 (204), 1931–2 (101), 1932–3 (57), 1933–4 (68), 1934–5 (46), 1935–6 (19), 1936–7 (15), 1937–8 (14), 1938–9 (4).

113. Azcárate was replaced in 1934 with a longtime Danish member and critic of the section, Helmer Rosting, who was forced out two years later by Avenol and Azcárate for insubordination (LNA Personnel file, "Rosting," 3045); Rosting's successor, another Dane, Peter Shou, served but one year, from July 1936 to July 1937, leaving the section under an interim director, a British member of the Political Section, Gerald Abraham, until Skylstad took office in Jan. 1938. Krauel to AA, Geneva, June 9, 1937, Germ. PA AA R102270; Makins memorandum, Jan. 10, 1938, GB FO 371/22347. In 1939, in a cost-cutting measure, the Minorities Section was merged with the Political Section.

114. The number of section personnel (including the director, members, and office staff) fell from a high of thirteen in 1929, to ten in 1933, to seven in 1938. LNOJ (1929–38). Reported annually in October, the Minority Section's budget (which also included the Department of Administrative Commissions) fell from a high of 332,559 Swiss francs in 1929, to 251,296 in 1933, to 171,179 in 1938; ibid.

115. Reports of the meeting in Germ. PA AA R102269, and FMAE SDN 443. The Congress met in Aug. 1938 at the University of Stockholm, indicating not only its straitened finances but also its new political orientation; reports from Berlin (May 17, Aug. 30, 1938) and Stockholm (Sept. 1, 1938), FMAE Z (Pologne) 371.

116. Details in Hadler, *Weg von Österreich!*

117. Walters to Makins, Geneva, May 21, 1938, GB FO 371/21700.

118. Chodacki to MSZ, Prague, May 30, July 8, 1936, AAN MSZ 6964.

119. LNOJ (1937), pp. 607–9.

This routine Geneva solution masked a dangerous problem. Henlein's original appeal, overshadowed by the crises over Ethiopia, the Rhineland, and Spain, had been handled personally by the secretary general to avoid antagonizing Berlin, despite Nazi Germany's abandonment of the League.[120] On Paris's advice, the Czechs had dragged their feet until the Locarno powers had worked out their new strategic relationship after the Reich's *coup de main* in the Rhineland. But once the committee of three dropped the Henlein petition in May 1937, Prague agreed to publication as a sign of its remaining clout in Geneva as much as its compliance.[121]

Just six months later, on November 5, 1937, the very day of the Nazi–Polish declarations, Hitler privately revealed his plan to attack Austria and Czechoslovakia.[122] Austria, a victim without allies, was easily overpowered in March 1938. To isolate Czechoslovakia from its western protectors, Berlin suddenly launched a major propaganda campaign against the "mistreatment of its racial comrades."[123] Drawing on two decades of criticism of the peace treaties, the minority states, and the League – but also ignoring its own persecution of the Jews and omitting Poland from its list of malefactors – the Third Reich unfurled the banner of minority champion, declaring that "national consciousness exists as an ethical right which cannot be denied."[124]

Hitler's prime target, Eastern Europe's only democracy, was a multinational state with several restive minorities. In addition to its large numbers of Germans, Hungarians, and Ruthenians, there were the Poles in Teschen and groups of Slovaks demanding autonomy from Prague's central control.[125]

Czechoslovakia's fifty-four-year-old-president, Eduard Beneš, once the youthful sage of Great-Power conclaves, was now a beleaguered Small-Power statesman menaced as much by his friends as by his foes. Trusting the mirage of collective security, Beneš neither dealt directly with Hitler nor called the Führer's bluff by moving promptly to assuage the Sudeten Germans' demands.[126] Lulled by the Reich's retreat in May, Prague failed to recognize the grim signals: Its neighbors' eagerness for its demise, Stalin's equivocal backing, Hitler's unalterable resolve to conquer Bohemia, and, above all, the Entente's determination to prevent the Czechs from defending

120. Krauel to AA, Geneva, Aug. 5, 1936, Germ. PA AA R102269.
121. Krauel to AA, Geneva, May 25, 1937, Germ. PA AA R102237. The German consul based his reports on an informant inside the secretariat.
122. DGFP, Ser. D Vol. 1, No. 19. Poland, the "screen" for Hitler's aggression against Czechoslovakia, was deliberately omitted as one of his impending victims. Weinberg, *Foreign Policy of Hitler's Germany: Starting World War II*, pp. 193–203.
123. *The New York Times*, Jan. 18, 1938.
124. Henderson to FO, Berlin, Mar. 29, 1938, GB FO 371/21700.
125. Lacroix to Delbos, Prague, Jan. 19, 1938, FMAE SDN 526.
126. Lacroix to FMAE, Prague, Mar. 31, 1938, FMAE SDN 526.

Photograph 11.3. Eduard Beneš (reproduced with the permission of the League of Nations Section of the United Nations Library, Geneva, Switzerland).

themselves and dragging Europe into war. This time there was no question of a "League solution."[127] Unlike its larger neighbors, the Prague government could neither threaten to expel its troublesome minority nor handle the alleged grievances without outside interference.

At the Munich Conference in September 1938, the four Locarno powers delivered the *coup de grâce* to the minority treaties. In bowing to Nazi Germany's threats, the Powers not only transferred the Sudetenland to the Third Reich without consulting Czechoslovakia or holding a plebiscite; they also left one of their 1919 creations helpless before the irredentist demands of its neighbors Poland and Hungary and the separatist claims of the Slovaks. Moreover, despite their pledge to defend the rump state, Britain and France

127. The British left, reversing its traditional internationalist stance on minority questions, now called for an "internal" solution to the Sudeten German problem. Parliamentary questions, Apr. 13, June 15, 1938, Roberts, Minute, June 11, 1938, GB FO 371/22547; *Manchester Guardian*, May 17, 1938, a position the Prague government strongly maintained. Raschhofer, *Völkerbund und Münchener Abkommen*, pp. 142–4.

were unprepared to stop Hitler from fulfilling his goal of marching into Prague six months later.[128]

Precisely the situation forseen and dreaded in Paris nineteen years earlier had come about. A powerful and expansionist state – one with a wretched record of persecuting its own citizens – used the pretext of defending minority rights to destroy its tiny, vulnerable neighbor. Almost twenty years of unremitting propaganda against the "injustices" of the peace settlement clouded the official deliberations and public debate over the fate of Czechoslovakia. The moribund League was ignored. Czechoslovakia's once-great sponsor, the United States, with "no political entanglements" and no ties to the treaties, urged a peaceful solution to the crisis.[129] And on September 29, 1938, three of the minority treaty's authors, Britain, France, and Italy, acquiesced in Hitler's sham in order to preserve European peace a few more months.[130]

Shortly afterwards, on November 9, 1938, with the unleashing of the *Kristallnacht* pogroms in Germany, Austria, and the Sudetenland, a horrendous new era of destruction and death had begun.

POSTMORTEM

At the end of World War II, the reestablishment of international minority protection in Eastern Europe was briefly considered and rejected by the Great Powers and by the new United Nations. Not only was the League's system almost universally judged a failure; the murder of almost 6 million Jews, the impending transfer of millions of *Auslandsdeutschen*, and the border shifts dictated by Stalin in Eastern Europe all indicated that an international system of guarantee was no longer needed.[131] Despite the hopes of the remaining Jews in the world, no power endorsed the insertion of a special minority clause in the UN Charter.[132] There was also no support for

128. Duroselle, *Politique étrangère de la France*, pp. 401–4.
129. Offner, *American Appeasement*, pp. 257–71.
130. Sharp, "Britain and the Protection of Minorities," p. 184. Lacaze, *La France et Munich*, and Taylor, *Munich: The Price of Peace*, are detailed studies of decision-making.
131. Ward memoranda (2), Mar. 5, 1945, Troutbeck memorandum, Mar. 14, 1945; unsigned memorandum, "Minority Protection under the League of Nations," Apr. 26, 1945, C. A. Macartney, memorandum, n.d.; unsigned memoranda, May 16, June 8, 1945, GB FO 371/50873.
132. Robinson et al., *Were the Minorities Treaties a Failure?*; Instructions for UK Delegation, July 11, 1945, GB FO 371/50873; hearings before the U.S. Senate Committee on Foreign Relations on the U.N. Charter, Sept. 13, 1945, pp. 309–12.

   Indeed, based on the Nazis' distortions, there was some sentiment in Allied and UN circles for gaining protection *against* minorities and their champions.

rebuilding the machinery for collective interference in any of the postwar states of Eastern Europe in the name of minority rights.[133] For almost forty years, until the collapse of the Soviet Empire and the outbreak of ethnic conflicts in Eastern Europe, there was practically no international interest in reviving the minority treaties.

133. "The minorities committees of the Council are perhaps the only institution of the League of which no trace appears in the structure of the United Nations," Walters, *History of the League of Nations*, p. 175; also p. 813.

CONCLUSIONS

"States are the subject of international law . . . individuals enjoy some special rights, but . . . groups are largely ignored."[1]

"It cannot be wrong for me to barge into my neighbor's house if my neighbor is just about to take an ax to his children."[2]

Are there any "lessons" to be learned from this melancholy history of international pressure and resistance, compromise agreements and ill-coordinated enforcement, timorous guarantors and ardent defenders, resistant target states and aggressive manipulators? Was international minority protection a premature initiative in a world not ready to embrace human rights and diminish state sovereignty, or simply a poorly conceived and executed idea? These are provocative, but unanswerable questions.

This book has examined a unique sixty-year period between 1878 and 1938 of Conservative and Liberal, Fascist and Communist Europe, between the age of Bismarck and Hitler, Disraeli and Chamberlain, Waddington and Daladier, Gorchakov and Stalin.[3] It was a time when Great Britain and France reached the peak of their imperial power but suddenly were faced with two new rivals, the United States and Japan, and with resistance by their subjects as well as by the growing unrest in Central, Eastern, and Southern Europe to which they reluctantly responded. It was a time when four multinational empires devolved into small, polyglot, and mostly authoritarian and quarrelsome states in Eastern Europe wedged precariously between

1. Gurr and Harff, *Ethnic Conflict in World Politics*, p. 143.
2. Roth, *The Wandering Jew*, p. 135.
3. It also spans the presidencies from Rutherford B. Hayes, the Ohio Republican governor whose contested 1876 election brought the end of Radical Reconstruction in the U.S. South along with the negotiations to restrict Chinese immigration, to Franklin Delano Roosevelt's neo-isolationist New Deal.

Germany and Russia and where two world wars would erupt. It spans a time of rapid economic change and modernization as well as global depression, conditions that greatly intensified intragroup rivalries. It was a time of rising racism that targeted minority groups, and of the spread of Bolshevism that attracted minorities and also tarred them as subversive elements. This was also a time when a few ardent Jewish advocates, not always unified in their efforts, attempted to enlist the West's power on behalf of the East's potential victims.

The quest for international minority protection in Eastern Europe involved the fusing of two powerful opposites: the attainment and maintenance of full national independence versus the expansion of outside control. The "Berlin precedent," which laid the groundwork for the League system, created an informal basis of limited sovereignty and foreign intervention; the Paris Peace treaties, building on Berlin's failures, created an elaborate system requiring enforcement and compliance. In both cases, at Berlin and at Paris, the authors of international minority protection were responding to domestic clamor over the threats and realities of violence in Eastern Europe. In both instances, they constructed stopgap measures, cautiously worded, limited in their reach, vulnerable to manipulation, and totally dependent on the cooperation of the treaty states.

The history of the Berlin and the League systems is a study of five interacting elements. First, there were the Great Powers, which, never questioning their right to dictate minority obligations, shaped two postwar orders in Eastern Europe. Despite their inability to control local conditions and their general disinclination to intervene, they drove European diplomacy into the complex, uncharted realm of human rights.

However, the problems were patent. Implicitly in 1878 and explicitly in 1919, the peacemakers refused to establish *universal* standards of minority rights. Hence they undermined the moral as well as political basis for outside interference and gave the treaty states ample opportunity to criticize, subvert, and ultimately opt out of the international protection system. In addition, the Powers failed to concert their enforcement, either informally before World War I or, more energetically, through the League of Nations. No sooner was the ink dry than the signatories, all moved by different motives as well as by different political and diplomatic agendas, shied away from collective minority protection.

To be sure, this was an era before any form of joint, public humanitarian intervention had ever been practiced. Moreover, there were huge practical and logistical impediments to enforcing treaty clauses – particularly in remote areas of Eastern Europe over which the western powers had no physical control and also in the "gray areas" where the facts were ambiguous. Add to this the dense web of local and foreign enmities and entanglements. The result was a mixed record of Great-Power performance, of audacity and irresponsibility clothed in humanitarian and *Realpolitiker* garb.

The second debilitating element was the revisionist powers, which throughout this period used minority protection for irredentist purposes. Despite their own negligent or oppressive internal policies, imperial, Weimar, and Nazi Germany, along with tsarist and Bolshevik Russia, kept the international waters churning. Germany in particular, as Europe's foremost champion of minority rights, combined propaganda campaigns with covert and overt threats against its vulnerable and culpable neighbors. After World War I, the Reich was joined not only by Hungary, Bulgaria, Lithuania, and Albania as advocates for their lost kin but also by liberal, left wing, and pacifist organizations defending the victims of Versailles.

Great- and Small-Power revisionism, which pervaded pre-1918 Europe, poisoned the political and international atmosphere of the interwar period. It is doubtful whether Germany or the Soviet Union would ever have accepted their substantial territorial and population losses after World War I even had the League applied more stringent international control over the minority states, had the two entered the League earlier, or had they been appeased with border adjustments.

Weimar Germany's minorities crusade between 1926 and 1933 exemplified the underlying threat of a Great Power's overweening expectations and derisory accomplishments within the constraints of a confined international system. The republic's unrelenting revisionism in the name of minority rights weakened the League and provided a pretext for Hitler's aggression. In the wake of the Nazis' atrocities in the name of German racial domination, the victors in World War II ostensibly settled Eastern Europe's minorities problem once and for all by redrawing frontiers and evicting millions of the former "master races." For more than a generation, the international community ignored the claims of "national homelands," until the end of the Cold War suddenly brought new threats and new violence by aggressive mother states.[4]

Element three was the succession states, formed and developed after 1878 and 1919 under the weight of international surveillance and tutelage of their internal affairs. Not necessarily victims of the Great Powers or abject subjects of the League, states such as Romania and Poland, although submitting to dictated terms, were both militant and vulnerable. By expanding beyond

4. Brubaker, "National Minorities," discusses the violence provoked by Serbia's "homeland politics."

their ethnic borders, they made themselves susceptible to internal unrest and foreign criticism. With a volatile mix of nationalism and self-defense, their governments, all declaring the goal of "national consolidation," strove to reduce the political, economic, social, and cultural power of former dominant peoples. Largely ignoring their minorities' complaints and their neighbors' pressure, they were nonetheless encumbered by an often-erratic combination of threats and cajolery to bring their domestic conditions in line with Western practices.

Needless to say, none of the minority states fully accepted their servitude, none ceased to protest the double standard applied to them, and none collaborated wholeheartedly with outsiders. Too late, Czechoslovakia recognized that its minority treaty was also a shield against its revisionist neighbors, Germany, Poland, and Hungary; but by then, this polyglot state and its long-evaded obligation, along with the rights of other subject peoples, were all but destroyed at Munich.

Element four were the Jews. Throughout these sixty years their spokesmen in Western Europe and the United States were the main nongovernmental proponents of international minority protection in Eastern Europe. Behind their efforts lay practical as well as humanitarian convictions, the effort to stave off an uncontrolled emigration along with the hope of preserving Jewish life in the ancient homelands. Building on historical precedents and using their political connections and access to the press and public forums as well as their supposed financial and economic influence, Jewish representatives negotiated with the Great Powers, with revisionist states, and with the minority states; they occasionally collaborated with labor, pacifist, and women's groups, with international jurists and parliamentarians, and with officials of the League of Nations.

There were numerous impediments to the Jews' minority diplomacy. Foremost were their own internal social and political divisions, their conflicting national loyalties, and particularly their long, bitter struggle over Zionism.[5] Whereas the Zionists, convinced of the permanent hostility of the non-Jewish world, could stay neutral from Europe's internecine quarrels, minority-rights advocates, thrust into the maelstrom, were completely dependent on the good will of non-Jews. Modest in their numbers and political experience, Jewish leaders exerted only a limited influence over Great-Power diplomacy and world public opinion.[6]

5. As Wise lamented in a letter to John Haynes Holmes, Apr. 16, 1926, "We Jews have infinitely much to learn in the way of tolerance to one another, and until that time, I wonder whether we have the right to count upon the understanding of the world, which sees a minimum of difference between Jew and Jew and lumps us all together with very much more justice than we Jews separate ourselves from one another"; *Stephen S. Wise*, p. 139.

6. Frankel, "The Paradoxical Politics of Marginality."

Between 1878 and 1938, Jewish diplomacy was also weighed down by political factors, by the growing domestic racism, anti-Semitism, and anti-Bolshevism that restrained all but their bravest, most secure spokesmen. Their tactics were also weak. Not only were Jewish leaders unable to forge long-term, equal alignments with other groups; they were also ambivalent and thus ineffectual in pursuing the cause of universal minority protection. Above all, their efforts were damaged by the fundamental cleavage within the ranks of Jewish minority defenders between the "western" idea of citizenship that stressed individual rights and duties and the "eastern" reality of separate religious and ethnic groups that were competing for resources and survival. Throughout this period, the Jewish program for international minority protection never achieved more than an uneasy compromise between the minimal goals of full citizenship and personal freedom and the larger aspirations for national recognition and group autonomy.

Fifth, there were the emerging internationalist, humanitarian, and pacifist movements, which included a growing support for minority rights, that contested the hegemony of traditional diplomacy centered on the European state system. After World War I, these forces endorsed the League of Nations as a revolutionary forum to promote peace and justice. The League disappointed them. With its restricted membership and limited charter, it remained a timid compact among sovereign states. Despite Geneva's ambitious civil servants, the organization lacked the means and desire to encroach on its members' prerogatives in any important area, whether it be disarmament, economic cooperation, the governance of mandates, or the protection of minority rights.

Were there alternatives to the hollow multinational treaties written in Berlin and in Paris? Probably not. Behind these formal agreements lay the old structure of a Great-Power condominium that controlled Eastern Europe. This assumption was challenged during the Balkan Wars and undermined, but not destroyed, by the bilateral agreements after World War I, which localized and contained minority problems, but also favored the strong over the weak and ignored the most endangered people who lacked a protector. On the other hand, this Great-Power structure was ostensibly stabilized by the population exchanges before and especially after World War I, aimed at removing elements of internal disturbance. Nonetheless, these population exchanges created only a temporary illusion of ethnic homogeneity and local peace; moreover, as in the case of Salonika, the minority problem was exported elsewhere.

In 1933, just fourteen years after the Paris Peace Conference, the fate of Eastern Europe's 6 million Jews looked exceedingly bleak, although its horrendous scale could scarcely be anticipated. Spread over fourteen states and caught in a vise between economic dislocation and poverty on one side and religious and national prejudice on the other, this minority had few places to flee to and scant means of local or outside protection. With breathtaking speed, Nazi Germany demolished the old Concert of Europe along with the hopes of world public opinion for a fairer and more just international order. With its persecution, spoliation, and compulsory migration, the Third Reich imposed the rule of force all over Eastern Europe and raised havoc throughout the world. International minority protection, constructed by Bismarck and manipulated by Ludendorff and Stresemann, was one of Hitler's many victims.

For more than four decades after World War II, Europe's leaders eschewed minority rights and focused on human rights, on the individual and not the group. However, throughout this period, on both sides of the Iron Curtain, minority persecution continued as did the pleas from within and without for protection and special rights.[7] West Germany, the penitent heir of the Third Reich, which had placed itself squarely in the western camp, restricted its external minority policy in the East to negotiating the emigration of ethnic Germans to the FRG.[8]

Post-Cold War Europe, which shares some similarity with post-1919 Europe, witnessed the revival of that era's internationalism and has made some strides in minority protection. After experiencing the ravages of an imploding Soviet Union and of "ethnic cleansing" in Yugoslavia, Europe neither revived the Berlin or League systems nor turned strictly to bilateralism. Instead, the continent has developed a dense variety of laws and practices, agencies, and structures to ensure international minority protection; and these are no longer confined to Eastern Europe.[9] The new post Communist governments of Eastern Europe, aspiring to join their Central and West European neighbors, have at least temporarily accepted outside control.[10] The United Nations, which long stayed aloof, has also assumed a measure of responsibility for Europe's minorities. The most dramatic extension occurred in 1999, when the United States and NATO applied an unprecedented use of force on behalf of the Albanians in Kosovo.[11]

7. Baron, *Ethnic Minority Rights*, pp. 22–47; Jackson Preece, *National Minorities*. pp. 95–120.
8. Wolff, "Changing Priorities or Changing Opportunities?," especially, pp. 189–91.
9. Council of Europe, *The Protection of Minorities*; Miall, *Minority Rights in Europe*; Julita Agnieszka Rybczynska, "Righting Wrongs? Problems of Protecting National Minorities in Central and Eastern Europe," paper delivered at a conference, "Constructing Identities: National Minorities in the 'New' Europe," Rutgers University, Nov. 1998.
10. Not only in the drafting of their constitutions, but also in practice, as when the Czech Republic, responding to European protests, removed the wall surrounding the gypsy habitations in Ústi nad Labem (formerly the largely German Elbe port, Aussig, in the Sudetenland).
11. Jackson Preece, *National Minorities*, pp. 123–64, ably reviews this period.

In this new century and millennium, Europe's minority problems have indeed grown rather than receded. Religious and ethnic minorities, many of recent arrival and some of recent creation, have manifested themselves, joined hands across borders, and raised large political demands, while older minorities, long suppressed or silent, citizens and non-citizens, are also speaking out.

The questions of the past still remain pertinent: How will Europe's old and new governments adjust their local and national power to enable minorities to survive and flourish? How will minorities regulate their demands within the framework of a democratic state? How will Germany, Russia, and other "mother states" frame minority questions in their relations with their neighbors? And how will a unifying Europe maintain the balance between justice and political realities; issues of local and continental concern; and the interests of diminishing sovereign states and the growing international stake in minority rights?

The Jews of Europe, who now constitute only a tiny percentage of the continent's population of 350 million, remain a subject of concern. Six decades after the Holocaust, there has not only been a slow, steady revival of Jewish life in Central and Eastern Europe but also new threats to its existence throughout the continent. Once more, outside Jewish intercessors, including the government of Israel, have begun to mobilize. Using new paths of persuasion and pressure, in private and in public, they participate in local and transnational humanitarian organizations, negotiate with governments, and appear in the forums of international diplomacy. Once more, in the shadows of hatred and violence in the Middle East, these intercessors plead for the rights and well-being of the remaining Jews of Europe.

Bibliography

1. PRIMARY SOURCES

A. Unpublished

Governmental Archives

Czech Republic, Archive of the Foreign Ministry, Prague (AMZV)
  Records of the Paris Peace Conference
Czech Republic. Military Historical Archive, Prague (Vojensko-historický archiv)
  Archives of the T. G. Masaryk Institute
France. Ministry of Foreign Affairs, Paris (FMAE)
  N. S. Guerre, 1914–18
  Series A: Paix
  Series B: Amérique, 1918–40
  Series E: Levant, 1918–29, especially Sionisme
  Series Y: Internationale, 1918–40
  Series Z: Europe, 1918–40
  Société des Nations [League of Nations] (SdN)
  Papiers d'Agents (PA-AP): Henri Bergson, Léon Bourgeois, Aristide Briand, Jules Cambon, Georges Decrocq, Jean Goût, Jules Jusserand, André Tardieu (Tardieu)
Germany. Archive of the Foreign Ministry, Bonn, now Berlin, Politisches Abteilung (PA AA)

Weltkrieg
Abteilung III Prof. Sobernheim, Jüdische Angelegenheiten
Friedensabteilung
Deutsche Friedensdelegation
Büro des Staatssekretär
Stresemann Nachlass
Germany. Bundesarchiv Berlin (formerly Zentralarchiv of the GDR)
Büro des Reichspräsidenten
Auswärtiges Amt: Nachrichten und Presseabteilung
Waffenstillstandskommission
Zentralstelle für Auslandsdienst
Reichsministerium des Innern
Great Britain. Public Record Office, Kew (GB)
Cabinet (CAB) records
War Cabinet
Paris Peace Conference
Regular Files
PREM Prime Minister's Office: Correspondence and papers
Foreign Office (FO) records
FO 371, FO 395 (News), FO 608 (Paris Peace Conference)
FO 800: Private Papers of George Nathaniel Curzon, Robert Cecil, Eyre Crowe, Noel Baker, Sir Eric Drummond, Arthur James Balfour, Marquess of Reading, Sir Mark Sykes, Harold Nicolson
Italy. Ministry of Foreign Affairs, Rome (IMAE)
Records of the Paris Peace Conference (Segretario)
Minoranze
Palestina
Commissione dei nuovi Staati
Political and cabinet records
Japan. Foreign Ministry Archive, Tokyo
Kokusai Renmei: Jinshu sabetsu teppai [League of Nations: Abolition of Racial Inequality] 1, 2, Nov. 1918–Apr. 1919
Poland, Archiwum Akt Nowych [Modern Documents Archive], Warsaw (AAN)
Polish Foreign Ministry (MSZ) records
Cabinet records (PRM)
Polish National Committee (KNP) records
Ignacy Paderewski papers (Paderewski)
Erazm Piltz papers
Leon Wasilewski papers
United States. National Archives, College Park, MD (NA)
Records of the State Department (USDS)
Captured records of the German Foreign Ministry 1867–1945 on microfilm (Germ. AA T-120)

International Organizations
United Nations Library, Geneva
League of Nations Archive (LNA)
Secretariat

Minutes of Directors' Meetings
Minorities Section
Paul Mantoux papers
Personnel files
United Nations Library, New York
Central Files. Human Rights Matters
Henry Schachter papers

Private Collections and Personal Papers
Alliance Israélite Universelle (AIU), Paris
Records concerning France, Great Britain, Greece, Poland, Romania, the United States
American Jewish Archives (AJA), Hebrew Union College, Cincinnati, OH
Louis Marshall papers (LM)
Jacob Schiff papers (Schiff)
Nachman Syrkin papers
Felix Warburg papers (Warburg)
American Jewish Committee (AJC), Archives, New York
Records of the American Jewish Committee
Cyrus Adler diary and papers (Adler, Diary; Adler papers)
Louis Marshall papers (LM)
American Jewish Historical Society Archives, Center for Jewish History, New York
Stephen S. Wise papers (microfilm edition) (Wise)
Board of Deputies of British Jews (BDBJ), London
Records of World War I, the Peace Conference, the Minorities Committee
Joint Foreign Committee Minute Book
British Library, London
Arthur James Balfour papers
Robert Cecil diary
George Nathaniel Curzon papers
Central Archives for the History of the Jewish People, Hebrew University, Givat Ram, Jerusalem (CAHJP)
Natan Gelber papers
Central Zionist Archive, Jerusalem (CZA)
Zionist Organization, Berlin, Copenhagen, London, Paris
Papers of (and concerning) Julius Berger, Israel Cohen, Jacob DeHaas, Nathan Feinberg, Felix Frankfurter, Yitzhak Grynbaum, Victor Jacobson, Julian Mack, Leo Motzkin, Lewis Namier, Paul Nathan, Nahum Sokolow, André Spire, Hermann Struck, Felix Warburg, Max Warburg, Otto Warburg, Stephen Wise, Lucien Wolf, Israel Zangwill, Arnold Zweig
Churchill College, Cambridge University
Sir James Headlam-Morley papers (HM CC)
Georgetown University, Washington, DC
Richard Crane papers
Harvard University, Law School Library, Cambridge, MA
Manley Hudson papers (Hudson)

Hoover Institute on War, Revolution, and Peace, Stanford, CA
Hugh Gibson papers (Gibson)
Herbert Hoover Presidential Library, West Branch, IA (Hoover)
American Relief Administration: European operations (ARA)
ARA Bulletin
Fridtjof Nansen materials
House of Lords Library, London
Lloyd George papers (LGP)
Joint Distribution Committee Archive, New York, NY (JDC)
Documentation on Pinsk
Library of Congress, Manuscript Division, Washington, DC (LC)
American Peace Commission
Papers of Newton Baker, Ray Stannard Baker, Tasker Bliss, Stephen Bonsal, Norman H. Davis, Leland Harrison, Edith Helm, Robert Lansing, David Hunter Miller, Henry Morgenthau (Morgenthau), Oscar Straus, Arthur Sweetser, Henry White (White), Woodrow Wilson (WWP), Henry Morgenthau, Diary
National Diet Library, Tokyo
Makino Nobuaki papers
Piłsudski Institute of America, New York, NY (PIA)
Akta Adjutantury Generalnej Naczelnego Dowództwa, 1918–1922 [(Records of the Polish Supreme Command 1918–1922) (AGND)]
Michał Mościcki papers
Michał Sokolnicki papers
Princeton University, Seeley G. Mudd Manuscript Library, Princeton, NJ
Allen W. Dulles papers (Dulles)
University of London, Mocatta Library, London
Lucien Wolf diary (Wolf, Diary)
University of Ulster at Coleraine
Sir James Headlam-Morley papers (HM UU Col.)
Yale University Library, New Haven, CT
Edward House papers, Edward House Diary (House, Diary), Arthur Bliss Lane papers, Frank Lyon Polk papers, William Wiseman papers
YIVO Institute for Jewish Research, Center for Jewish History, NY (YIVO)
Hermann Bernstein papers
Lucien Wolf/David Mowschowitch papers (W/M)

B. Published Primary Sources

Government Papers: National and International

Austria-Hungary. Ministerium des K. und K. Hauses und des Äussern. *Diplomatische Aktenstücke betreffend die Ereignisse am Balkan: 13 August 1912 bis 6 November 1913.* Vienna: Aus der K. K. Hof-und Staatsdruckerei, 1914.

France. Ministère des Affaires Étrangères. *Conférence de la Paix, 1919–1920. Receuil des actes de la conférence.* Parts 1–8, 45 vols. Paris: Imprimerie Nationale, 1922–35. (*Receuil*)

Documents Diplomatiques Français (1871–1914). 1re Série, 1871–1900. Paris: Imprimerie Nationale, 1929. (*DDF*)

Documents Diplomatiques: Affaires d'Orient: Congrès de Berlin 1878. Paris: Imprimerie Nationale, 1878. (*DD/CB*)

Documents Diplomatiques: Les Affaires Balkaniques, 1912–14. Paris: Imprimerie Nationale, 1922.

Documents Diplomatiques. Question de la reconnaissance de la Roumanie. Paris: Imprimerie Nationale, 1879.

Germany. *Akten der Reichskanzlei: Weimarer Republik. Das Kabinett Scheidemann 13. Februar bis 20 Juni 1919*. Ed. Hagen Schulze. Boppard am Rhein: Boldt, 1971.

Germany. Auswärtiges Amt. *Akten zur Deutschen Auswärtigen Politik*, Series A, 1918–1925. Göttingen: Vandenhoeck & Ruprecht, 1982–95, Series B, 1925–33. Göttingen: Vandenhoeck & Ruprecht, 1966–83. Series D, 1937–40. Baden-Baden: Imprimerie Nationale, 1950–56; Frankfurt-am-Main, Kepler, 1961–63. (ADAP)

Documents on German Foreign Policy, Series C, 1933–1937. Washington, D.C.: U.S. Government Printing Office, 1957–1983, Series D, 1937–45. Washington, D.C.: U.S. Government Printing Office, 1949–64. (DGFP)

Die Grosse Politik der Europäische Kabinette, 1871–1914. Ed. Johannes Lepsius, Albrecht Mendelssohn Bartholdy, Friedrich Thimme. 40 vols. Berlin: Verlagsgesellschaft für Politik und Geschichte, 1927.

Germany. Reichstag. *Verhandlungen des Reichstags, Stenographische Berichte: Verhandlungen der Verfassunggebenden Deutschen Nationalversammlung*. Berlin: Reichsdrückerei, 1932.

Verhandlungen des Reichstags, Stenographische Berichte. Berlin: Reichsdrückerei, 1920–33.

Great Britain. Foreign Office. *British Documents on Foreign Affairs: Reports and Papers from the Foreign Office Confidential Print*. Ed. Kenneth Bourne and D. Cameron Watt. Part I, Series A ("Russia, 1859–1880"). Frederick, MD: University Publications of America, 1983. Series H. Frederick, MD: University Publications of America, 1989. (Bourne and Watt, *British Documents*)

British Documents on the Origins of the War. Ed. G. P. Gooch and Harold Temperley. 11 vols. London: His Majesty's Stationery Office, 1934. (Gooch and Temperley, *Origins of the War*)

British and Foreign State Papers. Vol. 48 (1857–1858). London: Government Printing Office, 1866.

British and Foreign State Papers. *Correspondence Relative to the Recognition of the Independence of Romania, 1879–1880*. London: Ridgway, 1887.

Documents on British Foreign Policy, 1919–1939. Series 1, 1919–25. London: His/Her Majesty's Stationery Office, 1947–86. Series 1A, 1925–1929. London: Her Majesty's Stationery Office, 1966–1975. (DBFP)

Great Britain. House of Commons. *Debate in the House of Commons, 19 April 1872 on The Condition and Treatment of the Jews of Roumania & Servia*. London: Wertheimer-Lee, 1872.

Italy. Ministero del Affari Esteri. *I Documenti Diplomatici Italiani*. Ser. 2, 1870–1896. Rome: Istituto Poligrafico e Zecca dello Stato, 1960–2000. Ser. 6, 1918–1922. Rome: Libreria dello Stato, 1956–. (*DDI*)

League of Nations, *Official Journal*. Geneva: League of Nations, 1920–1939. (LNOJ)

League of Nations. Secretariat. *The League of Nations and Minorities*. Geneva: League of Nations Information Section, 1923.

League of Nations. Secretariat, Information Section. *The League of Nations and the Protection of Minorities of Race, Language, and Religion.* Rev. ed. Geneva: League of Nations, 1927.

Romania. Ministère des Affaires Étrangères. *Documents Diplomatiques: Les Événements de la péninsule Balkanique. L'action de la Roumanie, 20 Septembre 1912–1 Août 1913.* Bucharest: Imprimeria Stabului, 1913.

Le traité de paix de Bucharest du 28 juillet (10 août) 1913. Bucharest: Imprimerie de l'État, 1913.

United States. *Congressional Record.*

United States. Department of State. *Foreign Relations of the United States. 1919.* 2 vols. Washington, DC: Government Printing Office, 1920.

Foreign Relations of the United States: The Paris Peace Conference. 13 vols. Washington, D.C.: Government Printing Office, 1942–1947. (FRUS PPC)

Papers Relating to the Foreign Relations of the United States: 1902. Washington, DC: Government Printing Office, 1902.

Foreign Relations of the United States: 1938, Vols. 1–2. Washington: Government Printing Office, 1955.

Proceedings of the Brest-Litovsk Peace Conference: The Peace Negotiations between Russia and the Central Powers 21 November 1917–3 March 1918. Washington: Government Printing Office, 1918.

Texts of the Russian "Peace". Washington, D.C.: U.S. Department of State, 1918.

Other Documentary Collections

Adler, Cyrus and Aaron M. Margalith. *With Firmness in the Right: American Diplomatic Action Affecting Jews, 1840–1945.* New York: AJC, 1946.

Alliance Israélite Universelle. La question juive devant la conférence de la paix. Paris: Siège de la Société, 1919.

Arnim, Otto [Alfred Roth]. *Die Juden im Heere: Eine statistische Untersuchung nach amtlichen Quellen.* Munich: Deutscher Volks-Verlag, 1919.

Bridge, F. R. ed. *Austro–Hungarian Documents Relating to the Macedonian Struggle,* 1896–1912. Thessalonika: Institute for Balkan Studies, 1976.

Browder, Robert Paul and Alexander Kerensky, eds. *The Russian Provisional Government, 1917: Documents.* Stanford, CA: Stanford University Press, 1961.

Caminetti, Anthony. *Annual Report of the Commissioner General of Immigration.* Washington, DC: U.S. Government Printing Office, 1914.

Carnegie Endowment for International Peace, *Report of the International Commission to Inquire into the Causes and Conduct of the Balkan Wars.* Washington, DC: Carnegie Endowment, 1914.

Chasanowich, L. *Les pogromes anti-juifs en Pologne et en Galicie en novembre et décembre 1918: Faits et documents.* Stockholm: Bokförlaget Judäa A.-B., 1919.

Chasanowich, L. and Leo Motzkin, eds. *Die Judenfrage der Gegenwart Dokumentensammlung.* Stockholm: Bokförlaget Judäa A.-B., 1919.

Deutscher Geschichtskalender, Von Waffenstillstand bis zum Frieden von Versailles. Berlin: Reichsdruckerei, 1919.

Flournoy, Richard W., Jr. and Manley O. Hudson, eds. *A Collection of Nationality Laws of Various Countries as Contained in Constitutions, Statutes and Treaties.* New York: Oxford University Press, 1929.

Iancu, Carol. *Bleichröder et Crémieux: Le combat pour l'émancipation des juifs de Roumanie devant le Congrès de Berlin: Correspondance inédite, 1878–1880.* Montpellier: Centre de Recherches et d'Études Juives et Hébraïques, Université Paul Valéry Montpellier, 1987.

Le combat international pour l'émancipation des juifs de Roumanie: Documents et témoignages. Vol. 1 (1913–19). Jerusalem: Graphit, 1994.

"Benjamin Franklin Peixotto, L'Alliance Israélite Universelle et les juifs de Roumanie, correspondance inédite, 1871–76." *Revue des Études Juives* (1978): 77–147.

"Races et nationalités en Roumanie: Le problème juif à travers les documents diplomatiques français (1866–1880). *Revue d'Histoire Moderne et Contemporaine* 27 (1980): 391–472.

Joint Foreign Committee. *The Jews of Poland.* London: JFC, 1926.

Kapiszewski, Andrzej, ed. *Hugh Gibson and a Controversy over Polish-Jewish Relations after World War I: A Documentary History.* Cracow: Nakładem Uniwersytetu Jagiellońskiego, 1991.

Kohler, Max J. and Simon Wolf. *Jewish Disabilities in the Balkan States: American Contributions Toward Their Removal, with Particular Reference to the Congress of Berlin.* New York: AJC, 1916.

Kohler, Max J. *Jewish Rights at the Congresses of Vienna (1814–1815) and Aix-La-Chapelle (1818).* New York: AJC, 1918.

Kumaniecki, Kazimierz, ed. *Odbudowa Państwowsci Polskiej: Najwazniejsze dokumenty, 1912–1924* [*The Restoration of the Polish State: The Most Important Documents*]. Warsaw: Czernecki, 1924.

Lange-Akhung, Nadine. *The Macedonian Question, 1893–1908, From Western Sources.* Trans. Gabriel Topor. Boulder, CO: East European Monographs; New York: Columbia University Press, 1998.

Link, Arthur S., ed. and trans. *The Deliberations of the Council of Four, March 24–June 28, 1919: Notes of the Official Interpreter Paul Mantoux.* 2 vols. Princeton, NJ: Princeton University Press, 1992. (*Council of Four*)

Luckau, Alma. *The German Delegation at the Paris Peace Conference.* New York: Fertig, 1971.

Luzzatti, Luigi. *God in Freedom: Studies in the Relations Between Church and State.* Trans. Alfonso Arbib-Costa. New York: Macmillan, 1930.

Martens, G. Fr. de. *Nouveau receuil général de traités.* Leipzig: Weicher, 1921.

Miller, David Hunter. *My Diary at the Conference of Paris.* 21 vols. New York: Appeal Publishing Co., 1924; Microfilm ed., New York: Columbia University, 1940. (Miller, *Diary*)

The Drafting of the Covenant. 2 vols. New York: Putnam's, 1928. (Miller, *Covenant*)

Miller, Susanne, ed. *Die Regierung der Volksbeauftragten, 1918/19.* 2 vols. Düsseldorf: Droste, 1969.

Müller, Klaus. *Quellen zur Geschichte des Wiener Kongresses, 1814/1815.* Darmstadt: Wissenschaftliche Buchgesellschaft, 1986.

Novotny, Alexander. *Quellen und Studien zur Geschichte des Berliner Kongresses 1878.* Graz/Cologne: Hermann Bühlaus Nachf., 1957.

Report of the Delegation of Jews of the British Empire on the Peace Conference. London: BDBJ, 1919.

Report of the Secretary and Special Delegate of the Joint Foreign Committee on Questions of Jewish Interest at the Seventh Assembly of the League. London: JFC, 1926.

Schwabe, Klaus, ed. *Quellen zum Friedenschluss von Versailles*. Darmstadt: Wissenschaftliche Buchgesellschaft, 1997.

Sitzungsbericht der ersten Konferenz des Kongresses der organisierten nationalen Gruppen in den Staaten Europas im Jahre 1925 zu Genf. Geneva: no publisher, n.d.

Statistisches Jahrbuch für das deutsche Reich. Berlin: Puttkammer & Mühlbrecht, 1930.

Truhart, Herbert von. *Völkerbund und Minderheitenpetitionen*. Vienna: Braumüller, 1931.

Union des Nationalités. *Compte rendu sommaire de la IIIième conférence des nationalités réunie à Lausanne, 27–29 juin 1916*. Lausanne: Office de L'Union des Nationalités, 1916.

Webster, C. K. *British Diplomacy, 1813–1815: Select Documents Dealing with the Reconstruction of Europe*. London: Bell and Sons, 1921.

Wilson, Woodrow. *The Papers of Woodrow Wilson*. 69 vols. Ed. Arthur S. Link. Princeton, NJ: Princeton University Press, 1966–94. (*PWW*)

The Public Papers of Woodrow Wilson. 6 vols. Ed. Ray Stannard Baker and William E. Dodd. New York: Harper, 1925–27.

Winkler, Wilhelm. *Statistisches Handbuch der europäischen Nationalitäten*. Vienna: Braumüller, 1931.

Wolf, Lucien. *Notes on the Diplomatic History of the Jewish Question: With Texts of Protocols, Treaty Stipulations, and Other Public Acts and Official Documents*. London: Jewish Historical Society of England, 1919.

Diaries, Letters, Memoirs, Personal History

Adler, Cyrus. *Cyrus Adler: Selected Letters*. Ed. Ira Robinson. Philadelphia/New York: Jewish Publication Society of America, 1985.

Louis Marshall: A Biographical Sketch. New York: AJC, 1931.

Baker, Ray Stannard, ed. *Woodrow Wilson, Life and Letters*. 8 vols. Garden City, NY: Doubleday, 1927–39.

Woodrow Wilson and World Settlement. 3 vols. New York: Doubleday, Page, 1922.

What Wilson Did at Paris. Garden City, NY: Doubleday, 1919.

Baranowski, Władisław. *Rozmowy z Piłsudskim, 1916–1931*. Warsaw: Biblioteka Polska, 1938.

Beck, Colonel Józef. *Dernier rapport: Politique polonaise, 1926–39*. Brussels: Éditions de la Baconnière, 1951.

Bicknell, Ernest. *With the Red Cross in Europe, 1917–1922*. Washington: ARC, 1938.

Blumenfeld, Kurt. *Erlebte Judenfrage*. Stuttgart: Deutsche Verlags-Anstalt, 1962.

Bonsal, Stephen. *Suitors and Suppliants: The Little Nations at Versailles*. 2nd ed. New York: Prentice-Hall, 1946.

Unfinished Business. Garden City, NY: Doubleday, 1944.

Brockdorff-Rantzau, Graf Ulrich K. *Dokumente und Gedanken um Versailles*. Berlin: Verlag für Kultur-Politik, 1925.

Cambon, Jules. "*La paix* (notes inédites, 1919)." *Revue de Paris* (Nov. 1, 1937): 5–38.

Cecil, Viscount [Lord Robert]. *A Great Experiment: An Autobiography*. New York: Oxford University Press, 1941.
Clemenceau, Georges. *Grandeur and Misery of Victory*. Trans. Frederick M. Atkinson. New York: Harcourt, Brace, 1930.
Curtius, Julius. *Sechs Jahre Minister der deutschen Republik*. Heidelberg: C. Winter, 1948.
Dmowski, Roman, *Polityka polska i odbudowanie państwa*. 2 vols. Hannover: Schlütersche CDH, 1947.
Dubnow, Simon. *Mein Leben*. Berlin: Jüdische Buchvereinigung, 1937.
Ebert, Friedrich, *Schriften, Aufzeichnungen und Reden*. Dresden: C. Reissner, 1926.
Goldmann, Nahum. *The Autobiography of Nahum Goldmann*. New York: Holt, Rinehart & Winston, 1989.
Grey, Edward. *Twenty-Five Years, 1892–1916*. New York: Stokes, 1925.
Grove, William R. *War's Aftermath (Polish Relief in 1919)*. New York: Field, 1940.
Hanotaux, Gabriel. *Carnets (1907–1925)*. Ed. Georges Dethan and Georges-Henri Soutou. Paris, Pedone, 1982.
Hardinge, Lord Charles. *Old Diplomacy: The Reminiscences of Lord Hardinge of Penshurst*. London: Murray, 1947.
Headlam-Morley, Sir James. *A Memoir of the Paris Peace Conference, 1919*. Ed. Agnes Headlam-Morley, Russell Bryant, and Anna Cienciala. London: Methuen & Co., 1972. (Headlam-Morley, *Memoir*)
Herzl, Theodor. *The Diaries of Theodore Herzl*. Ed. and trans. Marvin Lowenthal. Gloucester, MA: Peter Smith, 1978.
Hindenburg, Marshall Paul von. *Out of My Life*. Trans. F. A. Holt. London: Cassell and Co., 1920.
Howard, Esme. *Theater of Life*. 2 vols. London: Hodder and Stoughton, 1935–6.
Jedrzejewicz, Wacław. *Kronika życia Józefa Piłsudskiego*. London: Polska fundacja Kulturalna, 1977.
Jones, Thomas. *Whitehall Diary, 1916–1925*. Ed. Keith Middlemas. London: Oxford University Press, 1969.
Kessler, Harry, Count. *In the Twenties: The Diaries of Harry Kessler*. Trans. Charles Kessler. New York: Holt, Rinehart & Winston, 1971.
Tagebücher, 1918–1937. Frankfurt: Insel, 1982.
Keynes, John Maynard. *Collected Writings*. Vol. 16: *Activities, 1914–1919, The Treasury and Versailles*. Ed. Elizabeth Johnson. London/Basingstoke: Macmillan, 1971.
Kremnitz, Marie Charlotte. *Aus dem Leben König Karls von Rumänien: Aufzeichnungen eines Augenzeugen*. 4 vols. Stuttgart: Verlag der Cotta'schen Buchhandlung, 1894–1900.
Lansing, Robert. *The Big Four and Others of the Peace Conference*. Boston: Houghton Mifflin, 1921.
The Peace Negotiations: A Personal Narrative. Boston: Houghton Mifflin, 1921.
Lloyd George, David. *Memoirs of the Peace Conference*. 2 vols. New Haven, CT: Yale University Press, 1939.
The Truth About the Peace Treaties. London: V. Gollancz, 1938.
War Memoirs. 6 vols. Boston: Little, Brown, 1933–7.

Loucheur, Louis, *Carnets secrets, 1908–1932*. Brussels: Brepols, 1962.
Marshall, Louis. *Louis Marshall: Champion of Liberty: Selected Papers and Addresses*. Ed. Charles Reznikoff. 2 vols. Philadelphia: Jewish Publication Society of America, 1957.
Narbut-Luczyński, Aleksander J. *U kresu wędrówki. Wspomnienia*. London: Gryf, 1966.
Nicolson, Harold, *Peacemaking 1919*. London: Constable, 1933.
Paderewski, Ignacy. *Archiwum polityczne Ignacego Paderewskiego*. Ed. Halina Janowska. 4 vols. Wrocław: Zakład Narodowy im. Ossolińskich, 1973–4.
Piłsudski, Józef. *Pisma zbiorowe*. Warsaw: Instytut Józefa Piłsudskiego, 1937–38.
Poincaré, Raymond. *Au service de la France: Neuf années de souvenirs*. 11 vols. Paris: Plon-Nourrit et cie., 1926–74.
Riegner, Gerhart M. *Ne jamais désespérer: Soixante années au service du people juif et des droits de l'homme*. Paris: Cerf, 1999.
Romer, Eugeniusz. *Pamiętnik paryski (1918–1919)*. Ed. Andrzej Garlicki and Ryszard Świętek. Wrocław: Zakład Narodowy imienia Ossolińskich, 1989.
Ropp, Friedrich von der. *Zwischen Gestern und Morgen: Erfahrungen und Erkenntnisse*. Stuttgart: Steinkopf, 1961.
Schiff, Jacob H. *Jacob H. Schiff: His Life and Letters*. Ed. Cyrus Adler. Garden City, NY: Doubleday, Doran and Co., 1929.
Seager, Robert and Doris D. Maguire, eds. *Letters and Papers of Alfred Thayer Mahan*. 3 vols. Annapolis, MD: Naval Institute Press, 1975.
Seymour, Charles, ed. *The Intimate Papers of Colonel House*. Boston/New York: Houghton Mifflin, 1928.
Shotwell, James T. *At the Paris Peace Conference*. New York: Macmillan, 1937.
Switalski, Kazimierz, ed. "Listy Józefa Piłsudskiego." *Niepodległość*. n.s., 7 (1962): 29–30.
Tumulty, Joseph P. *Woodrow Wilson As I Know Him*. Garden City, NY: Doubleday, 1921.
Vos, Carl Hermann, ed. *Stephen S. Wise: Servant of the People*. Philadelphia: Jewish Publication Society of America, 1970.
Waddington, Francis. "La France au Congrès de Berlin (Juin-Juillet 1878)." *Revue Politique et Parlementaire* 156 (July–Sept. 1933): 449–84.
Warburg, Max. *Aus meinen Aufzeichnungen*. Glückstadt: Augustin, 1952.
Weizmann, Chaim. *The Letters and Papers of Chaim Weizmann*. Series B. Papers, Vol. 1. Jerusalem/New Brunswick, NJ: Israel Universities Press/Transaction Books, 1983.
Trial and Error: The Autobiography of Chaim Weizmann. London: East and West Library, 1950.
Wise, Stephen S. *Stephen S. Wise: Servant of the People. Selected Letters*. Ed. Carl Hermann Voss. Philadelphia: Jewish Publication Society of America, 1970. (*Stephen S. Wise*)
Challenging Years: The Autobiography of Stephen Wise. New York: Putnam's, 1949.

Contemporary Writing on International Questions

Alcalay, I. *The Jews of Serbia*. Philadelphia: The Jewish Publication Society of America, 1918.

Ansky, S. "The Destruction of Galicia: Excerpts from a Diary." *The Dybbuk and Other Writings*. Trans. Golda Werman. New York: Schocken, 1992.

Azcárate, Pablo de. *League of Nations and National Minorities: An Experiment*. Trans. Eileen E. Brooke. Washington: Carnegie Endowment for International Peace, 1945.

La Société des Nations et la protection des minorités. Geneva: Centre Européen de la Dotation Carnegie pour la Paix Internationale, 1969.

Bauer, Otto. *The Question of Nationalities and Social Democracy*. Trans. Joseph O'Donnell. Minneapolis, MN: University of Minnesota Press, 2000.

Bendow, Josef [pseudonym Joseph Tenenbaum]. *Der Lemberger Judenpogrom (November 1918–Jänner 1919)*. Vienna/Brno: M. Hickl Verlag, 1919.

Benson, F. E. *The White Eagle of Poland*. New York: Doran, 1919.

Birnbaum, Nathan. *Ausgewählte Schriften zur jüdischen Frage*. Czernowitz: Birnbaum & Kohut, 1910.

Bowman, Isaiah. *The New World: Problems in Political Geography*. New York: World Book, 1921.

Buber, Martin. *A Land of Two Peoples: Martin Buber on Jews and Arabs*. Ed. Paul R. Mendes-Flohr. New York: Oxford University Press, 1983.

Bujak, Franciszek. *The Jewish Question in Poland*. Paris: Leve, 1919.

Bülow, Bernhard von. *Imperial Germany*. Trans. Marie A. Lewenz. London: Cassell, 1914.

Caro, Jecheskiel. *Geschichte der Juden in Lemberg*. Cracow: J. Fischer, 1894.

Churchill, Winston. *The World Crisis*. 5 vols. New York: Scribner's, 1923–30.

Cohen, Israel. *A Report on the Pogroms in Poland*. London: Central Office of the Zionist Organisation, 1919, 36 pp.

Coolidge, Archibald Cary. *Ten Years of War and Peace*. Cambridge, MA: Harvard University Press, 1927.

Council of Europe. *The Protection of Minorities*. Strasbourg: Council of Europe Press, 1994.

D'Avril, Adolphe. *Négociations relatives au Traité de Berlin et aux arrangements qui ont suivi, 1875–1886*. Paris: Ernest Leroux, 1886.

Dillon, E. J. *The Inside Story of the Peace Conference*. New York: Harper & Brothers, 1920.

Dubnow, Simon. *Nationalism and History: Essays on Old and New Judaism*. Ed. Koppel S. Pinson. Philadelphia: Jewish Publication Society of America, 1958.

Durkheim, Émile. "Rapport sur la situation des russes en France." *Genèses* (Dec. 2, 1990): 168–77.

Egert, B. P. *The Conflict Between the United States and Russia*. St. Petersburg: B. P. Egert, 1912.

Felinski, M. *The Ukrainians in Poland*. London: Reynolds, 1931.

Feinberg, Nathan. *La question des minorités à la conférence de la paix de 1919–1920*. Paris: Rousseau, 1929.

Fouques Duparc, Jacques. "Le développement de la protection des minorités." *Revue de Droit Internationale et de Législation Comparée* 5 (1926): 509–24.

La protection des minorités de race, de langue et de religion: Étude de droit des gens. Paris: Dalloz, 1922.

Gabrys, Juoszas. *La lithuanie sous le joug allemand, 1915–1918*. Lausanne: Librairie Centrale des Nationalités, 1918.

La question lithuanienne. Lausanne: Librairie Centrale des Nationalités, 1916.
Le problème des nationalités et la paix durable. Lausanne: Librairie Centrale des Nationalités, 1917.
Lithuania and the Autonomy of Poland. Paris: Lithuanian Information Bureau, 1915.
Ober Ost: Le plan annexionniste allemand en Lithuanie. Lausanne: Bureau d'Information de Lithuanie, 1917.
Hankey, Lord Maurice. *The Supreme Control At the Paris Peace Conference 1919: A Commentary*. London: Allen and Unwin, 1963.
Haskins, Charles Homer and Lord Robert Howard. *Some Problems of the Peace Conference*. Cambridge, MA: Harvard University Press, 1920.
Hope Simpson, John. *Refugees: A Review of the Situation Since September 1938*. London: Royal Institute of International Affairs, Oxford University Press, 1939.
House, Edward M. and Charles Seymour, eds. *What Really Happened at Paris*. New York: Scribner's, 1921.
Herzl, Theodor. *A Jewish State: An Attempt at a Modern Solution of the Jewish Question*. Trans. Sylvia d'Avigdor. New York: Federation of American Zionists, 1917.
Kahn, Bernhard and Joseph Rosen. *Report on the Activities of the Joint Distribution Committee*. Chicago: JDC, 1927.
Keynes, John Maynard. *The Economic Consequences of the Peace*. New York: Harcourt, Brace and Howe, 1920.
Kierski, Kazimierz. "Die Lage der Minderheiten in Polen nach der Septembererklärung." *Zeitschrift für Osteuropäisches Recht* 1 (Nov. 1934): 231–46.
Kollenscher, Max. *Aus der deutsch–polnischen Übergangszeit: Jüdisches Posen 1918–1920*. Berlin: "Ewer" Buchhandlung Hans Werner, 1925.
Krstich, Dragolioub. *Les minorités, l'état et la communauté internationale*. Paris: Rousseau, 1924.
Laroche, Jules. *La Pologne de Pilsudski*. Paris: Flammarion, 1953.
Loëb, Isidore. *La situation des israélites en Turquie, en Serbie et en Roumanie*. Paris: Baer, 1877.
Lugan, A. *Les problèmes internationaux et le congrès de la paix: Vue d'ensemble*. Paris: Bossard, 1919.
Machray, Robert. *The Poland of Pilsudski*. London: Allen and Unwin, 1936.
Mack, Julian W. *Americanism and Zionism*. New York: Federation of American Zionists, 1918.
Miller, David Hunter. "The Origins of the Mandates System." *Foreign Affairs* 6 (1928): 277–89.
Motzkin, Leo. "Les revendications nationaux des juifs." In *Les droits nationaux des Juifs en Europe Orientale*. Ed. Comité des délégations juives auprès de la conférence de la paix. Paris: Beresniak et fils, 1919, pp. 7–25.
Namier, Lewis. *Diplomatic Prelude*. London: Macmillan, 1948.
Europe in Decay. London: Macmillan, 1950.
Nawratzki, Kurt. *Die jüdische Kolonisation Palästinas*. Munich: Verlag Ernst Reinhardt, 1914.
Nicholson, Harold. *Peacemaking 1919*. London: Constable, 1933.
Nowak, Karl. *Der Sturz der Mittelmächte*. Munich: D. W. Callwey, 1921.
Oppenheimer, Franz. *Die Judenstatistik des preussischen Kriegsministeriums*. Munich: Verlag für Kulturpolitik, 1922.

Paléologue, Maurice. *La Russie des tsars pendant la grande guerre*. Paris: Plon, 1921.

Renner, Karl. *Das Selbsbestimmungsrecht der Nationen in besonderer Anwendung auf Oesterreich*. Leipzig/Vienna: Franz Deuticke, 1918.

Die Nation: Mythos und Wirklichkeit. Manuskript aus dem Nachlass. Vienna: Europa Verlag, 1964.

Report on the Work of the Zionist Organization, 1915–1919. Copenhagen: Zionist Organization, 1920.

Rogers, Lindsay. "The League of Nations and the National State." In *The League of Nations: The Principle and the Practice*. Ed. Stephen Duggan. Boston: Atlantic Monthly Press, 1919.

Robinson, Jacob, Oscar Karbach, Max Laserson, Nehemiah Robinson, M.V. Vishniak. *Were the Minorities Treaties a Failure?* New York: Institute of Jewish Affairs of the American Jewish Congress and the World Jewish Congress, 1943.

Roth, Joseph. *The Wandering Jews*. Trans. Michael Hoffmann. New York/London: Norton, 2001.

Santoro, Cesare. *Through Poland During the Elections of 1930*. Geneva: Kundig, 1931.

Schurman, Jacob. *The Balkan Wars, 1912–1913*. Princeton, NJ: Princeton University Press, 1914.

Seymour, Charles. *Geography, Justice, and Politics at the Paris Peace Conference of 1919*. New York: American Geographical Society, 1951.

Sidebotham, Herbert. *British Imperial Interests in Palestine*. Letchworth, England: The British Palestine Committee, 1937.

Smuts, Jan C. *The League of Nations: A Practical Suggestion*. London: Hodder & Stoughton, 1918.

Straus, Oscar S. "Humanitarian Diplomacy of the United States." *The American Spirit*. New York: Century, 1913.

Strong, Josiah. *Our Country: Its Possible Future and its Present Crisis*. New York: Baker and Taylor, 1885.

Swystun, Wasyl. *Ukraine: The Sorest Spot of Europe*. Winnipeg: Ukrainian Information Bureau, 1931.

Taft, William Howard. *The Presidency: Its Duties, Its Powers, Its Opportunities, and Its Limitations*. New York: Scribner's, 1916.

Tardieu, André. *La Paix*. Paris: Payot, 1921.

The Truth About the Treaty. Indianapolis, IN: Bobbs-Merrill, 1921.

Temperley, H. W. V., ed. *History of the Peace Conference of Paris*. 6 vols. London: H. Frowde and Hodder & Stoughton, 1920–24.

Troeltsch, Ernst. *Spektator-Briefe: Aufsätze über deutsche Revolution und die Weltpolitik, 1918–1922*. Tübingen: Mohr, 1924.

Trotsky, Leon. *The Balkan Wars, 1912–13: The War Correspondence of Leon Trotsky*. Trans. Brian Pierce. Ed. George Weissman and Duncan Williams. New York: Monad, 1980.

Ubicini, A. *La question des principautés devant l'Europe*. Paris: E. Dentu, 1858.

Unity in Dispersion: A History of the World Jewish Congress. 2nd rev. ed. New York: Institute of Jewish Affairs of the World Jewish Congress, 1948.

The World Jewish Congress: An Answer to the American Jewish Committee. New York: American Jewish Congress, June 1936.

2. SECONDARY SOURCES

Abramsky, Chimen. "Lucien Wolf's Efforts for the Jewish Communities in Central and Eastern Europe." *Jewish Historical Studies: Transactions of the Jewish Historical Society of England* 29 (1982–6): 281–95.

War, Revolution and the Jewish Dilemma. London: Lewis, 1975.

Adelson, Roger. *London and the Invention of the Middle East.* New Haven, CT: Yale University Press, 1995.

Adler, Selig. "The Palestine Question in the Wilson Era." *Jewish Social Studies* 10 (1948): 303–34.

Agnoletto, Attilio. *La tragoedia dell'Europa cristiana nel 16. secolo.* Milan: Istituto di Propaganda Libraria, 1996.

Ajnenkiel, Andrzej. "The Establishment of a National Government in Poland, 1918." In *The Reconstruction of Poland, 1914–1923.* Ed. Paul Latawski. London: Macmillan, 1992, pp. 133–43.

Alcock, Antony. *A History of the Protection of Regional Cultural Minorities in Europe: From the Edict of Nantes to the Present Day.* Basingstoke, England: Macmillan; New York: St. Martin's, 2000.

Alderman, Geoffrey. *Modern British Jewry.* Oxford: Clarendon, 1992.

Alonso, Harriet Hyman. *Peace as a Women's Issue.* Syracuse, NY: Syracuse University Press, 1993.

Ambrosius, Lloyd E. *Wilsonian Statecraft: Theory and Practice of Liberal Internationalism During World War I.* Wilmington, DE: Scholarly Resources, 1991.

Anastassiadou, Meropi. *Salonique, 1830–1912: Une ville ottomane à l'âge des réformes.* Leiden: Brill, 1997.

Anderson, Benedict. *Imagined Communities.* London: Verso, 1983.

Andrews, E. M. *The Anzac Illusion: Anglo–Australian Relations During World War I.* Cambridge: Cambridge University Press, 1993.

Angress, Werner. "The German Army's *Judenzahlung* of 1916: Genesis-Consequences-Significance." *Leo Baeck Institute Year Book* 23 (1978): 117–37.

"Juden im politischen Leben der Revolutionszeit." In *Deutsches Judentum in Krieg und Revolution, 1916–1923.* Ed. Werner Mosse. Tübingen: Mohr, 1971, pp. 137–315.

Apelt, Willibalt. *Geschichte der Weimarer Verfassung.* Munich: Biederstein, 1946.

Aptiev, Sabit J. *Das deutsche Reich und die mazedonische Frage, 1908–1918.* Neuried: Hieronymous, 1985.

Aronsfeld, C. C. "Jewish Enemy Aliens in England during World War I." *Jewish Social Studies* 18 (1956): 273–83.

Badinter, Robert. *Libres et égaux . . . L'émancipation des juifs sous la révolution française (1789–1791).* Paris: Fayard, 1989.

Baechler, Christian. *Gustave Stresemann (1878–1929).* Strasbourg: Presses Universitaires de Strasbourg, 1996.

Bagley, Tennent H. *General Principles and Problems in the International Protection of Minorities: A Political Study.* Geneva: Imprimeries Populaires, 1950.

Balch, Emily Green. *Approaches to the Great Settlement.* New York: Huebsch, 1918.

Bankier, David, ed. *Probing the Depths of German Antisemitism: German Society and the Persecution of the Jews, 1933–1941.* Jerusalem: Yad Vashem and Leo Baeck Institute; New York/Oxford: Berghahn, 2000.

Barnard, Harold. *The Forging of an American Jew: The Life and Times of Judge Julian W. Mack*. New York: Herzl Press, 1974.

Baron, Salo. *Ethnic Minority Rights: Some Older and Newer Trends*. Oxford: Centre for Postgraduate Hebrew Studies, 1985.

Die Judenfrage auf dem Wiener Kongress. Vienna and Berlin: R. Löwit Verlag, 1920.

Basch, Françoise. *Victor Basch ou la passion de la justice*. Paris: Plon, 1994.

Baumgart, Winfried. *The Peace of Paris, 1856: Studies in War, Diplomacy, and Peacemaking*. Trans. Ann Pottinger Saab. Santa Barbara, CA: ABC-Clio, 1981.

Bein, Alex. *The Jewish Question: Biography of a World Problem*. Trans. H. Zorn. Rutherford, NJ: Fairleigh Dickinson Press, 1990.

Beloff, Max. *The Role of the Palestine Mandate in the Period of Britain's Imperial Decline*. Haifa: University of Haifa, 1981.

Ben-Avram, Baruch. "Das Dilemma des Zionismus nach dem Ersten Weltkrieg." *Historische Zeitschrift* 244 (June, 1987): 605–31.

Ben-Israel, Hedva. "Nationalism in Historical Perspective." *Journal of International Affairs* 45 (1992): 367–97.

Ben Sassoon, H. H. *A History of the Jewish People*. Cambridge, MA: Harvard University Press, 1976.

Berkowitz, Michael. *Western Jewry and the Zionist Project*. Cambridge: Cambridge University Press, 1997.

Berman, Myron. *The Attitude of American Jewry Towards East European Jewish Immigration*. New York: Arno, 1980.

Best, Gary Dean. *To Free a People: American Jewish Leaders and the Jewish Problem in Eastern Europe, 1890–1914*. Westport, CT: Greenwood, 1982.

Beyrau, Dietrich. "Antisemitismus und Judentum in Polen, 1918–1939." *Geschichte und Gesellschaft* 8 (1982): 205–32.

Bierzanek, Remiguisz. "La Pologne dans les conceptions politiques des puissances occidentales en 1918–1919." *Revue d'Histoire Moderne et Contemporaine* 15 (1968): 273–303.

Birnbaum, Pierre. *Anti-Semitism in France*. Trans. Miriam Kochan. Oxford: Blackwell, 1992.

Biskupski, Mieczyslaw B. "Re-Creating Central Europe: The United States Inquiry into the Future of Poland in 1918." *International History Review* 12 (1990): 224–79.

"War and the Diplomacy of Polish Independence, 1914–1918." *Polish Review* 35 (1990): 5–17.

"The Wilsonian View of Poland: Idealism and Geopolitical Traditionalism." In *Wilsonian East Central Europe: Current Perspectives*. Ed. John S. Micgiel. New York: Piłsudski Institute, 1995, pp. 123–39.

Blackbourn, David. *The Long Nineteenth Century: A History of Germany, 1780–1918*. New York: Oxford University Press, 1998.

Black, Edwin. *The Transfer Agreement: The Untold Story of the Secret Agreement Between the Third Reich and Jewish Palestine*. New York: Macmillan, 1984.

Black, Eugene C. "Lucien Wolf and the Making of Poland: Paris, 1919." *Polin* 2 (1987): 5–36.

The Social Politics of Anglo-Jewry, 1880–1920. Oxford: Oxford University Press, 1988.

Bled, Jean-Paul. "La question de Bosnie-Herzegovine et la fin de l'ère libérale en Autriche." In *Der Berliner Kongress von 1878*. Ed. Ralph Melville and Hans-Jürgen Schröder. Wiesbaden: Steiner, 1982, pp. 259–70.

Bloom, William. *Personal Identity, National Identity, and International Relations*. Cambridge: Cambridge University Press, 1990.

Bobroff, Ronald. "Behind the Balkan Wars: Russian Policy Toward Bulgaria and the Turkish Straits, 1912–13." *Russian Review* 59 (2000): 72–95.

Bornemann, Elke. *Der Frieden von Bukarest 1918*. Frankfurt am Main: Lang, 1978.

Brecher, Frank W. *Reluctant Ally: United States Foreign Policy Toward the Jews from Wilson to Roosevelt*. New York: Greenwood, Press, 1991.

Bredin, Jean-Denis. *The Affair: The Case of Alfred Dreyfus*. Trans. Jeffrey Mehlman. New York: Braziller, 1986.

Breyfogle, Nicholas. *Heretics and Colonizers: Religious Dissent and Russian Empire-Building in the South Caucasus, 1830–1900*. Ithaca, NY: Cornell University Press, 2004.

Bronner, Stephen E. *A Rumor About the Jews: Reflections on Antisemitism and the Protocols of the Learned Elders of Zion*. New York: St. Martin's, 2000.

Broszat, Martin. "Aussen- und Innenpolitische Aspekte der preussisch–deutschen Minderheitenpolitik." In *Politische Ideologien und Nationalstaatliche Ordnung*. Ed. Kurt Kluxen and Wolfgang J. Mommsen. Munich: Oldenbourg, 1968, pp. 359–76.

Browning, Christopher. *The Final Solution and the German Foreign Office*. New York: Holmes and Meier, 1979.

Brubaker, Rogers. "Aftermaths of Empire and the Unmixing of Peoples: Historical and Comparative Perspectives." *Ethnic and Racial Studies* 18 (1995): 189–218.

"National Minorities, Nationalizing States, and External National Homelands in the New Europe." *Daedalus* 124 (Spring 1995): 107–32.

Brunet, René. *The New German Constitution*. Trans. Joseph Gollomb. New York: Knopf, 1927.

Burkman, Thomas W. "Japan, the League of Nations, and the New World Order, 1918–1920." Ph.D. dissertation, University of Michigan, 1975.

Burks, R. V. "Romania and the Balkan Crisis of 1875–1878." *Journal of Central European Affairs* 2 (1942): 119–34, 310–20.

Burns, Michael. "Disturbed Spirits: Minority Rights and New World Orders, 1919 and the 1990s." In *New European Orders, 1919 and 1991*. Ed. Samuel F. Wells, Jr. and Paula Bailey Smith. Washington, DC: Woodrow Wilson Center Press, 1996, pp. 41–61.

Bykofsky, Joseph. *The History of the American National Red Cross*. Washington, DC: American National Red Cross, 1950.

Calder, Kenneth J. *Britain and the Origins of the New Europe, 1914–1918*. Cambridge: Cambridge University Press, 1976.

Cameron, Rondo E. *France and the Economic Development of Europe, 1800–1914*. Princeton, NJ: Princeton University Press, 1961.

Caron, Vicki. *Between France and Germany: The Jews of Alsace-Lorraine, 1871–1918*. Stanford, CA: Stanford University Press, 1988.

Uneasy Asylum. Stanford, CA: Stanford University Press, 1999.

Castlebajac, Ghislain de. "La France et la question polonaise (1914–1918)." In *Recherches sur la France et le problème des nationalités pendant la première guerre mondiale (Pologne, Ukraine, Lithuanie)*. Ed. Ghislain de Castelbajac, Sébastien de Gasquet, and Georges-Henri Soutou. Paris: Presses de l'Université de Paris-Sorbonne, 1995, pp. 39–104.

Cesarini, David. "An Embattled Minority: The Jews in Britain During the First World War." *Immigrants and Minorities* 8 (1989): 61–81.

Chazan, Naomi, ed. *Irredentism and International Politics*. Boulder, CO: Rienner, 1991.

Chiriţă, Grigore. "România şi Conferinţa de la Paris, februarie–iunie 1866." *Revista de Istorie* 38 (1985): 967–86; 38 (1985): 1075–1100.

Chirot, Daniel. *The Congress of Berlin, Romanian Anti-Semitism, and the Dissociation of Liberalism and Nationalism Throughout Europe*. Berkeley, CA: Center for German and European Studies, n.d., Working Paper 6.62.

Social Change in a Peripheral Society: The Creation of a Balkan Colony. New York: Academic, 1976.

Chojnowski, Andrzej. *Koncepcje polityki narodowościowej rządów polskich w latach, 1921–1939*. Wrocław: Zakład Narodowy imienia Ossolińskich, 1979.

Chouraqui, André. *Cent ans d'histoire: L'Alliance Israélite Universelle et la renaissance juive contemporaine*. Paris: AIU, 1965.

Claude, Innis L. *National Minorities: An International Problem*. Cambridge, MA: Harvard University Press, 1955.

Cloarec, Vincent. *La France et la question de Syrie, 1914–1918*. Paris: Centre National de la Recherche Scientifique, 1998.

Cohen, Aharon. *Israel and the Arab World*. New York: Funk & Wagnalls, 1970.

Cohen, Israel. *Vilna*. Philadelphia: Jewish Publication Society of America, 1943.

Cohen, Lloyd A. "The Jewish Question During the Period of the Romanian National Renaissance and the Unification of the Two Principalities of Moldavia and Wallachia, 1848–1866." In *Romania Between East and West: Historical Essays in Memory of Constantin Giurescu*. Ed. Stephen Fischer-Galati, Radu Florescu, George Ursul. Boulder, CO: East European Monographs, distributed by New York: Columbia University Press, 1982, pp. 195–216.

Cohen, Michael. *Palestine, Retreat From the Mandate: The Making of British Policy, 1936–1945*. New York: Holmes and Meier, 1978.

Cohen, Naomi Wiener. "Abrogation of the Russo-American Treaty of 1832." *Jewish Social Studies* 25 (1963): 3–41.

Not Free to Desist: The American Jewish Committee, 1906–1966. Philadelphia: Jewish Publication Society of America, 1972.

Contee, Clarence G. "Du Bois, the NAACP, and the Pan-African Congress of 1919." *Journal of Negro History* 57 (Jan. 1972): 13–28.

Conze, Werner. *Polnische Nation und Deutsche Politik im Ersten Weltkrieg*. Cologne: Böhlau, 1958.

Corti, Egone Cesare. "Bismarck und Italien am Berliner Kongress 1878." *Historische Vierteljahrsschrift* 23 (1926): 456–71.

Costa, Nicholas J. *Albania: A European Enigma*. Boulder, CO: East European Monographs; distributed by New York: Columbia University Press, 1995.

Curtiss, J. S. *Russia's Crimean War*. Durham, NC: Duke University Press, 1979.

Czernin, Count Ferdinand. *Versailles, 1919*. New York: Putnam, 1964.

Dadrian, Vahakn N. "The Armenian Question and the Wartime Fate of the Armenians as Documented by the Officials of the Ottoman Empire's World War I Allies: Germany and Austria–Hungary." *Journal of Middle East Studies* 34 (2002): 59–85.

"The Documentation of the World War I Armenian Massacres in the Proceedings of the Turkish Military Tribunal." *International Journal of Middle East Studies* 23 (1991): 549–76.

German Responsibility in the Armenian Genocide. Watertown, MA: Blue Crane Books, 1996.

The History of the Armenian Genocide. Providence, RI: Berghahn, 1995.

Dakin, Douglas. *The Greek Struggle in Macedonia, 1897–1913*. Thessalonika: Institute for Balkan Studies, 1966.

Danford, Loring M. *The Macedonian Conflict*. Princeton, NJ: Princeton University Press, 1995.

Daniels, Roger. *The Politics of Prejudice*. New York: Atheneum, 1973.

Darques, Régis. *Salonique au XXe siècle: De la cité ottomane à la métropole grecque*. Paris: Centre National de la Recherche Scientifique, 2000.

Davies, Norman. *God's Playground: A History of Poland*. New York: Columbia University Press, 1982.

Great Britain and the Polish Jews, 1918–1920," *Journal of Contemporary History* 8 (April 1973): 119–42.

"The Poles in Great Britain, 1914–1919." *Slavonic and East European Review* 50 (1972): 63–89.

White Eagle, Red Star: The Polish-Soviet War, 1919–20. London: MacDonald, 1972.

Debo, Richard K. *Survival and Consolidation: The Foreign Policy of Soviet Russia, 1918–1921*. Montreal: McGill-Queen's University Press, 1992.

d'Encausse, Hélène. *The Great Challenge: Nationalities and the Bolshevik State, 1917–1930*. Trans. Nancy Festinger. New York: Holmes and Meier, 1992.

Dianoux, Hughes Jean de. "L'émancipation des juifs de Roumanie." *Revue d'Histoire Diplomatique*. 103 (3–4) (1989): 285–338.

Dickinson, Frederick R. "Japan's Asia in the Politics of a New World Order, 1914–1919." In *The Japanese Empire in East Asia and its Postwar Legacy*. Ed. Harald Fuess. Munich: Iudicium-Verlag, 1998, pp. 27–48.

War and National Reinvention: Japan and the Great War, 1914–1919. Cambridge, MA: Harvard University Press, 1999.

Dinnerstein, Leonard. *The Leo Frank Case*. New York: Columbia University Press, 1968.

Dioszegi, István. "Die Anfänge der Orientpolitik Andrássys." In *Der Berliner Kongress von 1878*. Ed. Ralph Melville and Hans-Jürgen Schröder. Wiesbaden: Steiner, 1982, pp. 245–58.

Djordjevic, Dimitrije and Stephen Fischer-Galati. *The Balkan Revolutionary Tradition*. New York: Columbia University Press, 1981.

Dockrill, Michael L. and J. Douglas Goold. *Peace without Promise: Britain and the Peace Conferences, 1919–23*. London: Batsford, 1981.

Doty, Madeline Z. "The Central Organization for a Durable Peace (1915–1919)." Doctoral thesis, University of Geneva, 1945.

Drozdowski, Marian M. "The National Minorities in Poland in 1918–1919." *Acta Poloniae Historica* 22 (1970): 226–51.

Ignacy Jan Paderewski: A Political Biography. Trans. Stanisław Tarnowski. Warsaw: Interpress, 1979.

Duda, Helge. *Nationalismus, Nationalität, Nation: Der Fall Albanien unter Berucksichtigung*. Munich: Vogel, 1991.

Duff, John B. "The Versailles Treaty and the Irish-Americans." *Journal of American History* 55 (1966): 596–616.

Duker, Abraham. "Jews in the World War." *Contemporary Jewish Record* (Sept.–Oct. 1939): 6–29.

Dumont, Paul. "La structure sociale de la communauté juive de Salonique à la fin du dix-neuvième siècle." *Revue Historique* 263(2) (1980): 351–93.

Durman, Karel. *The Time of the Thunderer: Mikhail Katkov, Russian Nationalist Extremism, and the Failure of the Bismarckian System, 1871–1887*. Boulder, CO: East European Monographs; New York: Columbia University Press, 1988.

Duroselle, Jean-Baptiste. *Clemenceau*. Paris: Fayard, 1988.

Politique étrangère de la France: La décadence, 1932–1939. Paris: Imprimerie Nationale, 1979.

East, W. G. *The Union of Moldavia and Wallachia*. Cambridge: Cambridge University Press, 1929.

Egerton, George W. *Great Britain and the Creation of the League of Nations: Strategy, Politics, and International Organization, 1914–1919*. Chapel Hill, NC: University of North Carolina Press, 1979.

Éléments d'histoire de la communauté israélite de Thessaloniki. Salonika: CIS, 1978.

Emerit, Marcel. *Victor Place et la politique française en Roumanie à l'époque de l'union*. Bucharest: Institut de Arte Grafice, 1931.

Engel, David, "Lwów: The Transmutation of a Symbol and its Legacy in the Holocaust." In *Contested Memories: Poles and Jews During the Holocaust and its Aftermath*. Ed. Joshua D. Zimmerman. New Brunswick, NJ and London: Rutgers University Press, 2003, pp. 32–44.

Esposito, David. "Imagined Power: The Secret Life of Colonel House." *The Historian* 60 (1998): 741–56.

Evans, Laurence. *United States Policy and the Partition of Turkey, 1914–1924*. Baltimore: Johns Hopkins University Press, 1965.

Farrar, L. L., Jr. *Divide and Conquer: German Efforts to Conclude a Separate Peace, 1914–1918*. Boulder, CO: East European Quarterly; New York: Columbia University Press, 1978.

Feilchenfeld, Werner, Dolf Michaelis, and Ludwig Pinner. *Haavara-Transfer nach Palästina und Einwanderung deutscher Juden 1933–1939*. Tübingen: Mohr, 1972.

Feldman, Eliyahu. "The Question of Jewish Emancipation in the Ottoman Empire and the Danubian Principalities after the Crimean War." *Jewish Social Studies* 41 (1979): 41–74.

Feldman, Louis. *Jew and Gentile in the Ancient World*. Princeton, NJ: Princeton University Press, 1993.

Ferguson, Niall. *The House of Rothschild: The World's Banker, 1849–1999*. New York: Viking, 1999.

Fest, Wilfred. *Peace or Partition: The Habsburg Monarchy and British Policy, 1914–1918*. London: Prior, 1978.

Fifield, Russell H. *Woodrow Wilson and the Far East*. Hamden, CT: Archon, 1965.

Finestein, Israel. *Anglo-Jewry in Changing Times: Studies in Diversity, 1840–1914*. London: Vallentine Mitchell, 1999.

Fink, Carole. "'As Little a Surprise as a Murder Can Well Be': Ausländische Reaktionen auf den Mord an Walther Rathenau." In *Die Extreme berühren sich: Walther Rathenau, 1867–1922*. Ed. Hans Wilderotter. Berlin: Argon, 1993, pp. 237–46.

"Between the Second and Third Reichs: The Weimar Republic as Imperial Interegnum." In *The End of Empire*. Ed. Karen Dawisha and Bruce Parrott. Armonk, NY/London: Sharpe, 1997, pp. 261–85.

"Defender of Minorities: Germany in the League of Nations, 1926–1933." *Central European History* 5 (1972): 330–57.

"Franz Kafka and the Dilemma of Ethnic Nationalism." *Canadian Review of Studies in Nationalism* 8 (1981): 17–36.

"Germany and the Polish Elections of November 1930: A Study in League Diplomacy." *East European Quarterly* 15 (1981): 181–207.

"Germany's 'Revisionspolitik,' 1919–1933." *Canadian Historical Papers* (Spring 1987): 134–45.

"The Great Powers and the New International System, 1919–1923." In *From War to Peace: Altered Strategic Landscapes in the Twentieth Century*. Ed. Paul Kennedy and William I. Hitchcock. New Haven, CT/London: Yale University Press, 2000, pp. 17–35, 257–65.

The Jews and Minority Rights During and After World War I. The University of Cape Town, South Africa: Kaplan Centre for Jewish Studies and Research, Occasional Paper No. 3, 2001.

"Minority Rights as an International Question." *Contemporary European History* 9 (Spring 1995): 197–205.

"The Minorities Question." In *The Treaty of Versailles: A Reassessment After 75 Years*. Ed. Manfred F. Boemeke, Gerald D. Feldman, and Elisabeth Glaser. Cambridge: Cambridge University Press, 1998, pp. 249–74.

"The Problem of Minority Rights and Democracy in Eastern Europe From the Paris Peace Conference to the Fall of the Soviet Empire: The International Dimension." In *L'Europe au XXe siècle: Éléments pour un bilan*. Ed. Tomasz Schramm. Poznań: Instytut Historii UAM, 2000, pp. 333–46.

"Stresemann's Minority Policies." *Journal of Contemporary History* 14 (July 1979): 403–22.

The Weimar Republic as the Defender of Minorities, 1919–1933: A Study of Germany's Minorities Diplomacy and the League of Nations System for the International Protection of Minorities. Ann Arbor, MI: University Microfilms, 1969.

Finney, Patrick B. "'An Evil for All Concerned': Great Britain and Minority Protection after 1919." *Journal of Contemporary History* 30 (1995): 533–51.

Fischer-Galati, Stephen. "Romanian Nationalism." In *Nationalism in Eastern Europe*. 2nd ed. Ed. Peter F. Sugar and Ivo John Lederer. Seattle, WA: University of Washington Press, 1994, pp. 373–95.

Fischer, Fritz. *Germany's Aims in the First World War*. Trans. James Joll. New York: Norton, 1967.

Fishman, Joshua A., ed. *Studies in Polish Jewry, 1919–1939*. New York: YIVO, 1974.

Fitzhardinge, L. F. "W. M. Hughes at the Paris Peace Conference, 1919." *Journal of Commonwealth Political Studies* 5 (1967): 130–42.

Fitzhardinge, L. F. *William Morris Hughes: A Political Biography*. Sydney: Angus & Robertson, 1979.

Floto, Inga. "Colonel House in Paris: The Fate of a Presidential Adviser." *American Studies in Scandinavia* 6 (1–2) (1973–4): 21–45.

Colonel House in Paris: A Study of American Foreign Policy at the Paris Peace Conference 1919. Aarhus: Universitetsforlaget, 1973.

Frankel, Jonathan, *The Damascus Affair: "Ritual Murder," Politics, and the Jews in 1840*. Cambridge: Cambridge University Press, 1978.

"The Dilemmas of Jewish National Autonomism: The Case of Ukraine, 1917–1920." In *Ukrainian-Jewish Relations in Historical Perspective*. 2nd ed. Ed. Howard Aster and Peter J. Potichnyj. Edmonton: Canadian Institute of Ukrainian Studies, 1990, pp. 263–79.

"The Paradoxical Politics of Marginality: Thoughts on the Jewish Situation During the Years 1914–1921." *Studies in Contemporary Jewry* 4 (1988): 3–21.

Prophecy and Politics: Socialism, Nationalism, and the Russian Jews, 1862–1917. Cambridge: Cambridge University Press, 1981.

Fredrickson, George M. *The Black Image in the White Mind: The Debate on Afro-American Character and Destiny, 1817–1914*. New York: Harper & Row, 1971.

Freiberg, Walter. *Sudtirol und der italienische Nationalismus*. 2 vols. Innsbruck: Wagner, 1989–90.

French, David. *British Strategy & War Aims, 1914–1916*. London: Allen and Unwin, 1986.

Frentz, Christian Raitz von. *A Lesson Forgotten: Minority Protection Under the League of Nations: A Case of the German Minority in Poland, 1920–1934*. New York: St. Martin's, 1999.

Friedländer, Saul. "Die politischen Veränderungen der Kriegszeit." In *Deutsches Judentum in Krieg und Revolution, 1916–1923*. Ed. Werner Mosse. Tübingen: Mohr, 1971, pp. 27–65.

Friedman, Isaiah, ed. *Germany, Turkey and Zionism, 1914–1918*. New York: Garland, 1987.

The Question of Palestine: British–Jewish–Arab Relations: 1914–1918. 2nd ed. New Brunswick, NJ: Transaction Publishers, 1992.

ed. *The Rise of Israel*. 12 vols. New York: Garland, 1987.

Funderburk, David. "United States Policy Toward Romania, 1876–1878." *Revue Roumaine d'Histoire* 16 (1977): 309–17.

Gainer, Bernard. *The Alien Invasion: The Origins of the Aliens Act of 1905*. New York: Crane, Russak, 1972.

Garai, George, ed. *40 Years in Action*. Geneva: World Jewish Congress, 1976.

Garlicki, Andrzej. *Józef Piłsudski, 1867–1935*. Trans. John Coutouvidis. Brookfield, VT/London: Ashgate Publishing, Scolar Press, 1995.

Gartner, Lloyd P. *The Jewish Immigrant in England, 1870–1914*. 3rd ed. London: Vallentine Mitchell, 2001.

"Roumania, America and World Jewry: Consul Peixotto in Bucharest, 1870–1876." *American Jewish Historical Quarterly* 53(1) (Sept. 1968): 25–117.

Gatrell, Peter. *A Whole Empire Walking: Refugees in Russia During World War I.* Bloomington, IN: Indiana University Press, 1999.

Geiss, Imanuel. "Die jüdische Frage auf dem Berliner Kongress 1878." *Jahrbuch des Instituts für Deutsche Geschichte* (Tel Aviv) 10 (1981): 413–22.

Die polnische Grenzstreifen, 1914–1918. Hamburg: Matthiesen, 1960.

Gelber, N. M. "An Attempt to Internationalize Salonika, 1912–1913." *Jewish Social Studies* 17 (1955): 105–20.

"The Intervention of German Jews at the Berlin Congress, 1878." *Leo Baeck Institute Year Book* 5 (1960): 221–48.

"The Problem of the Rumanian Jews at the Bucharest Peace Conference, 1918." *Jewish Social Studies* 12 (1950): 223–46.

"La question juive en Bulgarie et en Serbie devant le Congrès de Berlin." *Revue des Études Juives* 122 (1964): 85–90.

Gelfand, Lawrence E. "David Hunter Miller." *American National Biography*. Ed. John Garraty and Mark C. Carnes. New York: Oxford University Press, 1999.

The Inquiry: American Preparations for Peace, 1917–1919. New Haven, CT: Yale University Press, 1963.

Gellner, Ernest. *Nations and Nationalism.* Oxford: Blackwell, 1983.

George, Alexander L. and Juliette L. George. *Woodrow Wilson and Colonel House: A Personality Study.* New York: Dover, 1964.

Georgévitch, V. "La Serbie au Congrès de Berlin." *Revue d'Histoire Diplomatique* 5 (1891): 483–552.

Gerolymatos, Andre. *The Balkan Wars: Myth, Reality, and the Eternal Conflict.* Toronto: Stoddart, 2001.

Gerson, Louis. *Woodrow Wilson and the Rebirth of Poland.* New Haven, CT: Yale University Press, 1953 (reprinted Hamden, CT: Archon, 1972).

Geyer, Dietrich. *Russian Imperialism.* Trans. Bruce Little. Hamburg: Berg, 1986.

Gilam, Abraham. "The Leeds Anti-Jewish Riots 1917." *Jewish Quarterly* 29 (1981): 34–7.

Gilbert, Martin. *The First World War: A Complete History.* New York: Holt, 1994.

Golczewski, Frank. *Polnisch–Jüdische Beziehungen, 1881–1922.* Wiesbaden: Franz Steiner, 1981.

Goldstein, Erik. *Winning the Peace: British Diplomatic Strategy, Peace Planning, and the Paris Peace Conference, 1916–1920.* Oxford: Clarendon, 1991.

Goldstein, Judith S. *The Politics of Ethnic Pressure: The American Jewish Committee Fight Against Immigration Restriction, 1906–1917.* New York: Garland, 1990.

Goraíainov, Serge. *La question d'orient à la veille du Traité de Berlin.* Paris: Institut d'Études Slaves, 1948.

Gottlieb, Amy Zahl. *Men of Vision: Anglo-Jewry's Aid to Victims of the Nazi Regime, 1933–1945.* London: Weidenfeld & Nicolson, 1998.

Gottlieb, W. W. *Studies in Secret Diplomacy During the First World War.* London: Allen and Unwin, 1957.

Green, Nancy L. *The Pletzl of Paris: Jewish Immigrant Workers in the "Belle Époque."* New York: Holmes and Meier, 1986.

Greenberg, L. S. *The Jews in Russia.* New Haven, CT: Yale University Press, 1965.

Grosfeld, Leon. *Polityka państw centralnych wobec sprawy polskiej w latach pierwszej wojny światowej* [The Policy of the Central Powers with Regard to the Polish Question During the First World War.] Warsaw: Państwowe Wydawn. Naukowe, 1962.

Gurr, Ted Robert and Barbara Harff. *Ethnic Conflict in World Politics.* San Francisco: Westview, 1994.

Gütterman, Christoph. *Das Minderheitenschutzverfahren des Völkerbundes.* Berlin: Duncker und Humblot, 1979.

Hadler, Frank. "Peacemaking 1919 im Spiegel der Briefe Edvard Beneš von der Pariser Friedenskonferenz." *Berliner Jahrbuch für Osteuropäische Geschichte* 1(1) (1994): 213–55.

Weg von Österreich! Das Weltkriegsexil von Masaryk und Beneš im Spiegel ihrer Briefe und Aufzeichnungen auf den Jahren 1914 bis 1918. Berlin: Akademie Verlag, 1995.

Hagen, William W. *Germans, Poles, and Jews: The Nationality Conflict in the Prussian East, 1772–1914.* Chicago: University of Chicago Press, 1980.

"Murder in the East: German–Jewish Liberal Reactions to the Anti-Jewish Violence in Poland and Other East European Lands, 1918–1920." *Central European History* 34 (2001): 1–30.

Hall, Richard C. *The Balkan Wars, 1912–13: Prelude to the First World War.* London: Routledge, 2000.

Halpern, Ben and Jehuda Reinharz. *Zionism and the Creation of a New Society.* New York: Oxford University Press, 1998.

Harris, David. *Britain and the Bulgarian Horrors of 1876.* Chicago: University of Chicago Press, 1939.

Hartley, Stephen. *The Irish Question as a Problem in British Foreign Policy, 1914–18.* London: Macmillan, 1987.

Haselsteiner, Horst. "Zur Haltung der Donaumonarchie in der orientalischen Frage." In *Der Berliner Kongress von 1878.* Ed. Ralph Melville and Hans-Jürgen Schröder. Wiesbaden: Steiner, 1982, pp. 227–43.

Hassiotis, I. K. ed. *Queen of the Worthy: Thessaloniki, History and Culture.* 2 vols. Salonika: Paratiritis, 1997.

Hastaoglou-Martinidis, Vilma. "On the State of the Jewish Community of Salonica after the Fire of 1917." In *The Jewish Communities of Southeastern Europe: From the Fifteenth Century to the End of World War II.* Ed. I. K. Hassiotis. Thessaloniki: Institute for Balkan Studies, 1997, pp. 147–71.

Hausmann, Kurt Georg. "Piłsudski und die Mission des Grafen Kessler in Polen." In *Geschichte und Gegenwart. Festschrift für Karl Dietrich Erdmann.* Ed. Hartmut Boockmann, Kurt Jürgensen, and Gerhard Stoltenberg. Neumünster: Wachholtz, 1980, pp. 233–73.

Heater, Derek, *National Self-Determination: Woodrow Wilson and his Legacy.* New York: St. Martin's, 1994.

Heilbrunn, Rudolf. "Bismarcks blinder Hofjude." *Jahrbuch des Instituts fur Deutsche Geschichte* (Tel Aviv) 10 (1981): 283–317.

Helmreich, Ernst C. *The Diplomacy of the Balkan Wars, 1912–1913*. Cambridge, MA: Harvard University Press, 1938.

Helmreich, Paul C. *From Paris to Sèvres*. Columbus: Ohio State University Press, 1974.

Henrard, Kristin. *Devising an Adequate System of Minority Protection*. The Hague: Nijhoff, 2000.

Henry, Paul. *L'abdication du Prince Cuza et l'avènement de la dynastie des Hohenzollern au trône de la Roumanie*. Paris: F. Alcan, 1930.

Herlihy, Patricia. *Odessa: A History, 1794–1914*. Cambridge, MA: Harvard University Press, 1986.

Herrmann, David G. *The Arming of Europe and the Making of the First World War*. Princeton, NJ: Princeton University Press, 1996.

Higham, John. *Strangers in the Land*. 2nd ed. New York: Atheneum, 1973.

Hildesheimer, Esriel. "Die Versuche zur Schaffung einer jüdischen Gesamtorganisation während der Weimarer Republik, 1919–1933." *Jahrbuch des Instituts für Deutsche Geschichte* (Tel Aviv) 8 (1979): 334–64.

Hitchins, Keith. *Rumania, 1866–1947*. Oxford: Clarendon, 1994.

Hobsbawm, Eric. *The Age of Empire, 1875–1914*. London: Weidenfeld & Nicolson, 1987.

Hoffmann-Holter, Beatrix. *"Abreisendmachung": Jüdische Kriegsflüchtlinge in Wien 1914 bis 1923*. Vienna: Böhlau, 1995.

Holmes, Colin. *Anti-Semitism in British Society, 1876–1939*. London: Arnold, 1979.

Horak, Stephan M. *The First Treaty of World War I: Ukraine's Treaty with the Central Powers of February 9, 1918*. New York: Columbia University Press, 1988.

Poland and Her National Minorities, 1919–1939. New York: Vantage, 1961.

Horne, John N. and Alan Kramer. *German Atrocities, 1914: A History of Denial*. New Haven, CT: Yale University Press, 2001.

Hovannisian, Richard G. "The Allies and Armenia, 1915–18." *Journal of Contemporary History* 3 (1968): 145–68.

Hovi, Kalevo. *Cordon sanitaire ou barrière de l'est*. Turku, Finland: Turun Yliopisto, 1975.

Howard, Harry N. *The King–Crane Commission*. Beirut: Khayats, 1963.

The Partition of Turkey. Norman, OK: University of Oklahoma Press, 1931.

Hunczak, Taras. "Sir Lewis Namier and the Struggle for Eastern Galicia, 1918–1920." *Harvard Ukrainian Studies* 1 (1977): 198–210.

Hurewitz, J. C. *The Struggle for Palestine*. New York: Greenwood, 1968.

Hyman, Paula. *From Dreyfus to Vichy: The Remaking of French Jewry, 1906–1939*. New York, Columbia University Press, 1979.

Iancu, Carol. "Adolphe Crémieux, l'Alliance Israélite Universelle et les juifs de Roumanie au début du règne de Carol Hohenzollern Sigmaringen." *Revue des Études Juives* 133 (1974): 481–502.

"Adolphe Crémieux et la défense des droits des juifs au XIXe siècle." In *Armand Lunel et les juifs du Midi*. Ed. Carol Iancu. Montpellier: Centre de Recherches et d'Études Juives et Hébraïques, Université Paul Valéry, 1986, pp. 245–75.

L'émancipation des juifs de Roumanie (1913–1919). Montpellier: Centre de Recherches et d'Études Juives et Hébraïques, 1992.

Les juifs en Roumanie (1866–1919): De l'exclusion à l'émancipation. Aix-en-Provence: Éditions de l'Université de Provence, 1978.

Les juifs en Roumanie (1919–1938): De l'émancipation à la marginalisation. Paris and Louvain: Peeters, 1996.

"Napoléon III et la politique française à l'égard de la Roumanie." *Revue d'Histoire Diplomatique*, Nos. 1–2 (1974): 59–85.

Jackson, J. Hampden. *Clemenceau and the Third Republic.* London: Hodder & Stoughton, 1946.

Jackson Preece, Jennifer, *National Minorities and the European Nation-States System.* Oxford: Clarendon Press, 1998.

Janowsky, Oscar I. *The Jews and Minority Rights (1898–1919).* New York: Columbia University Press, 1933.

Jaworski, Rudolf. "The German Minorities in Poland and Czechoslovakia in the Interwar Period." In *Ethnic Groups in International Relations: Comparative Studies on Governments and Non-Dominant Ethnic Groups in Europe, 1850–1940.* Ed. Paul Smith. New York: New York University Press, 1991, Vol. 5, pp. 169–85.

Jelavich, Barbara. *A Century of Russian Foreign Policy, 1814–1914.* New York: Lippincott, 1964.

History of the Balkans. Cambridge: Cambridge University Press, 1983.

"Romania at the Congress of Berlin." In *Der Berliner Kongress von 1878.* Ed. Ralph Melville and Hans-Jürgen Schroeder. Wiesbaden: Steiner, 1982, pp. 189–204.

Russia's Balkan Entanglements, 1806–1914. Cambridge: Cambridge University Press, 1991.

Jochmann, Werner. "Die Ausbreitung des Antisemitismus." In *Deutsches Judentum in Krieg und Revolution, 1916–1923.* Ed. Werner Mosse. Tübingen: Mohr, 1971, pp. 409–510.

Gesellschaftskrise und Judenfeindschaft in Deutschland, 1870–1945. Hamburg: Christians, 1988.

Jonca, Karol. "Jewish Resistance to Nazi Racial Legislation in Silesia, 1933–1937." In *Germans Against Nazism. Non-Conformity, Opposition and Resistance in the Third Reich.* Ed. Francis R. Nicosia and Lawrence D. Stokes. New York: Berg, 1990, pp. 77–86.

Judd, Robin. "The Politics of Beef: Animal Advocacy and the Kosher Butchering Debates in Germany." *Jewish Social Studies* (Fall 2003): 117–50.

Judge, Edward H. *Easter in Kishinev: Anatomy of a Pogrom.* New York: New York University Press, 1992.

Kadish, Sharman. *Bolsheviks and British Jews: The Anglo-Jewish Community, Britain, and the Russian Revolution.* London: Frank Cass, 1992.

Kann, Robert A. *The Multinational Empire: Nationalism and National Reform in the Habsburg Monarchy, 1848–1918.* 2 vols. New York: Columbia University Press, 1950.

Keiger, John F. V. "Raymond Poincaré and the Ruhr Crisis." In *French Foreign and Defence Policy, 1918–1940: The Decline and Fall of a Great Power.* Ed. Robert Boyce. London: Routledge, 1998, pp. 49–70.

Kent, Marian. "Asiatic Turkey, 1914–1916." In *British Foreign Policy Under Sir Edward Grey*. Ed. F. H. Hinsley. Cambridge: Cambridge University Press, 1977, pp. 436–51.

Kertzer, David I. *The Kidnapping of Edgardo Mortara*. New York: Knopf, 1997.

Kimmich, Christoph. *Germany and the League of Nations*. Chicago: University of Chicago Press, 1976.

Kirby, David. *War, Peace and Revolution: International Socialism at the Crossroads, 1914–1918*. New York: St. Martin's, 1986.

Kitchen, Martin. *The Silent Dictatorship: The Politics of the German High Command under Hindenburg and Ludendorff, 1916–1918*. London: Croom Helm, 1976.

Klieman, Aaron S. "Britain's War Aims in the Middle East in 1915." *Journal of Contemporary History* 3 (1968): 237–51.

Klier, John. "The Jews." In *Critical Companion to the Russian Revolution 1914–1921*. Ed. Edward Acton, Vladimir Iu. Cherniaev, and William Rosenberg. Bloomington, IN: Indiana University Press, 1997, pp. 693–705.

"The Pogrom Tradition in Eastern Europe." In *Racist Violence in Europe*. Ed. Tore Björgo and Rob Witte. New York: St. Martin's, 1993, pp. 128–38.

Klier, John D. and Shlomo Lambroza, eds. *Pogroms: Anti-Jewish Violence in Modern Russian History*. Cambridge: Cambridge University Press, 1992.

Knock, Thomas J. *To End All Wars: Woodrow Wilson and the Quest for a New World Order*. New York: Oxford University Press, 1992.

Kocka, Jürgen. *Facing Total War: German Society, 1914–1918*. Trans. Barbara Weinberger. Cambridge, MA: Harvard University Press, 1984.

Komarnicki, Titus. *Rebirth of the Polish Republic*. London: Heinemann, 1957.

Korn, Itzhak. *El Congreso Judio Mundia: 40 años de lucha por los derechos del pueblo Judio*. Trans. Marcelo Sneh. Buenos Aires: Congreso Judio Latinoamericano, 1975.

Korzec, Pawel. *Juifs en Pologne*. Paris: Presses de la Fondation Nationale des Sciences Politiques, 1980.

"Polen und der Minderheitenschutzvertrag (1919–1934)." *Jahrbücher für Geschichte Osteuropas* 4 (1975): 515–55.

"The Ukrainian Problem in Interwar Poland." In *Ethnic Groups in International Relations: Comparative Studies on Governments and Non-Dominant Ethnic Groups in Europe, 1850–1940*. Ed. Paul Smith. New York: New York University Press, 1991, Vol. 5, pp. 187–210.

Koufa, Kalliopi K. and Constantinos Svolopoulos. "The Compulsory Exchange of Populations Between Greece and Turkey: The Settlement of Minority Questions at the Conference of Lausanne, 1923, and Its Impact on Greek–Turkish Relations." In *Ethnic Groups in International Relations: Comparative Studies on Governments and Non-Dominant Ethnic Groups in Europe, 1850–1940*. Ed. Paul Smith. New York: New York University Press, 1991, Vol. 5, pp. 275–308.

Kraut, Alan M., Richard Breitman, and Thomas W. Imhoof. "The State Department, the Labor Department, and German Jewish Immigration, 1930–1940." *American Jewish History* 7 (1998): 23–56.

Krekeler, Norbert. *Revisionsanspruch und geheime Ostpolitik der Weimarer Republik: Die Subventionierung der deutschen Minderheit in Polen, 1919–1933*. Stuttgart: Deutsche Verlags-Anstalt, 1973.

Krüger, Peter. "Zur europäischen Dimension der Aussenpolitik Gustav Stresemanns." In Karl Heinrich Pohl ed. *Politik und Bürger: Gustav Stresemann und seine Zeit.* Göttingen: Vandenhoeck und Ruprecht, 2002, pp. 194–228.

Kułakowski, Mariusz. *Roman Dmowski w swietle listów i wspomnień.* London: Gryf, 1972.

Kusielewicz, Eugene F. V. "The Teschen Question at the Paris Peace Conference." Ph.D. dissertation, Fordham University, 1963.

Lacaze, Yvon. *La France et Munich.* Berne: Lang, 1992.

Landau, Philippe-E. *Les juifs de France et la grande guerre: Un patriotisme républicain.* Paris: Centre National de la Recherche Scientifique, 1999.

Lapidoth, Ruth. *Autonomy: Flexible Solutions to Ethnic Conflicts.* Washington, DC: United States Institute of Peace Press, 1996.

Latawski, Paul. "The Dmowski–Namier Feud." *Polin* 2 (1987): 37–49.

"Roman Dmowski, the Polish Question, and Western Opinion, 1915–18: The Case of Britain." In *The Reconstruction of Poland, 1914–23.* Ed. Paul Latawski. New York: St. Martin's, 1992, pp. 1–12.

Lauren, Paul Gordon. *The Evolution of International Human Rights: Visions Seen.* 2nd ed. Philadelphia: University of Pennsylvania Press, 2003.

"Human Rights in History: Diplomacy and Racial Equality at the Paris Peace Conference." *Diplomatic History* 2 (1978): 257–78.

Lebzelter, Gisela C. *Political Anti-Semitism in England, 1918–1939.* London: Macmillan, 1978.

LeDonne, John P. *The Russian Empire and the World, 1700–1917.* New York/ Oxford: Oxford University Press, 1997.

Lemke, Horst. *Allianz und Rivalität: Die Mittelmächte und Polen im Ersten Weltkrieg.* Vienna: Böhlaus Nachf., 1977.

Lentin, Antony "Several Types of Ambiguity: Lloyd George at the Paris Peace Conference." *Diplomacy and Statecraft* 6 (Mar. 1995): 223–51.

Lerski, George J., comp. *Herbert Hoover and Poland.* Stanford, CA: Stanford University Press, 1977.

Leslie, R. F., Antony Polonsky, Jan M. Ciechanowski, and Z. A. Pelczynski. *The History of Poland Since 1863.* Cambridge: Cambridge University Press, 1980.

Lestschinsky, Jacob. "Dubnow's Autonomism and His 'Letters on Old and New Judaism.'" In *Simon Dubnow: The Man and His Work.* Ed. Aaron Steinberg. Paris: French Section of the World Jewish Congress, 1963, pp. 73– 91.

Levene, Mark. "Frontiers of Genocide: Jews in the Eastern War Zones, 1914–1920 and 1941." In *Minorities in Wartime: National and Racial Groupings in Europe, North America, and Australia during the Two World Wars.* Ed. Panikos Panayi. Providence, RI: Berg, 1993, pp. 83–117.

"Lucien Wolf: Crypto-Zionist, Anti-Zionist or Opportunist *par-excellence*?" *Studies in Zionism* 12 (1991): 133–48.

"Nationalism and Its Alternatives in the International Arena: The Jewish Question at Paris, 1919." *Journal of Contemporary History* 28 (1993): 511–31.

War, Jews, and the New Europe: The Diplomacy of Lucien Wolf, 1914–1919. Oxford: Oxford University Press, 1992.

Lewandowski, Józef. *Federalizm: Litwa i Bialoruś w polityce obozu belwederskiego, XI 1918–VI 1920.* Warsaw: Pánstwowe Wydawn. Naukowe, 1962.

"History and Myth: Pińsk, April 1919." *Polin* 2 (1987): 5–36.

Lewis, Bernard. *The Jews of Islam.* Princeton, NJ: Princeton University Press, 1984.

Lindemann, Albert S. *The Jew Accused: Three Anti-Semitic Affairs (Dreyfus, Beilis, Frank), 1894–1915.* Cambridge: Cambridge University Press, 1991.

Link, Arthur S. *Wilson.* 5 vols. Princeton, NJ: Princeton University Press, 1947–65.

Linke, Horst Günter. *Das zarische Russland und der Erste Weltkrieg.* Munich: Wilhelm Fink, 1982.

Linke, Uli. *Blood and Nation: The European Aesthetics of Race.* Philadelphia: University of Pennsylvania Press, 1999.

Lipman, V. D. *A History of the Jews in Britain Since 1858.* Leicester: Leicester University Press, 1990.

Lohr, Eric. "The Russian Army and the Jews: Mass Deportation, Hostages, and Violence During World War I." *Russian Review* 60 (2001): 404–19.

Lohrmann, Klaus. *Zwischen Finanz und Toleranz: Das Haus Habsburg und die Juden.* Graz: Styria, 2000.

Lord, Robert Howard. "The Congress of Berlin." In Charles D. Hazen, William R. Thayer, and Robert H. Lord, *Three Peace Conferences of the Nineteenth Century.* Cambridge, MA: Harvard University Press, 1919.

Lory, Bernard. "1912, les hellènes entrent dans la ville." In *Salonique, 1850–1918.* Ed. Gilles Veinstein. Paris: Éditions Autremont, 1993, pp. 247–53.

Lossoski, Piotr. *Stosunki polsko–litewskie w latach, 1918–20.* Warsaw: Książka i Wiedza, 1966.

Luke, Henry Charles and Edward Keith-Roach. *The Handbook of Palestine and Trans-Jordan.* London: Macmillan, 1930.

Lundgreen-Nielsen, Kay. *The Polish Problem at the Paris Peace Conference.* Trans. Alison Borch-Johansen. Odense: Odense University Press, 1979.

"Woodrow Wilson and the Rebirth of Poland." In *Woodrow Wilson and a Revolutionary World, 1913–1921.* Ed. Arthur S. Link. Chapel Hill, NC: University of North Carolina Press, 1982, pp. 105–26.

Macartney, C. A. *National States and National Minorities.* London: Royal Institute of International Affairs, 1934. 2nd ed., London: Russell & Russell, 1968.

Macartney, C. A. and A. W. Palmer. *Independent Eastern Europe: A History.* London: Macmillan, 1966.

Machray, Robert. *Poland, 1914–1931.* London: Allen and Unwin, 1932.

MacKenzie, David. *Imperial Dreams, Harsh Realities: Tsarist Russian Foreign Policy, 1815–1917.* Fort Worth, TX: Harcourt, Brace, 1994.

The Serbs and Russian Pan-Slavism. Ithaca, NY: Cornell University Press, 1967.

Magocsi, Paul R. *The Rusyn-Ukrainians of Czechoslovakia: An Historical Survey.* Vienna: Braumüller, 1983.

Mamatey, Victor S. *The United States and East Central Europe.* Princeton, NJ: Princeton University Press, 1957.

Manual, Frank. *The Realities of American-Palestine Relations.* Washington, DC: Public Affairs Press, 1949.

Marcus, Ernst. "The German Foreign Office and the Palestine Question in the Period 1933–1939." *Yad Vashem Studies* 2 (1958): 179–204.

Marcus, Joseph. *Social and Political History of the Jews in Poland, 1919–1939.* Berlin: Mouton, 1983.

Markovits, Andrei S. and Frank E. Sysyn. *Nationbuilding and the Politics of Nationalism: Essays on Austrian Galicia.* Cambridge, MA: Harvard University Press, 1982.

Marrus, Michael. *The Unwanted: European Refugees in the Twentieth Century.* New York: Oxford University Press, 1985.

Marshall, Philip R. "William Henry Waddington: The Making of a Diplomat." *The Historian* 38 (1975): 79–97.

Marston, F. S. *The Peace Conference of 1919: Organisation and Procedure.* Oxford: Oxford University Press, 1944.

Matkovski, Aleksandar. *A History of the Jews in Macedonia.* Trans. David Arney. Skopje: Macedonian Review Editions, 1982.

Maurer, Trude. *Ostjuden in Deutschland, 1918–1933.* Hamburg: Hans Christians Verlag, 1986.

Mayer, Arno. *Political Origins of the New Diplomacy.* New Haven, CT: Yale University Press, 1959.

Politics and Diplomacy of Peacemaking: Containment and Counterrevolution at Versailles. New York: Knopf, 1967.

McCagg, William O. *A History of Habsburg Jews, 1670–1918.* Bloomington, IN: Indiana University Press, 1989.

Medlicott, W. N. *The Congress of Berlin and After: A Diplomatic History of the Near Eastern Settlement, 1878–1880.* 2nd. ed. London: Frank Cass, 1963.

"The Recognition of Roumanian Independence, 1878–1880." *Slavonic and East European Review* 11 (1932): 354–72, 572–89.

Meisl, Josef. *Die Durchführung des Artikels 44 des Berliner Vertrages in Rumänien und die europäische Diplomatie.* Berlin: No publisher, 1925.

Melson, Robert. *Revolution and Genocide: On the Origins of the Armenian Genocide and the Holocaust.* Chicago: University of Chicago Press, 1992.

Mendelsohn, Ezra. *Zionism in Poland: The Formative Years, 1915–1926.* New Haven, CT: Yale University Press, 1981.

Miall, Hugh, ed. *Minority Rights in Europe: The Scope for a Transnational Regime.* London: Pinter, 1994.

Mick, Christoph. "Nationalisierung in einer multiethnischen Stadt: Interethnische Konflikte in Lemberg, 1890–1920." *Archiv für Sozialgeschichte* 40 (2000): 113–46.

Milojković-Djurić, Jelena. *Panslavism and National Identity in Russia and in the Balkans.* Boulder: East European Monographs; New York: Columbia University Press, 1994.

Minc, Mattiyahu. "Kiev Zionists and the Ukranian National Movement." In *Ukrainian–Jewish Relations in Historical Perspective.* 2nd ed. Ed. Howard Aster and Peter J. Potichnyj. Edmonton: Canadian Institute of Ukrainian Studies, pp. 247–61.

Mitchell, Pearl Boring. *The Bismarckian Policy of Conciliation with France, 1875–1885.* Philadelphia: University of Pennsylvania Press, 1935.

Molho, Rena. "The Jewish Community of Salonika and Its Incorporation into the Greek State (1912–1919)." *Middle Eastern Studies* 24 (1988): 391–403.

"Venizelos and the Jewish Community of Salonika, 1912–1919." *Journal of the Hellenic Diaspora* 13 (1986): 113–23.

Mosse, Werner. "Die Krise der europäischen Bourgeoisie und das Deutsche Judentum." In *Deutsches Judentum in Krieg und Revolution, 1916–1923*. Ed. Werner Mosse. Tübingen: Mohr, 1971, pp. 1–26.

Motzkin, Gabriel. "Leo Motzkin and Minority Rights, 1914–1919." Honor's B.A. thesis, Harvard University, 1967.

Mrocza, Ludwik. "Przyczynek do kwestii żydowskiej w Galicji u progu Drugiej Rzeczpospolitej." In Feliks Kiryk, ed. *Żydzi w Małopolsce: Studia z dziejów osadnictwa i życia społecznego*. Przemyśyl: Południowo-Wschodni Instytut Naukowy w Przemyślu, 1991, pp. 297–308.

Munro, Henry F. *The Berlin Congress*. Washington, DC: Government Printing Office, 1918.

Nahayewski, Isidore. *History of the Modern Ukrainian State, 1917–1923*. Munich: Ukrainian Free University, 1966.

Namier, Lewis. *1848: The Revolution of the Intellectuals*. New ed. Oxford: Oxford University Press, 1992.

Nere, Jacques. *The Foreign Policy of France, 1914–1945*. London: Routledge & K. Paul, 1975.

Nicault, Catherine. *La France et le sionisme, 1897–1948*. Paris: Calmann-Lévy, 1992.

Nicosia, Francis R. "Arab Nationalism and National Socialist Germany, 1933–1939: Ideological and Strategic Incompatibility." *International Journal of Middle East Studies* 12 (1980): 351–72.

The Third Reich & the Palestine Question. New Brunswick, NJ: Transaction, 2000.

Niewyk, Donald. *The Jews in Weimar Germany*. Baton Rouge, LA: Louisiana State University Press, 1980.

Nolte, Claire E. "The New Central Europe of Thomas Garrigue Masaryk." In *Wilsonian East Central Europe: Current Perspectives*. Ed. John S. Micgiel. New York: The Piłsudski Institute, 1995, pp. 7–24.

Norman, Theodore. *An Outstretched Arm: A History of the Jewish Colonization Association*. London: Routledge & K. Paul, 1985.

Offner, Arnold. *American Appeasement: United States Foreign Policy and Germany, 1933–1938*. New York: Norton, 1969.

O'Grady, Joseph P., ed. *The Immigrants' Influence on Wilson's Peace Policies*. Lexington, KY: University of Kentucky Press, 1967.

Oldson, William O. *A Providential Anti-Semitism: Nationalism and Polity in Nineteenth Century Romania*. Philadelphia: American Philosophical Society, 1991.

Opalski, Magdalena and Israel Bartal. *Poles and Jews: A Failed Brotherhood*. Hanover, NH: Brandeis University Press, University Press of New England, 1992.

Otetea, Andrei, ed. *The History of the Romanian People*. Trans. Eugenia Farca. New York: Twayne, 1970.

Panayi, Panikos. "Dominant Societies and Minorities in the Two World Wars." In *Minorities in Wartime*. Ed. Panikos Panayi. Oxford: Berg, 1993, pp. 3–26.

Pauley, Bruce F. *From Prejudice to Persecution: A History of Austrian Anti-Semitism*. Chapel Hill, NC: University of North Carolina Press, 1992.

Pazdur, Jan. *Dzieje Kielc do 1863*. Wrocław: Zakład Narodowy im Ossolińskich, 1967.

Dzieje Kielc, 1864–1939. Wrocław: Zakład Narodowy im Ossolińskich, 1971.

Pearson, Raymond. *National Minorities in Eastern Europe, 1848–1945*. London/Basingstoke: Macmillan, 1983.

Pease, Neal. *Poland, the United States, and the Stabilization of Europe, 1919–1933*. New York: Oxford, 1986.

Perman, Dagmar. *The Shaping of the Czechoslovak State: Diplomatic History of the Boundaries of Czechoslovakia*. Leiden: Brill, 1962.

Perry, Duncan. *The Politics of Terror: The Macedonian Liberation Movements, 1893–1903*. Durham, NC: Duke University Press, 1988.

Pieper, Helmut. *Die Minderheitenfrage und das Deutsche Reich, 1919–1933/34*. Hamburg: Institut für Internationale Angelegenheiten der Universität Hamburg, 1974.

Pinson, Koppel S. "The National Theories of Simon Dubnow." *Jewish Social Studies* 7 (1948): 335–58.

Plaut, Joshua E. *Greek Jewry in the Twentieth Century, 1913–1983*. Madison, NJ: Fairleigh Dickinson University Press, 1996.

Polvinen, Tuomo. *Imperial Borderland: Bobrikov and the Attempted Russification of Finland, 1898–1904*. Trans. Steven Huxley. Durham, NC: Duke University Press, 1995.

Porath, Yehoshua. *The Palestinian Arab National Movement, 1919–1939*. London: Frank Cass, 1977.

Posener, S [Solomon]. *Adolphe Crémieux: A Biography*. Trans. Eugene Golob. Philadelphia: Jewish Publication Society of America, 1940.

Posey, John P. "David Hunter Miller and the Far Eastern Question at the Paris Peace Conference, 1919." *The Southern Quarterly* 7 (1969): 373–92.

"David Hunter Miller as an Informal Diplomat: The Fiume Question at the Paris Peace Conference, 1919." *The Southern Quarterly* 5 (1967): 251–72.

"David Hunter Miller and the Polish Minorities Treaty, 1919." *The Southern Quarterly* 8 (1970): 163–76.

Pulzer, Peter G. J. *Jews and the German State: The Political History of a Minority, 1848–1933*. Oxford: Blackwell, 1992.

The Rise of Political Anti-Semitism in Germany and Austria. Rev. ed. Cambridge, MA: Harvard University Press, 1988.

Pundeff, Marin V. "Bulgarian Nationalism: Roots of National Consciousness." In *Nationalism in Eastern Europe*. 2nd ed. Ed. Peter F. Sugar and Ivo John Lederer. Seattle, WA: University of Washington Press, 1994, pp. 93–165.

Quinlan, Paul D. "Early American Relations with Romania, 1858–1914." *Canadian Slavonic Papers* 22 (1980): 187–94.

Rabinowitch, Wolf Zeev. *Studies in Pinsk Jewry*. Haifa: Association of the Jews of Pinsk in Israel, 1983.

Raschhofer, Hermann. *Völkerbund und Münchener Abkommen*. Vienna: Olzog, 1976.

Ratliff, William G. "Julius Curtius, the Minorities Question of 1930–31, and the *Primat der Innenpolitik*." *German Studies Review* 12 (1989): 271–88.

Reichmann, Eva G. "Der Bewusstseinswandel der deutschen Juden." In *Deutsches Judentum in Krieg und Revolution, 1916–1923.* Ed. Werner Mosse. Tübingen: Mohr, 1971, pp. 511–612.

Renouvin, Pierre. "Les buts de guerre du gouvernement français, 1914–1918." *Revue Historique* 235 (1966): 1–37.

Reznikoff, Charles. *Louis Marshall: Champion of Liberty.* 2 vols. Philadelphia: Jewish Publication Society, 1957.

Riccardi, Luca. *Alleati non amici: Le relazioni politiche tra Italia e l'intese durante la prima guerra mondiale.* Brescia: Morcelliana, 1992.

Rich, Norman. *Great Power Diplomacy, 1814–1914.* New York: McGraw-Hill, 1992.

Riker, T. W. *The Making of Roumania: A Study of an International Problem, 1856–1866.* London: Oxford University Press, 1931.

Rollet, Henry. *La Pologne au XXe siècle.* Paris: Pedone, 1984.

Roos, Hans. *Geschichte der polnische Nation, 1918–1978.* 3rd ed. Stuttgart: Kohlhammer, 1979.

Rose, Norman. *Chaim Weizmann.* New York: Viking, 1986.

Rosenstock, Morton. *Louis Marshall, Defender of Jewish Rights.* Detroit, MI: Wayne State University Press, 1965.

Rosenthal, Jerome C. "The Public Life of Louis Marshall." Ph.D. dissertation, University of Cincinnati, 1983.

Rosillo, Matilde Morcillo. "Essai sur la communauté séfardie de Salonique durant le premier tiers du XXe siècle." In *Jewish Communities of Southeastern Europe From the Fifteenth Century to the End of World War II.* Ed. I. K. Hassiotis. Thessaloniki: Institute for Balkan Studies, 1997, pp. 351–64.

Rossini, Daniela. "'Alleati per caso': Il colonnello House, la diplomazia americana e l'Italia durante la grande guerra." *Storia delle Relazioni Internazionali* 11–12 (1996–7): 3–38.

Roth, Norman. *Jews, Visigoths, and Muslims in Medieval Society.* Leiden: Brill, 1994.

Rothschild, Joseph. *East Central Europe Between the Two World Wars.* Seattle, WA: University of Washington Press, 1974.

Rothwell, V. H. *British War Aims and Peace Diplomacy, 1914–1918.* Oxford: Clarendon, 1971.

Rouland, N., S. Pierre-Caps, and J. Poumarède. *Droit des minorités et des peuples autochtones.* Paris: Presses Universitaires de France, 1996.

Rudin, Harry. *Armistice 1918.* New Haven, CT: Yale University Press, 1944.

Rutland, Suzanne D. "Australia and Refugee Migration, 1933–1945: Consensus or Conflict?" *Menorah* 2 (Dec. 1978): 77–91.

Sachar, Howard M. *A History of Israel.* New York: Knopf, 1988.

Sanders, Michael, *British Propaganda During the First World War, 1914–18.* London: Macmillan, 1982.

Saul, Norman E. *Concord and Conflict: The United States and Russia, 1867–1914.* Lawrence, KS: University Press of Kansas, 1996.

Scheidemann, Christiane. *Ulrich Graf Brockdorff-Rantzau (1869–1928): Eine politische Biographie.* Frankfurt am Main: Peter Lang, 1998.

Schleunes, Karl A. *The Twisted Road to Auschwitz: Nazi Policy Toward German Jews, 1933–1939.* Urbana, IL: University of Illinois Press, 1970.

Schmitt, Bernadotte E. and Harold C. Vedeler. *The World in the Crucible, 1914–1919.* New York: Harper & Row, 1984.

Schot, Bastian. *Nation oder Staat? Deutschland und der Minderheitenschutz.* Marburg/Lahn: J.G. Herder-Institut, 1988.

Schottenstein, Isaac Morris. "The Abrogation of the Treaty of 1832 between the United States and Russia." M.A. thesis, Ohio State University, 1960.

Schroeder, Paul. *Austria, Great Britain, and the Crimean War: The Destruction of the European Concert System.* Ithaca, NY: Cornell University Press, 1972.

Schwabe, Klaus. *Woodrow Wilson, Revolutionary Germany, and Peacemaking, 1918–1919.* Trans. Rita and Robert Kimber. Chapel Hill, NC: University of North Carolina Press, 1985.

Schwarz, Isaac I. *25 Years in the Service of the Jewish People.* New York: World Jewish Congress, 1957.

Sevenster, Jan. *The Roots of Pagan Antisemitism.* Leiden: Brill, 1975.

Shanafelt, Gary W. *The Secret Enemy: Austria–Hungary and the German Alliance, 1914–1918.* New York: Columbia University Press, 1985.

Sharp, Alan. "Britain and the Protection of Minorities at the Paris Peace Conference." In *Minorities in History.* Ed. A. C. Hepburn. London: Arnold, 1978, pp. 170–188.

"The Genie That Would Not Go Back into the Bottle: National Self-Determination and the Legacy of the First World War and the Peace Settlement." In *Europe and Ethnicity: World War I and Contemporary Ethnic Conflict.* Ed. Seamus Dunn and T. G. Fraser. London/New York: Routledge, 1996. pp. 10–29.

The Versailles Settlement: Peacemaking in Paris, 1919. New York: St. Martin's, 1991.

Sherman, A. J. *Island Refuge: Britain and the Refugees From the Third Reich, 1933–1939.* Berkeley, CA: University of California Press, 1973.

Shimazu, Naoko. *Japan, Race and Equality: The Racial Equality Proposal of 1919.* London: Routledge, 1998.

Sicker, Martin. *Reshaping Palestine.* Westport, CT: Praeger, 1999.

Silbermann, Alphons. "Deutsche Juden oder jüdische Deutsche? Zur Identität der Juden in der Weimarer Republik." In *Juden in der Weimarer Republik.* Ed. Walter Grab and Julius Schoeps. Stuttgart: Burg, 1986, pp. 347–55.

Skendi, Stavro. *The Albanian National Awakening, 1878–1912.* Princeton, NJ: Princeton University Press, 1967.

Skordylès, Kostas E. "Réactions juives à l'annexion de Salonique par la Grèce." In *Jewish Communities of Southeastern Europe From the Fifteenth Century to the End of World War II.* Ed. I. K. Hassiotis. Thessaloniki: Institute for Balkan Studies, 1997, pp. 501–15.

Smith, Charles D. *Palestine and the Arab-Israeli Conflict.* New York: St. Martin's, 1988.

Sontag, Raymond J. *European Diplomatic History, 1871–1932.* New York: Appleton-Century-Crofts, 1933.

Sowards, Steven W. *Austria's Policy of Macedonian Reform.* Boulder, CO: East European Monographs; New York: Columbia University Press, 1989.

Spear, Sheldon. "The United States and the Persecution of the Jews in Germany, 1933–1939." *American Jewish History* 7 (1998): 72–98.

Spector, Sherman D. *Rumania at the Paris Peace Conference*. New York: Bookman, 1962.

Stachiw, M. and J. Sztendera. *Western Ukraine at the Turning Point of Europe's History, 1918–1923*. New York: Shevchenko Scientific Society, 1969.

Stachura, Peter D. "National Identity and the Ethnic Minorities in Early Inter-War Poland." In *Poland Between the Wars, 1918–1939*. Ed. Peter D. Stachura. Houndsmill/London: Macmillan, 1998, pp. 60–86.

Starr, Joshua. "Jewish Citizenship in Rumania." *Jewish Social Studies* 3 (Jan. 1941): 57–80.

Staudenraus, P. J. *The African Colonization Movement, 1816–1865*. New York: Columbia University Press, 1961.

Stein, Leonard. *The Balfour Declaration*. London: Vallentine Mitchell, 1961.

Stern, Fritz. *Gold and Iron: Bismarck, Bleichröder, and the Building of the German Empire*. New York: Random House, 1977.

Sternhell, Zeev. "The Roots of Popular Anti-Semitism in the Third Republic." In *The Jews in Modern France*. Ed. Frances Malino and Bernard Wasserstein. Hanover, NH: University Press of New England, 1985, pp. 103–34.

Stevenson, David. *The First World War and International Politics*. Oxford: Oxford University Press, 1988.

Stillschweig, Kurt. *Die Juden Osteuropas in den Minderheitenverträgen*. Berlin: Jastrow, 1936.

Stone, Daniel. "Polish Diplomacy and the American Jewish Community between the Wars." *Polin* 2 (1987): 74–94.

Stone, Julius, *International Guarantees of Minority Rights*. Oxford: Oxford University Press, 1932.

Regional Guarantees of Minority Rights. New York: Macmillan, 1933.

Straus, Hannah A. *The Attitude of the Congress of Vienna Toward Nationalism in Germany, Italy, and Poland*. New York: Columbia University Press, 1949.

Strauss, Herbert A., ed. *Hostages of Modernization: Studies on Modern Antisemitism, 1870–1939*. 2 vols. Berlin and New York: Walter de Gruyter, 1992–93.

Strazhas, Abba. *Deutsche Ostpolitik im Ersten Weltkrieg: Der Fall Ober Ost, 1915–1917*. Wiesbaden: Harrassowitz, 1993.

Stresemann, Wolfgang. *Mein Vater Gustav Stresemann*. Munich: Herbig, 1979.

Sukiennicki, Wiktor *East Central Europe During World War I: From Foreign Domination to National Independence*. New York: Columbia University Press, 1984.

Sumner, B. H. *Russia and the Balkans, 1870–1880*. Oxford: Oxford University Press, 1937.

Suny, Ronald G. "Nationality Policies." In *Critical Companion to the Russian Revolution, 1914–1921*. Ed. Edward Acton, Vladimir Iu. Cherniaev and William Rosenberg. Bloomington, IN: Indiana University Press, 1997, pp. 659–66.

Surface, Frank M. and Raymond L. Bland. *American Food in the World War and Reconstruction Period: Operations of the Organizations under the direction of Herbert Hoover, 1919–1924*. Stanford, CA: Stanford University Press, 1931.

Sykes, Christopher. *Crossroads to Israel*. Bloomington, IN: Indiana University Press, 1973.

Szajkowski, Zosa. "The Attitude of American Jews to East European Immigration (1881–1893)." *Publications of the American Jewish Historical Society* 40 (1951): 221–80.

"East European Jewish Workers in Germany During World War I." [in Hebrew], In *Salo Wittmayer Baron Jubilee Volume on the Occasion of his 80th Birthday*. Ed. Saul Lieberman. New York: Columbia University Press, 1974, pp. 887–918.

"Jewish Diplomacy: Notes on the Occasion of the Centenary of the *Alliance Israélite Universelle*." *Jewish Social Studies* 22 (1960): 131–58.

Jews, Wars, and Communism. New York: Ktav, 1972.

"The Struggle for Yiddish During World War I. The Attitude of German Jewry." *Leo Baeck Institute Year Book* 9 (1975): 131–58.

Szporluk, Roman. "Polish–Ukrainian Relations in 1918: Notes for Discussion." In *The Reconstruction of Poland, 1914–1923*. Ed. Paul Latawski. Houndmills, Basingstoke, Hampshire: Macmillan, 1992, pp. 41–54.

Taylor, A. J. P. *The Struggle for Mastery in Europe*. Oxford: Oxford University Press, 1957.

Taylor, Telford. *Munich: The Price of Peace*. Garden City, NY: Doubleday, 1979.

Teich, Mukuláš and Roy Porter. *The National Question in Europe in Historical Context*. Cambridge: Cambridge University Press, 1993.

Ther, Philipp. "Chancen und Untergang einer multinationalen Stadt: Die Beziehungen zwischen den Nationalitäten in Lemberg in der ersten Hälfte des 20. Jahrhunderts." In *Nationalitätenkonflikte im 20. Jahrhundert*. Ed. Philipp Ther and Holm Sundhaussen. Wiesbaden: Harrassowitz, 2001, pp. 132–45.

Thompson, John M. *Russia, Bolshevism, and the Versailles Peace*. Princeton, NJ: Princeton University Press, 1966.

Thornberry, P. *International Law and the Rights of Minorities*. Oxford: Oxford University Press, 1991.

Tomaszewski, Jerzy. "Lwów, 22 listopada 1918." *Przegląd historyczny* 75 (1984): 279–81.

"Pińsk, Saturday 5 April 1919." *Polin* 1 (1986): 227–51.

Tomaszewski, Leszek. "Lwów – Listopad 1918. Niezwykłe losy pewnego dokumentu." ["Lwów – November 1918: The Unusual Vicissitudes of a Document".] *Dzieje Najnowsze Rocznik* 25 (1993): 163–73.

Tonini, Carla. *Operazione Madagascar: La questione ebraica in Polonia, 1918–1968*. Bologne: CLUEB, 1999.

Toscano, Mario. *South Tirol: Italy's Frontier with the German World*. Baltimore: Johns Hopkins University Press, 1975.

Treue, Wilhelm. "Zur Frage der wirtschaftlichen Motive in deutschen Antisemitismus." In *Deutsches Judentum in Krieg und Revolution, 1916–1923*. Ed. Werner Mosse. Tübingen: Mohr, 1971, pp. 387–408.

Troen, Selwyn Ilan and Benjamin Pinkus, eds. *Organizing Rescue: National Jewish Solidarity in the Modern Period*. London: Frank Cass, 1992.

Trumpener, Ulrich. *Germany and the Ottoman Empire, 1914–1918*. Princeton, NJ: Princeton University Press, 1968.

Turczynski, Emanuel. *Geschichte der Bukowina in der Neuzeit*. Wiesbaden: Harrassowitz, 1993.

Turner, Henry. "Eine Rede Stresemanns über seine Locarnopolitik." *Vierteljahrshefte für Zeitgeschichte* 15 (1967): 412–36.

Vermeil, Edmond. *La constitution de Weimar et le principe de la démocratie allemande*. Paris: Istra, 1923.

Viefhaus, Erwin. *Die Minderheitenfrage und die Entstehung der Minderheitenschutzverträge 1919*. Würzburg: Holzner, 1960.

Vital, David. "European Jewry, 1860–1919: Political Organisation and Trans-State Political Action." In *Ethnic Groups in International Relations*. Ed. Paul Smith. New York: New York University Press, 1991, Vol. 5, pp. 39–57.

The Origins of Zionism. Oxford: Clarendon, 1975.

Vogt, Dietrich. *Der grosspolnische Aufstand 1918/1919*. Marburg/Lahn: J. G. Herder-Institut, 1980.

Volovici, Leon. *Nationalist Ideology and Antisemitism*. Trans. Charles Kormos. Oxford: Pergamon, 1991.

Waller, Bruce. *Bismarck at the Crossroads*. London: Athlone, 1974.

Walters, F. P. *A History of the League of Nations*. London: Oxford, 1965.

Walworth, Arthur. "Considerations on Woodrow Wilson and Edward M. House." *Presidential Studies Quarterly* 24 (1994): 79–86.

Wilson and His Peacemakers. New York: Norton, 1986.

Wandycz, Piotr. *August Zaleski: Minister Spraw Zagranicznych RP 1926–32 w świetle wspomnień i dokumentów*. Paris: Instytut Literacki, 1980.

"Dmowski's Policy at the Paris Peace Conference: Success or Failure?" In *The Reconstruction of Poland*. Ed. Paul Latawski. New York: St. Martin's, 1992, pp. 117–32.

"The French *barrière de l'est* or *cordon sanitaire*." In *Wilsonian East Central Europe: Current Perspectives*. Ed. John S. Micgiel. New York: Piłsudski Institute, 1995, pp. 113–22.

The Lands of Partitioned Poland, 1795–1918. Seattle, WA: University of Washington Press, 1974.

Polish Diplomacy, 1914–1945: Aims and Achievements. London: Orbis, 1988.

"Polish Foreign Policy: An Overview." In *Poland Between the Wars, 1918–1939*. Ed. Timothy Wiles. Bloomington, IN: Indiana University Polish Studies Center, 1989, pp. 65–73.

"The Polish Question." In *The Treaty of Versailles: A Reassessment After 75 Years*. Ed. Manfred F. Boemeke, Gerald D. Feldman, and Elisabeth Glaser. Cambridge: Cambridge University Press, 1998, pp. 313–35.

Soviet–Polish Relations, 1917–21. Cambridge, MA: Harvard University Press, 1969.

The Twilight of French Eastern Alliances, 1926–1936. Princeton, NJ: Princeton University Press, 1988.

Wapiński, Roman. "Postawy i Oczekiwania: Kilka uwag o zachowaniach społeczeństwa polskiego w pierwszych miesiącach niepodległości (listopad 1918 – styczeń 1919)" ["Attitudes and Expectations: A Few Observations on the Behavior of Polish Society during the First Months of Independence (November 1918–January 1919)"]. *Kwartalnik Historyczny* 95(3) (1989): 73–85.

Warman, Roberta. "The Erosion of Foreign Office Influence in the Making of Foreign Policy, 1916–1918." *Historical Journal* 15 (1972): 133–59.

Weinberg, Gerhard. *The Foreign Policy of Hitler's Germany: Starting World War II, 1937–1939*. Chicago: University of Chicago Press, 1980.

ed. *Transformation of a Continent: Europe in the Twentieth Century*. Minneapolis, MN: Burgess, 1975.

Welter, Beate. *Die Judenpolitik der rumänischen Regierung, 1866–1888*. Frankfurt am Main: Peter Lang, 1989.

Wengst, Udo. *Graf Brockdorff-Rantzau und die aussenpolitischen Anfänge der Weimarer Republik*. Berne: Herbert Lang, 1973.

Wentling, Sonja P. "The Engineer and the *Shtadlanim*: Herbert Hoover and American Jewish Non-Zionists, 1917–28." *American Jewish History* 88 (2000): 337–406.

Wertheimer, Jack. *Unwelcome Strangers: East European Jews in Imperial Germany*. New York: Oxford University Press, 1987.

Wheeler-Bennett, John W. *The Forgotten Peace: Brest–Litovsk, March 1918*. New York: Morrow, 1939.

Wilson, Duncan. *Gilbert Murray 1866–1957*. Oxford: Clarendon Press, 1987.

Winckler, Martin. *Bismarcks Rumänienpolitik und die Durchführung der Artikels 44 des Berliner Vertrages (1878–1880)*. Ph.D. dissertation, Ludwig Maximilians-Universität zu München, 1951.

"Bismarcks Rumänienpolitik und die europäischen Grossmächte 1878/79." *Jahrbücher für Geschichte Osteuropas*. New Series 2 (1954): 53–88.

Wischnitzer, Mark. *To Dwell in Safety: The Storm of Jewish Migration since 1800*. Philadelphia: Jewish Publication Society of America, 1949.

Wolff, Stefan. "Changing Priorities or Changing Opportunities? German External Minority Policy, 1919–1998." In *German Minorities in Europe*. Ed. Stefan Wolff. New York/Oxford: Berghahn, 2000, pp. 183–203.

Woodward, C. Vann. *The Strange Career of Jim Crow*. 2nd ed. New York: Oxford University Press, 1966.

Wright, Jonathan. *Gustav Stresemann: Weimar's Greatest Statesman*. Oxford: Oxford University Press, 2002.

Yahil, Leni. "Madagascar: Phantom of a Solution for the Jewish Question." In *Jews and Non-Jews in Eastern Europe, 1918–1941*. Ed. Bela Vago and G. L. Mosse. New York: Wiley, 1974, pp. 315–34.

Yisraeli, David. "The Third Reich and Palestine." *Middle Eastern Studies* 7 (1971): 343–53.

Zake, Louis J. *The National Department and the Polish American Community, 1916–1923*. New York: Garland, 1990.

Zaklynski, Myron. "The November Overthrow and Battles for Lviv." In *Lviv: A Symposium on its 700th Anniversary*. New York: Shevchenko Scientific Society, 1962, pp. 191–202.

Zamoyski, Adam. *Paderewski*. New York: Atheneum, 1982.

Żarnowski, Janusz. *November 1918*. Trans. Jan Sek. Warsaw: Interpress, 1984.

Żbikowski, Andrzej. *Dzieje Żydów w Polsce*. Warsaw: Żydowski Instytut Historyczny w Polsce, 1994.

Zechlin, Egmont. *Die deutsche Politik und die Juden im Ersten Weltkrieg*. Göttingen: Vandenhoeck & Ruprecht, 1969.

Zelmanovits, L. *Origin and Development of the World Jewish Congress*. London: British Section of the World Jewish Congress, 1943.

Zeman, Z. A. B. *The Gentlemen Negotiators: A Diplomatic History of the First World War*. New York: Macmillan, 1971.

Zunkel, F. "Die ausländische Arbeiter in der deutschen Kriegswirtschaftspolitik des Ersten Weltkriegs." In *Entstehung und Wandel der modernen Gesellschaft*. Ed. G. A. Ritter. Berlin: De Gruyter, 1970, pp. 280–311.

3. NEWSPAPERS, JOURNALS (SELECTED)

Allgemeine Zeitung des Judenthums
American Hebrew
American Israelite
American Jewish Chronicle
American Jewish Yearbook
Basler Nationalzeitung
Berliner Börsenzeitung
Berliner Tageblatt
Chicago Tribune
Collier's
Daily Express
Daily Mail
Daily Telegraph
Der Abend
Der Schild
Deutsche Allgemeine Zeitung
Deutsche Israelitische Zeitung
Deutsche Stimmen
Deutsche Zeitung
Echo de Paris
Gazette de Lausanne
Germania
Hamburger Fremdenblatt
Hamburger Nachrichten
Het Volk
Izvestia
Japan Times
Japan Weekly Chronicle
Jewish Chronicle
Jewish Daily Bulletin
Jewish Morning Journal
Journal de Genève
Journal des Débats
Jüdische Rundschau
Kurjer Polski
L'Oeuvre
L'Univers Israélite
La Suisse
La Tribune Juive
Le Figaro
Le Matin

Le Petit Parisien
Le Progrès
Le Temps
Leipziger Neueste Nachrichten
L'Humanité
Manchester Guardian
Morning Post
Nation und Staat
National Review
Neue Freie Presse
Neue Jüdische Monatshefte
Neue Zürcher Zeitung
New Statesman and Nation
New York Herald
Nieuwe Rotterdamsche Courant
Nowy Dzjennik
Ostdeutsche Morgenpost
Pall Mall Magazine
Prager Presse
Pravda
Review of Reviews
Robotnik
Tägliche Rundschau
The Economist
The Literary Digest
The Nation
The New Republic
The New York Times
The Times [London]
The World
Tribune de Genève
Völkischer Beobachter
Vorwärts
Vossische Zeitung
Westminister Gazette
Wiener Morgenzeitung

Index